REPRESENTATION

THE LIBRARY OF CONTEMPORARY ESSAYS IN GOVERNANCE AND POLITICAL THEORY

Series Editor: Richard Bellamy and Antonino Palumbo

Titles in the series

Political Theory and the European Union
Edited by Richard Bellamy and Joseph Lacey

Representation
Edited by Christopher Lord and Johannes Pollak

Models of Deliberative Democracy
Edited by Antonino Palumbo

Transnational Citizenship and Migration
Edited by Rainer Baubock

Representation

Edited by

CHRISTOPHER LORD AND JOHANNES POLLAK
*University of Oslo, Norway, Institute for Advance Studies, Vienna
and Webster University, Austria*

THE LIBRARY OF CONTEMPORARY ESSAYS IN GOVERNANCE
AND POLITICAL THEORY

LONDON AND NEW YORK

First published 2018
by Routledge
2 Park Square, Milton Park, Abingdon, Oxon OX14 4RN

and by Routledge
711 Third Avenue, New York, NY 10017

Routledge is an imprint of the Taylor & Francis Group, an informa business

Editorial material and selection © 2018 Christopher Lord and Johannes Pollak; individual owners retain copyright in their own material.

All rights reserved. No part of this book may be reprinted or reproduced or utilised in any form or by any electronic, mechanical, or other means, now known or hereafter invented, including photocopying and recording, or in any information storage or retrieval system, without permission in writing from the publishers.

Trademark notice: Product or corporate names may be trademarks or registered trademarks, and are used only for identification and explanation without intent to infringe.

British Library Cataloguing in Publication Data
A catalogue record for this book is available from the British Library

Library of Congress Cataloging in Publication Data
A catalog record for this book has been requested

ISBN: 978-1-4724-3112-7 (hbk)

Typeset in Times New Roman MT by
Servis Filmsetting Ltd, Stockport, Cheshire

Contents

Acknowledgements ·   ix

Introduction   1

1. Jane Mansbridge, 'Rethinking Representation', *American Political Science Review* 97, 4, 2003, 515–527.   21

2. Heinz Eulau and Paul D. Karps, 'The Puzzle of Representation: Specifying Components of Responsiveness', *Legislative Studies Quarterly* 2, 1977, 233–254.   35

3. David Plotke, 'Representation is Democracy', *Constellations* 4, 1997, 19–34.   57

4. John Ferejohn and Frances Rosenbluth, 'Electoral Representation and the Aristocratic Thesis', in I. Shapiro et al. (eds), *Political Representation* (Cambridge University Press, 2009), pp. 271–303.   73

5. Russell Hardin, 'Representing Ignorance', *Social Philosophy and Policy* 21, 2004, 76–99.   107

6. Andrew Rehfeld, 'Towards a General Theory of Representation', *The Journal of Politics* 68, 1, 2006, 1–21.   131

7. Philip Pettit, 'Varieties of Public Representation', in I. Shapiro et al. (eds), *Political Representation* (Cambridge University Press, 2009), pp. 61–89.   153

8. Suzanne Dovi, 'Preferable Descriptive Representatives: Will Just Any Woman, Black, or Latino Do?', *American Political Science Review* 96, 4, 2002, 745–754.   183

9. Anne Phillips, 'Democracy and Representation: Or, Why Should it Matter Who Our Representatives Are?', in Anne Phillips (ed.), *Feminism and Politics* (Oxford University Press, 1998), pp. 224–240.   199

10. Iris Marion Young, 'Deferring Group Representation', in Will Kymlicka and Ian Shapiro (eds), *Ethnicity and Group Rights* (New York University Press, 1986), pp. 349–376.   217

11. Jane Mansbridge, 'Should Blacks Represent Blacks and Women Represent Women? A Contingent "Yes"', *The Journal of Politics* 61, 3, 1999, 628–657.   245

12. Andrew Rehfeld, 'The Concepts of Representation', *American Political Science Review* 105, 3, 2011, 631–641.   275

13. Christopher Lord and Johannes Pollak, 'Representation and Accountability: Communicating Tubes?', *West European Politics* 33, 5, 2010, 968–988.   287

14. Lisa Disch, 'Toward a Mobilization Conception of Democratic Representation', *American Political Science Review* 105, 1, 2011, 100–114.   309

15. Hanna Fenichel, 'Representation and Democracy: Uneasy Alliance', *Scandinavian Political Studies* 27, 3, 2004, 335–342.   325

16. Jane Mansbridge, 'A "Selection Model" of Representation', *Journal of Political Philosophy* 17, 4, 2009, 369–398.   333

17. Philip Pettit, 'Representation, Responsive and Indicative', *Constellations* 17, 3, 2010, 426–434.   363

18. Michael Saward, 'Mapping the Representative Claim', in *The Representative Claim* (Oxford University Press, 2010), pp. 35–57.   373

19. Christopher Lord and Johannes Pollak, 'The Pitfalls of Representation as Claims-Making in the European Union', *Journal of European Integration* 35, 5, 2013, 517–530.   395

20. John S. Dryzek and Simon Niemeyer, 'Discursive Representation', *American Political Science Review* 10, 24, 2008, 481–493.   409

21. James Bohman, 'Representation in the Deliberative System', in John Parkinson and Jane Mansbridge (eds), *Deliberative Systems: Deliberative Democracy at the Large Scale* (Cambridge University Press, 2013), pp. 72–94.   423

22. Nadia Urbinati, 'Representation as Advocacy: A Study of Democratic Deliberation', *Political Theory* 28, 6, 2000, 758–786.	447
23. Sofia Näsström, 'Democratic Representation beyond Election', *Constellations* 22, 1, 2015, 1–12.	477
24. Laura Montanaro, 'The Democratic Legitimacy of Self-Appointed Representatives', *Journal of Politics* 74, 4, 2012, 1094–1107.	489
25. Mark E. Warren, 'Citizen Representatives', in J. H. Nagel and R. M. Smith (eds), *Representation. Elections and Beyond* (University of Pennsylvania Press, 2013), pp. 269–294.	503
26. David E. Apter, Notes for A Theory of Nondemocratic Representation, Nomas X, Chapter 19, 1968, 278–317.	523
27. Michael Saward, 'Shape-Shifting Representation', *American Political Science Review* 108, 4, 2014, 723–736.	563
28. Nadia Urbinati and Mark E. Warren, 'The Concept of Representation in Contemporary Democratic Theory', *Annual Review of Political Science* 11, 2008, 387–412.	577
29. Mark Warren and Dario Castiglione, 'The Transformation of Democratic Representation', *Democracy and Society* 2, 1, 2004, 20–22.	603
Index	607

Acknowledgements

The chapters in this volume are taken from the sources listed below. The editor and publishers wish to thank the authors, original publishers or other copyright holders for permission to use their material as follows.

Cambridge University Press for permission to reprint Jane Mansbridge, 'Rethinking Representation', *American Political Science Review* 97, 4, 2003, 515–527.

John Wiley & Sons for permission to reprint Heinz Eulau and Paul D. Karps, 'The Puzzle of Representation: Specifying Components of Responsiveness', *Legislative Studies Quarterly* 2, 1977, 233–254.

John Wiley & Sons for permission to reprint David Plotke, 'Representation is Democracy', *Constellations* 4, 1997, 19–34.

Cambridge University Press for permission to reprint John Ferejohn and Frances Rosenbluth, 'Electoral Representation and the Aristocratic Thesis', in I. Shapiro et al. (eds), *Political Representation* (Cambridge University Press, 2009), pp. 271–303.

Cambridge University Press for permission to reprint Russell Hardin, 'Representing Ignorance', *Social Philosophy and Policy* 21, 2004, 76–99.

The University of Chicago Press for permission to reprint Andrew Rehfeld, 'Towards a General Theory of Representation', *The Journal of Politics* 68, 1, 2006, 1–21.

Cambridge University Press for permission to reprint Philip Pettit, 'Varieties of Public Representation', in I. Shapiro et al. (eds), *Political Representation* (Cambridge University Press, 2009), pp. 61–89.

Cambridge University Press for permission to reprint Suzanne Dovi, 'Preferable Descriptive Representatives: Will Just Any Woman, Black, or Latino Do?', *American Political Science Review* 96, 4, 2002, 745–754.

Oxford University Press for permission to reprint Anne Phillips, 'Democracy and Representation: Or, Why Should It Matter Who Our Representatives

Are?', in Anne Phillips (ed.), *Feminism and Politics* (Oxford University Press, 1998), pp. 224–240.

New York University Press for permission to reprint Iris Marion Young, 'Deferring Group Representation', in Will Kymlicka and Ian Shapiro (eds), *Ethnicity and Group Rights* (New York University Press, 1986), pp. 349–376.

The University of Chicago Press for permission to reprint Jane Mansbridge, 'Should Blacks Represent Blacks and Women Represent Women? A Contingent "Yes"', *The Journal of Politics* 61, 3, 1999, 628–657.

Cambridge University Press for permission to reprint Andrew Rehfeld, 'The Concepts of Representation', *American Political Science Review* 105, 3, 2011, 631–641.

Taylor & Francis for permission to reprint Christopher Lord and Johannes Pollak, 'Representation and Accountability: Communicating Tubes?', *West European Politics* 33, 5, 2010, 968–988.

Cambridge University Press for permission to reprint Lisa Disch, 'Toward a Mobilization Conception of Democratic Representation', *American Political Science Review* 105, 1, 2011, 100–114.

John Wiley & Sons for permission to reprint Hanna Fenichel, 'Representation and Democracy: Uneasy Alliance', *Scandinavian Political Studies* 27, 3, 2004, 335–342.

John Wiley & Sons for permission to reprint Jane Mansbridge, 'A "Selection Model" of Representation', *Journal of Political Philosophy* 17, 4, 2009, 369–398.

John Wiley & Sons for permission to reprint Philip Pettit, 'Representation, Responsive and Indicative', *Constellations* 17, 3, 2010, 426–434.

Oxford University Press for permission to reprint Michael Saward, 'Mapping the Representative Claim', in *The Representative Claim* (Oxford University Press, 2010), pp. 35–57.

Taylor & Francis for permission to reprint Christopher Lord and Johannes Pollak, 'The Pitfalls of Representation as Claims-Making in the European Union', *Journal of European Integration* 35, 5, 2013, 517–530.

Cambridge University Press for permission to reprint John S. Dryzek and Simon Niemeyer, 'Discursive Representation', *American Political Science Review* 10, 24, 2008, 481–493.

Cambridge University Press for permission to reprint James Bohman, 'Representation in the Deliberative System', in John Parkinson and Jane Mansbridge (eds), *Deliberative Systems: Deliberative Democracy at the Large Scale* (Cambridge University Press, 2013), pp. 72–94.

Sage Publications for permission to reprint Nadia Urbinati, 'Representation as Advocacy: A Study of Democratic Deliberation', *Political Theory* 28, 6, 2000, 758–786.

John Wiley & Sons for permission to reprint Sofia Näsström, 'Democratic Representation beyond Election', *Constellations* 22, 1, 2015, 1–12.

The University of Chicago Press for permission to reprint Laura Montanaro, 'The Democratic Legitimacy of Self-Appointed Representatives', *Journal of Politics* 74, 4, 2012, 1094–1107.

University of Pennsylvania Press for permission to reprint Mark E. Warren, 'Citizen Representatives', in J. H. Nagel and R. M. Smith (eds), *Representation. Elections and Beyond* (University of Pennsylvania Press, 2013), pp. 269–294.

Cambridge University Press for permission to reprint Michael Saward, 'Shape-Shifting Representation', *American Political Science Review* 108, 4, 2014, 723–736.

Annual Reviews for permission to reprint Nadia Urbinati and Mark E. Warren, 'The Concept of Representation in Contemporary Democratic Theory', *Annual Review of Political Science* 11, 2008, 387–412.

The authors for permission to reprint Mark Warren and Dario Castiglione, 'The Transformation of Democratic Representation', *Democracy and Society* 2, 1, 2004, 20–22

Disclaimer

The publishers have made every effort to contact authors/copyright holders of works reprinted in *Representation*. This has not been possible in every case, however, and we would welcome correspondence from those individuals/ companies whom we have been unable to trace.

Publisher's Note

The material in this volume has been reproduced using the facsimile method. This means we can retain the original pagination to facilitate easy and correct citation of the original essays. It also explains the variety of typefaces, page layouts and numbering.

Introduction

The many faces of representation

Christopher Lord and Johannes Pollak

Relational differences and substantial commonalities

Representation means the 'making present *in some sense* of something which is nevertheless *not* present' (Pitkin 1967: 8). It occurs when some people stand in for, speak up for, or act on behalf of others. Of course these are frustratingly broad definitions. Yet their breadth is itself revealing. No 'essentialist' definition is likely to capture all the ways in which the word 'representation' is used. Representation has no 'essence' or fixed substance. Rather it is a relational concept: a relationship that means different things to different people. The sparse idea that representation somehow involves acting for others is as about as far as we can get towards capturing the very different conceptions people have of what representatives can or should do.

Indeed, we know what is meant when we talk about being represented by a lawyer or when parents are said to represent their underage children. However, political representation is conceptually more challenging. The essential role of moral autonomy in Western thinking demands that we are the authors of the laws to which we are subjected. Given the impracticability of direct democracy in modern mass-societies and the ever rising complexity of organising our living together, representation is a practical means to arrange politics (see already Noah Webster 1787; John S. Mill 1820; Thomas Hare 1873).

Yet means, ends and concepts of representation differ from polity to polity. Practices of representation are everywhere sensitive to contextual conditions. Concepts of representation are subject to change, refinement, new questions and further discussion. The enormously rich literature on representation since the Middle Ages is proof of the richness of the concept. To name but a few of the types identified in the literature, representation can be *constitutional* (Sieyès 1789/1981); *factual, virtual* or *traditional* (Burke 1887); *substantial, descriptive* or *symbolic* (Pitkin 1967); *appropriated, estate-bound, imperative* or *free* (Weber 1956); *authoritative, consultative* or *mixed* (Kincaid

1999); *ascriptive* (Griffiths and Wollheim 1960); *sovereign* or *non-sovereign* (Leibholz 1966); *municipal* (Heller 1934); *real* and *fictitious* (Sterne 1869); *delegated, microcosmic* or *electoral* (Birch 1971); *sociological* (Sartori 1968); *social* (Holmberg 1999); *monolithic* (Rogowski 1981); *dynamic* (Stimson et al. 1995); *promissory, anticipatory, gyroscopic or surrogate* (Mansbridge 2003, 2005); *collective* or *dyadic* (Weissberg 1978); *institutional* (Jackson and King 1989); *executive, parliamentary, functional* or *territorial* (Marsh and Weßels 1997); *upstream* or *downstream* (Crum 2008); *synecdochical* and *metaphorical* (Ankersmit 2015), or *systemic* (Kuyper 2016).

All these adjectives serve as analytical crutches in an attempt to make at least some sense of the varieties, elements and levels of representation. We can differentiate between adjectives pointing to the object of representation (e.g. microcosmic, descriptive, virtual, collective, institutional), adjectives referring to the activity of representing (e.g. dynamic, constitutional), and adjectives used to describe the process of authorisation and selection of representatives (e.g. electoral, delegated, anticipatory, gyroscopic). Transversal adjectives refer to geographically and politically defined spaces: territorial, and local. And finally, some of the adjectives disclose information about the institutional system of representation (institutional, executive). As much as the delicate fine-tuning of the concept of representation with the help of adjectives is to be admired, conceptual clarity is hard to find.

Still, most forms of representation have at least some possibilities and problems in common. At some point representatives may feel that they can no longer represent: that they have reached the limits of the relationship beyond which they can no longer take a decision, make a commitment or state a view without the approval of those they represent. Not the least reason for such caution is that representatives are often accused of saying or agreeing to things they have no right to say or agree to in their role as representatives. Nor does that complaint just come from the represented. Often it comes from other representatives, eager to defend a particular conception of representation, or just to undermine the claims of their opponents to represent anything or anyone worthy of being represented.

If, though, representation is difficult, it also seems unavoidable, and not just as a practical means of arranging politics. Neither individuals, nor groups, nor whole societies are likely to manage very well without representation. Often, people need representatives to fill gaps in their own expertise. People may be able to make their own case in a court of law without making complete fools of themselves, and yet still be fools not to have access to the further expertise that comes from representation by a lawyer.

Yet, the need for representation goes beyond expertise. Several members of an academic department may be equally able to represent it in a university committee. Indeed, it is quite likely that the person who ends up representing the department is *not* the person who has the most expertise. No one can do everything. Labours have to be divided. And those who can divide labours between representatives and the represented may be able to achieve things that would be unthinkable without representation. To re-iterate the point that politics, polities, economies or societies of any size or ambition may be impossible without representation, individuals would stand little chance of developing a body of laws with the detail, complexity and scope needed to base modern societies on the rule of law if they had to control the making, amendment and administration of all their laws themselves. Representation relaxes that constraint. Representative bodies can be proliferated and sub-divided – as is common, for example, in parliaments where representatives themselves represent one another in specialist committees – until the 'supply' of representation is brought into line with 'demands' on representatives.

If, however, representation expands our scope to agree matters together, to take collectively binding decisions, to solve co-ordination and collective-action problems, and to arbitrate or adjudicate differences, it becomes all the more important that we can accept the practices by which we are represented. Some forms of representation may be difficult for some groups of people to accept. Some forms of representation may simply not be available to some societies or political systems. Thus, Arend Lijphart (1984: 4) has famously argued that majoritarian forms of democratic representation are probably only possible in societies that are sufficiently homogeneous for minorities to feel no great disadvantage or danger to themselves if representatives of major-ities get to dominate most decisions for four or five years at a time in systems where 'winner takes all'. Yet that feeling of security seems unlikely in divided or even more 'plural' societies, where representation is more likely to require some kind of a consensus, rather than a mere majority, of representatives.

As the majoritarian and consensus distinction suggests, representation can be variously a source of conflict, a means of mediating and managing conflict, and a way of building agreement. Some of the greatest conflicts in human his-tory have been fought over conflicting claims to represent peoples, religions or identities. Yet even settled forms of representation typically articulate and identify conflict as much as they mediate, moderate and decide it. This Janus-faced role in both politicising conflict – in putting conflicts and contrasting choices on to the political agenda in the first place – and in building agree-ment on shared laws and the provision of public goods is in a sense the mis-sion impossible of political representation. We might agree that democratic institutions should be neutral to – and equally able to represent – all values that are themselves compatible with the democratic process (Rawls 2003). Yet political science tells us that systems of representation typically 'mobilise bias' (Schattschneider 1960). There are limits to the ways in which electoral systems can be designed, and to the dimensions of co-operation and conflict along which a party system can structure voter choice. Whatever electoral system is used – whatever the dimensions along which political co-operation

4 REPRESENTATION

and competition are organised – will prejudice the kind of representation provided by any one political system.

If, finally, representation is relational and normative – if it depends on what people expect and value in any relationship between representatives and the represented – concepts and practices of representation are likely to be changeable, constructed and endogenous to representation itself. Indeed, we will argue later that profound changes are underway in a once standard understanding of representation. First, though, we need to grasp how a standard version of anything as fluid as representation ever emerged at all. That story involves both the pre-democratic roots of representation and the role representation has played in making mass democracy possible at all.

Representation before democracy

Today, representation and democracy have become synonymous, interchangeable, and almost pleonastic. This is all the more remarkable given the history of the two concepts and their political application. Democracy and representation started as explicit opposites, the latter invented to prevent the former (Urbinati 2004). Qualifications of class, wealth, gender, race and education were for centuries used to limit access to representative positions, and to prevent rather than implement democracy, which was identified with mob rule. Indeed, for much of its history, representation has had more to do with rule by the few than rule by the many: more to do with aristocratic than democratic forms of government (Manin 1997). Representation has been justified on the grounds that it is better to leave decisions and debate to a 'better' kind of person. Even amongst those thinkers who began to make the transition between pre-democratic and democratic forms of representation, James Madison assumed that representation is a necessary 'refinement of public views' (1787, Federalist No. 10), whilst John Stuart Mill hoped that representation would reconcile democracy with rule by the able.

Concepts of representation originally developed and refined in nondemocratic contexts have therefore been adapted to democratic ones. As Bernard Manin notes (1997: 3), many of the 'institutional choices' made by pre-democratic 'founders of representative government' have been carried over into contemporary democratic practice. As he puts it, 'several arrangements have remained the same, such as those governing the way representatives are selected and public decisions are made'. We can discern five basic continuities (see Przeworski et al. 1999): (1) those who govern are selected through territorially based elections; (2) while free to discuss and criticize at all times, citizens cannot give binding instructions to the government; (3) rulers are subject to periodic, free and fair elections; (4) public decisions undergo the trial of debate (Mill 1972); and finally (5) representatives have to justify their choice of action.

Indeed, by the mid twentieth century Joseph Schumpeter (1942) could still understand democracy as a political competition between elites, albeit one decided by popular vote. By then election of representatives by universal suffrage became the principal marker of democracy and the main way of distinguishing representative from direct democracy. Yet putting elections at the centre of representation has also created problems. Firstly, in Hanna Pitkin's words '[w]hat seems important is less what the legislature does than how it is composed' (1967: 61). Secondly, the multiple forms of non-elective representation in democracies are easily overlooked, be it new ways of interest aggregation by social movements or interest groups, or representation by delegation, e.g. by bureaucracy. And thirdly, the importance of responsiveness is limited to an act of election or, at best, campaigning for election; whilst, on the contrary, representation in democracies requires a constant striving for responsiveness, a constant renewal of a representative's mandate by different audiences (see below).

We will return to these difficulties below where we discuss crises in modern systems of representation and in what were once standard understandings of representative democracy. For the moment, though, it is important to state which burdens modern mass systems of representation have inherited from their pre-democratic past.

Consider two major functions of representation. First, representation allows citizens to pursue their private ends after they have delegated authority to elected politicians thereby enabling them, for a limited period, to govern the authoritative allocation of values. Thus, one major function of representation is the organisation of rule. It is an 'institutional technique by which power is structured in a political society [providing] a multilevel system capable of making public action possible' (Schwartz 1988: 23). Individual representatives may come and go but the system of representation outlasts them. Representation thus combines flexibility with stability and continuity. It provides a means of removing particular political leaderships whilst continuing with an underlying system for allocating legislative and executive power that publics can accept as legitimate in spite of the failures of this or that government. Indeed, more generally and most obviously, representation organises rule by providing a means of forming and controlling government by the people via elections, responsiveness, and accountability, a quality that makes it decisive for the maintenance of a democratic structure.

Yet the role of representation in organising the polity creates a problem, already noted by Jean-Jacques Rousseau (2012). In order to achieve the capability to act, citizens transfer individual sovereignty, thereby limiting their very own freedom. From Thomas Hobbes onwards this loss was thought to be justifiable since it delivers security and the protection of life and property. In modern democratic systems it is the very competition for votes – and the very act of voting for representatives – that has to be good enough to justify a mandate, or at least a licence, for governments and parliaments to rule on behalf of citizens. That is clearly one demanding test that any system of mass representation needs to be able to pass.

Secondly, representation has a major role in building identity. Representative bodies have long been understood as the nation or the polity assembled. As early as the fourteenth century the House of Commons understood the task of making the 'absent present' as one in which:

> Every Englishman is intended to be there present, either in person or by procuration and attorneys, of what pre-eminence, state, dignity or quality so ever he be, from the prince to the lowest person in England. And the consent of parliament is taken to be everyone's consent.
>
> (Smith 2013 [1583]: 46)

Thomas Hobbes would later argue that 'It is the Unity of the Representer, not the Unity of the represented, that makes the Person One' (1968: 220).

Indeed, Frank Ankersmit has argued that historically 'political reality only comes into being after the nation has unfolded itself in a represented and in a representation representing the represented'. This, moreover, goes for democratic politics too. As Ankersmit continues: 'without representation no democratic politics' (2002: 115). If anything, democracy is usually dependent on the idea that it is only after and through a process of representation that anything can be agreed within or about a polity and its identity. The irreducible plurality of interests and values in modern democracies – together with a commitment of democracy itself to treat those values as no better or worse than others save as individuals freely choose between them as equals – means that political agreement in democracies is necessarily only synthetic, procedural and temporary. In other words, it is, once again, such things as equal voting and deliberation in choosing representatives from time to time – and equal voting and deliberation between representatives themselves in choosing laws – that allow a democratic polity to reach procedural agreement even in the everyday absence of substantive agreement.

But can people really identify with a process of representation, especially one that must be rather mechanical, procedural and neutral if, in a democracy, it is to avoid affirming substantive positions of value? Perhaps 'yes' where people are able to recognise the acts of representatives as their own and where the representation of a plurality of values is the one thing that a society of plural values can have in common. But for as long as people have thought about the problem of representation they have come up with very different answers to the question of what representation must do if people are to recognise the actions of representation as their own.

One answer that many find intuitively appealing is that representative bodies should somehow mirror those they represent: that body is representative that contains as many women as men; as many young as old people as there are in society; as many butchers, bakers and candlestick makers and so on. In 1776 John Adams wrote 'a representative legislature should be an exact portrait, in miniature, of the people at large, as it should think, feel, reason and act like them' (in Peek 1954: 68; see also Birch 1993: 72). That view has been shared by thinkers as diverse as Robert Yates from the Anti-Federalists (see Bailyn 1993: 320) to Comte de Mirabeau (see Schmitt 1969: 189). Yet it has been opposed by most modern theorists. As J.R. Pennock (1979) sharply put it: 'no one would argue that morons should be represented by morons' (see also Pitkin 1967; Crane 1995). Indeed, the idea that representation should somehow be aesthetic and creative – that it should interpret the represented – hardly seems compatible with the view that it should just 'mirror' the society represented. Indeed, according to a very different view, representatives should definitely *not* be like the represented: they should be chosen for their skills in representing, skills that are peculiar to a few.

In any case representation necessarily creates a distance between the representative and the represented wherever it allows for deliberation and reflection. That deliberation is supposed to go beyond the immediateness and individuality of opinions held by individual citizens or groups of citizens: to confront those opinions with one another and to encourage those who hold any one view to justify it in relation to all other views, to transcend their own parochial horizons and thereby inform their political judgement.

No democracy without representation

So far we have shown how representation without democracy has been common for most of the history of representation. What, though, of the converse claim that democracy is not possible without representation? At first that claim seems implausible. After all, it is common to contrast representative with direct democracy, where citizens take decisions for themselves without the help of representatives. That surely implies representation has no monopoly on democracy?

Yet Robert Dahl (1970: 67–8) has famously illustrated how quickly any political process is likely to run into the limits of direct or participatory democracy. In a participatory democracy, Dahl observed, all the people would ideally speak for themselves. After all, allowing others to speak for us already begins to sound a bit like representation. Now, Dahl continued, assume everyone is given ten minutes' speaking time and a community sets aside ten hours a day to take decisions. That community would only be able to take one decision a day, even if it only has 60 members. Hence, citizens of any political community that is large enough to be viable are unlikely to be able to govern themselves directly. In contrast representation 'scales

8 REPRESENTATION

up "democracy"' and makes it 'possible in large polities' (N. Webster 1787, printed in Bailyn 1993: 130).

Still, it is possible to see representative democracy as a poor relative, to regard direct democracy as a pure and ideal form of democracy and representative democracy as a 'second-best'. However, that view is also contestable. Many arguments can and have been made that representative democracy is not just a regrettable necessity. Rather it can even be preferable to direct democracy in so far as representation acknowledges the dual nature of human beings as *citoyen* and individual person. Contrary to antiquity, we have the right to be un-political without being inhuman or divine. Representation allows for the realisation of individual ideas of the good life. George Kateb (1994) writes that the institution of representation is the source of the 'moral distinctiveness' of modern democracy, and the sign of its superiority to direct democracy. Representation allows for a greater degree of individual freedom in the banal sense of freeing the citizen of the cumbersome burden of attending *agora* meetings. Representation may also be morally required if it offers the best practical chances of meeting standards of deliberation and of temporally deferring decisions until they have been adequately deliberated (Young 1997).

If, however, democracy is the only standard of legitimacy available to societies that assume their citizens are free and equal, if democracy is unlikely without representation, and if democracy may even be better in some ways with representation than without it, representation will need to get things right. Just what core democratic standards must any system of representation deliver at a minimum? We would suggest three, as follows.

1. Public control. Without some public control of representatives, representation itself becomes autocratic, and a means of securing power, rather than of exercising it on behalf of the represented. More than that, representation will need to ensure public control if it is to satisfy core justifications for democracy itself. Consider two different understandings of what justifies democracy. According to one, democracy is justified by ideals of autonomy, as the one form of government in which individuals can autonomously shape their own lives and govern themselves. Others argue that that ideal is hopelessly utopian. There is no procedure that can allow individuals to govern themselves in modern democracies. The best that can be hoped for is that decisions which determine the terms by which those individuals live together (Bohman 2007) should depend in some reliable and non-arbitrary way on the people as a whole, not on some privileged section of the people, not on diktats of governments that cannot be challenged or reversed by citizens themselves.

However, both justifications of democracy presuppose public control. Individuals plainly cannot be as autonomous as possible in making their own life plans and writing their own laws – subject only to the greatest possible autonomy of all other individuals – unless those individuals also have as much control as possible over their own laws. No less self-evidently, law-making cannot depend on the people – rather than on how power-holders arbitrarily choose those laws for reasons of their own – where the public cannot control the making, amendment and administration of its own laws (Beetham 1994; Weale 1999: 14; Bohman 2007: 2), which, we have argued here, it can only realistically do through representatives. None of this, however, means that representatives need to make all – or even many – public decisions. But what it must mean is that there can be no law that the public cannot ultimately control and revise through its representatives if it wants to do so.

2. Political equality. Were some people to have much more weight than others in the formation of representative bodies, there would not be a straightforward rule of the people. Rather there would be an element of rule of some of the people by others of the people (Estlund 2008: 37). Political equality in the election of representatives is also essential to the autonomy of the democratic political process. It is only in so far as representatives follow a highly unusual and artificial incentive structure when they compete for election on a principle of strict political equality – namely, 'one person, one vote' – that modern democracies even have a slender chance of promoting policies and laws that do not merely follow economic and social inequalities. Yet structuring representation so that it ensures political equality is surprisingly difficult; although a necessary condition 'one person, one vote' is far from sufficient for political equality. First, equal votes have to be accompanied by equal apportionment of representatives to votes. That, in turn, is difficult to achieve perfectly wherever a political system is subdivided into constituencies, itself an important and valued quality of many forms of representation (Rehfeld 2005). Second, there may be no system for turning votes into representation and representation into decisions that does not make some voters and some represenatives more strategic – or pivotal – to outcomes than others.

3. Justifications for decisions. However, even public control with political equality is not enough. Imagine representatives who – though they can control governments and can, in turn, be controlled by citizens with equal votes – do not justify their decisions. Why would that be a problem? One too often forgotten difficulty is that democracy is itself a coercive form of political rule. What democracy lacks in cruelty, moreover, it makes up for in the scope and ambition of the decisions it takes on behalf of its citizens. As John Dunn (2005: 19) puts it:

> Like every modern state, the democracies of today demand obedience and insist on a very large measure of compulsory alienation of judgement on the part of their citizens. When they make that demand in their

citizens' own name, they do not merely add insult to injury ... they close the circle of civic subjection.

If, however, power is only non-arbitrary to the extent that it is justified to those over whom it is exercised, then even freely elected democratic majorities owe rights of justification for why those whose views have been outvoted should also be collectively bound by laws (Forst 2007). Moreover, democracy rests on the idea that 'losers' consent to the collectively binding decisions of democratic majorities because they themselves have a right to form the alternative majorities that would allow them to undo unwanted policies and laws. But to do that they need to know what arguments for any existing policy or law need to be countered if that measure is no longer to be justified.

Perhaps it was John Stuart Mill who best identified why even a democratically enacted law would be arbitrary if an elected representative could not ask for a public justification for it (1972 [1861]: 239):

> The Parliament has an office to be a Congress of Opinions; an arena in which every opinion can produce itself in full light to be tested in adverse controversy ... where those whose opinion is overruled can feel that it is set aside *not by a mere act of will* (our italics) but for reasons that commend themselves to representatives of a majority.

Of course, this might seem anachronistic: a hymn to a heroic age of representation that never was. Yet there is still one form of public justification – quite different from justifications through the media, Twitter or Facebook – that only formally elected representative bodies can provide; namely, justification during procedures for enacting laws themselves. Indeed, at this point we can draw together all the reasons why only elected and deliberative forms of representation can provide public control *with* political equality and justification. As Habermas has put it (1996: 170–1), only the 'parliamentary principle' can ensure all the following: (1) representatives elected on a basis of 'one person, one vote' who can (2) test justifications for laws in public, (3) during the course of law-making itself, all (4) within institutions that have some encompassing control over the making, amendment and subsequent administration of laws.

The standard version of representation and beyond

Given that democracy without representation seems inconceivable in modern societies, and representation itself needs to satisfy core conditions if it is to deliver democracy, it is perhaps unsurprising that a standard understanding (Castiglione and Warren 2006) of democratic representation developed as follows: representation was invented in order to render democracy possible in large political communities; we select and authorise individuals via elections to make decisions on our, the people's, behalf. Depending on the political system, representatives enjoy different degrees of discretion, ranging from delegates to trustees; they show different forms of responsiveness and are subjected to multiple forms of accountability, the most important being legal/constitutional and electoral. Yet, whatever its variations, representation standardly allows citizens to rule themselves as equals where (1) they belong to well-defined political communities of individuals who (2) have equal votes in (3) regular election, re-election or removal of representatives, who are, in turn, able (4) to control the making, amendment and administration of all laws on behalf of those they represent.

This particular twinning of representation and democracy was responsible for a remarkable advance in democracy in the second half of the twentieth century, not least in reaction to experiences with non-democratic forms of representation before 1945 and 1989. The end-of-history argument that democracy had won everywhere as the 'single world-wide name for the legitimate basis of political authority' (Dunn 2005: 15) to the point at which even its enemies had had to develop claims of their own to use the word was in many ways a victory for the standard model; or at least the absence of that model was widely seen as delegitimising many political systems after 1989.

Nor is it hard to see the appeal of the standard model. First, it specifies how the single act of voting representatives in and out can support complex systems by which the represented can indirectly control public policies, laws and political leaderships. Jane Mansbridge has single-handedly identified important ways in which this can work through her promissory and anticipatory selection models of representation (Mansbridge 2003; 2009). Representatives can be mandated and sanctioned so that they carry out *promises* to voters; or they can be incentivized to *anticipate* what voters are likely to want in future elections; or – even where representatives cannot be easily monitored and, therefore, sanctioned or incentivized – they can be *selected* on the basis of their pre-existing beliefs and the likelihood that those beliefs will shape the way in which they decide and deliberate on behalf of voters.

Second, 'one person, one vote' in the selection of representatives is an easily understood and intuitively fair way of institutionalising political equality. As Robert Dahl (2006: 32) has put it:

> some of our most distinguished philosophers have placed too much weight on the strength of human reason as a force for justice and fairness. What drives the search for fairness is not pure reason but emotions and passions which range from compassion, envy, anger and hatred.

The core aspect of political equality is 'one person, one vote' within a system in which voters themselves choose and dismiss their own governments. 'One person, one vote' is a compelling principle which is easy enough for everyone to understand. It appeals to the simplest and most intuitive ideas of fairness. Most people assume that allocating the same number of votes to each person is 'naturally' fair in the same way as it is 'naturally' fair to share a cake between dinner guests by cutting it into slices of equal size. Any other solution might well trigger some measure of compassion, envy, anger or hatred.

The role of political equality in supporting acceptance of collective decision-making with a simple principle of fairness is all the more extraordinary for the fact that most systems of human rule have historically assumed its opposite: namely, that some individuals just are better than others and that gives them a right to rule over others. Doubtless those systems are sometimes quite good at sustaining their own legitimacy by convincing their citizens of their own inferiority. Once a population comes to expect equality of recognition, however, even small deviations from equality of treatment may be seen as deeply offensive in so far as they imply that some people are of less worth than others. Since the act of voting is the nearest thing to the sacred in secular democratic practice, equality in the election of representative bodies has a special place in defining the individual as a citizen rather than as a subject. Unjustified inequalities in how votes are translated into representation are amongst the most serious inequalities of recognition that any polity can visit on its own population. Those who feel that they are not recognised as equals may feel that they do not belong. Thus, inequalities of representation are likely to corrode political community and to inhibit the formation of a *demos* that is accepted by all as entitled to make decisions binding on all.

Yet democracy today is widely perceived as being in crisis (e.g. Crouch 2004, Mair 2013; Streeck 2014; Tormey 2015). Moreover, this is specifically a crisis of the standard model of mass representative democracy. It is as much a crisis of that model as events after 1989 were seen as its vindication. The globalisation of problems from climate change to the borderless flow of money in unprecedented and incomprehensible volumes, the development of transnational decision arenas outside the easy control of any one democracy, the delegation of huge swathes of public policy to the unelected, the rise of private actors who can buy and arbitrarily dominate whole democratic processes, the fracturing of political communities by growing inequalities between rich and poor, all seem to make a mockery of the core claim of the standard model that individuals really can govern themselves as equals by electing representatives in well-defined political communities.

Three of these challenges to the standard version need singling out.

1. Social complexity. The standard version of mass democratic representation has always been deeply problematic. Pierre Rosanvallon (2007) shows that as soon as political systems even began to approximate to the standard model, they began to search for ways round its evident difficulties, adding extra elements of impartiality, reflexivity and proximity to the simple aggregation of views through systems of mass representation. But to long-established problems with the standard form of representation, new ones have been added by the greater complexification of society. The idea is that a single set of representatives elected at a single time once every four or five years in a contest structured around a manageably simple contest works best where the represented have simple representative needs. Yet even individuals have complex representative needs in modern societies where they engage simultaneously with the polity as citizens, members of occupational groups, consumers, as someone's relative, in sickness and in health, and so on. In any one polity there may be many different cleavages – cultural, territorial or sociological (Rokkan et al. 1999) – all of which citizens care very much should be represented in the institutions that make collective decisions on their behalf. On top of all that, many different values may be involved in satisfying each of the many needs that any one individual has for a system of collective choice. However, any one process of representation works through drastic simplification. Any one person has but one vote every few years.

Complex forms of representation have to some degree evolved precisely to meet the foregoing difficulty. Formal representation can be subdivided into separate representative bodies (chambers of a legislature) or offices (chief executive) elected at different times, in different ways, and at different levels (local or centre). Informal representation likewise has a role in dealing with social complexity. One well-known difficulty is that individuals don't just differ in their values. They also differ in the intensity with which those values are held. We might find it easy to agree that democratic representation is the best way to represent diffuse interests but find it less than self-evident that it is the best way to represent intense values, given that democracy's commitment to political equality puts the person whose life can be turned upside down by a particular decision on a level with those who are only remotely affected. Informal representation responds to the latter difficulty, since it is, of course, precisely those with intense interests who are most likely to organise themselves to influence a polity by means over and above those afforded by formal channels of representation.

2. Hollowing out of the democratic state. Unprecedented degrees of complexity, an increasing economic inequality, and the rise of anti-democratic parties have challenged tenets of representative democracy from within the state: elections are often perceived as unlikely to change the course of a polity, as empty shells without real meaning that offer few substantial policy alternatives. Political elites remodel themselves as a homogeneous professional class, withdrawing into state institutions that offer stability in a world of fickle voters. Meanwhile, non-democratic agencies and practices reminiscent of the age of representation without democracy proliferate and gain credibility

(Mair 2013). This development leads to a withdrawal of citizens and politicians into an anti-political sentiment. It leads to a distance between representatives and represented where even the brittle band of elections is interpreted as a hindrance and not a pillar of democracy. This rising scepticism meets a world populated by transnational players and decision-making arenas that are ever further removed from traditional representational institutions.

3. Globalisation and challenges to well-defined political communities. As Castiglione and Warren (2006: 18) put it, 'democratic legitimacy has not only to do with the relative equality of representation, but with the universalisation of inclusion' (Rehfeld 2005). As mentioned previously, democratic representation serves three purposes: it preserves the moral autonomy of the individual, it allows for collective-identity building, and it organises rule under conditions that enable public control and require justification for decisions. Nonetheless, this catalogue of functions lacks one vital aspect: an exact delimitation of who is represented in the polity. Certainly, at the time of the city-state, or, indeed, in more recent historical periods of, say, open-air rallies in small political constituencies from the Rhine to the Thames and from the Seine to the Danube, the lack of formal denomination of the body politic may have been sustainable. The body politic was visible and immediate and amenable to constant tension-diluting political debate about its own definition. However, aggregated democratic expression has expanded over ever larger geographic units and has similarly been channelled through evermore complex and differentiated structures determining, amongst other things, the various levels of democratic aggregation.

Thus, it seems that the standard model is overtaken by a new social reality that combines the transnationalisation of challenges with the demand for more participatory models of democratic decision-making. This poses enormous challenges for the study of representation. Three areas of research seem to us important responses to these challenges.

1. Representation as claims-making. Arguably, Michael Saward's (2006; 2010) procedural understanding of representation as constant claims-making is one of the most original and important contributions in the recent theoretical literature on representation. He convincingly develops the notion that 'good representation' is a fluid and endogenously defined standard in which some actors – be they parliamentarians, NGOs, interest groups, civil society associations, etc. – make claims to represent others which are, in turn, accepted, amended or rejected by various (sometimes overlapping) social groups or audiences. Together with the idea that representatives are 'shape-shifting' (Saward 2014) Saward's approach underlines the constructivist notion and creative function of representatives. It is a construction because representatives according to constraints and opportunities can occupy the role of trustee, delegate, surrogate, etc. They are many things to the many. It fulfils a constructivist function because it goes beyond the age-old discussion of what the object of representation is. It is not a given people, a territory, a general will; it is a constantly changing offer by representatives of how they interpret their political community, its needs, demands and ideas.

2. Formal and informal forms of representation. From the new complexity of modern mass-societies leads a direct path to representation as claims-making, and from there to the ubiquity of claims. While the standard model defines authorisation in the form of election as the *differentia specifica* of representation, a representative claim can be raised by everyone. As long as one audience grants an air of legitimacy to the claim by accepting it as a valid description of its demands, an informal representative is born. Such a complex mix of formal and informal representation may correspond much better to the above-charted complexities of modern societies. The 'right of justification' (Forst 2007) may well be better delivered by complex forms of representation. First, the formal organisation of the polity for different kinds of representation – ideological, territorial, institutional, and so on – will widen the criteria in terms of which proposals have to be justified and, indeed, increase the probability that they have to be justified to very different kinds of majority. Second, mutually suspicious representative institutions which compete with one another for power, public attention or resources may have every incentive to explore weaknesses in the justifications offered by the others. Third, formal and informal representation lend themselves to different forms of justification. Since formally representative institutions make collective binding laws, they are obvious sites for offering universal justifications for why a particular measure should in principle apply to all members of the polity. In contrast, informal representation challenges the polity as a whole to justify the implications of its measures for sectors and persons.

The multiplication of formal and informal structures and opportunities for democratic representation leads to a rising number of representative claims. Rather than raise the quality of representation, such claims may collide. This will most obviously happen where one claim to representativeness undermines another; where, for example, two conflicting majorities have equal claim to regard themselves as democratically elected representatives and equal claim to trump the other in deciding a law affecting the lives of the represented; or where a claim to represent some special need refuses to bow down to a claim to represent the public as a whole.

Various formal and informal claims – each with equal demand to being legitimated by the citizens – may all call to be better placed than others to represent citizens in the making of policies: closer to what happens on the ground, able to consider the larger picture, in touch with real political communities supported by real citizen movements and real unmediated debates, are just some of the contrasting claims typically made by different representatives for why their level is the best one at which to link the citizen to political decision-making. Representative institutions – with equally legitimate claim to representativeness – might only block one another and thus produce 'joint-decision traps'. They may also only encourage mutual insensitivity or incomprehension, since, throughout its history, theorists have cautioned against the organisation of representative democracy in such a way that one class, one group or one cultural segment develops interests of their own which are at odds with those of their fellows (Rousseau 2012 [1762]; Dunn 2005). The represented may thus find themselves with some of the costs of complex systems – notably the added cost of identifying who is responsible for what – without the full benefits of having different representatives competing to satisfy their needs and expectations.

3. Representation beyond the state. Here the study of representation needs to investigate the predicament that democratic representation beyond the state may be both necessary and impossible. Consider first why some element of democratic representation beyond the state may be needed. Bodies such as the EU make laws, and – as we have repeatedly argued here – individuals must be able to control their own laws through representatives if citizens are to be free and equal. Yet it is likely to be difficult to develop systems of representative democracy beyond the state. A long and demanding set of conditions may be needed for democracy to work well, including (1) freedoms and rights; (2) a form of political competition that offers voters choices relevant to the control of the political system; (3) a civil society in which all groups have equal opportunity to organise to influence the polity; (4) a public sphere in which all opinions have equal access to public debate; and (5) a defined *demos*, or, at least, agreement on who should have votes and voice in the making of decisions binding on all. Achieving all these conditions simultaneously may be hard for a body such as the EU that operates from beyond the state and is not, therefore, itself a state. The capacity of the state to concentrate power, resources and legal enforcement has been useful in all kinds of ways to democracy: in ensuring that the decisions of democratic majorities are carried out; in guaranteeing rights needed for democracy; in drawing the boundaries of defined political communities; and in motivating voters and elites to participate in democratic competition for the control of an entity which manifestly affects their needs and values.

If, then, it is difficult to make bodies that take decision-making beyond the state democratic, it might seem better to secure their democratic control through the democratic institutions of their participating states. Yet that may not allow single democracies to govern themselves by solving their collective-action problems either. If any national democracy has an interest in harming its neighbours or in free-riding on the efforts of others to maintain economic, ecological or security systems, then its own system of representation – its own electorate and parliament – is also likely to have an interest in behaving in those ways.

Outline of the volume

This volume brings together some seminal essays that have formed the debate on political representation up to the present day. They are grouped together in six sections that demonstrate both the difficulty of grasping what representation actually is and the paradoxes that have made it a central puzzle of political theory for over 2,500 years. We are convinced that the paradoxes have remained much the same since the first claims to represent were raised. However, answers to those paradoxes, as well as practical normative expectations – logics of appropriateness in representation – have changed. For example, demands for descriptive representation have appeared and failed numerous times in different contexts. One aim of this collection of essays is to place representation firmly in the context of democracy – not an easy task, given the long history of representation outside democracy. Pairing representation with accountability and legitimacy provides this firm ground that should serve as the normative basis for judging what good representation is. The challenges to the standard version of political representation are becoming ever more demanding, given the erosion of democracy as a form of rule legitimated by election.

Selecting the 'right' articles out of a myriad of papers necessarily reflects our own very personal bias. Doing justice to such an enormous body of literature is impossible. We wanted to provide a guide for the reader, but as everyone knows such guides, like travel guides, become outdated very quickly. New paths are opening up, old buildings are demolished, new ones occupy a much larger space and underground currents are at work all the time. As such, political representation is truly shape-shifting.

References

Ankersmit, F.R. (2002) *Political Representation.* Stanford, CA: Stanford University Press.

Ankersmit, F.R. (2015) 'Vom Mittelalter zur Demokratie und wieder zurück', in Paula Diehl and Felix Steilen (eds), *Politische Repräsentation und das Symbolische. Historische, politische und soziologische Perspektive.* Wiesbaden: Springer VS, pp. 107–133.

Apter, D. (1968) *Some Conceptual Approaches to the Study of Modernisation.* Englewood Cliffs, NJ: Prentice-Hall.

Bailyn, B. (1993) *The Debate on the Constitution. Federalist and Antifederalist Speeches, Articles, and Letters during the Struggle over Ratification. Part One: September 1787 to February 1788.* New York: The Library of America.

Beetham, D. (1994) *Defining and Measuring Democracy.* London: Sage and ECPR.

Birch, A.H. (1971) *Representation.* New York: Praeger.

Birch, A.H. (1993) *The Concepts and Theories of Modern Democracy.* London: Routledge.

Bohman, J. (2007) *Democracy across Borders: From Demos to Demoi.* Cambridge, MA: MIT Press.

Burke, E. (1887) 'A Letter to Sir Hercules Langrishe on the Subject of the Roman Catholics in Ireland, and the Propriety of Admitting them to the Elective Franchise, Consistently with the Principles of the Constitution, as Established at the Revolution (1792)', in *The Works of the Right Honourable Edmund Burke,* vol. 4. London: John Nimmo (1899), pp. 241–306.

Castiglione, D. and Warren, M. (2006) 'Rethinking democratic representation: Eight theoretical issues', paper presented at Rethinking Representation Conference, University of British Columbia, Vancouver, 18–19 May 2006.

Crane, T. (1995) 'Representation', in T. Hondrich (ed.), *The Oxford Companion to Philosophy.* Oxford: Oxford University Press.

Crouch, C. (2004) *Post-Democracy.* London: John Wiley & Sons.

Crum, B. (2008) 'The EU Constitutional Process: A failure of Political Representation?', *RECON Online Working Paper* 2008/08.

Dahl, R.A. (1970) *After the Revolution?* New Haven, CT: Yale University Press.

Dunn, J. (2005) *Setting the People Free: The Story of Democracy.* London: Atlantic Books.

Estlund, D. (2008) *Democratic Authority: A Philosophical Framework.* Princeton, NJ, and Oxford: Princeton University Press.

Eulau, H. (1978) 'Changing Views of Representation', in H. Eulau and J.C. Wahlke (eds), *The Politics of Representation: Continuities in Theory and Research.* Beverly Hills, CA, and London: Sage, pp. 31–54.

Forst, R. (2007) *Das Recht auf Rechtfertigung. Elemente einer konstruktivistischen Theorie der Gerechtigkeit.* Frankfurt am Main: Suhrkamp Verlag.

Griffiths, P.A. and Wollheim, R. (1960) 'How Can One Person Represent Another?', *Aristot Soc Suppl Vol.* 34(1), pp. 187–224.

Habermas, J. (1996) *Between Facts and Norms.* Cambridge: Polity.

Hare, T. (1873) quoted in Fairlie, J.A. (1968), 'Das Wesen politischer Repräsentation', in H. Rausch (ed.), *Zur Theorie und Geschichte der Repräsentation und Repräsentativverfassung.* Darmstadt: Wissenschaftliche Buchgesellschaft (1st edn 1940), pp. 28–73.

Heller, H. (1986 [1934]) *Staatslehre,* in der Bearbeitung von G. Niemeyer, 6th edn. Tübingen: Mohr.

Hobbes, T. (1968) *Leviathan.* London: Penguin.

Holmberg, S. (1999) 'Wishful Thinking among European Parliamentarians', in H.

Schmitt and J. Thomassen (eds), *Political Representation and Legitimacy in the European Union*. Oxford: Oxford University Press.

Jackson, J.E. and King, D.C. (1989) 'Public Goods, Private Interests, and Representation', *American Political Science Review* 83(4), pp. 1143–1164.

Kateb, G. (1994) *The Inner Ocean: Individualism and Democratic Culture*. Ithaca, NY, and London: Cornell University Press.

Kincaid, J. (1999) 'Confederal Federalism and Citizen Representation in the European Union', *West European Politics* 22(2), pp. 34–58.

Kuyper, J. (forthcoming 2016) 'Systemic Representation: Democracy, Deliberation, and Non-Electoral Representatives', *American Political Science Review*.

Leibholz, G. (1966) *Das Wesen der Repräsentation und der Gestaltwandel der Demokratie im 20. Jahrhundert*, 3rd edn. Berlin: Walter de Gruyter.

Lijphart, A. (1984) *Democracies: Patterns of Majoritarian and Consensus Government in Twenty-One Countries*. New Haven, CT: Yale University Press.

Mair, P. (2013) *Ruling the Void: The Hollowing of Western Democracy*. London: Verso.

Manin, B. (1997) *Principles of Representative Government*. Cambridge: Cambridge University Press.

Mansbridge, J. (2003) 'Rethinking Representation', *American Political Science Review* 97(4), pp. 515–528.

Mansbridge, J. (2005) 'The Fallacy of Tightening the Reins', *Sonderheft der Österreichischen Zeitschrift für Politikwissenschaft* 34(3), pp. 233–248.

Marsh, M. and Weßels, B. (1997) 'Territorial Representation', *European Journal of Political Research* 32(2), pp. 227–241.

Mill, J.S. (1972 [1861]) *Utilitarianism: On Liberty and Considerations on Representative Government*. London: Dent.

Pennock, J.R. (1979) *Democratic Political Theory*. Princeton, NJ: Princeton University Press.

Pitkin, H. (1967) *The Concept of Political Representation*. Berkeley, CA: University of California Press.

Przeworski, A., Stokes, S.C. and Manin, B. (eds) (1999) *Democracy, Accountability, and Representation*. Cambridge: Cambridge University Press.

Rawls, J. (2003) *Justice as Fairness: A Restatement*. Harvard, MA: Belknap Press, University of Harvard Press.

Rehfeld, A. (2005) 'Towards a General Theory of Political Representation', *Journal of Politics* 68(1), pp. 1–26.

Rogowski, R. (1981) 'Representation in Political Theory and in Law', *Ethics* 91(3), pp. 395–430.

Rokkan, S., Flora, P., Kuhle, S. and Unwin, D. (1999) *State Formation, Nation Building and Mass Politics in Europe*. Oxford: Oxford University Press.

Rosanvallon, P. (2007) *Democracy Past and Future*. Columbia, NY: Columbia University Press.

Rousseau, J.J. (2012 [1762]) *The Social Contract, or Principles of Political Right*, 2nd edn. London: Penguin.

Sartori, G. (1968) 'Representational Systems', in David L. Sills (ed.), *International Encyclopedia of the Social Sciences*. New York: Macmillan.

Saward, M. (2006) 'The Representative Claim', *Contemporary Political Theory* 5(3), pp. 297–318.

Saward, M. (2010) *The Representative Claim*. Oxford: Oxford University Press.

Saward, M. (2014) 'Shape-Shifting Representation', *American Political Science Review* 108(4), pp. 723–736.

Schattschneider, E.E. (1960) *The Semi-Sovereign People: A Realist View of Democracy in America*. New York: Holt.

Schmitt, E. (1969) *Repräsentation und Revolution. Eine Untersuchung zur Genesis der kontinentalen Theorie und Praxis parlamentarischer Repraesentation aus der Herrschaftspraxis des Ancien régime in Frankreich (1760–1789)*. Munich: Beck.

Schumpeter, J.A. (1942) *Capitalism, Socialism, and Democracy*. New York: Harper.

Schwartz, N.L. (1988) *The Blue Guitar: Political Representation and Community*. Chicago, IL: University of Chicago Press.

Sieyès, E.J. (1981 [1789]) 'Dire de l'abbé Sieyès sur la question du veto royal, 7.9.1789', in E. Schmitt and R. Reichardt (eds), *E.J. Sieyès, Politische Schriften 1788–1790*, 2nd edn. Vienna and Munich: Oldenbourg.

Smith, T. (2013 [1583]) *De Republica Anglorum: A Discourse on the Commonwealth of England*. Cambridge University Press.

Sterne, S. (1869) *Representative Government: Its Evils and Their Reform. A Lecture Delivered 1869, at the Invitation and under the Auspices of the Trustees of the Cooper Union*. New York: C.S. Wescott & Co.

Stimson, J.A., Mackuen, M.B. and Erikson, R.S. (1995) 'Dynamic Representation', *American Political Science Review* 89(3), pp. 543–565.

Streeck, W. (2014) *Buying Time: The Delayed Crisis of Democratic Capitalism*. London: Verso.

Tormey, S. (2015) *The End of Representative Politics*. London: Polity.

Urbinati, N. (2004) 'Condorcet's Democratic Theory of Representative Government', *European Journal of Political Theory* 3(1), pp. 53–75.

Voegelin, E. (1966) *The New Science of Politics*. Chicago, IL: University of Chicago Press.

Weale, A. (1999) *Democracy*. Basingstoke: Macmillan.

Weber, M. (1956) *Wirtschaft und Gesellschaft*, edited by J. Winckelmann, 4th edn. Tübingen: Mohr.

Webster, N. (1993 [1787]) 'A Citizen of America: An Examination into the Leading Principles of the Federal Constitution', reprinted in B. Bailyn (ed.), *The Debate on the Constitution. Federalist and Antifederalist Speeches, Articles, and Letters during the Struggle over Ratification. Part One: September 1787 to February 1788*. New York: The Library of America, pp. 129–163.

Weissberg, R. (1978) 'Collective vs. Dyadic Representation in Congress', *American Political Science Review* 72(2), pp. 535–547.

Young, I.M. (1997) 'Deferring Group Representation', in I. Shapiro and W. Kymlicka (eds), *Ethnicity and Group Rights, Nomos* XXXIX. New York: New York University Press, pp. 349–376.

1

Rethinking Representation
JANE MANSBRIDGE

A *long with the traditional "promissory" form of representation, empirical political scientists have recently analyzed several new forms, called here "anticipatory," "gyroscopic," and "surrogate" representation. None of these more recently recognized forms meets the criteria for democratic accountability developed for promissory representation, yet each generates a set of normative criteria by which it can be judged. These criteria are systemic, in contrast to the dyadic criteria appropriate for promissory representation. They are deliberative rather than aggregative. They are plural rather than singular.*

Over the past two decades empirical political scientists have developed increasingly sophisticated descriptions of how American legislators relate to their constituents. Yet although the empirical work has often been motivated by normative convictions that one way of relating is better than another, the normative theory of what constitutes "good" representation has not kept pace with current empirical findings. This paper seeks to narrow the gap.

The traditional model of representation focused on the idea that during campaigns representatives made promises to constituents, which they then kept or failed to keep. I call this *promissory representation*. In addition, empirical work in the last 20 years has identified at least three other forms of representation, which I call "anticipatory," "gyroscopic," and "surrogate" representation. *Anticipatory representation* flows directly from the idea of retrospective voting: Representatives focus on what they think their constituents will approve at the next election, not on what they promised to do at the last election. In *gyroscopic representation*, the representative looks within, as a basis for action, to conceptions of interest, "common sense," and principles derived in part from the representative's own background. *Surrogate representation* occurs when legislators represent constituents outside their own districts.

These are all legitimate forms of representation. None, however, meets the criteria for democratic accountability developed for promissory representation. I argue that the appropriate normative criteria for judg-

ing these more recently identified forms of representation are systemic, in contrast to the dyadic criteria appropriate for promissory representation. The criteria are almost all deliberative rather than aggregative. And, in keeping with the conclusion that there is more than one way to be represented legitimately in a democracy, the criteria are plural rather than singular.

The forms of representation identified here do not map well onto the traditional dichotomy of "mandate" and "trustee." Both mandate and trustee forms can appear as versions of promissory representation (or, alternatively, the trustee concept can figure as a subset of gyroscopic representation), but the new concepts of representation implied by recent empirical work do not have an obvious relation to the earlier dichotomy.

In practice, representative behavior will often mix several of these forms. One cannot always tell by looking at a specific behavior what dynamics lie behind it. Yet analyzing each form separately makes it possible to identify the underlying power relation in each form, the role of deliberation in each, and the normative criteria appropriate to each. These normative criteria are goals toward which to strive ("regulative ideals"), not standards that can be fully met. Conceiving of democratic legitimacy as a spectrum and not a dichotomy, one might say that the closer a system of representation comes to meeting the normative criteria for democratic aggregation and deliberation, the more that system is normatively legitimate.

Addressing the norms appropriate to a system of representation assumes that representation is, and is normatively intended to be, something more than a defective substitute for direct democracy.[1] Constituents choose representatives not only to think more carefully than they about ends and means but also to negotiate more perceptively and fight more skillfully than constituents have either the time or the inclination to do. The difference between representation and direct democracy creates a need for norms designed particularly for democratic representation. Yet democratic representation comes in different forms, with norms appropriate to each.

This paper has evolved over time. Most recently I am grateful for the suggestions of Douglas Arnold, David Brady, Martha Minow, Mark Moore, Dennis Thompson, and participants in seminars at Center for Advanced Study in the Behavioral Sciences, Princeton University, the University of California Los Angeles, Stanford University, and the University of Toronto. For excellent suggestions on earlier versions I thank William Bianco, Carol Swain, Melissa Williams, Iris Marion Young, and participants in seminars at the Institute of Governmental Studies at Berkeley, the Ohio State University, Nuffield College Oxford, Indiana University, Princeton University, the University of California San Diego, Harvard University, and Northwestern University. I particularly thank Benjamin Page for his close reading and incisive comments at an early stage, and the insightful reviewers for this journal. This paper, begun with support from the Institute for Policy Research at Northwestern University, was completed while the author was a Fellow at the Center for Advanced Study in the Behavioral Sciences. I am grateful for financial support provided by National Science Foundation Grant SBR-9601236.

---

[1] Although deliberative forms of direct democracy can be effective methods of democratic governance in many circumstances, representative forms of democracy have their own uses, functioning not just as "transmission belts" for constituent opinion (Schwartz 1988; see also Achen 1978, 476, Hibbings and Theiss-Morse 2002, Manin 1997, and Pitkin [1967] 1972).

515

REPRESENTATION

PROMISSORY REPRESENTATION

Promissory representation, the traditional model, follows the classic principal–agent format. The problem for the principal (in Bristol or Ohio) is one of keeping some control over the agent (in London or Washington). The problem in politics does not differ greatly from the problem of keeping any economic agent responsive to the desires of the principal. Economic history and theory have focused recently on the problem of long-distance trade when there was no governmental infrastructure to enforce contractual arrangements. In the Mediterranean in the fourteenth century, this situation necessitated either kinship ties or above-market payment rates to ensure that ships loaded with the surplus value of thousands of workers actually returned with the goods received in trade (see Greif 1993). When control (as in a seabound ship) or information (as in relations with an expert) is asymmetric, the problem for the principal is to make sure that the agent (the captain, the lawyer, the accountant) acts to further the interests of the principal (the merchant, the client). So too in political representation, both descriptive and normative writers have perceived the problem as one of the voters in a district keeping legal or moral control over their distant representatives. The normative understanding of accountability in promissory representation is that the representative is "responsible to," "answerable to," "bound," and even "bound by" those voters.[2] In the "mandate" version of the model, the representative promises to follow the constituents' instructions or expressed desires; in the "trustee" version the representative promises to further the constituency's long-run interests and the interests of the nation as a whole.

In promissory representation, the power relation from voter to representative, principal to agent, runs forward in linear fashion. By exacting a promise, the voter at Time 1 (the election) exercises power, or tries to exercise power, over the representative at Time 2 (the governing period):

$$V_{T1} \rightarrow R_{T2}.$$

Promissory representation thus uses the standard forward-looking concept of power, as in Robert Dahl's (1957) intuitive "A has power over B to the extent that he can get B to do something that B would not otherwise do" (202–203). Indeed, any definition of power derived, like Dahl's, from Weber ([1922] 1978, 53) will imply this kind of forward-looking intentionality. Dahl's "get" implies both that A acts with intention and that B's action will occur in the future. The power relation follows the simplest version of a principal-agent model, with the voter as principal, statically conceived, trying to exercise power over the representative as agent.[3]

Promissory representation works normatively through the explicit and implicit promises that the elected representative makes to the electorate. It works prudentially through the sanction the voter exercises at the next election (Time 3). That sanction is a reward or punishment for acting or failing to act according to the promise made at the previous election (Time 1). Both normatively and prudentially, the electoral audit at Time 3 focuses on whether or not the promises at Time 1 were kept. George Bush thus angered his supporters deeply by breaking an explicit campaign promise ("Read my lips: No new taxes").[4]

Promissory representation has the advantage that, at least in its more mandated versions, it reflects in a relatively unmediated manner the will (although not necessarily the considered will) of the citizenry. It comes closer than any other model to an ideal in which the simple imprint of the voter's will is transmitted through institutions to an equal exertion of power on the final policy. Although promissory representation has never described actual representation fully, it has been and remains today one of the most important ways in which citizens influence political outcomes through their representatives.

Promissory representation thus focuses on the normative duty to keep promises made in the authorizing election (Time 1), uses a conception of the voter's power over the representative that assumes forward-looking intentionality, embodies a relatively unmediated version of the constituent's will, and results in accountability through sanction.

How we conceive of representation begins to change, however, when we consider the implications of instituting a sanction at Time 3.

ANTICIPATORY REPRESENTATION

For more than a generation now, empirical political scientists have recognized the significance in the representative system of "retrospective voting," in which the voter looks back to the past behavior of a representative in deciding how to vote in the next election. Yet the normative implications of this way of looking at representation have not been fully explored. Returning to the model of promissory representation, it seems obvious that the power exercised in that model works through the voter's potential to vote a representative out of office at Time 3. This is "retrospective voting." From the representative's perspective, however, retrospective voting does more than provide the potential retribution for broken promises. It also

---

[2] See, e.g., Pitkin [1967] 1972, 55ff. Traditional accountability theory incorporates two analytically separable strands, usually intertwined. In the first, accountability means only that the representative has an obligation to explain ("give an account of") his or her past actions, regardless of the system of sanctioning (e.g., Behn 2001, 220 n. 12, and Guttman and Thompson 1996). The second focuses only on the capacity for imposing sanctions for past behavior (e.g. Manin, Przeworski, and Stokes 1999, 8–10). See Fearon 1999, 55, and Goodin 1999. This analysis employs the second meaning.

[3] Except when discussing Nagel's (1975) definition of power at its highest level of generality (see below p. 517), I mean by "power" here and elsewhere "coercive power," a subtype of Nagel's more general power. Coercive power, in contrast to "influence," involves either the threat of sanction or the use of force (see below p. 519 and footnote 8).

[4] I thank Douglas Arnold for this example. As Manin (1997) points out, however, no polity has ever legally compelled its representatives to abide by their electoral promises.

REPRESENTATION

generates what I call "anticipatory" representation, in which the representative tries to please future voters. Whereas in promissory representation the representative at Time 2 (the period in office) represents the voter at Time 1 (the authorizing election), in anticipatory representation the representative at Time 2 represents the voter at Time 3, the next election. [5]

In anticipatory representation, what appears to the representative to be a "power relation" thus works not forward, but "backward," through anticipated reactions, from the voter at Time 3 to the representative at Time 2:

$$R_{T2} \leftarrow V_{T3}.$$

Strictly speaking, the *beliefs* of the representative at Time 2 about the future preferences of the voter at Time 3, not the actual preferences of the voter at Time 3, are the cause of the representative's actions at Time 2. A later event cannot cause an earlier event. Indeed, the representative's beliefs may turn out to be mistaken. Nevertheless, from the perspective of the representative, the entity that exerts the sanction and thus the control appears to be the voter at Time 3.

The model of anticipatory representation thus requires a concept of power different from traditional, forward-looking, intention-based concepts such as Dahl's or Weber's. It requires a concept of power that can include "anticipated reactions." We find early formulations of this idea in the writings of Carl Friedrich (1937, 16–17, 1958, 1963, ch. 11), Peter Bachrach and Morton Baratz (1963), and Stephen Lukes (1974). The best formulation for the purposes of this analysis comes from Jack Nagel (1975, 29), who defined power, at the highest level of generality, as a "causal relation between the preferences of an actor regarding an outcome and the outcome itself." The neutrality of this definition in regard to intention and time make it compatible with anticipatory representation. Unlike Dahl's definition, Nagel's definition allows the anticipated preferences of the voter at Time 3 (that is, the representative's beliefs about those preferences) to cause the actions of the representative at Time 2.

Anticipatory representation directs empirical attention away from the relation between Time 1 (the authorizing election) and Time 2 (the representative's period of service), and toward the relations that arise between the beginning of Time 2 (the representative's period of service) and Time 3 (the next election). When preferences are stable over time, there is no important difference between the voter at Time 1 and Time 3 (Miller and Stokes 1963, 50; Nagel 1975, 24ff.) But when preferences are unstable or emergent, the representative has incentives to search during Time 2 for the characteristics of the voter at Time 3. Because this anticipation usu-

ally poses an extremely difficult information problem (Stimson, Mackuen, and Erikson 1995, 545), the search prompts attention to public opinion polls, focus groups, and gossip about the "mood of the nation" (Kingdon 1984, 153; Stimson, Mackuen, and Erikson 1995, 544). It also prompts attempts to change the voter at Time 3 so that the voter will be more likely to approve of the representative's actions.

This temporal shift has three implications for empirical description and analysis. First, the model becomes more deliberative. The space between Time 1 and Time 3 becomes filled with reciprocal attempts at the exercise of power and communication, much of it instigated by the representative:

$$R_{T2a} \leftrightarrow V_{T2a} \leftrightarrow R_{T2b} \leftrightarrow V_{T2b} \leftrightarrow \text{etc.} \leftrightarrow V_{T3}.$$

Second, anticipatory representation prompts attention to underlying interests as well as present preferences. Benjamin Page (1978, 221–22), for example, points out that a theory of democracy based on the representative's anticipation of reward and punishment "orients government responsiveness toward fundamental needs and values of the people rather than toward ephemeral or weakly held policy preferences." Douglas Arnold writes that the representative is better off thinking of the voters in the next election as having "outcome" preferences rather than "policy" preferences (1990, 17, 1993, 409). James Stimson (1995, 545) and his colleagues similarly argue that the information problem involved in rational anticipation encourages representatives to aim at general rather than specific knowledge. If we add to these formulations the idea that voters can change their preferences after thinking about them, we can find a place in empirical theory for the concept of "interests" (defined as enlightened preferences) in what would otherwise be a purely preference-oriented model of political behavior.[6]

Third, following from the first two points, anticipatory representation encourages us to think of voters at Time 3 as educable (or manipulable). Between Time 1 and Time 3 the voters can be "educated" not only by the representative, who seeks and prepares "explanations" of his votes (Fenno 1978; Kingdon 1981), but also—critical for the practice of democracy—by parties, interest groups, media, opposition candidates, and other citizens (Arnold 1990, 1993, 409; Kuklinski and Segura 1995, 15–16; Young 2001). (In the following diagram, groups, media, opposition and other citizens are all demarcated as "G" for "Groups." The arrow indicates both power and communication.)

---

[5] The concept of anticipatory representation is thus a corollary to the concept of retrospective voting (as in Fiorina 1981). With early formulations in Downs 1957, Key 1961, and Fiorina 1974, 32–33, 1977, 1981 (see Page 1978, 32), the concept of retrospective voting has now become standard in American empirical political science. For related views on anticipation, see Fiorina 1989, 5–6, Goodin 1999, Manin, Przeworski, and Stokes 1999, and Zaller 1994.

[6] In this analysis the preferences and interests into which deliberation should provide insight may be self-regarding, other-regarding, or ideal-regarding. I thus use the word "interest" in its American, rather than European, sense to include foundational (that is, identity-constituting) ideal-regarding commitments as well as material needs and wants. Because transforming identities transforms interests, interests can be seen both as "enlightened preferences" (with "enlightenment" seen as the product of experience and emotional understanding as well as of simple cognition) and as changeable and contested.

$$R_{T2a} \leftrightarrow V_{T2a} \leftrightarrow R_{T2b} \leftrightarrow V_{T2b} \leftrightarrow \text{etc.} \leftrightarrow V_{T3}$$
$$G_{T2a} \leftrightarrow G_{T2ab} \leftrightarrow G_{T2b}$$

Arnold (1993), Stimson et al. (1995), and others have drawn the attention of empirical political scientists to this form of representation. They have done so, however, without emphasizing its deliberative side. Arnold's "alternative control model," which otherwise describes well the process I call "anticipatory representation," does not fully capture the crucial elements of continuing communication and potentially changing voter preferences. Arnold (1993, 410) describes citizens in the model statically, as acting "more like spectators who register their approval or disapproval at the end of a performance." Yet Arnold (1993) himself recognizes that anticipatory representation can be intensely interactive with citizens when he notes that legislators "learn from interest groups, committee hearings, staff members, and other legislators about the policy consequences and the political consequences of specific decisions" (412). Interest groups and committee hearings are both institutions by which citizens communicate their evolving interests and opinions (although not without intervening biases introduced by the selection and medium of communication).

Arnold also describes legislators statically, as "controlled agents." Although he is right in saying the legislators are not "instructed delegates," his phrase "controlled agents" does not capture the legislators' role as potential initiators and educators. In contrast, the model of anticipatory representation is in most instances interactive and more continually reflexive. Anticipatory representation derives from a marketplace model, which Arnold (1993, 412) himself adopts when he writes that "movie makers, auto makers, and real estate developers attempt to anticipate and satisfy consumers' preferences." In the marketplace, customers are not mere "spectators"; nor are entrepreneurs "controlled agents." Rather, customers actively (if not intentionally) exert power and influence on the marketplace, and entrepreneurs too are active, in searching out and sometimes even creating preferences. Like the customer/entrepreneur relation in the marketplace, the voter/representative relation in anticipatory representation is best conceived as one of reciprocal power and continuing mutual influence.

The temporal shift produced by anticipatory representation has parallel implications for normative theory. Most prominently, it undermines the traditional understanding of accountability. It therefore demands new normative criteria in its place.

The traditional concept of accountability, focusing on the relationship between Time 1 and Time 2, asks whether the representative is doing what the statically conceived constituent wanted the representative to do at Time 1. By substituting the voter at Time 3 for the voter at Time 1, anticipatory representation makes the voter at Time 1 irrelevant. If we think of the representative as an entrepreneur, anticipating future customers' preferences, the forces that make the representative "accountable" are all forward looking. Yet it would seem strange to say that the representative was accountable to the voter at Time 3.

The argument that anticipatory representation undermines traditional notions of accountability will seem counterintuitive, because, of all the models I introduce here, anticipatory representation is most intimately related to those traditional notions. The desire for reelection is usually, and quite reasonably, interpreted as simply a mechanism for insuring the fidelity of the representative to the voter's wishes, making no distinction between the voter at Time 1 and the voter at Time 3. Indeed, if the voter at Time 3 does not differ from the voter at Time 1, then we can think of the voter at Time 3 as simply doling out the reward or punishment to enforce the power relation in promissory representation.

Most theorists and most members of the public still envision representation through the traditional model of promissory representation, in which the voter's power works forward and the representative's attention looks backward. The public's advocacy of term limits, for example, adopts this static feature of the traditional model. The voters fear that the farther away the representative gets from home, literally and figuratively, the weaker the tether that holds that representative to them. The voters want their "hooks" in the representative to be strong. In the intensity of that desire, they seem willing to forgo the reelection incentive. Their implicit calculus seems not to include the incentives built into Time 3.

But the shift in temporal emphasis in anticipatory representation brings unexpected normative changes in its wake. To the degree that we think of the legislator as representing the voter at Time 3, we turn the legislator into a Shumpeterian entrepreneur, motivated to try to attract the votes of future customers. As we have seen, in this conception, strictly speaking, the traditional principal–agent model disappears. We do not think of an economic entrepreneur as an agent, with the future customers as principals. A representative trying to anticipate the desires of voters at Time 3 has a prudential, not a moral, relationship to those voters. To the degree that the representative wants to be reelected, he or she will see pleasing the voters (and funders) at Time 3 as the means to that end. Whereas in traditional accountability, we would say that the representative "ought" to do what he or she had promised the voters at Time 1, we do not say that the representative "ought" to try to please the voters at Time 3. In this respect, purely prudential incentives have replaced a combined moral and prudential imperative.

Replacing morality with prudence in the incentive structure of anticipatory representation leads us to judge the process with new normative criteria. It makes us shift our normative focus from the individual to the system, from aggregative democracy to deliberative democracy, from preferences to interests, from the way the legislator votes to the way the legislator communicates, and from the quality of promise-keeping to the quality of mutual education between legislator and constituents.

Anticipatory representation forces normative theory to become systemic. In most anticipatory

REPRESENTATION

representation, the better the communication between voter and representative in the interval between Time 1 and Time 3, the better the representation. A representative could in theory accurately anticipate the desires of the voter at Time 3 without any mutual communication. In practice, representatives usually initiate and welcome the opportunity to communicate with voters, both to anticipate their preferences at Time 3 and to influence them. The quality of that mutual communication then depends only in small part on the dyadic efforts of the representative and the constituent. It depends much more on the functioning of the entire representative process—including political parties, political challengers, the media, interest groups, hearings, opinion surveys, and all other processes of communication. Each of these has important functions in an overall process of what might be called "continuing representation." Normative theory should ask, and empirical political science should try to answer, how well the entire representative system contributes to ongoing factually accurate and mutually educative communication (see Williams 1998 and Young 2000, 128, 130 on interaction; Thompson 1988 on representation over time).

Focusing on the changes in voter and representative between Time 1 and Time 3 also underlines the deliberative function of representation. Recognizing that the representative's initiatives have the potential to change as well as to anticipate voters at Time 3, normative theorists should be able to help empirical political scientists ask whether those changes are best described as "education" or "manipulation."[7]

Manipulation may be distinguished by the intent to deceive or create conditions of choice leading others to make a choice not in their interests (see Lukes 1974). Beyond nonmanipulation, the quality of education can be judged by the deliberative criteria of whether the mutual interaction between Time 1 and Time 3 makes the voters at Time 3 (1) more or less aware of their underlying interests and the policy implications of those interests and (2) more or less able to transform themselves in ways that they will later consider good (including, when appropriate, becoming more concerned with the common interest).

Education, in short, is a form of what I will call "influence" and manipulation a form of what I will call "coercive power." Within Nagel's broad understanding of power as preferences causing outcomes, we may distinguish analytically between these two forms. Influence, marked by (relatively) common interests on the issue between influencer and influenced, is exercised through arguments on the merits. Coercive power, marked (except in paternalism) by a conflict of interest between power exerciser and recipient, has two subtypes: "The threat of sanction," which involves the will of the actor subject to power, and "force," which includes not only physical force but any structuring of alternatives that

constrains the choices of the actor subject to power regardless of that actor's will. "Education" may be conceived as a form of influence, as it works through arguments on the merits and is by definition in the recipients' interests. "Manipulation" may be conceived as a form of force, as it occurs, by definition, against the recipients' interests without their recognizing characteristics of the situation that might have led them to take another action.[8] None of these forms of power is easy to operationalize, because their definitions involve contests over what is and what is not in an individual's interests.

Normative theorists are currently working to define the appropriate standards for the use of coercive power and influence. Regarding coercive power, the normative theory appropriate for aggregative models of democracy mandates that each voter's preferences should have roughly equal coercive power over the outcome. In deliberation, in contrast, the ideal is the absence of coercive power.[9] In deliberation, influence can legitimately be highly unequal (at least under conditions in which the unequal exercise of influence does not undermine a rough equality of respect among participants, foreclose further opportunities to exercise equal power, or deny any of the participants the opportunity to grow through participation). Knight and Johnson (1998) argue convincingly for an ideal of "equal opportunity of access to political influence" in democratic deliberation. But even that ideal is a default position, holding *unless* good reasons can be given for unequal access to influence. In formal representation, for example, citizens for good reasons place the representative in a position of greater potential influence and coercive power than most constituents. When a representative uses that greater coercive power in a deliberation, e.g., to set the agenda, that act is not automatically normatively wrong (as suggested by both ideals of equal access to influence and absence of coercive power) but should be judged by the three criteria, appropriate to deliberation, of nonmanipulation, illuminating interests, and facilitating retrospectively approvable transformation.

Unfortunately for analyses that try to be purely "objective," questions regarding voters' interests, in contrast to their preferences, are not susceptible to certain

---

[7] Cf. Jacobs and Shapiro 2000. "Education" in this context intrinsically requires distinguishing what people actually want from what they ought to want (and therefore should be "educated" to want) with regard to both means and ends.

[8] See Bachrach and Baratz 1963 and Lukes 1974. These stipulative definitions, useful analytically, do not encompass all of the ordinary meanings of these terms. In this section, in order to avoid confusion with Nagel's broad definition of power, I have labeled "coercive power" what elsewhere in the paper (along with many others) I simply call "power." This analysis omits any discussion of positive incentives, which pose a thorny problem of categorization in these terms (see, e.g., Barry [1975] 1991 and Nozick 1972). For other interpretations of power, see, e.g., Wartenberg 1990.

[9] For the aggregative ideal of equal coercive power (a regulatory ideal that cannot be reached in practice), see, e.g., Lively 1975 and Mansbridge [1980] 1983 (but cf. Beitz 1989). For the deliberative ideal of absence of (coercive) power, see, e.g., Habermas [1984] 1990, 235. (This regulatory ideal also cannot be reached in practice, because no exercise of influence can be separated fully from the exercise of coercive power, which will always affect the background conditions of the discussion, the capacities of those in the discussion, and the implementation of the decision.)

26

REPRESENTATION

resolution. They are "essentially contested" (Gallie 1962). They are nevertheless the right questions to ask. These questions force the observer to consider whether the process of mutual communication with the representative deepens the base on which the voters' preferences rest, or instead introduces misleading considerations or emphases that, given adequate information and the time for adequate reflection, the voters would reject.

At the moment, the existing representative apparatus in the United States does not facilitate well the processes of mutual education, communication, and influence. For example, when William Bianco (1994, 51) asked members of Congress whether they thought they could explain to their constituents a vote (against the repeal of Catastrophic Coverage for health insurance) that they considered a vote for good public policy, many found that their attempts at education only made their constituents angry.[10] In this case, some constituents (whose private policies covered much of what the bill would provide) had far greater access to influence than others. Some political entrepreneurs deceived the public, probably intentionally (King and Scott 1995). Critically, representatives had neither the political space nor the time to explain their reasoning to their constituents and be educated in turn. The citizens did not have forums in which they could discuss together all aspects of the matter. The deliberative process thus fell far short of meeting not only the criteria of equal opportunity for access to influence and nonmanipulation but also the criteria of interest clarification and (less relevantly here) retrospectively approvable transformation, which might have justified unequal access.

In the case of Catastrophic, political parties, the media, and the relevant interest groups played only minor roles in rectifying distortions in the process of representation. Yet in a polity the size of the United States, these intermediaries play a crucial role in the larger system of representation. By emphasizing the distance between the representative and the voter, the traditional model of promissory representation puts little weight on the quality of communication between the two. In contrast, the incentive structure behind anticipatory representation has created an entire apparatus of opinion polling, focus group, and interest group activity that deserves closer normative scrutiny. Rather than treating opinion polls and focus groups as tools of manipulation and interest groups as no more than the tool of "special interests," an empirical analysis driven by appropriate normative concerns should ask how well these institutions, along with opposition candidates, political parties, and the media, avoid the biases of unequally funded organizational forms and how well they serve the nor-

matively worthy purposes of mutual communication and education.[11] Such a focus would inevitably draw one away from the dyadic representative–constituent relation and toward the larger system of multi-actor, continuing representation.

In short, if in anticipatory representation the representative simply anticipated the preferences of the voter at Time 3 and made no move to change those preferences, the aggregative norms of equal power per voter that underlie the promissory model would need no supplementation. But if, as seems to be the case in almost all actual instances, representatives use their power and influence to affect the preferences of voters at Time 3, the norms of good deliberation must come into play, and we must ask whether the criteria of nonmanipulation, interest clarification and retrospectively approvable transformation that justify unequal access to influence are being met or at least approached.

Anticipatory representation thus focuses on the prudential incentive to please the voter in the next election (Time 3), uses a conception of the voter's power over the representative that allows anticipated reactions, replaces the constituent's transmission of will with the representative's desire to please, and shifts normative scrutiny from the process of accountability to the quality of deliberation throughout the representative's term in office.

GYROSCOPIC REPRESENTATION

I have given the label "gyroscopic representation" to a conception of representation that not only differs from, but is to some degree incompatible with, anticipatory representation. Others have called this representation by "recruitment" (Kingdon 1981, 45), by "initial selection" (Bernstein 1989), or by "electoral replacement" (Stimson et al. 1995).[12] In this model of representation, voters select representatives who can be expected to act in ways the voter approves *without* external incentives. The representatives act like gyroscopes, rotating on their own axes, maintaining a certain direction, pursuing certain built-in (although not fully immutable) goals. As in the other new models of representation introduced here, these representatives are not accountable to their electors in the traditional sense. In this case, the representatives act only for "internal" reasons. Their accountability is only to their own beliefs and principles.

This model can take several forms. In all forms the representative looks within, for guidance in taking action, to a contextually derived understanding of interests, interpretive schemes ("common sense"),

---

[10] See also other examples in Bianco 1994, 50, and Kingdon 1981, 48 (e.g.: "Very frankly, if I had a chance to sit down with all of my constituents for 15 minutes and talk to them, I'd have voted against the whole thing. But I didn't have that chance. They wanted [x]. If I voted against it, it would appear to them that I was against [x], and I wouldn't have had a chance to explain myself.) Richard Fenno concurs: "... If education is a home activity that by definition has to hurt a little [in asking people to change their minds], then I did not see a great deal of it" (1978, 162; Bianco 1994, 51).

[11] Taking these intermediary institutions seriously as vehicles of mutual learning suggests expanding and enhancing the interest group universe in ways that increase political equality (see, e.g., Cohen and Rogers 1995, Crosby 1995, Dahl 1997, Fishkin 1991, 1995, 1996, Nagel 1992, and Schmitter 1995).

[12] Miller and Stokes 1963 (50) also described their "first" means of constituency control as "for the district to choose a Representative who so shares its views that in following his own convictions he does his constituents' will." Their second means was a form of anticipatory representation.

conscience, and principles. In the United States, a voter may select the narrowest version of the type, dedicated to a single issue such as the legalization of abortion. Or a voter may select the broadest version, a person of integrity with a commitment to the public good. In general, people often try to select what Fearon (1999, 68) calls a "good type," with the characteristics of (1) having similar policy preferences to the voter, (2) being honest and principled, and (3) being sufficiently skilled. They explain their choices, for example, with the phrase, "He's a good man" or "She's a good woman" (Fenno 1978, 55; Miller and Stokes 1963, 54).

Character, including adherence to principle, is an important feature on which voters select. But it is not the only feature. In the United States, voters also use descriptive characteristics, along with party identification and indicators of character, as cues by which to predict the representative's future behavior (Popkin 1994). Legislators themselves often adopt this understanding of representation, seeing themselves as having an attitudinal identity with a majority of their constituents (Bianco 1994, 39; Fenno 1978, 115; Kingdon 1981, 45–47). Thus the two principal features that Fearon (1999) enunciates, of having policy preferences similar to the constituent's and being honest and principled, are analytically separable but entwined in practice, because similar policy preferences will not suffice if the representative can be bribed.[13]

In the "party discipline" models characteristic of much of Europe, representatives look within to a set of principles and commitments that derive partly from their own ideals and partly from their commitment to the collective decisions of the party. The representative is also subject to party sanctions for not obeying the party, and the party in turn is subject to sanctions from the voters. I focus here only on the model of gyroscopic representation that prevails in the United States.

In all versions of gyroscopic representation, the voters affect political outcomes not by affecting the behavior of the representative ("inducing preferences," as in promissory or anticipatory representation), but by selecting and placing in the political system representatives whose behavior is to some degree predictable in advance based on their observable characteristics. Whereas in promissory and anticipatory representation the representative's preferences are induced, in this model the representative's preferences are internally determined. Whereas in promissory and anticipatory representation the voters (at Time 1 or Time 3) cause changes in the representative's behavior, in gyroscopic representation the voters cause outcome changes first in the legislature and more distantly in the larger polity not by changing the direction of the representative's behavior but by placing in the legislature and larger polity

(the "system") the active, powerful element constituted by this representative. The voters thus have power not over the representative, but over the system:

$$V_{T1} \rightarrow SYSTEM_{T2}.$$

In this form of representation, the representative does not have to conceive of him or herself, in Pitkin's ([1967] 1972) terms, as "acting for" the constituent, at either Time 1 or Time 3. The motivations of the representative can remain a black box. The voter selects the representative based on predictions of the representative's future behavior derived from past behavior and other cues. We may envision the candidates vying for election as a set of self-propelled and self-directed thinking, feeling and acting machines, from which the voter selects one to place in the system. After the selection, the self-propelled machine need have no subsequent relation to the voter. The key to the voter–representative relationship in this model is thus not traditional accountability but deep predictability, in the sense of predicting an inner constellation of values that is, in important respects, like the constituent's own. In some electoral systems, the political party is often far more predictable and easier for voters to relate to their own interests than are individual politicians. In the United States, a politician's personal reputation, descriptive characteristics, and character (as the voters judge it) provide deep predictability above and beyond the predictor of party identification.

In the United States, gyroscopic representation forms a relatively large part of the representative process. As John Kingdon (1981, 45) writes, "The simplest mechanism through which constituents can influence a congressman is to select a person initially for the office who agrees with their attitudes." Approximately three-quarters of the time Kingdon (1981, 45) found no conflict between what a majority of the constituency wanted and the personal attitudes of their member of Congress. Gyroscopic representation (or representation by recruitment) could therefore comprise as much as three-quarters of the dynamic of representation in the United States Congress. Robert Bernstein (1989) agrees with this assessment, dubbing the prevailing fixation on what I call promissory representation and anticipatory representation "the myth of constituency control." In the most elegant analysis to date, Stimson et al. (1995) provide data suggesting that in the United States Senate and presidency, gyroscopic representation (their "electoral replacement") is the most important mechanism by which the representatives respond to public opinion changes. In the House of Representatives, their data suggest, the most important mechanism is anticipatory representation (their "rational anticipation").

Like anticipatory representation, gyroscopic representation has some ties to the traditional form of accountability postulated in promissory representation, but there are also crucial differences. In gyroscopic representation, the representatives do have a normative responsibility to their constituents not to lie about the characteristics on which they are being selected at

---

[13] Fearon's "good type" thus differs subtly from the virtuous and wise representative whom James Madison (along with James Wilson and many other Federalists) wanted selected (Manin 1997, 116–19), in being based more on similarity in preferences than on a universalistic understanding of and commitment to the public good. In emphasizing voters selecting on virtuous character, Brennan and Hamlin (1999, 2000) also omit similarity in preferences or interests. See also Lott 1987, 183.

election time. But in the gyroscopic model the deeper accountability of the representatives is to themselves or (particularly in electoral systems outside the United States) to the political party with which they identify. They are not expected to relate to their constituents as agents to principals. As Kingdon (1981, 46) puts it, in this model the member of congress "never even takes [the constituency] into account." Or, as Fearon (1999, 56) writes, "electoral accountability is not necessary." The fiduciary component to the relation is weak. The tether to the voter at Time 1 is almost nonexistent.

Gyroscopic representation also differs from Burke's "trustee" form of representation. Burke ([1774] 1889) envisioned the representative as a statesman, concerned with interests rather than mere preferences and with the interests of the entire nation rather than the district.[14] Yet in gyroscopic representation, the voter may select a representative only because both voter and representative share some overriding self-interested goal, such as lowering taxes. Or the voter may select a representative with many of the voter's own background characteristics, on the grounds that such a representative will act much the way the voter would if placed in the legislature. The point for the voter is only to place in the system a representative whose self-propelled actions the voter can expect to further the voter's own interests. Burke's "trustee" conception thus comprises one subset within the larger concept of gyroscopic representation.

The gyroscopic model does resemble Burke's trustee conception in one important respect. Having decided that the representative already wants, for internal reasons, to pursue much the same course as the one the voter wants, the voter often expects the representative (or the party) to act with considerable discretion in the legislature. This expectation opens the door to creative deliberation and negotiation at the legislative level. Compromises, changes of heart, and even the recasting of fundamental interests are all normatively permitted.

As we have seen, traditional accountability is irrelevant in the gyroscopic model. In the pure form of the model, as Kingdon points out, the representative never takes the constituency into account and is not expected to do so. The quality of ongoing communication between representative and constituent is also irrelevant. In the pure form of the model, as Kingdon also points out, the ongoing communication between the representative and the constituent can, even ideally, be nil. The normative process of judging this form of representation thus requires criteria that differ from those of traditional accountability.

One critical criterion, deliberation at authorization, requires normatively estimating the quality of deliberation among constituents and representatives before and at Time 1, the authorizing election. Good deliberation at this moment would result in voters achieving

both developed understandings of their own interests and accurate predictions of their chosen representatives' future behaviors. Good deliberation requires that representatives not intentionally deceive the public as to their future behavior. The voter's aim is to discern and select on the criterion of commonality of interests between the representative and the constituent (see Bianco 1996).

A second criterion, ease of maintenance and removal, requires that the voters be able at periodic intervals to reenter the system, either perpetuating its current direction by maintaining their self-propelled representatives in office or changing that direction by removing one representative and inserting another. Term limits, which make sense in a model of promissory representation, make little sense either for anticipatory representation or for gyroscopic representation. Term limits make it impossible to maintain one's chosen representative in the system.

In short, the normative criteria appropriate for gyroscopic representation are good systemwide deliberation at the time of selection (the authorizing election) and relative ease in maintaining one's selected representative in office or removing that representative and placing another in the system. Gyroscopic representation stresses the representative's own principles and beliefs, sees the voter as having power not over the representative but over the system (by inserting the representative in that system), and shifts normative scrutiny from traditional accountability to the quality of deliberation in the authorizing election.

SURROGATE REPRESENTATION

Surrogate representation is representation by a representative with whom one has no electoral relationship—that is, a representative in another district. As with the other forms of representation, I am not the first to notice the importance of this kind of representation in the United States today. Robert Weissberg described it in 1978 as "collective representation," and John Jackson and David King in 1989 called something similar "institutional" representation. Edmund Burke had a version he called "virtual" representation, but Burke's concept focused on morally right answers, wisdom rather than will, relatively fixed and objective interests, and the good of the whole, which is only one of many possible goals for surrogate representation.[15]

In the United States today, individuals and interest groups representing individuals often turn to surrogate representatives to help advance their substantive interests, including their ideal-regarding interests. A member of Congress from Minnesota, for example, may lead the Congressional opposition to a war opposed by significant numbers of voters in Missouri and Ohio whose own representatives support the war. The situation has changed from the time when territorial representation

---

[14] For a standard interpretation, see Miller and Stokes 1963, 45: "Burke wanted the representative to serve the constituency's *interest* but not its *will*" (emphasis in original). More fully, see Pitkin [1967] 1972.

[15] Burke [1792] 1871. Pitkin ([1967] 1972, 174ff) discusses these and other ways in which Burke's concept of virtual representation differs from modern concepts. For a related concept, see Gutmann and Thompson 1996, 144ff. on 'moral constituents.'

REPRESENTATION

captured many of a voter's most significant interests, but in the United States the representational system has not changed with it. In the United States, surrogate representation—a noninstitutional, informal, and chance arrangement—is the preeminent form of nonterritorial representation.

For the affluent (or the organized, e.g., through labor unions), surrogate representation is greatly enhanced by the possibility of contributing to the campaigns of representatives from other districts. Individual candidates, political parties, and many other political organizations as a matter of course solicit funds from outside their districts. Citizens with ample discretionary income find many of their most meaningful instances of legislative representation through what one might call "monetary surrogacy."

Surrogate representation, both state- and nationwide, plays the normatively critical role of providing representation to voters who lose in their own district. Because both federal and state electoral systems use single member districts, with first-past-the-post, winner-take-all majority elections, citizens whose preferred policies attract a minority of voters in their own districts could theoretically end up with no representation at all in the legislature. Yet with sufficient geographic clustering, the interests and perspectives that lose in one district will win in another, so that voters in the minority in District A will have surrogate representation through the representative of District B. In electoral systems structured this way, the accidental supplement to existing institutions provided by surrogate representation is crucial to democratic legitimacy. As we shall see, if serendipity did not produce enough surrogate representation to meet systemic criteria for legitimacy, the electoral system as a whole would not withstand normative scrutiny.

In the kind of surrogate representation that is not anchored in money or other contributions ("pure" surrogate representation), there is no relation of accountability between the representative and the surrogate constituent. Nor is there a power relation between surrogate constituent and representative:

$$V_{TI} \to 0.$$

The only power relation (in the sense of the threat of sanction or the use of force) arises between those who contribute money or other goods and the representatives to whose campaigns they contribute. In a relation of monetary or contributing surrogacy, the contributor exerts power through exacting promises as in traditional representation, through anticipated reactions as in anticipatory representation, and through placing in the system a legislator who will predictably act in certain ways as in gyroscopic representation. Because all the power that is exercised in any surrogate representation works through monetary or other contributions and through contributors rather than voters, surrogate representation in the United States today embodies far more political inequality than does even the traditional legislator–constituent relation.

Yet even without the fear of losing monetary or other contributions, and without any formal accountability, surrogate representatives sometimes *feel* responsible to their surrogate constituents in other districts. Legislators deeply allied with a particular ideological perspective often feel a responsibility to nondistrict constituents from that perspective or group.

That sense of surrogate responsibility becomes stronger when the surrogate representative shares experiences with surrogate constituents in a way that a majority of the legislature does not. Representatives who are female, African American, or of Polish ancestry, who have a child with a disability, or who have grown up on a farm, in a mining community, or in a working-class neighborhood, often feel not only a particular sensitivity to issues relating to these experiences but also a particular responsibility for representing the interests and perspectives of these groups, even when members of these groups do not constitute a large fraction of their constituents. Feelings of responsibility for constituents outside one's district grow even stronger when the legislature includes few, or disproportionately few, representatives of the group in question.[16]

Representative Barney Frank, a Democrat from Massachusetts, consciously sees himself as a surrogate representative for gay and lesbian citizens throughout the nation. Frank, who is himself openly gay, has a sympathetic district constituency: "My constituents at home understand my position. Issues concerning gay and lesbian discrimination are important to me." He points out that he is able to play this role because it does not take a great deal of time and therefore does not detract much from what he does for his district. Frank takes his surrogate responsibilities seriously. He believes that his surrogate constituents nationwide "know I understand their concerns. ... I have a staff with three openly gay, talented lawyers who feel committed to helping this problem at large."[17] He receives mail from gay and lesbian citizens across the nation "regarding their concerns about gay rights and discrimination," and he feels a special responsibility to that group, because he is one of the few openly gay members of Congress. In his case, this sense of responsibility is increased because the constituents who write him from around the nation are often not in a position, due to prejudice against them, to become politically active on their own.[18]

The relation of a surrogate representative with surrogate constituents can also be somewhat deliberative.

---

[16] For African American members of Congress see, e.g., Swain 1993, 218; for women see, e.g., Carroll 2002; Congressional Quarterly 1983, 76; Dodson et al. 1995, 15 21; Thomas 1994, 74; and Williams 1998, 141. For the political psychological effects of belonging to a group, see Conover 1988. For increased feelings of responsibility in the absence of other potentially responsible actors, see Latane and Darley 1970. For more on norms of "descriptive" representation, see Mansbridge 1999, Phillips 1995, and Williams 1998. The feelings of responsibility grow particularly strong when the disproportionately small number of descriptive representatives can be traced to past or present acts of injustice against the group.

[17] Interview with Representative Barney Frank, April 14, 1997, in DiMarzio 1997.

[18] Personal communication from Barney Frank, May 15, 1998.

30

REPRESENTATION

In addition to their contributions of money, in-kind services, and volunteer time, which foster a form of power relation, groups represented in surrogate fashion may provide information and expertise. (The moral approbation or disapproval that they also provide may be conceived in part as information and in part as an exercise of power.) Surrogate representatives may consult with group members, particularly those who have some formal or informal claim to represent others of the group, so that information and insights flow both ways.

Although dyadic, district-based, representative–constituent accountability is completely absent in pure surrogate representation, we can nevertheless develop normative criteria to judge the degree to which, on a systemic basis, that surrogate representation meets democratic standards. The most obvious criterion is that the legislature as a whole should represent the interests and perspectives of the citizenry roughly in proportion to their numbers in the population. But to this larger criterion we must enter certain caveats.

First, the aggregative aims of democracy require that the most conflictual interests be those on which most effort is made to achieve proportionality in representation. When interests conflict in ways that cannot be reconciled by deliberation, the Anglo-American theory of democracy that has evolved since the seventeenth century rests the fairness of the conflict-resolving procedure on some approximation to equal coercive power among the parties. The norm of "one person/one vote" implies the equal individual power of a vote in a direct democracy and equal proportional power in a representative democracy. The more important the conflict, the more vital becomes a proportional representation of the relevant interests.

Second, the deliberative aims of democracy require that the perspectives most relevant to a decision be represented in key decisions. Such perspectives do not necessarily need to be presented by a number of legislators proportional to the number of citizens who hold those perspectives.[19] The goal is to produce the best insights and the most relevant information, through mutual influence, which in deliberation may legitimately be unequal, not through coercive power, which ideally should be absent.

Deliberative goals may also justify some of the inequality currently characteristic of surrogate and other forms of representation. When the deliberative mechanisms built into an electoral system work well, they should select, through "the force of the better argument," against, at the very least, the least informed political positions in the polity. Accordingly, the representatives in the legislature who advocate these positions should be fewer proportionately than the number of citizens who hold that position. Good deliberation should work through the electoral process as well as through other processes of mutual education to winnow out the least informed ideas, leaving the best in active contest.[20]

The current surrogate selection process in the United States departs significantly from the democratic standard. Although existing electoral systems do to some degree select the best ideas, surrogate systems, even more than direct elections, select primarily for the best financed ideas and interests. In the United States inequalities of this sort are often justified on the grounds that they reflect freedom of "speech," as conveyed through monetary contribution. But unequal contributions to surrogate representatives are, I would argue, not justified on the grounds of either adversary fairness (providing proportional representation to conflicting interests) or deliberative efficacy (providing some representation for relevant perspectives on a decision).[21]

The normative questions to be asked with regard to surrogate representation differ from the questions posed by traditional accountability. In surrogate representation, legislators represent constituencies that did not elect them. They cannot therefore be accountable in traditional ways. As in gyroscopic representation, the legislators act to promote their surrogate constituencies' perspectives and interests for various reasons internal to their own convictions, consciences, and identities. Or they act to assure the continuous flow of dollars into their campaigns. The normative question for surrogate representation is not, therefore, whether representatives accurately reflect the current opinions or even the underlying interests of the members of their constituencies. Rather, it is whether, in the aggregate, each conflicting interest has proportional adversary representation in a legislative body (Weissberg 1978, esp. 542) and each important perspective has adequate deliberative representation. Such a normative analysis must involve a contest regarding what interests most conflict (and therefore most deserve proportional representation) in aggregation and what perspectives count as important in deliberation.[22]

In short, surrogate representation must meet the criteria for proportional representation of interests on relatively conflictual issues (an aggregative criterion) and adequate representation of perspectives on matters of both conflict and more common interest (a deliberative criterion). Surrogate representation thus focuses not on the dyadic relation between representative and constituent but on the systemwide composition of

---

[19] Kymlicka 1993, 77–78, 1995, 146–47, Phillips 1995, 47, 67ff, and Pitkin [1967] 1972, 84, point out that deliberation generally requires only a "threshold" presence of each perspective to contribute to the larger understanding. Important exceptions to this general rule come when greater numbers guarantee a hearing, produce deliberative synergy, or facilitate divergences, interpretations, and shades of meaning within a perspective (Mansbridge 1999). The underlying criterion remains, however, the contribution a perspective can make to the decision rather than strict proportionality.

[20] For "the force of the better argument," see Habermas [1977] 1984, 22ff, summarized in Habermas [1984] 1990, 235. One would expect good deliberation also to reduce or even eliminate the least moral positions in the polity. The normative issues raised by what one might call "deliberative winnowing," with its tension between respecting "remainders" (Honig 1993) and provisionally recognizing some arguments as better than others, require fuller discussion elsewhere.

[21] For a supporting argument, see Sunstein 1990.

[22] A deliberation among all potentially affected participants, marked by a minimal intrusion of power and by better rather than worse arguments, should ideally decide which interests most conflict and which perspectives are most crucial.

REPRESENTATION

TABLE 1. Forms of Representation

	Promissory	Anticipatory	Gyroscopic	Surrogate
Focus	Authorizing election	Reelection and preceding term	Authorizing election	Composition of legislature
Direction of voter power	Over the representative (forward looking)	Over the representative ("backward" looking)	Over the system	None for voters; only for contributors
Normative criteria	Keeping promises	Quality of rep/constituent deliberation during term	Quality of deliberation during authorizing election	1. Representation of conflicting interests in proportion to numbers in population
			Ease of selection, maintenance, and removal	2. Significant representation of important perspectives
Traditional accountability	Yes	No	No	No

the legislature, sees the represented as exercising no power over either the representative or the system except when the represented makes a (usually monetary) contribution to the representative, and shifts normative scrutiny from constituent-oriented accountability to systemic inequities in representation.

DELIBERATIVE, SYSTEMIC, AND PLURAL NORMATIVE CRITERIA

Table 1 summarizes some of the characteristics of these different forms of representation.[23] When empirical political scientists want to answer the question of how well a political system meets democratic norms, they need a democratic theory that will clarify those norms in ways that make it easier to tell when real-world situations conform to or violate them. In the field of United States legislative studies, the democratic norms regarding representation have often been reduced to one criterion: Does the elected legislator pursue policies that conform to the preferences of voters in the legislator's district? This criterion is singular, aggregatively oriented, and district-based. In contrast, this analysis advocates plural criteria (cf. Achen 1978; Beitz 1989). It further suggests that some of these criteria should be deliberatively-oriented and systemic.

From a deliberative perspective, even promissory representation requires good deliberation to ascertain whether or not representatives have fulfilled their promises or have persuasive reasons for not doing so. Anticipatory representation requires good deliberation between citizens and representatives in the period of communication between elections whenever—as is almost always the case—a representative tries to

influence the voter's preferences by the time of the next election. Gyroscopic representation requires good deliberation among citizens and between citizens and their representatives at the time the representative is selected. Surrogate representation requires not only equal gladiatorial representation of the most important conflicting interests in proportion to their numbers in the population but also good deliberative representation of important perspectives.

Each form of representation should also be judged by its contribution to the quality of deliberation in the legislature. In anticipatory representation, a good quality of communication among citizens, groups, and representatives between elections probably improves the quality of deliberation within the legislature. In contrast, one form of gyroscopic representation—based on voters' choosing a representative whom they expect to pursue a vision of the public interest—facilitates good legislative deliberation not by mutual continuing contact and education but by selecting individuals likely to deliberate well and leaving them free to pursue that goal as they think fit. Surrogate representation contributes to good legislative deliberation by making it more likely that varied and important perspectives will be included.

Although a normative judgment on each of these forms of representation involves judging the quality of the deliberation that they produce or that produces them, political theorists are currently only gradually working out what the criteria for good deliberation should be. The standard account is that democratic deliberation should be free, equal, and rational or reasonable. As we have seen in the case of equality, however, each of these characteristics needs greater specification, because not all of the ordinary language meanings of these words ought to apply to the deliberative case. Democratic deliberation should be free in the sense of open to all relevant participants (much hangs here, as elsewhere, on the definition of "relevant"). It should ideally come as close as possible (in a world created by and suffused by power) to a situation in which coercive

---

[23] Table 1 presents in a crude form some of the major points in this analysis. It does not pretend to incorporate all of the normative criteria relevant to judging the quality of representation (e.g., "clean" elections, equal votes). Nor does it incorporate all of the considerations presented in the text.

32 REPRESENTATION

power has no role and the only "force" is that of the better argument. It should ideally allow equal opportunity of access to influence for all constituents, except where good reasons can be given for unequal opportunity. It should facilitate the expression and processing of relevant emotions as well as cognitions. It should be nonmanipulative. And it should both clarify and appropriately transform individual and collective interests in the directions of both congruence and conflict.[24]

None of these criteria replace the criterion of constituent-representative congruence. They add to it. Indeed, congruence of a sort is a factor in each of the forms of representation. It is most obvious in promissory representation, where one would expect explicit promises to reflect points of congruence between constituent preferences and a representative's future actions. It applies in anticipatory representation to the re-election, where one would expect constituents to have moved both toward and with the representative's positions and the representative to have moved similarly both toward and with the constituents. In gyroscopic representation one would expect greater congruence to the extent that the representative was elected descriptively to duplicate the median voter but less to the extent that the representative was elected to behave as a principled notable. In surrogate representation, norms of congruence, when applicable, apply to the polity as a whole.

None of the recently identified forms of representation, however, involves accountability in its classic form. In anticipatory representation, strictly interpreted, the representative acts only as entrepreneur, preparing to offer and offering a product to a future buyer. In gyroscopic representation, strictly interpreted, the voter selects a representative who then acts purely autonomously. In pure surrogate representation, there need be no relation at all between the representative and the individual constituent. These three forms of representation supplement the traditional model of promissory representation, which does involve accountability in its classic form. They do not replace the traditional model; nor do they replace the concept of accountability. As legitimate and useful supplementary forms of representation, however, they require separate normative scrutiny.

In most respects, these models of representation are compatible with one another and with promissory representation. They have complementary functions for different contexts and can, thus, be viewed as cumulative, not oppositional. Compatibly, they direct attention to deliberation at different points in the representative system: to the moment of election, between elections, and in the legislature. Compatibly, they all require each voter's interests to have equal weight in contexts of conflicting interests, although promissory representation comes closest to the normative standard of direct democracy, in which the people themselves rule. Compatibly, surrogate representation provides at the national level elements required for systemic democratic legitimacy that the other three forms do not provide. Gyroscopic representation is most appropriate for uncrystalized interests and changing situations but requires considerable constituent trust, which many situations may not warrant. Promissory representation requires little open-ended trust but works badly in situations of rapid change. Anticipatory representation requires little trust and easily accomodates change, but produces incentives for short-term thinking and manipulation focused on the next election.

In a few respects, the models come in conflict. Most importantly, promissory representation restricts the representative's action after election, while gyroscopic representation frees it. Anticipatory representation attracts entrepreneurs; gyroscopic representation, public-spirited notables. Certain functions that might be thought compatible in a division of labor (e.g., gyroscopic representation requiring considerable constituent trust and anticipatory representation relatively little trust) might, from another point of view, be considered conflicts (institutions that assume little trust sometimes drive out institutions that assume greater trust). Other conflicts may become visible over time.

These forms of representation are not mutually exclusive. Moreover, they may interact over time with one another. An anticipatory representative may become a promissory representative at the next election. A legislator may start as a gyroscopic representative and, wings clipped and some trust lost, become a promissory representative. The preferences that constituents express at Time 1 in promissory representation may be the product of earlier anticipatory, gyroscopic, or surrogate processes.[25]

Although in some respects the normative criteria for judging these forms of representation are additive, the plural criteria of this analysis do not require the models to be fully congruent with one another, any more than the separate normative mandates of freedom and equality need to be congruent. As a consequence, what representatives ought to do when faced with constituent preferences that are not in the constituents' long-term interests or not compatible with the good of the whole is, from the perspective of representational theory, indeterminate. Representatives may legitimately act in several ways, as long as they respect moral norms and the norms appropriate for the model, or combination of models, they are following.

---

[24] The criteria listed are not intended to exhaust the criteria for good deliberation. For the early 'standard account' of criteria for democratic deliberation linked to a theory of democratic legitimacy, see Cohen 1989. For criticisms, further criteria and discussion see, e.g., Applbaum 1999, Gutmann and Thompson 1996, Thompson 1988, Young 2000, and, from a more empirical perspective, Braybrooke 1996, Entman 1989, Herbst 1993, and Page 1996. For positive views of transformations in the direction of the common good, see Barber 1984 and Cohen 1989. For appropriate cautions, see Knight and Johnson 1994, 1998 and Sanders 1997.

REFERENCES

Achen, Christopher H. 1978. "Measuring Representation." *American Journal of Political Science* 22 (August): 475–510.

---

[25] I thank Dennis Thompson for this point.

REPRESENTATION

American Political Science Review

Applbaum, Arthur Isak. 1999. *Ethics for Adversaries: The Morality of Roles in Public and Private Life.* Princeton, NJ: Princeton University Press.

Arnold, Douglas R. 1990. *The Logic of Congressional Action.* New Haven, CT: Yale University Press.

Arnold, Douglas R. 1993. "Can Inattentive Citizens Control Their Elected Representatives?" In *Congress Reconsidered.* 5th ed., ed. Lawrence Dodd and Bruce Oppenheimer. Washington, DC: CQ Press.

Bachrach, Peter, and Morton Baratz. 1963. "Decisions and Non-Decisions: An Analytical Framework." *American Political Science Review* 57 (September): 632–42.

Banfield, Edward C. 1961. *Political Influence.* Glencoe, IL: Free Press.

Barber, Benjamin R. 1984. *Strong Democracy: Participatory Politics for a New Age.* Berkeley: University of California Press.

Barry, Brian. [1975] 1991. "Power: An Economic Analysis." In *Democracy and Power: Essays in Political Theory I.* Oxford: Oxford University Press.

Behn, Robert D. 2001. *Rethinking Democratic Accountability.* Washington, DC: Brookings Institution Press.

Beitz, Charles R. 1989. *Political Equality: An Essay in Democratic Theory.* Princeton, NJ: Princeton University Press.

Bernstein, Robert A. 1989. *Elections, Representation, and Congressional Voting Behavior: The Myth of Constituency Control.* Englewood Cliffs, NJ: Prentice Hall.

Bianco, William T. 1994. *Trust: Representatives and Constituents.* Ann Arbor: University of Michigan Press.

Bianco, William T. 1996. "A Rationale for Descriptive Representation: When Are Constituents Better Off Electing 'Someone Like Us.'" Presented at the Annual Meeting of the Midwest Political Science Association.

Braybrooke, David. 1996. "Changes of Rules, Issue-Circumscription, and Issue-Processing." In *Social Rules: Origins; Character; Logic; Change,* ed. David Braybrooke. Boulder, CO: Westview Press.

Brennan, Geoffrey, and Alan Hamlin. 1999. "On Political Representation." *British Journal of Political Science* 29 (January): 109–27.

Brennan, Geoffrey, and Alan Hamlin. 2000. *Democratic Devices and Desires.* Cambridge: Cambridge University Press.

Burke, Edmund. [1792] 1889. "Letter to Sir Hercules Langriche." In *The Works of the Right Honorable Edmund Burke,* Vol. 3. Boston: Little, Brown.

Burke, Edmund. [1774] 1889. "Speech to the Electors of Bristol." In *The Works of the Right Honorable Edmund Burke.* Vol. 2. Boston: Little, Brown.

Carroll, Susan J. 2002. "Representing Women: Congresswomen's Perceptions of their Representational Roles." In *Women Transforming Congress,* ed. Cindy Simon Rosenthal. Oklahoma City: Oklahoma University Press.

Cohen, Joshua. 1989. "Deliberation and Democratic Legitimacy." In *The Good Polity: Normative Analysis of the State,* eds. Alan Hamlin and Philip Pettit. Oxford: Basil Blackwell.

Cohen, Joshua, and Joel Rogers. 1995. "Secondary Associations and Democratic Governance." In *Associations and Democracy,* ed. Eric Olin Wright. London: Verso.

Congressional Quarterly Weekly. 1983. "Varied Legislative Styles, Philosophies Found Among Congress' 23 Women." 41 (April 23): 784–5.

Connolly, William A. 1972. "On 'Interests' in Politics." *Politics and Society* 2 (Summer): 459–77.

Conover, Pamela Johnston. 1988. "The Role of Social Groups in Political Thinking." *British Journal of Political Science* 18 (January): 51–76.

Crenson, Matthew A. 1971. *The Un-Politics of Air Pollution A Study of Non-Decisionmaking in the Cities.* Baltimore: Johns Hopkins.

Crosby, Ned. 1995. "Citizen Juries: One Solution for Difficult Environmental Problems." In *Fairness and Competence in Citizen Participation,* ed. Ortwin Renn et al. Norwell, MA: Kluwer Academic.

Dahl, Robert A. 1957. "The Concept of Power." *Behavioral Science* 2 (July): 201–15.

Dahl, Robert A. 1997. "On Deliberative Democracy." *Dissent* 44 (Summer): 54–8.

DiMarzio, Amy. 1997. "Surrogate Representatives: A Congressional Voice for Minorities." Undergraduate paper. Harvard University.

Dodson, Debra L., et al. 1995. *Voices, Views, Votes: The Impact of Women in the 103rd Congress.* New Brunswick, NJ: Center for the American Woman and Politics, Rutgers University.

Downs, Anthony. 1957. *An Economic Theory of Democracy.* New York: Harper and Row.

Entman, Robert M. 1989. *Democracy Without Citizens.* New York: Oxford University Press.

Fearon, James D. 1999. "Electoral Accountability and the Control of Politicians: Selecting Good Types versus Sanctioning Poor Performance." In *Democracy, Accountability, and Representation,* ed. Adam Prezworski, Bernard Manin, and Susan C. Stokes. Cambridge: Cambridge University Press.

Fenno, Richard F., Jr. 1978. *Home Style: House Members in their Districts.* Boston: Little, Brown.

Ferejohn, John. 1986. "Incumbent Performance and Electoral Control." *Public Choice* 50 (Fall): 5–25.

Fiorina, Morris P. 1974. *Representatives, Roll Calls, and Constituencies.* Lexington, MA.: Lexington Books.

Fiorina, Morris P. 1977. "An Outline for a Model of Party Choice." *American Journal of Political Science* 21 (August): 601–25.

Fiorina, Morris P. 1981. *Retrospective Voting in American National Elections.* New Haven, CT: Yale University Press.

Fishkin, James. 1991. *Democracy and Deliberation.* New Haven, CT: Yale University Press.

Fishkin, James. 1995. *The Voice of the People.* New Haven, CT: Yale University Press.

Fishkin, James. 1996. *The Dialogue of Justice.* New Haven, CT: Yale University Press.

Friedrich, Carl J. 1937. *Constitutional Government and Politics.* New York: Harper and Bros.

Friedrich, Carl J. 1958. "On Authority." In *Authority: NOMOS I,* ed. Carl J. Friedrich. Cambridge, MA: Harvard University Press.

Friedrich, Carl J. 1963. *Man and His Government.* New York: McGraw–Hill.

Gallie, W. B. 1962. "Essentially Contested Concepts." In *The Importance of Language,* ed. Max Black. Englewood Cliffs, NJ: Prentice Hall.

Gaventa, John. 1980. *Power and Powerlessness.* Urbana: University of Illinois Press.

Goodin, Robert E. 1999. "Accountability." In *The International Encyclopedia of Elections,* ed. Richard Rose. Washington, DC: Congressional Quarterly Press.

Greif, Avner. 1993. "Contract Enforceability and Economic Institutions in Early Trade: The Maghiribi Traders' Coalition." *American Economic Review* 83 (June): 525–48.

Gutmann, Amy, and Dennis Thompson. 1996. *Democracy and Disagreement.* Cambridge, MA: Harvard University Press.

Habermas, Jürgen. [1968] 1971. *Knowledge and Human Interests.* Trans. Jeremy J. Shapiro. Boston: Beacon Press.

Habermas, Jürgen. [1977] 1984. *The Theory of Communicative Action. Vol. 1. Reason and the Rationalization of Society.* Trans. Thomas McCarthy. Boston: Beacon Press.

Habermas, Jürgen. [1984] 1990. "Justice and Solidarity: On the Discussion Concerning 'Stage 6.'" Trans. Shierry Weber Nicholsen. In *The Moral Domain: Essays in the Ongoing Discussion between Philosophy and the Social Sciences,* ed. Thomas E. Wren. Cambridge, MA: MIT Press.

Herbst, Susan. 1993. *Numbered Voices.* Chicago. University of Chicago Press.

Hibbings, John R., and Elizabeth Theiss-Morse. 2002. *Stealth Democracy.* Cambridge: Cambridge University Press.

Honig, Bonnie. 1993. *Political Theory and the Displacement of Politics.* Ithaca, NY: Cornell University Press.

Jacobs, Lawrence R., and Robert Y. Shapiro. 2000. *Politicians Don't Pander: Political Manipulation and the Loss of Democratic Responsiveness.* Chicago: University of Chicago Press.

Jackson, John E., and David C. King. 1989. "Public Goods, Private Interests, and Representation." *American Political Science Review* 83 (December): 1143–64.

Key, V. O., with Milton C. Cummings. 1961. *The Responsible Electorate.* New York. Vintage Press.

King, David, and Esther Scott. 1995. "Catastrophic Health Insurance for the Elderly." Cambridge, MA: Kennedy School of Government Case C18-95-1278.0.

34 REPRESENTATION

Kingdon, John W. 1981. *Congressmen's Voting Decisions*. New York: Harper and Row.

Kingdon, John W. 1984. *Agendas, Alternatives, and Public Policies*. Boston: Little Brown.

Knight, Jack, and James Johnson. 1994. "Aggregation and Deliberation: On the Possibility of Democratic Legitimacy." *Political Theory* 22 (May): 277–96.

Knight, Jack, and James Johnson. 1998. "What Sort of Political Equality Does Democratic Deliberation Require?" In *Deliberative Democracy*, ed. James Bohman and William Rehg. Cambridge, MA: MIT Press.

Kuklinski, James H., and Gary M. Segura. 1995. "Endogeneity, Exogeneity, Time, and Space in Political Representation." *Legislative Studies Quarterly* 20 (February): 3–21.

Kymlicka, Will. 1993. "Group Representation in Canadian Politics." In *Equity and Community: The Charter, Interest Advocacy, and Representation*, ed. F. L. Siedle. Montreal: Institute for Research on Public Policy.

Latane, Bibb, and John M. Darley. 1970. *The Unresponsive Bystander*. Englewood Cliffs, NJ: Prentice–Hall.

Lively, Jack. 1975. *Democracy*. Oxford: Blackwell.

Lott, John R. 1987. "Political Cheating." *Public Choice* 52 (2): 169–86.

Lukes, Stephen. 1974. *Power: A Radical View*. London: Macmillian.

Manin, Bernard. 1997. *Modern Representative Government*. Cambridge: Cambridge University Press.

Manin, Bernard, Adam Prezworski, and Susan C. Stokes. 1999. "Elections and Representation." In *Democracy, Accountability, and Representation*, ed. Adam Prezworski, Bernard Manin and Susan C. Stokes. Cambridge: Cambridge University Press.

Mansbridge, Jane. [1980] 1983. *Beyond Adversary Democracy*. Chicago: University of Chicago Press.

Mansbridge, Jane. 1999. "Should Blacks Represent Blacks and Women Represent Women? A Contingent 'Yes.'" *Journal of Politics* 61 (August): 628–57.

Mill, John Stuart. [1859] 1974. *On Liberty*. New York: Pelican Books.

Mill, John Stuart. [1861] 1969. "Utilitarianism." In *Essays on Ethics, Religion and Society*, ed. J. M. Robson. Toronto: University of Toronto Press.

Miller, Warren E., and Donald E. Stokes. 1963. "Constituency Influence in Congress." *American Political Science Review* 57 (March): 45–56.

Nagel, Jack H. 1975. *The Descriptive Analysis of Power*. New Haven, CT: Yale University Press.

Nagel, Jack H. 1992. "Combining Deliberation and Fair Representation in Community Health Decisions." *University of Pennsylvania Law Review* 140 (May): 2101–21.

Nozick, Robert. 1972. "Coercion." In *Philosophy, Politics and Society*, 4th ser., ed. Peter Laslett, W. G. Runciman, and Quentin Skinner. Cambridge: Blackwell.

Page, Benjamin I. 1978. *Choices and Echoes in Presidential Elections: Rational Man and Electoral Democracy*. Chicago: University of Chicago Press.

Page, Benjamin I. 1996. *Who Deliberates: Mass Media in Modern Democracy*. Chicago: University of Chicago Press.

Phillips, Anne. 1995. *The Politics of Presence*. Oxford: Oxford University Press.

Pitkin, Hanna Fenichel. [1967] 1972. *The Concept of Representation*. Berkeley: University of California Press.

Popkin, Samuel L. 1994. *The Reasoning Voter*. Chicago: University of Chicago Press.

Rogowski, Ronald. 1981. "Representation in Political Theory and in Law." *Ethics* 91 (April): 395–430.

Sanders, Lynn M. 1997. "Against Deliberation." *Political Theory* 25 (June): 347–76.

Schmitter, Philippe. 1995. "The Irony of Modern Democracy and the Viability of Efforts to Reform its Practice." In *Associations and Democracy*, ed. Joshua Cohen. New York: Verso.

Schwartz, Nancy L. 1988. *The Blue Guitar: Political Representation and Community*. Chicago: University of Chicago Press.

Stimson, James A., Michael B. Mackuen, and Roberts S. Erikson. 1995. "Dynamic Representation." *American Political Science Review* 89 (September): 543–65.

Sunstein, Cass R. 1990. *After the Rights Revolution*. Cambridge, MA: Harvard University Press.

Swain, Carol M. 1993. *Black Faces, Black Interests: The Representation of African Americans in Congress*. Cambridge, MA: Harvard University Press.

Thomas, Sue. 1994. *How Women Legislate*. New York: Oxford University Press.

Thompson, Dennis. 1988. "Representatives in the Welfare State." In *Democracy and the Welfare State*, ed. Amy Gutman. Princeton, NJ: Princeton University Press.

Young, Iris Marion. 2000. *Inclusion and Democracy*. New York: Oxford University Press.

Wartenberg, Thomas E. 1990. *The Forms of Power: From Domination to Transformation*. Philadelphia: Temple University Press.

Weber, Max. [1922] 1978. *Economy and Society*, ed. Guenther Roth and Claus Wittich. Berkeley: University of California Press.

Weissberg, Robert. 1978. "Collective vs. Dyadic Representation in Congress." *American Political Science Review* 72 (June): 535–47.

Williams, Melissa S. 1998. *Voice, Trust, and Memory: Marginalized Groups and the Failings of Liberal Representation*. Princeton, NJ: Princeton University Press.

Zaller, John. 1994. "Strategic Politicians, Public Opinion, and the Gulf Crisis." In *Taken By Storm: The Media, Public Opinion and U.S. Foreign Policy in the Gulf War*, ed. W. Lance Bennett and David L. Paletz. Chicago: University of Chicago Press.

HEINZ EULAU
PAUL D. KARPS

2

The Puzzle of Representation: Specifying Components of Responsiveness

This study examines the conceptualization of representation, particularly the problems resulting from conceiving of it simply in terms of congruence between the attitudes of constituents and of representatives on policy questions. It examines critically some of the work that followed the innovative study of Miller and Stokes. Regarding representation as responsiveness, it identifies four components of this concept: policy, service, allocation, and symbolic responsiveness.

The puzzle: "We have representative institutions, but like the Greeks we do not know what they are about" (Eulau, 1967).

With the publication in 1963 of "Constituency Influence in Congress" by Miller and Stokes, the direction was set for a novel approach to the study of political representation.[1] The virtue of this original study notwithstanding, the approach had some quite unexpected consequences for subsequent theoretical development and empirical research. Much of this development and research was due less to the impact of Miller and Stokes' innovative approach as such than to its vulgarization. The questions addressed in this paper are two: first, we propose to unravel the continuing puzzle of representation which was probably made even more puzzling by the thoughtless use of the concept of "congruence" which Miller and Stokes had introduced into discourse about representation; and second, we propose to explicate the concept of "responsiveness" by decomposing it into four components which seem to correspond to four targets of representation.

The Miller-Stokes Model

Miller and Stokes (1963) themselves were well aware of the broader context of theory and research on representation,[2] but the focus of their particular analysis was a more limited one than "representation." They were interested in the degree to which "constituency control," rather than "party voting," determined congressional roll call behavior: "The fact that

LEGISLATIVE STUDIES QUARTERLY, II, 3, August 1977   233

Heinz Eulau and Paul D. Karps

our House of Representatives . . . has irregular party voting does not of itself indicate that Congressmen deviate from party in response to local pressures" (p. 45). The analysis addressed an old question: which factor, party or constituency, contributes more to variance in roll-call voting (all other things being equal)? The question had been previously asked in numerous studies relying, of necessity, on aggregate surrogate indicators of presumed district predispositions, most of them demographic or ecological.[3]

Miller and Stokes' research was a giant stride in the study of representation because it freed analysis from dependence on surrogate variables as indicators of constituency attitudes or predispositions. Miller and Stokes interviewed a sample of congressional constituents (voters and non-voters) and their respective congressmen (as well as non-incumbent candidates) whose attitudes in three broad issue domains they compared with each other, with congressmen's perceptions of constituency attitudes, and with corresponding roll call votes. Their tool of analysis was the product moment correlation coefficient and their mode of treatment was "causal analysis," which was then being introduced into political science. Miller and Stokes found the relationships among the variables of their model to vary a good deal from issue area to issue area, being strongest in the case of civil rights, weaker in the case of social welfare, and weakest in the case of foreign involvement. They concluded:

> The findings of this analysis heavily underscore the fact that no single tradition of representation fully accords with the realities of American legislative politics. The American system *is* a mixture, to which the Burkean, instructed-delegate, and responsible-party models all can be said to have contributed elements. Moreover, variations in the representative relation are most likely to occur as we move from one policy domain to another (p. 56).

We have no quarrel with this general conclusion concerning the American system. We are bothered by the definition of what Miller and Stokes call "the representative relation" and its operational expression. This "relation" is the similarity or, as it is also called, the "congruence" between the four variables of the causal model that serves the purposes of analysis.[4] This specification of congruence as the expression of the representative relation has had great influence on later researchers, both those working in the tradition of, or with the data made available by, the Michigan group and those working independently with fresh data of their own.[5] The concern here is not this influence as such but rather the gradual erosion of alternative theoretical assumptions about representation of which Miller and Stokes themselves are fully cognizant. As a result of this erosion, what for Miller and Stokes (1963, p. 49) was only "a starting point for a wide range of analyses" became an exclusive definition of representation: high

The Puzzle of Representation

congruence was interpreted as evidence of the presence of representation, and low congruence was taken as proof of its absence.

Whatever congruence may be symbolizing, it is not a self-evident measure of representation. Later researchers, poorly tutored in theories and practices of representation, tended to ignore this. Miller and Stokes, in order to use congruence as a measure, had stipulated three conditions for constituency influence or control. First, control in the representational relationship can be exercised through recruitment—constituents choose that representative who shares their views so that, by following his "own convictions," the representative "does his constituents' will." Second, control can be obtained through depriving the representative of his office—the representative follows "his (at least tolerably accurate) perceptions of district attitude in order to win re-election." And third, "the constituency must in some measure take the policy views of candidates into account in choosing a Representative" (pp. 50-51).

The electoral connection is of course only one of the links between representative and represented. And it should by no means be taken for granted that it is the most critical, the most important, or the most effective means to insure constituency influence on or control over public policies and the conduct of representatives. It is so only if one or all of the conditions for constituency control specified by Miller and Stokes are satisfied. This is also precisely the reason why attitudinal or perceptual congruence is not an exclusive measure of representation; it is simply the "starting point," as Miller and Stokes knew, in the puzzle of representation. Anyone who has the least sensitivity to the representative process recognizes that representatives are influenced in their conduct by many forces or pressures or linkages other than those arising out of the electoral connection and should realize that restricting the study of representation to the electoral connection produces a very limited vision of the representational process. Miller and Stokes themselves were eminently aware of this, as their "Conclusion" indicated. Yet, only three years after publication of their analysis, when two other analysts (Cnudde and McCrone, 1966), subjecting the Miller-Stokes data to an alternative causal analysis, found no support for recruitment as a condition of representation, constituency control was reduced to a purely psychological function in the representative's mind, and the danger of limiting the "representative relation" to attitudinal and perceptual congruence was demonstrated. Moreover, these analysts altogether ignored Miller and Stokes' important third condition for constituency influence through the electoral connection: constituents' taking account of the candidate's policy views in choosing the representative.

Indeed, Miller and Stokes themselves had the most trouble with

236 Heinz Eulau and Paul D. Karps

this last condition. The overwhelming evidence of their research and that of others denies the condition: most citizens are not competent to perform the function which the model assumes—that elections are in fact effective sanctioning mechanisms in the representational relationship. Miller and Stokes gave a number of "reasons" for why representatives seem to be so sensitive about their voting records—for if voters do not know the record, this sensitivity is surely puzzling. They suggested that the voting record may be known to the few voters who, in close contests, make the difference between victory or defeat, and that the Congressman is "a dealer in increments and margins." They also speculated that the voting record may be known to opinion leaders in the district who serve as gatekeepers and conveyors of evaluation in a two-step flow of communication. But there is no evidence for this in their own research.[6]

The Crisis in Representational Theory

It would not yield further theoretical dividends to review in any detail the empirical studies of representation that, in one way or another, are predicated on the attitudinal-perceptual formulation of congruence that had served Miller and Stokes as a starting point but that, for most of their successors, became a terminal point. Most of these studies are distinguished by lack of historical-theoretical knowledge of representation and of independent theoretical creativity. In particular, they are cavalier in regard to a number of dilemmas that, by the middle sixties, had forced themselves on the attention of scholars interested in theoretical understanding of the problem of representation. That these dilemmas were articulated by different scholars at about the same time was probably coincidental, but the coincidence is important because it emphasized the possibility of alternative research directions.

First, representational theory made assumptions about citizen behavior that were negated by the empirical evidence. Wahlke, examining the role of the represented in the representational relationship, concluded that the evidence did not justify treating citizens as significant sources of policy demands, positions or even broad orientations that could be somehow "represented" in the policy-making process. Citizens simply lack the necessary information for effective policy choices to be communicated to their representatives, even if they were to make the effort to communicate. This being the case, Wahlke concluded that the "simple demand-input model" of representation was deficient. This is of course precisely the model that Miller-Stokes had in fact constructed in order to organize and explain their data. Wahlke suggested that a "support-input model" might be more appropriate.[7]

The Puzzle of Representation

237

Second, given the limited capacity of the represented to formulate policy, a viable theory could no longer ignore the asymmetry of the representational relationship. Eulau suggested, therefore, that research should proceed from the structural assumption of a built-in status difference between representative and represented in which the former rather than the latter give direction to the relationship. Representational theory would have to deal with the tensions arising out of status differentiation rather than deny their existence (Eulau, 1967). Once status is introduced as a variable into the representational equation, the model of the representational relationship can be recursive, and the causal ordering of the relevant variables is likely to be reversed.

Finally, in a linguistic study of the concept of representation, Pitkin (1967) found the traditional theories of representation flawed. She advanced the proposition that representation, referring to a social relationship rather than to an attribute of the individual person, could be meaningfully conceptualized only as a systemic property. Representation might or might not emerge at the level of the collectivity, the criterion of emergence being the collectivity's potential for "responsiveness." Political representation "is primarily a public, institutionalized arrangement involving many people and groups, and operating in the complex ways of large-scale social arrangements. What makes it representation is not any single action by any one participant, but the over-all structure and functioning of the system, the patterns emerging from the multiple activities of many people" (pp. 221-222). Moreover, after considering every conceivable definition, Pitkin concluded that political representation means "acting in the interest of the represented, in a manner responsive to them" (p. 209). However, there is also the stipulation that the representative "must not be found persistently at odds with the wishes of the represented without good reason in terms of their interest, without a good explanation of why their views are not in accord with their interests" (pp. 209-210).

Pitkin's formulation creates many measurement problems for empirical research. Concepts like "wishes," "good reason," "interest," or "views," are difficult to operationalize. She provides no clues as to how "responsiveness" as a systemic property of the political collectivity can be ascertained and how, indeed, it can be measured in ways enabling the scientific observer to conclude that representation has in fact emerged at the level of the political system. Pitkin's treatment seems to stress the condition in which the representative stands ready to be responsive when the constituents do have something to say. A legislature may, therefore, be responsive whether or not there are specific instances of response. In other words, Pitkin emphasized a potential for response rather than an act of response. There are

238 Heinz Eulau and Paul D. Karps

considerable difficulties in empirically working with a concept stressing the possibility of an act rather than the act itself. Moreover, the formulation ignores Wahlke's injunction to jettison the demand-input model. Nevertheless, Pitkin's work had an almost immediate and profound effect on subsequent empirical research. (See Prewitt and Eulau, 1969; Muller, 1970; Peterson, 1970.)

Research on representation following the watershed year of 1967 has taken two major innovative routes. First, taking their cue from Wahlke's critique of the demand-input model, Patterson, Hedlund,and Boynton (1975) have used a support-input model that makes fewer requirements on the capacity of the represented to play a role in the representational process. However, their model continues to be based on congruence assumptions. Their analysis, conducted at the level of the individual, largely consists of comparison of the represented and representational elites in terms of relevant attitudes, perceptions and behavior patterns.

Second, taking a cue from Pitkin, Eulau and Prewitt (1973) transformed data collected at the level of individuals into grouped data, and conducted their analysis of representation at the macro level of small decision-making groups (city councils). In contrast to Patterson and his associates, Eulau and Prewitt stressed actual rather than potential response to constituent inputs, whether of the demand or support variety. In retrospect, it appears, they were harnessing "reactive" behavior rather than responsive behavior in Pitkin's sense, for they ignored the direction of the response— whether it was in fact "in the interest of" the constituents at the focus of representation. But these retrospective musings only suggest that the problem of conceptualizing representation in terms of responsiveness remains on the agenda of theory and research. As Loewenberg (1972, p. 12) has summed up the situation more recently:

Representation . . . is an ill-defined concept that has acquired conflicting meanings through long use. It may be employed to denote any relationship between rulers and ruled or it may connote responsiveness, authorization, legitimation, or accountability. It may be used so broadly that any political institution performs representative functions or so narrowly that only an elected legislature can do so. To a surprising extent, the Burkean conceptualization of the representative function is still in use, and Eulau's call for a concept adequate to modern concerns about the relationship between legislators and their constituencies has not been answered.

Responsiveness as Congruence

Although the expectations or behavioral patterns to which the term "responsiveness" refers were implicit in the concept of "representative government,"[8] the term as such had not been used by Miller and Stokes or others as the defining characteristics of representation. By 1967, when Pitkin's work was published, the term struck an attractive chord as the ideals of "participatory democracy" were once more being revived in neo-populist movements that had intellectual spokesmen in the social sciences. Even though one should not expect a close affinity between the vocabulary of participation and the vocabulary of representation on logical-theoretical grounds, a term like responsiveness stemming from considerations of representative democracy could easily blend in with considerations of participatory democracy. When analysts of political participation like Verba and Nie (1972) came to pay attention to empirical work on representation, they had little trouble in linking, by way of an adaptation of the assumption of congruence, the concept of responsiveness to their work on participation. Interestingly, although they did not cite or refer to Pitkin's linguistic analysis, Verba and Nie found, on the one hand, that "responsiveness, as far as we can tell, rarely has been defined precisely, almost never has been measured, and never has been related to participation" (p. 300). On the other hand, they acknowledged Miller and Stokes, who had not used the term: "Miller and Stokes in their analysis of the relationship between constituency attitudes and Congressmen, do deal with responsiveness in ways similar to ours" (p. 300, ft. 3).

Indeed, in examining and seeking to explain the effects of different degrees of citizen participation on the responsiveness of community leaders, Verba and Nie present a rechristened version of the congruence assumption of representation which they call "concurrence":

Our measure of congruence depends on how well the priorities of the citizens and the leaders match. Several types of concurrence are possible . . . our measure of the concurrence between citizens and community leaders measures the extent to which citizens and leaders in the community choose the same "agenda" of community priorities (p. 302).

But they immediately raise the critical problem of causality: "whether we have the warrant to consider our measure of *concurrence* to be a measure of responsiveness. Just because leaders agree with citizens and that agreement increases as citizens become more active, can we be sure that it is citizen activity that is causing leaders to *respond* by adopting the priorities of the citizen?" (p. 304).

In order to test for the causal relationship, Verba and Nie compared the correlation coefficients obtained for the relationship between "citizen activeness" and concurrence, on the one hand, and between "leader activeness" and concurrence, on the other hand. Finding that the correlations for citizens are "much stronger" than those for leaders, Verba and Nie concluded that their measure of concurrence "seems to be a valid measure of responsive-

240 Heinz Eulau and Paul D. Karps

ness to leaders" (pp. 331-332). But this mechanical comparison is not a test of causality at all in regard to the direction of responsiveness. In fact, it amounts to a false interpretation of the data. The correlations for citizens simply mean that more active citizens see things (priorities to be done in the community) more like leaders do than is the case with less active citizens; the correlations for leaders simply mean that the more active leaders see things more like citizens do than is the case with less active leaders. The strength of the coefficients, all of which are positive for both citizens and leaders, does not prove anything about the direction of causality—whether citizens influence leaders or leaders influence citizens, or whether citizens are responsive to leaders or leaders to citizens. It cannot be otherwise because Verba and Nie's measure of concurrence, like Miller and Stokes' measure of congruence, is neutral as to direction and requires that the direction of the relationships involved in the model be theoretically stipulated. There is no such stipulation in the Verba-Nie application of the concurrence measure to the question of linkage between leaders and led.

Causal analysis, then, does not free the analyst from defining his terms—be they power and influence, or be they responsiveness—in advance and stipulating the direction of expected relationships in advance.[9] The mechanical application of statistical tests of a possible causal structure does not necessarily model real-world relationships if the operational definitions of the model's components make no theoretical sense. Verba and Nie's two-edged use of the responsiveness, operationalized in terms of the directionless concept of concurrence, is intrinsically characterized by ambiguity. If concurrence is a measure of responsiveness of leaders to citizens, it cannot be a measure of responsiveness of citizens to leaders. If one were to take their comparison of the correlations between participation and concurrence for citizens and leaders as an indication of anything, it would have to be that leaders are responsive to citizens and citizens are responsive to leaders, varying in degree with degree of participation.

Pitkin, it was noted, had raised the importance of responsiveness as the critical characteristic of representation, but she had left the term undefined. Representatives, in order to represent, were to be responsive to their constituents, but Pitkin did not specify the content or target of responsiveness. Verba and Nie had taken a step forward by specifying public policy issues as the target of responsiveness. In focusing exclusively on congruence or concurrence in regard to policy attitudes or preferences, they ignored other possible targets in the relationship between representatives and represented which may also give content to the notion of responsiveness. By emphasizing only one component of responsiveness as a substantive concept, they reduced a complex phenomenon like representation to one

The Puzzle of Representation 241

of its components and substituted the component for the whole. But if responsiveness is limited to one component, it cannot capture the complexities of the real world of politics. It is necessary, therefore, to view responsiveness as a complex, compositional phenomenon that entails a variety of possible targets in the relationship between representatives and represented. How else could one explain that representatives manage to stay in office in spite of the fact that they are *not* necessarily or always responsive to the represented as the conception of representation as congruence or concurrence of policy preferences requires?

It deserves mention that Miller and Stokes (1963) had themselves realized that there are possible targets of responsiveness other than policy issues. They emphasized the "necessity of specifying the acts *with respect to which* one actor has power or influence or control over another." Their target, they conceded, was only the set of issues lying within the three policy areas of civil rights, social welfare and foreign involvement. But significantly they added, "We are not able to say how much control the local constituency may or may not have over *all* actions of its Representative, and there may well be pork-barrel issues or other public matters of peculiar relevance to the district on which the relation of Congressman to constituency is quite distinctive" (p. 48). Miller and Stokes did not specify what they referred to as "other public matters." It is the task of the rest of this paper to suggest what some of these other targets of responsiveness might be.

Components of Responsiveness

There are four possible components of responsiveness which, as a whole, constitute representation. While each component can be treated as an independent target of responsiveness, all four must be considered together in the configurative type of analysis which, it seems to us, the complexity of the representational nexus requires. The first component is, of course, *policy responsiveness* where the target is the great public issues that agitate the political process. Second, there is *service responsiveness* which involves the efforts of the representative to secure particularized benefits for individuals or groups in his constituency. Third, there is *allocation responsiveness* which refers to the representative's efforts to obtain benefits for his constituency through pork-barrel exchanges in the appropriations process or through administrative interventions. Finally, there is what we shall call *symbolic responsiveness* which involves public gestures of a sort that create a sense of trust and support in the relationship between representative and represented. It is possible that there are other targets of responsive conduct which, in composition with the four here tapped, constitute the matrix of representational relationships. But the main point we are trying to make is this: responsiveness refers not just to "this" or "that" target of political activity on the part of the representative but to a number of targets. Only when responsiveness is viewed as a compositional phenomenon can the approach to representation-as-responsiveness recommended by Pitkin be useful. It is the configuration of the component aspects of responsiveness that might yield a viable theory of representative government under modern conditions of societal complexity.

Policy Responsiveness

How the representative and the represented interact with respect to the making of public policy lies at the heart of most discussions of responsiveness. Responsiveness in this sense refers to the structure in which district positions on policy issues, specified as some measure of central tendency or dispersion, are related to the policy orientation of the representative—attitudinal or perceptual—and to his subsequent decision-making conduct in a given field of policy.

The premise underlying the specification of policy responsiveness is the presence of a meaningful connection between constituent policy preferences or demands and the representative's official behavior. This is what Miller and Stokes called "congruence" and what Verba and Nie called "concurrence." Whatever the term, the operational definition is the same: if the representative and his constituency agree on a particular policy, no matter how the agreement has come about, then the representative is responsive. There are, as has been noted, several problems with the model of representation built on the operationalization of responsiveness as congruence, notably the problem that congruence is neither a necessary nor a sufficient condition for responsiveness. The representative may react to constituency opinion, and hence evince congruent attitudes or behavior, yet not act in what is in the best interest of the constituency as he might wish to define that interest, thereby being in fact unresponsive. Further, the representative may make policy in response to groups and interests other than his constituents, including executive and bureaucratic agencies. Whether such conduct is also in the interest of his district as he sees it is an empirical question. But whatever the formulation and findings, it cannot be denied that policy responsiveness is an important component of representation.

The notion of policy responsiveness is implicit in some of the classic theories of representation. First of all, the controversy over mandate versus independence, whether the representative is a delegate or a trustee, though considered obsolete by Eulau (1967, pp. 78-79) and in

The Puzzle of Representation 243

many respects resolved by Pitkin (1967, ch. 7, pp. 144-167), is still intriguing and relevant to the present discussion. For the debate is over whether the representative should act according to what *he* thinks is in the "best interest" of the constituency, regardless of constituency "wants," or whether he should follow the "expressed wishes" of the district, regardless of how he personally feels. The debate really turns on the competence of the citizenry in matters of public policy. For while the citizenry may know what it wants, it may not know what it needs. Secondly, therefore, an appropriate definition of policy responsiveness will be related to the classic issue of "district interest" as against "district will." There is no denying that the notion of policy responsiveness pervades empirical research on legislative decision-making, even when the issue of representation as a theoretical one is not raised. (For recent research, see Turner and Schneier, 1970; Kingdon, 1973; Clausen, 1973; Jackson, 1974; Matthews and Stimson, 1975.) However, precisely because this is the case, it is important not to ignore other components of responsiveness in the representational relationship. Exclusive emphasis on the policy aspects of responsiveness may give a one-sided view and may not help in solving the puzzle of representation.

Service Responsiveness

A second target for responsiveness to define the representational relationship concerns the non-legislative services that a representative actually performs for individuals or groups in his district. Service responsiveness, then, refers to the advantages and benefits which the representative is able to obtain for particular constituents. There are a number of services that constituents may expect and that the representative considers an intrinsic part of his role. Some of them involve only modest, if time consuming, requests, such as responding to written inquiries involving constituents' personal concerns, or facilitating meetings and tours for visitors from the home district. Newsletters or columns in local newspapers may be used to inform constituents of legislation that may be of interest and use to them. Much of this work is routine and carried out in regular fashion.

Another link in the chain of service responsiveness is often referred to as case work. (See Clapp, 1963.) Given his official position and presumed influence, the representative is in a position to solve particular problems for members of his constituency. The representative intervenes between constituents and bureaucrats in such matters as difficulties with a tax agency, delays in welfare payments, securing a job in government, and so on. Providing constituent services and doing case work constitute for many representatives more significant aspects of their representational role than does

244 Heinz Eulau and Paul D. Karps

legislative work like bill-drafting or attending committee hearings. These "errand boy" functions deserve more theoretical attention than they have been given in contemporary research. In some important situations the representative may actually serve as an advocate and even lobbyist for special interests in his district vis-à-vis the legislature, departmental bureaucracies or regulatory agencies. This type of responsiveness is indeed crucial in trying to understand modern representative government.

This notion of service responsiveness seemed to underlie Eulau and Prewitt's (1973, pp. 424-427, 649-650) operational definition of responsiveness. In their study of San Francisco Bay Area city councils, they initially divided these small representative bodies into those which seemed to be somehow responsive to constituent needs or wants and those which did not seem to be responsive. They then distinguished among the former councils those which were responsive to important standing interests in the community or attentive publics, and those which more often were responsive only to temporary alliances having a particular grievance or request. This conception of responsiveness, then, is based on the kind of group or individuals whom the representative perceives as being primarily served by his activities. Zeigler and Jennings (1974, pp. 77-94), in a study of school boards, present a similar conception of responsiveness, conceptually distinguishing more sharply between "group responsiveness" and "individualized responsiveness." Both of these research teams, then, defined responsiveness in terms of the significant recipients of representational services.

That service responsiveness is an important element in representation should be apparent. Moreover, there is every reason to believe that it is increasing rather than declining. Until the middle sixties, it was generally assumed that case work and the advocacy of special interests bring advantages and benefits only to those who take the initiative in soliciting the representative's help. But as Fiorina (1977, p. 180) has recently pointed out, at least with reference to the federal level, increased bureaucratic activity in the wake of increased federal largesse to all kinds of population groups has also motivated congressmen to "undoubtedly stimulate the demand for their bureaucratic fixit services." The representative does not just respond to demands for his good offices and services; he has become a kind of hustler who advertises and offers them on his own initiative.[10]

This explication of service responsiveness has been entirely focused on the relationship between the representative and particular constituents. The representative can also be responsive in his unique role as a middleman in the allocation of more generalized benefits. We refer here to what has been traditionally called "pork-barrel politics" and to what we shall refer, for lack of a better term, as "allocation responsiveness." Both service respon-

The Puzzle of Representation

siveness, whether initiated by the representative or not, and allocation responsiveness, which is always initiated by him, are important elements of representational behavior and important pillars in the representational relationship.

Allocation Responsiveness

It has long been recognized that pork-barrel politics in legislative allocations of public projects involves advantages and benefits presumably accruing to a representative's district as a whole. Although traditionally these allocations were seen as "public goods," with the expansion of the government's role in all sectors of society—industry, agriculture, commerce, health, education, welfare, internal security, and so on—the distinction between public and private benefits is difficult to maintain. Again, as Fiorina (1977, p. 180) has felicitously put it in connection with federal politics, "The pork-barreler need not limit himself to dams and post offices. There is LEAA money for the local police; urban renewal and housing money for local officials; and educational program grants for the local education bureaucracy. The congressman can stimulate applications for federal assistance, put in a good word during consideration, and announce favorable decisions amid great fanfare." Such allocations may benefit the district as a whole, or they may benefit some constituents more than others because they make more use of the benefits. The critical point to be made is that in being responsive as an "allocator," whether in the legislative or bureaucratic processes, the representative seeks to anticipate the needs of his clients and, in fact, can stimulate their wants.

Legislators' committee memberships sometimes serve as indicators of allocation responsiveness, as revealed in Fenno's (1973) studies of legislative conduct in committees of the U. S. House of Representatives. A representative from a district that has a particular stake in a committee's jurisdiction will often seek a post on a parent committee but also on a particularly suitable sub-committee; such membership presumably enables him to act in a manner responsive to the best interests of his district and some or all of his constituents.

However, one cannot automatically assume that a legislator serving on a committee "not relevant" to his district is necessarily unresponsive and not interested in securing allocations. Legislators often seek preferment on important committees like Rules, Appropriations, or Ways and Means not because these committees are directly "relevant" to the interests of their constituents, but because they place members in positions of power and influence vis-à-vis administrative agencies which distribute benefits, such

246 Heinz Eulau and Paul D. Karps

as the Army Corps of Engineers, the Park Service, or the Veterans Administration. These secondary bonds are probably as critical in securing benefits for the district as are the primary bonds resulting from "relevant" committee assignments. However, the secondary bonds have less symbolic value than do the primary bonds. And symbolic pay-offs, we shall see, are an important fourth component of representational responsiveness.

Symbolic Responsiveness

The fourth component of responsiveness is more psychologically based than the others. The first three components all somehow tap a behavioral aspect of representation: policy responsiveness is oriented toward the decision-making behavior of the representative in matters of public controversy; while service and allocation responsiveness are oriented toward particularized or collective benefits obtained through the acts of the representative. The representational relationship is not, however, just one of such concrete transactions, but also one that is built on trust and confidence expressed in the support that the represented give to the representative and to which he responds by symbolic, significant gestures, in order to, in turn, generate and maintain continuing support.

The notion of symbolic responsiveness has been alluded to by Wahlke (1971) in examining the role of the constituency in the representational relationship. He found little evidence for presuming that a district makes specific policy demands on its representative. Rather, he suggested the relevance of Easton's concept of diffuse support (1965, pp. 247-340) as a key component in the relationship between the represented and their representative. He states that the "symbolic satisfaction with the process of government is probably more important than specific, instrumental satisfaction with the policy output of the process" (Wahlke, 1971, p. 288). The important question then becomes, ". . . how do representative bodies contribute to the generation and maintenance of support?" (p. 290).

In an era of cynicism about the functioning of representative institutions, the ways in which representatives manipulate political symbols in order to generate and maintain trust or support become critical aspects of responsiveness. Edelman (1964, 1971), following the earlier work of Merriam, Lasswell, and Smith (1950), has emphasized the importance of symbolic action in politics. The need for giving symbolic reassurance is being demonstrated by the "reach out" efforts of the new President of the United States—walking down Pennsylvania Avenue after his inauguration, fire-side chats, telephonic call-a-thons, visits to economically stricken areas, being "Jimmy" Carter, and so on. The purpose of all of these symbolic

The Puzzle of Representation

acts is to project an image that the President is truly the people's representative and ready to be responsive to them. By mobilizing trust and confidence it is presumably easier to go about the job of representation than would otherwise be the case.

Fenno (1975), in a paper on "Congressmen in their Constituencies," emphasizes the importance of political support in the representational relationship. The representative's "home style"—how he behaves *in* his constituency—is designed not just to secure constituent support and re-election but also to give the representative more freedom in his legislative activities when he is away from home. Symbolic politics has the purpose of building up credit to be drawn on in future contingencies. Although Fenno does not cite Wahlke at all, it is significant that his analysis approximates the "support-input model":

> . . . congressmen seek and voters may give support on a non-policy basis. They may support a "good man" on the basis of his presentation "as a person" and trust him to be a good representative. So, we might consider the possibility that constituent trust, together with electoral accountability, may also provide a measure of good representation. The point is not that policy preferences are not a crucial basis for the representational relationship. They are. The point is that we should not start our studies of representation by assuming that they are the only basis for a representational relationship. They are not (p. 51).

Fenno's comments are all the more germane to the argument of this paper because it is interesting to note that this most eminent of legislative scholars deflates the prevailing obsession with policy responsiveness as the *sine qua non* of representation. In fact, much of what may appear to be policy responsiveness is largely symbolic responsiveness. From session to session, legislators on all levels of government—federal, state, and local— introduce thousands of bills which have not the slightest chance of ever being passed and, more often than not, are not intended to be passed. Yet representatives introduce these bills to please some constituents and to demonstrate their own responsiveness.[11]

Responsiveness and Focus of Representation

Once the concept of representation-as-responsiveness is decomposed, policy responsiveness appears as only one component of representation and, perhaps, as by no means the dominant link between representative and represented. There is no intrinsic reason why responsiveness in one component of representation cannot go together with unresponsiveness in another. An individual or group may disagree with the representative's position and behavior on an issue of public policy and, as a result, may be unrepresented in this sense; yet, the same individual or group may be well represented by a person who is responsive by attending to their particular requests for some type of service. Similarly, it is possible for a representative to be responsive with regard to securing public goods for his constituency, while simultaneously being quite unresponsive with respect to issues of public policy. Finally, what matters in symbolic responsiveness is that the constituents feel represented, quite regardless of whether the representative is responsive in his policy stands or the services or public goods he provides for his constituency.

Moreover, even if attention is given only to policy responsiveness, research cannot simply neglect some of the classical questions of representational theory, such as the issue of representing the district's will as against its interest, or the issue of the focus of representation. It is easily conceivable that being responsive to a district's will—the wants of its people—may involve being unresponsive to a district's interest—the needs of its people. With regard to the focus of representation, being responsive to the electoral district may produce unresponsive behavior in the larger unit of which the district is a part and, of course, vice versa.[12]

In fact, a closer look at the question of representational focus will reveal further the potentially multidimensional character of the phenomenon of responsiveness. The representative can perceive his "constituency" in a multitude of ways,[13] thereby making the number of foci quite large. One might organize these possible foci into three categories. The first category entails a geographic focus; the representative may perceive his constituency in terms of nation, region, state, district, or any other territorial level of society. The second category would include particular solidary or functional groupings like ethnic, religious, economic, and ideological groups, whether organized or not. Finally, the representational relationship may have as foci individual persons ranging from distinguished notables to unknown clients in need of help and to personal friends.

Representational focus, then, can differ a great deal in each of these three ways. The crucial point, however, is that the focus of representation might vary with each of the four components of responsiveness. While one might find particular foci, according to the three categories, for policy responsiveness, one might find altogether different foci in regard to any of the other components of responsiveness. Any empirical combination is possible within relevant logical constraints. Empirical research has yet to address the relationship between modes of responsiveness and foci of representation, and untangle the web of complexity created by the relationship.

The Puzzle of Representation 249

Responsiveness versus Response

The generally confused and confusing use of "responsiveness," especially when linked to notions of "concurrence," is only symptomatic of a malaise that has come to characterize the "scientific" study of politics. The malaise is to substitute "theory construction" as a technique for substantive theory or theorizing. A younger scholar in the field, Fiorina (1974, p. 24), after reviewing the empirical research on representation of recent vintage, has come to a similar conclusion. We quote him precisely because he is not ignorant of or inimical to the new technological dispensations of our time:

> Too often it seems that the increasing availability of electronic computing facilities, data banks, and canned statistical packages has encouraged a concomitant decline in the use of our own capabilities. Rather than hypothesize we factor analyze, regress, or causal model. We speak of empirical theory as if it miraculously grows out of a cumulation of empirical findings, rather than as a logical structure one must carefully construct to explain those findings.

When Fiorina identifies "data banks" as one of the villains, he presumably implies that the user of these facilities has grown increasingly remote from his subjects of observation and lost touch with the humanity he is supposed to understand. Indeed, there are today users of survey research who have never interviewed a single person in their lives. Not surprisingly, therefore, causal models are being reified as if they described reality rather than being abstractions from reality. In the case of representational responsiveness, for instance, the causal direction has been assumed to point from the represented to the representative; the latter has been assumed to be the object of stimuli to which he responds (or does not respond) in the fashion of Pavlov's famous dog. But such a model, even if one provides for intervening attitudinal or perceptual processes, does not approximate representational relationships which are, above all, transactions not necessarily structured in the ways of the S-O-R paradigm.

To appreciate the complexity of representational relationships as transactions, it is simply erroneous to assume that responsiveness—whatever component may be involved—is somehow the dependent variable in a causal structure. "Responsiveness" and "response" are not the same thing. On the contrary, a representative whose behavior is purely *reactive*—a condition that is hard to conceive on reflection but one that the "concurrence model" postulates—is the very opposite of a politically responsive person in Pitkin's sense. As that person has been chosen, elected, or selected from the multitude or mass to be a representative, that is, as he occupies a superior position in the relationship by virtue of his "elevation," one should expect him not merely to be reactive but to take the initiative. Whether he does or not is, of course, an empirical question; but the question cannot be answered by simply substituting an inappropriate model of causation for empirical observation and a viable theory of representation that would guide both observation and analysis.

As already suggested, the attractiveness of the notion of responsiveness in the most recent period has been due in part to the fusion of participatory and representational ideas about democracy. But in the participatory theory of democracy the leader—insofar as the model admits of leadership at all—is largely a reactive agent guided by the collective wisdom of the group. He is at best the executor of the group's will, indeed a human facsimile of Pavlov's dog. He reacts, presumably, but he is not responsive. One is in fact back to the "instructed-delegate" model in which there is no room for discretion in the conduct of the representative. A causal model of representation that draws its arrows only in recursive fashion from the represented to the representative cannot capture, therefore, the meaning of responsiveness in Pitkin's sense. It excludes *ab initio* what is yet to be concluded.

It is a grievous error, against which Fiorina warned, to assume and to act as if the assumption were valid, that "causal analysis" will automatically yield "theory," or that by simple inversion of causal assumptions something meaningful will come out of a causal analysis. Theorizing involves something more than arbitrarily inverting the causal directions on the assumption that the resultant statistical structure will somehow reflect reality. It involves *giving reasons* and *justifying* the assumptions one brings into the causal analysis. It involves "going out on a limb," as it were, and saying something substantive about the phenomena being investigated, rather than hiding behind the artifactual "findings" of a causal analysis that may be inappropriate in the first place.

A next step in the study of representation as responsiveness must take off from the compositional nature of the phenomenon. This step cannot be limited to simplistic measures like congruence or concurrence in connection with one component of a complex set of transactional relationships. Any inferences one may make about the functions of any one component of responsiveness in "representative government" must be related to inferences one may make about the functions of other components. Otherwise the puzzle of representation—having representative government but not knowing what it is about—will continue to bewilder the political imagination.

NOTES

An earlier version of this paper was presented at the annual meeting of the Western Political Science Association, March 31-April 2, 1977.

The Puzzle of Representation 251

1. Miller and Stokes (1963). A revised version is included in Campbell, Converse, Miller, and Stokes (1966, pp. 351-372). We shall be citing the original article because we are only interested here in the theoretical aspects of the analysis which remained unaffected by the revision. The particular analysis was part of a much larger study of representation conducted in connection with the 1958 congressional elections.

2. In footnote 2 of their original article Miller and Stokes refer to Eulau, Wahlke, Buchanan, and Ferguson (1959); Hanna F. Pitkin's then unpublished Ph.D. dissertation (1961), which presumably led to her later *The Concept of Representation* (1967); de Grazia (1951); and Fairlie (1940).

3. The two most significant studies of the fifties in this genre were: Turner (1951) and MacRae (1958).

4. The operational definition was expressed as follows: "In each policy domain, crossing the rankings of Congressmen and their constituencies gives an empirical measure of the extent of policy agreement between legislator and district." The measure itself was expressed as follows: "To summarize the degree of congruence between legislators and voters, a measure of correlation is introduced" (Miller and Stokes, 1963, p. 49 and ft. 10).

5. See, e.g., Stone (1976, p. 8), where one finds the bland statement: "Representation is conceived as congruence or agreement between the behavior of the legislator and the opinion of the constituency on comparable policy dimensions." Compare this also with Clausen (1973, p. 128): "Given the principal orientation of this book, the policy orientation, representation is further defined as the congruence of the policy requirements of the constituency with the policy decisions of the representative."

6. Instead, to illustrate the constituency's sanctioning power through elections, Miller and Stokes relied on data for a single Congressional district in a case which is both inappropriate and deviant, involving the defeat of Congressman Brook Hays in the Fifth Arkansas District where all *voters* in the sample (N=13) had read or heard "something" about Hays and his write-in opponent. But, as Miller and Stokes admit, the case was inappropriate: the voters probably knew little about Hays' legislative record in the previous Congress but punished him for his non-legislative role in the Little Rock school crisis. The Hays case indicated the power of an aroused electorate in an unusual situation; but even if they knew the legislative records of their representatives, electorates are rarely so aroused over any one of the many legislative issues with which representatives deal.

7. Wahlke (1971). The core ideas of this article were first presented by Wahlke in a 1967 paper before the Seventh World Congress of the International Political Science Association in Brussels, Belgium.

8. We could cite here, of course, as extensive "institutional" literature which has come to be neglected by "behavioral" students of representation. For a particularly useful recent introduction that paints a broad canvas, see Birch (1971).

9. The problem with causal analyses of phenomena like influence or responsiveness is that the direction of the relationships to which they presumably refer cannot be inferred from the causal structure of the statistical model that may be applied. The statistical model assumes the existence of a conceptual isomorphism between its ordering of the variables and their real-world ordering. The existence of a *possible* isomorphism between the direction of a political relationship and a causal relation between two variables in a statistical model was brought to the attention of political scientists in a series of papers by Herbert A. Simon. Attempting to define political power, Simon found that "the difficulty appeared to reside in a very specific technical

Heinz Eulau and Paul D. Karps

point; influence, power, and authority are all intended as asymmetrical relations." It seemed to him that "the mathematical counterpart of this asymmetrical relation appeared to be the distinction between independent and dependent variables—the independent variable determines the dependent, and not the converse." But, he pointed out in a significant passage that causal analysts seem at times to overlook, "in algebra, the distinction between independent and dependent variable is purely conventional—we can always rewrite our equations without altering their content in such a way as to reverse their roles." The problem, then, is one of giving operational meaning to the asymmetry that is implied in the definition of influence or power: "That is to say, for the assertion, 'A has power over B,' we can substitute the assertion, 'A's behavior causes B's behavior.' If we can define the causal relation, we can define influence, power, or authority, and *vice versa*." See Simon (1957, p. 5). The most significant term in Simon's explication of the causal relation is "vice versa." It suggests that the definition of the "causal relation" and the definition of the phenomenon to be causally treated (here influence) are interdependent events. In other words: "If we can define influence, we can define the causal relation."

10. Unfortunately Fiorina then characterizes the new-style Congressman as an "ombudsman." This attribution is inappropriate because an ombudsman, though presumably available for the settlement of grievances, is not the kind of "hustler" whom Fiorina sees as coming on the stage of representation. Of course, both roles seem to be involved—that of ombudsman and that of hustler.

11. For example, Froman (1967, p. 36) found that in the 88th Congress (1963-1964) 15,299 bills and resolutions were introduced in the House of Representatives, whereas only 1,742, or a little over 11 percent, were reported by committee.

12. For the distinction between "style" and "focus" of representation, see Eulau, Wahlke, Buchanan, and Ferguson (1959).

13. Fenno (1975) has also seen the need to decompose the concept of constituency. He suggests that congressmen perceive several distinct types of constituencies to which they respond in different ways.

REFERENCES

Birch, A. H. 1971. *Representation*. London: St. Martin's Press.

Campbell, Angus, Converse, Philip E., Miller, Warren E., and Stokes, Donald E. 1966. *Elections and the Political Order*. New York: Wiley.

Clapp, Charles. 1963. *The Congressman: His Job as He Sees It*. Washington: Brookings Institution.

Clausen, Aage R. 1973. *How Congressmen Decide*. New York: St. Martin's Press.

Cnudde, Charles F., and McCrone, Donald J. 1966. "The Linkage between Constituency Attitudes and Congressional Voting: A Causal Model," *American Political Science Review* 60 (March, 1966): 66-72.

de Grazia, Alfred. 1951. *Public and Republic*. New York: Knopf.

Easton, David. 1965. *A Systems Analysis of Political Life*. New York: Wiley.

Edelman, Murray. 1964. *The Symbolic Uses of Politics*. Urbana: University of Illinois Press.

————. 1971. *Politics as Symbolic Action*. Chicago: Markham.

Eulau, Heinz. 1967. "Changing Views of Representation," in Ithiel de Sola Pool, ed., *Contemporary Political Science: Toward Empirical Theory*. New York: McGraw-Hill.

The Puzzle of Representation 253

Eulau, Heinz, Wahlke, John C., Buchanan, William, and Ferguson, LeRoy C. 1959. "The Role of the Representative: Some Empirical Observations on the Theory of Edmund Burke," *American Political Science Review* 53 (September, 1959): 742-756.

Eulau, Heinz, and Prewitt, Kenneth. 1973. *Labyrinths of Democracy: Adaptations, Linkages, Representation, and Policies in Urban Politics.* Indianapolis: Bobbs-Merrill.

Fairlie, John S. 1940. "The Nature of Political Representation," *American Political Science Review* 40 (April-June, 1940): 236-248, 456-466.

Fenno, Richard F. 1973. *Congressmen in Committees.* Boston: Little, Brown.

————. 1975. "Congressmen in their Constituencies." Prepared for delivery at the annual meeting of the American Political Science Association.

Fiorina, Morris P. 1974. *Representatives, Roll Calls, and Constituencies.* Lexington, Mass.: D. C. Heath.

————. 1977. "The Case of the Vanishing Marginals: The Bureaucracy Did It," *American Political Science Review* 71 (March, 1977): 177-181.

Jackson, John E. 1974. *Constituencies and Leaders in Congress.* Cambridge, Mass.: Harvard University Press.

Kingdon, John W. 1973. *Congressmen's Voting Decisions.* New York: Harper and Row.

Lasswell, Harold D., Merriam, Charles E., and Smith, T. V. 1950. *A Study of Power.* Glencoe, Ill.: Free Press.

Loewenberg, Gerhard. 1972. "Comparative Legislative Research," in Samuel C. Patterson and John C. Wahlke, eds., *Comparative Legislative Behavior: Frontiers of Research.* New York: Wiley.

MacRae, Duncan, Jr. 1958. *Dimensions of Congressional Voting.* Berkeley: University of California Press.

Matthews, Donald R., and Stimson, James A. 1975. *Yeas and Nays: Normal Decision-Making in the U. S. House of Representatives.* New York: Wiley.

Miller, Warren E., and Stokes, Donald E. 1963. "Constituency Influence in Congress," *American Political Science Review* 57 (March, 1963): 45-56.

Muller, Edward N. 1970. "The Representation of Citizens by Political Authorities: Consequences for Regime Support," *American Political Science Review* 64 (December, 1970): 1149-1166.

Patterson, Samuel C., Hedlund, Ronald D., and Boynton, G. R. 1975. *Representatives and Represented: Bases of Public Support for the American Legislatures.* New York: Wiley.

Peterson, Paul E. 1970. "Forms of Representation: Participation of the Poor in the Community Action Program," *American Political Science Review* 64 (June, 1970): 491-507.

Pitkin, Hanna F. 1961. "The Theory of Representation." Ph.D. dissertation, University of California, Berkeley.

————. 1967. *The Concept of Representation.* Berkeley: University of California Press.

Prewitt, Kenneth, and Eulau, Heinz. 1969. "Political Matrix and Political Representation: Prolegomenon to a New Departure from an Old Problem," *American Political Science Review* 63 (June, 1969): 427-441.

Simon, Herbert A. 1957. *Models of Man.* New York: Wiley.

Stone, Walter J. 1976. "Representation in the United States House of Representatives." Ph. D. dissertation, University of Michigan.

Turner, Julius. 1951. *Party and Constituency: Pressures on Congress*. Baltimore: Johns Hopkins University Press.

Turner, Julius, and Schneier, Edward V., Jr. 1970. *Party and Constituency*. Baltimore: Johns Hopkins University Press.

Verba, Sidney, and Nie, Norman H. 1972. *Participation in America: Political Democracy and Social Equality*. New York: Harper and Row.

Wahlke, John C. 1971. "Policy Demands and System Support: The Role of the Represented," *British Journal of Political Science* 1 (July, 1971): 271-290.

Zeigler, L. Harmon, and Jennings, M. Kent, with G. W. Peak. 1974. *Governing American Schools*. No. Scituate, Mass.: Duxbury Press.

3

REPRESENTATION IS DEMOCRACY

David Plotke

Complaints about the quality of representation appear widely in contemporary politics. Angry citizens assail representatives for acting in elitist and narrowly self-interested ways. Some critiques target the inefficiency of legislative procedures. Others blame elected officials and interest groups for creating dense, corrupt networks of influence that prevent action on crucial matters. Participatory democrats and postmodern radicals often reject representation altogether in favor of immediacy and direct control.

My argument takes a different direction. I will first discuss how debates about representation took shape during the Cold War, and how the end of that conflict changes the terms of debate. Then I propose a view of representation which differs in crucial ways from the main views advocated during the Cold War.

I argue that the opposite of representation is not participation. The opposite of representation is exclusion. And the opposite of participation is abstention. Rather than opposing participation to representation, we should try to improve representative practices and forms to make them more open, effective, and fair. Representation is not an unfortunate compromise between an ideal of direct democracy and messy modern realities. Representation is crucial in constituting democratic practices. "Direct" democracy is not precluded by the scale of modern politics. It is unfeasible because of core features of politics and democracy as such.

I. After the Cold War

In the late 1980s and early 1990s most Communist regimes fell apart. The shape of their replacements was not clear. An economic debate ensued – how fast should the transition to a market economy occur, and what sort of market economy should be built? Parts of the Western left made a useful contribution by arguing that the most rapid and thorough shift to a market economy was not always optimal for growth, political stability or equity.

In politics, the idea was that Communist states should be replaced by liberal parliamentary regimes. Here the Western left had little of interest to say about this process or its aims. Why?

At a recent meeting of political scientists, a prominent political theorist spoke on a panel whose members had been asked to respond to the events of the last

Constellations Volume 4, Number 1, 1997

decade in Eastern Europe. He said that those events are not very compelling, because dismantling old-fashioned tyrannies is not our problem ("our" meant democrats in the ex-West). To focus on the demise of the Communist regimes might even misdirect our attention, turning us away from the intricate forms of unfreedom that confine politics in the ex-West.

There is a connection between these two episodes – one large and one small. Democrats who are mainly skeptical of representative institutions tend not to have much of interest to say about how such institutions should be built and developed in countries which previously lacked them. To explain why this is so requires looking once again at the Cold War.

The Cold War was partly a political argument, and the defeat of the Soviet Union and its allies was a political defeat. Well before the end of the Cold War, the political failure of the Communist side appeared in the *demoralization* of Communist elites – in their lack of commitment to the Communist order and eventually in their notable unwillingness to fight for it.

A repeated logic of political argument helped to shape the outcome of the Cold War. First, Communist regimes and theorists rejected Western democracy as hollow and false. They claimed to be establishing a fuller and higher form of democracy.

Second, defenders of Western regimes responded with an account of what can fairly be called minimal democracy. This view was formulated sharply by Joseph Schumpeter in the 1940s. He argued that democracy means choosing political leaders through elections – period:

> . . . the democratic method is that institutional arrangement for arriving at political decisions in which individuals acquire the power to decide by means of a competitive struggle for the people's vote.[1]

Proponents of minimal democracy did not simply restate Schumpeter's claim. They often stressed the intrinsic value of political liberties (which Schumpeter derived from the notion of a free electoral competition). Some advocates of minimal democracy also claimed that political socialization could bolster democracy. Yet most theorists of minimal democracy put electoral competition for leadership at the center of democratic practices.

This view was highly effective in political and theoretical battles during the Cold War, when all parties claimed to uphold democracy. Politically, it allowed critics of Communism to ask blunt and effective questions: How are leaders chosen in these higher democracies? Who decides if they should be replaced? These questions were powerful weapons among Western publics and, it would appear, in weakening support for Communist regimes among their political and social elites. (They remain effective today, as in the political competition between the regimes in China and Taiwan.)

Theoretically, Schumpeter's formulation was compelling in a now familiar way. He explained an important result (democracy) as the unintended result of self-interested action in a particular institutional setting (seeking power via elections). Here is Schumpeter again:

> . . . [T]he social meaning or function of parliamentary activity is no doubt to turn out legislation and, in part, administrative measures. But in order to understand how democratic politics serve this social end, we must start from the competitive struggle for power and office and realize that the social function is fulfilled, as it were, incidentally – in the same sense as production is incidental to the making of profits.[2]

In the third part of the Cold War dynamic, critics of minimal democracy in the West rejected it as pseudodemocratic. Proponents of a participatory left saw themselves as caught between corrupt critiques of minimal democracy made by apologists for Communist regimes and restrictive notions of democracy proposed as quasi-official doctrine in the West.

In the Cold War, nonCommunist left critics of minimal democracy tended to define their positions by reversing the latter's claims. For example, Communist regimes extolled high levels of participation in their countries. Proponents of minimal democracy responded by insisting that this participation was coerced. They argued that the right to participate entails the right to refrain from politics. When some went on to suggest that, given basic freedoms, low levels of political participation show satisfaction with the overall course of politics, they took a complacent and even apologetic view of participation in the West.

Given this unappetizing menu, critics of minimal democracy advocated a sharp and sustained increase in political participation. They did not propose that coercion be used. Yet they paid little attention to the limits to participation that exist in a democratic regime, notably time constraints and varied preferences for political activity.

Critics of minimal democracy claimed they were sincerely democratic, not pro-Communist. This rationale for participatory and neorepublican positions has largely disappeared, as there are no more Communists against which radical proposals look reasonable because they are not manifestly authoritarian. The end of the Cold War undermines the implicit basis of such proposals, which went something like this: Given the political and ideological rigidity of the Cold War, there is no prospect of our proposals being implemented. Consider them as provocations about what might be done in a very different political climate. Now a different political context has appeared, and participatory democrats have had little to say beyond warning democrats in the ex-Communist countries not to get too excited about their new parliamentary institutions.

The political dynamic I have outlined recurred in the four decades of the Cold War. Figure 1 summarizes some of the main arguments in which the participatory left rejected and often tended to invert the positions taken by minimal democrats. On most fronts, proponents of minimal democracy won these arguments about politics. They dominated crucial debates, such as those about how to connect and

Constellations Volume 4, Number 1, 1997

distinguish political and social life (by affirming separation); about the forms and extent of agreement required for political stability (agreement on political procedures and procedural norms); and about the appropriate form of the state (regulation rather than planning). Over time, advocates of Communism appeared sinister or stupid while participatory democrats seemed naive or disruptive.

Today all three Cold War positions have unraveled. Communism has disappeared as a political and theoretical force. The views of the participatory left have not recently yielded major new political or theoretical initiatives. The fragmentation of minimal democracy is well advanced, as libertarians, cultural conservatives, social liberals, and social democrats clash and redefine their positions.

II Arguments about Representation

I want to explore this dynamic of Cold War argument through the important case of representation. During the Cold War, leaders and theorists of Communist regimes vigorously criticized "Western" representative politics while claiming:

Communist leaders function as wise trustees for the nation, making decisions in everyone's long-run interests.

All legitimate social interests are represented politically within the leading party.

Figure 1. Cold War Conflicts

	Minimal Democracy	Communism	Participatory Left
Forms of representation	Elite competition, linked to parties and interest groups	Pure trustee (Leninism)	Replace with participation
Links between social and political life	Social pluralism and separation between politics and society	Integrate society into politics (vertical and horizontal)	Integrate politics into society
Agreement needed for political stability	Agreement on procedures and procedural norms	Political and moral agreement on the direction and meaning of history	Republican unity in a political and social community
Appropriate form of the state	Decentralized within a political system; aimed at regulation	Ultracentralist; aimed at controlling social and economic outcomes	Welfarist; aimed at redistribution

Representation is Democracy: David Plotke

The party and quasipolitical organizations (trade unions, neighborhood associations, women's groups) overcome the Western separation between citizens and politics and allow people to influence governance directly.

The first claim linked quasi-Burkean notions of representation to left-authoritarian practices. It turned on judgments of long-run interests about which there was no agreement. Critics of Communism showed that the second and third claims were not true. Advocates of the Communist regimes were thus vulnerable to the charge that citizens had no way to make their own decisions about the degree of their leaders' wisdom.

Proponents of minimal democracy, stressing regular and open elections, did not have to claim much to win the day. For this view, representation appears as what elites must have been doing to keep themselves in power. If elections occur regularly, representatives who refuse to pay attention to constituents will be pushed out of office. The fear of electoral defeat constrains the choices of officials and stirs their interest in the opinions and welfare of their constituents.

The Communist account of representation in state socialist regimes was so weak that it could be defeated by almost any account of representation in the West, all of which compared favorably with a Communist reality in which trustees told constituents what to do with little fear of sanctions. Minimal democracy faced a stronger critique from parts of the nonCommunist left. The claim was that conventional representative procedures, based on a fragmented and disinterested electorate, replaced or blocked political participation and left most people powerless. In the 1960s and 1970s, this participatory argument intersected a neorepublican critique of representation that extolled the virtues of political action and public life. While the participatory critique underlined the *lack of power* of those who were only represented, the republican argument stressed the *deprivation* suffered by those who did not spend their time exercising public freedom.

These critiques of representation made strong points against proponents of a scheme in which citizens had little role between elections and did little more than assent to choices prepared and defined by elites. But critics offered no compelling alternative. Participatory democrats advocated that everyone participate actively in deciding everything important for their lives. Neorepublicans depicted public life as not only a good thing, but as the primary source of real accomplishment and happiness. Such proposals were vulnerable to rejoinders by minimal democrats: Everyone cannot always participate everywhere, and not everyone should value public life above other goods. Proponents of minimal democracy dominated this field of argument so easily that their thin notions of representation became political common sense.

After the Cold War, complaints about the quality of representation have become louder. The critique of representation has been taken up vigorously by a renovated right in the United States and elsewhere. Doubtful that representatives can be made to act more responsibly, conservative critics of political representation try to constrain representative bodies by limiting the number of terms that elected officials can serve, decentralizing control of important matters (block grants), limiting spending (a balanced budget amendment), and narrowing government intervention through deregulation. The conservative critique contrasts political representation with communal networks and markets, where individuals can have real power and live virtuously. This critique regards political decisionmaking as inferior to markets and communal associations, which are held to be simpler, more efficient, and more respectful of individuals' autonomy.

At a time when populist criticism of legislatures and representation is angry and insistent, we should recognize that urgent calls for direct and simple political relations have often been made by democratic movements. Yet successful democratic movements most often make politics more complex and less direct. This may not be the immediate experience of those involved. Women who gain the vote can speak more directly on public matters. Workers who build independent unions and blacks who dismantle segregation become more directly involved in making political decisions.

When democratic movements win, however, politics as a whole tends to become more complex. Direct personal domination is replaced by procedures that rely on more general and abstract relations among political agents. Democratic successes expand the number of voices in conversations about what to do and thereby make decisions more complicated.

If democratic movements tend to increase political complexity, we should not identify democracy with simplicity or directness per se – even if those same movements rightly say that democratic reform will make politics more directly accessible for them. Obviously to claim that increased complexity causes democratization is not plausible. But complexity and democracy can often be compatible and even interdependent, as they are in many forms of representation. Thus while a particular representative scheme may be unnecessarily complicated and deserve criticism, there is nothing democratic in principle about criticizing representation for being complex or abstract.

In fact, representation has a central positive role in democratic politics. To develop this view, I next assess a proposal for democracy without representation. Then I discuss key elements of the concept of representation. I emphasize the relational and active dimensions of representation, as opposed to conceptions that begin by identifying representation with the absence or passive role of the one represented.[3]

I should underline that I do not intend to reject participation. My point, again, is that the opposite of representation is not participation: the opposite of representation is exclusion. And the opposite of participation is abstention. Rather than opposing participation to representation, we should try to improve and expand representative practices. On that basis, a number of the most valuable aspects of participation should be considered as part of a reformed scheme of representation.

III The Critique of Representation

Calls for participatory democracy played a positive and provocative role during the Cold War by underlining the narrowness of prevalent conceptions of minimal democracy. After the Cold War this role no longer exists. To say one's critique of conventional democratic forms is not authoritarian is not a resonant claim when there are no Communists to play the role of undemocratic radicals. Advocates of participatory democracy now face a setting where their ideas might be taken seriously as practical choices – no wartime unity precludes it.

Benjamin Barber's influential critique of representation illustrates the limits of those ideas. Barber advocates "strong" democracy, meaning:

> politics in the participatory mode where conflict is resolved in the absence of an independent ground through a participatory process of ongoing, proximate self-legislation and the creation of a political community capable of transforming dependent, private individuals into free citizens and partial and private interests into public goods.[4]

He adamantly rejects representation:

> Representation is incompatible with freedom. . . . Representation is incompatible with equality . . . Representation, finally, is incompatible with social justice. . . .[5]

When Barber outlines a "strong" democracy he proposes:

> 1. A national system of NEIGHBORHOOD ASSEMBLIES of from one to five thousand citizens; these would initially have only deliberative functions but would eventually have local legislative competence as well.[6]

The assembly presumably includes all adults in the neighborhood. If not, there is no point in further discussion, as we are already in a representative situation.

To give life to this assembly, imagine that it is charged with deliberating and then choosing policies about local primary and secondary education. Two problems immediately arise, probably with enough force to stop the project as direct democracy. One is the problem of attendance. In the deliberative stage, consider that most people prefer to attend. But circumstances make a number of people unable to do so: illness, work schedules, responsibility for children. Others are ambivalent – students who prefer to study, artists who want to complete their day's work in the evening, and so forth. In direct democracy, everyone needs to attend. Could this be done without coercion for a sequence of meetings?

The second problem arises if time scarcity were somehow managed and sufficient resources were expended to allow everyone to attend. At this meeting of (say) one thousand people, who gets to talk first? And last? Imagine an open floor at one of the first meetings, when an agenda for deliberation is shaped. Presume a long evening meeting of 2.5 hours. Interventions average three minutes, including applause and pauses between speakers. Fifty speakers get the floor. (The meeting has conversational elements, so there are forty separate speakers and ten people speak twice.)

Are the other 960 members of the assembly participants or highly interested spectators at a political event? If "direct" means more than being physically present, in what sense would this 96% of the assembly be engaged in strong or direct democracy? Barber's critique of representation would surely apply to the relation between the 4% of the room with a voice and the 96% with eyes and ears only.

Somehow these problems are surmounted and we continue to regard the assembly as engaged in direct democracy. Consider a sequence of such meetings on education policies. Imagine an enthusiastic assembly willing to deliberate weekly for between six months and a year before moving toward choices on policies. Then the meeting arrives when the assembly becomes a legislative body.

Prior deliberations give everyone a good knowledge of models of education and their community's needs. For legislative purposes people now have two choices. They can discuss overall models one at a time. Or they can consider component policies individually. Presume that time constraints encourage a choice to address the main issues in order: hiring school directors; selecting the teaching staff; defining the curriculum; choosing sites for schools and deciding how to build them; organizing transportation; and funding all the above. This list marks a decision point: coercion, collapse, or representation.

Why? The assembly would have two main options for its new legislative meetings. It could meet as a whole in a sequence of meetings to take up each issue in turn. This sequence would probably have to be much longer than the first set of deliberative meetings in order to make the required decisions. It is unimaginable that unanimous attendance would persist, due to time constraints, exhausted resources, and varied preferences. Sustaining attendance would probably require coercion as the meetings went to a second year. If the assembly rejected coercion, and a diminishing part of the neighborhood attended, it would head toward collapse due to a lack of legitimacy (and collective action problems).

A committee system, based on policy areas, would most likely be the preferred alternative to another series of general meetings. These committee meetings would make a clear transition to a representative model. Someone very interested in choosing school directors would sacrifice their lesser interest in curricular issues. One might reasonably hope to have a vote in the final integration of policies decided by the subcommittees. But by then the whole process would have a frankly representative character, if it survived.

Barber or an advocate of similar views might object that I am taking his proposal too literally. Yet it is not persuasive to say that Barber's proposal would be workable with less stringent criteria – say 60 percent of the adult members of the neighborhood attend half the meetings, while others attend occasionally. Such meetings would be a *de facto* representative assembly with no legitimate basis for selecting members or making decisions.[7]

It takes only a small number of citizens and a routine issue (education) to rule out a nonrepresentative democracy. Direct democracy is implausible – not a desirable but difficult goal, nor an attractive horizon that may be out of reach. Little is gained by proposals to integrate two types of democracy, representative and direct. The intent of such proposals may be to shake up minimal democratic forms, to expand participation and address new issues. Yet proposing to combine representative and direct democracy offers to mix a flawed reality with an implausible construct. We should instead try to improve representative practices and develop new ones.

"Direct" democracy is not precluded by the scale of modern politics, but because of core features of democracy as such. This is true because democratic premises include sufficient autonomy for individuals to develop and sustain different preferences, including different preferences for political involvement, and because democratic forms include a commitment to reaching decisions.[8]

The image of a direct and simple democracy relies on a misconceived effort to substitute participation for representation. But representation is not an unfortunate compromise between an ideal of direct democracy and messy realities. It is crucial in constituting democratic practices.

IV Elements of Representation

What does representation mean, especially in politics? Hannah Pitkin's start, in her valuable and influential book on the subject, is misleading: ". . . [R]epresentation, taken generally, means the making present *in some sense* of something which is nevertheless not present literally or in fact."[9]

Formulations like Pitkin's are often used to get discussions of representation off the ground. Thus Ernesto Laclau recently writes that representation is "[e]ssentially the *fictio iuris* that somebody is present in a place from which he or she is materially absent."[10] From Pitkin to Laclau there is a loss of nuance (the notion that representation makes something "present in some sense" is gone). But Laclau's formulation is basically equivalent to Pitkin's because she focuses on literal, physical presence.

For Pitkin *presence* and *representation* seem mainly to be opposites. This downplays the *relational* and *abstract* elements of political representation. In a typical dictionary listing the first meaning of representation is "to stand for" – not replace or omit.[11] That is a reasonable starting point. Yet when we refer to social relations, if we say to *represent is to stand for* we need to add *in a relation of mutual interest.*

To understand political representation we can first look at other forms of that relation. With representation among objects, the first meaning is signification – to represent something is to stand for it, without replacing it.

28 *Constellations Volume 4, Number 1, 1997*

To say x represents y entails several claims. First, there is a claim of nonidentity. We do not say that my chair represents my chair, though we might say that a particular chair represents chairs in general.

Second, there is a claim of a meaningful rather than a natural connection, so that a symbol is *recognized*. Let this piece of chalk represent a division of an army as I portray a famous battle, let this wine represent the blood of Christ. When x and y share a property and are thus similar – oranges and lemons, or lions and tigers – we do not say they represent each other.

Third, claims of representation are contextual. A red sign at a streetcorner represents an instruction to comply with a law against going through the intersection without stopping.

These elements remain when we ask about representation in a market setting. If we say that person a represents person b in an exchange, we mean a is not identical to b; their relationship is a function of social understandings (about how contracts can be made); and this relationship is contextual (one's real estate agent is not entitled to announce one's conversion to a new religion).

New features appear. My representative in the market is *authorized* to make certain agreements. He or she is presumed to make *truthful depictions* of my aims and capacities (e.g., I can buy the building in question). In turn I am *obligated* by his or her actions. I communicate with my representative, and I can replace him or her.

These new elements indicate the presence of *agency* in market representation. For the participatory view, to say x represents y is to say that x does something to y. But a market relation contains agency on both sides. The active side of the agent's behavior is sometimes noted – and criticized as a form of domination or alienation – in participatory accounts. What is not taken seriously in such accounts, and usually not even noted, is the agency of the principal, i.e., the person being represented. If x represents y, y is guiding and constraining x, enabling and authorizing her or him.

In political representation all these elements persist. Nonidentity, relations of meaning, and contextuality are all features of political representation. Nonidentity is a very important dimension of any democratic notion of representation. Concepts of representation that claim a merging and full identity between a representative and those who seek representation are often deployed in authoritarian populist regimes: Peron, or Castro, or even Mussolini represents you because he is like you, understands you, is even identical to you as a part of the people. You are, in effect, represented by the presence of a superior version of yourself in government.

As in a market context, my representative is *authorized* to vote on legislation. He or she is presumed to be intending to be truthful, e.g., if he or she claims that a majority in their district supports a measure, they have good reason to think so. I accept the outcomes of the voting process in the relevant legislative setting as *binding*, unless they are changed by authorized procedures. I express my preferences, minimally through voting, and could act (along with others) to replace my representative.

A major new emphasis appears in political representation. Imagine that I instruct my economic agent to buy space for a factory to produce an item whose manufacture is highly profitable but whose production is very destructive of the environment. She returns from her business to say that because of that prospect she decided to make a different purchase (or donate the money to a worthy charity). I would be entitled to dismiss her as my representative, subject to the terms of our contract. It is presumed that my expressed preferences should define the course of her actions. A market agent can adjust his or her actions to take account of unanticipated events, but sweeping reinterpretations of preferences are not permitted, certainly not without consultation between principal and agent.

A political representative looks toward the preferences of those they represent, toward others' preferences, and toward their own view of overall welfare. Political representatives recognize the existence of competing and general interests alongside those of their constituents. And they consider whether their constituents' choices are the best way to get what those constituents want. In political representation dialogic elements between principal and agent expand, as does the latter's room for maneuver.

Political representation, like market forms of representation, authorizes agents to act, presumes a reliable report of aims, entails communication, produces decisions that are binding for the person represented, and is revocable. Political representation includes a substantial role for the judgment of the representative in choosing how to act as a responsible agent. The preferences of the person being represented are subject to interpretation – making them clear requires dialogue. And preferences other than those of the person represented need recognition, if only for strategic reasons.

For participatory critics of representation, and many others who rely on Pitkin's analysis, representation is linked with absence. In a more recent essay, Pitkin follows this logic and depicts participation as the preferred alternative to representation:

> As long as politics is equated with government, and government regarded as a means for achieving private purposes and reconciling conflicting claims in a generally acceptable manner, rightly designed representative institutions may serve its purposes very well. But if its real function is to direct our shared, public life, and its real value lies in the opportunity to share in power over and responsibility for what we, jointly, as a society, are doing, then no one else can do my politics 'for' me, and representation can mean only the exclusion of most people from its benefits most of the time.[12]

The key phrase, "do my politics," signals the convergence of libertarian and participatory critiques of politics in an image of self-expression and self-realization. What disappears is any sense that representation is a *relation*, one in which both parties are active. To gain representation, I communicate preferences about how social relations should be ordered to someone else. My aim is to achieve those preferences, with the proviso that they might change in the course of communication about how to do so.

Thinking of representation as absence is apt to lead to rejecting the concept and the practice. If *X* represents *Y* in politics, is *Y* present? We could simply say yes, because we are already in a political realm where everyone is in principle present as citizens. But that answer seems almost glib, given what we know about rates of voting and other forms of political participation in many democratic countries. It would be better to change the meaning of the question a bit: Physical persons and relations of political representation exist at different analytical levels. Even though these levels are intertwined in actual situations they are not the same. Thus it is plausible to say that in a given context, someone is present politically but not physically.

The distinction between physical presence and political presence can be clarified by a nondemocratic example. Think of a slaveowners' polity, when citizens assemble to decide on common matters. The citizen slaveowners bring their slaves to the assembly, where they serve their owners and wait near them for instructions. We would hesitate to say that the slaves were present in a political sense, because we do not really think that physical and political presence are the same thing.

I gain political representation when my authorized representative tries to achieve my political aims, subject to dialogue about those aims and to the use of mutually acceptable procedures for gaining them. I may or may not be physically present when my representative engages in various activities, but in a political sense I am forcefully present throughout the representative process. This conception underlines the agency of both participants in the relationship, the strategic elements of their interaction, and the need for communication between them.[13]

V Democracy as Representation

Representation helps constitute democratic capacities and practices. In principal-agent relations in a market context, we do not assume an opposition between acting and being represented. Instead we presume that the principal is both active and represented. Both market and political notions of representation presume the agency of the principal, so to speak. "I represent *X*" most often means that I act as a representative for *X*. But "I represent" also means that I claim to have certain capacities and interests. Thus I represent myself politically, to and through a representative. These uses of representation signal its active side for the person who often appears as a predicate [*B* represents me in Congress] or a passive subject [I am represented by *B*].

Here I will return to the dimensions of representation outlined earlier in order to indicate their positive elements with regard to democratic practices. First, to

Representation is Democracy: David Plotke 31

say that I am represented makes a claim of nonidentity. To assert that one is represented by *B* is a claim not of dependence but of mutuality, which presumes real autonomy from *B*.[14]

Second, my representation is a relation that requires others' recognition. Part of the basis for recognition is the act of political choice that I have made in selecting a representative. Thus I am recognized as being able to participate in a relationship of representation.

Third, representation is contextual: *B* is my political representative. My understanding of this shows I can distinguish among practices.

These elements of representation help constitute a political person with a significant degree of autonomy; the capacity to choose a representative; and the capacity to make and sustain distinctions between political and other practices.

What I have identified as the market dimension of representation helps to constitute competent agents. When I take on an agent who can make agreements – when I represent myself through an agent – I expand my ability to make such agreements. The idea that I am obligated by my agent's acts attests to my capacity to meet such obligations (if I were not capable, he or she might not have agreed to represent me). These forms of power to set and attain objectives have a *potentially* democratic meaning insofar as I represent my interests and abilities truthfully and accurately through my agent, and I communicate effectively with him or her during our relationship.

Crucial democratic features of representation emerge with its most specifically political elements. A political representative (by convention and often by law) cannot be subject to binding mandates, however strong their commitment may be to the preferences of constituents. That lack of closure creates a permanent need for representatives and those who are representing themselves to negotiate their relationship. Both parties know that while the person who wants representation has preferences, those are not the only relevant factors. Other constituents may have different preferences, and the representative has his or her own aims.

These features of representation encourage a person who wants good representation to take account of others' preferences and to recognize complexity (and scarcity) of many types. In reporting a preference to a representative with any prospect of success, I have to be able to step back from my experience far enough to describe a problem in terms that someone who does not share that experience can understand. I have to be able to define the relations in which that problem is located and evaluate its causes in ways that are plausibly connected to remedies I might propose. I also have to make a decision about what to propose that my representative do, in a context where I know that other projects are underway: I have to persuade my representative how to act.

Democratic politics is *constituted* partly through representation. Representation is constructive, producing knowledge, the capacity to share insights, and the ability to reach difficult agreements. It entails a capacity for recognizing social relations in order to consider changing them. Representation also helps to constitute democratic institutions. It requires procedures for taking decisions, and there have to be ways of sustaining those decisions over time.

As with forms of representation, democratic politics in general is a process of more or less artful construction. The "unnatural" qualities of democracy make it vulnerable to critiques as thin, formal, and abstract. Such criticism is partly true and basically misleading. Democracy is abstract when it treats citizens as equal. It is abstract in sustaining decision procedures that are part of the process through which majorities are built. It is formal in insisting on the nonnegotiable character of rights and procedures (e.g., freedom of expression and voting). And democracy means compromises of principle because it is a way to make decisions where resources are limited and preferences are strong. The misleading core of participatory and populist criticism is the idea that we could get rid of the formality and the complexity and still have democracy, much less a purer form of it.

VI Choices about Representation

My aim here is not to endorse any particular set of representative forms, but to insist that a democratic politics has to be a politics of and about representation. I will close by proposing positions in difficult debates about appropriate forms of representation.

A system of representation should not be a pure expression of any single mode of trustee, interest, identity or any other form of representation.[15] In a complex polity with functional and territorial divisions, several modes of representation have a legitimate role to play. Choices are usually about weighing gains and losses from giving one or another mode of representation a primary role in a particular setting.

Yet the starting point in a democratic view of representation should be interest representation. Interest representation gives greater weight to the activities of citizens in seeking to understand, clarify, and achieve their preferences than do alternative models of representation. Thus it emphasizes the active and reflective elements of seeking representation. A system based exclusively on interest representation would have notable defects, which critics have often pointed out (too much bargaining, too little deliberation, too little room for actions aimed at the general or public interest). Despite these problems, any overall system of representation without a large element of interest representation would probably not be feasible for long as a democratic process.

What do citizens do in interest representation? Their first aim is to clarify their own preferences. Then they seek to select representatives who will try to produce suitable results. When their electoral efforts succeed, constituents seek to press their representatives to take positive steps. Constituents need to be diligent because of the strong presence of competing interests within and outside their district. What do representatives do? They seek to win results that match the expressed preferences of their constituents. In relations with other representatives there is much bargaining (along with at least some deliberation – it is hard to strike a good bargain on an important matter without deliberation about what that bargain means). Representatives remain close to their initial positions, changing them mainly as a result of trades that can be justified to constituents (a highway in our district next year rather than two bridges this year).

In interest representation, representatives seek primarily to pursue their constituents' interests as defined by their expressed preferences. As binding interest representation (fully mandated representation) is illegitimate in democratic polities, we are considering forms of representation that contain general elements. A representative cannot say only: I support Y because I am bound to do so by an agreement with my constituents. He or she must say: Y, which is a matter of great concern to my constituents, is crucial to the public good. Political debate contests that claim.

Starting with interest representation rules out a view of democratic reform as primarily a matter of expanding the autonomy of representatives from their constituents, to improve parliamentary deliberation or for some other purpose. The aim should be to improve these links, for example by increasing deliberative elements within them. Taking interest representation as a starting point also means little sympathy for populist or libertarian assaults on interest group politics, as though the political terrain would be better swept clean in favor of "the people" or the market.

Starting with interest representation opens up promising areas of practical inquiry: expanding participation in representative forms; enhancing communication between representatives and constituents; increasing effective participation by previously excluded or underrepresented groups; and increasing sites and modes of representation. Such efforts will meet strong resistance, from people who believe politics is already too complex and from people who regard such reforms as an undesirable expansion of politics *per se*.

What about the episodes with which I began? Most of the Western left has had little to say about political choices in East and Central Europe because political forces in those countries have aimed mainly to establish stable forms of minimal democracy, not to criticize or overcome them. This has put the left in general and the participatory left in particular in an uncomfortable position. Often nothing at all is said about some of the most important political changes of the last few decades. Alternatively, what is said appears to diminish the accomplishment of getting rid of the communist regimes and starting to build democratic political orders. An effort to rethink and reconstruct representative practices is a better place for democrats to start, though it promises much conflict at a time when the main political positions of the Cold War have come apart.

NOTES

* Parts of this article were presented at a general seminar of the Graduate Faculty, New School for Social Research, and at the Graduate Institute in Cracow, Poland, in the summer of 1996. Thanks for comments to: Andrew Arato, Jeffrey Goldfarb, James Miller, and members of the Cracow course.

34   *Constellations Volume 4, Number 1, 1997*

1. Joseph Schumpeter, *Capitalism, Socialism, and Democracy* (New York: Harper, 1950), 269.
2. Ibid., 282.
3. Like everyone who writes about representation, I have benefited from Hannah Fenichel Pitkin's *The Concept of Representation* (Berkeley: University of California Press, 1972).
4. Benjamin Barber, *Strong Democracy: Participatory Politics for a New Age* (Berkeley and Los Angeles: University of California Press, 1984), 132.
5. Ibid., 135, 145–46.
6. This proposal is the first and crucial element in a program of 12 points that Barber claims "does not illustrate strong democracy; it is strong democracy." Ibid., 307.
7. His proposal has further problems – for example, it pays little attention to the possibility that those deliberating about education would develop strong differences through the process of considering the issues, extending deliberations and making policy decisions much harder to reach.
8. Here my argument intersects that of Jane Mansbridge in *Beyond Adversary Democracy* (Chicago and London: University of Chicago Press, 1983). She contrasts a unitary conception of democracy based on shared or common interests to an adversary conception based on conflicting interests. To use her terms, I would say that any feasible democracy contains decisive elements of the adversarial model, less because of the size of the units involved than because differing preferences and pressures to reach decisions exist in virtually all political settings.
9. Pitkin, *The Concept of Representation*, 9.
10. Ernesto Laclau, "Power and Representation," *Emancipation(s)* (London and New York: Verso, 1996), 97.
11. *The American Heritage Dictionary of the English Language – New College Edition* (Boston: Houghton Mifflin Company, 1980).
12. Hannah Fenichel Pitkin, "Representation," in Terence Ball et. al. eds., *Political Innovation and Conceptual Change* (Cambridge: New York, 1989), 150.
13. This conception might be called abstract. Yet democratic politics is by its nature abstract with regard to people's direct social experience: it entails selective description, critical reflection, and making decisions under constraints. Any account of direct experience entails considerable abstraction from the vast amount of data that could be described. A second abstraction occurs because politics entails reflection on how to organize social life, not a thick redescription of what people experience. Individuals and groups choose what to discuss and how to evaluate it, and then compare and argue for their evaluations. A third abstraction results from the need for decisions among political actors, who are never political actors alone (time scarcity), disagree deeply, and are in principle equal. To make a decision in these circumstances means considering alternatives. This in turn means abstracting key features of complex settings in order to compare prospective outcomes.
14. This autonomy precludes any closure in which principal and agent become one – either one. Nondemocratic concepts of representation allow a reversal of terms so that representatives incorporate their principals. Two important versions of representation as incorporation in American political and legal history were coverture in marriage law and Southern accounts of slavery as part of republican politics.
15. In trustee representation, the representative aims to achieve what he or she imagines to be the best outcome for an individual, without necessarily acting in accord with that person's expressed preferences. A good trustee is a wise judge of his or her constituents' needs and how to meet them. What do trustee representatives do among themselves? In the best case they jointly pursue the public good while seeking to sustain the conditions of political freedom that make such inquiry possible. They are colleagues in a deliberative enterprise. For deliberation to matter, representatives must be open to changing their initial positions in response to persuasive arguments. And they must be prepared to defend those changes to constituents who are willing to accept them when they disagree. Burke is an obvious referent for one type of trustee representation; Lenin for another. These referents suggest the difficult relationship between a pure trustee model and democratic norms. Identity representation has recently been defended strongly in Anne Phillips, *The Politics of Presence* (Oxford and New York: Oxford University Press, 1995). Her aim is to show that the adequate representation of certain kinds of minorities or previously excluded groups requires a large presence of members of those groups in decision making bodies.

4

Electoral representation and the aristocratic thesis

John Ferejohn and Frances Rosenbluth

I. Introduction

A modern democracy is conducted by a small body of elected officials who make the laws and control the state. This fact has been taken by some to mean that modern democracy is really a kind of elite rule. In its strong form, this claim implies that modern democratic governments pursue the interests of an elite or aristocracy; the weak form claims no more than the evident fact that government is run by a relatively narrow class of people and leaves open the question of whose interests may be served by this arrangement. Strong form elite theorists do not necessarily reject the possibility that the people may have some influence in picking and choosing which parts of the elite class control government. But they typically stress how weak and ineffective such controls are, especially when it comes to getting the elite to pursue public interests. If public interests are served, on the strong account, they are served gratuitously, by leaders who happen to be publically motivated, and not because of any strong incentive leaders may have to govern for the people.

Versions of the elitist view were stated by Schumpeter years ago and have been developed in various ways by Przeworski, Manin, and Dunn. The emphases of these theories vary quite a bit but all concur in seeing elections as devices for picking an elite and not an instrument by which the people exercise real control over these leaders. All of them reject the democratic idea that government is, in any intelligible sense, "by" the people. The core idea shared by these thinkers – that a government of elected representatives is necessarily aristocratic in some sense – is quite ancient, dating back at least to Aristotle. And the common conclusion of this view is that electoral democracy is really nothing at all like direct democracy as was practiced, for example, by the Athenians.

Two typical complaints about Athenian-style direct democracy are often run together but they are independent of one another. One, attributable to Thucydides, is that democratic rule is turbulent and unstable. Emblematic of this worry is the example he gives of the Athenian assembly deciding to put an uppity city to the sword and then, a few hours later, reversing the decision, dispatching a fast ship to stop the slaughter. Another example was the rash decision to attack Syracuse. The idea is that there is something about direct rule by a large assembly that makes it vulnerable to demagogic oratory and other kinds of deliberative failures. Madison summarized this worry when he remarked that even if the Athenian assembly was made up of copies of Socrates it would still have been a mob.

The second complaint, due to Aristotle, is that direct democracy is rule by the poor who are more numerous, and it systematically reflects their class interest. Democracy's defect on this account is not that it is willful or arbitrary but that it is biased to prefer one part of the city. These two complaints, while they may be held by the same person (as they were in the case of Madison, for example), would seem to have different kinds of remedies.

For the first complaint – turbulence, unsteadiness, emotionality – the best remedy according to Kant (and Montesquieu and Madison among others) was to ensure that government is indirect or conducted by representatives, rather than by the sovereign people themselves.[1] Many writers hoped that in an indirect or representative government power would be exercised by a better sort of person – by those skilled in leadership, or at least by educated people, or people who specialized in government. But many of them thought that, even if none of that was true, indirect government would minimize or eliminate appeals to the public that might corrode governmental stability and rule of law. Arguably, changes in Athenian government in the fourth century provide an example: while every citizen could attend the assembly or be selected to most executive offices, certain kinds of vital decisions (military and financial) were reserved to elected magistrates. In this respect even democratic Athens came to practice a degree of indirect government.

The second complaint may require a different sort of remedy. Assuming the poor are actually a majority, Aristotle thought that either the electoral franchise ought to be restricted, or else that the other interests in the city be given some voice or check on what policies should be pursued.[2] Essentially, each of these is a strategy of representation: in the first case, by disenfranchising some of the poor, political representation

---

[1] The sovereign we are speaking of here is, of course, the people, but Kant saw that the argument also implied that a monarchy, if it is to avoid despotism, ought to work through representatives rather than through the direct imposition of the will of the monarch.

[2] There is a third option. The majority may be motivated to pursue common rather than class interests but it seems unrealistic to rely on that motivation in designing political institutions of a large heterogeneous polity.

will tend to weigh the interests of the wealthy more heavily. The second strategy gives institutional roles to people with wealth that permit them to project and protect their interests; in this sense the wealthy are over-represented in the corridors of power. This second strategy amounts to a kind of mixed government strategy and is exemplified by the system of institutional checks of the kind that Polybius admired in the Roman constitution.

The strategy of mixed government has been especially attractive in modern democratic conditions where franchise restrictions are generally hard to justify. Aristotle himself proposed both strategies at various points in the *Politics*, sometimes favoring a restriction on citizenship, and some-times favoring a kind of mixed democracy. And many other classical and modern writers have done so as well. Interestingly, one of the institutions that Aristotle thought could help moderate democracy into a good form of government (*politeia*) was election. So for Aristotle it seems that the two evils of democracy — turbulence and class bias — may yield to the same remedy.

While the idea of a government conducted by elected representatives has become commonplace in the modern world, it has two distinct fea-tures that Madison, Rousseau, and many others have noticed. First, if representatives are drawn from an elite class, they may pursue the inter-ests of that elite, at least to some extent. This is, of course, exactly what those who favored mixed government anticipated and endorsed. Second, and more problematically, whether or not representatives come from a distinct social class, they may themselves constitute a class of a certain kind and would be expected to some extent to pursue their own interests at least some of the time. If they do, then there is a natural sense in which we could understand representatives to be a kind of oligarchy, united in pursuing their own interests rather that those of the public. Nowadays we call this a problem of agency, and it seems to us to form an alternative basis for the aristocratic hypothesis.

Political representation is prone to a distinctive class of agency prob-lems for several reasons. In ordinary agency relations the concern is to design a "contract" — or incentive system – for agents who want to pursue private remuneration or leisure. This is ordinarily done by establishing a system of rewards and punishments for the agent which are condi-tioned on some measure of her actions. But the actions of political agents are very hard to observe, and elections, the typical way of disciplining political agents, are a crude and imperfect way to control officials; they happen infrequently and they can usually only punish or reward officials by withholding or awarding office. Second, representatives have a wide range of possible motivations: like ordinary agents they may desire to increase their own wealth and leisure but they may also desire to pursue ideological goals. Finally, there is a reluctance on the part of many people to see elected representatives as employees hired to pursue the interests of the public. Elected officials of course foster this view, claiming not to be mere servants but to be leaders who symbolize the dignity of the public and who ought to be trusted to exercise their own vision and resourcefulness.[3] Such deferential attitudes towards elected officials may further limit the kinds of electoral "contracts" that are available for selecting and incentivizing leaders; and they may limit the willingness of voters to enforce such contracts by punishing poor behavior. For these reasons, elected representatives usually have a great deal of latitude to pursue their own goals. On the surface, then, there appears be a great opportunity for a kind of aristocratic rule — rule by elected officials — under the cloak of nominally democratic procedures.

There are, however, countervailing forces. Because elective office offers so many attractive options, we expect there to be intense competition for it. In equilibrium, we expect the value of office to be dissipated in this competition; indeed, in some models, one would expect aspirants to willingly incur in campaign costs the full expected value of the office, discounted by their chance of winning it. Or they might promise post-election benefits that would reduce their (private) value of winning office. Aspiring office-holders might be expected to provide benefits to electors such as by bribing them with favors prior to the election, as was described in Lewis Namier's (1929) wonderful study of eighteenth-century England. Mark Kishlansky (1981) has documented such activities in the previous century, as has Gordon Wood (1991) during the early years of the American republic. More generally, we expect campaigns to be based on promises of future rewards for voters, sometimes private, sometimes public. Such practices will not always benefit voters, but they will tend to erode any gains from office that might otherwise accrue to the elected officials. Rather, policies are likely be chosen that will please those who have effective control over access to office such as contributors and activists.

---

[3] Perhaps this phenomenon is not confined to political agents. Potential agents have a generic incentive to reduce interagent competition, and to some extent high-status agents (usually labeled "professionals") have succeeded in getting state assistance in doing this by imposing entry restrictions in the form of licensing or training requirements. Such professional requests are always, more or less plausibly, based on concerns to protect the health or safety of the public (i.e. the potential principals), but they invariably result in conceding more freedom of action for agents. Often part of the price for getting the public to go along with such regulations is a more or less credible commitment on the part of the profession to self-regulate by means of a code of conduct or something of that sort.

Election and the aristocratic thesis 275

The point is that competition can limit the capacity of the elected officials to rule in their own interest.

The thrust of our argument is not, on balance, very supportive of any strong form of the aristocratic hypothesis. While political agents have a great deal of scope for autonomy while in office, they are unlikely to gain much from it. The potential agency gains are liable to be competed away by other aspirants to public office.[4] Instead, political agency is likely to favor those in society – voters and contributors – who have a comparative advantage in monitoring the actions of representatives. Insofar as there is a political aristocracy, it is to be found in those privileged principals rather than among the agents.

II. Democracy

Definitions of democracy are inherently controversial because any definition involves value judgments. One kind of definition focuses on particular institutions and how they function. In the classical period the focus was on the use of lottery to choose officials, and direct rule by popular assemblies. More recently, many have followed Dahl (1971) in requiring well-functioning competitive elections as the defining feature. Another approach emphasizes democracy's connection with equality and requires that everyone have an equal opportunity to rule. (Aristotle's notion was that democracy is a system in which everyone takes turns ruling and being ruled.) As we want to leave open the possibility that a government of elected officials may (or may not) be democratic, our definition of democracy focuses on whose interests guide governmental policy. We claim that a government is democratic if its policies reliably track the interests of a majority, and that this tracking is accomplished through the agency of the citizens.

In a representative government, our definition requires that government policy generally follows the public's opinion about what its interests are, at least at times before elections. Political leaders may to some extent shape or persuade the public, but if they fail at this, leaders may have to give up on a policy altogether – at least eventually. Other background conditions must of course be satisfied as well so that the desires of the majority may reasonably be counted as expressing the views of a large part of the people as a whole. The specifics here seem historically variable but nowadays we would insist that both the franchise and

---

[4] This suggests that those who have good outside opportunities have little reason to choose a career as a representative, so that selection into the political occupation may be drawn from among the others.

eligibility for office be open to (virtually) every adult, that information circulate quite freely, that elections are frequent, and that votes be counted equally.

Admittedly this definition is weaker than the idea that the people rule themselves directly, as the Athenians were supposed to have done when they determined policy in their popular assembly or decided verdicts in their popular courts. But, as we emphasized above, even the Athenians eventually chose to leave the most important matters to elected officials, and they also relied extensively on mechanisms of legal accountability to ensure that, generally speaking, all officials (however they were chosen) had reason to act for the general interest.[5] Our definition is not the mere requirement that policy track the interests of a majority or of the people as a whole. That might as well be accomplished by a wise, poll-taking, and benevolent monarch. We insist that the best account of why policy tracks majority or popular interests must be that voters have some way of motivating their leaders to take their opinions as to their interests into account. This implies that leaders have reason to pay attention to what the voters actually want (their opinions) and not only what is thought to be best for them (their interests). Democracy can be a poor form of government if citizens tend to have defective views about what is in their own interests and if its policies therefore do not reflect their real interests. This is, in fact, what Schumpeter and Aristotle thought.[6]

How leaders will respond to public opinion depends on the structure of the democracy in question. Elected officials may, in some systems, be held personally accountable before voters in single-member districts (or open-list systems), or be collectively responsible to them as members of a party. Either way, as long as voters have a real opportunity to demand such an account at regular intervals, we would say the system is democratic. This opportunity must be real, of course. Elected officials or parties must face a prospect of losing office and this "reality" test implies that elections

---

[5] The use of mechanisms of accountability in Athens was ubiquitous and far more pervasive than anything in the modern world. For one thing, the terms of office were very short — only a year — and there was a requirement that officials be examined before assuming office, and especially upon leaving it. Then too, officials could be impeached before the assembly or before the courts. And anyone carrying out a public function, whether elected as an official or selected by lot, or simply acting on his own initiative to push a proposal before the assembly, was subject to legal liability before the courts. Finally, there was always the possibility that someone (any citizen) could simply be ostracized for no stated reason at all, though as far as we know the reason almost always amounted to getting "too big for one's britches."

[6] This was also Churchill's view when he remarked in 1945 upon being voted out of office, "In my country the people can do as they like, although it often happens that they don't like what they have done" (Gilbert 2007: 864).

Election and the aristocratic thesis

must generally be competitive.[7] And what that requires depends on the institutional structure in various ways. But if those conditions are fulfilled, it seems to us that a system could be democratic while being governed by a small class of potential aspirants for office. That small class might well be described as an aristocracy in some circumstances, such as if membership in it were determined by heredity or wealth or education. What is critical is that each leader or party be genuinely vulnerable to the judgments of the electorate.

We think it is a ubiquitous fact about modern democracies that positions of leadership are precarious. While journalists often complain of an insulated and protected political class, the fact is that public officials are always in danger of losing their jobs, and they know it. If you want to be, or remain, in public office you need public approval, and no matter how far you have debased yourself in its pursuit, you can never be sure that you have enough to survive the next test. Fear of losing office is an existential fact of political life. We need only recall a few prominent political careers, such as that of Richard Nixon, to see how realistic that fear is, and to imagine the lengths to which leaders might go to cope with it. American scholars of congressional elections have long observed that nearly every congressman has, at one time or another, suffered defeat or at least a close call that she did not expect. From the perspective of governing officials in a democracy, then, public life is characteristically a treacherous business. Perhaps this is less so today than for the Athenians: Themistocles, the creator of the fleet that destroyed the Persian armies and brought about the possibility of a vast Athenian empire, was ostracized from the city. And even Pericles himself suffered the loss of office. The point is that, in a democracy, political leaders can never forget that they serve at the pleasure of a fickle and unpredictable master.

This "democratic condition" implies that even if politicians as a class share some interests in common, which of course they do, it is exceedingly dangerous for them to try to pursue these interests if that pursuit would risk support among the people. Moreover, even if elected and appointed officials share some interests, the democratic condition forces them to compete with each other for scarce political rewards, and this gives them reason to undercut and double-cross each other. Elected officials may be described as an aristocracy in virtue of possessing or seeming to possess

---

[7] It is too much to ask that every election be genuinely competitive; rather what is required is that control of government be competitive among parties or leaders. Therefore, as is the case in all democracies, the seats of many backbench members of parliament may be quite securely held even if control of government is insecure.

rare and valuable skills, but they are likely to have a very hard time converting these advantages into personal or class gains. That is not to say they cannot succeed, but success in pursuing private interests is not guaranteed, and from a certain perspective looks doubtful.

III. Representation

As our purpose is to analyze a feature of representative government rather than studying representation in general, we shall not follow Pitkin's (1967) lead in trying to unravel the concept of representation.[8] We shall work instead with a stipulative definition that we think illuminates the "core" aspects of political representation. Specifically, we take what Pitkin calls a formalistic view and focus on the relationships of authorization and accountability to try to understand the constraints on official representatives and ask whether or in what sense representatives can be characterized as an elite. There are two separate ideas here: a person is authorized to act for a group by being given authority prior to taking action. Moreover, a person is accountable for her actions on behalf of a group if she can be rewarded or punished for those actions if they fail to respond to the group's interests (by some entity, not necessarily by the group itself).

The authorization/accountability view significantly narrows our focus, in that it marginalizes certain normative claims that may work within practices of representation, such as the idea that a representative is supposed to mirror the represented. But such views are only marginalized as potential definitions. There may still be reasons for a representative to try to, or claim to, mirror her constituents in some way or other.[9] Doing so may help her to get selected and to hold onto office, or even to make wise decisions. And it may make her constituents more inclined to take her words and acts as authoritative for them.

Election is one way that a representative may be authorized. Representatives could, alternatively, be appointed as Senators are in Canada, or selected by lotteries as in classical Athens, or inherit their office as do members of the House of Lords. Such officials are rightly regarded as representatives as long as it is accepted that those chosen owe duties to

---

[8] We take the analysis in her book to demonstrate the extreme difficulty of such an endeavor. In any case, if it is true that representation is essentially contested, any such effort must fail.

[9] In fact, the agency view can illuminate such appeals by showing when they might be persuasive. If potential agents can differ in the degree to which they resemble principals, perhaps in the sense of sharing their preferences, there is a competitive reason for each of them to be seen as similar to the principal as possible.

Election and the aristocratic thesis 279

advance certain interests of the represented in appropriate contexts.[10] To be a representative is, in this sense, to be selected according to a conventionally accepted scheme and thereby to be embedded in a certain kind of normative relationship with a group.[11] This normative relationship may be to represent the desires or opinions of the group (to act as its ambassador or delegate) or to represent its interests (to act as a trustee).

A representative may be accountable for his failure to fulfill his normative obligation to represent. Duties to represent might be enforced, if they are enforced at all, directly by those to whom the duties are owed – in which case the representative is made accountable before the represented – or they may be enforced by whoever has the authority to select the representative. For example, while a representative may have a duty to pursue the common interests of the people, she may be selected by voters in a particular geographic district. This is another form of political accountability. As before, the representative is or is not reelected according to the will of a majority. Alternatively, as in the case of fiduciary duties, duties might be enforced by a third party or by courts of law, according to some legal or normative standard.[12] We call this an instance

[10] Regarding representation as a normative relation of a certain kind has the additional advantage of making sense of "informal" claims to represent, such as when someone claims to speak for a group or subset of the population. Such claims remain informal because there is no accepted convention for conferring authority, and because informal representatives are not entitled to exercise state authority.

[11] We are employing an interpretive construct here in order to facilitate institutional comparisons. If a people has a set of practices that can best be explained by positing their possession of a unified concept that supports the idea, then they actually have something like that concept even if they have no single word for it. For example, the Athenians had an extraordinary range of practices of holding public figures to account. They required magistrates (whether selected by lottery or election) to give an ex post account of their official behavior before a court (and sometimes in the assembly as well). They exposed anyone proposing decrees or laws to public law prosecutions. And they exposed everyone to ostracism (and this must have been most dangerous for public leaders). Moreover, the content of these interrogations – the questions posed – appeared to relate mostly to whether the official had acted in ways that served the common interests of the city as expressed in its laws. That the magistrates and other public figures owed duties to act in the interest of the city, and that, in addition, these duties were enforced through making them accountable to the people, suggests that the magistrates were expected to act as representatives. This is obviously a kind of functional definition and is situation-specific.

[12] Legal accountability is one mode of enforcement, and traces of it remain in impeachment procedures in modern politics. The Athenian requirement was not only legal but also popular or political since the courts were popular institutions without professional judges or lawyers. Modern systems tend to rely mostly on political rather than legal accountability, a practice the Athenians had largely abandoned by the end of the fourth century. Impeachment and criminal sanction remain supplementary forms of accountability relations as well, even if they are used rarely in practice. We emphasize that duties may not be enforceable at all: duties can sensibly exist that cannot be enforced. Moral duties are an example. Where duties cannot be enforced or enforced very well, it is important that the people select representatives who are likely to have a kind of moral

of "legal" accountability. When an agent is politically accountable to the represented, the representatives are free to decide to retain her or not, according to their will. When an agent is legally accountable before a tribunal, the agent may be removed only for cause: for failing to perform up to some legal or normative standard. Persuasive reasons have to be given to the tribunal to justify the removal.

Traces of legal accountability remain in the impeachment procedures in modern polities, and in the fact that political officials are not completely immune to prosecution for criminal acts. But mostly modern governments rely on political accountability to select and de-select representatives. We can appreciate this by contrasting it with Athenian practices. Democratic Athens required its officials and other public actors to account for their actions in legal as well as political forums and, after 403 BC the balance was heavily toward legal rather than political accountability. Their courts were themselves popular institutions without professional judges or lawyers, so the difference between the two forms is perhaps less sharply etched than in modern polities.[13] But they did retain some distinctly political forms, permitting impeachment before the assembly and ostracism as well.[14]

We emphasize that some duties may not be enforceable at all. Moral duties often are not. Indeed, we think representatives have moral duties to constituents even if, and especially if, their actions cannot be observed by their constituents. Where duties to represent cannot be enforced or enforced very well, the people have reason to select representatives who are likely to have some kind of internal motivation to pursue their interests. Perhaps this is best done by choosing representatives whose private interest and/or ideology are correlated somehow with the public interest they are to serve. But perhaps there is a residual need for public officials to have moral motivations.

The expression "representative" government is usually used to refer to a government made up of representatives selected according to

> motivation to pursue their interests. Perhaps this is best done by choosing representatives whose private interest is correlated somehow with the public interest they are to serve.

[13] Still, there was a distinction in that legal judgments are supposed to be based on reasons (of law and fact), whereas political judgments can be more or less arbitrary.

[14] The emblematic case of this is the story of the poor and nearly illiterate farmer struggling to spell a name on a pottery shard (*ostraca*). The philosopher Aristedes (who was generally known as Aristedes the Just) asked if he could help: "Whose name are you trying to write?" The farmer replied "Aristedes." "But why?" asked the philosopher. The farmer snorted in reply, "I am sick and tired of hearing of this 'Aristedes' always being called 'the Just'." Ostracism was often aimed not so much at those who abused power or popular trust, it seems, but simply at the famous who had grown perhaps too big for the city.

Election and the aristocratic thesis 281

conventionally accepted procedures for allocating offices. It is often used descriptively, though there are some who think that calling a government representative is a kind of praise. When "representative" is used as a qualifier of "democracy," as in the expression "representative democracy," the normative terrain is more divided: some people take it to indicate a kind of qualification or even a negation of the real thing (genuine democracy), made necessary by the scale and complexity of the modern nation-state.[15] Others regard representative government as a kind of improvement over direct democracy, either by making democracy more attractive by moderating its democratic aspect, or by making it more rational or deliberative (in Madison's expression: representatives were expected to "refine and enlarge" public opinion).

Everyone agrees that representatives, as political agents, are supposed to act in the interests of the people in settings where they are authorized to act and, as a means of achieving this, to be answerable to them in some way. But citizens have only meager means for disciplining their representatives. Representatives' actions are hard to observe; the occasions for demanding an account are few, and are shared by a heterogeneous group of people. For that reason, elected officials do not seem to be on a very tight leash. Why is this? Perhaps we think of political officials differently than we do other kinds of agents: as leaders rather than servants. Because of this we may want to provide them with a fair amount of autonomy to take the kinds of actions that might best advance our interests. So we may not insist, as we might in other agency relations, on being able to audit their actions closely.

These "distortions" in the agency relation remind us that political agency may be distinctive in permitting political agents a lot of slack or autonomy. Elite theorists, starting with Aristotle, think that giving leaders the chance to take independent action can increase the prospects for beneficial policy choices and stability in government. The distinctive slack in political agency is what makes room for the aristocratic hypothesis. Those with more popular sympathies worry that slack will allow official corruption or the capture of government by private interests. Discussions of political agency are marked therefore by controversy over how much scope should be permitted to an agent and how agency duties are best enforced or at least encouraged.

---

[15] Kant and Madison and legions of modern writers have thought representation constitutes an improvement over direct democracy because it introduces non-democratic elements in a kind of mixed government, which moderates populist impulses and produces reasonable or moderate policy. Others have argued that genuinely democratic rule must be representative for other reasons: for example, representatives are better able to deliberate effectively and to pursue common interests than the people would be.

IV. Political agency

We argue that, suitably modified, the agency model – a version of what Pitkin has called the authorization/accountability model – captures the central aspects of formal representation.[16] We hire an official by means of an election and expect her to employ her legal authority to pursue our interests in government. We hire a private lawyer for similar reasons: we expect that lawyer to advance the interests we entrust to her within the confines of legality and professional norms. In both cases we retain some degree of control over our representative both ex ante and ex post: before the fact we make it known what we expect, sometimes implicitly by voting for the candidate who makes the most attractive offer; and after the fact we can punish or reward her for her performance. In both cases, our representative is expected to act in our interest, to be accountable to us, to warrant our trust, and to explain and justify her behavior when she appears to fall short.[17] And she runs risks of being fired or not paid (or sued) if she fails to fulfill our expectations.[18]

We do not deny, of course, that the word "representation" is used in other ways to describe other activities: as metaphor or synecdoche, as a theory of meaning or a concept of mind, or as a particular way of drawing or painting. Some thinkers have sought to put some of these other meanings on a par with the idea of representation as authorization, arguing that political representation must make sense of these other usages. Within political life, people sometimes make claims that someone can speak for another only insofar as he is "like" the other in some way. Sometimes this is applied to elected representatives and sometimes to competitors for leadership. Such claims may be persuasive in various contexts – usually they are aimed to persuade – but they are essentially normative arguments aimed at influencing action, or perhaps undercutting claimed authority, rather than conceptual claims. Moreover, such

[16] Pitkin's criticism of this view is that it focuses too narrowly on aspects of representation – that the agent has been given authorization to take certain actions – to the exclusion of others: she lists several including "having one's actions attributed to another" and "having the right to command another" (Pitkin 1967: 51). Neither of these is a part of the agency view at all as far as we can see, and neither seems necessarily a part of representation either, unless the principal somehow authorizes them. This may or may not occur.

[17] The best ethnographic account of this relationship, as it appears to the representative, is still Richard Fenno (1978).

[18] This does not imply that agents can easily be removed for non-performance. The typical situation in agency relations is, indeed, that some non-performance occurs in equilibrium. And we do not deny that punishment is harder in political settings, but it is hard in many non-political settings as well. The difference is not a matter of degree, and depends on specific features of the agency relationship, political or non-political.

Election and the aristocratic thesis

arguments are not confined to the political realm: you might want to have as a doctor someone of your own age or gender. But those wants count only as normative reasons for choosing between doctors. In the end, the actual picking remains the crucial thing: until you actually do that you do not have a doctor at all. And once you have picked a doctor she will be authorized to make certain choices on your behalf, whether or not she happens to share your gender or age.

We used the expression "suitably modified" to signify that the kind of agency relations found in public life may differ from agency relations in the private sphere. In what we shall call the standard model, the agency "contract" provides ongoing incentives for the agent by attaching rewards or punishments to her actions. Such contracts also serve to screen or filter potential agents by making the role of agent more or less valuable to different kinds of people. There are really two distinct ideas here: agents, having different preferences than the principal, need to be given incentives to take actions that are in the principal's interest. And, some potential agents are better than others for the principal in some way: they may be more competent, more ethical, or have preferences more like those of the principal. These two ideas correspond to the "moral hazard" and "adverse selection" perspectives. In the first, the focus is on controlling an agent's actions while she is in office; in the second it is on selecting the right kind of agent in the first place.

In either case, there will normally be more slack in political agency relations than in other kinds of agency relations. One reason for this is that political principals tend to be collectivities rather than individuals. This requires that there be some way of making collective decisions — elections, for example — for resolving disputes among principals who may disagree about what they want their common agent to do. Virtually every way of making such decisions creates problems of collective action of various kinds and opportunities for agents to exploit.[19] Second, political agency "contracts" are typically crude, in that it is not only costly or impossible for voters to observe most activities done by their representatives,

[19] Both of these features of political agency are explored in Ferejohn (1986), in the context of a very simple model. In that paper, the principal's only way of controlling the policymaker was the possibility of firing her. Even so, as long as the policy space is one-dimensional so that there is a median voter, the principal could exert some degree of control on the agent. But in higher dimensions the agent is basically uncontrollable unless the principals could somehow agree to judge the agent using a one-dimensional performance criterion. In effect, only if the principals can solve the collective action problem and act as a kind of "person" can they hope to get the agent to pursue or represent their interests. That model was extreme in limiting the tools available to the principals to control the agent, but the logic of the situation will carry over to much more complex settings.

284   *John Ferejohn and Frances Rosenbluth*

but it is also impossible to make rewards and punishments sensitively contingent even on observed differences. Voter opportunities for expressing disapproval are limited to infrequent elections and perhaps by some legal institutions that permit impeachment or criminal accusation.[20] So, for various reasons, we are unable to treat officials differently depending on the actions they take or the outcomes that result. Finally, political agency relations may be subject to relatively weak competitive pressures. Normally we would expect that a person would refrain from hiring an agent whose behavior she has little control over. But, as we pointed out earlier, a citizen cannot really refuse to enter the relationship if its terms seem unattractive. Such a refusal requires costly efforts at coordination.

In market settings one expects that competition among agents will lead to the creation of more attractive agency contracts — that is, contracts that can be conditioned on a finer description of events and that are more effective in motivating and screening agents. But this process is often blocked in the political sector (and it is occasionally blocked in markets as well). Why is this? Political agency relationships differ from ordinary agency relations in a way that does not really seem to track any formal feature of agency models. When someone hires an agent, one might think that a kind of hierarchical relationship is established: the agent is an employee, a hireling, whose duty it is to do what the principal wants and whose compensation depends on performance in some way. Think of hiring a person to mow your lawn or fix your car or sell your home. This model breaks down a bit in the case of high-status professions such as surgeons, but for reasons that seems to have nothing to do with the agency relation. No doubt surgeons have skills and information that permit them to do things for us that we cannot do for ourselves; and, in the course of surgery, our ability to monitor the physician's actions is probably compromised. And maybe in certain areas of surgery, the important skills are rare and there is little competition among potential agents. Anyway, someone who needs surgical services probably is in a hurry, which places further limits on competition. But these circumstances are not special to surgeons. Think of having your car break down on an isolated road with only one garage in the vicinity. Remember, a couple of centuries ago people thought of surgeons as on a par with barbers and mechanics.

---

[20] In market settings one expects that competition among agents can improve this situation. But even there, competition may not eliminate problems. The reason we see doctors and lawyers and other professionals adopting ethical codes and organizational modes of enforcing them is precisely because agency relations are imperfectly policed by incentive contracts, and potential agents seek efficiency gains through self-policing or governmental regulation.

Election and the aristocratic thesis

Perhaps officials in a democracy enjoy an especially high status because, though they may be our employees, they are expected to "lead" us, to direct or command our actions. Why would that matter? Possibly, it is a matter of psychology: it may be difficult to accept orders from a subordinate, so people may psychologically "elevate" political agents, projecting onto them some undeserved superiority. Another answer is to say that elected officials are not "our" servants as collections of individuals but are servants of our collective interest. We elect them not to subordinate ourselves but because we think they have special political skills that make them better able to discern what is in our collective interest than we, as disparate individuals and groups, would be. These seem plausible enough answers, but dangerous ones, and we doubt that robust democracies could concede so much to their leaders. Another possibility, one that seems more consonant with a democratic culture, is that elected leaders enjoy a kind of democratic deference out of respect for elections: that representatives who have been chosen in orderly and fair elections may be due a special degree of respect that is traceable not to them as individuals but to the people.

The belief that political leaders are somehow above individual citizens may explain why we are reluctant to demand more effective agency contracts concerning them. This may account for why elected officials enjoy relatively long terms, why popular recall is rarely available, and why binding instructions to elected officials are almost never countenanced. To restrict the terms or employment conditions of our elected officials may be to express a kind of contempt and not only for them as officials, but also for the people who elected them. To be sure, these are all variables rather than constants because there is nothing that dictates the appropriate length of a term, for example. Therefore, if we are right, hierarchical beliefs are probably variable as well. The Athenians, for example, permitted officials to serve only a year and required them to undergo ex ante oaths as well as stringent ex post audits, and subjected them to a number of other ongoing checks on their official performance. Of course many of their officials were ordinary citizens chosen by lottery, and people may have thought they had to be kept on a short leash. But their elected officials were constrained in the same way.

It seems significant that most of the restrictions on the agency contract are not in any sense "natural," but are actually imposed on us by our political agents. Political manipulation rather than deference may explain the distance at which politicians hold voters at bay. In competitive settings one would expect agents who offer poor contract terms to disappear, so one expects agency contracts to be attractive. But typically the restrictions on political agency are imposed collectively and not individually.

Sometimes they are placed in the constitution: the Bonn Constitution forbids binding instructions on representatives and the American Constitution has been interpreted to resist term limitations, to take two examples. More often, agents set the rules by statutes or chamber rules that govern how observable their actions are and the extent to which their rewards and punishments can be made to depend on them. These practices limit the extent to which contract terms can be subjected to competitive pressures that might force them to be more favorable to principals. Sometimes competitors do try to offer new and more attractive terms – such an offer was the basis of the "Contract with America," with its pledge of term limits and the like – but such offers are neither credible nor, if they are accepted by gullible voters, actually implemented.

V.   Representative government and aristocratic rule

Madison thought that part of the genius of American government was that it was indirect: the sovereign power, the people, had no actual role in government (*Federalist* 63). Governing is done by delegates who obtain grants of power from voters, through election, and are entitled for a period of time and within certain limits to exercise it on behalf of the people. There is no doubt that Madison thought this feature of the new Constitution – the fact that the people had no direct role in government – was not an unhappy compromise forced upon it by the size or extent of the new republic, but an essential feature of a good form of popular government.[21]

[21] He voiced apprehension of a direct appeal to the people in *Federalist* 49 as well, where he explained that such appeals would undermine the development of popular veneration for the new Constitution. That Madison worried about direct popular involvement does not make him anti-democratic in the way that term is used nowadays. His preference was explicitly for a republican government in which all authority was drawn directly or indirectly from the people. He thought, however, that direct popular involvement in government would undermine the possibility of stable republican government by unleashing passionate appeals to transient majority sentiment. In fact Madison went much further than this in seeking to limit the indirect influence of popular majorities in government. He thought the more dependent a government was on the people, the more dangerous it was, and the more need there was to control and check its power. The state legislatures were dangerous to liberty precisely because of their popular proximity, and the federal House of Representatives similarly dangerous, though less so, for the same reason. For that reason the legislative branch, which was necessarily close to the people, posed a powerful threat to republican rule: Madison said that the legislative "vortex" was the chronic source of turbulence, irrationality and danger to stability. His central arguments for establishing a national government (in *Federalist* 10), for federalism (in *Federalist* 45–46), for checks and balances (*Federalist* 51), all aimed at restraining popular influence. Finally, in what seems the direct expression of a desire for a kind of aristocratic rule, albeit of the republican kind associated with Rome, he argued that by adopting large

Election and the aristocratic thesis 287

Madison was not alone in thinking that a government of representatives was to be preferred to a direct democracy. Kant also thought that democratic government – by which he meant a direct democracy – was necessarily will-driven and for that reason despotic.[22] "Every form of government that is not representative is properly speaking without form, because one and same person can no more be at one and same time the legislator and executive of his will (than the universal proposition can serve as the major premise in a syllogism at the same time as be the subsumption of the particular under it in the minor premise)" (Kant 1970 [1795]: 114). A government of representatives was much more likely to be able to act under the control of reason and therefore to be moderate or temperate.

Kant's reasons for preferring representative government have nothing to do with representatives being in some sense "better" or more virtuous than the people. Rather, his argument is based on the defining feature of indirect rule: the person who takes action – the representative – is not the one source of valuation or preference. He is an executive who acts on the interests, passions, preferences, or opinions of others rather than on his own valuations and he is, for that reason, better able to act rationally. This is a kind of separation-of-powers argument in which the passions and emotions of the people are acted on, and disciplined by, their representatives. One sees in it echoes of Plato's division of the soul (Plato 1987), where the rational part controls the appetitive and passionate parts. In that respect, it also echoes Montesquieu's idea that the separation of legislative (evaluative) and executive powers is necessary to avoid tyrannical rule, by which he meant rule by passions rather than reason. But Kant argues here for a vertical (between people and their representatives) rather than a horizontal (between departments of government) separation of powers.

Several Greek writers had already expressed similar misgivings about direct democracy. Thucydides chronicled the passionate and turbulent politics of democratic Athens during the Peloponnesian War which he attributed partly to the effects of democratic rule. Xenophon,

---

constituencies for the House of Representatives one could hope that elections would tend to choose virtuous leaders who would be likely to "refine and enlarge" on public opinion.

[22] "[D]emocracy, in the proper sense of the term, is necessarily a despotism" (Kant 1970: 114). By "proper" democracy Kant meant direct democracy, and he went on to specify what was defective about direct rule (whether democratic or not). Kant, like Madison, favored a popular component in government but insisted that the authority of the people be exercised only through representatives. He went on to criticize the ancient republics – surely referring to Rome and possibly to Athens as well – for failing to understand this and therefore degenerating into despotism.

condemning the popular reaction to an attempt to introduce legal process into the famous trial of the generals, quoted an incensed member of the assembly as saying, "It is outrageous to say that the people cannot do whatever they want." Unmediated or direct democracy was seen as impulsive and subject to bouts of irrationality. Indeed, there is reason to think that even ordinary Athenians thought there was reason to temper or moderate direct rule: after the democracy was restored at the end of the fifth century, the Athenians embraced various judicial institutions that could limit and control the actions taken by the assembly.[23]

Aristotle's normative views were complex. He did not reject democracy as such but sought ways to ensure that a democratic government would act moderately. In Book VI of *Politics*, for example, he expressed admiration for an agrarian democracy in which most of the people lived outside the city and were too busy farming to take much interest in politics, and would therefore prefer to use elections to select their leaders (rather than choosing them by lottery as the Athenians did).[24] He had already defined democracy as a kind of government in which the citizens actually rule in some direct sense, whether they take turns ruling as in a good constitution, or rule at the same time as in Athens. He did not expect either kind of direct rule in an agrarian democracy. Elections would be employed to choose magistrates and would select only certain kinds of people into office. Possibly these would be especially able or wealthy which might conduce to a better government. In any case, electing the able or the wealthy would recruit them into public service rather than leaving them outside of government where they could cause trouble. We imagine that he thought it a saving feature of Athenian democratic practice that some of its officials – the most important ones – were chosen by election rather than by lottery.[25] That, at least, permitted the selection of officials with

---

[23] Even in the heyday of direct democracy in the fifth century, Athenian government had important elements of mixture that incorporated the rich and upper middle-class governmental institutions. Election of the generals was an important kind of mixing – the generals tended to come from those who had military or naval equipment and experience as far as we know – as was the extension of elections to choose financial officers.

[24] Aristotle (1962: Book VI, ch. 4).

[25] While we present the argument from "competence" here it is by no means clear that that is the reason the Athenians used elections to pick generals throughout their history, and to pick financial magistrates in the fourth century. It may also be that elections allowed the state to harness potentially dangerous people with private armies. The powerful families that produced Themistocles, Cleisthenes, Pericles, and others would have been a danger to the state if they were not in its service. Indeed, Themistocles ended his life in exile. The oligarchic coups of 411 and 404 were led by such people who may have been eclipsed or threatened by parvenus. And the creation of elected financial offices may have been an attempt to enlist wealth-holders in the service of the state rather than any recognition of competence or superiority.

Election and the aristocratic thesis

the ability to make reasoned policy decisions in complex and dangerous policy domains, though it did not guarantee that they would.

Later thinkers, such as Schumpeter, have put a somewhat different spin on their preference for a government of representatives. Schumpeter (1942) thought that ordinary people, being unfamiliar with political life and issues of public policy, would be incompetent to make reasonable political choices. Public officials may or may not be talented in this respect but their day-to-day experience would at least lead them to acquire some skills relevant to governing. So he argued that the people ought to confine their involvement in politics to choosing a government and perhaps removing it later if they did not like the results. While he did not argue this directly, he probably thought that the comparative advantage of elected elites partly explains why it is that modern democracy takes the representative form that it does.

We imagine a representative government can become a system of elite rule in two different ways. Michels (1915) claimed in his "iron law of oligarchy" that any organization will devolve ruling authority on a small set of people. Michels thought elite rule could be an emergent feature of any organization irrespective of the beliefs or values of the organization's members or of the mechanisms for choosing leaders. Schumpeter appears to have shared a similar view, since his arguments do not seem to turn directly on the use of election itself, though we admit it is less than clear from his writings. On this view we would expect to see elite rule within the lottery-selected Athenian boule as well as in an elected assembly.

Against this view, we may contrast theories that claim that an organization is elite-dominated if it employs a method of leadership selection that tends to choose leaders who have special qualities. That is to say, certain selection processes may "recognize" certain people with special qualities relevant for leadership. Madison and Aristotle entertained theories of this kind and so does, with qualifications, Bernard Manin (1997). Aristotle and Manin thought that the electoral mechanism was a device for elite selection. Madison thought that elections in large districts would perform in this way.

Manin appears to accept the idea that elected representatives will govern differently than ordinary citizens would if they were rotated into office. It is not that he thinks that representatives are likely to be a better sort of person. Nor does he claim, like Schumpeter, that elected representatives are likely to be more competent in matters of policy and government. Manin argues that it is simply the use of elections as the device for selecting leaders that produces aristocratic tendencies, locating its critical feature in the tendency of voters to make choices based on certain kinds of considerations. He sought "to deduce the inegalitarian and aristocratic effects [directly] from an abstract analysis of election" (ibid.: 135). By doing this he hoped to drive home the conclusion that these effects are intrinsic to the electoral mechanism itself.[26] However, he acknowledged that his deductive argument depended on certain empirical (contingent) assumptions – essentially that voters will tend to elect those they think are superior in some relevant way: "The dynamics of choice and cognitive constraints usually leads to the election of representatives perceived as superior to those who elect them" (ibid.: 145).[27] So he could not reach all the way to the analytic conclusion he sought.[28] Still he thought these contingencies were likely to be satisfied in most circumstances of modern democracy.

We agree. The most that can be said is that voters tend to choose those whom they believe to possess some valuable characteristic for political leadership, and they may well be wrong both in the value of the characteristic and who are likely to possess it. Second, whether this constitutes an aristocratic tendency seems to depend on the idea that the characteristics in question are somehow valuable or attractive in some wider sense. Third, we have to think that these characteristics are fixed prior to election and not conferred by the fact of being elected. After all, if elite characteristics were automatically attributed to those who happen to be elected, election would simply *constitute* an aristocracy. It may be true that marks of superiority are not too mutable, at least not deliberately so, in a variety of circumstances, but we doubt that that it is anything like universally true. Moreover, to say that contingent factors matter is to

[26] Manin presents his argument as a kind of completion of a project begun by Aristotle, showing that elections are an aristocratic device and are, for this reason, incompatible with democracy. In the case of Aristotle we are not yet persuaded. Aristotle could be read as speaking merely of tendencies or statistical regularities – that lottery tends to be employed in democracies and election in oligarchies – or else as making something like a constitutive claim – that something is not a democracy if it uses elections for important offices. But Aristotle plainly thought that Athens was democratic and it employed election for significant offices. Moreover, the constitutive claim seems even harder to defend in light of *Politics*, VI, 4 where he discusses (agrarian) democracies that employ elections. In any case, both the constitutive claim (that democracies necessarily employ lottery) and the statistical claim are distinct from the claim that we think Manin wants to make: that democracies have good reason to employ lottery and that they will therefore tend to make that choice. This seems a causal claim and Manin's "deduction" is an attempt to elucidate the causal elements of that story. And, of course, it is no defect of a causal argument that contingencies play an essential part.

[27] And even here he qualifies the sense of "superiority" as being only in respect to relevant qualities for government. There is little sense that the elected are more virtuous in any moral sense or even more competent except with respect to political skills – or, rather, reputed political skills.

[28] The four assumptions are these: the unequal treatment of candidates by voters which says that voters *may* choose candidates in an arbitrary fashion; distinction of candidates due to the circumstance of choice, which says that voters choose candidates thought to have some mark of superiority; that certain persons are more salient or visible than others; and that it is costly to secure public recognition. We agree, of course, that these factors make it unlikely that as a matter of fact election will treat everyone equally.

REPRESENTATION

Election and the aristocratic thesis

leave open which factors actually matter and how likely they are to arise in practice. Perhaps other contingent factors operate to defeat the effects of the contingent factors that Manin cites.

In any case, the qualities of the candidates may not be as important for the aristocratic hypothesis as what the governmental officials actually do and what policies they produce. Thucydides' criticism of Athens was based at least partly on his judgment that disastrous or unstable policies were chosen and other writers seem largely to agree. No doubt Thucydides thought that there was some connection between the quality of the officials and their policies, but after all it was Pericles who led Athens into the war with Sparta (whose qualities Thucydides would not have doubted), and Alcibiades (another highly capable leader, even if he was a flawed character) who convinced the Athenians to undertake the disastrous Sicilian expedition. One has to be open to the possibility that that connection between capable leaders and good policy is uncertain. Why not, instead, ask the policy question directly? Doing this may indeed support an alternative version of the aristocratic hypothesis: the idea is that, even if elections do not produce better officials, the policies produced tend to support the public interest or perhaps the interest of some elite.

VI.   Policies in representative v. direct democracy

Athenian democracy had three characteristic institutional features. The first was what is now called direct democracy: any citizen who wanted to could attend the assembly and vote or speak on any issue. Second, every citizen was eligible to be chosen by lottery to serve in the magistracies that governed the city. Third, every citizen was eligible to be selected a juror, again by lottery, in the very powerful court system. In these respects everyone could take (equal) turns in ruling the city. In this section we want to compare direct democracy – where the people choose policies by some kind of popular referendum – with representative democracy.

Since the appearance of Downs's (1957) work half a century ago, many positive political theorists have shared the intuition that majority rule tends to perform similarly in different institutional settings, independently of whether people are choosing between policies or candidates.[29]

---

[29] This intuition is supported by the median voter theorem which is thought of as a general tendency of majority rule in a one-dimensional setting. However, to be accurate, the statement needs to be qualified by saying it represents a kind of intuition. After all, it is easy to create game theoretic specifications in which majority rules are extremely sensitive to institutional details in the sense of departing from the preferred outcome of the median voter.

292   *John Ferejohn and Frances Rosenbluth*

If additional institutional structure matters, it is only because these additional details introduce some kind of bias that constrains the majoritarian property. In a one-dimensional world this intuition is supported in median voter models, in which the preferences of the median voter determine the outcome, assuming that distorting institutional frictions, such as monopoly agenda control, are absent.

For example, in two-candidate competition over a one-dimensional policy space, under very weak assumptions, both candidates "converge" on the position of the median voter. And, in an open-agenda legislature (where anyone is free to make proposals), the legislative outcome will be at the same point. The median voter theorem may not hold in some settings, such as when someone has agenda control or if candidates are insufficiently motivated to seek office or are not somehow free to pick winning platforms. Except for imperfections or frictions of this sort, the intuition is that the majoritarian aspect of the institution will dominate.

At least in some special cases results of this kind extend to higher dimensions, though many complications arise that define such extensions, since in many models equilibria frequently do not exist. But when an equilibrium does exist in a "legislative game" in which people are free to propose alternative policies under an open agenda, then a two-candidate equilibrium exists as well in which both candidates propose the legislative outcome. So there is at least some support for the majoritarian intuition even in this unpromising setting.

In the same spirit, we can sensibly ask the comparative institutional question posed in the introduction: when will an elective/representative democracy produce similar policies to a direct democracy? Let us assume, to begin, a one-dimensional policy space and direct democratic rule with an open agenda, as in the Athenian *ekklesia*, where everyone is free to propose whatever they want. Such an institution would tend to select policy at the preferred position of the median voter. Assume, now, the simplest possible representative government: one person is elected who then is to set policy, and this person is elected in a two-person election (we leave details aside for now). As argued above, the two candidates will have reason to promise to implement the preferred policy of the median voter. In this simple case, therefore, the Downsian intuition is satisfied. One can imagine extending this argument to a multidistrict setting if, for example, the districts are ideologically identical to the voting population so that each representative will advocate policies at the median position of her constituency. In that case the representatives will all have preferred policies at the population median. It is easy to see that this result could be further extended (a bit) by permitting constituencies to vary as long as the median legislator is located at the population median.

Election and the aristocratic thesis

And, again in somewhat special cases, one could devise extensions to higher dimensions.

Ideas of this kind have been pursued further in two-stage models, which take account of how representatives would campaign for legislative office. When standing for election, a legislative candidate cannot plausibly claim that she alone would set policy if elected. Rather, she could only argue that she will play a more or less predictable part in producing legislation. Such models contemplate that the voters form beliefs as to the consequences of electing one representative rather than another – in effect, voters are assumed to have a model of the legislative process that allows them to assess the policy consequences of electing one or another candidate – and then vote based on a full assessment of the policy effects of their vote. One such model was developed by Austen-Smith and Banks (1988) in which they establish a connection between the preferred policy of the median voter in the population – which we could assume would be chosen in a direct democracy – and equilibrium in the representative democracy game. Their results depend on a number of other quite restrictive assumptions about the structure of elections and about the kind of electoral competition that takes place. But their basic finding is that equilibrium policy is related to the position of the median voter.

These arguments sidestep problems of political agency which we have discussed earlier by assuming that representatives will do as they promise after the election. If that assumption is relaxed it is not clear how constrained representatives are by having to compete for election. It is easy to imagine models in which it is a powerful constraint: a world where a single elected official wants to stay in office, faces frequent elections, and can choose among policies contained in a one-dimensional space, for example. In that world, if information about the official's actions is sufficiently available to voters, and sufficiently easy to interpret, it might be hard for the official to stray far from the preferred policy of the median voter. But these informational assumptions are stringent, as is the notion that the space of policy has such a simple structure. And, as we depart from drastically simplifying assumptions of this model, by permitting numerous politicians to make decisions, allowing the policy space to be complex and to map uncertainly into a multidimensional space of outcomes, the reelection constraint facing the representatives probably diminishes in its force. Once account is taken of these considerations, the theoretical perspective adopted here, therefore, seems unlikely to support the idea that representative and direct democracy will generally produce the same or similar policy outcomes. So we turn, for now, to examine empirical evidence that may bear on this issue.

294   *John Ferejohn and Frances Rosenbluth*

To examine the question of policy convergence, some authors have asked about the effects of introducing direct democratic mechanisms – the referendum or the initiative – into representative democracies. While the resulting literature is somewhat diverse, the basic finding so far is that the introduction of such devices tends to push policies in the direction of the median voter (Frey 1994; Gerber 1999; Matsusaka 2004; Funk and Gathmann 2005). This effect sometimes is direct: a popular initiative is enacted that moves policy in the direction of the median on that issue. And sometimes it is indirect in that the legislature in initiative states may tend to produce policies nearer the median, presumably out of worry that failure to do so would provoke popular policymaking. Indeed, sometimes one can actually observe such thinking at work where the legislature enacts a law after seeing initiative petitions being gathered; or where the legislature puts a referendum on the same ballot as the initiative in an effort to undercut support for the initiative (Gerber, Lupia, McCubbins, and Kiewiet 2001).

These phenomena suggest that states without the initiative tend to produce systematically different policies than states with such an option. In effect they lend support to the idea that representative democracy chooses different policies than direct democracy would. Of course, the comparison is very imperfect as we are forced to make an extrapolation from those polities permitting popular initiatives to a polity that makes all its policies in this way. That is a very long extrapolation indeed, and so evidence of this kind can only be suggestive.

In any case, from a normative viewpoint it is not very reassuring to learn that our government will tend to do whatever the median voter happens to want. After all, the median voter is, like the rest of us, a private person occupied with making a living or raising a family and probably not very familiar with the world of policy. As Schumpeter worried, her policy preferences are likely to be influenced by superficial beliefs and emotional responses rather than being well thought out or consistent.

There is reason to think, both theoretically and empirically, that direct and indirect democracies tend to choose different policies, except in the special circumstances we have outlined. This difference seems to be systematic rather than random: direct democracy, as far as we can see, tends to pick out median voter outcomes and representative governments depart from that in some direction or another. And the difference seems regularly related to how purely representative the government is: partial systems, which include some institutions of direct democracy, exhibit policies closer to the position of the median voter. Finally, we do not have any idea whether these differences are properly traceable to the use of elections as such or to the specifics of how elections are implemented

Election and the aristocratic thesis   295

(e.g. the absence of rotation, term limits, instructions, and the presence of many incumbent-favoring features).

The evidence seems weaker when it comes to the question of whether the policies of representative government favor the interests of an elite rather than the general interest. Madison, for example, would have expected systematic differences of the kind we discuss but thought that, in the right constitutional setting, these policies may simply have been better at advancing the common good than the median voter's preferred policy. But there is some evidence on this issue and it will be discussed in the conclusion.

VII.   Election or lottery

Bernard Manin reminds us that until the eighteenth century, educated people thought that lottery was the selection mechanism most compatible with democracy. The assumption was that officials chosen by lottery would be more likely to pursue policies that most citizens (who were poor) would want, whereas elected officials would tend to choose systematically different policies. We saw in the previous section that recent empirical evidence suggests that elected leaders probably do choose differently than the people themselves when asked to choose policies directly. But would elected officials choose differently than officials selected by lottery? We do not know a way to examine this issue empirically, so we shall resort to theory.

Let us start with Aristotle's political ontology which divides the city into wealth classes – sometimes he speaks only of the rich and the poor, but sometimes he refers to a middle class (*mesoi*) – and assumes that each class will necessarily seek to pursue its own interest. And, in his two-class model, assuming that the poor are much more numerous than the rich, a democratic government will tend to be a government of the poor. Aristotle had two ideas for moderating this tendency: one was to impose a property requirement for citizenship that was sufficiently high that the new democracy would tend to choose moderate policies for the whole city (including those who were not permitted to be citizens). Such a strategy could work, of course, only if there were a middle class: otherwise franchise restrictions would have no effect or else would shift authority directly from the poor to the rich. The Athenians, who we assume had a large middle class, attempted to achieve something like this following the oligarchic coup of 411, when there was an effort to reduce the number of citizens to 5,000, but this effort collapsed quickly and the democracy was restored.

296   *John Ferejohn and Frances Rosenbluth*

Aristotle's second idea was more robust to social circumstances and could work, in principle, even if the city was strictly divided between the rich and the poor. It was to devise institutions that would permit the rich to take part in ruling the city along with the poor. It is in this context that he saw election as a device by which the rich could participate in government, while lottery would tend to select the poor. If some offices were chosen according to each principle, that would implement a kind of balance in government. Overall policy would then be a kind of moderate compromise that was likely, he thought, to approximate, to the common interest, an interest that neither class would pursue if it monopolized the government. He recognized, of course, that neither class would be satisfied and thought that, in his own day, the establishment of democracy (rule by the poor) was more or less inevitable, partly because there were so many poor people in every city. But he thought it was partly inevitable too because of the kind of deep egalitarianism of Greek popular culture at the time.

Aristotle framed the aristocratic hypothesis by comparing elections and lottery as a device for picking officials. We can make this comparison by using citizen candidate models, in which any citizen is free to stand for election, and so election, like lottery, is simply a device for selecting leaders. The question posed is this: who (or which kinds of people) will be selected as a representative out of the population, and which will tend to be chosen by lottery? Citizen candidate models allow us to examine the aristocratic hypothesis in a particularly precise manner since every other feature of the city is held constant in the comparison. Of course this precision is won within the context of very simple and stylized models.

To begin, it seems plausible to think that lottery will pick a person whose characteristic is an unbiased estimate of the mean of the population distribution. And these models also allow us to ask whether, or when, election by itself will produce officials who might plausibly be regarded as an elite in some way. We do not offer a definition of "elite" at this point, leaving the idea to emerge from the specific model (hopefully) intuitively.

In many of the early models, voters had complete information about each other's characteristics and each had to decide whether to stand for election. This can be seen as a very simple kind of agency model in which voters have no ex post control over the behavior of an official and can achieve their ends only by selecting agents with the right kind of (internal) motivation. In the simplest two-period model, plurality rule is used to elect a single official (Osborne and Slivinski 1996; Besley and Coate 1997) who, after being elected in the first period, sets policy in the second. Citizens differ only in their policy preferences in a one-dimensional policy space and these are commonly known. Any voter is

Election and the aristocratic thesis

free to declare her candidacy in period 1 and declared candidates (voters) pay an entry cost. Once entry decisions are made, the election takes place under a plurality rule with ties broken by a fair random device. In the second (policymaking) period the official will necessarily choose her most preferred policy. Any first-period promise to do otherwise would not be credible. The fact that promises are not credible is what permits voters to form preferences between the declared candidates and to decide how to vote.

In this setting, depending on entry costs and the benefits of winning office, only a small number of citizens will declare candidacy (how many depends on the cost of entry), and each will receive the same number of votes. If entry costs are high enough, there will be two-candidate equilibria, and we confine our discussion to those. In a two-candidate equilibrium, policy positions of the leading vote-getters will be moderate (not "too far" from the median) and will be symmetrically situated around the position of the median voter (in the sense that the median voter must not prefer one candidate over the other). The intuition is that their positions are close enough to the median that no one near the median would find it worthwhile to enter the election, but sufficiently separated that no one at either extreme would want to enter either. Many pairs of candidates can actually satisfy this condition so there are many such equilibria, and in each one the leading vote-getters must receive the same number of votes. And the policies of the leaders will be moderate (not too far from the median) but separated from each other.[30]

It is a little hard to see how this kind of result could support the aristocratic hypothesis, for two reasons. First, the set of electable candidates is different from the kind of voter likely to be picked in a lottery. A lottery pick in this model has an expected value at the mean of the distribution of the population over the issue space. If we think of the electoral elite as the set of all voters who could be office-holders in some equilibrium, this elite will be symmetrically arranged around the position of the median voter. So if the mean and the median are identical – as they would be in a symmetric voter distribution – there is a sense in which election and lottery picks would both be centered on the mean of the population distribution. Roemer (2001) has shown that the set of electable candidates is of the same dimensionality as the original issue space, so it is, in this respect, a large subset of the population, and this set is centered at the

---

[30] The trick in these models is accomplished by the assumption that candidates cannot commit to a policy different from their ideal point. So candidates can merely decide whether or not to enter and not which position to offer. This may be sensible in a single election but is less so when elections take place over time. And it is less sensible where there is incomplete information.

mean of the population. While it is true that the set of people who could be picked by lottery is even larger (it includes everyone), the most likely lottery choices are close to the mean/median in the symmetric setting and resemble in policy terms those who are electable. In this setting it is hard to see how the electables can be seen as an elite in any interesting sense.

There is a natural interpretation of this model that is still more damaging to the aristocracy hypothesis. Assume that voters have identical preferences over consumption of a single commodity, but differ only in their initial wealth levels. The collective decision to be made is to set a uniform wealth tax, with the proceeds to be distributed on an equal per capita basis, perhaps with some attenuation. In this model policy preferences are wholly determined by initial wealth, with the richer voters preferring lower tax rates and the poorer ones higher taxes. In a two-candidate equilibrium, the candidates will be located near the median, with one a bit richer than the median voter and the other a bit poorer. In each equilibrium, the expected policy outcome is at the median. Moreover, if we assume that the wealth distribution is skewed in the way that wealth distributions generally are – so that the median income is less than the mean – in each equilibrium the candidates will be two relatively poor citizens (relative to the mean of the distribution). But, in this model, the lottery pick is centered at the mean and so will tend to be richer than the citizen elected. Again, it is hard to see policy as manifesting any kind of elite bias; what bias there is seems to be in another direction. Moreover, Roemer's argument shows that the set of people who could be the elite will be large, as well as relatively poor.

Something like an aristocratic tendency may be observed in a slightly more complex model of the political economy.[31] Suppose a two-period model in which capital investment is productive and that people have identical utility functions but different wealth endowments. In the first period each person has to decide how much to invest, which will yield a second-period return, and to consume what remains. Assume the government has an option to set the second-period tax rate and to redistribute the proceeds on an equal per capita basis. In the second period, the investment decisions have been made and the government could tax productive returns in a non-distortionary manner. But if it is expected to set second-period tax rates too high it will discourage investment, leading to low levels of redistribution. So the government (i.e. the median

---

[31] The model in this section is a simplification of one in Chapter 7 of Persson and Tabellini (2002). In their more complex settings they reach similar general conclusions.

voter) would want to commit to optimally low second-period taxes. Let us assume for illustrative purposes that the median voter has no wealth endowment so that all of her income comes from redistribution. Then she needs to assure high-income voters, credibly, that second-period taxes will not be set too high. One way to do this might be to give the power to set second-period tax rates to a voter with sufficient wealth to want to set the rate at the optimal level.[32] One might be tempted to say that in this model an "aristocrat" is given the power to make policy in her own interest. Of course that is true, but the policy she chooses is the best policy from the standpoint of the median voter, who is poor. While there is a kind of aristocracy in this model, the aristocrats are forced by a kind of invisible hand to do the bidding of the median voter.

In view of these results, it is not clear that anything like an aristocratic tendency can be generated in simple settings of the kind that have been studied in these models, but we do not want to belabor results of this kind that are set in very sparse environments. Citizen-candidate models are of potential interest because they allow us to focus on how elections select candidates. Citizen-candidate models suggest that elections generate something like a weak median voter outcome even if voters lack the power to monitor and punish their behavior in office. But these models abstract away the strategic complexity introduced by multiple principals and multiple agents, which we take to be the core problem of political agency.

In a somewhat more complex model where information is not complete about some relevant characteristic which we may call "competence," voters would like to choose highly competent candidates but it is hard to identify them. Given the difficulty of measuring competence, one would expect that if office is valuable, people with low levels of competence will try to imitate more highly competent types. And, assuming that the electoral mechanism can create only very imperfect incentives for screening candidates (as we have argued), some of these imitators will be expected to succeed in equilibrium. Moreover, which people find it worthwhile to become candidates for office depends importantly on their other opportunities. If good political leaders are those that have skills with a high market value and poor ones do not, then one expects talented leaders to avoid running for office and the resulting pool of potential

---

[32] Doing this entails another credibility problem: how can the median voter commit to not taking back the power to set policy in the second period? One could imagine various "solutions" but none is really fully satisfying. Perhaps the policymaker could be given the control of the military. This is a kind of neo-Hobbesian solution but it is still vulnerable to ex post revolution.

candidates to be mediocre. If that assumption is right, then the election mechanism, taken as a whole, will be likely to select inferior candidates – candidates who voters would agree are inferior if they could directly observe their attributes. Elections will, in short, select the mediocre and not the aristocratic, if that term is used to refer to high-quality potential officials.

Of course we are not claiming that such a sweeping and dismal conclusion is actually warranted. Possibly the talented will sometimes choose to run out of a desire to serve. Or perhaps political skills are not marketable and competent political leaders have poor outside prospects. In any case it seems possible that the important qualities can be learned after election and that, even if elections have a tendency to choose those with meager inherited gifts, those who take office will tend to form a professional elite and get better with practice. Thus it seems possible that under some circumstances elections may select different and better candidates. But the circumstances in which this may happen seem fairly special.

VIII. Conclusions

The Romans thought that elections could not be trusted to produce or reproduce the kind of elite that they thought was central to the stable and conservative rule of the Republic. They fretted mightily, as far as can be inferred from their practices, over the details of the voting procedures that were employed in their lawmaking assemblies (*comitia*). They were careful to assemble voting classes so that the rich and well-armed had greater voting weight, to manage tribal membership, and to ensure that the poor of Rome were "packed and stacked" into a small subset of tribes. And they tried to ensure that the order and procedure of voting were such that the elite would get the results they wanted (Staveley 1972). As far as we know, usually this worked as expected. But there were several notorious exceptions where laws were enacted over the objections of the elites.

In modern times, things are arranged less bluntly. But probably they may still be arranged in ways that permit the reliable reproduction of an elected elite of some kind. Almost everywhere the representatives get to choose the details of the electoral system by which they get and hold their jobs, and to change it if they think it is working unacceptably. They have nearly universally avoided term limitations and instructions from their constitutions and usually too the institutions of direct democracy. Almost everywhere they have succeeded in gaining or keeping working conditions that make them hard to monitor and control even by the most attentive

Election and the aristocratic thesis

voters and interest groups.[11] These are "aristocratic" achievements of a sort. But are they traceable to elections as such or to many additional restrictions on the way that election is employed? More importantly, is there any reason to think that the benefits of their achievements are kept by political incumbents?

Political office is valuable precisely because of these (slack producing) achievements, and so one would expect this value to be the object of intense competition. Competition for office makes political aspirants dependent on the favor of those who can help them to get it and keep it. Sometimes this forces dependence on parties or on others who can help mobilize voters. More recently, however, the dependence seems to run in the direction of those with disposable wealth. Martin Gilens (2001) and Larry Bartels (2002) have presented evidence that seems, on the face of things, to support this view. They argue that representatives tend to respond disproportionately to those from upper income groups who have greater access to the tools of political influence, and that policy exhibits a kind of class bias as a result. To the extent that representatives are forced to compete away the privileges that they would want to reserve to themselves, rendering them beholden to those who control the means to put them in office and keep them there, the elected are a strange and dependent kind of aristocracy.

BIBLIOGRAPHY

Aristotle. 1962. *The Politics of Aristotle*, ed. and trans. Ernest Barker. New York: Galaxy Books.

Austen-Smith, David, and Jeffrey Banks. 1988. "Elections, Coalitions, and Legislative Outcomes." *American Political Science Review* 82 (2): 405–22.

Bartels, Larry. 2002. "Economic Inequality and Partisan Politics." Paper presented at the Annual Meeting of the American Political Science Association, September, Boston.

Besley, Timothy. 2006. *Principled Agents? The Political Economy of Good Government.* New York: Oxford University Press.

Besley, Timothy, and Stephen Coate. 1997. "An Economic Model of Representative Democracy." *Quarterly Journal of Economics* 112 (1): 85–114.

Dahl, Robert. 1971. *Polyarchy: Participation and Opposition*. New Haven, CT: Yale University Press.

---

[11] For a qualification to this argument see John Ferejohn (1999). That paper argues that under certain conditions elected officials may voluntarily increase the degree to which they may be monitored in order to induce people to support a larger public sector. In effect, this argument, like others in this chapter, cuts against any strong form of the aristocratic hypothesis.

302 *John Ferejohn and Frances Rosenbluth*

Disch, Lisa. 2006. "Rethinking Re-presentation." Paper prepared for delivery at the Annual Meeting of the American Political Science Association, September, Philadelphia, PA.

Downs, Anthony. 1957. *An Economic Theory of Democracy*. New York: Harper and Row.

Dunn, John. 2005. *Setting the People Free: The Story of Democracy*. London: Atlantic Books.

Fenno, Richard. 1978. *Home Style*. Boston: Little, Brown.

Ferejohn, John. 1986. "Incumbent Performance and Electoral Control." *Public Choice* 50: 5–25.

——— 1999. "Accountability and Authority: Toward a Political Theory of Electoral Accountability," in *Democracy, Accountability, and Representation*, ed. Adam Przeworski, Susan Stokes, and Bernard Manin. New York: Cambridge University Press, 131–53.

Frey, Bruno. 1994. "Direct Democracy: Politico-Economic Lessons from Swiss Experience. *American Economic Review* 84 (2): 338–42.

Funk, Patricia, and Christina Gathmann. 2005. "Estimating the Effect of Direct Democracy on Policy Outcomes: Preferences Matter." Working paper, Stanford University Department of Economics.

Gerber, Elisabeth. 1999. *The Populist Paradox: Interest Group Influence and the Promise of Direct Legislation*. Princeton, NJ: Princeton University Press.

Gerber, Elisabeth, Arthur Lupia, Mathew McCubbins, and Roderick Kiewiet. 2001. *Stealing the Initiative: How State Government Responds to Direct Democracy*. Upper Saddle River, NJ: Prentice Hall.

Gilbert, Martin. 2007. *Churchill: A Life*. New York: Henry Holt.

Gilens, Martin. 2001. "Political Ignorance and Collective Policy Preferences." *American Political Science Review* 95 (2): 379–96.

Hamilton, Alexander, John Jay, and James Madison. 1961. *The Federalist*, ed. Jacob E. Cooke. Middletown, CT: Wesleyan University Press.

Kant, Immanuel. 1970 [1795]. "Perpetual Peace," in *Kant's Political Writings*, ed. Han Reiss. New York: Cambridge University Press.

Kishlansky, Mark. 1981. *Parliamentary Selection*. New York: Cambridge University Press.

Manin, Bernard. 1997. *The Principles of Representative Government*. New York: Cambridge University Press.

Matsusaka, John. 2004. *For the Many or the Few: The Initiative, Public Policy, and American Democracy*. Chicago: University of Chicago Press.

Michels, Robert. 1915 [1911]. *Political Parties: A Sociological Study of the Oligarchical Tendencies of Modern Democracy*, English trans. Eden Paul and Cedar Paul. New York: The Free Press.

Montesquieu, Charles de Secondat. 2002. *The Spirit of the Laws*. Amherst, NY: Prometheus Books.

Namier, Lewis. 1929. *The Structure of Politics at the Ascension of George III*. London: Macmillan.

Osborne, M. J. and A. Slivinski. 1996. "A Model of Political Competition with Citizen Candidates." *Quarterly Journal of Economics* 111 (1): 65–96.

Election and the aristocratic thesis

Persson, Torsten, and Guido Tabellini. 2002. *Macroeconomic Policy, Credibility and Politics*. London: Routledge.

Pitkin, Hanna. 1967. *The Concept of Representation*. Berkeley: University of California Press.

Plato. 1987. *The Republic*. London: Penguin Classics.

Rousseau, Jean-Jacques. 1968. *The Social Contract*. London: Penguin Books.

Schumpeter, Joseph. 1942. *Capitalism, Socialism, and Democracy*. New York: Harper Colophon Books.

Staveley, E. S. 1972. *Greek and Roman Voting and Elections*. Ithaca, NY: Cornell University Press.

Wood, Gordon. 1991. *The Radicalism of the American Revolution*. New York: A. A. Knopf.

5

REPRESENTING IGNORANCE*

By Russell Hardin

I. Introduction

If we wish to assess the morality of elected officials, we must understand their function as our representatives and then infer how they can fulfill this function. I propose to treat the class of elected officials as a profession, so that their morality is a role morality and it is functionally determined. If we conceive the role morality of legislators to be analogous to the ethics of other professions, then this morality must be functionally defined by the purpose that legislators are to fulfill once in office. Hence, the role morality of legislators will largely be determined by our theory of representation. We will need not a normative account of their role, but an empirical explanatory account. In David Hume's terms, the morality of role holders is one of "artificial" duties, that is to say, duties defined by their functional fit with the institutional purposes of a profession.[1] Our most difficult problem, therefore, is to understand the role of our elected representatives.

This problem is severely complicated by the nature of democratic choice and participation in a modern, complex society. A central problem of democratic theory for such a society is the general political ignorance of the citizens. In *Capitalism, Socialism, and Democracy* (1942), Joseph Schumpeter argues that citizens have no chance of affecting electoral outcomes and, therefore, no reason to learn enough about politics even to know which candidates or policies would serve their interests. He writes, "[W]ithout the initiative that comes from immediate responsibility, ignorance will persist in the face of masses of information however complete and correct."[2] If the problem of knowing enough to judge elected government officials is already hard, the lack of incentive to correct this problem is

---

* I am indebted to my fellow contributors to this volume, to participants in the Monday Night Theorists at New York University, and to Ellen Frankel Paul for comments on an earlier draft of this essay.

[1] Russell Hardin, "The Artificial Duties of Contemporary Professionals," *Social Service Review* 64 (1991): 528–43. Hume distinguishes "natural" from "artificial" virtues in David Hume, *A Treatise of Human Nature* (1739–40), ed. L. A. Selby-Bigge and P. H. Nidditch, 2d ed. (Oxford: Oxford University Press, 1978), bk. 3, pt. 2, sec. 1. Acting from a natural duty produces a good directly, and more or less immediately. Acting from an artificial duty, such as the duty of justice, produces good only through the mediation of a social institution or norm.

[2] Joseph A. Schumpeter, *Capitalism, Socialism, and Democracy* (1942), 3d ed. (New York: Harper, 1950), 262.

devastating. Indeed, the costs of knowing enough about government to be able to vote intelligently in one's own interest surely swamp the modest costs, for most people in the United States and other advanced democratic nations, of actually casting a vote, at least on commonplace issues of public policy outside moments of great crisis. Therefore, an economic theory of knowledge or "street-level epistemology" weighs against knowing enough to vote well because the incentives cut heavily against investing in the relevant knowledge.[3] The typical voter will not be able to put the relevant knowledge to beneficial use.[4]

One response to the problem of citizens' incompetence to judge how they should be governed is government by Burkean representatives. Throughout his writings, Edmund Burke (1729-97) supposes that only members of an elite are competent to govern, and the mass of the citizenry ought to turn government over to them to do what they think best.[5] I will suppose that we resort to representative government for a very different, structural reason. It is impossible for the entire polity of a large state to make policy directly or to implement it.[6] We therefore have specialized bodies to do these things. It is this structural fact that wrecks our incentive to know much about the politics that governs much of our lives. Still, we want representative government genuinely to represent us, to adopt the policies that we would adopt if we had relevant knowledge and power. Any actual representative government may have many problems that get in the way of its serving us in such a manner,[7] but I will ignore those problems and focus on the ethics of the representative in trying to

---

[3] Russell Hardin, "The Street-Level Epistemology of Democratic Participation," *Journal of Political Philosophy* 10, no. 2 (2002): 212–29; reprinted in James Fishkin and Peter Laslett, eds., *Philosophy, Politics, and Society*, vol. 7 (London: Blackwell, 2003), 163–81. The argument here is essentially from the logic of incentives and it casts no blame on anyone. Others hold the political system, the poor educational system, or politicians responsible for the seeming incompetence of voters. See, for example, Matthew A. Crenson and Benjamin Ginsberg, *Downsizing Democracy: How America Sidelined Its Citizens and Privatized Its Public* (Baltimore, MD: Johns Hopkins University Press, 2002).

[4] Martin P. Wattenberg argues that, additionally, there are obstacles even to casting one's vote correctly in the United States, where the act of voting can be almost as difficult as taking a college entrance examination. See Martin P. Wattenberg, *Where Have All the Voters Gone?* (Cambridge, MA: Harvard University Press, 2002), chap. 6.

[5] See, for example, Edmund Burke, "Speech to the Electors of Bristol" (1774), in Hanna Fenichel Pitkin, ed., *Representation* (New York: Atherton Press, 1969), esp. 174–75; and Edmund Burke, "Appeal from the New to the Old Whigs" (1791), in *The Works of Edmund Burke* (London: George Bell & Sons, 1890-1906), 3:85–87. For later views, see Michael Oakeshott, *Rationalism in Politics and Other Essays* (New York: HarperCollins, 1962), esp. Oakeshott's essay, "On Being a Conservative."

[6] Even in a not so modern polity—England and Wales in 1754—the electorate was about two hundred and eighty thousand out of a population of roughly eight million. See Bernard Manin, *The Principles of Representative Government* (Cambridge: Cambridge University Press, 1997), 82. In the United States at the time of ratification of its constitution in 1788, the electorate was about one million out of a population of a little more than three million. Thus, even these relatively small populations, by modern standards, required representative government or some other device for making decisions without involving all citizens at once.

[7] Ibid.

78   RUSSELL HARDIN

represent others in the face of both gross ignorance on the part of voters and harsh limits on information for the representative.

I will not assume the position of those who view representative democracy as a forum for deliberation on "the truth." In *The Principles of Representative Government* (1997), Bernard Manin states that political scientist Carl Schmitt (1888–1985) holds this view, namely, "that truth must 'make the law,' " and that "debate is the most appropriate means of determining truth, and therefore the central political authority must be a place of debate, that is, a parliament."[8] I will not deal with this vision here, because I think it largely irrelevant. Parliamentary debate does not often approach "truth," and, in any case, politics is far more about interests than it is about truth.[9] If there is a truth to be discovered and demonstrated, then after sufficient debate there should be consensus and each of us should grasp the truth. In that case, the Schmitt thesis would make sense. When there is a conflict of interests, however, there is no truth of the kind Schmitt envisions. Deliberation on interests is as likely to lead to dissensus as to consensus.[10] I should also note that Schmitt's justification of a parliamentary body does not require that the body actually be representative of the various groups in a society, but only that it be the political decision-making body for the society.

In general, the tasks of representatives will be easiest when they merely represent interests of fairly basic kinds on issues, for example, of economic policy or welfare provision. Their tasks might also seem to be straightforward when they deal with hotly contested issues over which public views are relatively forcefully asserted, as with the contemporary debate over abortion in the United States. Indeed, for any controversial matter such as abortion, representatives might often think of themselves as delegates because they would not expect to get reelected if they reneged on their electioneering commitment to take one side or the other on the issue (although there might be intermediate positions on which they could compromise). The most difficult issues for representatives will generally be those for which clarity is lacking, at least in the sense that citizens do not know where they stand or, rather, where their interests lie. As John Stuart Mill says, individuals distort many issues with their idiosyncratic beliefs, and they tend to discount the future, so that individuals' claims of what their interests are can be distorted.[11]

---

[8] Ibid., 185. See also Carl Schmitt, *The Crisis of Parliamentary Democracy* (1923), trans. Ellen Kennedy (Cambridge, MA: MIT Press, 1988), 35, 43.

[9] Geoffrey Brennan and James M. Buchanan, *The Reason of Rules: Constitutional Political Economy* (Cambridge: Cambridge University Press, 1985); and Russell Hardin, "Deliberation: Method, Not Theory," in Stephen Macedo, ed., *Deliberative Politics: Essays on Democracy and Disagreement* (New York: Oxford University Press, 1999), 103–19.

[10] See Hardin, "Deliberation: Method, Not Theory"; and Cass Sunstein, "Deliberative Trouble? Why Groups Go to Extremes," *Yale Law Journal* 110 (2000): 71–119.

[11] John Stuart Mill, *Considerations on Representative Government* (1861), in John Stuart Mill, *Essays on Politics and Society*, vol. 19 of *Collected Works of John Stuart Mill*, ed. J. M. Robson (Toronto: University of Toronto Press, 1977), 444–45.

II. Voter Ignorance

If, in general, we make the effort to know something in large part *because we think it will serve our interest to know it*, then we cannot expect people to know very much about what their representatives do. In the argument of the "economic theory of democracy," a citizen typically does not have very much interest in voting. One vote has a miniscule chance of making a difference, so miniscule that, even when it is multiplied by the value of making a difference and getting one's preferred candidate or policy, the expected value of the vote is vanishingly slight. Therefore, if there is any real cost involved in casting a vote, this cost swamps the expected benefit to the voter of voting. Hence, there is little point in knowing enough actually to vote well.

Most of the research on and debate over voting since Schumpeter's *Capitalism, Socialism, and Democracy* and Anthony Downs's *An Economic Theory of Democracy* (1957)[12] has focused primarily on the incentive to vote rather than the incentive to know enough to vote intelligently.[13] The latter is at least logically derivative from the former, because it is the lack of incentive to vote that makes knowledge of how to vote well virtually useless, so that mastering such knowledge violates the pragmatic understanding of knowledge. Since my vote has miniscule causal effect on democratically determined outcomes, there is no compelling reason for me to determine how to vote intelligently. Or, to put this the other way around, the fact that I would benefit from policy X does not give me reason or incentive to know about or to understand the implications of policy X unless I can somehow affect whether policy X is to be adopted.

In what follows, I will simply take for granted that typical citizens do not master the facts they need to know if they are to vote their interests intelligently. There is extensive evidence on this claim, although there is, of course, also great difference of opinion on its significance for electoral choices. For example, political scientist Samuel Popkin canvasses problems of voter ignorance in American presidential elections and then refers to "low-information rationality," which is rationality despite abysmal factual ignorance.[14] He also argues for a 'Gresham's law' of political information: bad facts drive out good facts. According to this law, "a small amount of personal information [on a candidate] can dominate a large amount of historical information about a past record."[15] The personal information might be some minor fact that comes up during a campaign. However, the effect of Gresham's law might often run against Popkin's claim for low-information rationality by driving out the little bit of policy-

---

[12] Anthony Downs, *An Economic Theory of Democracy* (New York: Harper, 1957).

[13] Hardin, "The Street-Level Epistemology of Democratic Participation." (Passages in the next two pages are taken from pages 217–19 of this essay.)

[14] Samuel L. Popkin, *The Reasoning Voter: Communication and Persuasion in Presidential Campaigns*, 2d ed. (Chicago, IL: University of Chicago Press, 1994).

[15] Ibid., 73.

RUSSELL HARDIN

relevant information the voter has. If the personal information seems to be politically relevant, however, its dominance over other information might not matter so much. For example, Italy's prime minister, Silvio Berlusconi, has been caught up in an ongoing scandal over accusations that he bribed his way to wealth and, thence, to political power. Sociologist Renato Mannheimer says, "Italians don't understand the contents of the processes against him, so they make their judgments according to their political leanings."[16] But some voters might judge him for his use of office to serve his own interests.[17]

Manin argues that the form representative democracy now takes is "audience democracy."[18] The trouble with the large amount of historical information that is, at least in principle, available is that voters do not typically know much about it because it would be silly for them to invest the time needed to acquire such information. Hence, in this age of media and celebrity, we vote for personalities rather than for policies and thereby give an outsized role to personal information.

As evidence of how seldom voters even seek better information before voting, consider the difficulty that candidates have in getting their message across to voters. Congressional scholar Richard Fenno elegantly portrays the burden that candidates for the U.S. House of Representatives face in merely finding people to talk to.[19] Even professional political scientists, who have a strong interest in knowing more about politics than their mere interest in the outcome of elections would suggest, find it hard to keep up with much of what happens. Weekly tallies of votes in the U.S. House of Representatives and Senate, for example, are reported in some newspapers, but with such brevity that only specialists on a particular issue would find them meaningful.

Results of referenda on even relatively simple issues suggest astonishing misunderstanding by voters. California voters displayed cavalier irresponsibility in a 1994 referendum (Proposition 184) on a so-called three-strikes sentencing law that mandates harsh minimum prison terms for repeat offenders.[20] Consider two early cases to which the law was applied. The first involved a thief with a prior record, who was sentenced to a term of twenty-five years to life, with no possibility of parole before serving at least twenty years, for his "felony petty theft" of one slice of pizza.[21] In the second case, Russell Benson was sentenced to a similar

---

[16] Quoted in Frank Bruni, "Italy, a Land of Tolerance, Even to Prime Ministers," *New York Times*, May 28, 2003, late edition-final, sec. A, p. 4, col. 3.

[17] He pushes legislation that would directly benefit him as an oligopolistic media owner. See "Italian Leader Faces Dissent over Control of the Media," *New York Times*, April 6, 2003, late edition-final, sec. A, p. 4, col. 1.

[18] Manin, *The Principles of Representative Government*, 218–32.

[19] Richard F. Fenno, Jr., *Home Style: House Members in Their Districts* (Boston, MA: Little, Brown, 1978).

[20] Susan Estrich, *Getting Away with Murder: How Politics Is Destroying the Criminal Justice System* (Cambridge, MA: Harvard University Press, 1998).

[21] "25 Years for a Slice of Pizza," *New York Times*, March 5, 1995, sec. 1, p. 21.

term for shoplifting a twenty-dollar carton of cigarettes.[22] The three-strikes referendum was provoked by some truly gruesome crimes, yet it is so badly framed that it brutalizes petty felons.

California voters also apparently displayed complete misunderstanding of a 1998 referendum (Proposition 3) to undo a prior referendum (Proposition 198 of 1996) on open primaries. The prior referendum, passed by the voters in presumable ignorance of its consequences, would stupidly have disallowed California representation at the national Republican and Democratic Party nominating conventions in the year 2000. After the electorate failed to pass Proposition 3, administrative devices were used to enable the state to distinguish Democratic and Republican voters in its presidential primary elections, thereby securing representation at the two party conventions.[23] In this failure to enact Proposition 3, democracy was a charade and, when it failed due to ignorance and widespread misunderstanding, a knowledgeable bureaucrat, California Secretary of State Bill Jones, intervened against the democratic result. (In a subsequent suit by the major parties against the law, the U.S. Supreme Court overturned Proposition 198 as a violation of the constitutional right of the political parties to assemble.)[24]

III. Madisonian Representatives

Edmund Burke supposes that constituents are apt not to understand what would serve the public good and, therefore, he suggests that representatives should act in the true interest of the public rather than as their constituents might want them to act.[25] He further supposes that constituents should recognize the superiority of their representatives to carry out the task of serving the public interest. His view is not contrary to Schmitt's, and it would allow the selection of members of a parliament by criteria other than representativeness of the polity. On this view, all representatives represent everyone, or the public as a whole. Virtually no one supposes this today, however, and from U.S. constitutional debates forward, we generally assume that representatives primarily represent merely the interests of their constituencies and of those who supported their campaigns.

Let us drop two of Burke's views: that representatives ought to be concerned with the overall public good and that representatives are or should be superior individuals, imbued with character and values that only hereditary elites can acquire. A national party or a national executive might claim to fulfill the first, although parties are invariably partisan and national executives are commonly partisan. On the second, contrary to

[22] Elisabeth R. Gerber et al., *Stealing the Initiative: How State Government Responds to Direct Democracy* (Upper Saddle River, NJ: Prentice Hall, 2001), 64.

[23] Ibid., 71–74.

[24] *California Democratic Party v. Jones*, 530 U.S. 567 (2000).

[25] See also Mill, *Considerations on Representative Government*, 511–12.

what Burke wants, what might set legislators apart is that they become competent at politics, legislation, and governance through their specialized roles. Our representatives even tend, in Manin's characterization, to become aristocratic in that they must have relatively high levels of competence and achievement to attain and hold their offices.[26] They clearly do not represent their constituents in the sense of being like them. There are, for example, almost no working-class representatives in modern democratic governments, and lawyers are radically overrepresented in U.S. legislative bodies. Representation of groups must often be through so-called active representation by people who themselves do not directly share the interests of the groups they represent. For example, Senator Ted Kennedy (D–MA) often represents the interests of union members and the poor, although he has no experience of either status in his own life.

An obvious but painful implication of the Schumpeterian world, in which the public exhibits a general political ignorance, is that representatives can take advantage of citizens. This is true not merely in the manner of Italy's Berlusconi, who has used his official power to enact laws that specifically benefit him by helping him avoid trial for bribery, an offense that he has implicitly admitted.[27] It is true more fundamentally in the sense that, even without such overt actions as Berlusconi's, government personnel can be parasitic on the larger society, making themselves wealthier than they otherwise could have been in any other profession, giving themselves prerogatives far beyond their ordinary emoluments, and securing long tenure for themselves and often even their relatives. In a sense well beyond Manin's, they become an aristocratic class apart from the society that they both govern and represent.

Even the slightest Madisonian or Humean view of human nature as self-interested yields this implication. Political sociologist Robert Michels (1876–1936) claims that democratic government within political parties—especially European socialist parties—produced an aristocracy with great power over rank-and-file members.[28] This claim is true more generally of democratic governments, although they may typically be subjected to greater scrutiny that might impede some of the worst excesses of oligarchic power. In Michels's famous slogan, "Who says organization says oligarchy." Perversely, who says representative democracy evidently also says oligarchy.

---

[26] Manin, *The Principles of Representative Government*, chap. 4.

[27] Members of Berlusconi's party in the Italian Parliament introduced legislation to exempt the top five government officials from facing trial while they hold office (Jason Horowitz, "World Briefing/Europe: Berlusconi Immunity Plan," *New York Times*, May 30, 2003, late edition–final, sec. A, p. 8, col. 5). Berlusconi previously pushed through legislation to reform the courts in ways that might have permitted him to avoid prosecution for bribery, complaining that "to search for, and single out, individual culprits [is] disingenuous and inherently unjust" when there is so much suspicious activity to go around (Bruni, "Italy, a Land of Tolerance").

[28] Robert Michels, *Political Parties: A Sociological Study of the Oligarchal Tendencies of Modern Democracy* (1911), trans. Eden and Cedar Paul (Glencoe, IL: Free Press, 1949).

According to the Manin and Michels theses of an aristocracy of leadership, in some sense it is not the individual elected officials but the class of them that is problematic. As John C. Calhoun (1782–1850) writes: "The advantages of possessing the control of the powers of the government, and thereby of its honors and emoluments, are, of themselves, exclusive of all other considerations, ample to divide . . . a community into two great hostile parties." [29] As a class, the political aristocracy is parasitic on the society that it ostensibly serves and that has the power of election over it. Although some representatives may be very well grounded in their constituencies, many representatives are far more likely to view their fellow "aristocrats" as their reference group than their respective electorates. The supposedly mighty citizenry with its power of election over officials does not have the power to refuse to elect any of them; it can only turn out the occasional overtly bad apple. The electorate usually does not have the temerity to overcome incumbents' advantage. Burke believes that citizens should be deferential to their aristocratic leaders. Few people would argue for such social deference today, although there is pervasive deference to the power of elected officials and to their celebrity, which is a peculiarly ugly aspect of modern democracies, perhaps uglier and more pervasive in the United States than in other advanced democracies.

The U.S. Constitution does not explicitly say either that elected officials have a special status or that they have a duty to represent their constituents. *It is essentially a social convention that they should represent their constituents.* Social conventions generally are not morally binding except through considerations other than the fact that they are conventions. Moreover, there is no constitutionally determined principle of representation to which elected officials are bound. The range of possible principles is so large and various that all officials could claim to be living up to one or another principle. For example, a legislator could claim to represent some part of a particular geographical constituency and to support whatever the leaders of the relevant interest groups in that constituency want.

Add to various visions of the nature of representation the problem of citizens' ignorance. This is a problem that does not bother a Burkean, because Burke's arguments are grounded in the presumption of citizens' ignorance and their deep incapacity to decide what policies their government should adopt. It is also not a problem for Schmitt's views, because he supposes that the role of the representative body is not to represent but to find truth; that citizens do not know truth is taken for granted in the very structure and purpose of legislative government. In both Burke's and Schmitt's views, elected representatives might suppose that they should do for citizens what citizens do not even know they want done. Indeed, citizens might not even want it done once they had given it some

---

[29] John C. Calhoun, *A Disquisition on Government and Selections from the Discourse* (1851), ed. C. Gordon Post (Indianapolis, IN: Bobbs-Merrill, 1953), 14–15.

thought because, virtually by definition, they are not in the places of the Burkean or Schmittian representatives who have superior capacities for determining what should be done.

Although Madison's views include some of the elitism of Burke and others, he is, with Manin, more focused on the way things actually work than on a recommendation that we create a deliberately elitist system. Mill stands somewhere between these theorists in that he supposes that elected parliamentarians should be elite in their qualifications but not, as Burke supposes, via birthright. Mill is also less interested in representation per se, so that he would allow extra votes (which he calls plural votes) to such people as fellows at Oxford and Cambridge Universities, because they would likely be better qualified to vote intelligently.[30] He, too, seems more driven by some (extremely vague and underarticulated) sense of the public good than by concern with representation of varied interests. Perhaps it is the fact that Madison is engaged in actually creating a representative government that makes him the most realistic and focused of all these theorists. His realism is driven in part by his concern to deal with the divisiveness of factions that seemed to fracture the political affairs of several of the states in the United States under the Articles of Confederation.

Madison wants representatives to represent moderately large communities, so that they will not be too focused on narrow issues. (In this, he opposes the Anti-Federalists, who want representation down to the small community level.) But he does not have a conception of "the" public good, and he does not expect the legislature to work for any such good. It would, rather, somehow aggregate diverse interests. One might argue that serving constituency interests would be a way of discovering the collective good in a Madisonian system. This good would not be the true good, as Schmitt would want, but only the product of a compromise of interests negotiated by legislators.

Madison is concerned with at least two overriding issues that he might have thought of as part of the public good. One of these is simply order, and the other is a relatively uniform national economic system that would encourage, or at least enable, economic growth and prosperity by facilitating trade, especially by preventing states from placing restrictions on interstate trade and by standardizing tariffs on foreign trade. There were parties who would have preferred to keep the economic system diverse so that they could free-ride on the anticompetitive practices of others. For example, the antinationalists of Rhode Island benefited from the high tariffs that Massachusetts imposed on goods from England and the Caribbean. Traders in Rhode Island imported goods from these places without tariffs, and then transshipped the goods to Massachusetts, where they could undercut the prices of both domestic and imported goods even while making a substantial profit.

[30] Mill, *Considerations on Representative Government*, chap. 8.

Henceforth, I will focus on what we might call 'Madisonian', 'Humean', or 'Schumpeterian' representatives (or, with more criticism for the unreality of his vision, 'Millian' representatives). I will also discuss (in Section VB) the nature of representation in the current era of audience democracy. Although they have intellectual appeal, 'Burkean' and 'Schmittian' representatives are not part of our political world and we need not dwell on their conceptions. Madisonian representatives are strongly driven by their interests, and they work for the interests of their constituents not because they necessarily share those interests, but because they will be rewarded for doing so. Representatives elected by parties have an analogous interest in supporting their parties' positions on behalf of the parties' electorates. There appears to be no analogous sense in which politicians of audience democracy have an interest that mirrors that of their constituents.

IV. AUSTRIAN SOCIAL THEORY

So far the focus has been on the ignorance of citizens. Another similarly pervasive and important problem is that central government and its agents cannot know enough to devise good policies in many realms. Much of the relevant knowledge is decentralized to smaller organizations and to citizens. The knowledge relevant to governing is, therefore, extremely dispersed. There are things I know that you do not know, and so forth, and things that each of us knows that no one in government can know. This fact of the nature of our knowledge is clearly of fundamental importance for the prospect of a centralized economy. Indeed, much of the main debate over socialist economic organization during the first half of the twentieth century was about how demand functions could be determined so that they could be matched with supply that was set entirely by central authorities.

Suppose we do not have a centralized economy in anything like the form that existed in the socialist economies of the former Soviet bloc. We have central fiscal policy, centrally determined regulations for many activities, and central oversight of civil liberties. Many of these central determinations of policy seem not only to work reasonably well, but better than the lack of such central controls. Clearly, central authorities ought to oversee or regulate many activities, but not others.

The nearest equivalent to Madisonian theory in the twentieth and early twenty-first centuries has been Austrian economics, as represented by F. A. Hayek among others.[31] Although it is ostensibly an economic theory, its most cogent insights apply to broader social theory. An especially odd aspect of the current hegemony of Austrian and Madisonian views of politics and society—even without these labels attached—is that they were almost purely theoretical when enunciated. In the past, there was no

---

[31] Russell Hardin, "Seeing Like Hayek," *The Good Society* 10, no. 2 (2001): 36–39.

way to test Austrian views on the ground. But now they have been and are being tested, and they seem to be acquitting themselves very well, although shenanigans at Enron, WorldCom, and so on are attributed by some to the loosening of government regulation. Madison himself was not willing to practice his theory once he was in office, and perhaps if they had gained office, Hayek and others of the Austrian School would not have been either. But the example of the Soviet world, admittedly a bad version of socialist statism, compared to the freer but partially trammeled markets of the more prosperous West, gave us a chance to see a crude, perhaps second-best test of the Austrian-Madisonian theses.

Of course, my assessment is made while we are in the midst of extensive changes, and it might turn out to be grossly optimistic, a mere extrapolation from the most positive aspects of current appearances. But for the moment, the Austrian and Madisonian schools seem to have the right vision. This is a stunning turn, even more stunning to those on the traditional Left than to Millian libertarians. The most impressive consequence is the reversal of the long historical trend toward ever increasing state hegemony over the economy, and all else when the state fell into bad hands, such as Stalin's or Hitler's.

The centerpiece of the Austrian-Madisonian vision is that the knowledge to run a society is widely distributed and most of it cannot become available to a central government. Hence, a central government should not attempt to manage society in detail, and it should not attempt a massive redesign of society. Austrian economists typically worry about central control of the economy, but they could just as well worry about central control of social relations more generally. Political scientist James Scott especially deplores what Hayek calls "Cartesianism" and what Scott calls the "high modernism" of arrogant redesign of major parts of society, as in the effort to design cities in supposedly more rational ways,[32] or to reorganize peasants into collective farms in the Soviet Union or into Ujamaa villages in Tanzania.[33]

Austrian constraints mean that legislators cannot know in detail what their constituents want. On average, a member of the U.S. Congress has a district of nearly six hundred and fifty thousand people, and a senator from all but a handful of states represents millions of people. These representatives cannot know their constituents. Survey research at its best (as it seldom is) cannot determine very clearly what people want from government or what would benefit them if government acted in relevant ways. Commonly, when government tries to benefit citizens through attention to their narrow interests, it is not by directly providing benefits, but only by regulating, prohibiting, or enabling various activities. Of

---

[32] James C. Scott, *Seeing Like a State: How Certain Schemes to Improve the Human Condition Have Failed* (New Haven, CT: Yale University Press, 1998), chap. 4.

[33] Ibid., chaps. 6 and 7.

course, there are exceptions, as evidenced by the astonishing scale of government largesse toward agriculture both in the United States and the European Union. It is only on relatively big issues that public preferences are likely to be known, and very often even for such issues—for example, health care—understanding is radically defective, so that it is virtually impossible to know what would serve constituents well, much less what would serve them best.

V. Theories of Representation

The two most rigorous accounts of representative government that are relevant to actual practice in modern democracies are those of Mill and Manin. Each focuses much of his discussion on representatives, and each has some sense of the "Austrian" constraints that I discussed above. Let us briefly canvass Mill's and Manin's theories in order to set up an account of what the functions of representatives should be and, from that, infer their role morality. I will not provide a full rendition of the views of Mill and Manin, but only of those aspects that are especially relevant to understanding the role morality of representatives.

A. Mill

In his *Considerations on Representative Government* (1861), Mill supposes that a good government must provide order and progress. For this, a sine qua non is obedience (but not excessive obedience). The requisites of order and progress are much the same, because of the dynamism of the problems that human beings face (387).[34] For government to work well, the most important consideration is the quality of citizens (389). Hence, the most important tasks of government are to promote the virtue and intelligence of citizens (390) and to organize what virtue and intelligence already exist (392). Of course, Mill is a welfarist, and therefore his central claim is that government must enable the people to do well. For this and for progress more generally, liberty and individuality are fundamentally important (396–97).[35]

Mill notes that it is historically commonplace to assert that the best form of government is benevolent dictatorship (chapter 3). He says on the contrary that, for example, the benevolent despotism of Augustus set up Romans for the "more odious" reign of Tiberius (403). Moreover, an autocratic government cannot know enough (399) to run the society well. Mill essentially presumes an Austrian social theory. He also anticipates

---

[34] In this section only, citations to pages and chapters in Mill's *Considerations on Representative Government* will be given in parentheses. See note 11 for complete bibliographic information.

[35] Mill gives a compelling consequentialist justification for liberty, without which progress is eventually stifled.

Schumpeter's main point, that a voter's incentive is to be ignorant because, as Mill puts it, "a person must have a very unusual taste for intellectual exercise in and for itself who will put himself to the trouble of thought when it is to have no outward effect" (400). Mill holds an essentially pragmatic view of knowledge. He also reinforces this view when he says that no one will take an interest in government who cannot participate (469). This suggests that almost no one will take much interest in government, because almost no one can participate to any significant extent. But Mill's point in this passage seems to have been intended to suggest that people could be motivated to participate through education. Unfortunately, education might sooner lead one to understand just how massive are the obstacles to real participation most of the time. Mill himself concludes that there is very little opportunity for holding office in the central government (chapter 15). Local government, with its smaller scale and higher proportion of office holding, helps (535–36), but even local government in modern democracies is commonly carried out by representatives who have constituencies numbering in the thousands and even hundreds of thousands, so there cannot be very much participation even here.

In a continuation of his quasi-Austrian views, Mill says that what a legislative body is competent to do is quite limited (chapter 5). It can adopt not very precise legislation—for example, in our time, tax policy or environmental regulation. To do much more, it must delegate such things to expert advisers and to committees (430). Even then, laws will tend to become inconsistent over time because no one will have massive oversight of the whole body of law (a task performed by the Nomothetae in ancient Athens [431]). Hence, the proper function of a legislature is the very limited one of watching and controlling the administrative branches of government (432).

Mill famously claims that it is especially useful to engage in debate (433). This is not the "deliberative democracy" of current visions, although Mill's authority is often invoked in its support. His claim may partly suggest Schmitt's concern with deliberation as a device for finding the truth. Against Schmitt, however, Mill thinks that genuine representativeness is required, because it enables the legislature "to indicate wants, to be an organ for popular demands, and a place of adverse discussion for all opinions relating to public matters . . . ; and, along with this, to check by criticism, and eventually by withdrawing their support, those high public officers who really conduct the public business" (433).

Mill attributes the infirmities of representative government to two general causes (chapter 6). First, there is the quasi-Austrian general ignorance and incapacity of government and its agents; second, there is the danger of being under the influence of interests not identical to the general welfare of the community (436). He supposes that the main comparison to be made is between government by bureaucracy and government by representative democracy (438–39). Autocracy and aristocracy are too obviously flawed to merit consideration.

Against the danger of class legislation, Mill optimistically supposes that the few individuals who are public-spirited combined with those whose own interest happens to coincide with the public interest can collude in a majority to carry the day for the public interest (446–47). This is Panglossian. He should have read Madison more attentively. Indeed, he should have read himself more attentively.

In chapter 8 Mill discusses the extent of the suffrage and his view that it should generally be extended and should include women (479–81). Mill argues that fully representative democracy is the only true democracy (467). In keeping with his general view that citizens must be required to be intelligent enough to see their own interests if they are to gain the franchise, he proposes educational requirements on suffrage, because voters must be able to read, write, and do arithmetic if they are to vote intelligently on their own interests. For him this seems to be little more than a definitional implication of the idea of democracy: universal teaching must precede a universal franchise (470).

Mill especially worries about the fact that the large majority of citizens in his England are manual laborers. He supposes that they might abuse their power through their democratic majority to enact class legislation. He was largely wrong about this empirical point, because manual workers in his time were a diverse lot with conflicting interests. Manual laborers included farmers as the largest group, factory workers (who only became the bare majority of the English work force several decades after Mill wrote), and a miscellany of service workers, especially in urban areas. (In the United States in his time farmers were the overwhelming majority of all workers.) These quite diverse groups had little in common. Indeed, the only interest that they might have shared was in redistribution from the middle and upper classes, which in any case was not a viable political program in Mill's day. (Madison, too, worries about the possibility that the poor majority could combine to dispossess the wealthy of their property, a worry that made some sense empirically in his time, but not in ours, when evidence says it does not happen.)

Mill advocates universal but unequal suffrage (473–74). Uniquely among democratic theorists up to his time, he proposes intelligence, not property, as the qualification for extra weight (478). He grants, however, that unequal suffrage may not be a practical suggestion (476). He is also inclined to contrive devices that give greater weight to some voters over others, as through the use of gerrymanders to block workers from achieving a parliamentary majority by concentrating their votes in certain districts that they would win overwhelmingly while diluting their strength elsewhere (477). (This is what he calls a "fully representative democracy.") He gives a not very convincing causal claim in support of such voter inequality. He says that the best incentive to the growth of intelligence is rising to power, not having achieved it (479). This claim is a pointless fallacy of composition: the class might rise to power but almost none of its members would. Thus, although the class of workers might rise to power, individual workers generally cannot. Mill thinks that a constitution should not declare ignorance to be entitled to as much political power as knowledge—as the U.S. Constitution virtually does declare (478). He therefore excoriates the American system.

B. Manin

In the first two chapters of his *The Principles of Representative Government*, Manin gives an account of the great transformation from direct to representative democracy.[36] In Athens, there was general representation of all by all in certain bodies of government, coupled with selection by lot of people to serve in more restrictive bodies. Now democracies are with rare exception systems of elected representative bodies. For Madison and Emmanuel-Joseph Sieyes, the great constitutional thinkers of the American and French democratic revolutions, respectively, representative democracy was a new and, for its time, preferable form of government.

Manin's main thesis on the development of representative government is that it inherently tends toward aristocracy of an odd and familiar kind. Membership in the class of aristocrats is determined by citizens through elections, and the characteristics that earn entry into this class have changed over time, from something like social distinction in Madison's time and earlier in colonial America and England, to something more nearly like celebrity today. This aristocratic tendency of elected representative government was already foreseen by the ancient Greeks, who preferred to select officeholders by lot, considering it more genuinely representative (27). By lot, even the lowliest citizen could be selected for a government position. Montesquieu famously observed that there is a close link between lot and democracy and between election and aristocracy (70). Manin says that rotation in office and selection by lot reflect deep distrust of the professionalism that would follow from specializing in holding office over a long period. Madison and Sieyes, however, want professionalism (32). They worry that democracy could entail putting power in the hands of amateurs (33). They believe that officeholders should be more distinguished than the ordinary run of citizens (94). In actual democracies, wealth, property, and the payment of taxes have often been employed as qualifications for running for office (97-98), and wealth in our time is often still very useful for gaining office by spending lavishly on one's campaign.

---

[36] In this section only, citations to pages and chapters in Manin's *The Principles of Representative Government* will be given in parentheses. See note 6 for complete bibliographic information.

In the Constitutional Convention of 1787, and in the state ratifying conventions and the debates leading up to them, the Anti-Federalists held that representatives should fairly closely mirror their constituents (109). Representation was not a matter of giving representatives mandates but of having the diverse U.S. population represented by their own types (109). Anti-Federalist Samuel Chase pointed out that the great majority of the population—farmers and ordinary workers—could never be elected (112). Before early fascist or corporatist guilds, the Anti-Federalists were probably the only true advocates of genuinely representative democracy by station in life rather than by geographical location, and there has been no further debate on the aristocratic nature of election after the Anti-Federalist arguments of 1787–88 (132). Manin concludes that, for solid causal reasons, "election cannot, by its very nature, result in the selection of representatives who resemble their constituents" (149). In the end, however, power is not earned by distinctive traits or capacities but by agreement among the electorate about what traits constitute superiority (158). Apart from his being the son of a former president, one would be very hard pressed to account for the traits that put George W. Bush in the presidency, but one can give an account of how support coalesced around him at various stages in the 2000 election cycle. Still, Manin notes that the principles of distinction and salience that make for election do not violate norms of equality and political right, although the constraint of wealth does (159). Mill thought that American political leaders in his time were woefully undistinguished.[37]

In the traditional view, members of the British Parliament represented the nation as a whole and not merely their constituencies (163), as in the views of Burke and, to some extent, Mill. This view has given way, first to party democracy, in which a party gains control of parliament and governs for its term (206–18), and then to what Manin calls "audience democracy" (218–32), which is substantially formed by the media and the capacity of individual candidates to appeal to the voters.

Against Schmitt's view that deliberation is valued for giving us access to truth, Manin concludes, "It is the collective and diverse character of the representative organ, and not any prior or independently established belief in the virtues of debate, that explains the role conferred on discussion" (187). What makes some resolution of legislative debate a law is some form of consent, not discussion of it or its truth value (189). Moreover, the requisite consent is typically merely majority agreement, whereas truth should command unanimous consent once it is established.

In keeping with Manin's thesis on audience democracy and "celebrity," the great playwright Arthur Miller (1915–) analyzes the acting abilities of

---

[37] John Stuart Mill, "De Tocqueville on Democracy in America, II," in John Stuart Mill, *Essays on Politics and Society*, vol. 18 of *Collected Works of John Stuart Mill*, ed. J. M. Robson (Toronto: University of Toronto Press, 1977), 175.

modern American presidents, going back to Franklin Roosevelt.[38] Miller evaluates the acting ability of these presidents as he would assess how and why an actor succeeds on the screen or on the stage. He especially notes the peculiar differences between live and screen performances; in the latter, close-up cameras could turn more intense expressions into something baroque or rococo. In the television age, candidates must be flat; they cannot be orators in the grand style of, say, William Jennings Bryan. Miller argues that successful politicians tend to master performing before the camera and that we the voters value them in part for this success. Miller's analysis is far more sophisticated in its appreciation of the theatricality of politics than we are accustomed to from pundits, who typically lack his professionalism. Miller himself came to appreciate the difference between screen and stage from participating in the filming of *The Misfits* (1961). Clark Gable, the film's star, explained to Miller that he had to play his part very low key. Roosevelt might partly be Miller's favorite from the cast of modern presidents because he politicked in the era before television, which allowed him a florid acting style, rather than the flat affect favored by presidents in the television era.

VI. THE ROLE MORALITY OF REPRESENTATIVES

Carl Schmitt holds that democracy is the identity of ruler and ruled, and this is not compatible with representation; Rousseau believes that representative democracy is slavery.[39] Schmitt's is merely a definitional move. If we suppose Schmitt's identity, it is pointless for us to talk about the role morality of the rulers with respect to the ruled. The issue only arises because there is not an identity between the ruler and the ruled in a representative democracy. Similarly, if representative democracy is a form of slavery, it is silly to speak of a role morality for the overseers of the slaves. Against both these views, elected officials are, by a complex formula, both the agents and the rulers of the citizenry.

My purpose is to analyze the role morality of elected representatives in the light of the more credible theories of representation that I have canvassed: Madisonian constituency representation, party representation, and representation in Manin's audience democracy. I propose that we define the morality of representatives as artificial duties derived from their roles.

There are two other ways that we might proceed. We might apply something like conventional morality to the roles of representatives. Apart from intuitionists, no moral philosopher would do this, but we might suppose that, empirically, there is a broadly expected—therefore conventional—morality for elected officials. One measure of such a con-

[38] Arthur Miller, *On Politics and the Art of Acting* (New York: Viking, 2001).

[39] Manin, *The Principles of Representative Government*, 151, 1. Rousseau specifically discusses England in the eighteenth century. He wrote, of course, before the rise of representative democracy in its fuller forms.

ventional morality might be gleaned from surveys on why people vote against someone whom they previously supported. I doubt that there is a standard, widely accepted conventional morality for elected officials, but there might be, or there might have been in some eras. Insofar as there is such a conventional morality, it seems likely to be related to the functional role moralities that I will canvass below.

Although it seems unlikely that there is even the hint of a consensus on any broad conventional morality for elected officials in modern democracies, there might be nearly a consensus that our officials should not use their offices to work for their private benefit against the interests of their constituencies or of the larger public. There is a standard moral constraint on agency relationships in general, which bars the agent from taking any action that would be a conflict of interest. Agents should not use their position of acting on the authority of others to take advantage of them. While this principle is seemingly simple in the contexts of many agency relationships—in our dealings with lawyers, doctors, accountants, and so forth—articulation of such a principle for elected officials is complex, as I shall argue below.

A. Functionally determined morality

The role morality of a doctor is to see to the patient's health because this is the function for which the doctor's services are sought; the role morality of a lawyer is, analogously, to see to winning the client's case or giving beneficial legal advice. If we wish to determine what the role morality of elected officials is—by analogy to professional ethics—we must first settle on what the function of an elected official is in relation to a constituent. This depends on our explanatory (not normative) theory of representation. Clearly, there cannot be a generally correct role morality for political representatives in the way that there is for doctors, because there are many theories of representation and these require different principles of action by elected officials.

We have at least three practical theories of representation that are quite distinct from one another. First, there is the *quasi-Madisonian theory* that focuses on individual legislators as agents of their constituencies. Second, there is the *political party theory* that makes elected officials the agents of their parties, and parties the agents of their partisan constituencies, which typically are broadly defined classes rather than geographical constituencies. Third, there is *Manin's audience democracy*, in which it is not clear that elected officials are agents of anyone other than themselves. The first two theories yield relatively straightforward principles of role morality for representatives. Historically, the role morality that seems most commonly stipulated by citizens in many democracies is that representatives be seen as agents of their constituents or as party loyalists. Given that representatives cannot know in detail what their constituents' wants are, representatives can knowledgeably only address their constituents' interests as fairly broadly conceived. Therefore, the role morality of an elected lawmaker is to see to the broadly defined interests of his or her constituents. We can call this the 'Madisonian role morality' of elected legislators, which had its greatest influence in the early United States. We can call it 'party role morality' in systems organized by parties, although in a party system, service to one's constituency is rendered indirectly through service to one's party, which serves all relevant constituencies.

If we consider the current stage of development of representation, Manin's audience democracy, we may wonder whether any role morality still applies to elected officials. One might assert a role morality, but the voters are unlikely to be concerned with it, except perhaps when a representative is grossly out of line. Suppose we do not elect our officials on the ground of how we expect them to handle their role in office, but primarily on the ground of who they are, including whether they happen to be celebrities. Then they would seem to have no mandate beyond continuing to be themselves. If media mastery is the route to election, then it might also be the route to renown while in office. It would be perverse for the electorate to complain that their officials are very good at precisely the skills that got them elected.

We might still think that the role morality of representatives is to represent, to work as agents for their constituents' interests, sometimes to seek the larger public good, and sometimes to defend civil liberties. But in America our moral expectations evidently do not explain or even correlate with how we vote to select our representatives. It was a happy fact of both Madisonian individual and later party systems that our interests coincided with our moral expectations for our representatives. In audience democracy, they do not correlate well.

Voters sometimes do hold candidates accountable for lack of media appeal, as in the case of Al Gore and George Bush in 2000, or for loss of it, as in the case of Gary Condit in 2002. Gore was often ridiculed for his stiff, dull manner (with at least one popular comedian comparing him to a wooden cigar store Indian). Bush, who barely won a close election over Gore, had likewise been satirized for his frequent verbal clumsiness. Prior to 2002, Condit had been reelected several times, even though his legislative impact was nil throughout his time in office. When he became the furtive man who refused to speak to the press about his reputed affair with his murdered former intern, his career was doomed, even if it could have been shown that he had played no role in her murder, and even though mere revelation of his affair, had the woman not been murdered, might not have blocked his continued reelection. By appearing indifferent, if not sinister, he simply lost much of the personal appeal that had repeatedly won him reelection.

If personality and media success are the grounds for election, then the electorate is likely to be divided on most politicians just because different personalities are likely to appeal to different voters. It seems probable, for example, that the astonishing divergence of views on Bill Clinton had much to do with divergent responses to his personal style. Even as he shifted the Democratic Party toward the center of American politics, he was detested by the American Right as perhaps no one since Franklin Roosevelt. In keeping with Manin's thesis on the evolution from Madisonian to audience democracy, Roosevelt seems to have been despised for his political positions, Clinton for being Clinton.

The development of audience democracy raises the question of whether personality might correlate with political positions to a sufficient degree as to yield the cues that Popkin and others need for their argument that voters base their votes on low-information rationality. There are two interlocking sets of correlations: first, on the side of the candidates and, then, on the side of the voters. Candidate personality must correlate with candidate position, and, given this correlation, candidate appeal must correlate with the voters' positions on issues. These correlations are tenuous reeds for us to hold onto in the hope for rational politics, if we have indeed entered an era of audience democracy. Against even such a slim hope for rationality, it seems likely that audience democracy is a response to the combination of voter ignorance of policy and government and of politicians' ignorance of voters' interests other than in broad terms. If we put the Schumpeterian vision of the limited capacities of voters together with the Austrian vision of the limited capacities of the state, we have representatives who cannot know much about their constituents trying to represent constituents who do not even know their interests in many areas and who, in any case, know very little about their government, its policies, and its officials.

B. Conventionally determined morality

Beyond any role morality that is functionally determined by our theory of representation, we might insist on several other "moral constraints" (that derive from conventional morality) on what our representatives do in office. There is one fairly broad, general concern that representatives are commonly expected to address: the political equality of citizens. This is a concern that seems to follow from the nature and purpose of democracy. We might fundamentally disagree about the extent to which economic inequality is good (as in the theory of justice of John Rawls, who allows inequalities — which might be extreme — that redound to the benefit of the worst off), but we do not generally argue in public that political inequality is good, although some, including Mill and Texas oilman H. L. Hunt, are notable exceptions. Exactly what it takes to make individuals politically equal is not easily determined, but some elements seem clear enough.[40] Anything that is an obstacle to political participation, such as extremely poor education, and that might be affected by public policy is an issue that we might ex-

---

[40] For discussion, see Thomas Christiano, *The Rule of the Many: Fundamental Issues in Democratic Theory* (Boulder, CO: Westview Press, 1996).

pect our representatives to take on, even though it goes beyond our own interests and beyond their representation of our interests.

As noted earlier, Mill supposes that two of the most important tasks of government are to promote the virtue and intelligence of citizens, and to organize what virtue and intelligence already exist.[41] These two functions are of such salience for him because he supposes that the most important consideration in creating and running government is the "quality" of citizens,[42] which might be partly a concern with political equality. (Against such generosity of interpretation, however, we know that Mill strongly defends inequality of political power grounded in intellectual qualifications.) If we thought that citizens played a substantial and active role in government, then we might agree with this claim, but it is prima facie false that citizens play a great role. They might occasionally mobilize effectively and bring about a change in government policy, as may have happened in the civil rights and anti–Vietnam War movements in the United States. But such activism is surely a rare activity for citizens, who generally attend to their own lives, acquiesce in government's discretion to determine and carry out public policy, and even acquiesce to the extreme as millions are sent off to fight and die in "great" wars.

One might contrive an argument that, say, broader education would redound not only to the benefit of those educated by this new policy, but also to the benefit of more or less all citizens through the creation of a more productive or otherwise more appealing society. But in general, it seems likely that a representative who works for such an egalitarian policy for the whole society will risk harming the interests of his or her constituents, who may not directly benefit from, but may directly pay for, the programs that enhance educational equality. Some things that a representative might seek for his constituents can most readily be attained if they are provided for all those in the relevant class. For example, the best way to guarantee a minimum wage for my constituents might be to legislate it for the entire nation. Hence, I might act in a way that is similar to the actions of a Burkean or Millian representative concerned with the general welfare and not merely with the welfare of my own constituents.

We could stipulate other "moral constraints" on representatives, such as seeing to the constituents' moral development or their religious beliefs. These two purposes were ruled out by the American constitutionalists, although they have been stipulated to be a large part of the mandate of government by many other regimes. In American politics there have been major movements that advocate the use of government for other purposes, for example, the social-agenda crowd that wants regulation of values, the mercantilist-statist Right that wants government to protect business interests, or the socialist-statist Left that wants government to restructure society to achieve greater economic equality.

[41] Mill, *Considerations on Representative Government*, 390, 392.
[42] Ibid., 389.

Additionally, we can probably claim that part of the role morality of some government officials in the United States is to defend individual liberties, such as those defined in the Bill of Rights. For many officials, such as legislators, the defense of liberties requires merely refraining from infringing them, although, on occasion, legislators might be called upon to devise new protections, and other officials, especially those in the justice system, might be expected to defend liberties against official abuse. It is primarily the judiciary that has the function and, therefore, the role morality to defend civil liberties. Elected officials and appointed officials, such as the U.S. Attorney General, frequently find civil liberties an annoyance.

Finally, we might wish to press upon legislators as part of their role morality the more general purpose of working for the interest of the entire public, and not merely for their constituents. In a variant on my example of education, many legislators who represent districts in which education meets reasonably high standards might be expected, nevertheless, to vote for legislation mandating such standards for the entire nation, not in order to enhance political competence (as in my original example), but to enrich the life prospects of those who would benefit from the new programs. The votes of these legislators would serve not the interests of their own constituents, but only, in some sense, the broader public good or even only the interests of other citizens outside their constituency, possibly even at a substantial cost to their own constituents. If the policy were seen as a public good, then support for it could easily be justified on Burkean or Millian grounds, but it might sometimes also be argued on the ground of concern for political equality, in which case it would be an outgrowth of a conventional morality.

Clearly, none of these conventional moral principles for legislators is strongly backed by the electorates of many democratic nations. These are in many cases idiosyncratic views endorsed by activists of various stripes, not views inferred from the logic or nature of representation. Some of them might be backed by particular moral theories, such as utilitarianism, which might also back the institutions of representative government, but the principles are still not inherent in the nature of representation.

C. Conflicts of interest

Finally, we ought to consider one aspect of the role morality of anyone who acts as an agent for anyone else. All agents must avoid conflicts of interest that could lead them to benefit themselves at the expense of their principals. If our elected officials are our agents, then they must adhere to this constraint. The problem of conflicts of interest raises what is apparently the most striking difference between traditional professional ethics and any plausible ethics for elected officials: both the traditional professional and the elected official are agents on our behalf, and we want them to act in our interests, but the politician's position is far more complex than that of the traditional professional. For example, every doctor to whom I go as a patient should be my agent. But a representative can be seen as my agent and not yours in a meaningful and important sense if I voted for this representative while you voted against her. You cannot claim that she should work for your interests in the same way that I can, because she should act for the majority who elected her, including me, more than for those who opposed that majority.

Moreover, you might want to have her removed from office if she engages in practices that seem to benefit herself at public expense. I might not want her to be removed because I suspect that any replacement would be less committed to serving my interests. Consider the complications that might factor into opposition or support for a politician aside from the merits of any charges against him. As a real-world example, consider the positions of those who supported or opposed the impeachment of President Clinton and his removal from office. (The concern in his case was not over any abuse of office for his own interest.) Obviously, there was a substantial correlation between one's position on these moves and one's interest in having Clinton continue in office. Similarly, supporters of Berlusconi and his Northern League have argued that court actions to try him for bribery are politically motivated and opportunistic and, as I previously noted, they support legislation that would protect him from prosecution.[43]

If we are legislating in advance, when there is no political valence to corruption, then we might all agree that acting from certain classes of conflict of interest should be punished by removal from office. When there is an actual case, you might favor removal while I do not, because your interests are served by removal and mine are not. The role morality for the officeholder will then be whatever we have stipulated by law and will not be colored by our own interests in removal or retention of a particular person in office. We could sensibly say that there is a public interest in blocking certain classes of conflict of interest.

VII. Conclusion

If democracy were strictly representative, then government would be an epiphenomenon determined by the wants and interests of citizens, as in the view of political scientist Arthur Bentley (1870-1957).[44] It is not merely an epiphenomenon, though, because citizens' interests and demands are only weakly determinative. Government takes on a life of its own that has much to do with the elevation of political leaders to a peculiar aristocracy. This aristocracy is not the oligarchy of Michels, because its members are far more subject to election, and they can occasionally be unelected by the larger public. Michels's oligarchs were subject to control only within their organizations, not by the larger public.

---

[43] Bruni, "Italy, a Land of Tolerance."

[44] Arthur F. Bentley, *The Process of Government* (Chicago, IL: University of Chicago Press, 1908).

A saving grace of aristocratic representative democracy is that, in any case, democracy works at all only where there is fairly broad consensus on political order and, commonly, civil liberties. This consensus means that most citizens need merely acquiesce in allowing government to run or intrude into large parts of their lives. As political scientist Robert Dahl says, "In a sense, what we ordinarily describe as democratic 'politics' is merely the chaff. It is the surface manifestation, representing superficial conflicts. [These] disputes over policy alternatives are nearly always disputes over a set of alternatives that have already been winnowed down to those within the broad area of basic agreement."[45] This is roughly Tocqueville's view as well: "When a community actually has a mixed government—that is to say, when it is equally divided between adverse principles—it must either experience a revolution or fall into anarchy."[46]

We should qualify Dahl's claim with the note that "the broad area of basic agreement" need only be an area in which the politically effective groups are in agreement. Indeed, it need merely be an area in which the aristocratic political class is in agreement while the rest of the population basically acquiesces.[47] We might revise the Dahl and Tocqueville view to fit current conditions and say that much of the chaff of politics today is more nearly a part of the image than of real policy-oriented concern in its own right. For example, the chaff of Gary Condit's life dominated the media for weeks until it was reduced to its properly trivial status by the terrorist attacks of September 11, 2001.

Finally, note the irony that it is only because citizens began to be somewhat educated that representative democracy could arise in a large state (although the state's capacity to take a census and its technological capacity to collect votes have also played roles).[48] Yet it is the limits of citizens' understanding that makes it difficult for us to assess the quality of the very representatives we elect and, in particular, to determine whether they live up to any role morality we might assign to them. In the face of current trends in electoral motivations, it seems unlikely that the electorate consistently has in mind any role morality, either conventional or functional, for the media masters we put in office.

Politics, New York University, and Political Science, Stanford University

---

[45] Robert A. Dahl, *A Preface to Democratic Theory* (Chicago, IL: University of Chicago Press, 1956), 132–33.

[46] Alexis de Tocqueville, *Democracy in America*, 2 vols. (1835, 1840; reprint, New York: Knopf, 1945), 1:260.

[47] Russell Hardin, *Liberalism, Constitutionalism, and Democracy* (Oxford: Oxford University Press, 1999), chap. 4.

[48] Scott argues that a state's capacity to keep records on us or, in his term, to make us 'legible' allows the state to control us in various ways, such as by raising taxes and armies. This capacity also makes it possible to determine just who is to be represented in a modern democracy. Indeed, the U.S. Constitution requires a periodic census primarily for the purpose of allocating seats in the House of Representatives according to state populations so that representation is relatively equal.

6

Towards a General Theory of Political Representation

Andrew Rehfeld

Nondemocratic "representatives" increasingly act on the global stage, as "representatives" of their dictatorships to the United Nations, or when an NGO represents prisoners of war. Standard accounts of political representation depend upon democratic institutions (like elections) and a certain kind of proper activity (like deliberation and constituent accountability) and thus cannot explain how these people are representatives at all. I argue that the standard account of political representation is thus inadequate to explain political representation throughout the globe. I offer a general theory of political representation which explains representation simply by reference to a relevant audience accepting a person as such. When audiences use democratic rules of recognition, the familiar cases arise. When audiences use nondemocratic rules of recognition, nondemocratic cases arise. The result is that political representation, per se, is not a democratic phenomenon at all. The account offers a more parsimonious explanation of political representation, providing a tool for analysis of political representation throughout the globe.

". . . whatever else the political philosopher may do, one obvious project is the examination of the languages of political discussion and legitimation, the critique of various of the assumptions from which those languages start, the exploration of how far the languages cohere with one another and with the languages of other times and places, and the search for new and broader terms in which to frame political debate."—Phillip Pettit, *Republicanism* (Pettit 1997, 2)

On 27 July 2004, just after the World Trade Organization (WTO) had decided to allow Libya to negotiate for membership, Ms. Najat Mehdi Al-Hajjaji addressed the General Council of the organization. Al-Hajjaji said that Libya "look[ed] forward to WTO membership . . . for the accomplishment of economic development for all."[1] Officially, Al-Hajjaji was the "permanent representative" to the WTO of the Libyan Araba Jamahiriya, and if we asked, "who represented Libya in front of the WTO on that date?" we would correctly identify Al-Hajjaji as that person. Yet Al-Hajjaji was not elected by the people of Libya, nor should we have any confidence that she represented the interests of its people. Even if she merely represented the Araba Jamahiriya, their choice of her was likely dictated by that nation's military dictator,

Muammar Qadhafi. Al-Hajjaji purported to be a political representative (whether of Libya or merely the Araba Jamahiriya) despite not having been freely and fairly elected by those she purportedly represented and whose interests she may or may not in fact pursue. In what sense, then, *is* she a political representative at all?

This kind of case of institutionalized *nondemocratic* representation is familiar in global institutions. In the United Nations, for example, individuals purporting to be political representatives act on behalf of their nations' interests whether or not they were selected according to democratic procedures. Other less formal cases raise a similar set of issues. Leaders of nongovernmental organizations (NGOs) like the International Red Cross purportedly represent the interests of prisoners of war even when those individuals have had no say in the selection of their representatives. In other cases, like that of environmental groups, the interests represented are not even human ones.[2] Given the lack of any democratic structures by which those represented can authorize and hold these actors to account, given the fact that they may or may not actually be pursuing the interests of those they

---

[1]Information in this paragraph taken from the web site of the World Trade Organization, accessed on 9 March 2005 at http://www.wto.org/english/news_e/news04_e/libya_stat_27july04_e.htm.

[2]These are "nonhuman" interests only to the extent to which they have "intrinsic" value. If they are valued *because* humans value them, that is another matter.

The Journal of Politics, Vol. 68, No. 1, February 2006, pp. 1–21

purportedly represent, are these even cases of political representation?

The question is critical because contemporary accounts of political representation explain why one *is* or why one *fails to be* a representative *at all* by reference to democratic norms: a representative is purportedly someone who looks out for the substantive interests of those who elected them through free and fair elections. Yet, when Nikita Khrushchev slammed his shoe on the podium at the United Nations observers had no problem recognizing that he was the representative of the Soviet Union (whether of the nation or of its government) despite his failing to have conformed to any reasonably democratic norms. Similarly, many who believe that George W. Bush became president of the United States in 2001 by deception or other means nevertheless recognized that he was the representative of that nation from 2001 to 2005.[3] If political representation is explained by democratic norms and institutions, then it would seem that Bush and Khrushchev were not representatives of their nations, a result as strange as it is false.

What other conditions might explain why Sue, but not Tom, is the political representative of some group? What could "political representation" be if it does not necessarily depend on notions of accountability, authorization, and "acting for another's interests?" And if the concept is simply a nonnormative description of a set of facts about the political world, what precisely is it descriptive of? In short, how do we explain political representation if not by an appeal to democratic legitimacy? These are the questions of this article.

I argue here that political representation has a robust nonnormative descriptive sense, that is, it describes facts about the political world without necessarily appealing to normative standards of legitimacy or justice. Political representation, I argue, results from an audience's judgment that some individual, rather than some other, stands in for a group in order to perform a specific function. The audience uses a set of "rules of recognition" to judge whether a claimant is a representative in any particular case.[4]

When audiences use democratic rules to guide their judgment, the democratic, but special, case arises. Indeed, these are the cases we are most familiar with—democratic audiences judging whether to accept a particular person as their legislative representative using rules that follow from a normative account of legitimacy. When audiences use rules of recognition that do not conform to democratic norms, however, nondemocratic cases arise. These cases are particularly salient in the international sphere, where audiences regularly use rules like "whoever has control of the military" (in the case, say, of Pervez Musharref in Pakistan) or "whoever has the power to act" (in the case, say, of the head of the Red Cross) to determine who is the political representative of a group. By referencing the rules of recognition that any particular audience uses rather than any substantive evaluation about those rules we can thus explain how political representation *qua* representation arises. The standard, democratic account thus turns out to be merely a special case of the more general phenomenon: political representation arises simply by reference to a relevant audience accepting a person as such. Thus, political representation, per se, is not a particularly democratic phenomenon at all.

In the remainder of this introduction I develop in more detail the problem that gives rise to the present account, I explain what is at stake, and I provide a road map by which I proceed.

Development of the Problem

The questions in this article may appear to be settled or uninteresting. Political representation has been extensively used and discussed for over two millennia.[5] It entered pre-modernity with *Magna Charta* (Fasolt 1991), was limited by Hobbes (1994, 101–105), extolled by Madison (Hamilton, Jay, and Madison 1949, 56–65), repudiated by Rousseau (1978, 101–104), equalized by Cady Stanton (Keyssar 2000, 172–221), institutionalized by Mill (1991), vitalized by Dewey (1954), criticized by Schmitt (1996), and pluralized by Dahl (1956). Contemporary accounts begin

---

[3]Bush was reelected in 2004 without much controversy.

[4]"Rules of recognition" are adopted directly from H. L. A. Hart's treatment of law (Hart 1997). They function in a similar way only to the extent that they indicate that audiences need to reference rules in order to determine whether this, but not that, is the object in question. Hart's object was "law," mine is "representation." There are certain other similarities not developed here, including the role of first-order and second-order rules, and an account of the emergence of the rules in the first place. But the fact that our objects of analysis are so different means that the use of rules of recognition may be an adequate explanation of one phenomenon without explaining the other. Thus, even if critics of Hart are right, these rules may still serve an important function in other contexts. An extended discussion of this point will be important to the extended development of the present argument, but it is tangential to our concerns here.

[5]The claim by some of the American founders that political representation was "discovered" by the moderns is as erroneous as it is repeated. See Manin (1997) for a good summary of the evidence of its use in Ancient Greece.

with Pitkin's (1967) analysis of this history establishing what I call the "standard account" of political representation: political representation purportedly involves, *inter alia*, authorization, accountability, and the looking out for another's interests.[6]

Consider how closely the dimensions of the standard account fit with accounts of normative legitimacy, that is, the conditions by which a group has the *right* to make and enforce laws that bind others.[7] Under the standard account, a political representative purportedly has *substantive* obligations to act on behalf of another's interests as *ipso facto* what it means to be a political representative.[8] Political representation must arise and be maintained through a set of *procedural* standards of *authorization and accountability* usually by way of *free and fair* elections.[9] The fact

[6]Despite some important disagreements around symbolic and descriptive representation, few historical treatments have been so completely accepted as a standard account of a concept in all areas of political science. Pitkin's work quickly became the point of departure for anyone writing on the topic, whether in political theory or elsewhere in the field, and has shaped the debate ever since it was published. This achievement is all the more impressive given the enormous democratization internationally and the post-Voting Rights Amendment debates in the United States that fully emerged only after her work was published.

[7]Normative legitimacy differs from "sociological legitimacy" (also called "empirical legitimacy") which often equates "legitimacy" with "public approval." The "group" that makes binding rules has usually been the government (in particular, the legislature) of a nation-state, but in the context of global institutions other groups are making rules that claim to bind governments and their citizens. Because political representatives are the ones who write and pass these rules, I take the legitimacy of any political representative to be a necessary but insufficient condition for the normative legitimacy of the rules they pass. (For more, see Rehfeld 2005, 13–16). By framing legitimacy in terms of a right to make and enforce law, I thus agree with Wellman who has argued, ". . . political legitimacy is distinct from political obligation; the former is about what a state is permitted to do, and the latter concerns what a citizen is obligated to do. Although I believe these two are related, clearly they are not identical" (Wellman 1996, 212).

[8]Another's interests may be identical to the representative's own interests, but the obligation to represent the former accrues only by virtue of their interests being someone else's. A more complex case arises when the representative is part of the group whose interests she is representing. This is not terribly difficult to understand as a case in which the representative *qua* representative is not representing her own interests but rather the interests of the group of which she, as a citizen, happens to be a member.

[9]No less familiar, if less clearly distinguished, are disagreements about the epistemic source of these interests: should constituents or the nation *determine* the content of those interests, or should the representative's own wisdom be her guide? A representative might believe that her job is to pursue her constituents' interests, but nevertheless believe that she knows what is best for them. Similarly, she might take the national interest as her goal, but believe that asking her constituents what they think is the national interest is the best way to find out what it is. Thus this epistemic question should be differentiated from the more familiar *delegate/trustee* distinction. (See Rehfeld 2005, 202–204).

that the standard account of political representation and analyses of legitimacy use the same kinds of standards is no coincidence: these obligations and standards are quite plausibly what render any case of political representation *legitimate*. But if we use the same criteria to judge whether a person is a representative *at all* we cannot then explain the kinds of cases described above, cases of purportedly illegitimate representation.

If Pitkin's treatment established the seminal treatment of the standard account, subsequent work has only expanded, without seriously questioning, Pitkin's fundamentals. Of this next generation, Young (1990), Phillips (1995) and Williams (1998) all expanded on the standard view and offered different arguments for the inclusion of certain kinds of groups. In addition to these, Amy (1993), Bohman (Bohman and Rehg 1997), Bybee (1998), Cohen (1989), Fishkin (1991), Gutmann and Thompson (1996), Habermas (1996, 287–328 and 463–90), James (2004) and many, many others have argued for more legitimate or better representation through accountability (mostly through deliberation), authorization (mostly through electoral reform), and the pursuit of interests. Manin (1997) has argued that representative government is properly viewed as an elective aristocracy but, again, animated by the norms Pitkin described. Reinforcing these norms, Mansbridge's terrific critique of empirical research on political representation argues these forms fail to meet "the criteria for democratic accountability" (Mansbridge 2003, 515). And Dryzek (2000) and Kuper (2004) (to name just two) have argued in favor of democratic institutions for global purposes that rely on particular views of political representation, again tied closely to deliberative legitimacy and democratic justice respectively.

By wedding representation with the conditions that render it legitimate, the standard account is doing double duty: not only does it tell us when a representative is legitimate or democratic, it also purportedly tells us when a person is a political representative at all. By simultaneously defining conditions by which someone becomes a political representative and the conditions for her legitimacy we are unable to explain how the cases of illegitimate representation I illustrated above arise. Indeed, under the standard account, the question, "What makes Smith a representative but not Jones?" becomes impossible without an appeal to facts about the legitimacy of Smith's claim.

Cases of illegitimate political representation are not mistakes of classification or cases in which the representative simply fails to achieve an ideal: political representation in, say, the early modern period in

England, was less about legitimizing practices as about a practical way for the monarchy to extract taxes from the people (Fasolt 1991). Similarly, in many nations over the last 50 years, whether in Africa, South America, or Eastern Europe and the republics of the former Soviet Union, we see nations filled with political representatives, but whose elections, conduct, and other criteria do not meet any plausible account of legitimacy. NGOs now send their representatives who purportedly "represent" nonstate actors and causes on the world stage. And, as I said above, between 2001 and 2005 there were many Americans who viewed their president as the illegitimate occupant of his office. Nevertheless, they called him "Mr. President" if they saw him and felt pride or shame as he acted *as their representative* in the international realm. If political representation entails its own legitimacy, it is hard to see how these things can be so.

What is at Stake: Who Cares?

There are two main benefits of a general theory of political representation. First, if this account is accurate it will explain how political representation operates as a political phenomenon in democratic and nondemocratic, formal and informal contexts. It will thus provide an extremely useful tool to study political representation in nonnational, global arenas where nondemocratic and informal representation increasingly occurs. We can explain why people can be political representatives despite there having been no free and fair elections that selected them, nor their plausibly acting in the interests of "their people." The account shifts our attention from democratic norms to the more generally important rules of recognition that different audiences use to judge whether this person, but not that one, is a representative. The account also allows us to explain why and how the same audience will use very different rules of recognition in different cases. This alone would justify the treatment.

The second value of a general theory of political representation is that it helps explain and illustrate how norms are introduced into the political world. When we do not adequately distinguish the concept of political representation from underlying norms of legitimacy we allow ourselves to avoid the hard questions of what makes institutions just or legitimate. This is a familiar enough critique of empirical social scientists who uncritically adopt normative judgments into their purportedly "value free" research; for example, those who equate "legitimacy" with public opinion (rather than right). But in the case of the theoretical literature, "political representation" has now emerged as a normative category all its own. Thus do theorists argue about what "real representation" is, rather than what *legitimate* political representation might be. This obscures the fact that political representation need not be just, legitimate, equal, fair, or otherwise deserving of approval without failing to be any less "real" or "true" a case of representation.

The account here does not deny that normative judgments play a part in the recognition of political representation. Quite the opposite: a general theory of political representation allows us to specify precisely how and where normative arguments enter the political world. In the case of representation, it is the rules that audiences use to recognize representatives rather than the institutions or practices of representatives themselves that explain why they are, or fail to be, legitimate or just.[10] Representation *really does happen* whenever a particular audience recognizes a case that conforms to whatever rules of recognition it uses, regardless of whether these rules are just or unjust, fair or unfair, legitimate or illegitimate. By demonstrating the conceptual limits of political representation, I mean to implicate the normative arguments that underlie its use in a more direct and uncompromising way, a point I will return to at the close of this account.

The article continues over five more sections. In the second section, I state the general theory. I explain in the third section the "rules of recognition" and how the audience operates in greater detail, answering some initial objections to the general account. I then describe how the terms of representation combine into necessary and sufficient conditions for representation to obtain. In the fifth section, I show how this account is formally related to—but need not assume—conceptions of normative legitimacy. Finally, I conclude with a description of the concept as spanning substantive and formal dimensions.

A General Theory of Political Representation

In this section, I lay out a general theory of political representation that depends not on institutional facts, but rather on an audience's judgment. Most of this section merely states the general theory without objection. In later sections, I defend it against important concerns.

[10] As we will see, the rules of recognition an audience uses may happen to correspond closely with the conditions for legitimate institutions.

Two things are trivially true of *all* representational relationships (including political, symbolic, artistic, and linguistic): there is purported to be some thing (loosely defined) to be represented and some thing (loosely defined) that represents it. Call the object of representation the *Represented*.[11] Call that which represents it the *Representative*. Formally, the *Representative* is a set, the members of which stand for the *Represented*. In many cases, there is only one member of that set (the single-member district, or the symbol that represents the artist formerly known as Prince).[12] In other cases, the Representative contains more than one member (possibly a multimember political district, or the many different symbols that represent "God" in art.)

Descriptively, the audience uses a set of rules to denote the *Representative*. These rules specify a *Selection Agent* who uses a *Decision Rule* to select a representative from a *Qualified Set*. In most democratic systems, the *Selection Agent* is "voters within an electoral district," the *Decision Rule* is some variant of "majority rule," and the *Qualified Set* from which the *Representative* must come is "citizens who reside in the district above a certain age." In most democratic systems the Selection Agent and the Represented overlap considerably; in nondemocratic representation, the Selection Agent differs from the Represented. For example, the *Represented* might be "the people of England," and the set of rules might be "Whomever (*Qualified Set*) the king (*Selection Agent*) desires (*Decision Rule*)."

Rules alone do not create representation; they are what an audience uses to recognize a claimant as a representative in the following way. First, an *Audience* must take these rules to be valid and appropriate given the case. Second, the *Audience* must recognize that the rules in fact denote an individual claimant. When an *Audience* recognizes that the rules it uses designate a particular claimant, that claimant becomes the *Representative*. This happens whenever an *Audience* recognizes that a particular claimant meets *whatever* set of rules it uses, whether these rules are arbitrary, *merely* pragmatic or normatively justifiable.

I briefly note that the use of the terms "qualified," "valid," and "appropriate" within the rules of recognition may appear to introduce normative claims that are not merely descriptive. These terms describe how the Audience views the rules that they use; that the Audience takes them to be "qualified," "valid" and "appropriate." But they do not imply that the rules *in fact* are what *should* count as "qualified" "valid" or "appropriate." For example, as long as an Audience takes "white men" to be the appropriate Selection Agents, then only claimants selected by "white men" will be Representatives, no matter how unjust that would be. Similarly, if an Audience takes "Mickey Mouse" to be the appropriate selection agent, only claimants selected by Mickey Mouse will be Representatives. (I will defend this claim in Section 5.)

The *Selection Agent, Decision Rules*, and *Qualified Set* simply describe the substantive content of the rules of recognition that any audience will use to judge who is, in fact, a political representative. A representative cannot represent something *simply* because some agent selected it; the Audience must recognize the Selection Agent through the rules it uses. Importantly, because representation relies on the correspondence between a claimant and an *Audience's* rules of recognition, we can explain cases in which we think a claimant *is* in fact a representative, despite the Audience's rejection of him, and those in which we think a claimant is not a representative despite the Audience's acceptance of him. These cases are ones in which an audience makes a mistake relative to rules it uses (a point I develop in Section 4.).

Who counts as the Audience? The Audience is the relevant group of people who must recognize a claimant as a representative, and the relevance of the group will always depend on the particular *Function* of a case of representation. Representation is always in service to some purpose or function; it is never "had" just to have it—a representative does not *merely* "stand for" another, she "stands in for another *in order to perform a specific function*." The *Function* of any particular case of representation describes the substantive activity a *Representative* is to do when "standing for" the *Represented*: "vote on laws"; "propose trade regulations"; "advocate for the environment"; etc. The Function thus also defines who counts as the relevant Audience in any particular case: if the Function is "to vote on laws *in the national legislature*" then the relevant Audience will be "the national legislature." As we'll see towards the end of the account, the *Function* plays a critical role in generating substantive,

---

[11]The word "constituent" might seem to be more natural here than "Represented." But "constituent" has a technical sense that is tied too closely to democratic theory to be of help. Further, "constituent" often refers only to that subset of represented individuals who register to vote, actually vote, or vote for the winning candidate. In the case of symbolic political representation there are no "constituents" represented, even though there is a thing (loosely defined) that is represented. Thus I have decided on the less familiar term "Represented" to denote that which is represented. For more on "constituency" see Rehfeld (2005).

[12]I thank Emily Hauptmann for her astute contribution to this point.

136 REPRESENTATION

Box 1: Definition of Terms

The Function	= the purpose of representation defining the job the Representative is supposed to do.
The Represented	= some person, group or thing represented.
The Representative	= some set of persons or things that stands in for the Represented.
The Audience	= the relevant parties before whom the Representative claims to stand in for the Represented and act as defined by the Function.
Rules of Recognition:	= the three rules the Audience uses to decide whether a claimant is a Representative.
Qualified Set	= the claimant(s) must be a member of a set the Audience recognizes as qualified.
Decision Rule	= the claimant must have been picked by the Decision Rule the Audience recognizes as valid.
Selection Agent	= the person(s) who employed the Decision Rule must be one the Audience recognizes as appropriate.

Box 2: Necessary and Sufficient Conditions for Representation to Obtain

Representation obtains in case:

R1: There is some Function that requires a Representative.
R2: A particular claimant is a member of the Qualified Set.
R3: The claimant was selected using the Decision Rule.
R4: The Selection Agent used the Decision Rule to pick a member of the Qualified Set.
R5: If applicable, the Representative accepts the charge.
R6: The Audience, in fact, recognizes that R2–R4 have obtained (that a member of the Qualified Set was selected by the Selection Agent to represent the Represented according to the Decision Rule.)

evaluative criteria against which we can say whether a representative is doing her job well or poorly.[13]

Box 1 summarizes the initial terms of this account. Box 2 summarizes how representation obtains, the details and defense of which I treat in the remainder of this article.

The Audience and its Rules of Recognition

In this section I explain the Rules of Recognition ("Qualified Set," "Decision Rule," and "Selection

---

[13]This account is an illustration of how representation forms a social institution that imposes what Searle has called a "status-function" upon people (Searle 1991). With Searle, to say that representation "*really* exists" means referring to individual collective intentions concerning a group activity. Whether one *is* a representative is a fact of the matter that corresponds to whether an audience recognizes a claimant as such. As a claim about the social world, it is thus no more nor less true than the "brute fact" (in Searle's terms) that Mount Everest exists independent of our language representations of it. I say this only to indicate the underlying foundations upon which this account rests: far more is needed to substantiate this important but presently tangential point.

Agent") in greater detail. I also illustrate what I mean by the "Audience", explain why it is necessary given the other features of this account, and consider preliminary objections to that term.

The Three Rules of Recognition

The Qualified Set

Qualified Set = the claimant(s) must be a member of a set the Audience recognizes as qualified.

The "Qualified Set" indicates the group of which a claimant must be a member in order for her to be recognized as a Representative by an Audience. Examples include the following:

- members of a particular gender (in contemporary France);
- property-owning white males (in Colonial America);
- individuals who nominate themselves to run (in Ancient Athens);
- district residents over the age of 25 (in the contemporary United States); and

- members of a minority group (in Canada and Bosnia-Herzegovina).

In most cases, the Qualified Set is a subset drawn from the Represented, but conceptually it may be identical to the Represented when all members of a professional organization, say, have the right to run for office. Members of the Qualified Set may also be entirely independent of the Represented, as is the case when, say, a child welfare advocate represents children—most audiences do not accept children in need of protection as themselves qualified—i.e., members of the Qualified Set. The Qualified Set can also be an almost trivial constraint when it is equivalent to "all humans on the planet" (though this would keep asses out of office).

The Decision Rule

The Decision Rule = the claimant must have been picked by the Decision Rule the Audience recognizes as valid.

A Decision Rule specifies the process through which some particular person or object (and not some other person or object) is chosen to be a representative. In this account the Decision Rule can be any rule that denotes a particular object(s). Decision Rules for selecting representatives have varied widely and may include:

- Voting (whether by plurality, majority or super-majority rules);
- Appointment;
- Divine Intervention;
- Imagination;
- Reasoning;
- Self-declaration;
- Duels; and
- Random selection.

Decision rules must pick out a discrete set of people (at least one) to be a representative. Since the Audience will have to view the rule as valid (whether or not it is actually defensible), in most democratic contexts this will significantly limit the range of possible decision rules. All that is required now is that some rule be used that picks out a particular person or group of people and that the Audience takes this rule to be valid, whether or not it actually is.

The Selection Agent

The Selection Agent = the person(s) who employed the Decision Rule must be one the Audience recognizes as appropriate.

TABLE 1   **Examples of Selection Agents (SA) in Some Familiar Cases of Representation**

- SA is a subset of the represented group, but not identical to it, when only some of the Represented vote.
- SA is identical to the represented group when all of the Represented vote.
- SA is not a member of the Represented in cases where a member of the U.S. Senate dies in office and the State governor appoints a replacement representative until the next election.*

*Formally speaking, the governor *in his role as governor* is not part of the Represented, even though as a citizen of the state he is part of the Represented.

The selection agent is a person or a set of people who use the specified Decision Rule to select a representative. In most political cases, decision rules require a Selection Agent.[14] Similarly, the selection agent is an insufficient condition for designating a representative. One can specify some agent(s) to pick a representative, but without any decision rule, a representative cannot be determined. Therefore, a selection agent and a decision rule (that the agent uses) are usually required (but insufficient) to denote a representative.

As an historical matter, Selection Agents have varied widely. The agent may be the board of the International Red Cross who appoints a representative for its group to testify before a panel at The Hague. It may be the Governor of State of Missouri who selects an interim representative to replace a deceased member of the U.S. Senate. And in the most familiar democratic case, the Selection Agent can be the adult citizens of a nation.

In Table 1 above I present illustrative examples of selection agents in three cases of purportedly *legitimate* political representation: where the agent is a subset of the represented, equivalent to the represented, or independent of the represented. Other permutations (an infinite number) are possible.

The Audience

As I claimed above, representation always denotes some kind of activity. In this way, representation is

[14]Some decision rules can seem to be self actuating and not dependent on any selection agents. For example, it appears that no selection agent is needed to pick out a single individual if we use the decision rule, "whomever survives a terrible illness first." But in this case the "we" that is using that purportedly self-actuating decision rule is the Selection Agent: whoever is the appropriate person(s) to choose "whomever survives" as the decision rule is the selection agent no more nor less than whoever uses ballots to choose a person. I thank Randy Calvert for raising this problem.

always in service to some function—whether to lobby a legislature, pass laws, or negotiate a peace settlement—and this function determines the Audience. The Audience is defined as *the relevant parties before whom a particular case of representation needs to be accepted.* In a legislature, for example, for Smith to "count" as a representative of some constituent group, *the other members of the legislature* are the relevant parties, because they must accept him as a representative before his vote will count.[15] It will not matter if anyone else accepts Smith as a representative, the legislature alone is the relevant party.

Notice that in this case, the constituent's (i.e., the Represented's) own judgment that Smith is their representative (as expressed, say, through majority vote) does not determine whether Smith is the representative of the group. The legislature's recognition of Smith is what matters, and it is this recognition that renders him, and not Jones, the representative of the group. Of course, when Smith comes before his constituents to explain what he did in the legislature, his constituents are now the Audience, and they often use the same rules of recognition that the legislature used to recognize him as their representative. In democratic systems, the legislature's recognition that Smith is the representative of a particular group *will* correspond closely, perhaps even exactly, to the group's own judgments, but this need not be and is only the case because each Audience is using similar rules of recognition.

In what follows, I will illustrate how the Audience uses its rules of recognition, explain why the Audience is necessary, and answer a preliminary objection to it based on role playing.

An Illustration of the Audience in Action: Negotiating Allowance. Imagine three children want to raise their allowance. Instead of going as a group to plead before their parents, they believe they would do better by having one represent the bunch. They select their youngest sister, Margaret, because they think she will be most persuasive in the situation. Margaret speaks

to her parents about a raise, explaining that she represents her siblings in the negotiation.

In such a case, given the Function of the representational relationship ("standing for the children in order to set allowance") the parents are the Audience, that is, they are the relevant parties because they are (by stipulation) the only ones who could change how much allowance the kids receive. The parents will thus have to recognize Margaret as their children's representative. If the parents failed, for whatever reason, to recognize Margaret as representing her siblings, she would not be their representative. Moreover, consider that it would not matter if *some stranger* believed that the eldest child, Sims, were the *proper* representative by virtue of his being the eldest child. Nor would it matter if some *other parent* as a matter of principle did not think children were qualified to be representative agents at all. It is necessary and sufficient that Margaret's parents, the parties before whom the relationship has any relevance, recognize their daughter as the representative of her siblings.

Variations on this example are illustrative. Imagine that, unbeknownst to his siblings, and after their agreement to present Margaret as their representative, Sims takes matters into his own hands, petitioning his parents directly. He argues that as the eldest son he has a right to represent his siblings. Imagine that his parents change their minds and accept Sims but for very crude and different reasons: they simply love Sims more than they love Margaret. The others now protest. "Dad, Sims doesn't speak for us; he may not argue on our behalf." Yet the parents disagree and hurtfully say, "*We* like Sims best, so he does represent you; our agreement with him is binding on you." Such a change—from Margaret to Sims—does not change the Audience; the Audience is still the parents. Nor does it change who the Represented are; they are still those children. A shift from Margaret to Sims does, however, signify a change in the Selection Agents that are part of the Audience's rules of recognition. In the first case, the selection agents were the siblings themselves who chose Margaret, in the latter case they were the parents who chose Sims. In both cases, the representative (Margaret or Sims) had to accept the charge. Critically, we can see that it is strictly up to the parents to set the conditions under which someone represents their children. Those conditions of acceptance might be distasteful (whom they love more) or more plausibly legitimate (whom the children want). Consider yet another case: the parents ask the children's cousin Owen to represent their children in the negotiation. The kids would be outraged. However, represent them Owen would.

---

[15]The fact that the legislature, rather than the home constituency, executive or judiciary, is the Audience in this case is a contingent fact about how legislatures tend to operate. For example, in the United States House of Representatives current members decide whether any one of them is a current member (Article 1, Section 5: "Each House shall be the Judge of the Elections, Returns and Qualifications of its own Members . . ."). In this case, the rule is circular because it presumes the very existence of the legislature in order to determine who its members are, that is, it presumes its own existence in order to determine whether it exists! The rule nicely illustrates that political representation often presumes a great deal of stability: although the rule would fail to resolve multiple simultaneous disputes, it functions perfectly well for occasional disputes of a few members.

In any particular case, the Function of representation specifies who the relevant parties are; that is, who is the Audience. The reverse is true, though not to the same extent: specify the Audience and a limited set of Functions follows. So if I specify "Margaret's parents" as the relevant parties, I've specified a range of functions of representation—from raising her allowance to changing her bedtime—but I've also limited them. Margaret couldn't represent her siblings before her parents (in their roles as parents) in order to get them into a good college or for the purposes of affecting national child welfare policy.

In sum, "relevant parties" or the Audience are the set of people who have the power to do whatever a Function of a particular case of representation specifies. The Audience uses *whatever* rules of recognition they do to determine whether this person, but not that one, is the representative.

The Illustration of Relevant Parties. Given that most accounts of political representation refer only to the content of what I am calling the "rules of recognition" without reference to the Audiences who use them, I need to illustrate the centrality of the Audience for representation. I will do this by working through an example in which I leave the Audience unspecified and demonstrate that without it we cannot tell whether a person is in fact a representative at all.

Imagine the other descriptive terms take on the following values:

The Represented = the City of Chicago
The Selection Agent = my mother
Qualified Set = anyone sitting around the table
The Decision Rule = "If my son wants to represent Chicago he should; if not I'll choose someone else."
The Representative = my mother's son (he wants the job)

Being my mother's son and wanting the job, I claim to be the representative of Chicago. To which the understandable response is, "Maybe in *your* mind and your mother's you represent the city of Chicago, but in no one else's." Similarly, "You only *think* you represent the city but you don't." So, why wouldn't I?

The answer lies in our background[16] assumptions about the Function of this case: we assume I would be laughed at (if not arrested) if I tried to act as a representative of Chicago before a trade union, the U.S.

[16]The background here functions in the way Searle (1991, 127–37) has described it.

Congress, or in front of a neighborhood council. If the Function of a representative in a certain case is to do certain things (like speak for the members of the city before this or that group), then the group before whom I act will have to view me as, in fact, representative of some other group for those purposes. As I demonstrated in the allowance example above, who the audience is depends entirely on what the Function of the case of representation is.

In the present example I've purposely left the Function unspecified: was it to represent parties to a contract, vote in the Illinois legislature, or speak on behalf of the city of Chicago at a trade association? Yet I suspect most people would have a stronger inclination to discount the role of Function here and say, *whatever the function of representation is* my mother is simply mistaken, I don't *really* represent Chicago on her say-so. Yet consider what happens if we make our background assumptions explicit and assert that the Function of representation in this case is "standing for the City of Chicago in order to play a board game." In the game, someone needed to determine who represented different cities and it was my mother's choice how to allocate positions to play. In that context, I certainly did represent Chicago, though for the very limited purposes of playing the game. The Function of the particular representative case determines the Audience (in this case it was my mother, since she was the referee of the game) and, once specified, the Audience must recognize a claimant as the representative.

Representing versus Role Playing: A First Objection to the Audience Function.[17] Playing a game entails role playing and on the surface it may seem inappropriate to draw analogies to the political sphere from that kind of a case. First, it may seem that that these particular rules of recognition (e.g., "if my son wants the job . . .") crop up in domestic, informal situations, and are not used in the political world. Of course, this is simply not true, even if today the use of such discretionary rules is limited. Kings and dictators have routinely used their children to represent their nations for reasons not much different than "because they wanted to." And most importantly, institutions like the WTO, the United Nations, and NGOs regularly use similar rules of recognition for figuring out who are the political representatives from, say, Libya, pre-2003 Iraq, and Syria. Only slightly more complex (if equally objectionable) rules of recognition explain how rep-

[17]The more serious objection that the Audience's judgments are simply judgments about legitimacy will be taken up in detail in the fifth section.

resentatives of the Soviet Union, China, and North Korea become representatives in international contexts. In all of these cases, the rules that world bodies use to determine who the representative is look very much like the rules my mother used in this example.

The more important general objection is that there is sphere confusion going on: political representation is a fundamentally different kind of *activity* from game playing and thus examples in one arena do not translate into the other. To specify this in more detail, the *Function* of political representation explains what kind of activity a representative will be engaged in and defines the audience by context. The Function of political representation takes on this form: "A Representative stands in for the *Represented* in order to do X" where X is some activity for which representation is needed. Now in the case of a game, "doing X" is simply "playing the game." In the cases of political representation most familiar to us, the *substance* of the Function is different but not its form: "advocate for a constituent's interests in the legislature" or "sign a global warming treaty to maximize a dictator's benefit." Structurally, then, the cases work in very similar ways.

Still there is a lingering sense that something is so substantively distinctive about each case as to preclude analogical reasoning from one to the other. As a last response, it will be useful here to work through Pitkin's objection to exactly these kinds of concerns. For Pitkin, when I play a game, I do not "represent" the player: I pretend *to be* the role I take on (Pitkin 1967, 26). In Pitkin's example, an actor does not "represent" Hamlet, he pretends "to be" (or not to be, I suppose) Hamlet. Similarly, I don't represent the City of Chicago when I play the game, I pretend "to be" the representative of the City of Chicago.[18]

Pitkin's distinction between players and actors depends on the purported fact that actors have not been "authorized" by those they represent, *and* that their activity is different from that of political representatives.

> Ordinarily the actor in a play does not claim or even pretend to be the authorized representative of anyone. He does not pretend to act on authority of Hamlet, but *to be* Hamlet. His entire manner and appearance are directed to creating the illusion that he is someone else, someone whom he is playing or, as we say, representing

on the stage. Conversely, an authorized representative does not, under ordinary circumstances, pretend to *be* the person he represents. The agent of the king does not dress or behave like the king, or try to pass himself off as his royal majesty. The West-coast representative of a national corporation does not try to pass himself off as that corporation itself. Nor, of course, does a Congressman pretend to be a large number of citizens. (Pitkin 1967, 26)

The actor's "situation" *seems* to be ". . . defined not by prior giving of right or accepting of responsibility, nor by pretense to these, but by the content and manner of what he does and how he acts" (Pitkin 1967, 27). So, for Pitkin, an actor is not a representative for two distinctive reasons: (a) unlike the political representative, the actor is not authorized by those he represents; and (b) unlike the political representative, the actor tries to "be" that which he represents. I will take each in turn.

What should we make of the claim that actors are not authorized by those whom they represent, but political representatives are? Well, it is certainly true that Hamlet (the quasi-historical figure) did not authorize any actor in the twenty-first century to play him on stage. But the general claim that political representation necessarily involves *being authorized by those you represent* is just false: even democratic political representatives represent people who did not authorize them to act, say those who voted for the losing candidate or those who did not vote at all. When representatives are appointed for a population, say in the example of the International Red Cross representing political prisoners, or a monarch appointing a representative to work for the good of his people, these are also representatives who, like the actor, have not been authorized by those they represent. Once we see the role that third parties regularly play, we can also rethink the acting example: the actor *is* authorized by a casting director, the producer, and/or the audience who watches and accepts the performance as a reasonable portrayal.

What should we make of the second claim that in theatrical representation an actor tries to be the character he represents and thus performs a different sort of activity from political representation? Here, this just seems mistaken on both sides. First, no sane actor really tries "to be" Hamlet, duping the audience into believing transubstantiation is occurring before their eyes. Instead, actors try to imitate salient features of Hamlet (how he spoke, fretted, hesitated, killed, etc.) in order to represent him on stage. Second, as an empirical matter, political representatives often do exactly the same sort of things with those they represent. When

---

[18]For the sake of symmetry I suppose I should say that when I play that game I do not *represent* Chicago, I pretend *to be* Chicago. Aside from being a meaningless statement, it is also not descriptive of the game. For by stipulation I am playing a representative of the city, able to negotiate its future success or demise based on decisions I make. So whether this playing counts as "representation" is exactly the matter at hand.

REPRESENTATION

deliberating and voting, for example, political representatives often ask themselves, "How would my constituents think about this matter?" trying out different modes of thought. In democratic contexts, when they campaign they often pretend to be something they are not, appearing more "of the people" then they really are. And similarly they are often criticized for not acting or being enough like the group they are supposed to represent. In neither the theatrical nor the political case are the representatives trying to existentially "be" those they represent, but in both cases the representatives are trying to model how those they represent *would* act in certain, if different, respects.

The problem can be resolved by precisely distinguishing "The Represented" from "The Selection Agent" and both from "The Audience." In the case of performing, each is actually a separate entity. The Represented is Hamlet, the Selection Agent is the casting director, the Decision Rule may be "the best available actor," and the Audience is some combination of the play's producer and audience *who must view the actor as representative of Hamlet for the role to be convincing.* It is representation with a very different function than the political case, but it is representation nonetheless. This example also illustrates the migration of normative judgments into the concept of "political representation." In this case, Pitkin introduced the necessity of "authorization" of a proper kind into the concept of representation: if the *actor* acted "on authority of Hamlet" then in some sense he *would* be a representative *of Hamlet* on stage. By analogy, the reason I fail to represent the mayor of Chicago in the example above, is *inter alia* because the Mayor did not authorize me. But as we said, this was not the case.

As long as representation is cast only in terms of its own legitimacy it is understandable why the three roles of Agent, Represented, and Audience remain undifferentiated: in democratic (that is, purportedly legitimate) systems these three roles are often identical. In democratic government, the Represented are said to be the constituents. The Agents that select the Representative are the Represented (at least a subset of them). And the Represented *are* often the Audience before whom the relationship must be taken as valid. By separating the roles that this same group (constituents) plays, we can see how in different cases independent individuals (or groups) may assume the roles. In such cases, all the necessary conditions are present for representation, but their content is vastly different. The account here parses out just how an actor represents the character he portrays, even if he represents that character in a very different way from the political case.

Specifying the Conditions for Political Representation

Earlier, I demonstrated the centrality of the Audience to a general theory of political representation. But if the conditions for representation boil down to whether the Audience accepts John as the representative of some other group, why do we need the rules of recognition at all? Strictly speaking, we don't: *as long as an audience accepts John as the representative of some group he is their representative.*[19] As a descriptive matter that's the end of the story and by itself explains why some cases of political representation fail any plausible test of legitimacy: when Audiences accept people as representatives for really bad reasons they often turn out to be illegitimate.

Why then do we need to bother with the rules of recognition at all? The rules of recognition explain what it is the audience is judging when they recognize (or fail to recognize) a particular claimant as a representative.[20] The rules they use will further allow us to say whether the case is a normatively good one, whether the representative is legitimate or not. And it is by reference to these three rules of recognition that we can explain why we sometimes believe Audiences make mistakes, failing to recognize a person we believe *should be* recognized as a political representative. As we'll see, such a case is one in which an Audience fails to follow its own rules.

In this section I complete this account by fleshing out these judgments. I will describe how the Audience comes to view a relationship as representational, what "accepting the charge" amounts to, and explain the importance of the "enabling condition" to explain how Audience mistakes can occur.

How the Audience Comes to View a Relationship as "Representational"

Recall the first four conditions that I said were necessary for representation to obtain:

R1: There is some Function that requires a Representative.

R2: A particular claimant is a member of the Qualified Set.

---

[19] I will refine this to account for Audience mistakes in the next section.

[20] I do not mean to say that audiences always self consciously use these rules with intention, although in most cases they do. At issue here are questions of intentionality as developed in Searle (1983) and Searle (1991), issues I will take up in a more sustained way at another time.

R3: The claimant was selected using the Decision Rule.

R4: The Selection Agent used the Decision Rule to pick a member of the Qualified Set.

R1 establishes the context and purpose of a case of representation. R2–R4 acknowledge that who the representative is and how she was selected *are* central to considering whether a person is a representative. These three separate conditions explain why relationships that we might want to call "representational" nevertheless are not.

To see the necessity of these conditions consider some examples where only two of the three conditions (R2-R4) obtain:

1) In 2005, the King of Morocco selects Grace Kelly (d. 1982) to be that nation's representative to the United Nations. (Condition R2 fails.)
2) Jim Drew (a living, adult citizen of Chicago), is selected by lottery to be the U.S. Senator from Illinois. (Condition R3 fails.)
3) In 2005, my book group elects Elizabeth Dole by majority rule to serve as the head of the Red Cross commission to represent Prisoners of War. (Condition R4 fails.)

In the first case, R2 alone explains why the UN does not recognize Grace Kelly (d. 1982) as the Moroccan representative to the UN, even though the appropriate agent (the King) used a valid decision rule (whomever the king wants) as his selection device.[21] Being dead, Kelly does not qualify for the position. Similarly, R3 explains why, in example 2, Jim Drew would fail to be the political representative of the state of Illinois: in 2005, the Audience (U.S. Senate) would not consider random selection to be a valid decision rule even though the case fits its other rules. Finally, R4 demonstrates how "appropriate selection agents" are critical to an audience's rules of recognition: few audiences are likely to accept "my book group" as the appropriate selection agent to select a representative of the Red Cross, even if we selected (by majority rule) Elizabeth Dole, a past president of that organization (purportedly meeting conditions R2 and R3).[22]

Less fanciful historical examples are readily available. Qualifying limits for representative candidates are made explicit (and some—like being a human being—implicit) in all political constitutions. Indeed, one of the more contentious matters in England during the seventeeth and eighteenth centuries was specifying who could decide qualifications for representatives in Parliament. The controversy lead to the inclusion of the first line of Article 1, Section 4, Clause 1 of the U.S. Constitution: "Each House shall be the Judge of the Elections, Returns and Qualifications of its own Members. . . ." For an example of rejecting a decision rule, we can imagine the start of labor negotiations. Although workers elected John to represent them, management rejects him as their representative because they elected him *viva voce*. Without a secret ballot, management (in this case, the Audience) argues, they do not accept him as the workers' representative.

Now consider a case many people would consider "illegitimate." The UN General Assembly accepts King Hussein as the representative of Jordan when he speaks before that body. They accept that he is qualified, that he was his own selection agent, and that the decision rule he used ("pick the king") was an appropriate one. Many would thus take King Hussein to be the valid political representative of Jordan for pragmatic reasons without necessarily conceding that he is that nation's legitimate representative.

Accepting the Charge

R5 was a conditional statement: "If applicable, the Representative accepts the charge" (see Box 2). R5 accounts for the fact that most, but not all, cases of political representation involve self-conscious human action and therefore require an individual who accepts her role as representative. A representative need not "accept the charge" when the representation involved is symbolic, and where the representative is an *inanimate object*, R5 does not apply. Importantly, if this account is correct, symbolic representation need not be any more or less political than other kinds of representation that are active or nonsymbolic.

Here are two examples to illustrate these exceptions.

1) **Symbolic representation:** Anatoly Sharansky is a representative of Soviet Refuseniks whether or not he accepts the charge.[23]

---

[21]As I said above, "valid," "qualified," and "appropriate" refer to an Audience's judgment, and they need not be normatively justifiable. See the next section for more.

[22]Note that in all cases I am assuming that the relevant parties (i.e., the Audience) reject examples 1–3 for the reasons I give. If they instead accepted dead people as qualified, random selection as valid, and my book group as the appropriate agents—then of course, representation would obtain. This only reinforces the centrality that these rules play in the establishment of political representation.

[23]Refuseniks were Soviet Jews who were refused permission to leave the Soviet Union and who often suffered persecution following their requests to leave. Anatoly Sharansky became one of

2) **The "Representative" is an inanimate object**: The Italian flag represents the hope and glory of Italians, whether or not it (the flag) accepts that charge.

In the first example, Sharansky *as a symbolic representative* need not have accepted the charge to represent Soviet Refuseniks because symbolic representation does not entail that he do anything. He might even explicitly reject that he was such a representative ("I'm just a guy who wants to leave the Soviet Union and that's all I am"). However, because the Function of this case of representation is to be a symbol and symbols are often symbolic simply by "being," it is not *necessary* that the symbol accept the charge. Thus, Sharansky was a symbol whether or not he wished to be simply because the Audience (before whom this symbol was relevant) took him to be symbolic. For analogous reasons, when the representative is an inanimate object (a flag), it can only be a symbolic representative and thus need not accept the charge (whatever that would mean).

The Enabling Condition: Explaining Audience Mistakes

The sixth condition puts the account all together, explaining how audiences use a set of rules to recognize a particular individual as being a Representative:

R6: The Audience, in fact, recognizes that R2–R4 have obtained (that a member of the Qualified Set was selected by the Selection Agent to represent the Represented according to the Decision Rule).

R6 explains how R1–R5 come together to form a case of political representation: an audience must in fact recognize that their rules have been met for representation to occur. In finally explaining how

the parts come together, R6 also accounts for two important kinds of audience mistakes (false positives and false negatives) that lead to anomalies of representation.[24]

First, audiences may mistakenly believe that a case conforms to their own rules of recognition when it does not (false positives). When this happens we can coherently, but imprecisely, claim, "Despite an audience's judgment, that person is no representative at all." More precisely, we'd mean, "That person does not meet the standards set by the audience's own rules of recognition, and they are making a mistake to recognize her as such." Second, audiences may fail to recognize, or mistakenly reject, cases that do conform to their own rules of recognition (false negatives). When this happens, we can coherently, but imprecisely, say "Despite an audience's judgment, that person really is a representative." More precisely we'd mean, "That person meets the standards set by the audience's own rules of recognition, and they are making a mistake not to recognize her as such." I will take each of these failures in turn and then clarify the issue of coherence and imprecision I just raised.[25]

Consider first a "false positive," a case in which an audience believes that a claimant conforms to their rules of recognition when, in fact, the claimant does not. Imagine that a person named "George" was selected through fraudulent election tactics and then claims to be the representative in front of an audience that purports to use a different set of decision rules or selection agents (i.e., "clear ballots," "all eligible voters," etc.). Since the fraud was unexposed to the audience, when George claimed to be the representative they mistakenly thought that his was a case that conformed to their rules. Knowing that fraud had occurred, we would coherently say, "George is no representative at all." But precisely we'd mean, "The audience is making a mistake; they should not recognize George as their representative because his case fails to conform to their own rules of recognition."

This case, of course, is similar enough to how many people viewed George W. Bush's claim, after the

---

the more celebrated cases and a rallying cry of the American Jewish community during the 1980s. His symbolic stature was reflected in the words of the song "Anatoly," written by Doug Mishkin, and sung at political rallies in the United States at the time: "Anatoly as long as you are there/We the people of Israel hear your prayer/Anatoly as long as you're not free/Neither are we" (Mishkin 1987). Sharansky finally immigrated to Israel where he took the Hebrew name, Natan, and became very active in electoral politics. In a preface to his song, recorded after Sharansky was released, Mishkin claimed that the "spirit" of "Anatoly" represents all who struggle against oppression. To the best of my knowledge, Sharansky never agreed to link his name (let along his story) to the cause (although he was present on at least one occasion where the song was sung, and given his involvement in electoral politics, one must assume he would welcome the linkage). Thus it is that symbolic representation arises independent of a claimant accepting the charge.

[24]I am grateful to Jennifer Rubenstein who, as a reader for *The Journal of Politics*, raised this issue. It led to a reconfiguration of the argument into its present form.

[25]A third kind of claim would reject the rules an audience uses because they are bad ones, say, "only men are appropriate selection agents." In such a case, we might be tempted to say, "That person is no representative at all because he was selected by an illegitimate rule." This would be a mistake for reasons that have motivated the present argument: the representative who is recognized using normatively bad rules may be illegitimate, but she is still the representative. See the first section for more on this; for the interaction between this model and normative evaluation, see Section 5.

election of November 2000, to be the President of the United States. The case helpfully illustrates that rules of recognition need not be simplistic and are often complex. Arguably, the rules that most Americans use to recognize who won the election began with those stipulated in the U.S. Constitution, albeit indirectly.[26] But they are supported by secondary rules that explain how conflicts are to be handled.[27] I suspect most Americans who believed that the election of 2000 was premised on unclearly constructed ballots in the state of Florida nevertheless accepted the role of the Supreme Court to intervene as a specification of their rules concerning "Selection Agents."[28]

Second, consider a "false negative," a case in which an audience fails to recognize that a person conformed to their rules of recognition: the claimant was a member of the Qualified Set, selected using a Decision Rule they purport to deem as valid, as it was employed by a Selection Agent they viewed as appropriate. For example, imagine that Joseph Ratzinger, a Cardinal of the Catholic Church (the Qualified Set), claimed that the College of Cardinals (the appropriate Selection Agent) had chosen him (the valid Decision Rule) to be Pope. He takes the name "Benedict XVI" (thereby accepting the charge) and goes on television to claim that he is the representative of God on earth. This is, of course, what happened in the Spring of 2005. But now, deviating from the actual event, imagine that Catholics rejected Ratzinger's claim to be Pope despite his conforming to all their rules of recognition. They respect this man as a Cardinal, but refuse to accept him as Pope.

What could explain this failure given, as I have described it, their own rules of recognition were met? Why wouldn't Ratzinger have been the Pope, that is, God's representative here on Earth? Imagine that in their excitement at the selection of a new Pope the Cardinals simply forgot to light the fire that produces white smoke in the Vatican chimney. Without the smoke, Catholics do not *believe* that the first three conditions were met and thus would mistakenly reject Ratzingers' claim.[29] Thus the other Cardinals might say coherently, "Ratzinger really *is* the representative of God on earth." Precisely, they'd mean, "Given the rules of recognition that Catholics use to determine who the representative of God on earth is, you *should recognize Ratzinger* as the Pope because he met these rules."

Both of these cases of mistakes emphasize that representation depends only upon the Audience's judgment of the case and *not* on the purported case itself independent of the Audience. In each of these cases, George and Benedict XVI will be (or will fail to be) representatives of their purported "Represented" case by case, dependent only on the rules of recognition used by a particular audience before whom they stand. In the case of George W. Bush, foreign governments and American citizens may well use very different rules of recognition to determine who the representative of the United States is. While U.S. citizens recognize representatives who conform to rules specified in the U.S. Constitution, foreign governments likely use a far more simplistic, pragmatic rule: "Whoever occupies the White House is the Representative of the United States." (These two rules of recognition will usually be extensionally equivalent, but they may not be in times of civil unrest.) In the case of Ratzinger, his claim to be the representative of God on earth will fail when made in front of non-Catholic audiences, simply because they do not use the same rules of recognition that Catholics use to recognize God's representative on earth. However, they will almost certainly recognize the Pope as the representative of the Vatican. Indeed, the fact that the Pope regularly fails to be recognized as the representative of God on earth before an audience of non-Catholics is a tangible example of the need for claimants to cohere to an audience's rules of recognition for them to be representatives at all.

---

[26]"Indirectly" because I suspect most people rely on the signals of their media sources to tell them who conformed with the rules they purportedly use, rather than knowing the rules themselves or whether, in fact, they were conformed to. In this way, "headlines" and "news reports" function in exactly the same way as "white smoke" does in the case of the selection of a new Pope—it signals that certain rules have been met but does not itself constitute the rule. I will take up the case of white smoke and the Pope in a moment.

[27]Hart (1997) uses secondary rules of recognition for similar purposes.

[28]If their rules were those specified in the U.S. Constitution, they may have made a mistake. Still, even if they should not have recognized Bush as President, as long as they do, he is their representative.

[29]In this example I am assuming that "white smoke from the Vatican chimney" signaled that that the rules had been met, rather than that the smoke was part of the Audience's rules of recognition. I suspect that is the correct description of the case, that the white smoke is merely a ritualized signal: if the Cardinals had issued a statement saying that the chimney broke down and Ratzinger was the new Pope, there would have been little confusion or argument. By contrast, consider that few Catholics would have accepted someone chosen in explicit violation of these rules, say, if the Cardinals announced that Rabbi Peter Schaktman (a Jewish, non-Cardinal) was the new Pope. This raises important questions of how rules emerge, evolve, and change, a question that must be deferred for now.

REPRESENTATION

Finally, I said that one coherent but imprecise response to a case in which an Audience makes a mistake would be, "That person should be considered a representative" or "That person is no representative at all." The reason such a statement is coherent is because we understand colloquially what that claim means. But it is imprecise because, consistent with this account *there is no representation* as long as the audience fails to recognize that a case conforms to its rules. Representation depends formally on the recognition by an audience, *not* on the coherence (or lack of coherence) of a purported case to a set of rules that the audience uses. In short, it is the beliefs of the Audience that matter, not whether those beliefs are true.

The fact that most audiences use a reasonably stable and public set of rules to which cases must conform explains why these statements then cohere if imprecise. For example, when a legislature fails to recognize as a representative an individual who met its own professed rules of recognition, and accepted someone who did not, we'd rightly say they made a mistake. But if they persisted in that mistake, and accepted, say, Libby as the representative instead of Florence, then Libby would be the representative simply on account of their recognition of Libby. As a matter of precision we'd want to say, *Florence should be considered the representative even though, in fact, Libby is the representative.* And to anticipate a worry here, the "should" in this sentence is a nonmoral, epistemic and conditional "should": *if* the audience wishes to recognize cases that conform to *these* rules, but not *those*, it should recognize *this* person, but not *that one* as the representative. When such cases do persist in the light of open exposure of the facts, there is good reason to believe that the rules of recognition have changed.[30]

Political Representation and Legitimacy

In real life, Audiences do not use any old rules of recognition. In democratic regimes they usually use rules that correspond closely, if not perfectly, to some normative account of legitimacy. The Selection Agents

they recognize as appropriate are usually some subset of "citizens," and the Decision Rules they take to be valid are usually some form of "majority rule." In other words, the rules of recognition an audience uses are usually, but not necessarily, derived from a normative theory of legitimacy or justice. Yet the claim I am making is that these rules and representation more generally can be explained without reference to any normative argument even though these rules appeal to "qualifications," "validity," and "appropriateness." These sound suspiciously like normative terms. It is time, then, to take on the objections to this account I raised earlier: the "Rules of Recognition" are just a smoke screen for some substantive idea of *legitimacy.*

The simplest way to address the objection is to repeat that the Rules of Recognition are meant to be descriptive only of how an audience decides whether this person *but not that one* is the Representative, and the terms (appropriate, qualified, and valid) are completely context-dependent. In any particular case, an Audience must view the claimant as a member of the Qualified Set; that in *this* particular circumstance they view some decision rules, but not others, as valid; and that in this particular case, they accept *that* group of individuals, *but not others* as the appropriate ones to decide. These need not be final judgments derived from a theory of right, but may instead be judgments of political expediency given the way things are.

Consider, for example, that in 2005 the United States Government accepted Pervez Musharef as the political representative of Pakistan, likely by reference to these rules:

Qualified Set: Any person or group who is likely able to control the military of Pakistan is qualified *given the context.*

Decision Rule: "Whoever, in fact, controls the military of Pakistan" is a valid decision rule, *given the context.*

Selection Agent: Whoever, in fact, took control of the military is the appropriate selection agent *given the context.*

Representation thus depends only on an Audience recognizing *that* a particular claimant matches a person denoted by these rules, whatever these rules happen to be. As such, despite using the terms "qualified," "valid," and "appropriate," this account stands no matter what the content of these rules turns out to be. The fact that in this context we use prudential rules to recognize that the commander of the Pakistani army is the political representative of

---

[30]A separate issue is how these rules emerge in the first place, change over time, whether they need to be formally acknowledged as such, and how, in the absence of formal rule changes, we come to know that they have changed at all. These are critical issues though I do not think there is anything special about these rules of recognition than for any other set of institutional rules. In any case, I cannot pursue this more complicated issue here.

that country does not mean that these rules are just or legitimate, though they may be. (Indeed, we may well believe other rules, more democratically legitimate rules, are morally preferable and work to change the context so that these will also be prudential ones to follow.) Nor does this account require that the Audience use any particular normative theory to establish the content of their own rules. To figure out who the Iraqi representative to the United Nations was from 1979 to 2003, an Audience may for very practical reasons choose to view "Whomever Saddam selected" as the *valid* decision rule. In short, the Audience merely judges *that* a claimant is a *member* of a qualified set, etc., without judging *whether* the qualifications, etc., established are legitimate or just.

The 2000 U.S. Presidential election provides a further example of how the three rules need not confer legitimacy onto a political representative despite their reference to "validity," "appropriateness," and "qualification." Here, I want to show how an audience could come to view these rules of recognition as having been met, even in a reasonably high functioning democracy, without conferring legitimacy on the representative.

To see this, I want to walk through a stylized example of the 2000 U.S. Presidential election using these four premises:

P1) Albert Gore, Jr. received a majority of the popular vote in the United States;

P2) The legitimate winner of an election is the candidate who receives the most popular votes;

P3) Gore was therefore the legitimate winner of the 2000 U.S. Presidential election;

P4) Bush is (nevertheless) accepted as a political representative, without error, by people who believe that premises P1–3 are true.[31]

I want to explain how the model here makes sense of "P4" given P1–P3. For the sake of the example, I want to assume the hard case: the audience before whom Bush is claiming to be a political representative is comprised exclusively of people who believe that premises P1–P3 are true. In other words, this Audience believes Gore won the most votes, believes he was the legitimate winner, *and* believes that Bush is the

representative of the United States. Again, the point is to show how a group of people could accept the conditions of representation as obtaining without acquiescing in the legitimacy of the case.

First, George W. Bush must have been a member of a *qualified set* (R2), though membership in the qualified set changed over time. Before election day, the qualified set included anyone who met the U.S. Constitutional requirements. After election day, as the returns were contested, the "qualified" set was reduced to two people: Bush and Gore. After that date, *only* one of these two would have been considered qualified to be the Representative. Imagine, for example, that in their decision that determined the outcome of the election, the U.S. Supreme Court ruled that Ralph Nader (a third-party candidate who received a small but strategically significant portion of the vote) was the victor. Even though Nader was part of the qualified set prior to Election Day, after the election he was no longer viewed as qualified *given the context*. In such a case, I believe most of those who can accept P1–P4 above, would reject that Nader could be the representative at all.

Second, to accept P4, an audience arguably had to view the Supreme Court as the appropriate selection agent to select the Representative (i.e., Bush).[32] This judgment of "appropriateness" describes whom the Audience accepted as the selection agent and does not necessarily confer legitimacy, although accounts of legitimacy often specify whom the Audience should or should not deem as appropriate. Before the election, the appropriate selection agents were the registered populations of each state, and this, it turns out, also plausibly rendered the winner legitimate.[33] After Election Day the situation changed and audiences would probably have deemed a number of selection agents as appropriate, only a subset of which they would have deemed legitimate. Candidates for appropriate selection agents might have been: the Florida Legislature, the U.S. House of Representatives, the U.S. Supreme

---

[31]This is a simplified and stylized account. The claim that Bush is illegitimate more often (and more plausibly) rests on the nature of the U.S. Supreme Court's intervention than it does on the popular vote. The fact that the U.S. Constitution permits the election of the loser of the popular vote through the institution of the electoral college creates an even more complicated case.

[32]I am simplifying the case. Since the Supreme Court's ruling in *Bush v. Gore* concerned whether certain ballots could or could not count, the Supreme Court more precisely served as the valid arbiter of the rules of recognition. This raises again the question of how rules of recognition for political representation get established and maintained, a subject beyond the scope of this article.

[33]Consistent with my claims, it is a commonplace to argue that low voter turnout renders the result suspect in terms of legitimacy, and illustrates the point: we don't normally deny John's claim to be our political representative because of low voter turnout, we dispute his legitimacy instead.

Court, and the Florida State Supreme Court.[34] None necessarily confers legitimacy on a candidate, but all would probably have been deemed as "appropriate" in the eyes of most audiences. By contrast, consider some "inappropriate" selection agents, including Barbara Bush (the President's mother), the Texas State Legislature, or The Members of the British House of Commons. If any of these people or groups announced *its* choice of Bush over Gore, most audiences would have rejected this fact as irrelevant to whether they should recognize Bush as the President of the United States.

Finally, for anyone to accept P4, the Audience must have deemed the decision rule that the selection agent used to select George W. Bush to be "valid," that is, valid in this case. Before the election, that decision rule was just "following the constitutionally mandated rules" by which a variant of majority rule elected the president. *After* the election, assuming the Supreme Court was taken to be the appropriate selection agent, the valid decision rule appears to have been "a set of reasoned arguments supported by a majority of the court." Had the Supreme Court *merely* announced, "Bush is President because we like him better," I suspect that Bush's very claim to the Presidency would have been seriously questioned (and not merely the legitimacy of their decision) because *in this context* "we like him better" would not have been taken to be a valid decision rule. (Note that "we like him better" is taken to be perfectly valid in other contexts, particularly when candidates are selected by popular vote.) Validity thus functions similarly to its technical role in philosophical analysis, as a check on internal consistency: something may be valid (internally consistent) but still false. Similarly, the audience might even view the decision as a reasonable attempt at legitimacy (well intended and plausible) but one that in the end was wrong. But again, validity merely expresses a pragmatic consequence. Few would accept "hereditary rule" as a selection rule that confers legitimacy, yet many accept it as valid to determine who represents the Jordanian people on the world stage.

The Two Dimensions of Political Representation: Being versus Activity

If the account I have offered of political representation is descriptively correct it explains how it is we can determine *whether* a person is a political representative or not. But this account has (so far) failed to explain the activity of political representation. Another way to say this is that while the account explains how representatives as nouns or beings are created by a set of beliefs that audiences have, we have given no account of what representation as a verb or activity is. And this gives rise to the first of two very important objections: without reference to activity there appears to be no way of distinguishing between being a "political representative" and "holding a political office" more generally.[35] Here I would answer by saying that any particular case of representation is always context-limited: it is defined by the Function towards which it aims, and that Function always specifies that "The Representative *stands for* the Represented in order to do X." When "holding a political office" does not entail *standing for* anyone else, but merely enforcing orders, executing law, or some other thing, we can reject this as not a case of representation at all.

But this raises a second more serious problem. By separating the *fact* of *being* a representative from the *activity* representation, the general theory of political representation does not appear to admit of degree: it explains *whether* this is a case of representation but not *how well* that representative is doing her job.[36] This is a problem because we regularly and understandably say "John did a poor job representing his community," and yet there is no way to account for this judgment in the explanation of representation I have given thus far. Indeed, it might even appear that we are finally forced into accepting a substantive standard of legitimacy, as if the activity of representation were somehow necessarily connected to "looking out for another's interests."

I do not deny that these are meaningful statements for which any description of representation must

---

[34] In the case of the 2000 U.S. Presidential election, the political battle hinged on who the "appropriate" selection agents would be, and all parties focused on the state of Florida and a few other states where the popular vote was very close. At various points in the five-week saga, the Florida state legislature, state popular vote, the intentions of those who voted, and the state Supreme Court all were claimed to be the proper selection agents. Because of the democratic norms of the United States, "proper" mapped closely to procedural and substantive accounts of legitimacy.

[35] I am grateful to an anonymous reviewer at the *Journal of Politics* for raising this objection.

[36] Pitkin puts the problem this way. "In each of the views discussed so far, a theorist attempts to draw conclusions about the proper conduct for a representative, or the proper way of institutionalizing representative government. Yet the definitions we have examined do not lend themselves to the drawing of such conclusions; they are not suitable for telling a representative what to do, or for telling us how to judge his performance" (1967, 112).

account. But I think a better explanation of these evaluations is made by reference to the stated Function of a particular case. In this way we could think of the "role" of representative as having very separable descriptive and performative features: the general account explains how a person comes to be a representative, and also how the performative (and evaluative) features of representation arise and are differentiated case by case. But it is the particular function or purpose for which representation is used that establishes what "representation as activity" is. Similarly, it is a normative standard of judgment that we employ about what it means to do that particular function well against which we judge whether a representative performed well or poorly. Formally, then, "representation" is a dichotomous variable: either one has it by having a Representative or one does not have it.[37] I will try to explain this complicated point briefly.

To begin with, we can separate the insight that representation admits degree (i.e., we evaluate a representative's activity as good or bad representation), from any judgment concerning the substantive activity that we should judge or the standard we should use in making our judgment. For representation to admit degree assumes only a prior commitment to some specified function or goal, but not any *particular* goal, let alone a particular normative standard on the basis of which we should evaluate the achievement of that goal. *The acknowledgment that representation will always admit degree—that we can say John was a bad representative relative to some goal and using some normative standard—is a separate matter from specifying the particular goal or standard that he will have to uphold.* These standards are thus not part of the *formal concept* of representation, any more than "going really fast" is part of the *formal concept* of "automobile." Rather, these standards constitute a second *substantive* dimension of representation, the ends at which any particular instance of representation is aiming but not actually part of what it means to represent.

[37]I acknowledge that if representation is a dichotomous variable then our ordinary language use of the terms "over-" and "under-represented" are imprecise and misleading. Indeed, I think when we say a constituency is over or underrepresented we are imprecisely conjoining these two different ideas: *having* representation *and either* (1) the power that that representative has relative to other representatives or (2) the relative value of an individual's preferences compared to the preferences of other people who chose a different representative. A constituency is thus not actually *over* or *under* represented per se, although that is what we say. Rather, some representatives and selection agents have more power than others. All of which is suggestive; a full defense of this claim requires far more elaboration.

As I said earlier, the Function of representation takes the form, "a Representative 'stands for' the Represented *in order to do X*" and thus specifies its own activity that will differ depending on context. Thus the descriptor "good" or "bad" is not modifying the *activity* of representation per se, it is modifying a particular case of it. Representation always involves *standing for* the Represented, but what it means to stand for the Represented will vary dramatically depending on *the purpose of* the case. When we critique a representative's activity we are making a judgment about how well or poorly she is acting relative to the goal as stated by the Function. We are not actually passing a judgment about "the quality of representation" itself, but the quality of representation *given a goal and given a normative theory about how representatives should act*. The ends specify *what* the representative will *do*, the Function of the case of representation, and thus imply the goal *we will* judge.

So the first thing is to realize that Function determines who counts as the relevant parties and what activity should be done to accomplish a particular representational aim. This means that our judgments about the quality of representation are in fact judgments about the quality of a particular activity specified by the function given a particular context. And this judgment will depend on a normative theory quite apart from "representation." So, for example, what it means to represent "well" or be a "good representative" in, say, a legislature will likely refer to democratic norms of autonomy, equality, and respect: a representative ought to consider the views of all his constituents not *because* he is a representative, but *because he "stands for" in order to democratically make law*. By contrast, we will presumably judge whether a political advocate was a good or bad representative by reference to a normative account of advocacy in the context of a pluralist society: a representative of an interest group ought to push as hard as she can to get the laws favorable to her group not *because* she is a representative, but *because she "stands for" in order to advocate within a pluralist society*.

We can now give an account of why previous theories of political representation have been so closely aligned with theories of legitimacy. Historically, the study of political representation has been done within the context of democratic (or increasingly democratic) regimes. This means that the rules of recognition that democratic audiences use are closely related to, if not identical with, the internal conditions required for legitimacy (free and fair elections, etc.). And similarly, in terms of our evaluations of political representatives, they have historically been done

FIGURE 1 Sequence of Political Representation

Function→ [Audience → Who Uses Rules of Recognition to Recognize a Claimant→ Representative]→
Performance

FIGURE 2 Connecting the Formal and Substantive Dimensions of Political Representation

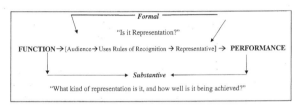

against a democratic context, in which the Function of representation has meant *standing for in order to democratically make law*. This has made it hard to ask what representation is apart from the democratic contexts in which it has been studied.

We can now connect the formal and substantive dimensions of representation. Reading from left to right in Figure 1 above, once the aims of the relationship are specified (Function), the Audience is determined. The Audience then must judge whether a particular claimant meets its three rules of recognition; if so, she becomes a Representative. Assuming she accepts her charge, the Representative then goes about doing her job (labeled "Performance"), as specified by the Function.

Figure 2 above describes how the formal and substantive dimensions of representation relate to each other and thus explain how representation might admit degree. The formal relationship obtains in the bracketed space between "FUNCTION" and "PERFORMANCE." Representation occurs (or fails to occur) in this middle area, if you will. The substantive dimension—the ends of representation and whether or not they are achieved—address the relationship between the Function of the case and the Performance of the job by the Representative. One cannot step into the formal dimension of representation until one specifies the Function of the (yet to be created) relationship and thus has a standard by which to judge. Yet one cannot get to the substantive matter of representation, in which a representative performs some Function, until one goes through the formal steps. The question, "Is *this* a case of representation?" refers only to the conditions specified by the bracketed terms in the middle. And thus, the substantive question, "How well did John represent his constituents?" can only be understood as a question about the relationship between Function and Performance. The two dimensions go hand in hand, even as neither determines the other.

To illustrate this formal structure, we can now reconsider the example with which this article began: Libya's representation in the World Trade Organization (WTO). This illustration is schematic and incomplete, but should help flesh out and summarize the general theory.

First, we must specify the Function of this case. Arguably, the Function here is, "To stand for Libya *in order to express policy preferences before the voting members of the WTO*." As stated, the Function indicates the Audience and it is here the WTO, who in turn must accept that Al-Hajjaji, and not someone else, is the representative of Libya. Further, the activity or performance of representation in this case is also indicated by its Function: "To express policy preferences of Libya before the voting members of the WTO."

The WTO uses rules of recognition to determine that Al-Hajjaji is the representative of Libya. It decides whether the selection agents (*Araba Jamahiriya* and Qadhafi) were the appropriate ones and, given the authority of these bodies, the WTO accepts them as appropriate. They decide whether the decision rule used by these agents were valid. And in this case the WTO probably uses very broad standards of validity, including "whomever Qadhafi likes." But there are some important limits. For example, the WTO would probably reject as invalid the decision rule, "whoever sits in the Oval Office in Washington D.C. is the representative of Libya," even if the other conditions were met, that is, even if Qadhafi were to approve of the U.S. President as his nation's representative. Finally, the WTO decides whether the claimant is a member of the Qualified Set in this case. Here, again, their judgment will be very broad, perhaps no more than a judgment of mental competency. This explains why the WTO might not accept someone with severe mental retardation as the Libyan representative even if the other rules of recognition were met.

Importantly, at no point in this process does the WTO have to appeal to facts about the legitimacy of the representative (let alone elections, accountability or proper activity) for representation to occur. But the account does allow us to see where norms enter politics and political institutions. Here, for example, Najat Mehdi Al-Hajjaji's job is "to stand for Libya *and express policy preferences before the voting members of the WTO.*" A normative theory of the good, right or just will specify what counts as praiseworthy activity given this context. For example, we might say she was a good representative if, among other things, she *accurately* expressed the policy preferences of Libya. Importantly, we'd have to also say something about what constitutes a "policy preference of Libya": is it what Qadhafii wants, what his legislature desires, or the general good of the people? That would have to be specified in order to evaluate how well or poorly she did her job.

Conclusion

Standard, contemporary accounts beginning with Pitkin's analysis are useful in explaining the conditions under which political representation becomes legitimate. Consider how this is done, in this case by Rogowski endorsing Pitkin's enmeshment.

> On the one hand, as Pitkin has pointed out, representation cannot mean mere agency: the lawyer who does only what I, in my ignorance of the law, would do in her place does not represent me well. On the other hand, and crucially, B's claim to represent A is always rebuttable: if, in some relevant domain, a client researches the facts and the law thoroughly and finds that, so informed, he would have acted very differently from his lawyer, he has strong reason to claim that he has been badly represented. (Rogowski 1981, 396–97)

Rogowski, like Pitkin, can only argue that "representation" does not mean mere agency (a claim regarding the formal dimension) only by saying the lawyer did a bad job (a claim regarding the substantive dimen-

sion). Of course, that lawyer will represent you in case a court (the relevant party here) recognizes that she meets their rules of recognition (she has the right license, etc.). And if "acting like you in all your ignorance" does not disqualify the lawyer according to these rules, he'll even represent you acting in that way. Yes, we want to say "the lawyer only represents me formally." That is precisely the point.

To the extent that contemporary accounts collapse these two dimensions of representation they lose a fair amount of clarity in the process. Given the rise of global institutions that rely on nondemocratic representatives, the need for an account of political representation that does not depend on democratic norms, institutions, or activity is particularly important. Doing so allows us to see that arguments about political representation are most often either: (1) arguments about the content of the rules of recognition that audiences use, or should use, to determine whether *this* person, but not that one, is a political representative; or (2) what is the morally preferable way to achieve the goals of a particular case of representation. Far from claiming that political representation in practice is "value free," a general theory of political representation becomes a useful tool for political analysis and a way to specify precisely how normative arguments play out in the political world.

Acknowledgments

Two anonymous referees for the *Journal of Politics* helped to reconfigure the argument in its present form, and I am indebted to them and the journal's editor for their careful reading and engagement. Jennifer Rubenstein deserves particular thanks for her forceful and insightful remarks that reshaped the entire argument. I am also grateful to participants in the September 2005 Legal Theory Workshop at Columbia University Law School—in particular Jean Cohen, Kent Greenawalt, Ira Katznelson, Andrzej Rapaczynski, and Jeremy Waldron—for their penetrating comments, only some of which could be responded to here. For comments on earlier versions I thank Randy Calvert, Chad Cyrenne, Mark Hansen, Emily Hauptmann, Jack Knight, Charles Larmore, Patchen Markell, Chris Rohrbacher, Sue Stokes, and Cass Sunstein.

Manuscript submitted 28 September 2004
Manuscript accepted for publication 23 June 2005

References

Amy, Douglas J. 1993. *Real Choices, New Voices: The Case for Proportional Representation in the United States*. New York: Columbia University Press.

Bohman, James, and William Rehg. 1997. *Deliberative Democracy: Essays on Reason and Politics*. Cambridge: MIT Press.

Bybee, Keith. 1998. *Mistaken Identity: The Supreme Court and the Politics of Minority Representation*. Princeton: Princeton University Press.

Cohen, Joshua. 1989. "Deliberation and Democratic Legitimacy." In *The Good Polity*, eds. Alan Hamlin and Philip Pettit. Cambridge: Basil Blackwell, pp. 17–34.

Dewey, John. 1954. *The Public and Its Problems*. Athens, OH: Swallow Press.

Dahl, Robert A. *A Preface to Democratic Theory*. Chicago: University of Chicago Press.

Dryzek, John. 2000. *Deliberative Democracy and Beyond: Liberals, Critics, Contestations*. New York: Oxford University Press.

Fasolt, Constantin. 1991. "Quod Omnes Tangit Ab Omnibus Approbari Debet: The Words and the Meaning." In *In Iure Veritas: Studies in Canon Law in Memory of Schaefer Williams*, eds. Steven B. Bowman and Blanch E. Cody. Cincinnati: University of Cincinnati College of Law, pp. 21–55.

Fishkin, James S. 1991. *Democracy and Deliberation: New Directions for Democratic Reform*. New Haven: Yale University Press.

Gutmann, Amy, and Dennis Thompson. 1996. *Democracy and Disagreement*. Cambridge: Belknap Press.

Habermas, Jurgen. 1996. *Between Facts and Norms: Contributions to a Discourse Theory of Law and Democracy*. Trans. William Rehg. Cambridge: MIT Press.

Hamiton, Alexander, John Jay, and James Madison. 1949. *The Federalist*. Middletown, CT: Wesleyan University Press.

Hart, H.L.A. 1997. *The Concept of Law*. 2nd ed. New York: Oxford University Press.

Hobbes, Thomas. 1994. *Leviathan*. Edwin Curley, ed. Indianapolis: Hackett.

James, Michael Rabinder. 2004. *Deliberative Democracy and the Plural Polity*. Lawrence: University of Kansas Press.

Keyssar, Alexander. 2000. *The Right to Vote: The Contested History of Democracy in the United States*. New York: Basic Books.

Kuper, Andrew. 2004. *Democracy Beyond Borders: Justice and Representation in Global Institutions*. New York: Oxford University Press.

Mansbridge, Jane. 2003. "Rethinking Representation." *American Political Science Review* 97 (4): 515–28.

Manin, Bernard. 1997. *The Principles of Representative Government*. New York: Cambridge University Press.

Mill, John Stuart. 1991. *Considerations on Representative Government*. Reprinted in *On Liberty and Other Essays*. New York: Oxford University Press, pp. 203–467.

Mishkin, Doug. 1987. "Anatoly." In *Woody's Children*. Washington: Quaker Hill Songs.

Pettit, Phillip. 1997. *Republicanism: A Theory of Freedom and Government*. Oxford: Oxford University Press.

Phillips, Anne. 1995. *The Politics of Presence*. New York: Oxford University Press.

Pitkin, Hanna Fenichel. 1967. *The Concept of Representation*. Berkeley: University of California Press.

Rehfeld, Andrew. 2005. *The Concept of Constituency: Political Representation, Democratic Legitimacy, and Institutional Design*. Cambridge: Cambridge University Press.

Rogowski, Ronald. 1981. "Representation in Political Theory and in Law." *Ethics* 91 (3): 395–430.

Rousseau, Jean-Jacques. 1978. *On the Social Contract*. Ed. Roger D. Masters. Trans. Judith R. Masters. New York: St. Martin's.

Schmitt, Carl. 1996. *The Crisis of Parliamentary Democracy*. Trans. Ellen Kennedy. Cambridge: MIT Press.

Searle, John R. 1983. *Intentionality: An Essay in the Philosophy of Mind*. New York: Cambridge University Press.

Searle, John R. 1991. *The Construction of Social Reality*. New York: Free Press.

Wellman, Christopher H. "Liberalism, Samaritanism, and Political Legitimacy." *Philosophy and Public Affairs* 25 (3): 211–37.

Williams, Melissa. 1998. *Voice, Trust and Memory*. Princeton: Princeton University Press.

Young, Iris Marion. 1990. *Justice and the Politics of Difference*. Princeton: Princeton University Press.

7

Varieties of public representation

Philip Pettit

I. Background and basics

Systems of representative government, I shall assume, are designed to give control over government to the people. Far from being an alternative to democracy, as some have taken them (Manin 1997), they embody an institutional framework – or rather a family of frameworks – for realizing the democratic ideal of giving *kratos* to the *demos*, power to the people. The distinction between a participatory and a representative system is not one between democracy proper and some faint approximation but a distinction between rival proposals for the implementation of democracy.

My focus in this chapter is on representation in this democratic, popularly enabling sense. Thus the target of the chapter is narrower than it might have been. As Hobbes in particular argues, the idea of representation may be used, not just of representatives who are subject to the continuing or periodic control of the people, but also of a hereditary, absolute monarch. The defenders of parliament in the 1640s tried to give its members a monopoly right on the use of the word (Skinner 2005), but Hobbes argued against them that it was absurd that a monarch who "had the sovereignty" over his subjects "from a descent of 600 years" should not be "considered as their representative" (Hobbes 1994: 19.3). His own view, to the contrary, was that "the King himself did . . . ever represent the person of the people of England" (Hobbes 1990: 120).

But though my focus is narrower than Hobbes's, it is broader than the target to which many contemporary theorists give their attention. As will appear, I use the notion of representation in such a way that any public authorities, and any citizens who assume a legitimate role in public

---

I benefited enormously from discussion at the Yale conference where a first version of the chapter was presented in November 2006; from discussion and commentary (by Ian McMullin) at a seminar in Washington University, St. Louis, in April 2008; from exchanges with Eric Beerbohm, Nate Kemp, Frank Lovett, Evan Oxman, and Andrew Rehfield; and from the comments of two anonymous referees. I am grateful to Bryan Garsten for directing me to expressions of the indicative ideal among anti-federalist writers.

62   *Philip Pettit*

discourse, may make a legitimate claim to represent the people (Richardson 2002). Others apply the notion, however, only to elected representatives – elected members of the legislature and, where relevant, of the executive and the judiciary. The concept of electoral representation is more tightly circumscribed than my looser concept of democratic representation, but I think that it does not offer the same generality of perspective.[1] I hope that this chapter may help to vindicate that claim.

There are three factors in any relationship or system of representation, whether in my sense of representation or in any other. First there are the representatives or, using a seventeenth-century word, the representers; I prefer this term since the other has an exclusively electoral connotation. Second, there are the represented or, as I shall say, the representees. And, third, there is the relationship that exists between those two parties: the representation that is exercised by representers on behalf of representees.[2]

Representers

Representers may be individual agents or groups of individual agents. And in the case where a group serves in this role, the members may each act for their own ends, according to their own judgments, or they may act on a shared intention to further this or that end. In this latter case the individuals will each intend that together they promote the agreed end and they will each do their bit for the promotion of the end, expecting that others will play their parts too (Bratman 1999); they will be a cooperative grouping, not a mere collection of individual agents.

The cooperative grouping that combines around a joint intention comes itself in two forms. The members may act for shared goals, now on this occasion, now on that, without ever forming a joint intention governing their continuation over time. Or they may form the special, shared intention that over time they together should constitute a corporate agent or agency: a body that simulates the performance of a single agent with a single mind. The intention shared in this case will be that they together cooperate in the organized pursuit of agreed ends according to agreed judgments. The ends will usually be an evolving set of ends selected under agreed procedures, and the judgments an evolving body of judgments selected under agreed procedures (Pettit and Schweikard 2006). The distinctions are mapped in Figure 3.1.

---

[1] For a very congenial and insightful account of representation in a broader sense than that of electoral representation, see Rehfeld (2006).

[2] On the emergence and development of the concept of representation in the late seventeenth and early eighteenth century, see Knights (2005).

Varieties of public representation

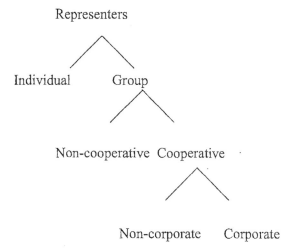

Figure 3.1 Representers.

These distinctions are readily illustrated. The member of the legislature who represents a certain constituency or the President who represents the people as a whole exemplifies the individual representer. And the legislature or the executive as a whole exemplifies the group representer. The members of such a group may behave as a collection of independent agents, each with their own brief, or as a cooperative grouping. And if they behave as a cooperative grouping, then they may or may not incorporate in the manner of a body with a coherent, evolving set of goals and judgments.

The US Congress might be seen as an unincorporated, cooperative grouping that does battle, now on this issue, now on that, looking in each case to see if a more or less ad hoc majority can be assembled to support a certain line. There is some concern with securing coherence between the lines supported over time, of course, as well as coherence with the Constitution. But this concern can take second place to the other concerns of members – say, their concern to display their colors back home. This will especially be so if in any case a presidential veto is likely, or if the Supreme Court is expected to reject or reinterpret the legislation.

The Westminster parliament might be seen, by contrast, as an incorporated, cooperative agency whose members assume a higher degree of responsibility for legislating on coherent lines, at least within the timeframe of a given parliament. The members acquiesce in a procedure whereby a fixed majority will be established and that majority – say, a

64   *Philip Pettit*

single, incorporated party – will bring forward a coherent program of legislation to be enacted after parliamentary discussion in the name of the parliament as a whole.

Representees

So much for the possibility of variation on the side of the representers in a democratic system. There is a corresponding degree of variation on the side of the representees. The representee may be a single individual, as when the member of a legislature takes up some cause on behalf of a constituent. Or the representee may be a group. The group represented may be cast as a mere collection, such as perhaps the electors in a given district, or they may have a more cooperative aspect. And the cooperative representee may be incorporated or unincorporated. In other words the distinctions on the side of the represented may correspond to those that we map on the side of the representing.

The loose pressure group or the ethnic minority that succeeds in finding a spokesperson in the legislature or elsewhere will often be an unincorporated entity whose members are united around just a single issue. But equally an entity with a corporate or quasi-corporate form of organization may figure as representee. The states that are represented by the Senate of the US or Australia are surely entities of this kind.

The ultimate representee in any democratic system will be the people as a whole: a body that might be taken as a mere collection but is usually depicted as an incorporated entity. It is of the essence of a democratic system that it is supposed to create a state that represents the people as a whole, acting in their name on the international stage and in dealings with individual citizens and groups of citizens (McLean 2004). Thus John Rawls (1999) says that the government in a well-ordered society – ideally, a liberal democratic society – will be "the representative and effective agent of a people" (ibid.: 38) – "the political organization of the people" (ibid.: 26). The disordered society where a small group usurps power, like the unordered society where political organization fails utterly, will be marked by the absence of precisely this system-wide level of representation.

Representation

Not only are there variations of these kinds in who are represented and who do the representing: that is, in the relata at either end of the representative relationship. There are also variations in the nature of the relationship. I argue that there are two fundamentally contrasting

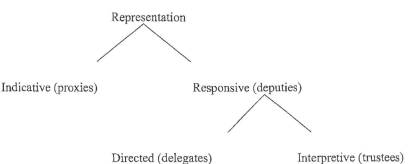

Figure 3.2 Representation.

varieties of representation, indicative and responsive. Indicative representers *stand for* the representees in the sense of typifying or epitomizing them; how they act is indicative of how the representees would act.[3] Responsive representers *act for* or *speak for* the representees, playing the part of an agent in relation to a principal; how they act is responsive to how the representees would want them to act. Both sorts of representation, so I shall assume, have to be authorized by the representees.

Authorized indicative representers I describe as proxies, authorized responsive representers as deputies. Deputies divide, in a traditional distinction, into delegates who are more or less explicitly directed by representees and trustees who have interpretive discretion in determining how to construe their representees. The distinctions appear in Figure 3.2.

Three metaphors have dominated the tradition of thinking about the meaning of representation (Skinner 2005). One of these metaphors is drawn from representation in the pictorial arts, and it maps onto indicative representation. As the painting is indicative of how the subject of the painting looks, so on this image should representers be indicative of representees: they should be proxies. The other two metaphors are drawn respectively from the courts and from the theater: from the way in which an attorney represents a client, and an actor represents a character. These reflect the two different modes of responsive or deputy-style representation: one directed, the other interpretive. As the attorney acts under the explicit or implicit direction of a client, so should

---

[3] Pitkin (1972) casts the indicative relationship as descriptive representation: as involving nothing more than the sort of relationship that holds between statistical sample and a population. But she misses the fact that a representee population may appoint a descriptive representer with a view to having things done as it would do them, or want them done; the possibility is nicely illustrated by the British Columbia citizens' assembly that I discuss later. It is only such controlled representation that I describe as indicative.

66   *Philip Pettit*

representers act under the explicit or implicit direction of their representees: they should be delegates. As the actor constructively interprets the mind of a character, so should representers interpret the mind of representees: they should be trustees.

The following two sections review these two conceptions of representation, looking at how they might apply with different sorts of representers and representees but focusing in particular on the representation of a people. The fourth section then asks how these forms of representation might be organized in a democracy, focusing on a particular problem that is raised by responsive representation of the interpretive kind. In order to illustrate the usefulness of the distinctions, the paper concludes with an appendix that considers issues of representation in the presidential and parliamentary systems that are exemplified respectively by Washington and Westminster.

II.   Indicative representation

The standard case

In the standard form of this first conception, the assumption is that there are a number of representers, that the representees are the people as a whole, and the indicative requirement is that the representers should be a reliable or representative sample of the representees. They should faithfully reproduce significant differences among the population, and reproduce them in proportion to their realization within the community. We are familiar nowadays with the idea of indicative representation in the context of statistics. The random sample that is polled in the statistical exercise is a representative sample in the sense of being a good indicator of the population as a whole.

This conception of representation goes naturally with the pictorial or figurative metaphor. As Quentin Skinner (2005: 163) argues, it appears in those parliamentarian writers in England of the mid-seventeenth century who look for a "speaking likeness" of the people in those who rule them, "describing Parliament as a 'representation' – a picture or portrait – of the body of the people."

The relationship that is envisaged between the body of representatives and the body of the people is certainly figurative, as in the likeness between a portrait and the subject of the portrait. But it might best be conceptualized as the relationship whereby a painting or sculpture, particularly one of an abstract kind, can exemplify a feature of the subject: the mass of a body, the elegance of a movement, and so on. As a tailor's swatch contains pieces of cloth that exemplify the purportedly significant

Varieties of public representation

features of various fabrics, so figurative works exemplify purportedly significant aspects of an object or substance or situation or whatever (Goodman 1969). And as figurative representations can play this part to an aesthetic purpose, so politically representative bodies ought to serve in a parallel, democratic role. They ought each to exemplify and indicate the presumptively significant aspects of the people they represent, reproducing salient variations amongst its members and in a proportion that corresponds to their distribution in the population.

The idea of indicative representation figures early in democratic theory, since it is the sort of representation that is achieved or is likely to be achieved under the lottery system that was favored by the Athenians and that also played an important part in later regimes such as those of the Italian city-republics (Waley 1988; Hansen 1991). This lottery system might be taken as a version of the technique of random sampling, but random sampling put to use in the service of advancing goals espoused by the people as a whole. While it may have been motivated by a desire to have a regular turnover in the representer body, the important thing from our viewpoint is that it would have ensured a degree of proportional and indicative representation.

The indicative idea also appears in the jury system, as that was developed in medieval Europe (Abramson 1994). To be subjected to the judgment of one's peers, whether in determining that there is a legal case to answer, or that one is legally liable, is to be exposed, not to a random arbiter – a chance enemy, perhaps – but to a body that stands in for the community as a whole. The idea is that the jurors should represent a cross-section of the community, or at least of the fully enfranchised members: in medieval Europe, the mainstream, propertied males.[4]

The ideal of indicative representation was entrenched in the thinking of many of those associated with the American War of Independence and the French Revolution. Melanchton Smith could write in 1788, in opposing the American Constitution: "The idea that naturally suggests itself to our minds, when we speak of representatives is, that they resemble those they represent; they should be a true picture of the people" (Ketcham 2003: 342). Again, it was powerfully endorsed in a speech given by Mirabeau to the French Constituent Assembly in January 1789, though he used the image of a map rather than a picture to get it across. According to this version of the model:

---

[4] It is significant that a supporter of the anti-federalist cause in 1787 could complain that in the enlarged United States there would not be a representative body in legislature or jury "which possesses the same interests, feelings, opinions, and views the people themselves would were they all assembled" (Ketcham 2003: 265).

68   *Philip Pettit*

a representative body is to the nation what a chart is for the physical configuration of its soil: in all its parts, and as a whole, the representative body should at all times present a reduced picture of the people – their opinions, aspirations, and wishes, and that presentation should bear the relative proportion to the original precisely as a map brings before us mountains and dales, rivers and lakes, forests and plains, cities and towns. (Pitkin 1969, 77)

With the growth of electoral machinery, the indicative idea was naturally applied to elections for the legislature, providing support for making the electoral system more and more proportional (Mill 1964). Is it also behind the practice of organizing the legislature around geographically dispersed districts? It is hard to believe that it did not play some role in justifying that practice but the evidence, according to Rehfeld (2005), is against this hypothesis. Still, districting does induce a similarity in one dimension – nowadays a fairly unimportant one – between the population as a whole and the legislature that represents it.

The indicative idea survives in the continuing enthusiasm for proportional representation and has been given new life in campaigns for supplementing electoral representation with novel, statistically representative bodies. It is there in the general policy of organizing citizens' juries that would review various policy issues (Stewart, Kendall, and Coote 1994). It is present in the notion of the deliberative opinion poll that is chosen as a random sample and then canvassed for its view on one or another issue at two separate times: first, before members of the sample make contact, and, second, after they come together to receive background information, to hear different points of view, and to debate the right line to take on the issue under consideration (Fishkin 1997). A particularly striking example appears in the citizens' assembly that was recently established in the Canadian province of British Columbia (Fung and Fagotto 2006; Ferejohn 2007). A more or less representative sample of 160 citizens was assembled and given the task, over much of 2004, of reviewing the existing electoral system in the light of various hearings and discussions, and making a recommendation on whether or not it should be amended. The group recommended a change that then went to referendum and won more than 50 percent support – just short of the quota required to trigger a change.[5]

The similarity between representer and representee does not mean, in itself, that the representee has any degree of control over the representer.

---

[5] Since everything is a perfect indicator of itself, a limit case of indicative representation is the participatory democracy where the whole population is present to vote, not just a sample. Far from being cast as the contrast point for indicative representation, the compulsory, participatory arrangement can be seen as a special case. The case is so special, however, and so infeasible, that I ignore it in this discussion.

Varieties of public representation 69

The connection between them is not one under which the representer has to track the dispositions of the representee, and respond by acting in conformity to those dispositions. Rather it is a connection under which the representer is a good indicator or model of how the representee might have been disposed to act or speak, if in the position of the representer. Thus the people of British Columbia did not control the citizens' assembly but, given that the assembly was a microcosm of the people, it might be thought to model the decision that the people as a whole would have made had it been given the same information.

But while the indicator relationship does not necessarily give control over representers to representees, it is possible for representees to exercise control by selecting suitable indicators as their representers, by subjecting them to constraints designed to ensure that they remain indicators, and by deselecting them if they fail to act appropriately. Such authorized, indicative representers, as indicated earlier, I describe as proxies of the representees; they stand in for those who determine their selection.

Suppose that I see someone who thinks like me, as we say, and is a good indicator in a certain domain of how I tend to respond on various issues. While I do not directly control what he or she does, I do assume a position of indirect control when I decide to authorize that person to act in my stead, say on a committee. By appointing that person rather than someone else, I make it more likely that the committee will act in a congenial manner: act, as they would have been led to act, had I myself been a member. And this indirect control can be further strengthened by additional measures. I may put other constraints or incentives in place that make it more likely that the person will simulate what I would have done on the committee: for example, I might take steps to insulate the person against special, warping motives. And I may retain the power of de-selecting the person, should he or she, for whatever reason, not serve my interests well. The person is my proxy, someone who takes my place, with my authority.

The extended case

These observations about the control that is possible with indicative representers should prompt us to recognize that while indicative representation has traditionally been associated with the proportional representation of groups, the model can also apply in very different contexts.

Consider the professional or quasi-professional public figures who are appointed by government, often under strict regulations and often with a (limited or unlimited) tenure that is independent of those who do the appointing. Obvious examples will be judges and prosecutors, public auditors and ombudsmen, agency heads and the members of public commissions. These figures will serve as proxies for the public, being appointed under public authorization because of the likelihood that they will serve the public well.

This likelihood may not be based on a similarity of nature between representers and representees, but it will be based on a similarity in the tendency of their wishes. There will be a convergence between the goals the representers are professionally constrained and motivated to implement – at least ideally – and the goals that the public would want to promote in the domain of their operation. The representers are recruited to public service, plausibly, on the grounds that their interests, if things go well, are likely to be indicative of the interests of the public. And they can be subjected to constraints that make it even more likely that this will be so. Such figures can be cast as proxy representers of the people on the same grounds that certain proportional bodies can be cast as proxies.

Think of those who serve on a central bank like the Federal Reserve in the US. Or think of those who are members of an election commission of the kind that is given responsibility in many countries, at arm's length from parliament, to draw the boundaries of electoral districts. Absent dependency on the elected officials who appoint them – absent reliance on those officials for continuing tenure, for example – such individuals may be moved by motives of professional reputation to act reliably in a manner that answers to the interest of the people as a whole. And this will be especially likely if their performance is subject to public check and commentary. It is surely more likely that an independent electoral commission would act in this way, for example, than that elected members of a parliament or congress would do so, since elected representatives would have special party interests in the shape of district boundaries (Pettit 2004).

The idea of appointing professional figures was not unknown to traditional democratic theory. A good example is provided by the official known as a "podesta," who played a very important role in the life of twelfth- and thirteenth-century Italian city-republics (Waley 1988). The podesta, who might serve at different times in different cities, was an outsider appointed for six months to a year in order to run a city's affairs. He was given a range of issues to control, was often forced to act without having contact with special interest groups within the citizenry, and was subjected to intense scrutiny at the end of his tenure. Since he might hope to be appointed as podesta by different cities at different times, he would also have been susceptible to reputational motives for doing his job to the satisfaction of the citizenry. Such a figure would have been a good example, in our terms, of an indicative representer: a proxy agent who takes the place of those he represents.

But it is not just public appointees who can count as indicative representers in the extended sense we are examining. For another sort of example, think of the whistle-blowers who can expose abuses in public life, or the "private attorneys general," as they have been called (Rabkin 1998), who serve the public well by challenging certain laws before the courts. The fact that the public or people give whistle-blowers protection, and the fact that they give private attorneys general a license to use the courts as they do, means that these figures are authorized to act in their characteristic manner. In the aggregate they serve the public well, by most accounts, acting as they do on convergent if not always identical interests. Their authorization by the public means that like formally appointed officials, they can be seen as representers who are employed in their characteristic roles, precisely because of the indicative relationship between their dispositions and the presumptive dispositions of the people as a whole.

III. Responsive representation

Directed responsiveness

Where the indicative idea is that a microcosm or model of the people should rule because it is likely to be a good indicator of how the people as a whole would decide the issues that come before it, the responsive idea takes the complementary line. In this conception the representer tracks what the representee wants and responds with appropriate action, playing a very different role from that of being a passive indicator of the representee's disposition.[6] The judicial metaphor in which the lawyer or attorney acts for the client offers an illustration of the idea in which the representee explicitly or implicitly directs the representer. As the lawyer tracks the client's wishes, so the responsive representer is to track the wishes of the representee.

---

[6] I take indicative and responsive representers to be indicative and responsive only in a positive mode. If an indicative agent pursues something, that indicates that it is something that the principal would favor; but if the agent does not pursue something, that does not indicate that it is something the principal would not favor. If a principal has an interest in something, the responsive agent will not have an interest in it but if the principal does not have an interest in something that does not mean that the responsive agent will not have an interest in it. This assumption means that a responsive agent may not be indicative, as an indicative agent may not be responsive.

72   *Philip Pettit*

Under the responsive conception of representation, the wishes of representees exercise a degree of control over how representers act, and they do this with the authorization of the representees themselves; the representative process materializes, if not at their initiative, at least with their knowledge and acquiescence. Indicative representers are recruited or licensed to act because they are or can be made to be indicative. Responsive representers are recruited or licensed to act because they are or can be made to be responsive. Where I describe representers who are authorized to serve in an indicative role as proxies, I describe representers who are authorized to serve in a responsive role as deputies. We shall see that apart from directed deputies who answer to the metaphor of the attorney, there are also interpretive deputies who answer better to the metaphor of the actor.

Responsiveness among representers may materialize spontaneously, as a result of a natural love or reverence or fear of the representees, or it may be manufactured by contextual incentives or constraints that elicit suitable attentiveness. Let the representees form an intention that something be done by the representers and, at least in the directed version of responsive representation, the representers will become disposed to do it. The representers may respond to instructions issued by the representees – that is, to the manifestations of their wishes – or they may not need any such instruction, being disposed to respond to the wishes that the representees manifestly hold. Such explicitly or implicitly directed deputies I describe, in a received term, as delegates of those they represent: they are agents who serve as voiceboxes for the represented (Pitkin 1972; but see Urbinati 2000).

The category of delegates is often taken to be illustrated – rightly or wrongly, as we shall see – by those who serve in the legislature, or perhaps the executive, in sensitivity to the wishes of the electorate.[7] The control that the people exercise over such public representers may take an active, hands-on form, as when the representees impose suitable constraints on representers or give them explicit instructions. But it may often be just virtual in character, constituting a sort of hands-off, arm's-length control (Pettit 2001); while this may also be possible with indicative representers, it is particularly salient with responsive ones. Hands-off control will materialize when the representers behave in a congenial fashion and the representees stand by, ready to reveal relevant attitudes, or impose relevant constraints, only in the event that the representers stop

---

[7] For a state-of-the-art assessment of political, responsive representation, see Mansbridge (2003). Mansbridge (forthcoming) defends congenial views on indicative representation, as I learned when this paper was in press.

Varieties of public representation

performing to their taste. In this case the representees ride herd on the representers, to use an image from cowboy life. They intervene in the affairs of the representers, eliciting suitable motivation or information, only on a need-for-action basis.[8]

Might the control of responsive representers be increased by ensuring that they are indicative as well as responsive? The hope that it can be increased in this way motivates the drive for ensuring proportionality among elected deputies. The case for proportional, electoral representation is made in John Stuart Mill's classic work on representation (1964 [1861]), as indicated earlier, and it is reinforced by contemporary theorists such as Anne Phillips (1995) and Thomas Christiano (1996). There are many reasons to think that salient divisions among a represented population should be reflected in an elected house of representatives. But it is not so clear that ensuring such proportionality will ensure the indicative reliability that we might expect, for example, in the British Columbia citizens' assembly.

The reason is that no matter how much proportionality is imposed on a parliament or congress, the fact that members are chosen by election from among those who are ready to stand at the polls introduces a framework of motivation that is going to undermine the prospect of parliament operating as a reliable model or microcosm of the people. Those who stand for election are not going to be typical of the society, and even if they are typical, their performance in the legislature is bound to be affected by a special motive: the interest in being elected and reelected. In order to constitute a model of the people, legislators would need to go about their business without a thought for anything but what by their lights it is best to do. And no elected officials can be expected to do that; they are bound to be subject to what from the point of view of the indicative model is a deeply warping influence.

As suggested, there is a serious question as to whether public, responsive representers really can serve as delegates who are explicitly or implicitly directed by their constituents. Directed, responsive representation supposes that the mind of representees is made up and manifested to representers. There are explicit or implicit directives available to express

---

[8] The notion of control employed across the distinctions we have made is quite univocal. We can say that one party, A, exercises control over another party, B, to the extent that A raises the probability – robustly raises the probability (Lovett 2007: 712–13) – that B will behave in a congenial manner above the level that that behavior might have had in A's absence (Dahl 1957; Pettit 2007). A will have such an effect if A actively elicits the deputy or proxy performance sought. But A will also have this effect in the case where A stands ready to intervene on a need-for-action basis. A will guard against the possibility that B has a change of mind and by raising the probability that B will behave congenially even in that case, A will raise the absolute probability of such behavior.

74 *Philip Pettit*

the mind of representers and the responsive representational job is to track those directives. The problem that we should now note, however, is that representees in the public worlds rarely provide representers with a fully formed, directive mind. Thus responsive representation often has to become interpretive or constructive in a manner that evokes the metaphor of the actor rather than that of the attorney.

Interpretive responsiveness

Where attorneys have to be guided by the explicit or implicit directives of clients, actors bear a much less constrained relationship to the scripted characters that they are required to play. The actor interprets the character, taking the spare lines of the dramatist and giving them life in a pattern of emphasis and presence that makes interpersonal sense; the interpretation lets the character portrayed be understood as a person amongst persons. Representation in this interpretive sense is described by Hobbes (1994: 16) as personation: an act in which the representer speaks with authority for another, in particular for another individual or group of individuals.

Like any form of responsive representation, the interpretive sort that answers to this metaphor has to be authorized by the representees, at least if it has democratic credentials. Representees have to authorize the representers to speak for them, even though they do not provide the representers with the words to use. Where responsive representers on the attorney model are voiceboxes of the people, as we might say, responsive representers on the actor model are spokespersons. Where I describe attorney-like deputies as delegates, I follow tradition in describing actor-like deputies as trustees (Pitkin 1972).

The authorization that representees give interpretive deputies means that those who speak for them do not report the mind of their constituents, as a journalist or opinion survey might report that mind. Subject perhaps to certain provisos, the representees are deemed to think what their authorized spokesperson – or body of spokespersons – says that they think. The authorization is not just a prediction to the effect that the representers will be a pretty good guide to what they think. It is a guarantee that, at least within certain limits and under certain conditions, they can be taken to be minded as the representing words portray them as minded. They can be held to those words.

Responsive representation has to be interpretive with an individual representee if that person is a minor – here authorization may be supplied by a court – or if the person does not express his or her mind on some particular issue where the representer needs to act. But the context in

Varieties of public representation

which responsive representation is most clearly required to be interpretive is one of political representation, where there are a number of individuals in the position of representees, and the representer is forced, at whatever level of grain, to ascribe a coherent, enactable set of attitudes to them – a single mind.

Suppose that one or more representers are acting for an unincorporated collection or multitude. Whatever control is exercised by the representees in the multitude it had better allow the representers to act for a consistent set of goals, according to a consistent set of judgments; otherwise the representative actions are liable to undercut one another. Or if that requirement is thought too strict, on the grounds that many agents fall short of consistency, then the control certainly ought to allow the representers to be responsive to charges of inconsistency. They should not be required to have to admit that what they hold or seek on behalf of their representees is an inconsistent package; else they and their constituents would be a laughing stock.

Might the representees impose an arrangement under which they control what the representers do in a goal-by-goal or judgment-by-judgment way, and still hope to satisfy such a coherence constraint? It turns out that they could not. And that suggests that the responsive representation of a multitude is bound at a certain point to become interpretive. Those who serve in such responsively representative roles will have to be spokespersons, not voiceboxes: they will have to be deputies in the trustee mould, not in the mould of the delegate.

The most obvious way in which a multitude might hope to control the actions of its representers would be by forcing those agents always to follow the majority vote of its members. But the "discursive dilemma" shows why this will not work in general (Pettit 2001: ch. 5). The votes of entirely consistent individuals on logically connected issues can generate a set of inconsistent positions on those issues. Suppose that A, B, and C want to establish a majority collective view on three issues: whether p; whether q; and whether p&q. They might be judges in a court who have to decide on whether a plaintiff in tort did harm (p), had a duty of care (q) and so was liable for damages (p&q) (Kornhauser and Sager 1993). It is perfectly possible for A, B, and C each to have a consistent set of views on these issues and yet for the group to be forced by majority voting into endorsing an inconsistent set.

That will happen, for example, if the votes that the individuals submit are as follows. A and B vote that p, C votes against; B and C vote that q, A votes against; and so only B votes that p&q. A and C vote that not-p&q, thereby giving a majority verdict that p, that q, and that not-p&q. The following matrix should make the pattern vivid.

	P?	Q?	P & Q?
A	Yes	No	No
B	Yes	Yes	Yes
C	No	Yes	No
Majority vote	Yes	Yes	No

This paradox is of general significance, since it turns out that no voting system is guaranteed to produce a consistent output from consistent inputs if it is to work with all patterns of input and if, roughly, it is to treat both individuals and issues even-handedly (List and Pettit 2002). The lesson is that if the representers of a multitude are required to enact a coherent mind, furthering a consistent set of goals according to a consistent set of judgments, then they cannot be controlled by representees on an issue-by-issue basis. Such control is liable to provide representers with an inconsistent set of attitudes to enact: a set of attitudes like the judgments that p, that q, and that not-p&q.

The lesson, put more positively, is that in a case like this responsive representation has to be interpretive or constructive. It has to involve, not the faithful reflection of a pre-given mind, but a constructive interpretation in virtue of which the multitude is imputed a coherent mind or mentality. When that occurs, the multitude will assume the status of a corporate agent.

The idea that the interpretive representation of a multitude can transform it into a corporate agent is present in Western thought from at least the fourteenth century. In 1354, Albericus de Rosciate could say that a collegial agent, although it is constituted out of many members, is one by virtue of representation: *collegium, licet constituatur ex pluribus, est tamen unum per representationem* (Eschmann 1946: 33, fn 145). The theme dominates the work of legal theorists of the time, such as Bartolus of Sassoferrato and his pupil, Baldus de Ubaldis, who make much of the way represented groups, in particular the represented people of a city, could figure as corporate agents or persons (Woolf 1913; Canning 1983). Arguing that the *populus liber*, the free people of a city-republic, is a corporate person, Baldus explains that this is because the council represents the mind of that people: *concilium representat mentem populi* (Canning 1987: 198).

The theme reappears in the writings of Thomas Hobbes in the seventeenth century. He makes representation, a term that he uses as an alternative to personation, central to the possibility of a group's creating and enacting a single mind. "A multitude of men are made one person, when they are by one man, or one person, represented." Where does the unity come from? From the fact that the representing individual – or body – will speak with one voice, thereby testifying to one mind in the group: "it is the unity of the representer, not the unity of the represented, that maketh the person one" (Hobbes 1994: 16.13).

IV. Representation and democracy

Varieties of democratic representation

Democracy, on the Lincolnian formula, is government of the people, by the people and for the people. Representation has to have a place in any democratic constitution insofar as it is only by courtesy of representers that government can hope to be by the people; popular participation is inevitably restricted to the occasional referendum.

There is obviously room in a democratic constitution for indicative representation, of both the standard and the extended kind. The British Columbia citizens' assembly exemplifies a standard variety of indicative representation that any democracy could usefully institute. And the extended variety of indicative representation is bound to have a place insofar as every plausible democracy requires some statutory officers and bodies, such as judges, ombudsmen, and electoral commissioners, as well as a possibility of contestation by public attorneys general and by other informal invigilators of government.

Equally clearly, there has to be room in a democratic constitution for responsive as well as indicative representation. In order for many reliably indicative representers to be appointed to office, as statutory officers will have to be appointed, there must already be elected and presumptively responsive representers in place. But in any case there are quite independent reasons why no plausibly democratic regime could operate on the basis of indicative representation alone. Such representation requires that people have a standing interest in decisions being made after a more or less determinate pattern, as in requiring judges to adjudicate cases according to established law. And in many cases there would be no such interest available to guide indicative authorities. Thus popular representation is bound to require a role for responsive as well as indicative representation.

Democracy has to make room, then, both for proxies and for deputies. This is not the place to investigate the best way of networking such different kinds of representers in a satisfactory democratic dispensation, nor the best way of frameworking their activities by suitable constitutional and other constraints. Some of the relevant issues will be highlighted

78   *Philip Pettit*

by the discussion in the appendix, which constitutes the final section of the chapter, on the operation of the Washington and Westminster systems. But in the remainder of this section I discuss one serious problem that may be raised about the democratic control of those responsive representers, those deputies, that operate in an interpretive rather than a directed mode. This is a telling issue since the argument at the end of the last section suggests that all public deputies will have to be interpretive trustees rather than directed delegates.

A problem

The medievals who spoke of the representation of a people – as I take it, their interpretive representation – generally appear to have had an intuitively democratic form of representation in mind, at least relative to a citizenry of mainstream, propertied males. They looked to a form of representation in which the individual people not only consented to being represented but exercised an influence over what representers said and did as a corporate spokesperson. They took it for granted that the council of a city-republic would be appointed, at least in good part, by voting and rotation – under the *regimen ad populum* – so that the city or people could be described, in Bartolus's words, as a *sibi princeps*, a prince unto itself (Woolf 1913: 155–60, 180).

Hobbes went beyond this in arguing that the interpretive representation whereby a people assumes the unity of a person might be practiced by a monarch with absolute powers or by a committee of aristocrats: and this with the authorization of members of the people. He did not think that there could be democracy with representation by others, arguing that democracy would require the people to self-represent, ruling themselves in a committee-of-the-whole; this theme was later taken up by Rousseau (1973). Mistakenly, in view of the discursive dilemma, he thought that this self-representation could be achieved under a regime of majority voting (Hobbes 1994: 16.15–17), as indeed did Locke (1960: Bk 2, ch. 8.96) and Rousseau (1973: Bk 4, ch. 2).

The issue as to whether interpretive representation can be democratized is important, given that interpretation is going to be unavoidable when a multitude is responsively represented. We took responsive representation, being a relationship of tracking the representees, to require the control of those representees. The question here is whether such control is available with interpretive representation as well as with responsive. How might interpreters – authorized interpreters, as we can assume – be subjected to the control of representees?

Varieties of public representation

Participation in the committee-of-the whole, as envisaged in Hobbes's vision, is not a feasible way of imposing democratic control. Contemporary societies are just too big to allow for a participatory regime, in particular the sort that would require members to adjust in face of majority support for inconsistent positions. And neither is an electoral regime going to provide an effective democratic discipline. Elected representatives cannot be responsively controlled by the majority attitudes of the population, since those attitudes may be incoherent. And if the only restriction on those members springs from the desire to be reelected, or from the fact of having to live under the laws proposed, still it will leave them free to construct the mind of the people in a relatively unconstrained fashion. So is there any alternative or supplementary discipline that might be imposed on interpretive representers?

A solution?

At the time of the civil rights disputes in the United States, as at many other junctures in American history, the protagonists made rival claims as to what was the way of thinking about racial relations that represented the mind of the American people. Was it the much-vaunted heritage of a state like Mississippi in which strict segregation had been enforced on public transport, in public schools, and in other public amenities? Or was it the message of equality and respect that had long been enshrined in the Constitution and its amendments? The division on this issue created a fault line that ran through the legislatures, the courts, the media, and out onto the streets. Ultimately the constitutionally supported message won out and became a theme around which citizens generally rallied. But did this victory constitute a democratic breakthrough: a win for the right interpretation of the people's mind over the wrong interpretation? Or was it a victory of what was morally right over what was morally wrong? Or was it just a victory for the stronger over the weaker, the more numerous over the less numerous?

I think that there is only one base on which the line taken in a case like this can be justified as the right rather than the wrong interpretation of the people's mind. This is the base provided by considerations in the family of what Rawls (1993, 1999) describes as public reasons. My own view is that the victory in the civil rights disputes can be cast as a democratic victory, so far as the line that emerged triumphant is the only line that had the support of such public reasons.

Central to the idea of a democratic polity is the assumption that citizens can debate with one another about what government and the state should do from positions of relative equality: positions in which they can see public action as action that they together license and support (Larmore 2003). So at any rate I assume. Given this assumption, it follows that any proposal as to what government is to do should be supported by the sorts of considerations that all can equally recognize as relevant, even if they weight them differently. If one group can argue for a certain policy only on the ground that it is good for its own members, or in line with their particular view of the world, then that cannot be expected to pass muster under the discipline of public debate – not, at least, unless the policy can also be shown to benefit other groups or not to do them any harm (Elster 1986a).

The existence of a political society in which members address one another in arguing for this or that public policy ought, under the assumption of equality, to generate a currency of public reasons. These will be reasons that get established in the course of debate and argument as considerations that are appropriately invoked in assessing public measures and initiatives. If the members of the society cannot find a fund of considerations on which to draw in argument about public policy – a fund of considerations that all will take to be relevant, even while they weight them differently – then the exchanges between them will degenerate into power struggles and they will live in the precincts of civil war.

The assumption of equal positioning in public debate makes it inevitable that certain core considerations are endorsed in any democratic society: in particular, the claim of each member to equal respect and concern. But there are many considerations that may receive endorsement in one society and not in another. One society might endorse considerations that support a system of more or less exclusively private ownership, for example, another considerations that support a system that allows for considerable public property. One society might foster considerations that promote the development of certain cultural norms, another promulgate considerations that provide support for quite different conventions. And so on.

The considerations acknowledged and valorized in any society will typically leave issues of detailed policy underdetermined, of course; what they rule out will be the policies that are unthinkable, certainly indefensible, in the discourse of the public sphere. But even when there are many candidate policies for dealing with a given issue, all of which pass muster in public debate, the public reasons acknowledged in that debate may support one or another procedure for resolving the tie. The supported procedure might involve a parliamentary vote, or reference to an expert committee, or resort to referendum, or even the use of a citizens' assembly.

Varieties of public representation

As a democracy grows, then, we may expect that the trial and error process whereby participants float considerations and find that they are accepted or rejected will generate a currency of considerations that all valorize, and valorize as a matter of common access. Those considerations will provide the blocks out of which any case for changing or conserving the way things are done will have to be built; they will indicate the sorts of presumptions or premises on the basis of which arguments in public policy are to be made. This observation is at the heart of Rawls's conception of public reasons, although he spells it out only occasionally. In one version, he says, "the political culture of a democratic society that has worked reasonably well over a considerable period of time normally contains, at least implicitly; certain fundamental ideas from which it is possible to work up a political conception of justice suitable for a constitutional regime" (Rawls 2001: 34–5).

Returning to our original question, then, how can one argue that the interpretations of the people's mind that are selected and given authority in public life really are the correct interpretations: the interpretations that are controlled in an appropriate sense by the representees? The only available base for arguing this in a large-scale democracy has to be that they are the interpretations that emerge in a process where public reasons are the primary selectional force. The interpretations may be uniquely consistent with considerations that are given the status of public reasons. But more likely they will be that particular set of interpretations, among the sets that are compatible with public reason, that are selected under procedures endorsed in public reason.

Go back, then, to the civil rights case. The argument of public figures in Mississippi and other southern states may have been in line with some local traditions. But it seems clear that in the opinion of the courts, the media, and the vast majority of US citizens those traditions conflicted with the requirements of the idea of equality as that figured and still figures in American law and culture. It is doubtful if the civil rights movement would have won the day had there not been a widespread acceptance that practices of segregation were not supported in the currency of public reasons that were accepted in the country. The inconsistency with public reasons may not have been enough on its own to bring about the changes that occurred in the 1950s and 1960s but, arguably, it was an essential prerequisite for the success of the civil rights movement.

It is time to sum up the overall argument of the chapter. We have seen that representers and representees may be individuals or groups and, if groups, that they may be mere collections, mere cooperatives, or full-scale corporate entities. We have also seen that the relations of representation come in two broad types, with representers figuring as indicative proxies under the first variety, responsive deputies in the other. And, focusing on issues of politics, we have argued that both sorts of representation are bound to have a place in a democratic regime; that responsive representation is likely to require interpretive trustees, not directed delegates; and that interpretive, responsive representation, however constructive, can be democratically controlled under a discipline of public reason.

But are these ideas and distinctions of any use in considering empirical systems? In order to vindicate their claim to significance I conclude with observations on two ideal types of system, one associated with Washington, the other with Westminster. The distinctions we have made enable us to mark a nice difference in representational priority between these two models: inevitably, these two rather toytown models. And that difference clearly matters.

V. Appendix: The Washington and Westminster systems[9]

Philip Pettit and Rory Pettit

The Washington model

The Washington system employs individual elected representers at a number of sites. Broadly speaking, members of the House represent districts, members of the Senate represent states, and the President represents the people as a whole. The representation at this level is responsive in character, with members of the House being apparently committed to the service of their districts, members of the Senate to the service of their state, and the President to the service of the nation or union.

Representation is practiced in this system, however, not just at the level of individuals, but also at the level where members of Congress cooperate with one another and with the President and other members of the administration. It is this group, Congress-cum-administration, that ultimately gets various measures into law, performing a representative function that parallels the representative work of the individuals in that group. Where individuals may serve their different constituencies in a responsive way, this group will be expected to serve the people as a whole in a responsive manner. What it promulgates as law and policy is meant to count, under suitable controls, as the law and policy supported by the people.

[9] This builds in some part on R. Pettit (2007).

Varieties of public representation

Given the complexity of views in any district or state, the individual representation of constituency is bound to be fundamentally interpretive. The member of the House or the Senator will have to construct the mind of the constituency he or she serves, operating as a trustee rather than a delegate. Since the views of the people as a whole are even more complex, the representation of the people by the Congress-cum-administration is also bound to be interpretive. But how can the Congress-cum-administration serve as an interpretive representer of the people – a reliable trustee – if it is composed of individuals who often have conflicting briefs? They have to serve as trustees both for their constituency and for the nation or people as a whole.

Congress-cum-administration does not constitute a corporate entity with a coherent set of goals and judgments. If it did, then that entity might be a reliable system-wide trustee, imposing constraints on its members to support suitable policies. Congress-cum-administration operates, rather, as a loose aggregation that provides a majority, now for this compromise and coalition, now for that. It has to get enough members on side in order to create the requisite support for any bill that passes into law. But the majority it musters in support of one bill may be different from the majority it musters in support of another. And in each case it will have to manufacture the majority by buying off various members with favors that will play well with their electors back home. In operating on this pattern, the Congress-cum-administration will be subject to various constitutional constraints, but it is not clear that these provide anything but the lightest level of regulative control.

In this system there is an inherent tension between two sorts of forces. There are pressures on individual members of Congress to represent their different constituencies responsively, on pain on not being reelected. And at the same time there is pressure at the group or system level to generate and maintain a body of law that has the coherence required, and the fit with system-wide public reasons, to pass as the voice of the people (Dworkin 1986).

These forces are quite likely to interact so as to produce laws that fail to fit with one another, and perhaps even with the Constitution. The laws themselves will often involve subclauses designed to pick up the support of swing voters, and such complexity can make the demands of coherence hard to identify. But even when those demands are obvious, the desire to strike a popular, electorally helpful posture is liable to generate support among members of Congress for laws that fail to fit with one another. In that case the buck passes to the President, who may veto the law. And, failing a presidential veto, the buck will pass to those members of the public who may combine to challenge the law and to the courts that will

84 *Philip Pettit*

adjudicate that challenge. If there is a coherent body of law emerging at the end of the process, that will be a product of this interplay of different factors, not the work of any single corporate body.

This result can be summed up by saying that the Washington system prioritizes the individual-level representation of constituencies at a possible cost to the group-level or system-level representation of the people as a whole. It allows members of Congress to serve as trustees for their constituencies, thereby raising a problem for how the administration-cum-Congress can serve as a trustee for the people as a whole. It is directed at ensuring not so much a representative government as a government of representatives – something that resembles what Edmund Burke (1999) described as a congress of ambassadors.

The Westminster model

The reason why the Washington system of representation prioritizes individual-level representation goes back to the fact that the executive or administration is elected directly, not by members of the Congress. This separation means that the fate of the administration does not depend on how the members vote. And so those members are free to vote as they wish, with party constraints serving only as a relatively light discipline, at least under normal conditions. This marks the crucial difference between the Washington and the Westminster regimes.

In the Westminster system the administration stands or falls with the support of the individual members of parliament, in particular the lower House. And that means that those parliamentary representatives who have succeeded in electing an executive – the members of the winning party or coalition – will have to stick together in order to maintain that executive in power. In effect, the party or coalition will have to be organized so that its members are forced to cleave to an agreed party line, on pain of losing party membership and the chance of being reelected. The party or coalition will become a self-policing corporate entity.

Given this pressure, the behavior of parliamentary representatives cannot be dictated by a desire to please those back in the constituency, and to promote the prospects of reelection; they cannot serve as trustee representatives for the constituency. If their party gets enough members into parliament to be able to select the executive, then members will be bound by the party whip to stick on most important matters to the party line. And if their party fails to do this, then they will be bound by the party whip to present a solid face of opposition to the party in power, playing by the same hard-ball rules. This necessity is manifest to voters, of course, so that legislators will be elected in great part on the grounds of which executive they promise to support in office – usually, an executive composed of members of their own party – not on the grounds of how well they are likely to serve the local constituency.

In the Westminster system, then, the individual-level representation of constituency gets put in a decidedly second place, since individual members will tend to vote as their party votes and will be expected even by those who elect them to vote that way. But if that is the weakness of the system, the strength is that the parliament will operate very efficiently to generate a body of legislation that can be expected to be internally coherent, to cohere with established law and principle, and to be generally responsive to the public reasons that carry weight among the people as a whole. The legislative program for any parliament will have to be planned by a corporate body: the party in power. This party will have had to ensure the coherence of its legislative program. It will have had to advertise the program as that which it would implement in office. And once in office it will have to stick to the program, at least in general outline. Short of being a minority or coalition government, it will have no excuse for departing from it and any departure will be subject to a powerful challenge from the opposition, the media, and the public.

We saw that the Washington system prioritizes the individual-level representation of constituency at a cost to the system-level representation of the people. These comments on the Westminster system show that things there are almost exactly the other way around. The system prioritizes the group-level representation of the people, giving parliament the cast of a corporate body, albeit a body controlled by members of the party that holds office. And it does this to the detriment of the individual-level representation of constituency. In contrast to the Washington model, it is directed at ensuring a representative government rather than a government of representatives.

Significance

The difference of representational priority has enormous implications for other aspects of the two systems, including implications that bear on the claims of each to be a satisfactory democratic regime.[10] The significance of the difference in representational priority comes out in differences of sensitivity to a variety of pressures. We can illustrate the point, somewhat speculatively, with reference to local pressures, expressive pressures, lobby pressures and the pressure of public opinion.

---

[10] Other assessments of the two systems tend not to focus on this issue of representational priority: see Shugart and Carey (1992); Linz and Valenzuela (1994).

86 *Philip Pettit*

Local pressures Under the Washington system members of Congress are bound to be influenced, for good or ill, by a concern for how their votes will play back home. This localism may occasionally bring real benefits to their district, as when members can secure legislative favors. The members of a Westminster parliament will have little occasion to think locally in this manner, since their votes will be controlled by the party; local efforts will be restricted to providing some local advisory services and to playing the part of a celebrity in local events.

Expressive pressures To act in a purely instrumental way is to act out of a concern for the outcome of what one does; to act purely expressively is to act out of a concern for the posture associated with acting in that manner (Brennan and Lomasky 1992). The members of Congress will often be in a situation where they cannot affect the outcome, even as part of an effective majority, and where relevant they will be motivated to take positions on an expressive basis. They will be tempted to grandstand on issues like prostitution and drugs and crime, for example, focusing on the symbolic rather than the substantive utility of doing so (Nozick 1994). The members of a Westminster parliament will be less exposed to this pressure. The party in power will always be able to affect outcomes, with the result that concern for outcome should balance if not eliminate the concern for posture and thereby reduce expressive motives. Something similar may be true of the party out of power, for it will always have to think about what to do if it wins office.

Lobby pressures The members of a Washington Congress, being more or less free to vote as they will, are going to be subject to intense lobby pressure for their vote, especially when the lobbies involved can provide campaign finance for those who vote congenially. The members of a Westminster legislature, not being free to vote against their party, will not be subject to the same lobbying pressure, at least not outside the ministry. Lobbies will have to buy over whole parties in order to have a legislative impact, not just the swing voters on any issue.[11]

Public opinion The members of Congress will not necessarily be responsive to a high level of public opinion in favor of a particular measure. Whether a response is forthcoming will depend, first, on how far

---

[11] The very fact that the party in power puts up a unified legislative program for the duration of a parliament may facilitate the influence of an opinion-forming elite in the process whereby that program is formed. And that particular danger may be relatively absent under the Washington system.

that opinion generates local pressure on the representer to do something; second, on how expressively beneficial or costly will be the posture of support; third, on how far lobby pressures are silent or supportive on the issue; and, fourth, on how far the transaction costs of getting a majority together in support of the measure are manageable. But if public opinion strongly supports a given measure, then the party in office under the Westminster system can usually be expected to back the measure. It will not be subject to the same local, expressive and lobbying concerns; there will be low transaction costs involved, since it will already be organized as a corporate entity; and, as an effective agent in power, it will be expected to respond to public opinion and will run an electoral risk if it fails to do so. The difference between the two models may help to explain why the public support for gun control that generally emerges in the wake of gun outrages routinely elicits a response in Westminster systems and routinely fails to do so under the Washington model.

If these thoughts are on the right lines, then the representational priority adopted in a system of government is going to have an enormous influence on how the system and the society as a whole works. Let the system go toward Washington and it will activate local, expressive, and lobby pressures and reduce the impact of aggregate public opinion. Let it go toward Westminster and it will reduce local, expressive, and lobby pressures and intensify the impact of public opinion.

These predictions should be qualified for variation in other factors, of course, and need to be tested against empirical observations. But assuming they are broadly on the right lines – and there is some evidence that they are (Foweraker and Landman 2002) – they emphasize the importance of the issue of representational priority. There are various normative standpoints possible on that issue, of course, so that some thinkers may favor the Washington model, some the Westminster. But no one is likely to think that the issue is insignificant. It demonstrates, if demonstration is needed, that the theory of representation matters.

BIBLIOGRAPHY

Abramson, J. 1994. *We, the Jury: The Jury System and the Ideal of Democracy.* New York: Basic Books.

Bratman, M. 1999. *Faces of Intention: Selected Essays on Intention and Agency.* Cambridge: Cambridge University Press.

Brennan, G. and L. Lomasky. 1992. *Democracy and Decision.* Cambridge: Cambridge University Press.

Burke, E. 1999. "Speech to the Electors of Bristol," in *Selected Works of Edmund Burke.* Indianapolis, IN: Liberty Fund.

88   *Philip Pettit*

Canning, J. P. 1983. "Ideas of the State in Thirteenth and Fourteenth Century Commentators on the Roman Law." *Transactions of the Royal Historical Society* 33: 1–27.

——— 1987. *The Political Thought of Baldus de Ubaldis*. Cambridge: Cambridge University Press.

Christiano, T. 1996. *The Rule of the Many: Fundamental Issues in Democratic Theory*. Boulder, CO: Westview Press.

Dahl, R. 1957. "The Concept of Power." *Behavioral Science* 2: 201–15.

Dworkin, R. 1986. *Law's Empire*. Cambridge, MA: Harvard University Press.

Elster, J. 1986a. "The Market and the Forum: Three Varieties of Political Theory," in *Foundations of Social Choice Theory*, ed. J. Elster and A. Hilland. Cambridge: Cambridge University Press, 103–30.

Eschmann, T. 1946. "Studies on the Notion of Society in St Thomas Aquinas: St Thomas and the Decretal of Innocent IV Romana Ecclesia, Ceterum." *Medieval Studies* 8: 1–42.

Ferejohn, J. 2007. "The Citizens' Assembly Model," in *Designing Deliberative Democracy: The British Columbia Citizens' Assembly*, ed. H. Perse and M. Warren. Cambridge: Cambridge University Press, 192–213.

Fishkin, J. S. 1997. *The Voice of the People: Public Opinion and Democracy*. New Haven, CT: Yale University Press.

Foweraker, J. and T. Landman. 2002. "Constitutional Design and Democratic Performance." *Democratization* 9: 43–66.

Fung, A. and E. Fagotto. 2006. "The British Columbia Citizens' Assembly." Kennedy School of Government, Harvard University. Cambridge, MA.

Goodman, N. 1969. *Languages of Art*. London: Oxford University Press.

Hansen, M. H. 1991. *The Athenian Democracy in the Age of Demosthenes*. Oxford: Blackwell.

Hobbes, T. 1990. *Behemoth or The Long Parliament*, ed. F. Toennies. Chicago: University of Chicago Press.

——— 1994. *Leviathan*, ed. E. Curley. Indianapolis, IN: Hackett.

Ketcham, R. (ed.). 2003. *The Anti-Federalist Papers*. New York: Signet Classic.

Knights, M. 2005. *Representation and Misrepresentation in Later Stuart Britain: Partisanship and Political Culture*. Oxford: Oxford University Press.

Kornhauser, L. A. and L. G. Sager. 1993. "The One and the Many: Adjudication in Collegial Courts." *California Law Review* 81: 1–59.

Larmore, C. 2003. "Public Reason," in *The Cambridge Companion to Rawls*, ed. S. Freeman. Cambridge: Cambridge University Press, 368–93.

Linz, J. J. and A. Valenzuela (eds.). 1994. *The Failure of Presidential Democracy*. Baltimore, MD: Johns Hopkins University Press.

List, C. and P. Pettit. 2002. "Aggregating Sets of Judgments: An Impossibility Result." *Economics and Philosophy* 18: 89–110.

Locke, J. 1960. *Two Treatises of Government*. Cambridge: Cambridge University Press.

Lovett, F. 2007. "Power," in *A Companion to Contemporary Political Philosophy*, ed. R. E. Goodin, P. Pettit, and T. Pogge. Oxford: Blackwell.

McLean, J. 2004. "Government to State: Globalization, Regulation, and Governments as Legal Persons." *Indiana Journal of Global Legal Studies* 10: 173–97.

Varieties of public representation

Manin, B. 1997. *The Principles of Representative Government*. Cambridge: Cambridge University Press.

Mansbridge, J. 2003. "Rethinking Representation." *American Political Science Review* 97: 515–28.

forthcoming, "A 'Selection Model' of Political Representation," *Journal of Political Philosophy*.

Mill, J. S. 1964. *Considerations on Representative Government*. London: Everyman Books.

Nozick, R. 1994. *The Nature of Rationality*. Princeton, NJ: Princeton University Press.

Pettit, P. 2001. *A Theory of Freedom: From the Psychology to the Politics of Agency*. Cambridge: Polity Press; New York: Oxford University Press.

2004. "Depoliticizing Democracy." *Ratio Juris* 17: 52–65.

2007. "Republican Liberty: Three Axioms, Four Theorems," in *Republicanism and Political Theory*, ed. C. Laborde and J. Manor. Oxford: Blackwell, 102–30.

Pettit, P. and D. Schweikard. 2006. "Joint Action and Group Agency." *Philosophy of the Social Sciences* 36: 18–39.

Pettit, R. 2007. "Reconceptualising Democratic Representation," BA honors thesis, Department of Philosophy, University of Sydney.

Phillips, A. 1995. *The Politics of Presence*. Oxford: Oxford University Press.

Pitkin, H. F. (ed.). 1969. *Representation*. New York: Atherton Press.

1972. *The Concept of Representation*. Berkeley: University of California Press.

Rabkin, J. A. 1998. "The Secret Life of the Private Attorney General." *Law and Contemporary Problems* 61: 179–203.

Rawls, J. 1993. *Political Liberalism*. New York: Columbia University Press.

1999. *The Law of Peoples*. Cambridge, MA: Harvard University Press.

2001. *Justice as Fairness: A Restatement*. Cambridge, MA: Harvard University Press.

Rehfeld, A. 2005. *The Concept of Constituency: Political Representation, Democratic Legitimacy, and Institutional Design*. Cambridge: Cambridge University Press.

2006. "Towards a General Theory of Political Representation." *Journal of Politics* 68: 1–21.

Richardson, H. 2002. *Democratic Autonomy*. New York: Oxford University Press.

Rousseau, J.-J. 1973. *The Social Contract and Discourses*. London: Dent.

Shugart, M. S. and J. M. Carey. 1992. *Presidents and Assemblies: Constitutional Design and Electoral Dynamics*. Cambridge: Cambridge University Press.

Skinner, Q. 2005. "Hobbes on Representation." *European Journal of Philosophy* 13: 155–84.

Stewart, J., E. Kendall, and A. Coote. 1994. *Citizens' Juries*. London: Institute of Public Policy Research.

Urbinati, N. 2000. "Representation as Advocacy: A Study of Democratic Deliberation." *Political Theory* 28: 758–86.

Walcy, D. 1988. *The Italian City-Republics*, 3rd edn. London: Longman.

Woolf, C. N. S. 1913. *Bartolus of Sassoferrato*. Cambridge: Cambridge University Press.

8

Preferable Descriptive Representatives: Will Just Any Woman, Black, or Latino Do?
SUZANNE DOVI

A body of theoretical literature has developed that explains why historically disadvantaged groups should be represented by members of those groups. Such representatives are commonly referred to as descriptive representatives. This literature has also endorsed various institutional reforms aimed at increasing the number of descriptive representatives, e.g., party list quotas, racial districting, and proportional representation. However, this literature does not articulate criteria that should guide the selection of descriptive representatives to serve in these institutional positions. Indeed, some thinkers claim that such criteria cannot, or at least should not, be articulated. I argue that some descriptive representatives are preferable to others and that criteria for selecting preferable descriptive representatives can, and should, be articulated. Moreover, I recommend one such criterion: Preferable descriptive representatives possess strong mutual relationships with dispossessed subgroups of historically disadvantaged groups.

Democratic political institutions are often evaluated by the gender, ethnicity, and race of elected representatives (e.g., Guinier 1994; Paolino 1995). Implicit in these evaluations is the assumption that democratic political institutions that lack any representatives from historically disadvantaged groups are unjust. Moreover, these evaluations often assume that an increase in the number of representatives from historically disadvantaged groups can contribute to the substantive representation of those groups (e.g., Thomas 1991). For example, 1998 was declared the "Year of the Woman" in the United States because in that year the number of women in the House leaped from 28 to 48, and that in the Senate from two to six. This method of evaluating democratic institutions often assumes that the more women, Blacks, and Latinos, the better for democratic institutions.[1]

These assumptions justify the political practice of setting aside certain political and institutional positions for members of historically disadvantaged groups. These positions are specifically designed to increase the number of representatives from historically disadvantaged groups—that is, the number of what I call "descriptive representatives." Contemporary political theorists have directly and indirectly supported these assumptions by offering several explanations for why political representatives for a historically disadvantaged group should come from that group (e.g., Mansbridge 1999; Phillips 1995; Sapiro 1981). In their terminology, they have advanced reasons to think that "descriptive representation," "group representation," "the politics of presence," or "self-representation" is important.[2]

Although the reasons they advance differ significantly, these theorists sound a common theme: To be fully democratic, a society that has denied full political membership to certain groups must be strongly committed to including those groups in its political life. Such a commitment, at least in many circumstances, requires society to take active steps to increase the number of descriptive representatives. On these grounds, these theorists endorse various institutional reforms such as party list quotas, caucuses, racial districting, and schemes for proportional representation. But these theorists have said remarkably little about the criteria that should guide democratic citizens in their choice of descriptive representatives.[3] The emphasis of this literature so far has been on establishing the *need for the presence* of some descriptive representatives, not on *investigating criteria for identifying preferable* descriptive representatives.

Which members of historically disadvantaged groups are preferable representatives for those groups? My primary aim is to argue for the need for criteria that will help answer this question. I take the value of having descriptive representatives in public positions as a given.[4] I advance existing discussions of group representation by explaining how democratic citizens should choose among various possible descriptive representatives. Toward this end, I propose one criterion for identifying preferable descriptive representatives: Preferable descriptive representatives have strong *mutual* relationships with *dispossessed* subgroups. I purposely set aside the question of whether descriptive representatives should be evaluated by the same or different criteria as other representatives in liberal democracies.[5] I focus on a different question: Are there any criteria for guiding

---

The author would like to thank Sigal Ben-Porath, Bernard Harcourt, Kristen Hessler, Jacob Levy, Melissa Williams and most of all, Houston Smit for their invaluable conversations, comments, and support. Thanks to Carrie Brennan, John Garcia, Cindy Holder, Patchen Markell, William Mishler, Jeff Spinner-Halev, John Schwarz, and Sue Thomas for reading and commenting on drafts of this paper. The author would, finally, like to thank the anonymous reviewers for their challenging and insightful comments.

[1] For an opposing view, see Cameron, Epstein, and O'Halloran 1996.
[2] I use these terms interchangeably in the rest of this paper.

---

[3] I use "democratic citizens" to refer to all citizens—that is, to both citizens who are members of historically disadvantaged groups and citizens who possess more privileged social locations.
[4] The need for institutional reforms aimed at increasing the number of descriptive representatives for a certain historically disadvantaged group may be temporary. These reforms may be dropped, if and when the society has advanced to the point where a historically disadvantaged group is no longer politically marginalized.
[5] I agree with Iris Marion Young's position (2000) that the difficulty in choosing descriptive representatives—what she calls the problem of one person representing the many—is a problem for all

729

184 REPRESENTATION

the appointment, nomination, or election of members of historically disadvantaged groups to positions that were created to increase the diversity of actors in the political arena and thereby the substantive representation of such groups? In other words, are there any principled reasons for preferring one *descriptive* representative to another? I offer my criterion to provide guidance for such decisions and to be more explicit about the political commitments that underlie a politics of presence. To put my position boldly, a commitment to a politics of presence would be more likely to support robust democratic relations if descriptive representatives were selected on the basis of their mutual relationships with dispossessed subgroups.

CONSTRUCTING A POLITICS OF PRESENCE: BUILDING AROUND A TENSION

Hannah Pitkin's classic work *The Concept of Representation* has set the terms of the debate over descriptive representation. For Pitkin, descriptive representation concerns what representatives "look like," rather than what they "do." For this reason, Pitkin (1967, 89) proclaimed that arguments for descriptive representation have "no room for representation as accountability." This line of reasoning—that a politics of presence is somehow incompatible with accountability—has defined the theoretical problem facing proponents of descriptive representation. Early attempts to articulate the need for members of historically disadvantaged groups to represent those groups focused on the conflicting interests of privileged and relatively less privileged groups. Most notably, Virginia Sapiro (1981) showed that trusting some groups to protect another group's interests, e.g., letting husbands take care of their wives' interests, was and continues to be foolhardy. The recurring betrayals of historically disadvantaged groups by relatively privileged groups partially explain why traditional mechanisms of accountability are insufficient. By emphasizing the conflicts between advantaged and disadvantaged citizens, Sapiro laid the theoretical groundwork for a politics of presence. She did so by standing Pitkin's point on its head: Democratic accountability sometimes requires descriptive representation.

Following Sapiro's lead, a rich theoretical literature has developed that defends the intuition that the chronic underrepresentation of women and ethnic minorities is a problem. Anne Phillips (1998, 228) has, very helpfully, laid out four groups of arguments about why descriptive representation matters. The first of these, which Phillips calls "the role model argument," claims that members of historically disadvantaged groups benefit from seeing members of their group in positions of power. Having a woman in office increases other women's self-esteem and their capacity to assume leadership roles. Second, Phillips maintains that descriptive representatives are needed to compensate for past and continued injustices toward certain groups. According to this second argument, past and present betrayals by privileged groups create a belief that trust can be given only to descriptive representatives. The presence of descriptive representatives can partially compensate for those betrayals. She refers to this second argument for presence as "the justice argument." The justice argument examines patterns of inequality to reveal the need for descriptive representation. Her third argument focuses on "overlooked interests." According to this argument, group representation allows historically excluded groups to get onto the political agenda their perspectives, issues, and interests that had been previously ignored. Deliberations about public policy will be improved by having a more diverse set of representatives. Finally, Phillips advances the "revitalized democracy" argument, which asserts that a commitment to diverse representation is necessary for increasing political participation and strengthening the legitimacy of democratic institutions.

Dismissing the role model argument as uninteresting and without bearing on democratic politics (Phillips 1995, 63),[6] Phillips devotes much of her attention to the remaining three arguments. Her work reflects a tendency in the literature on group representation as a whole to stress the value of group representation for considerations of justice, for deliberation, and for revitalization of democratic institutions. For present purposes, I focus primarily on justice arguments—that is, arguments that unfair patterns of inequality indicate a need for an institutionalized voice. These arguments appeal to evidence ranging from formal political exclusions (e.g., the disenfranchisement of certain groups) to economic disparities (e.g., mean incomes falling below the mean incomes of other groups). Such evidence challenges the assumption that all groups in liberal democracies enjoy the political equality that democratic commitments demand. Appealing to this evidence, theorists of group representation assert that justice demands paying particular attention to those in liberal democracies who are worse off. In doing so, they invoke the spirit of John Rawls's difference principle (1971).[7]

Theorists of group representation unambiguously acknowledge that despite the importance of descriptive representation, some descriptive representatives fail to further, and can even undermine, the best interests of historically disadvantaged groups. For instance, Melissa Williams (1998, 6) states that "it would be absurd to claim that a representative, simply

---

representation. The criteria for choosing descriptive representatives will overlap significantly with the criteria for choosing representatives more generally. However, descriptive representatives who have been appointed, nominated, or elected to positions aimed at increasing the substantive representation of historically disadvantaged groups have particular and unique obligations to those groups.

[6] In contrast, I maintain that the ability to inspire and to be an example of a political leader from a historically disadvantaged group could be crucial for mobilizing that group.

[7] Rawls's difference principle asserts that social and economic inequalities are just to the extent that they are necessary to the institutional structure that is the greatest benefit to the least advantaged in the distribution. See Rawls 1971, 60, 302.

REPRESENTATION

185

because she is a woman, therefore represents the interests or perspectives of women generally, or that an African-American representative is automatically representative of all African Americans. The mere presence of members of marginalized groups in legislatures is not *sufficient* for the fair representation of citizens from those groups, even though it is often *necessary.*" Similarly, Phillips (1995, 157) states that "if the presumption is that all women or all black people share the same preferences and goals, this is clearly—and dangerously—erroneous." In some circumstances, a politics of presence can be undesirable. Most theorists of group representation recognize that members of historically disadvantaged groups have diverse interests and beliefs and that a politics of presence by itself is insufficient for revitalizing democratic institutions.

A tension thus emerges in the literature on group representation. On the one hand, theorists of group representation have argued that certain patterns of inequalities justify having an institutionalized voice. Such arguments emphasize the *shared* obstacles facing certain members of particular groups. Highlighting how certain groups are unfairly excluded from political life substantiates their claims that certain policy remedies are desperately needed. On the other hand, these theorists increasingly acknowledge the diversity within historically marginalized groups. This diversity can seem to undermine the presumption that certain shared experiences of oppression justify giving some groups an institutionalized voice.

Generally speaking, the literature has responded to this tension by exploring its implications for the meaning of representation as a whole. In particular, it has emphasized that representation is a dynamic process that must negotiate seemingly contradictory demands. Here the literature makes some of its most insightful contributions to democratic theory. For instance, Williams shows how the contradictory demands placed on representatives lead to understanding representation as a kind of mediation. Williams (1998, 8) identifies three dimensions of political life that representatives must mediate: the dynamics of legislative decision-making, the nature of legislator–constituent relations, and the basis for aggregating citizens into representable constituencies. Williams's understanding of representation as mediation expands the traditional conception of representation, which focuses almost exclusively on the relationship between the representative and the represented.

Iris Marion Young also offers a revised understanding of representation in response to the problem posed by diversity within historically disadvantaged groups. Young warns that attempts to include more voices in the political arena can inadvertently suppress other voices. She (Young 1997, 350) illustrates this point using the example of a Latino representative who might inadvertently represent heterosexual Latinos at the expense of gay and lesbian Latinos. For Young (1997, 351) the suppression of differences is a problem for *all* representation. Representatives of large districts or of small communities must negotiate the difficulty of one person representing many. Because such a

difficulty is endemic to all representation, the legitimacy of a representative is not primarily a function of his or her similarities to the represented. Representation should not be characterized by a "relationship of identity."

Instead, Young uses Jacques Derrida's concept of *différance* to recommend reconceptualizing representation as *a differentiated relationship.* Derrida's concept of *différance* is both extremely radical and subtle. The basic idea underlying the concept of *différance* is the rejection of polarities or dichotomies, such as that of cause–effect. For those who think that certain distinctions are straightforward, it will be tempting to reject the concept of *différance* out of hand. But Young (2000, 127) finds this concept useful for capturing the dynamic process of representation: for this concept, she suggests, encourages thinking of oppositions "in terms of the trace, a movement of temporalization that carries past and future with it." Young further explains that the concept of *différance* promotes a way of thinking about entities in their "plurality without requiring their collection into a common identity .... Things are similar without being identical, and different without being contrary, depending on the point of reference and the moment in a process." Using this idea of *différance,* Young recommends understanding representation as a fluid relationship, instead of a "relationship of identity" between constituents and representatives.

Let me briefly explain how Young applies Derrida's concept of *différance* to the meaning of representation. The basic move is to argue that the differences between the represented and the representative need to be both acknowledged and affirmed. According to Young (2000, 127), "Conceptualizing representation in terms of *différance* means acknowledging and affirming that there is a difference, a separation, between the representative and the constituents." For Young, constituents should not look for representatives with their same identity; rather, they should look for traces of accountability and authorization. Representation should be understood as a dynamic process that moves between moments of authorization and moments of accountability (Young 2000, 129). For Young, the movement between these moments makes the process "democratic." A representative process is democratic to the degree that citizens authorize their representatives and then can hold them accountable. Assessments of representative processes will therefore partially depend on the past and future behavior of representatives. Young's description of the dynamic of representation emphasizes that citizens often cannot anticipate the issues that representatives will confront during their term in office. Democratic citizens should continuously suspend or "defer" their evaluations of representatives. Democratic citizens must assess representation dynamically, that is, assess the whole ongoing processes of authorization and accountability of representatives. Young would resist assessing a representative from any one point of reference.

Young is quite right that representation in general is a complex and dynamic process. However, something important is overlooked in the quick move from group

186

REPRESENTATION

representation to representation as a whole. Young's focus on the problems of all representation obscures the distinctive problems of representation facing historically disadvantaged groups. She loses sight of the fact that some differences between representatives and the represented are more politically relevant from the perspective of democratic theory. Some politically salient differences should not be affirmed, e.g., differences that result from unjust and systemic exclusion.[8] As Young herself pointed out in her earlier work, some groups face structural obstacles. In *Justice and the Politics of Difference*, she described real representation as consisting of "the self-organization of groups, the group generation of policy proposals in a context where decisions makers were required to be responsive to their perspectives and a group veto regarding specific policies that affect a group directly" (Young 1990, 184). In her later work, Young (1990, 372; 2000, 144, fn 27) "defers" the question of institutional supports for group representation. Her emphasis on the problems common to all representation downplays how particular institutional supports are necessary for overcoming some structural obstacles. Her admirable concern about the ways in which such institutional supports can suppress differences among historically disadvantaged groups leads her to retract her earlier commitment to certain institutional reforms, e.g., group vetoes. Young does continue to support multimember legislative jurisdictions, caucuses, and party list quotas. Reserved legislative seats should be used as "a last resort and temporary option for representing otherwise excluded perspectives" (Young 2000, 150). Young's desire to avoid excluding certain opinions, interests, or perspectives of historically disadvantaged groups thus weakens her initial support for institutional reforms aimed at increasing the real representation of those groups.

The degree to which Young has changed her mind is of less immediate interest than how the desire to avoid suppressing differences among members of historically disadvantaged groups can prevent theorists from articulating and defending reasons for preferring certain descriptive representatives over others. Simply to affirm all differences, as Young eventually does, ignores how certain politically salient differences between different groups in society (specifically between those who have been oppressed and those who have not) can justify the need for an institutionalized voice. Consider Young's example of the Asian American, who, she claims, has the perspective of an African American. This example shows how much she has weakened the claim that a historically disadvantaged group should be represented by members of that group. If one extends one's understanding of group membership so far as to include certain Asian Americans as members of

the African-American community,[9] then existing proposals for group representation, e.g., party list quotas, become untenable, for it is questionable whether such a person could contribute to the self-organization of an African-American community (or should count toward a party list quota for African Americans.) If Asian Americans can possess an African-American perspective and thereby satisfy the requirements of being descriptive representatives for African Americans, so can whites. Young's revised understanding of representation could legitimate an all-male (or all white) legislature as adequately representing women (or people of color) provided that they shared similar interests, opinions, and perspectives. The central claim of the literature on group representation—that historically disadvantaged groups need representatives from those groups—is seriously diluted by Young's notion of representation as a differentiated relationship.

Young's description of the dynamic of representation and her explicit recognition of the diversity within historically disadvantaged groups are useful contributions to theoretical debates about the general meaning of representation. But they provide little guidance to those confronted with the task of evaluating a particular descriptive representative. Such evaluations could be improved by articulating some general criteria for preferring some descriptive representatives to others.

JUSTIFYING THE SILENCE ABOUT CRITERIA

Silence about the criteria for evaluating descriptive representatives is not accidental. Theorists of group representation have offered two kinds of arguments to justify their silence. I call these two arguments the autonomy argument and the contingency argument.

According to *the autonomy argument*, members of historically disadvantaged groups should decide for themselves who is a preferable descriptive representative. This argument assumes that autonomy is best equated with being left alone—at least in the case of a group's choice of its representatives. According to this line of thinking, respecting the autonomy of historically disadvantaged groups requires theorists to refrain from advancing criteria for evaluating descriptive representatives. This argument has two main versions. The first suggests that articulating criteria for judging descriptive representatives attributes to historically disadvantaged groups a fixed identity. The second emphasizes the autonomy of the representative.

The first version of the autonomy argument asserts that any proposed criterion for evaluating descriptive representatives presupposes that a historically disadvantaged group has an essential nature. In other words, it presupposes that that such a group has a "fixed

---

[8] Democratic citizens should remain vigilant about preventing unjust and systemic exclusions. One way that they can do this is by assessing their choice of descriptive representatives in light of such exclusions. Institutional reforms aimed at increasing the number of descriptive representatives can revitalize democratic institutions if citizens select descriptive representatives based on an understanding of whose interests, perspectives, and opinions are being systemically marginalized.

[9] I assume here that Asian Americans are not typically considered part of the African-American community. I recognize that biracial and multiracial identities might complicate this assumption. My argument does not assume an essential identity to these groups but is based on existing, historically contingent understandings of group membership.

REPRESENTATION

essence given once and for all, and with traits that are homogeneously distributed among all the group members" (Gould 1996, 182). Such an assumption places undesirable constraints on the behavior of members of historically disadvantaged groups. According to Williams (1995, 6), "No defensible claim for group representation can rest on assertions of the essential identity of women or minorities; such assertions do violence to the empirical facts of diversity as well as to the agency of individuals to define the meaning of their social and biological traits." To explain why some members are less suitable descriptive representatives is to question the authenticity of those members' identity. Such explanations possess an implicit charge that "she isn't really a woman" or "he isn't really black." In this way, discussions about the criteria for selecting descriptive representatives are often interpreted as attacks on the "authenticity" of descriptive representatives. Not only are such discussions overly divisive (Jones 1993; Stasiulis 1993), but they prevent the group from determining its own boundaries. According to this first version of the autonomy argument, members of historically disadvantaged groups should define for themselves the meaning of their group identity, as well as choose their own descriptive representatives.

The second version of the autonomy argument emphasizes the autonomy of descriptive representatives. Phillips, in particular, argues that specifying the criteria for evaluating descriptive representatives would undermine the arguments for group representation. For Phillips, a politics of presence is justified because representatives have some political discretion about their political decisions. Because of this discretion, descriptive representatives should be present where political decisions are being made. To uphold standards of "strict accountability"—that is, to require descriptive representatives to act in certain ways, e.g., to endorse a particular policy— would undermine a primary reason for why certain historically disadvantaged groups need representatives from those groups: namely, that representatives are not mere puppets of their constituents but must exercise their own judgment. To suppose that there is a fixed set of criteria by which descriptive representatives should be judged is to fail to appreciate how the *autonomy* afforded to representatives justifies the politics of presence. According to this second formulation, it would be misguided to provide a laundry list of "good policies" that a female representative should support and to insist that preferable female representatives can vote only in ways consistent with that list. After all, male representatives could also vote according to a laundry list. The more one knows how a descriptive representative should act, the less it is necessary to have a descriptive representative. Such reasoning led Mansbridge (1999, 630) to conclude that descriptive representatives become less necessary when interests have crystallized.

The second kind of argument for remaining silent about the criteria for judging descriptive representatives is *the contingency argument*. According to this argument, it is impossible to articulate the criteria that should be used to evaluate descriptive representatives

because context matters. Some theorists of group representation, such as Williams (1998, 17), stress that particular historical developments play "an important role in defining the groups whose moral claims are strongest." Others stress that the experiences of historically disadvantaged groups defy generalizations. *A priori* proposals for criteria will either be irrelevant or do more harm than good. The variations across groups prevent adopting any one set of criteria. Mansbridge provides a particularly illuminating discussion of the relationship between descriptive representation and contingency. She identifies four contingent conditions that could justify preferring descriptive representatives to nondescriptive representatives: "(1) adequate communication in contexts of mistrust, (2) innovative thinking in contexts of uncrystallized, not fully articulated, interests, ... (3) creating a social meaning of 'ability to rule' for members of a group in historical contexts where the ability has been seriously questioned, and (4) increasing the polity's de facto legitimacy in contexts of past discrimination"(Mansbridge 1999, 628). For Mansbridge, descriptive representatives are needed when marginalized groups distrust relatively more privileged citizens and when marginalized groups possess political preferences that have not been fully formed. She emphasizes that descriptive representatives are necessary only under certain conditions—that is, when descriptive representatives perform certain functions in certain contexts. Mansbridge's discussion provides some important insights into evaluating when descriptive representation is necessary. Implicitly, her work offers some general criteria for evaluating descriptive representatives—that is, by their ability to satisfy these different functions. However, her emphasis on identifying the contingent conditions under which descriptive representation is preferable to nondescriptive representation makes the actual choice of descriptive representatives secondary, if not irrelevant.

In summary, theorists of descriptive representation refuse to specify any criteria for evaluating descriptive representatives for two good reasons. First, they see offering such criteria as violations of the autonomy of historically disadvantaged groups and/or their descriptive representatives, and second, they view such criteria as insensitive to contextual variation. For these reasons, theorists of descriptive representation avoid a tough question: Who is a preferable descriptive representative? Answering this question is not easy, because it requires privileging the interests, values, and perspectives of certain members of historically disadvantaged groups over those of other members. Answers to this question can therefore have the effect of downplaying, if not excluding, certain interests, values, and perspectives. For this reason, answers to the question of who is a preferable descriptive representative are more likely to be disputed than answers to the question, "Why have descriptive representatives?"

THE NEED FOR CRITERIA

Underlying both the autonomy and the contingency arguments is a legitimate concern about who gets to decide which criteria are best. The impulse to speak for others can be and often is paternalistic and imperialistic (Alcoff 1995). Standards for assessing political performance have often been used to disqualify historically disadvantaged groups from political participation. To articulate criteria for evaluating descriptive representatives runs the risk that those criteria can be used in unanticipated and possibly harmful ways. Some fear that articulating such criteria might also unduly influence members of historically disadvantaged groups.

Such concerns are understandable but ultimately unpersuasive. After all, to articulate such criteria is not necessarily to assume that all members of a historically disadvantaged group have some essential identity. In fact, the very real and politically relevant differences among members of historically marginalized groups point to the desperate need for a theoretical discussion of criteria. There is a difference between articulating particular policies that a descriptive representative must endorse to count as a legitimate descriptive representative and articulating general guidelines for identifying preferable descriptive representatives. For instance, theorists of group representation have agreed that institutional reforms are necessary because historically disadvantaged groups possess overlooked interests. To maintain that a descriptive representative should pay special attention to overlooked interests does not require that she possess a particular view about those interests.[10] Descriptive representatives have autonomy to the extent that she can reasonably interpret those interests in a variety of ways. However, to say that descriptive representatives can legitimately interpret their group's interests in multiple ways is not to say that anything goes. Descriptive representatives who denounce their group affiliations or who deny that they have any particular obligation to their group would fail to achieve the ends for which descriptive representation was introduced (cf. Phillips's four arguments). Descriptive representatives who claim to represent only the common good might be desirable representatives for other reasons; however, they do not satisfy Phillips's "overlooked interests" argument.

One can articulate criteria for evaluating descriptive representatives without violating the autonomy either of historically disadvantaged groups or of their descriptive representatives. To pose criteria for judging descriptive representatives is not the same as imposing those criteria on members of historically disadvantaged groups. Obviously, to impose criteria on such groups,

or on democratic citizens more generally, is wrongheaded. It is crucial according to my view that members of historically disadvantaged groups retain the ability to choose to adopt any proposed criterion.[11]

I would remind those who fear that articulating criteria for evaluating descriptive representatives might exercise an undue influence on a historically disadvantaged group that silence holds similar risks. After all, members of historically disadvantaged groups are not always the ones who select descriptive representatives. Privileged citizens are frequently in charge of selecting political appointees and nominating candidates for public office. To assume that not articulating the criteria for selecting descriptive representatives for committees or party lists is the best way to protect the autonomy of historically disadvantaged groups ignores the power that privileged groups currently hold. As Audre Lorde (1984, 41) aptly warned, "Your silence will not protect you." Silence about controversial subjects does not necessarily bring about desired outcomes.

Besides, citizens inevitably bring their general standards of representation to bear on their choice of representatives. Critically evaluating the standards for descriptive representatives can facilitate deliberations by democratic citizens, thereby "assisting, and not infringing on" the autonomy of historically disadvantaged groups.[12] Articulating criteria for assessing descriptive representatives does not make the exercise of judgment unnecessary; rather, deliberations about these criteria can refine those judgments. Theorists can offer criteria for choosing among descriptive representatives and still maintain that members of historically disadvantaged groups must determine for themselves whether a specific criterion is appropriate at any particular moment. This leads to the second argument for remaining silent: the role of contingencies in evaluations of descriptive representatives.

Context undeniably does matter. Evaluations of descriptive representatives, like arguments for a politics of presence (Phillips 1995, 46), depend on "historically specific analysis of the existing arrangements for representation." For instance, who is a preferable descriptive representative might depend on whose interests, opinions, and perspectives are currently being stigmatized and marginalized by existing political norms and institutional processes. "Because group identity is orchestrated and produced in part through political institutional processes" (Bickford 1999, 86), citizens should consider the unjust effects of those processes as relevant to assessments of preferable descriptive representatives. Which descriptive representatives are preferable might also depend on the reasons that descriptive representation is necessary, e.g., to increase the trust groups have in democratic institutions or to include overlooked interests on the policy agenda.

Espousing criteria is not the same as requiring that certain criteria be applied in all circumstances. Like

---

[10] Like representatives generally, good descriptive representatives should sometimes act as trustees and at other times act as delegates. The standards for good representation cannot be linked strictly to the policy preferences of the represented. Pitkin (1967, 166) expressed this point in the following way: "Neither 'follow their wishes' nor 'ignore their wishes' will do; the decision must depend on why they disagree ... but the standard by which he [the representative] will be judged as a representative is whether he has promoted the objective interest of those he represents. Within the framework of his basic obligation there is room for a wide variety of alternatives." My criterion for assessing preferable descriptive representatives does not assume one particular understanding of the objective interests of historically marginalized groups.

[11] A description of the conditions necessary for promoting this ability is clearly beyond the scope of this paper.

[12] I want to thank an anonymous reviewer for helping me formulate my position in this way.

REPRESENTATION

most theorists of descriptive representation, I share the suspicion of a cookie-cutter approach to evaluating descriptive representatives. It would be foolhardy to propose a set of criteria that did not consider context or that did not require individuals to use their own judgment to determine whether the criteria apply to the particular case at hand. To recognize the importance of particularities does not preclude articulating criteria for evaluation. It requires having criteria that are sensitive to those particularities.

My final argument for articulating criteria for evaluating descriptive representatives is based on my understanding of a particular role that political theory can and should play. Increasingly, the need for political theory to inform contemporary political controversies has been recognized (Isaac 1998, chap. 7). Contemporary politics is plagued by controversies about the representation of historically disadvantaged groups. Consider the controversies over the leadership of African Americans, such as Louis Farrakhan. Angela Dillard (2001, 4) notes that conservatives among women (e.g., Phyllis Schlafly) and minorities (e.g., Thomas Sowell and Richard Rodriguez) "have been dismissed as traitors, as sell-outs, as self-loathing reactionaries who are little more than dupes of powerful white, male, heterosexual conservatives." Recently, Lee Freed, a female president of the Manitoba chapter of the First Nations Accountability Coalition in Canada, accused the male tribal leadership of corruption and nepotism. Such contemporary controversies over the leadership of historically disadvantaged groups confirm that historically disadvantaged groups can possess different understandings about who should be their representatives. They also confirm the suspicion that simply having descriptive representatives is not sufficient to meet the requirements of a democratic commitment to the concerns of historically disadvantaged groups. Descriptive representation can fail to revitalize democratic institutions. It can also undermine democratic institutions if the ruling elites of historically disadvantaged groups use their institutional positions to control those groups instead of mobilizing those groups or bringing their overlooked interests onto the policy agenda (e.g., Cohen 1999). For these reasons, it is important to clarify the criteria for judging descriptive representatives. Evaluations of democratic institutions need to go beyond merely quantitative considerations—that is, the number of descriptive representatives. Evaluations of democratic institutions need to consider the extent to which preferable descriptive representatives are present. The criteria for identifying preferable descriptive representatives need to identify principled reasons for preferring some descriptive representative to others that are in line with the arguments for group representation. By failing to discuss criteria for assessing descriptive representatives, this theoretical literature ignores certain persistent debates about descriptive representation in contemporary politics. It also disregards the possible dangers and disappointments of a politics of presence to democratic politics.

THE CRITERION FOR EVALUATING DESCRIPTIVE REPRESENTATIVES

My criterion for evaluating descriptive representatives is a general one: Democratic citizens should consider the degree to which a descriptive representative has mutual relationships with dispossessed subgroups as relevant to identifying preferable descriptive representatives. Preferable descriptive representatives will have strong *mutual* relationships with *dispossessed subgroups*. This criterion is composed of two aspects. First, preferable descriptive representatives should possess a particular kind of relationship (mutual), and second, they should have this kind of relationship *with* certain subgroups of historically disadvantaged groups (dispossessed). I explicate both aspects of my criterion below.

Mutual Relationships

The importance of relationships to group identity is not a new claim. David Truman (1951, 24) maintained that "interactions, or relationships, give the group its molding and guiding power." Other theorists of group representation discuss relationships between representatives and their constituents (e.g., Williams 1998, chap. 6; Young 2000, chap. 4). However, these theorists typically examine these relationships primarily in terms of whether the constituents "trust" their representatives. Young (2000, 128–30) evaluates the *process* of representation by the extent to which the relationship between representative and constituents "avoids separation" and "renews connection." She does not address how to evaluate particular individuals engaged in the process of representation.

What is distinctive about my criterion is its specification that representatives and members of historically disadvantaged groups must *mutually* recognize each other. Mutuality requires an interactive relationship between representatives and citizens. Mutual relationships require a historically disadvantaged group to recognize its descriptive representatives in a particular way *as well as* a descriptive representative to recognize that group in a particular way. Such reciprocal recognition is necessary for descriptive representatives and their groups to coordinate consciously chosen political activities. Descriptive representatives without mutual relationships could be "representative" in the sense that their behavior responds to the policy preferences of their group, but such responsiveness is not sufficient to make the form of representation democratic. Kings could be representatives of their subjects, in this sense, if they sufficiently polled the preferences of their subjects.

Democratic relations demand effective participation on the part of citizens (Dahl 1989, 109). Democratic representation requires that citizens can access and influence political institutions. Descriptive representatives with mutual relations would improve democratic representation by enabling historically disadvantaged groups to influence the political decision-making process. In doing so, historically disadvantaged groups

190 REPRESENTATION

act in concert with their descriptive representatives. Democratic relationships are therefore ones "in which both parties are active" (Plotke 1997, 29).

In proposing this criterion, I am advocating a new approach to assessing the performance of descriptive representatives. Political scientists often evaluate descriptive representatives' performance by focusing exclusively on notions of interests as identified by policy preferences. Assessing descriptive representatives solely by the way they cast their votes can lead to the conclusion that it does not matter who represents historically disadvantaged groups (Schwarz and Shaw 1976; Swain 1993). This approach ignores other reasons for having descriptive representatives, e.g., introducing overlooked interests or building trust in the political institutions. Cathy Cohen's analysis (1999) of AIDS activism in the African-American community revealed the general failure of black elites to recognize the particular needs of certain subgroups in the African-American communities, that is, black gays and lesbians and IV drug users. Cohen showed that although black leaders often maintained a "good" voting record in terms of AIDS policies, they failed to transform the nature of the political debate in ways that address the particular interests of specific subgroups in the African-American community, e.g., needle exchange programs.

Good descriptive representatives therefore cannot be identified simply by examining voting records. Just as presidential performance is partially judged by the president's selection of staff, descriptive representatives should be judged by who does and does not interact with them. Assessments of descriptive representatives need to consider whether these representatives reach out to (or distance themselves from) historically disadvantaged groups. Preferable descriptive representatives facilitate social networks. Formal as well as informal ties provide the channels through which democratic relationships could work and thereby the means to revitalize democratic institutions. I introduce mutual relationships into discussions of descriptive representation because these discussions need to reflect the fact that what determines policy is not only what political actors do but also whom they know.

It is important to emphasize a consideration implicit in my claim that preferable descriptive representatives possess mutual relationships: The commitment to democratic representation requires that democratic citizens should not be apathetic. Preferable descriptive representatives will inspire their group to act in concert with them. Although it is possible that a descriptive representative could adequately "represent" the concerns of the apathetic insofar as the representative takes positions that reflect the interests or preferences of apathetic citizens, the descriptive representative's actions would not be democratic to the extent that apathetic citizens do not care about the activities of that representative. My criterion prefers descriptive representatives who can and do mobilize a historically disadvantaged group, encouraging the active engagement of that group. Requiring preferable descriptive representatives to have mutual relations is very demanding and therefore likely to support robust democracies.

To possess mutual relations, descriptive representatives must recognize and be recognized by members of a historically disadvantaged group in two ways. First, they must recognize each other as belonging to a historically disadvantaged group, and second, they must recognize each other as having a common understanding of the proper aims of a descriptive representative of the group. To recognize each other mutually in these two ways is to possess a mutual relationship.

Preferable descriptive representatives are those who recognize and are recognized by members of their historically disadvantaged group as being "one of us." In particular, they have a reciprocated sense of having a fate linked with that of other members of their group.[13] Michael Dawson (1994, 77) defines the notion of linked fate in reference to African Americans as "the degree to which African Americans believe that their own self-interests are linked to the interests of the race." To possess a sense of linked fate is to experience "the group interests . . . as a useful proxy for self-interest." In other words, individuals who believe that their fates are linked to a group believe that "what happens to the group as a whole affects their own lives."

The notion of linked fate reflects the fact that a person's range of choices—that is, his or her perceived opportunities and goals— is both subjective and social. Group identities are partially formed by "the political processes through which concrete notions of collective interest are shaped, . . . who participates in those processes and who is advantaged and disadvantaged by them" (Reed 1999, 45–46). Recent political theorists have also endorsed the view that the social world— what they call culture—limits the range of choices available to individuals. For example, Joseph Raz and Avishai Margalit (1994, 119) state that "familiarity with a culture determines the boundaries of the imaginable. Sharing in a culture, being part of it, determines the limits of the feasible." In this way, membership is both "something that you are 'born' into and that constitutes you as being who you are and is ascribed to you by others in a way that makes it involuntary from your point of view" (Gould 1996, 182). Thus, even individuals who object to their identities being defined largely in terms of their group membership or who are critical of the ways in which group membership can constrain their choices can still have a sense of sharing their fate with a historically disadvantaged group.

To have a sense of linked fate with a historically disadvantaged group partially entails having a substantive conception of that group that is relevantly similar to those held by other members of that group. Group membership can be based on shared visible characteristics, e.g., color of skin, or on shared experiences (Mansbridge 1999). The substantive content of group membership can vary. Some individuals can belong to more than one group and therefore experience conflicting allegiances to different groups. Members can also possess conflicting views on their group's politics. I am not denying such differences.

---

[13] For a discussion of how to measure this sense of linked fate using attitude and opinion surveys, see Dawson 1994, 77–80, 82–84.

REPRESENTATION

But preferable descriptive representatives for a given group share an understanding of the group's boundaries with that group. Descriptive representatives who possess a narrower (and more exclusive) understanding of those boundaries are unable, or at least less likely, to satisfy the arguments that justify group representation. For this reason, an African-American descriptive representative who denies that gay and lesbian blacks are members of the group (or who excludes conservatives, IV drug users, Muslims, or other religious African Americans) would be less preferable than one who includes those members in his or her understanding of the group.[14] After all, justifications for group representation tend to emphasize the extent to which descriptive representatives include overlooked interests, build trust, and foster deliberation. Descriptive representatives who overlook certain members of the group or who deem certain members "inauthentic" are less likely to fulfill these functions. Representatives who possess broader understandings of the group are more likely to overlap with the varied understandings of the represented and therefore satisfy the reasons for having an institutionalized voice.

Inclusive language also has its pitfalls (e.g., Cohen 1999; Minow 1990; Reed 1999, 17). Generalized notions of a group can be so abstract and all-encompassing that they ignore significant differences among members of the group. Hence, U.S. suffragists who claimed to speak for women were justifiably criticized for speaking from an unreflective bias of being middle-class or educated or white (Davis 1983). Abstract notions of the group can also prevent elites from being held accountable to specific people. Speaking about the "underclass," "women," or "Latinos" in general terms can create an illusory unity among members of those groups that can be used to the detriment of vulnerable members of those groups (Reed 1999, 5). For example, it is possible to diminish community support for policies aimed at helping vulnerable members of a community by portraying those policies as attacks on the community. Preferable descriptive representatives possess shared understandings of group membership that recognize salient differences of subgroups. I elaborate on my understanding of such salient differences in my discussion of dispossessed subgroups below.

To understand the importance of mutual recognition of belonging to the group for evaluating a descriptive representative, consider the following case. It is possible to imagine an African-American representative who grew up in a primarily white neighborhood, attended predominantly white private schools, has a white spouse, and has shown no demonstrable interest in the problems of other African Americans. In fact, such a representative could thrive politically by publicly distancing herself from the African-American community.[15] The point of this example is not to

question whether this woman is an "authentic" African American. I believe that she is.[16] Rather, it is to question whether such a representative could satisfy sufficiently the reasons that theorists for a politics of presence gave for increasing the number of descriptive representatives. After all, such a descriptive representative lacks the relationships necessary to satisfy these reasons. She might individually face certain obstacles and experience forms of discrimination because of her identity; however, she lacks the relationships with African Americans that could enable her to achieve mutual recognition with them. The extent to which she disavows her relationships to African Americans indicates the extent to which she is less likely to possess mutual relationships with them. African-Americans would be more likely to distrust her. She would also be less likely to advance overlooked interests of the African-American community and to mobilize that community. Who perceives that representative as "belonging" to the group and whom a representative claims to act on the behalf of are important considerations for evaluating the qualifications of descriptive representatives.

Individuals in mutual relationships not only recognize each other as belonging to the same group, but also recognize that they share an understanding of the proper aims of their representatives. To have shared aims is to possess a similar vision for the future direction of politics—one whose goal is the improvement of the social, economic, and political status of particular historically disadvantaged groups. My understanding of aims has two components: policy preferences and values.[17] A descriptive representative could disagree with members of a historically disadvantaged group about either component, yet still share aims.[18] Some

---

[14] As can be seen, descriptive representatives with mutual relations do not necessarily possess "progressive" or "liberal" policy agendas.
[15] My example bears a strong resemblance to Young's example of an Asian American who has an African-American perspective. However, my argument suggests that such an Asian American would be

---

a less preferable descriptive representative if those in the African-American community did not accept and identify him as a member of their community. Given the current divisions between racial groups, such a revised understanding of racial identity is possible, albeit unlikely. Note that Young's example is presented in a way that emphasizes its potential to be more inclusionary, while my argument suggests that relationships provide reasons for objecting to certain descriptive representatives for particular groups.
[16] To articulate reasons for preferring some descriptive representatives to others is not the same as questioning the authenticity of a descriptive representative's membership. A full discussion of the relationship between preferability and legitimacy is clearly beyond the scope of this paper. Here I purposely limit my discussion to the desirability of particular descriptive representatives, not their legitimacy. I recognize that all members of a historically disadvantaged group are in some sense legitimate descriptive representatives of that group. In other words, Reverend Jesse Jackson, Marian Wright Edelman, Shelby Steele, and Allan Keyes are all legitimate descriptive representatives for African Americans; however, who is a preferable descriptive representative for African Americans depends on who possesses strong mutual relationships with dispossessed subgroups. Such subgroups can include conservative and/or poor subgroups.
[17] For a discussion of the difference between measuring political values and policy preferences, see Stoker 2001 and Rasiniski 2001.
[18] To explicate the idea of an aim, it is necessary to differentiate an aim from what Young (2000, 134) calls the "modes of representation"—that is, three aspects of one's identity that need to be represented. Those three aspects are interests (policy preferences), opinions (values, priorities, and principles), and perspectives (starting points of conversations). While Williams (1998, 171) argues that interests and perspectives are more inextricably tied, Young stresses how these different aspects of a person's identity can conflict.

192

REPRESENTATION

Preferable Descriptive Representatives

December 2002

members might experience a descriptive representative advocating certain public policies as a litmus test for shared aims with that representative, e.g., their position on abortion or affirmative action, while others see shared aims as resulting from a particular combination of policy preferences and values. Individuals can and will have different conceptions of what is necessary for having shared aims. Nevertheless, a descriptive representative who did not share either component with a historically disadvantaged group does not share aims with that group.

In this way, my criterion recognizes that people who share similar political values can justifiably disagree about the desirability of certain public policies. It also recognizes that individuals with different political values can agree about certain public policies. Consequently, I do not always want people who agree with my political values or with my policy preferences. I do want someone who shares my aims. The notion of shared aims recognizes the importance of the interaction between policy preferences and values for selecting preferable descriptive representatives. For this reason, shared aims must be measured in degrees: Descriptive representatives share aims with a historically disadvantaged group to greater or less degrees.

This notion of aims as a kind of direction for politics interjects into discussions of group representation my belief that the actions of descriptive representatives do matter. Pitkin was wrong to draw such a firm distinction between what a representative looks like and what a representative does. My criterion for evaluating descriptive representatives offers one way to follow Phillips's recommendation to integrate a politics of presence with a politics of ideas. Descriptive representatives are preferable to the degree that their actions are perceived by members of a historically disadvantaged group as improving their linked fate. My notion of aims is meant to capture the fact that members of historically disadvantaged groups, despite having different policy preferences and values, can still share a political vision aimed at relieving the plight of their communities. Thus, the actions of descriptive representatives are not irrelevant to who should be considered a preferable descriptive representative. Preferable descriptive representatives recognize themselves, and are recognized by members of a historically disadvantaged group, as sharing the aims of that group.

The importance of shared aims is most readily apparent when one lacks a representative who shares one's aims. One is less likely to accept differences of opinions with those who have different aims than with those who share one's aims. My discussion of shared aims reflects evidence that African Americans tend to give their leaders the benefit of the doubt in the face of controversies, e.g., controversies over Louis Farrakhan. Historically disadvantaged groups are willing to "own" a representative with whom they disagree (Dawson 1994). The reason is that they possess a linked fate and shared aims with these leaders.

Both a sense of belonging to a group and shared aims are important for mutual relations, for individuals whose fates are linked can have different aims. For example, ultraorthodox Jewish women are forbidden from studying general subjects such as math and embrace their traditional role in the house. Moreover, many ultraorthodox women believe that women are incapable of making important decisions (such as voting). For some of these women, it is proper to arrange their social and political lives around the assumption that women are inferior. The presence of these ultraorthodox Jewish women in Israel affects how Israeli women (including Jewish secular or even Palestinian women) are perceived. Nonpracticing Jewish women, Palestinian women, and ultraorthodox Jewish women thus share fates in Israel, even though these different subgroups have contradictory policy preferences and values. This example demonstrates that members of historically disadvantaged groups can share fates, even though their aims differ.

Preferable descriptive representatives are those who possess mutual relationships with their constituents. But, as has been shown, this relationship consists in descriptive representatives and their historically disadvantaged groups recognizing each other as having a linked fate and sharing aims. This mutual recognition thus provides some substantive guidance both for which descriptive representative is preferable and for what a descriptive representative should be doing. In these ways, mutual relationships between a descriptive representative and a historically disadvantaged group provide that group with a stake in politics: They can influence the political agenda through acting in concert with their descriptive representatives.

Dispossessed Subgroups

I now clarify the second aspect of my criterion—what I mean by a dispossessed subgroup. Dispossessed subgroups should not be understood as those groups that literally do not possess any private property, possessions, or resources. Rather, I use the term dispossessed in a narrower way to refer to groups that are unjustly excluded from and/or stigmatized by the political process and consequently lack the political and economic resources necessary for effective representation. Often dispossessed subgroups suffer oppression not only as members of their overarching group but also as members of the subgroup. They are therefore members of historically disadvantaged groups, yet they face *further* political obstacles—what Cathy Cohen (1999, 70) describes as secondary marginalization—that is, the ways in which members of marginalized groups construct and police group identity as to regulate behavior,

---

For Young, the process of democratic representation relies on all three modes.

Young's analysis of the dynamic processes of representation, though, can divert attention from the proper standards for evaluating particular representatives. Individual representatives are less likely to satisfy all of these different modes of representation than are the processes of representation. I know of no representative who shares all of my interests, opinions, and perspectives. These modes of representation are too narrow to provide much guidance for identifying preferable descriptive representatives. For this reason, I argue that members of historically disadvantaged groups should seek descriptive representatives who share their aims.

REPRESENTATION

attitudes, and the public image of those groups. Perhaps it is in virtue of the combination of the forms of oppression that they lack the financial, time, and social resources necessary for political participation. Class, sexuality, drug use, geographic location, relationships to welfare, criminal records, and religion are all possible markers of dispossessed subgroups.

This second aspect of my criterion offers a way to return to the commitment found in the literature on group representation to those groups that *have been and continue to be* marginalized within the existing political system. A commitment to group representation entails a commitment to those whose interests have been overlooked, who have been and continue to be unjustly excluded from political participation, and whose presence could revitalize democratic institutions. Group representation therefore requires being vigilant about groups that lack a political voice. Preferable descriptive representatives would be those who seek out and establish mutual relationships with dispossessed subgroups.

To demonstrate the importance of mutual relationships with dispossessed subgroups, I focus on the ways in which class inequalities can constrain effective representation.[19] Such inequalities can undermine democratic citizens' political resources. My discussion of dispossessed subgroups is by no means limited to the experiences of poor subgroups of historically disadvantaged groups. Other subgroups that lack the political and economic resources for effective representation would also count as dispossessed. I use poor subgroups to illustrate my understanding of dispossessed subgroups for two reasons. First, this example highlights the necessity of mutual relationships for improving the substantive representation of historically disadvantaged groups. Second, this example demonstrates the interactions among different forms of oppression.

Theorists of group representation often implicitly recognize the importance of class in their arguments. Almost all proponents of group representation (e.g., Phillips 1999, 151; Williams 1998, 15–18; Young 2000, 92–99) appeal to the economic structural inequalities that certain marginalized groups face, e.g., the rates of victimization, of poverty, of housing, and of job discrimination, to justify group representation. In this way, they recognize that economic inequalities are one indicator that a group deserves a political voice.

Nevertheless, just as in previous times women and ethnic groups were considered adequately represented by the presence of white male representatives, theorists of self-representation do not adequately acknowledge problems with poor subgroups of historically disadvantaged groups being represented by economically more privileged members of their group. Some explicitly deny that class should be incorporated into political solutions for presence. For example, Phillips argues that the politics of presence should be treated as distinct from issues concerning class. Phillips offers several reasons for this distinction, e.g., the difficulty in defining class. However, Phillips (1995, 170–78) admits that these reasons for treating class separately are "insincere," stating that "when it comes down to it, the real reason for my silence on class is simply that it does not lend itself to the same kind of solutions."[20] This admission implies that considerations of class cannot be adequately incorporated into the types of institutional reforms necessary for increasing the number of descriptive representatives. Interestingly, this admission contradicts her arguments for a politics of presence. Phillips is quite explicit that a politics of presence is not a guarantee for a robust democratic politics. A democratic politics must balance the commitment to presence with another commitment: what Phillips calls "a politics of ideas." For Phillips, the politics of ideas refers to the commitment to particular opinions, preferences, and beliefs. The politics of ideas would include one's position on class issues. In contrast, a politics of presence is a commitment to the intuition that it matters who expresses those opinions, preferences, and beliefs. For Phillips, democratic practices will flourish when democratic citizens start integrating these two commitments. Phillips's claim that class should not be incorporated into a politics of presence violates her own understanding of the conditions necessary for robust democratic relations.

Others minimize the significance of socioeconomic factors by choosing examples that focus almost exclusively on only one form of oppression. Often these examples explore the ways that groups are formally excluded from political participation. For instance, Williams focuses on the structural obstacles faced by U.S. women and African Americans in their efforts to gain full political standing. She cites economic inequalities as indicators that institutional reforms are necessary, yet her proposed institutional reforms are aimed exclusively at formal political exclusions.

Williams's emphasis on formal political exclusions reflects the tendency among proponents of group representation to notice the oppressive nature of socioeconomic status without incorporating this observation into their arguments for group representation or into their proposed institutional reforms. These proponents also have not incorporated the insight that one must understand the interactions among multiple forms of oppression (e.g., Collins 1990; Higginbotham 1992; hooks 2000).[21] One cannot simply "add on" an analysis of class after advocating for increasing the

---

[19] I explicitly reject an understanding of class that is based on categories and classification schemes; rather, I am concerned with how class relations are produced and maintained through political institutions. Phillips argues that the category of class is substantively different from conceptions of race and gender. For example, one loses one's class when one becomes an elected official. For an alternative understanding of class, see Acker (2000, 197), who defines class as "social relations constructed through active practices, not as categories or classifications of people according to socioeconomic characteristics or occupational status."

[20] For her full discussion of class, see Phillips 1995, chap. 7.

[21] The failure of the literature on descriptive representation to incorporate this insight is readily apparent in its proposed institutional reforms, e.g., party quotas. For instance, these reforms do not specify whether Asian Americans should count as descriptive representatives for African Americans and therefore should count toward an African-American party quota, as Young's example implies. Nor do they provide any way for determining whether African-American

194 REPRESENTATION

representation of women and people of color. Deborah King illustrates the inability to add on class by noting that education can increase the income potential among different groups disproportionately. King (1993, 223–24) claims that the economic benefits "of a post-secondary education, a college degree or higher, are greater for black females than for white females while among those with less than a college degree, black females earn less than white females." In this way, King reveals that focusing too much on only one form of oppression can mask the obstacles faced by certain segments of historically disadvantaged groups.

Williams's analysis of self-representation would have benefited from an example in which the dynamic of multiple forms of oppression was considered. For instance, Margaret Wilkerson and Jewell Gresham (1993, 297) have argued that the "feminization of poverty" cannot be understood as distinct from the "racialization of poverty." Wilkerson and Gresham claim that the focus on the economic inequalities faced by women "negates the role played by racial barriers to black employment, particularly among males." Theorists of group representation tend to give examples in which the dynamics of race, class, and gender are prominent only a cursory treatment, if any treatment at all. They also tend to downplay how political norms and practices within the democratic institutions, e.g., recruitment practices, can marginalize certain subgroups. Consequently, their understandings of group representation ignore that inclusion in politics can promote instrumental political bargaining at the expense of transformative politics (Dryzek 1996; Reed 1999).

More specifically, theorists of group representation do not adequately address the particular barriers to effective representation experienced by poor subgroups of historically disadvantaged groups. For instance, given the practice of disenfranchising convicts, the high incarceration rates of poor blacks and Latinos cut off traditional avenues for seeking political representation:

> Every state but three imposes some type of ban on voting by those convicted of serious crimes. Most states bar voting by felons while in prison, but restore the right to vote once the individual has served his sentence or completed parole. In 14 states, a felony conviction can mean a permanent ban on voting. (Braceras 2000)

The current practice of disenfranchising convicts cast doubts on whether certain subgroups of historically disadvantaged groups should rely primarily on electoral procedures for achieving substantive representation. Theorists of group representation need to address the obstacles that are produced through the interactions among different forms of oppression and that unjustly constrain certain subgroups.

Theorists who emphasize electoral reforms that increase the number of descriptive representatives also

---

women should "count" under the number of all women or have their own quota in the party lists. The failure to address these issues in this literature reveals the failure to incorporate an interactive understanding of race, class, and gender.

tend to ignore the kinds of resources necessary for poor subgroups to advance their political agendas. Traditional means for getting policy preferences onto the political agenda—studies, public relations campaigns, lobbying efforts—advantage citizens who are financially better off and resource-rich. Being able to stay informed about political issues, let alone to participate in politics, requires time and economic resources. Elected officials increasingly spend their time fund-raising. Citizens with economic resources can buy access, but those without economic resources tend to have relatively less access. Consequently, those with economic resources do not necessarily need as much of an institutionalized voice as those who lack those resources.

Typically, citizens who lack economic resources need to register their preferences through non-institutional and confrontational tactics. Frances Fox Piven and Richard Cloward (1979, 3) have argued that "protest tactics which defied political norms were not simply the recourse of troublemakers and fools. For the poor, they were the only recourse." According to Piven and Cloward, poor citizens need alternative tactics, such as protests, for effective representation. These tactics depend on numbers and relationships. Piven and Cloward's position reflects the common belief in the literature on social movements that more disruptive tactics are more likely to be successful (e.g., McAdam 1983; Tarrow 1994; Tilly, Tilly, and Tilly 1975). The social networks surrounding descriptive representatives are therefore relevant to their preferability. A descriptive representative who possesses mutual relationships to poor subgroups of historically disadvantaged groups is more likely to have the political resources necessary for advancing those subgroups' interests. Such descriptive representatives also hold the promise of expanding the boundaries of political participation.

One should not assume that class "perspectives" are necessarily better represented if ethnicity, race, and gender are better represented in legislatures. After all, research has documented the economic disparities within various racial groups (e.g., Dawson 1994, chap. 2; Hochschild 1995; Wilson 1980). Such disparities are increasing. Although they continue as a group to be economically and socially worse off than whites, African Americans are increasingly economically divided in ways that affect housing, jobs, death rates, and the likelihood of being a victim of crime. Such disparities among African Americans have led some to conclude that black identity will increasingly be tied to considerations of class as opposed to race—what Kilson (1983) called "status deracialization" and Wilson (1980) titled "the declining significance of race."

For Dawson (1994), the economic polarization of blacks does not necessarily lead to political polarization. Economic polarization, though, does affect the extent to which poor blacks participate politically. After examining falling rates of political participation among poor blacks, Hochschild (1995, 50) concluded that "the worst-off in general are losing political influence, and the worst-off blacks in particular are losing most." This observation is especially troublesome when considered in conjunction with Cohen's (1997)

REPRESENTATION

American Political Science Review

claim that historically disadvantaged groups are policed internally. If Cohen is correct, then the choice of descriptive representatives is crucial for understanding why some dispossessed subgroups lack substantive representation. This choice is also crucial for the proposed institutional reforms, e.g., party list quotas and proportional representation, to be able to revitalize democratic practices.

Of course, low economic status is not the only reason that citizens do not participate in politics. Cohen (1999, 346) revealed that black gays and lesbians who were HIV-positive did not participate in AIDS protests from fear of being seen by other members of the black community. Such fears were particularly acute for members who relied on that community for support while sick. As Cohen's example demonstrates, other political norms and practices besides the formal exclusion of historically disadvantaged groups can exclude certain subgroups of historically disadvantaged groups. For this reason, preferable descriptive representatives can have mutual relationships with other types of dispossessed subgroups.

My criterion for evaluating descriptive representation should not be interpreted as arguing that the self-representation of women or of African Americans or other minorities is secondary to the representation of the poor. Such an argument would merely mimic the common claim that identity politics is divisive while class is more unifying (Gitlin 1995). Nor am I repeating claims that class is more politically salient than race (e.g., Loury 1987; Murray 1984; Sowell 1984). Instead, I maintain that who is a preferable descriptive representative depends on how different forms of oppression intersect, for example, how race can work in conjunction with class is relevant to determining who is a preferable descriptive representative. Democratic citizens need to evaluate descriptive representatives in ways that attend to how political institutions marginalize certain groups. Young was right that institutional reforms aimed at increasing the number of descriptive representatives can entrench certain interests, e.g., by privileging heterosexual Latinos at the expense of gay and lesbian Latinos. Moreover, evaluations of descriptive representatives are particularly messy when segments of a historically disadvantaged group reject a descriptive representative. For Young, the diversity within historically disadvantaged groups can be so great that schemes of group representation will necessarily result in the suppression of difference.

However, recognition of the diversity within historically disadvantaged groups does not change the fact that some groups are chronically underrepresented. In other words, it does not change the fact that some groups need institutional reforms to enhance their substantive representation. For the institutional reforms to work successfully, democratic citizens need to select descriptive representatives in ways that are sensitive to how institutional norms and practices unjustly marginalize dispossessed subgroups. My criterion offers one way to take into account the dynamic among different forms of oppression: Who is a preferable descriptive representative depends partially on

whose interests, opinions, and perspectives are being excluded. Recall that a descriptive representative's shared aims and sense of belonging to a group provide some substantive guidance for what that representative should be doing. In this way, my criterion depends on context. Those selecting descriptive representatives (for appointments, committees, or public office) need to attend to the mutual relationships that descriptive representatives possess with dispossessed subgroups. They should not assume that "just any woman will do" or that "just any black will do." Institutional reforms aimed at increasing the number of descriptive representatives are more likely to revitalize democratic institutions if citizens assess descriptive representatives using my criterion.

For this reason, I submit that when one has a choice between two descriptive representatives, one who has strong mutual relationships to dispossessed subgroups and another who does not, one should (*ceteris paribus*) prefer the former. I have so far avoided the question of what to do when choosing among descriptive representatives who possess mutual relationships to different dispossessed subgroups. Such moments do not have generalizable or easy answers. In such circumstances, citizens face tough choices that require exercising their own political judgment. To recognize that the dispossessed too can have diverse interests is to acknowledge that my criterion might not settle the question of who is a preferable descriptive representative. However, the refusal to examine the criteria being used for selecting descriptive representatives can reinforce the norms and practices that unjustly exclude dispossessed subgroups. Public deliberations about the proper criteria could therefore help refine those decisions and prevent such exclusions.

If historically disadvantaged groups do possess such deep divisions that they must consistently choose among interests, opinions, and perspectives of competing dispossessed subgroups, then those groups are less likely to be legitimately represented by only one representative. In other words, if certain groups possess intractable divisions, e.g., between liberal and conservative African Americans or between heterosexual and gay and lesbian Latinos, then such groups would need more than one descriptive representative. This observation affirms Young's conclusions (1999) about the need to pluralize group representation. The presence of multiple dispossessed subgroups indicates the need for more descriptive representation, not less. Unfortunately, there is often a limit to how many descriptive representatives a given group can have.[22] Such limits require principled criteria for selecting descriptive representatives. As we have seen, the refusal to articulate any criteria for preferring some descriptive representatives to others has led some theorists, such as Young, to weaken their commitment to the position that historically disadvantaged groups should be represented by

---

[22] This argument could lead to the proliferation of descriptive representatives. For a helpful discussion on how to identify historically disadvantaged groups, and thereby subgroups, that deserve group representation, see Williams 1998, 15–18.

members of their group. As I have also pointed out, this refusal could also prevent the proposed institutional reforms from revitalizing democratic institutions: Some descriptive representatives may perpetuate or even aggravate the marginalization of historically disadvantaged groups.

Proponents of group representation are likely to agree that it is important to attend to the relationships between descriptive representatives and dispossessed subgroups. In fact, my criterion arises from the same normative commitments that justify group representation. According to this logic, the extent to which a politics of presence can include those who have been systemically excluded from political life is also the extent to which a politics of presence can bolster democratic participation and the legitimacy of democratic institutions.

However, one needs to understand that democratic representation excludes as well as it includes. The act of excluding is not in itself objectionable on democratic grounds. After all, representative institutions require selecting some representatives at the expense of others. I introduce my criterion in an effort to provide some guidance for preferring certain descriptive representatives to others. I hope that others will expand on my criterion in ways that are sensitive to the reasons for supporting group representation and to data on the political marginalization of different groups. Introducing a criterion such as mine into existing discussions of group representation offers a principled way to balance a commitment to the diversity within historically disadvantaged groups with a commitment to group representation.

REFERENCES

Acker, Joan. 2000. "Revisiting Class: Thinking from Gender, Race, and Organizations." *Social Politics* (Summer): 192–213.

Alcoff, Linda. 1995. "The Problem of Speaking for Others." In *Who Can Speak*, ed. Judith Roof and Robyn Wiegman. Chicago: University of Illinois Press, 97–119.

Bickford, Susan. 1999. "Reconfiguring Pluralism: Identity and Institutions in the Inegalitarian Polity." *American Journal of Political Science* 43 (January): 86–108.

Braceras, Jennifer. 2000. "Massachusetts Shouldn't Let Convicts Vote." *The Boston Globe* (October 5): A27.

Cameron, Charles, David Epstein, and Sharyn O'Halloran. 1996. "Do Majority-Minority Districts Maximize Substantive Black Representation in Congress?" *American Political Science Review* 90 (December): 794–812.

Cohen, Cathy. 1997. "Straight Gay Politics: The Limits of an Ethnic Model of Inclusion." *Nomos XXXIX: Ethnicity and Group Rights*, ed. Ian Shapiro and Will Kymlicka. New York: New York University.

Cohen, Cathy. 1999. *The Boundaries of Blackness: AIDS and the Breakdown of Black Politics.* Chicago: University of Chicago.

Collins, Patricia. 1990. *Black Feminist Thought: Knowledge, Consciousness, and the Politics of Empowerment.* Boston: Unwin Hyman.

Dahl, Robert A. 1989. *Democracy and Its Critics.* New Haven, CT: Yale University.

Davis, Angela Y. 1983. *Women, Race & Class.* New York: Vintage Books.

Dawson, Michael C. 1994. *Behind the Mule: Race and Class in African-American Politics.* Princeton, NJ: Princeton University.

Dillard, Angela. 2001. *Guess Who's Coming to Dinner Now? Multicultural Conservatism in America.* New York: New York University.

Dryzek, John. 1996. "Political Inclusion and the Dynamics of Democratization." *American Political Science Review* 90 (September): 475–87.

Gitlin, Todd. 1995. *Twilight of Common Dreams.* New York: Metropolitan Books.

Gould, Carol. 1996. "Diversity and Democracy: Representing Differences." In *Democracy and Difference: Contesting the Boundaries of the Political*, ed. Seyla Benhabib. Princeton, NJ: Princeton University, 171–86.

Guinier, Lani. 1994. *The Tyranny of the Majority: Fundamental Fairness in Representative Democracy.* New York: Free Press.

Higginbotham, Evelyn. 1992. "African American Women's History and the Metalanguage of Race." *Signs* 17: 251–74.

Hochschild, Jennifer. 1995. *Facing Up to the American Dream: Race, Class, and the Soul of the Nation.* Princeton, NJ: Princeton University.

Hooks, Bell. 2000. *Feminist Theory: From Margin to Center.* Cambridge, MA: South End.

Isaac, Jeff. 1998. *Democracy in Dark Times.* Ithaca, NJ: Cornell University.

Jones, Kathleen. 1993. *Compassionate Authority: Democracy and the Representation of Women.* New York: Routledge.

Kilson, Martin. 1983. "The Black Bourgeoisie Revisited." *Dissent* (Winter): 85–96.

King, Deborah. 1993. "Multiple Jeopardy: The Context of a Black Feminist Ideology." In *Feminist Frameworks.* 3rd ed. Boston: McGraw–Hill, 220–36.

Lorde, Audre. 1984. *Sister Outsider.* Trumansburg, NY: Crossing Press.

Loury, Glenn. 1987. "Who Speaks for Black Americans?" *Commentary* 83 (January): 34–38.

Mansbridge, Jane. 1999. "Should Blacks Represent Blacks and Women Represent Women? A Contingent 'Yes.'" *Journal of Politics* 61 (August): 628–57.

McAdam, Doug. 1983. "Tactical Innovation and the Pace of Insurgency." *American Sociological Review* 48: 735–54.

Minow, Martha. 1990. *Making All the Difference.* Ithaca, NY: Cornell University.

Murray, Charles. 1984. *Losing Ground: American Social Policy, 1950–1980.* New York: Basic Books.

Paolino, Phillip. 1995. "Group-Salient Issues and Group Representation: Support for Women Candidates in the 1992 Senate Elections." *American Journal of Political Science* 39 (May): 294–313.

Phillips, Anne. 1995. *Politics of Presence.* New York: Clarendon.

Phillips, Anne. 1998. "Democracy and Representation: Or, Why Should It Matter Who Our Representatives Are?" In *Feminism and Politics.* Oxford: Oxford University, 224–40.

Pitkin, Hanna Fenichel. 1967. *The Concept of Representation.* Berkeley: University of California.

Piven, Francis Fox, and Richard Cloward. 1979. *Poor People's Movements: Why They Succeed, How They Fail.* New York: Vintage.

Plotke, David. 1997. "Representation is Democracy." *Constellations* 4 (November 1): 19–34.

Rasiniski, Kenneth. "Commentary: The Study of Values." In *Citizens and Politics: Perspectives from Political Psychology*, ed. James Kuklinski. New York: Cambridge University.

Rawls, John. 1971. *Theory of Justice.* Cambridge, MA: Belknap Press of Harvard University.

Raz, Joseph, and Avishai Margalit. 1994. "National Self-Determination." In *Ethics in the Public Domain: Essays in the Morality of Law and Politics*, ed. Joseph Raz. New York: Oxford University.

Reed, Aldoph. 1999. *Stirrings of the Jug.* Minneapolis: University of Minnesota.

Sapiro, Virginia. 1981. "When Are Interests Interesting?" *American Political Science Review* 75 (September): 701–21.

Schwarz, John E., and L. Earl Shaw. 1976. *The United States Congress in Comparative Perspective.* New York: Holt, Rinehart and Winston.

Sowell, Thomas. 1984. *Civil Rights: Rhetoric or Reality?* New York: Quill.

REPRESENTATION

Stasiulis, Daiva. 1993. "Authentic Voice: Anti-Racist Politics in Canadian Feminist Publishing and Literary Production." In *Feminism and the Politics of Difference*, ed. S. Gunew and Anne Yeatman. Sydney: Westview.

Stoker, Laura. 2001. "Political Value Judgments." In *Citizens and Politics: Perspectives from Political Psychology*, ed. James Kuklinski. New York: Cambridge University.

Swain, Carol M. 1993. *Black Faces, Black Interests: The Representation of African Americans in Congress.* Cambridge, MA: Harvard University.

Tarrow, Sidney. 1994. *Power in Movement.* Cambridge: Cambridge University.

Thomas, Sue. 1991. "The Impact of Women on State Legislative Policies." *Journal of Politics* 53 (November): 958–76.

Tilly, Charles, Louise Tilly, and Richard Tilly. 1975. *The Rebellious Century, 1830–1930.* Cambridge, MA: Harvard University.

Truman, David. 1951. *The Governmental Process.* New York: Knopf.

Wilkerson, Margaret, and Jewell Gresham. 1993. "The Racialization of Poverty" In *Feminist Frameworks.* 3rd ed. Boston: McGraw–Hill.

Williams, Melissa. 1998. *Voice, Trust, and Memory: Marginalized Groups and the Failings of Liberal Representation.* Princeton, NJ: Princeton University.

Wilson, William Julius. 1980. *The Declining Significance of Race: Blacks and Changing American Institutions.* 2nd ed. Chicago: University of Chicago.

Young, Iris Marion. 1990. *Justice and the Politics of Difference.* Princeton, NJ: Princeton University.

Young, Iris Marion. 1997. "Deferring Group Representation" In *Nomos XXXIX: Ethnicity and Group Rights*, ed. Ian Shapiro and Will Kymlicka. New York: New York University.

Young, Iris Marion. 2000. *Inclusion and Democracy.* Oxford: Oxford University.

9

Democracy and Representation: Or, Why Should it Matter Who our Representatives Are?

Anne Phillips

Though the overall statistics on women in politics continue to tell their dreary tale of under-representation, this under-representation is now widely regarded as a problem, and a significant number of political parties have adopted measures to raise the proportion of women elected. That the issue is even discussed marks a significant change. Even more remarkable is that growing support for a variety of *enabling* devices (day-schools, for example, to encourage potential women candidates) now combines with some minority backing for measures that *guarantee* parity between women and men. Parties in the Nordic countries took the lead in this, introducing gender quotas for the selection of parliamentary candidates from the mid-1970s onwards, but a quick survey across Europe throws up a number of parallel developments. Positive action to increase the proportion of women elected is now on the political agenda. It has become one of the issues on which politicians disagree.

In some ways, indeed, this is an area where those engaged in the practice of politics have edged ahead of those engaged in its theory. Gatherings of party politicians are significantly more likely to admit the problem of women's under-representation than gatherings of political scientists, for while the former remain deeply divided over the particular measures they will support, most can manage at least a lukewarm expression of 'regret' that so few women are elected. The pressures of party competition weigh heavily on their shoulders. In an era of increased voter volatility, they cannot afford to disparage issues that competitors might turn to electoral advantage. Hence the cumulative effect noted in Norwegian politics, where the Socialist Left Party first adopted gender quotas in the 1970s; this was followed in the 1980s by similar initiatives from the Labour and Centre

First published in *Schweizerisches Jahrbuch für Politische Wissenschaften* (1994), 63–76. Reprinted by permission of Editions Paul Haupt Berne. An expanded version of this argument is in *The Politics of Presence* (Oxford University Press, 1995).

DEMOCRACY AND REPRESENTATION

Parties; and was accompanied by substantial increases in the number of women selected by the Conservative Party as well (Skjeie 1991). Hence the impact of the German Green Party, which decided to alternate women and men on its list for the 1986 election; the threat of this small—but at the time, rapidly growing—party contributed to the Christian Democrats' adoption of a voluntary quota, and the Social Democrat's conversion to a formal one (Chapman 1993: ch. 9). Hence the otherwise surprising consensus that has emerged among Britain's major political parties—at central office level if not yet in local constituencies—in favour of selecting a higher proportion of women candidates (Lovenduski and Norris 1989). None of this would have happened without vigorous campaigning inside the political parties, but the campaigns have proved particularly effective where parties were already worried about their electoral appeal.

This pragmatically driven conversion contrasts with a more tough-minded resistance inside the political science community, where arguments range from a supposed lack of evidence that sex affects policy decisions, to a distaste with what is implied in saying that it should. Women's under-representation in politics is in one sense just empirical fact: they are not present in elected assemblies in the same proportions as they are present in the electorate. But the characteristics of those elected may diverge in any number of ways from the characteristics of those who elect them, and this is not always seen as a matter of democratic consequence. In a much cited article on representation, A. Phillips Griffiths (1960: 190) argued that some divergences are regarded as positively beneficial. We do not normally consider the interests of lunatics as best represented by people who are mad, and 'while we might well wish to complain that there are not enough representative members of the working class among Parliamentary representatives, we would not want to complain that the large class of stupid or maleficent people have too few representatives in Parliament: quite the contrary'. Feminists may find the implied parallels unconvincing, especially when we recall the many decades in which women were classified with children and the insane as ineligible for the right to a vote; but the general point remains. Establishing an empirical under-representation of certain categories of people does not in itself add up to a normative case for their equal or proportionate presence. It may alert us to overt forms of discrimination that are keeping certain people out, but does not yet provide the basis for radical change.

The contemporary version of Phillips Griffiths' argument takes

225

ANNE PHILLIPS

the form of the notorious 'slippery slope': if measures are proposed for achieving a fair 'representation' of the proportion of women in the electorate, why not also of homosexuals, of pensioners, of the unemployed, of people with blue eyes and red hair? Though usually raised with deliberately facetious intent, such questions combine with more serious work on representation which has tended to dismiss ideals of 'descriptive' or 'mirror' representation as a nostalgic yearning for direct democracy. In her influential work on *The Concept of Representation*, Hanna Pitkin (1967: 86) suggests that the metaphors of descriptive representation are most commonly found among those who regard representative democracy as a poor second-best, and who therefore look to more 'accurate' or pictorial representation of the electorate as a way of approximating the old citizen assemblies. Yet representatives, she argues, are supposed to act—what would be the point of a system of representation that involved no responsibility for delivering policy results?—and too much emphasis on who is present may divert us from the more urgent questions of what the representatives actually do. 'Think of the legislature as a pictorial representation or a representative sample of the nation, and you will almost certainly concentrate on its composition rather than its activities' (1967: 226). In Pitkin's preferred version, it is the activities rather than the characteristics that matter, and what happens after the action rather than before it that counts. Representing 'means acting in the interests of the represented, in a manner responsive to them' (1967: 209). Fair representation cannot be guaranteed in advance; it is achieved in more continuous process, which depends on a (somewhat unspecified) level of responsiveness to the electorate. The representatives may and almost certainly will differ from those they act for, not only in their social and sexual characteristics, but also in their understanding of where the 'true' interests of their constituents lie. What renders this representative is the requirement for responsiveness. 'There need not be a constant activity of responding, but there must be a constant condition of responsive*ness*, of potential readiness to respond' (1967: 233).

Radicals may challenge this resolution as allowing too much independence of judgement and action to the representatives, but the direction their criticisms take also lends little support to arguments for gender parity. The most radical among them will scorn what they see as a reformist preoccupation with the composition of political élites—and they may express some dismay that a once obsessively democratic women's movement could retreat to such

DEMOCRACY AND REPRESENTATION

limited ambitions. Others will give more serious consideration to reforms that increase the representative nature of existing national assemblies, but they will prefer mechanisms of accountability that minimize the significance of the individuals elected. The shift from direct to representative democracy has shifted the emphasis from *who* the politicians are to *what* (policies, preferences, ideas) they represent, and in doing so, has made accountability to the electorate the pre-eminent concern. We may no longer have much hope of sharing in the activities of government, but we can at least demand that our politicians do what they promised to do. The quality of representation is then thought to depend on tighter mechanisms of accountability that bind politicians more closely to the opinions they profess to represent. Where such processes are successful, they reduce the discretion and autonomy of individual representatives; in the process, they seem to minimize the importance of whether these individuals are women or men.

Consider, in this context, the guidelines that were introduced by the US Democrats in the early 1970s, to make their National Convention (which carries the crucial responsibility of deciding on the presidential candidate) more representative of the party rank and file. Dismay at the seemingly undemocratic nature of the 1968 Convention prompted the formation of a Commission on Party Structure and Delegate Selection, which recommended more extensive participation by party members in the selection of delegates, as well as quota guidelines to increase the proportion of delegates who were female, black, and young. As a result of this, the composition of the 1972 Convention was markedly more 'descriptive' of Party members than previous ones had been: 40 per cent of the delegates were women, 15 per cent were black, and 21 per cent were aged between 18 and 30. But the reforms pointed in potentially contradictory directions, for they simultaneously sought to increase rank and file participation in the selection of delegates, to bind delegates more tightly to the preferences of this rank and file, and to ensure a more descriptive representation according to age, gender, and race. As Austin Ranney (1982: 196)—one of the members of the Commission—later noted, the success of the first two initiatives undermined the importance of the third. By 1980, the overwhelming majority of delegates were being chosen in party primaries which bound them to cast their votes for one particular candidate; they became in consequence mere ciphers, who were there to register preferences already expressed. 'If that is the case,' Ranney argues, 'then it really doesn't matter very much who the delegates are.' The

ANNE PHILLIPS

more radical the emphasis on accountability, the less significance attaches to who does the work of representation.

Those engaged in campaigns for gender quotas have worked with some success on the electoral sensitivities of party politicians, but have made less headway among the tough-minded theorists of representation. My concern here is to address the latter, and to create maximum difficulties for myself I will focus on the stronger claim of gender parity, rather than the more modest claim for some more women elected.[1] This reflects what may be a naïve confidence on my part: that no one who seriously considers the matter could regard the current balance between the sexes as a fair process of representation. At the lowest points of women's under-representation (it was only in 1987 for example, that the British House of Commons lifted itself above the 5 per cent mark), one need only reverse the position of the sexes to demonstrate the democratic deficit. What would men think of a system of political representation in which they were outnumbered nineteen to one? At such gross levels of gender imbalance, rhetorical devices are all that we need—one would have to be a pretty determined patriarch to defend this as an appropriate state of affairs. But recent initiatives have raised the stakes considerably higher, insisting on positive action as a condition for effective change, and aiming at fifty/fifty parity, or a 40 per cent minimum for either sex. What are the arguments for this more radical position, and how do they engage with current conventions of accountability and representation?

Arguments for raising the proportion of women elected fall broadly into four groups. There are those that dwell on the role model successful women politicians offer; those that appeal to principles of justice between the sexes; those that identify particular interests of women that would be otherwise overlooked; and those that point towards a revitalized democracy that bridges the gap between representation and participation. The least interesting of these, from my point of view, is the role model. When more women candidates are elected, their example is said to raise women's self-esteem, encourage others to follow in their footsteps, and dislodge deep-rooted assumptions on what is appropriate to women and men. I leave this to one side, for I see it as an argument that has no particular purchase on politics *per se*. Positive role models are certainly beneficial, but I want to address arguments that engage more directly with issues of democracy and representation.

One final preamble. Though I deal here only with general issues of justification, there is a second order question, which is how legit-

DEMOCRACY AND REPRESENTATION

imate objectives can be best achieved. The emphasis on quota mechanisms and other such guarantees has aroused strong resistance even among those who claim to share the ultimate goal of women's equality in politics, and while some of this can be discounted as intellectual or political dishonesty, much of it relates to pragmatic judgements of what is possible in any particular context. The potential backlash against women is one consideration here, as are the difficulties some political parties claim to experience in finding enough women candidates. Some of the resistance depends on more general arguments against positive action; some of it reflects still unresolved tensions between gender and class; some relates to a familiar problem in political argument, which is that mechanisms proposed for achieving one desired goal can conflict with other desirable ends. Considerations of space prevent me dealing with this second order question, and I will merely note that there *are* pragmatic judgements to be made, which do not flow simply from the conclusions on general objectives. But if gender parity can be shown to matter, and existing structures can be shown to discourage it, this constitutes a case for positive action.

I. THE CASE FOR GENDER PARITY: THE JUSTICE ARGUMENT

One of the most powerful arguments for gender parity is simply in terms of justice: that it is patently and grotesquely unfair for men to monopolize representation. If there were no obstacles operating to keep certain groups of people out of political life, then we would expect positions of political influence to be randomly distributed between both sexes and across all the ethnic groups that make up the society. There might be some minor and innocent deviations, but any more distorted distribution of political office is evidence of intentional or structural discrimination (Phillips 1991). In such contexts (that is, most contexts!) women are being denied rights and opportunities that are currently available to men. There is a *prima facie* case for action.

There are three things to be said about this argument. One is that it relies on a strong position on the current sexual division of labour as inequitable and 'unnatural'. Consider the parallel under-representation of the very young and very old in politics. Most people will accept this as part of a normal and natural life-cycle, in

ANNE PHILLIPS

which the young have no time for conventional politics, and the old have already contributed their share; and since each in principle has a chance in the middle years of life, this under-representation does not strike us as particularly unfair. The consequent 'exclusion' of certain views or experiences may be said to pose a problem. But however much people worry about this, they rarely argue for proportionate representation for the over-70s and the under-25s.[2] The situation of women looks more obviously unfair, in that women will be under-represented throughout their entire lives, but anyone wedded to the current division of labour can treat it as a parallel case. A woman's life-cycle typically includes a lengthy period of caring for children, and another lengthy period of caring for parents as they grow old. It is hardly surprising, then, that fewer women come forward as candidates, or that so few women are elected. Here, too, there may be an under-representation of particular experiences and concerns, but since this arises quite 'naturally' from particular life-cycles it is not at odds with equality or justice.

I do not find the parallel convincing, but my reasons lie in a feminist analysis of the sexual division of labour as 'unnatural' and unjust. The general argument from equal rights or opportunities only translates into a specific case for gender parity in politics when it is combined with some such analysis; failing this, it engages merely with the more overt forms of discrimination that exclude women from political office, and cannot deliver any stronger conclusion. Justice requires us to eliminate discrimination (this is already implied in the notion of justice), but the argument for women's *equal* representation in politics depends on that further ingredient which establishes structural discrimination. Feminists will have no difficulty adding this. This first point then helps clarify what is involved in moving from a description of women's under-representation to an analysis of its injustice.

The second and third points are more intrinsically problematic, and relate to the status of representation as a political act. If we treat the under-representation of women in politics as akin to their under-representation in management or the professions, we seem to treat being a politician as on a continuum with all those other careers that should be opened up equally to women. In each case, there is disturbing evidence of sexual inequality; in each case, there should be positive action for change. The argument appeals to our sense of justice, but it does so at the expense of an equally strong feeling that being a politician is not just another kind of job. 'Career politician' is still—and rightly—a term of abuse; however accurately

DEMOCRACY AND REPRESENTATION

it may describe people's activities in politics, it does not capture our political ideals. If political office *has* been reduced to yet another favourable and privileged position, then there is a clear argument from justice for making such office equally available to women. Most democrats, however, will want to resist pressures to regard political office in this way. So while men have no 'right' to monopolize political office, there is something rather unsatisfying in basing women's claim to political equality on an equal right to an interesting job.

An alternative and more promising formulation considers the under-representation of women in elected assemblies as analogous to their under-representation in the membership of political parties or the attendance at political meetings, and thus treats the equal right to be an elected representative as part of an equal right to political participation. This provides a more theoretically satisfying foundation, for equality in participation is one of the criteria by which democracies are judged, and the systematic under-participation of particular social groups is normally regarded as a political problem (Verba, Nie, and Kim 1978; Parry, Moyser, and Day 1992). This is not to say that everyone must be equally enthralled by the political process: the interest in politics is unevenly distributed, as is the interest in sport or in jazz. But when the distribution coincides too neatly with divisions by class or gender or ethnicity, political participation is by definition unequal and political influence as a consequence skewed. The principle of a rough equality between various social groups is already implicit in our idea of participation, and too marked a deviation from this is already regarded as a political failing. Once gender is admitted as an additional and relevant imbalance, it is easy enough to argue for equal participation between women and men.

As applied to representation, however, the argument seems to assert what has still to be established: that representation is just another aspect of participation, to be judged by the same criteria. Yet many theorists of democracy proceed from just the opposite direction, and they have based much of their critique of direct or participatory democracy on precisely what differentiates representation from participation. Participation implies activity, and yet activity is always a minority affair. By setting the requirements for participation impossibly high, theorists of participatory democracy are said to promote a politics that becomes 'unrepresentative' and unequal, for while most citizens can manage an occasional foray into the polling booth, few are willing or able to take on more

ANNE PHILLIPS

continuous engagement, and the power then slips into the hands of those who most love politics. Representative democracy claims to solve this conundrum by removing the requirement for physical presence. As long as there is a minimal level of equality in the act of voting, then the representation can be said to be equal; we do not have to commit ourselves additionally to the hard labour of the political life.

Equality of presence—a rough approximation to the social groups that make up the society—is already implicit in the notion of participation. But it is not so obviously implicit in the notion of representation, which was, if anything, dreamt up to get round this bothersome condition. The two are, of course, related, for a society that provided genuinely equal access to participation in meetings and pressure groups and parties would almost certainly produce the same kind of equality among the people elected. In principle, however, they are separate, for in distancing itself from participating democracy, representative democracy has distanced itself from physical presence as the measure of political equality. Representative democracy claims, for example, to represent the competing interests of capital and labour by giving each of us an equal right to vote, and this is said to encourage a variety of parties to emerge that will speak to our different concerns. But representative democracy makes no claims about achieving a proportionate representation of working class people inside the legislative assemblies: workers, should be equally represented, but not necessarily by workers themselves. So while we can readily appeal to existing understandings of democracy as the basis for women's equal *participation*, the case for gender parity among elected representatives moves onto more unchartered ground.

What we can perhaps do is turn the argument around, and ask by what 'natural' superiority of talent or experience men could claim a right to dominate assemblies? The burden of proof then shifts to the men, who would have to establish either some genetic distinction which makes them better at understanding problems and taking decisions, or some more socially derived advantage which enhances their political skills. Neither of these looks particularly persuasive: the first has never been successfully established; and the second is no justification if it depends on structures of discrimination. There is no argument from justice that can defend the current state of affairs; and in this more negative sense, there *is* an argument from justice for parity between women and men. But there is still a troubling sense in which the argument overlooks what is peculiar to represen-

232

DEMOCRACY AND REPRESENTATION

tation as a political act. When democracy has become largely a matter of representing particular policies or programmes or ideas, this leaves a question-mark over why the sex of the representatives should matter.

II. THE CASE FOR GENDER PARITY: WOMEN'S INTERESTS

The second way of arguing for gender parity is in terms of the interests that would be otherwise discounted: this is an argument from political realism. In the heterogeneous societies contained by the modern nation state, there is no transparently obvious 'public interest', but rather a multiplicity of different and potentially conflicting interests which must be acknowledged and held in check. Our political representatives are only human, and as such they cannot pretend to any greater generosity of spirit than those who elected them to office. There may be altruists among them, but it would be unwise to rely on this in framing our constitutional arrangements. Failing Plato's solution to the intrusion of private interest (a class of Guardians with no property or family of their own) we must look to other ways of limiting tyrannical tendencies, and most of these will involve giving all interests their legitimate voice.

This, in essence, was James Mill's case for representative government and an extended franchise, though he notoriously combined this with the argument that women could 'be struck off without inconvenience' from the list of potential claimants, because they had no interests not already included in those of their fathers or husbands. (He also thought we could strike off 'young' men under forty years of age.) Part of the argument for increasing women's political representation looks like a feminist rewrite and extension of this. Women occupy a distinct position within society: they are typically concentrated, for example, in lower-paid jobs; and they carry the primary responsibility for the unpaid work of caring for others. There are particular needs, interests, and concerns that arise from women's experience, and these will be inadequately addressed in a politics that is dominated by men. Equal rights to a vote have not proved strong enough to deal with this problem; there must also be equality among those elected to office.

At an intuitive level, this is hard to fault. It takes what is a widely accepted element in our understanding of democracy and applies it

ANNE PHILLIPS

to women's situation. Looked at more closely, however, the argument from women's interests or women's concerns seems to rest on three conditions: that women have a distinct and separate interest as women; that this interest cannot be adequately represented by men; and that the election of women ensures its representation. As critics of gender quotas will be quick to point out, each condition is vulnerable to attack. The notion that women have at least some interests distinct from and even in conflict with men's is relatively straightforward (we can all think of appropriate examples), but this falls a long way short of establishing a set of interests shared by all women. If interests are understood in terms of what women express as their priorities and goals, there is considerable disagreement among women, and while attitude surveys frequently expose a 'gender gap' between women and men, the more striking development over recent decades has been the convergence in the voting behaviour of women and men. There may be more mileage in notions of a distinct woman's interest if this is understood in terms of some underlying but as yet unnoticed 'reality', but this edges uncomfortably close to notions of 'false consciousness', which most feminists would prefer to avoid. Indeed the presumption of a clearly demarcated 'woman's interest' which holds true for all women in all classes and all countries has been one of the casualties of recent feminist critique, and the exposure of multiple differences between women has undermined more global understandings of women's interests and concerns (see, for example, Mohanty 1992). If there is no clearly agreed and recognized 'women's interest', does it really matter if the representatives are predominantly men?

Definitive as this might seem, it does not seriously undermine the claim to gender parity; if anything, it can be said to strengthen it. Consider, in this context, Edmund Burke's rather odd understanding of interests as reflecting 'an objective, impersonal, unattached reality', which can then be represented by any sufficiently competent and honest individual (Pitkin 1967: 168). Odd as this is, it conveys a partial truth. The more fixed the interests, or the more definite and easily defined, the less significance attaches to who does the work of representation. So if women's interests were transparently obvious to any intelligent observer, there might be no particular case—beyond the perennial one of trust—for insisting on representatives who also happen to be women. We might feel that men will be less diligent in pressing women's interests or concerns, but if we all know what these are, it will be correspondingly easy to tell whether they are being adequately pursued. If, however, the interests are varied,

234

DEMOCRACY AND REPRESENTATION

unstable, perhaps still in the process of formation, it will be far more difficult to separate out what is to be represented from who is to do the representation. The greater problems arise, that is, where interests are not so precisely delineated, where the political agenda has been constructed without reference to certain areas of concern, or where much fresh thinking is necessary to work out the appropriate policies. To this extent, the very difficulties in defining what are in women's interests strengthen the case for more women as representatives.

The more decisive problem lies in the third condition. Does the election of more women then ensure their representation? Again, at an intuitive level, an increase in the number of women elected seems likely to change both the practices and the priorities of politics, increasing the attention given to matters of childcare, for example, or ensuring that women's poor position in the labour market is more vigorously addressed. This intuition is already partially confirmed by the experience of those countries which have changed the gender composition of their elected assemblies. But what does this mean in terms of political representation? Elections are typically organized by geographical constituencies, which sometimes coincide with concentrations of particular ethnic or religious groups, or concentrations of certain social classes, but which never coincide with concentrations of women or men. Elections typically take place through the medium of political parties, each of which produces candidates who are said to represent that party's policies and programmes and goals. In what sense can we say that the women elected through this process carry an additional responsibility to represent women? In the absence of mechanisms to establish accountability, the equation of more women with more adequate representation of women's interests looks suspiciously undemocratic. How do the women elected know what the women who elected them want? By what right do they claim responsibility to represent women's concerns?

Though this is rarely stated in the literature, the argument from women's interests implies that representatives will have considerable autonomy: that they do have currently, and by implication, that this ought to continue. Women's exclusion from politics is said to matter precisely because politicians do not abide by pre-agreed policies and goals. As any observer of the political process knows, policy decisions are *not* settled in advance by party programmes, for new problems and issues emerge alongside unanticipated constraints, and in the subsequent weighing of interpretations and priorities, it

ANNE PHILLIPS

matters immensely who the representatives are. Feminists have much experience of this, gained through painful years of watching hard won commitments to sexual equality drop off the final agenda. When there is a significant under-representation of women at the point of final decision, this can and does have serious consequences, and it is partly in reflection of this that feminists have shifted their attention from the details of policy commitments to the composition of the decision-making group. Political experience tells us that all male or mostly male assemblies will be poor judges of women's interests and priorities and concerns, and that trying to shore up this judgement by pre-agreed programmes has only limited effect. There is a strong dose of political realism here. Representatives *do* have considerable autonomy, which is why it matters who those representatives are.

It is worth dwelling on this point, for it highlights a divergence between current feminist preoccupations and what has long been the main thrust in radical democracy. Radical democrats distrust the wayward autonomy of politicians and the way they concentrate power around them, and they typically work to combat these tendencies by measures that will bind politicians more tightly to their promises, and disperse over-centralized power. Feminists have usually joined forces in support of the second objective: feminism is widely associated with bringing politics closer to home; and women are often intensely involved in local and community affairs. But when feminists insist that the sex of the representatives matters, they are expressing a deeper ambivalence towards the first objective. The politics of binding mandates, for example, turns the representatives into glorified messengers: it puts all the emphasis onto the content of the messages, and makes it irrelevant who the messengers are. In contesting the sex of the representatives, feminists are querying this version of democratic accountability.

The final point about the argument from interests is that it may not of itself justify equal or proportionate presence. In a recent discussion of demands for group representation in Canada, Will Kymlicka (1993) makes a useful distinction between arguments for equal or proportionate presence (where the number of women or aboriginal Indians or francophone Canadians in any legislative assembly would correspond to their proportion in the citizenry as a whole), and the case for a threshold presence (where the numbers would reach the requisite level that ensured each group's concerns were adequately addressed). When the group in question is a numerically small minority, the threshold might prove larger than their proportion in the population as a whole; when the group composes half the population, the threshold might be considerably lower. On this basis, there might be an argument for greater than proportionate representation of Indians, for example, but less than proportionate representation of women: not that women would be formally restricted to 25 or 30 per cent of the seats, but that they might not require any more than this in order to change the political agenda. It is the argument from justice that most readily translates into strict notions of equality; the argument from women's interests need not deliver such strong results.

III. THE CASE FOR GENDER PARITY: TOWARDS A REVITALISED DEMOCRACY

The third argument is less developed, and I offer it here as a way of dealing with some of the problems I identify above. The argument from justice works well enough on the limited ground that treats being a politician like any other kind of job, or on the negative ground that denies any just basis for a male monopoly. The argument from women's interests works well enough as a case for a threshold, but not necessarily equal, presence, but is best understood in terms of a realistic assessment of how rarely politicians abide by their pre-agreed programmes. These are powerful arguments, but they are not, on the whole, the kinds of arguments that feminists most admire: they are too much grounded in an impoverished experience of democracy to bear the full weight of feminist ambition. And they leave unresolved that recurrent radical concern about controlling wayward politicians. Apart from the argument that women should get an equal chance at a political career (which is a fair enough argument, but not intrinsically about democracy), we can only believe that the sex of the representatives matters if we think it will change what the representatives do. In saying this, we seem to be undermining accountability through party programmes. We are saying we expect our representatives to do more—or other—than they promised in the election campaign.

There is often an expectation, for example, that women politicians will operate on a cross-party basis, forging alliances to press for improvements in childcare provision or changes in the abortion laws. In her study of Norwegian representatives, Hege Skjeie (1991) records a number of such initiatives, but she notes that it is the

ANNE PHILLIPS

priorities of their party that finally dictate the way women politicians vote. If we are either surprised or disappointed by this, it must be because we see an increase in the number of women politicians as challenging the dominance of the party system or the tradition of voting along party lines. Those who feel that the tighter controls of party discipline have discouraged serious discussion and debate may be happy enough with this conclusion. But in the absence of alternative mechanisms of consultation or accountability, it does read like a recipe for letting representatives do what *they* choose to do.

What makes sense of this, I believe, is an additional presumption that is implicit in most feminist arguments, a conviction that changing the composition of existing elected assemblies is only part of a wider project of increasing and enhancing democracy. When the argument for gender parity is taken out of this context, it has to rely more heavily on arguments from political realism, and while these are powerful enough arguments in themselves, they fall short on some key concerns. Put back into its context, the argument often reveals a more ambitious programme of dispersing power through a wider range of decision-making assemblies, and changing the balance between participation and representation.

We might think here of the further initiatives that are so typical of women in politics: the use of the open forum, for example, as a way of consulting women in a local community; the report back to women's sections or women's conferences; or just the extraordinary energy so many women politicians devote to what they see as their responsibilities for representing women. Even among those most committed to party politics (and many women deliberately stay outside, in the more amorphous politics of women's movement groups and campaigns), the political party is frequently viewed as an inadequate vehicle for representation. In 1980s Britain, for example, there was a flowering of women's committees within the framework of local government (usually associated with more left-wing Labour councils), and these made extensive use of co-option or the open forum as a way of consulting women outside the political parties. Now you could think of this as a short term compensation for women's current under-representation among elected councillors, but there is little to support this view. More commonly, those associated with the development of women's committees saw the additional mechanisms of consultation and participation as always and everywhere desirable—even under some future scenario where women might hold 50 per cent of council seats. The women involved were querying the exclusive emphasis on the party as the

DEMOCRACY AND REPRESENTATION

vehicle for representation; they were pursuing complementary (sometimes conflicting) ways of empowering women to make their needs better known.

The case for gender parity in politics should, I believe, be understood within this broader context, and to this extent, it confirms Hanna Pitkin's intuition. The argument for more 'descriptive' or 'mirror' representation does move in close parallel with arguments for a more participatory form of democracy; and those concerned with the under-representation of women in politics do look to additional mechanisms of consultation and accountability and participation that would complement our occasional vote. We do not need this additional ammunition to argue for more women in politics; there are arguments enough from justice or interests that provide a basis for substantial change. But as a more profound set of issues about democracy and representation, the case for gender parity is at its strongest when it is associated with the larger dream.

Notes

1. I use the term parity to indicate a rough equality between the proportion of women and men elected. My use of this term should not be confused with the arguments that have recently surfaced within the Council of Europe for so-called parity democracy. See Outshoorn (1993) for a critical review of this literature.
2. There *are* parties which operate quotas for youth—as with my own example of the 1972 Democratic National Convention—but when it comes to parliamentary candidatures, few people worry about the paucity of those under 25.

References

Chapman, Jenny (1993), *Politics, Feminism, and the Reformation of Gender* (London: Routledge).

Grofman, B., Lijphart, A., McKay, R.B., Scarrow, H.A. (eds.) (1982), *Representation and Redistricting Issues* (Lexington, Mass.: D. C. Heath and Co.).

Kymlicka, Will (1993), 'Group Representation in Canadian Politics'. Paper prepared for IRPP project on 'Communities, the Charter and Interest Advocacy'.

Lovenduski, Joni and Norris, Pippa (1989), 'Selecting Women Candidates: Obstacles to the Feminisation of the House of Commons', *European Journal of Political Research*, 17, 533–63.

Mohanty, Chandra (1993), 'Feminist Encounters: Locating the Politics of Experience', in Michèle Barrett and Anne Phillips (eds.), *Destabilizing Theory: Contemporary Feminist Debates* (Cambridge: Polity Press), 74–92.

ANNE PHILLIPS

Outshoorn, Joyce (1993), 'Parity Democracy: A Critical Look at a "New" Strategy', paper prepared for workshop on 'Citizenship and Plurality', European Consortium for Political Research', Leiden.

Parry, Geraint, Moyser, George, and Day, Neil (1992), *Political Participation and Democracy in Britain* (Cambridge: Cambridge University Press).

Phillips, Anne (1991) *Engendering Democracy* (Cambridge: Polity Press).

Phillips Griffiths, A. (1960), 'How Can One Person Represent Another?' *Aristotelian Society*, Supplementary vol. xxxiv, 187–208.

Pitkin, Hanna F. (1967), *The Concept of Representation* (Berkeley: University of California Press).

Ranney, Austin (1982), 'Comments on Representation Within the Political Party System', in Grofman *et al.* (1982), 193–7.

Skjeie, Hege (1991), 'The Rhetoric of Difference: On Women's Inclusion into Political Elites', *Politics and Society*, 19/2, 233–63.

Verba, Sidney, Nie, Norman H., and Kim, Jae-on (1978), *Participation and Political Equality: A Seven National Comparison* (Cambridge: Cambridge University Press).

240

10

DEFERRING GROUP REPRESENTATION

IRIS MARION YOUNG

Women's movement activists and feminist scholars in many parts of the world have suggested that legislatures peopled almost entirely by men cannot be said properly to represent women. In response to such claims, some countries, such as Argentina, have enacted legislation requiring that party lists include a certain portion of women.[1] Even where there are no laws that require it, many parties around the world have decided that their lists are not properly representative without certain numbers of women, and they maintain quotas in their lists.

In the United States, similar discussions take place about the specific representation of racial or ethnic minorities. Some districts have been drawn or voting processes adjusted to make the election of African Americans or Hispanics more likely. Both the idea and practice of promoting specific representation of minorities are controversial, but the issue will not fade from the American public agenda. Many other countries of the world have schemes for specific social group representation, either in the form of reserved seats, party list rules, or voting schemes.

In earlier work, I argued for a principle of special representation for oppressed and disadvantaged groups in processes of political decision making.[2] Special representation is necessary only for oppressed and disadvantaged groups, I argued, because the dominant groups are already represented. Explicit processes for

349

ensuring the representation of oppressed or disadvantaged groups allows the expression of otherwise unheard interests and perspectives. Group representation, furthermore, relativizes the expression and perspectives of the dominant groups so that they are less able to assume that their ideas and policies are impartial and universal.

Policies, proposals, and arguments for group representation, however, face many objections. One of these I find particularly compelling because it comes from a commitment to attend to rather than to submerge social difference, in order to undermine domination and oppression. The idea of group representation, this objection claims, presumes that a group of women, or African Americans, or Maori, has some set of common attributes or interests which can be represented. But this is usually false. Differences of race and class cut across gender, differences of gender and ethnicity cut across religion, and so on. Individual members of a gender or racial group have life histories that often make them very different people with very different interests and outlooks. The unifying process required by group representation inappropriately freezes fluid relational identities into a unity, and can recreate oppressive segregations.[3] Group representation further implies that in expressing interests and taking public positions on issues, the dominant groups within the groups suppress or marginalize the perspectives of minorities. If Latinos were to be specially represented in American politics, for example, a heterosexual perspective would be likely to dominant their discourse and policy preferences, thus marginalizing gay and lesbian Latinos.[4]

In this essay, I consider these problems with the idea of group representation. I argue that the problem of how one person can speak for many, and the tendency to freeze those represented into a unity, is not an issue only for group representation but for all representation. Thus in order to respond to the intuition that there is something wrong with decision-making bodies from which women or cultural minorities are absent, but also to avoid essentializing and marginalizing consequences for a solution to this problem, it is necessary to think about the meaning and functions of political representation altogether.

I suggest that the objection that group representation freezes

Deferring Group Representation

the group into a unity assumes that the representative is or should be in a relation of identity with the constituents. Accounts of democracy which find direct democracy as the most authentic also tend to assume the representation relation as one of identity. I theorize representation as a differentiated relation whose most important moments are authorization and accountability, and show that this conceptualization dissolves some of the problems and paradoxes that sometimes appear in thinking about representation.

This chapter takes seriously, moreover, the claim that members of social groups usually vary greatly in their interests and opinions. I introduce and elaborate on a concept of social-group perspective, as distinct from interest or opinion, to give articulate meaning to the widely held intuition that social groups can and should be represented in some respect. I conclude by rearticulating the argument for special representation of oppressed or disadvantaged groups.

I. PARADOXES OF REPRESENTATION

Problems with group representation seem particularly stark when discussing the inclusion of women in politics. On the one hand, women as a group have been and continue to be largely excluded from decision-making power, and at the same time women continue to suffer serious social and economic disadvantages. Thus, it would seem that women and their interests ought to be represented in public decision making. On the other hand, women are everywhere, and differ so vastly along so many dimensions that it seems absurd to suggest that women who might attain positions as representatives can legitimately speak for other women.

This problem appears, however, with all forms of political representation. The legitimacy of a person elected in a district speaking and acting on behalf of the members of the district might appear even more questionable than a woman speaking for women. Congressional districts in the United States contain more than 500,000 people. How can one person possibly claim to speak in place of all those people, with their huge diversity of interests, experience, and needs? The legitimacy of a particular African American acting as a spokesman for other African Americans is often properly contested, again because there are so many different opinions and experiences among members of this group. Even interest-group representation can be challenged in this way. How can a handful of lobbyists and office staff be said to represent the diverse experience and perspectives of the members of, say, the Sierra Club?

Some theorists of democracy conclude that political representation is incompatible with strong democracy because, they claim, representatives are necessarily distant from constituents. Political inclusion must consist in people speaking and acting for themselves.[5] Direct democracy, where each citizen is himself present to and directly participates in the decisionmaking process, is real democracy. Representative democracy is at best a grudging concession to size or efficiency, and at worst simply not democracy at all.

I believe that this elevation of direct democracy to the apex, as the only "real" democracy, is mistaken, and that political representation is both necessary and desirable. Representative democracy in itself is not less democratic than direct democracy but is a specific structure of democracy that has its own degrees of more and less. Full argument for this claim deserves an essay of its own, so here I will only sketch some reasons.

Representation is necessary because the web of modern social life often ties the actions of some people and institutions in one place to consequences in many other places and institutions. No person can be present at all the decisions or in all the decision-making bodies whose actions affect her life, because there are so many and they are so dispersed. Though her aspirations are often disappointed, she hopes that others will think about her situation and represent it to the issue forum.[6]

One might object that this argument presupposes a large-scale society and polity which a preference for direct democracy rejects. A democracy without representation must consist of small, decentralized, self-sufficient units. Robert Dahl gives a compelling set of arguments, however, for how even this vision of decentralized direct democracy cannot avoid representation. The equal participation of everyone in political deliberation, he argues, can occur only in small committees. Even in assemblies of a few hundred people, most people will be more passive participants who listen

Deferring Group Representation

to a few people speak for a few positions, then think and vote. Beyond the small committee, that is, features of time and interaction produce de facto representation. But such de facto representation is arbitrary; in fact direct democracy often cedes political power to arrogant loud mouths whom no one chose to represent them. It is fairer and probably wiser to institute formal rules of representation. Dahl also argues, I think plausibly, that the ugly tendencies of power and competition that haunt human life imply that small decentralized political units are likely to grow larger either by means of conquest or coalition. As soon as scale returns, then, representation also returns.[7]

Not only is political representation inevitable in these ways, it is also positively desirable as a means to facilitate deliberation. I assume that a democratic process guided by public discussions which aim to arrive at the most just and wise solutions to political problems is better than a process that merely aggregates the private preferences of citizens.[8] Representation facilitates such discussions by reducing the number of discussants. More important for the deliberative model, a carefully and fairly designed system of representation can better ensure that unpopular, or minority, or weak participants have a voice in the discussion than could a free-for-all direct democracy. Representative bodies can enable people from diverse groups or across large geographical areas to communicate, indirectly to show one another their circumstances and needs, thus enlarging their understanding of social policies and their effects.

These arguments seem to leave us with the following paradox. The problem of the one and the many is impossible to solve. It is not possible for one person to stand for many people, to speak and act as they would. It is impossible to find the essential attributes of constituents, the single common interest that overrides the diversity of their other interests, experiences, and opinions. Representation understood in this way is impossible. Yet representation is both necessary and desirable. I suggest that this is a false paradox generated by an implicit assumption of the representative as in some sense identical with those represented. In the next section, I will expose this assumption and argue that representation should be understood in terms of *différance* rather than identity.

II. Representation as Differance

The conundrums about representation that I discussed above appear partly because the representative relation is often implicitly thought of as a relation of identity. Some of those who criticize representative systems because they lack women, blacks, or Muslims in significant proportions, for example, often assume a concept of "mirror" representation. They assume, that is, that a representative body should resemble the attributes of the social body. Mirror representation also seems to assume that a representative's sharing specific attributes with constituents—gender, class, race, religion, and so on—is sufficient to ensure that those constituents are properly represented.

A number of writers properly criticize this assumption that a person or group is legitimately represented when the representative identifies with specific group attributes. Having such a relation of identity or similarity with constituents says nothing about what the representative does.[9] The idea of mirror representation is also subject to the objection to group representation which I articulated earlier, namely that people with similar attributes of structural social position or cultural group nevertheless usually have very different interests and opinions.[10] Simply having certain group attributes that constituents can be said to share is not a ground for saying that the constituents are legitimately represented.

Those who object to the idea of group representation, however, also assume that representation entails a relation of identity. They object to group representation on the grounds that the social group cannot be reduced to a unity of will or condition for which the representative can speak and act. The objection seems to presuppose that in the absence of such a self-consciously unified group or interest or mandate, legitimate representation cannot occur.

I argued in the previous section, moreover, that few if any representative relations exhibit that sort of unity of the many constituents into a common will or interest for which the representative speaks and acts. Recognizing this problem that the constituency is rarely identical with itself, thus making it impossible to represent that identity, many conclude that representation is illegitimate. Direct democracy is the only real democracy, because no person can stand for another in the specificity of her experience and interests. Thus, this purism of direct democracy also assumes that representation is properly a relation of identity between the representative and constituents.

This identity assumption, I will now argue, misrepresents the meaning and function of political representation. I suggest that we adopt Jacques Derrida's critique of a metaphysics of presence, and conceptualize representation by means of his concept of *differance*.

The classical problem of the one and the many is produced by a metaphysics of presence, or a logic of identity. This metaphysics aims to capture the flowing temporality of movement and change in stable elements. It conceptualizes material processes in terms of self-identical substances, which underlie and remain the same through change, and which can be captured in a definition of their essential attributes. Individuals within a substantial category always vary in their particular attributes, but they belong to the same group because they share a common set of attributes.

This substance metaphysics of presence and identity sets up hierarchical dichotomies. One term is the substantial origin, underlying change in time, the other is the derivative supplement. Thus the hierarchical dichotomies of substance-accident, cause-effect, presence-absence polarize and freeze experienced differences. The aim is then to reduce the second pole to the first.

Derrida directs his critique of the metaphysics of presence also at a classical understanding of language and the relation of subjects to the world. This classical view of language privileges voice, the spoken word, as the origin of linguistic meaning. This philosophy implicitly takes the subject to be immediately and authentically present to listeners in speech. Writing, on this classical view, is a secondary, alienated form of language. Material marks aim to represent the authentic meaning of speech, but on this view writing is always a poor substitute, absent, ambiguous, and derivative.[11]

Derrida offers the term *differance* as the alternative for expressing experience and the operation of language. Differance has the double meaning of "to differ" and "to defer." Where the metaphysics of presence generates polarities because it aims to reduce the many to one identity, thinking of entities in terms of *differance* leaves them in their plurality without requiring their collection into a common identity. Things take their being and signs take their meaning from their place in a process of differentiated relationships. Things are similar without being identical, and different without being contrary, depending on the point of reference and the moment in a process.

Thus according to the second aspect of the meaning of *differance,* reality and meaning are best thought of as playing over intervals of space and time. Oppositions such as substance-accident, cause-effect, presence-absence, or reality-sign, locate authentic being in an origin, an always earlier time for which the present process is a derivative copy. Derrida proposes to rethink such oppositions in terms of the idea of the "trace," a movement of temporalization that carries past and future with it. This moment in the conversation, this moment in the being of the mountain, carries traces of the history of relationships that produced it, and its current tendencies anticipate future relationships.[12]

Derrida himself relates his critique of the classical account of the relation of substance and accident, sign and referent, to the context of political representation. The sign would thus be a deferred presence. Whether it is a question of verbal or written signs, monetary signs, electoral delegates, or political representatives, the movement of signs defers the moment of encountering the thing itself, the moment at which we could lay hold of it, consume or expand it, touch it, see it, have a present intuition of it.[13]

I suggest that many discussions of political representation assume a metaphysics of presence or a logic of identity through the following sort of image of the representative function. The representative is supposed to grasp and stand for "the will of the people." Ideally, "the people" meet in an original moment of presence, where they express their will, and choose a person to represent that will. In this original moment, the many become one. Representative bodies are necessary because the polity is large and requires decisions to be made by a manageable body of deliberators, in a central place from which most of the people are absent. The representative's responsibility is to be present in their place, to speak as they would speak, in their absence. His words

Deferring Group Representation

and deeds are effects only, with their cause in the original will of the people. On this model, representation is always derivative, secondary, distanced, ambiguous, and suspect. "Real" democracy consists in "the people" meeting face to face and in one another's presence making decisions for themselves. The legitimate representative tries to re-present this original moment of decision.

Of course I am constructing an image of political representation which I believe underlies rejection of representation as democratic grounds complaints that the representative cannot bring the many into one. There is a myth of authentic democratic moment when the people are present to themselves, and this myth impedes normative thinking about political representation. Instead of conceptualizing representation as some kind of relation of identity, in which the representative stands for a unified will of the constituents, I suggest that we conceptualize representation as a *differentiated relationship*.

This means, first, affirming that there is a difference, a separation, between the representative and the constituents. Of course no person can stand for and speak as a plurality of other persons. The representative function of *speaking for* should not be confused with an identifying requirement that the representative *speak as* the constituents would, to try to be present for them in their absence. It is no criticism of the representative that he is separate and distinct from the constituents, but the two aspects in their difference must be in a determinate relation to maintain legitimately the representative function.

Second, representation as differentiated relationship implies that there is no original "will of the people" to which the representative should give voice as mere effect. Because the constituency is internally differentiated from itself, the representative does not stand for or refer to a substance or essence of opinion or interest which it is his job to describe and for which he advocates.

Conceiving representation as differentiated relationship, finally, encourages a shift in thought from substance to process. What matters about representation is neither the attributes of the representatives nor the attributes of the constituency. Nor does it matter whether the representative properly depicts an originary will or essence. Representation, instead, is a *process* involving both the constituency and the representative, and normative political theory can evaluate the democratic character of this process along lines I will develop in the next section. In her classic work about representation, Hanna Pitkin argues against a tendency to conceive representation in terms of the identity of the representative rather than in terms of the actions of representation. Thinking of representation as process rather than substances agrees with this analysis.[14]

Pitkin also discusses the debate about whether the representative should only express a mandate from the constituents or instead should be autonomous from them and act according to his reasoned view of the common good. She argues that neither the view of the representative as delegate nor the view as trustee is adequate, but rather that the representative function involves both. Conceiving representation as differentiated relation helps fill out how and why the representative is both delegate and trustee. The representative is separate from the constituents, in a different place, in a setting of discussion and decision making with other representatives from which the constituents are absent. Even if the constituents could agree on a mandate, in the setting away from them there may be new issues that arise that make the mandate irrelevant, and the representative has no choice but to act as he thinks best. If the representative thinks of himself or is thought of as pure trustee, then the relationships between him and the constituency is severed, and the representative function dissolves. Representation as differentiated relationship entails a moving dialectic between a delegate and trustee function.

III. THE REPRESENTATIONAL RELATIONSHIP: AUTHORIZATION AND ACCOUNTABILITY

Much political theory and practice, I have suggested, implicitly brings representation under a metaphysics of presence. It mistakenly conceives the function of representation as making the voice of the absent present, speaking and deciding as they would. Thinking of representation in terms of *differance* emphasizes temporality, that representation is a process rather than a condition of substitution.[15] Representation is a deferring relationship between constituents and representative, moving between three moments of authorization, representation, and accountability. I will now

Deferring Group Representation

elaborate on each of these three moments in the process of representation, focusing on where each moment in the process bears traces of the others.

The processes of authorization, representation, and accountability, moreover, enact differance in three senses. They consist in a flow between the representative, who differs from the constituents, and also among the constituents, who differ from one another. Second, in the process the deciding mandate is always temporally deferred. The relationship of authorization and accountability, finally, implies a dialectic in which constituents and representative each defer to the judgment of the other.

The ideal of representing the "will of the people" presumes, that "the people" exist prior to and independently of the process of representation, as the original cause of the representative's act. It also presumes that this people can form a common will that they delegate to the representative. But this image defies the plurality of the constituency, which does not exist as a unity, and is not present to itself. In most situations calling for representative bodies, the constituency is too large, or the varying activities of its members are too dispersed, or its definition and borders too vague, to expect any process where the constituency in one moment arrives at a collective will.

Nevertheless, democratic representation requires a process of *authorization* which establishes a relationship between the constituency and the representative. In the process of authorization, the people anticipate the moment of representation that will take place, and this anticipation brings the dispersed constituency into a relationship with itself. There is no constituency prior to the process of representation, no people who form an original unity they then delegate onto the derivative representative. Without the motive of a political decision deferred onto another who is accountable to them through public procedures, "the people" might not go looking for each other in order to form a base of public opinion and account.[16]

In the process of authorization the constituency forms itself in light of the issues the people believe or desire will face a representative body. Ideally, this process consists in broad and inclusive public discussion of issues, and public criticism and contestation of the constituency with itself about the content of a decision-making agenda, the actions representatives should take, and who they should be. This discussion occurs over time, and thus the precise moment of authorization is always deferred. The process aims at agreement but is always open to further contest, and so agreement is always deferred. Democratic norms of authorization should include fair and public rules of election that constitute the relationship between constituency and representative. But just as important, the ideal of democratic representation should also include structured processes of issue discussion that allow constituents to listen and be heard. Systems are more or less democratic to the degree that they allow and even encourage inclusive participatory discussion. In representative democracy, however, decision making about these policies is deferred onto the representative.

In this process, the activity of representing ideally recollects and anticipates. The representative should maintain a connection between her speech and action and the constituency. But the representative cannot be a mere effect of a prior cause in the people's will. Instead, the representative process carries, or ought to carry, the *traces* of authorizing processes of discussion and decision making. At the same time, the representative ought to act with a view to a future moment when she will be called to account by the constituency, and will have to answer for her speech and actions.

The representative's action refers backward, to the process of authorization, and forward, to the moment of accountability. The representative is authorized to act, but his judgment is always in question. Whether he acted on authority is a question deferred to a later time, when he will be held accountable. Should the constituency find his action or judgment wrong, he must defer to their evaluation.

Thus the third moment, accountability, is as important as the other two. In the process of calling to account, the constituency can meet itself anew, reform itself, and engage in new debate and conflict. Such renewed opinion formation may bear the traces of the process of authorization, but it also has new elements because then the constituents did not know just how issues would be formulated in the representative body and what arguments would be offered there. The anticipation of holding accountable and of being called to account can condition the actions of both

Deferring Group Representation

constituents and representatives, to maintain a connection between them.

In most democracies today, the moment of accountability is weaker than the moment of authorization. Even more disturbingly, for many representatives, the only form of being held to account is reelection. Strong democracy requires some processes and procedures of constituencies calling representatives to account in addition to the processes that defer onto them representative authority. Without strong processes of accounting, the representative can effectively operate on her own, and the constituency need no longer be active after the process of authorization. This process of accountability should have the traces of authorization, but authorization itself should be conditioned by anticipation of the process of accounting. In this way there is no origin, no decisive moment when the judgment is made. Institutional means of accountability distinct from election campaigns can include citizen review boards, implementation studies, and periodic official participatory hearings that follow the process of policy making.

I describe the function of representation as a process that flows between constituents and representatives in a circle of authorization and accountability. This description has a normative dimension by indicating some criteria for evaluating degrees of democracy. Democracy is not an all or nothing affair; the idea of a pure and authentic democracy, in comparison to which everything else is a sham, is a dream. Instead, as Frank Cunningham argues, democracy is a matter of degree.[17] Representative processes can be more or less democratic. They should be normatively evaluated according to the degree to which they enable inclusive discussion among constituents, institute fair voting procedures that aim to promote political equality in influence and not merely number, and have independent mechanisms of accountability.

IV. MODES OF REPRESENTATION

The representative should not be thought of as a substitute for those he or she represents, I have suggested, nor should we assume that the representative can or should express and enact some unified will of the constituency. The representative can stand for neither the identity of any other person nor the collective identity of a constituency. There is an inevitable difference and separation between the representative and constituents, which always puts in question the manner and degree to which constituents participate in the process that produces policy outcomes. Yet representation is both necessary and desirable in modern politics. Rather than devaluing representation as such, participatory and radical democrats should evaluate the degree to which processes of authorization and accountability exist, are independent, and activate the constituency in inclusive participatory public opinion.

Another measure of the degrees of democracy, I suggest, is whether people are connected through relationships of authorization and accountability to a few or many representatives. The assumption that representatives should in some fashion be identical to constituents implicitly carries the impossible requirement that a person is only represented if everything about her potentially has a voice in the political process. Since no representative can stand for all the constituents in all the thickness of their individuality, direct democracy, in which each stands only for himself, wrongly appears to be as the only authentic democracy. The representative must be different from the constituents, and a democracy is better or worse according to how well those differentiated positions are related. Democracy can also be strengthened by pluralizing the modes and sites of representation. Systems of political representation cannot represent individuals in their individuality but rather should represent *aspects* of a person's life experience, identity, or activity where she or her has affinity with others. Potentially there are many such aspects or affinity groups. I propose to distinguish here three general modes through which a person can be represented: according to interest, opinion, and perspective. Within a particular political context, a person may be represented in several ways within each of these modes. Explication of what it means to represent perspective in particular will set the basis for a new argument for the special representation of oppressed or disadvantaged social groups.

What do I mean when I say that I feel represented in the political process? There are many possible answers to this question but three stand out for me as important. First, I feel represented when someone is looking after the interests I take as mine and share with some others. Second, it is important to me that the principles, values and priorities that I think should guide political decisions are voiced in discussion. Finally, I feel represented when at least some of those discussing and voting on policies understand and express the kind of social experience I have because of my social group position and the history of social group relations. I will discuss interest and opinion only briefly because these have been much discussed in political theory. I will focus more attention on representing perspectives because this idea is less familiar.

Interest. I define interest as what affects or is important to the life prospects of individuals, or the goal-oriented success of organizations. An agent, whether individual or collective, has an interest in whatever is necessary or desirable in order to realize the ends the agent has set for himself, herself, or themselves. These include both material resources and the ability to exercise capacities—e.g., for cultural expression, political influence, economic decision-making power, and so on. I define interest here as self-referring, and as different from ideas, principles, and values. The latter may help define the ends a person sets for herself, where the interest defines the means for achieving those ends.

Interests may and often do conflict, whether in the action of a single agent or between agents. Where agents need resources to accomplish a variety of ends, they are likely to find some of the resources they need to be relatively scarce. Sometimes the means one agent needs to pursue a certain end implies directly impeding another agent's ability to get what he needs to pursue his ends. It is important to note, however, that interests do not necessarily conflict. The pursuit of ends in society and the setting of political frameworks to facilitate that pursuit need not necessarily be structured as a zero-sum relationship among agents.

The representation of interest is familiar in political practice, and there exists more theory of interest representation perhaps than any other kind. I do not here wish to review the entire literature on interest groups and the means by which they can achieve political influence. I only note here that it is part of the free associative process of communicative democracy that people have the freedom to press politically for policies that will serve their interests and to organize together with others with similar interests in order to gain political influence.

Opinions. I define opinions as the principles, values and priorities held by a person as these bear on and condition his or her judgment about what priorities should be pursued and ends sought. This is the primary sphere of what Anne Phillips refers to as the "politics of ideas,"[18] on which much contemporary discussion of pluralism also focuses. Rawls's recent discussion of the principles and problems of political liberalism, for example, focuses on the existence of plural ideas and belief systems in modern societies, how these legitimately influence political life, and how people with differing beliefs and opinions can maintain a working polity.[19] By opinion, I mean any judgment or belief about how things are or ought to be, and the political judgments that follow from these judgments or beliefs. Opinions may be religious, or derive from religious reasons, or they may be culturally based in a worldview of the history of social practices. They may be based in disciplinary or knowledge systems, as might be political opinions derived from certain premises of neoclassical economics, or based in a set of normative principles such as libertarianism or radical ecology. While I doubt that most people's opinions on public matters all derive from a single "comprehensive doctrine," I do assume that most people make judgments about particular social and political issues with the guidance of some values, priorities, or principles that they apply more broadly than that case, if not to all cases. Opinions are certainly contestable, and often some can be shown to be more well founded than others. A communicative democracy, however, requires the free expression and challenging of opinions and a wide representation of opinions in discussions leading to policy decisions.

Political parties are the most common vehicle for the representation of opinions. Parties often put forward programs that less express the interests of a particular constituency, and more organize the political issues of the day according to principles, values, and priorities the party claims generally to stand for. Smaller or more specialized associations, however, can and often do form to represent opinions in public life and influence public policy. Traditionally, interest group theory has treated such associations as another kind of interest group, and for most purposes this is a

Deferring Group Representation

harmless conflation. I think it important to distinguish in general, however, between kinds of political association motivated by an instrumentalist interest, on the one hand, and kinds of association motivated by commitment to beliefs and values, on the other. Whereas the former sort of motivation is selfish, even if selfish for a group, the latter often takes itself to be impartial or even altruistic.

Perspective. Social perspectives involve the way people interpret issues and events because of their structural social locations. Structural social locations arise from group differentiations that exist in a society, collective attributions that have cultural and practical meanings for the way people interact or the status they have—such as age, gender, race, ethnicity, caste, religion, physical ability, or health status in some societies, sexuality in some societies, and so on. These structured relations of social action involve the differentiation of at least one category of people from others. In most societies these group differentiations structure some social inequalities of prestige, power, or access to resources. Many structural relations of differentiated groups, that is, are relations of privilege, on the one hand, and oppression or disadvantage on the other.

A well-developed theoretical discourse describes these sorts of social structures as "positioning" individuals. Individual actors find themselves located in certain positions in relation to others, in a web of social relations that varies across societies, and which changes in a particular social history.[20] Contemporary American society positions me as a woman, white, Anglo, professional, and so on. Without my choice, I find myself designated in certain ways by others that imply specific norms and status in relation to others. Any one of us finds ourselves positioned in multiple ways in modern societies. Others are similarly positioned with me who bear similar designations and for whom this implies similar relations with specific others. Social positioning conditions the lives of individuals by posing constraints on action and distributing benefits and burdens. It is a mistake to think that structural positioning forms the *identity* of persons, however. My life is conditioned by my social position of being a woman, but this hardly begins to say anything specific about who I am.[21] In our actions and self-formation, each of us takes an attitude toward the social positioning which both enables and constrains our social possibilities, the way others regard us, the way we regard them, the social norms that guide our conscious and unconscious interaction, and often the formal and bureaucratic status we do or do not have. But "who I am" is a product of my own particular history and active engagement with the multiple facts of social positioning that condition my life. Thus we may say that women or people of color, for example, are similarly positioned in a particular society without attributing to them a common identity.

Because of their social locations, people are attuned to particular kinds of social meanings and relationships to which others are less attuned. Sometimes others are not positioned to be aware of them at all. From their social locations people have differentiated knowledge of social events and their consequences. Because their social locations arise partly from the constructions that others have of them, and which they have of others in different locations, people in different locations may interpret the meaning of actions, events, rules, and structures differently, though not necessarily in incompatible ways. Structural social positions thus produce particular locationally relative kinds of experience and a specific knowledge of social processes and consequences.

Social *perspective*, then, refers to this experience, history and social knowledge derived from social position. To represent a social perspective means to approach public discussion and decision making with the experience and knowledge of those positioned in a structurally specific way. Representing an interest or an opinion, I suggest, usually entails promoting certain specific outcomes in the decision-making process. Representing a perspective, on the other hand, usually means promoting certain starting points for discussion. From a particular social perspective a representative asked certain kinds of questions, reports certain kinds of experience, recalls a particular line of narrative history, or expresses a certain way of regarding the positions of others. These vitally contribute to the inclusion of different people in the decision-making process and attention to effects that proposed policies may have on different groups. Expressing perspective, however, does not usually mean drawing a conclusion about outcomes.

I introduce the idea of social perspective, and the idea of representing a social perspective, in order to begin to address the

Deferring Group Representation

objection to the idea of group representation with which I began this essay. I wish to retain the intuition that social groups structured by gender, race, nationality, religion, ablement, sexuality, and so on, have some socially specific and politically relevant ways of experiencing and speaking about political issues. Nevertheless, I take seriously the claim that no such groups can be defined by a set of common interests, nor do all their members agree on principles and values to guide political discussion and decision making. African Americans in the United States, for example, have a large number of different and even conflicting interests, and adhere to a broad spectrum of political ideologies and opinions. For this reason, representing African Americans in political life cannot mean representing a particular set of interests or opinions. But I wish to retain the intuition that African Americans may have a reason to claim that they should be specifically represented in the political life of the United States. I believe that the structured position of African Americans in a historically racist society, and the specific social and cultural consequences of this history and position, provides African Americans with specific experiential background and knowledge of the workings of society which makes them attentive to certain issues, questions, or events that others tend not to think about. This is what I mean by perspective.

For more than fifty years, *The Pittsburgh Courier* has been an important newspaper for African Americans in the city of Pittsburgh and in other parts of the United States as well. I think that this newspaper illustrates well the difference between perspective, on the one hand, and interest and opinion, on the other. In the pages of this newspaper each week appear reports of many events and controversies that exhibit the plurality of interests, not all of them compatible, that African Americans in Pittsburgh and elsewhere have. On the opinion pages, moreover, appear editorials that cover the range from right-wing libertarian to left-wing socialism, from economic separatism to liberal integrationism. Despite this variety of interests and opinions, it is not difficult to identify how *The Pittsburgh Courier* nevertheless speaks an African American perspective. Most of the events discussed involve African Americans as the major actors, and take place at sites and within institutions which are are majority African American or otherwise specifically associated with them. When the paper discusses local or national events not specifically identified with African Americans, the stories usually ask questions or give emphases that are particularly informed by issues and experiences more specific to African Americans.

One might object that the idea of an African American perspective, or a female gendered perspective, is just as open to criticism as the idea of interest or opinion. Isn't it just as inappropriately reductive to talk about *one* Native American perspective as one interest? This is in fact so. Each person has his or her own irreducible history which gives him or her unique social knowledge and perspective. I think, however, that we must avoid the sort of individualism that would conclude from this fact that any talk of structured social positions and group defined social location is wrong or incoherent. It makes sense to say that nonprofessional working-class people have predictable vulnerabilities and opportunities because of their position in occupational structures. The idea of perspective is meant to capture that sensibility of group positioned experience without specifying unified content to what the perceptive sees. The social positioning produced by relation to other structural positions and by the social processes that issue in unintended consequences only provide a background and perspective in terms of which particular social events and issues are interpreted; they do not make the interpretation. So you can well have different persons with a similar social perspective giving different interpretations of an issue. Perspective is an approach to looking at social events, which conditions but does not determine what one sees.

I take interests, opinions, and perspectives to be three important aspects of persons that can be represented. None reduce to the identity of either a person or a group, but each is an aspect of the person. I do not claim that these three aspects are exhaustive of the ways people can be represented, moreover. There may well be other possible modes of representation, but I find these three particularly important in the way we talk about representation in contemporary politics and in answering the conceptual and practical problems posed for group representation.

None of these aspects of persons is reducible to the others.

Deferring Group Representation

They are logically independent in the sense that from a general social perspective one can derive neither a set of interests nor opinions. Within an individual life, it may be possible to explain why being socially positioned in a certain way has led a person to set certain goals or develop certain values, but such connection among interests, opinions, and perspectives can only be made at the level of the individual case.

Unlike interests or opinions, moreover, social perspectives cannot easily be thought of as conflicting. Put together they usually do not cancel each other out but rather offer additional questions and fuller social knowledge. Perspectives may often seem incommensurate, however. An account of postwar America from the perspective of those now in their eighties cannot be made in the same language and with the same assumptions as an account made from the perspective of those now in their twenties.

V. New Argument for Group Representation

We are now in a position to return to the problem with which I began this essay. Advocates of inclusive democracy are faced with a certain dilemma. On the one hand, in nearly every society an underrepresentation of less privileged structural social groups can be observed in many dimensions. Women are underrepresented everywhere, racial, ethnic, or religious groups often lack significant political influence, as do poor and working-class people. Many find such underrepresentation wrong, which leads to calls for mechanisms of special representation for excluded groups.

Implementing such measures of group representation, on the other hand, seems to imply that the represented group has or should have a common set of interests or opinions. The fact that such unity of interest or opinion almost never exists seems to imply that social group representation is impossible. The idea of representing the social group perspective, coupled with the argument that representation is a differentiated relationships rather than a condition of identity or substitution, aims to move democracy theory out of this dilemma. A structural social group does not exist as a unity prior to the moment of representation, with a clear set of interests and opinions with which it authorizes the representative's action. Rather, the very mechanisms of authorizing a representative activate members of the social group to discuss with one another their perspective on issues, and perhaps to formulate positions. Representing a social group consists primarily in representing the perspective members of the group have derived from their structured social positioning. Perspective concerns questions, assumptions, and particular experience more than answers or conclusions.

Thus a renewed argument for the special representation of oppressed or disadvantaged social groups runs as follows: Inclusive democracy implies that every structured social group perspective in the polity should be represented. Every perspective should be represented not only for reasons of political fairness but also to maximize the social knowledge needed to reach fair and wise decisions. In societies structured by group based privilege and disadvantage, political processes of procedural liberalism generally result in the dominance of the perspectives of privileged groups in political discussion and decision making. Democratic inclusion thus requires special measures to enable the representation of oppressed or disadvantaged structural social groups. Ensuring the representation of multiple perspectives gives voice to distinctive experiences in the society and relativizes the dominant perspectives which are assumed as normal and neutral.

Does this argument imply that minority or disadvantaged interests or opinions should be specially represented? Before deciding that the same sort of reasoning applies to interests and opinions, we should notice their differences from perspectives. Social perspectives arise from broad social structures that position many people in similar ways whether they like it or not. This makes social perspectives basic in a way that some interests and opinions are not. Interests and opinions may be shared with a large number of others, or they may be quite idiosyncratic. Many are voluntarily formed and organized, and their potential number in a given society is vast.

But the primary relevant difference between interests and opinions, on the one hand, and social perspectives, on the other, is that some asserted interests or opinions may be bad or illegitimate, whereas a social perspective is not in itself illegitimate. In a society of white privilege, for example, the social perspective of white people usually wrongly dominates the making of many pub-

Deferring Group Representation

lic discussions, and it should be relativized and tempered by the social perspectives of those positioned differently in the racialized social structures. But the social perspective of white people is not itself wrong or illegitimate. White supremacist opinions, on the other hand, which would call for the forced segregation of all people of color, are illegitimate. A liberal society in which such opinions are held by a small minority might be obliged to let them express the opinions, but it is not obliged to give any special support to them just because they are at a disadvantage in the marketplace of ideas.

In general, liberal principles of free speech and association govern the representation of interests and opinions. Everyone should have the freedom to express opinions and organize groups to publicize them. Everyone should be free to organize groups to promote particular interests. Both freedoms should be limited by rules that enable a similar freedom for others and which prohibit activities that wrongfully harm others. The content of this harm principle is notoriously contested, of course, and I will not enter that controversy here. The point is that on the whole maximizing liberty of speech and association should be the general principle guiding the representation of interests and opinions.

Some critics of interest group liberalism, however, rightly argue that unbridled freedom of expression and association leads to gross unfairness in an economic system where some interests and opinions have much greater access to resources than others. At this point, some of the reasoning used to argue for special measures to ensure that representation of perspectives might also support special measures to ensure the representation of interests or opinions in public debate. Political equality may require guaranteeing media access to groups with few resources, or limiting the ability of richer groups to dominate public influence. As Joshua Cohen and Joel Rogers suggest, moreover, a fair system of interest group representation ought to subsidize the ability to organize of those with legitimate interests but few resources.[22]

How should a principle of the special representation of silenced or excluded perspectives be implemented? Space permits only a brief answer to this important question. In my previous work on group representation, I argued that oppressed or disadvantaged social groups should be given resources to organize, have special representative seats, and veto power over some issues most directly affecting the lives of those associated with the group. This is a strong interpretation of the requirements of the representation of perspectives. While I do not retract this position, at the moment I will defer it, and here will consider other, weaker practical options for promoting the political inclusion of social perspectives.

Many writers and policy makers concerned with group representation look to legislative districts and/or voting procedures. I believe that it is not wrong to draw representative district boundaries in ways that will increase the likelihood that unrepresented social perspectives are represented. As Lani Guinier and others point out, however, it is nearly impossible to create a homogenous district, and group-conscious districting does tend wrongly to balkanize an electorate. Thus, I agree with her and others that various forms of proportional representation in voting schemes may be the best way to combine choice and fairness with a desire to maximize the representation of social perspective.[23]

It is important recognize that law-making bodies need not be the only governmental sites whose members are elected according to rules of representation. A more democratic representative government would have various layers and sites of elected, appointed, and volunteer bodies serving as agenda setting—advisory commissions and administrative review boards, as well as legislatures. In such bodies, it is possible to give specific representation to particular social group perspectives which might not otherwise be present in the policy-making and review processes. If more attention had been paid to special representation of oppressed or disadvantaged groups in the process of setting up the citizens's discussions that led to Oregon's health care rationing plan in 1990, for example, those citizen discussion groups would probably not have been so white middle-class and college educated.[24]

The processes of authorization and accountability that constitute the representative function, finally, should not be thought of as confined to official government bodies. I have already discussed how the free associative life of civil society is important for the formation and expression of interests and opinions. It is also an important site for the consolidation and expression of social perspectives. Deepening democracy means encouraging the

Deferring Group Representation   373

flourishing of associations that people form voluntarily according to whatever interests, opinions and perspectives they find important. A principle of the special representation of oppressed or disadvantaged social perspectives would apply to civil society by subsidizing the organization of members of oppressed or disadvantaged social groups and linking them to processes of policy formation. In order to ensure that the perspectives of migrant groups are represented in the policy-making process, for example, the Dutch government subsidizes the organization of migrant groups and regularly consults with them.[25]

I have argued that the worry that the representation of groups implies that all members of the group must have the same interests presupposes that the representative stands for everyone in the group or somehow unites the group. Conceiving representation as a differentiated relationship whose primary moments are authorization and accountability, I have suggested, helps dispel this logic of identity. Representation of social positions structured by gender, race, nation, class, age, and so on, moreover, should be thought of primarily in terms of perspective rather than interests or opinions. Representing a social perspective means bringing to discussion certain kinds of experiences, questions, and sensibilities, moreover, rather than making positive assertions about policy outcomes. Thus, representing perspectives is less unifying than representing interests or opinions, and a particular perspective may be compatible with a variety of interests and opinions. Special mechanisms for ensuring the representation of perspectives that would not otherwise be represented maximizes fairness and social wisdom.

NOTES

I am grateful to Linda Alcoff, David Alexander, Will Kymlicka, and Ian Shapiro for helpful comments on an earlier version of this paper. Earlier versions of this paper were presented at conferences sponsored by the Institute of Philosophy of the Czech Academy of Sciences and the Institute of Cultural Studies in Essen, Germany. I am grateful to Jean Cohen and Gertrud Koch for arranging my speaking on those occasions, and this paper benefitted from discussion at both conferences.

1. See Nelida Archenti, "Political Representation and Gender Interests: The Argentine Example," paper presented at the Sixteenth World Congress of the International Political Science Association, August 1994.

2. I. M. Young, "Polity and Group Difference: A Critique of the Ideal of Universal Citizenship," in *Throwing Like a Girl and Other Essays in Feminist Philosophy and Social Theory* (Bloomington: Indiana University Press, 1990); I. M. Young, *Justice and the Politics of Difference* (Princeton: Princeton University Press, 1990), chapter 6.

3. For versions of this objection, see Anne Phillips, *Democracy and Difference* (Cambridge: Polity Press, 1993); Chantal Mouffe, "Feminism, Citizenship, and Politics," in *The Return of the Political* (London: Verso, 1993).

4. See Maria Lugones, "Purity, Impurity, and Separation," *Signs: A Journal of Women in Culture and Society* 19:2 (Winter 1994): 458–79.

5. Benjamin Barber, *Strong Democracy* (Berkeley: University of California Press, 1984), 145–46; Paul Hirst, *Representative Democracy and Its Limits* (Oxford: Polity Press, 1990).

6. Linda Alcoff argues that the position that a person can and should speak only for herself is an abrogation of responsibility. It ignores the fact that people's lives are affected by the congruence of many distant actions, and that the participation of people in institutions here in turn affects others. See "The Problem of Speaking for Others," in *Cultural Critique* (Winter 1991–92): 5–32.

7. Robert Dahl, *Democracy and Its Critics* (New Haven: Yale University Press, 1989), chapter 16.

8. This is the general vision of deliberative democracy. See Joshua Cohen, "Deliberation and Democratic Legitimacy," in A. Hamlin and P. Pettit, ed., *The Good Polity* (London: Basil Blackwell, 1989), 7–34; John Dryzek, *Discursive Democracy* (Cambridge: Cambridge Univeristy Press, 1990); Iris Marion Young, "Communication and the Other: Beyond Deliberative Democracy," in Seyla Benhabib, ed., *Democracy and Difference* (Princeton: Princeton University Press, 1996).

9. This is Hanna Pitkin's criticism of mirror, or what she calls descriptive, representation. See *The Concept of Representation* (Berkeley: University of California Press, 1972); see also Will Kymlicka, *Multicultural Citizenship* (Oxford: Oxford University Press, 1995), chapter 7.

10. See Ann Phillips, *The Politics of Presence* (Oxford: Oxford University Press, 1995). See also Rian Voet, "Political Representation and Quotas: Hannah Pitkin's Concept(s) of Representation in the Context of Feminist Politics," *Acta Politica* (1992–94): 389–403.

11. See Jacques Derrida, *Of Grammatology* (Baltimore: Johns Hopkins University Press, 1974).

Deferring Group Representation

12. I derive my account of *differance* primarily from Derrida's essay of that title in *Speech and Phenomena and Other Essays in Husserl's Theory of Signs* (Evanston, Ill.: Northwestern University Press, 1973). My discussion of *differance* no doubt will be thought too simple by those familiar with Derrida's philosophy and perhaps too abstract by those who are not. My purpose is not to explicate Derrida but to borrow and perhaps transform as set of concepts that I believe help build a better description of the function of political representation.

13. Derrida, "Differance," 138. See also Derrida's essay, "Sendings: On Representation," translated by Peter and Mary Ann Caws, *Social Research* 49 (Summer 1982): 294–326.

14. Hanna Pitkin, *The Concept of Representation* (Berkeley: University of California Press, 1972).

15. See Claude Lefort, *The Political Forms of Modern Society* (Oxford: Oxford University Press, 1986), 305–25; see also Chantal Mouffe, "Democratic Citizenship and the Political Community," in *The Return of the Political* (London: Verso, 1993), 74–90.

16. See Brian Seitz, *The Trace of Political Representation* (Albany: State University of New York Press, 1995), especially chapters 4 and 5.

17. Frank Cunningham, *Democratic Theory and Socialism* (Cambridge: Cambridge University Press, 1987), chapter 3.

18. Anne Phillips, *The Politics of Presence* (Oxford: Oxford University Press, 1995).

19. John Rawls, *Political Liberalism* (New York: Columbia University Press, 1993). With the term "opinion," however, I do not necessarily intend something so all-encompassing and fundamental as what Rawls calls "comprehensive doctrine," partly because I doubt that most people in modern societies hold and have most or all of their moral and political judgments guided by a single comprehensive doctrine. See I. M. Young, "Rawls's *Political Liberalism*," in *Journal of Political Philosophy* 3:2 (June 1995): 181–90.

20. See Diana Fuss, *Essentially Speaking: Feminism, Nature, and Difference* (London: Routledge, 1989), chapter 1; Bill Martin, *Matrix and Line: Derrida and the Possibilities of Postmodern Social Theory* (Albany: State University of New York Press, 1992), 149–60.

21. I have developed at length a concept of social collectivity that aims to distinguish membership in socially positioned collectives from group identity. See "Gender as Seriality: Thinking about Women as a Social Collective," in *Signs: A Journal of Women in Culture and Society* 19:3 (1994): 713–38.

22. Joshua Cohen and Joel Rogers, "Secondary Associations and Democratic Governance," *Politics and Society* 20:4 (December 1992): 393–472.

23. Lani Guinier, "The Representation of Minority Interests: The Question of Single-Member Districts," *Cardozo Law Review* 14 (1993): 1135–74; "No Two Seats: The Elusive Quest for Political Equality," *Virginia Law Review* 77:8 (November 1991): 1413–1514. See also Center for Voting and Democracy, *Voting Democracy Report*, Washington, D.C., 1995.

24. See Michael J. Garland and Romana Hasraen, "Community Responsibility and the Development of Oregon's Health Care Priorities," *Business and Professional Ethics Journal* 9:3 and 4 (Fall 1990): 183–200.

25. See Yasemin Nohglu Saysal, *Limits of Citizenship: Migrants and Postnational Membership in Europe* (Chicago: University of Chicago Press, 1994), chapter 6.

11

Should Blacks Represent Blacks and Women Represent Women? A Contingent "Yes"

Jane Mansbridge

Disadvantaged groups gain advantages from descriptive representation in at least four contexts. In contexts of group mistrust and uncrystallized interests, the better communication and experiential knowledge of descriptive representatives enhances their substantive representation of the group's interests by improving the quality of deliberation. In contexts of historical political subordination and low de facto legitimacy, descriptive representation helps create a social meaning of "ability to rule" and increases the attachment to the polity of members of the group. When the implementation of descriptive representation involves some costs in other values, paying those costs makes most sense in these specific historical contexts.

In at least four contexts, for four different functions, disadvantaged groups may want to be represented by "descriptive representatives," that is, individuals who in their own backgrounds mirror some of the more frequent experiences and outward manifestations of belonging to the group. For two of these functions—(1) adequate communication in contexts of mistrust, and (2) innovative thinking in contexts of uncrystallized, not fully articulated, interests—descriptive representation enhances the substantive representation of interests by improving the quality of deliberation. For the other two functions—(1) creating a social meaning of "ability to rule" for members of a group in historical contexts where that ability has been seriously questioned, and (2) increasing the polity's de facto legitimacy in contexts of past discrimination—descriptive representation promotes goods unrelated to substantive representation.

In the contexts of group mistrust, uncrystallized interests, a history suggesting inability to rule, and low de facto legitimacy, constitutional designers and in-

This article was completed while the author was a Fellow at the Center for Advanced Study in the Behavioral Sciences. I am grateful for financial support provided by the National Science Foundation Grant #SBR-9601236 and the Institute for Policy Research at Northwestern University. I am also grateful for excellent suggestions, on versions of this and a more comprehensive study, from William Bianco, Carol Swain, Melissa Williams, Iris Marion Young, and participants in seminars at the Ohio State University, Nuffield College, Indiana University, Princeton University, the University of California at San Diego, Harvard University, Northwestern University, and Boston College. I would particularly like to thank Benjamin Page for his close reading and incisive comments on that work.

dividual voters have reason to institute policies that promote descriptive representation, even when such implementation involves some losses in the implementation of other valued ideals. As political parties, legislative committees, and voters weigh the pros and cons of descriptive representation, this analysis argues for attention to the specific historical contexts that make descriptive representation most useful.

The analysis will stress that the deliberative function of democracy requires descriptive representation far more than does the aggregative function. It is primarily when we ask how to improve deliberation—both vertically, between constituent and representative, and horizontally, among the representatives—that we discover the virtue of shared experience, which lies at the core of descriptive representation.

What Is "Descriptive" Representation?

In "descriptive" representation, representatives are in their own persons and lives in some sense typical of the larger class of persons whom they represent.[1] Black legislators represent Black constituents, women legislators represent women constituents, and so on.

Few commentators have noticed that the word "descriptive," modifying representation, can denote not only visible characteristics, such as color of skin or gender, but also shared experiences, so that a representative with a background in farming is to that degree a descriptive representative of his or her farmer constituents. This criterion of shared experience, which one might reasonably expect to promote a representative's accurate representation of and commitment to constituent interests, has a long history in folkways and even in law. Long-term residents in a town often argue for electing to office someone born in the town on the implicit grounds that lifetime experience increases the representative's common experiences with and attachment to the interests of the constituents. Similar arguments appear against "carpetbaggers" in state legislatures. The United States Constitution even requires that a president of the nation be born in the United States. "Being one of us" is assumed to promote loyalty to "our" interests.

Arguments against Descriptive Representation

Descriptive representation is not popular among normative theorists. Indeed, most normative democratic theorists have rejected descriptive representation relatively summarily, often with some version of Pennock's trenchant comment, "No one would argue that morons should be represented by morons" (Pennock 1979,

---

[1] Birch 1993, 72; see also 1964, 16. The term "descriptive representation" was coined by Griffiths and Wollheim (1960, 188) and adopted by Pitkin ([1967] 1972). I use this term instead of the simpler "mirror" representation because of a potential confusion: Many people expect representatives of all kinds to "mirror" the *views* of their constituents. In the two best recent treatments of the issue, Phillips (1995) uses the term "politics of presence" and Williams (1998) the term "self-representation."

630   *Jane Mansbridge*

314, based on Griffiths and Wollheim 1960, 190; see also Grofman 1982, 98; Pitkin [1967] 1972, chap. 4). Even among explicit advocates of group representation the ideal of descriptive representation finds little support. Will Kymlicka writes, "[T]he general idea of mirror [descriptive] representation is untenable" (1995, 139) and Iris Marion Young concurs: "Having such a relation of identity or similarity with constituents says nothing about what the representative does" (1997, 354).

Empirical political scientists studying women and Black legislators have had similar negative assessments. Irene Diamond, the first empirical political scientist to investigate in depth the actions of women legislators, reported, for example, that in New Hampshire, the state with the highest percentage (and also the highest absolute number) of women legislators, most women legislators did not see themselves as "acting for" women, in Pitkin's phrase. Rather, New Hampshire's low salary ($200 a year in 1972) and high representative/constituent ratio (with its consequent low competitiveness) brought to the legislature a high proportion of older homemakers. With little self-confidence or desire for a career in politics, they did not see themselves as representing women's interests (Diamond 1977). On the basis of this kind of evidence, women political scientists often concluded that descriptive female gender had no predictable relation to support for women's substantive interests (e.g., Schlozman and Mansbridge 1979).[2] The first empirical political scientist to investigate in depth the actions of Black members of Congress, Carol Swain, similarly concluded that in the U.S. Congress, "[m]ore black faces in political office (that is, more descriptive representation for African Americans) will not necessarily lead to more representation of the tangible interests of blacks" (1993, 5).

These normative theorists and empirical researchers make an important, incontrovertible point. The primary function of representative democracy is to represent the substantive interests of the represented through both deliberation and aggregation. Descriptive representation should be judged primarily on this criterion. When nondescriptive representatives have, for various reasons, greater ability to represent the substantive interests of their constituents, this is a major argument against descriptive representation.

The Costs of a Lottery: Lesser Talent

The most frequent criticism of descriptive representation charges that descriptive representatives will be less able than others to perform the task of the

---

[2] Sapiro (1981, 712), however, argued that in the case of women descriptive representation was "a necessary condition, but it is not sufficient." Her argument for necessity rested on the grounds that (1) having women rather than men in office demonstrably makes government somewhat more responsive to women's interests; (2) participation in government is intrinsically valuable; and (3) increased representation of women will undermine the perception that politics is a male domain. I will reproduce most of these arguments here, while both moving them from the domain of necessity to contingency and agreeing that the contingent circumstances that make some descriptive representation beneficial for women obtain now.

Should Blacks Represent Blacks and Women Represent Women?   631

substantive representation of interests: "No one would argue that morons should be represented by morons."

This criticism rests primarily on confusing two forms of descriptive representation, the "microcosmic" and the "selective" forms.[3] In "microcosmic" representation, the entire assembly is designed to form a microcosm, or representative sample, of the electorate. Microcosmic representation was the ideal of John Adams, James Wilson, Mirabeau, and certain other eighteenth-century theorists (Pitkin [1967] 1972), including particularly the American Anti-Federalists (Manin [1995] 1997, 109–14). Almost all of Hanna Pitkin's argument against descriptive representation, which has often been taken as dispositive, is explicitly or implicitly directed against this form (Pitkin [1967] 1972, chap. 4).

If microcosmic representation, achievable only by lottery or another form of representative selection, were to replace elected representative assemblies, one cost would indeed lie in the strong likelihood that choosing the members of a ruling assembly at random from the population would produce legislators with less ability, expertise, and possibly commitment to the public good than would choosing those legislators through election. In current electoral systems, many of those who run for election have chosen lawmaking as their vocation. They have spent much of their adult lives acquiring the skills needed for the job. The voters then select among these individuals, guided in part by the ability and training of the candidates in their chosen field. Representatives so selected arguably have greater abilities and training in this field than individuals selected through a representative sample.[4] Representatives who have chosen politics as a calling and who have been selected in competitive elections may also have a greater commitment to the public good than individuals chosen through a representative sample (see Madison [1788] 1987), although some election and reelection incentives work in the opposite direction.

My own experience with town meeting democracy (Mansbridge [1980] 1983) leads me to conclude that the ability, expertise, and commitment to the public good of ordinary members of the public are sufficient to make a relatively random

---

[3] The term "microcosmic" comes from Birch 1993, 72; the term "selective" is my own.

[4] Burnheim's (1985) suggestions for microcosmic representation reduce the potential costs of lesser talent with a process based on a mixture of nomination and lot. Manin ([1995] 1997) traces the different uses of lot in the political systems of ancient Greece, Rome, and the Italian republics of the Renaissance, specifying in each case the mechanisms that increased the likelihood of competent and responsible action on the part of the officeholder chosen by lot. He plausibly attributes the relatively sudden disappearance in the eighteenth century of political interest in the lot both to a concern that citizen *consent* be expressed in electoral participation and—among many writers in England, France, and the Federalists in America—to a desire for representatives to rank higher than most of their constituents in talent, virtue, and wealth. Representation by some forms of lot, he argues, was practicable even in polities as large as those of eighteenth-century England (82). For a general discussion of the uses of randomization, see Elster [1987] 1989.

sample of citizens a plausible, although by no means ideal, representative assembly. In contrast to Pitkin, who argued that there is simply "no room" in a descriptive concept of representation for "leadership, initiative or creative action" ([1967] 1972, 90), I do not find it hard to envision a representative sample of the U.S. population producing the kind of leadership, initiative, and creative action of which the average New England town meeting is capable. The capacities of such leaders, initiators, and creators would undoubtedly not reach the level of those who now guide the United States, but I am not sure that they would be incapacitatingly worse.

Nevertheless, because lawmaking in large states and at the national level usually requires considerable talent and acquired skill, the costs of replacing current elected assemblies with assemblies chosen simply by random selection from the population overwhelm the current benefits. Very few democratic theorists advocate substituting microcosmic representation for electoral representation. Even the Australian John Burnheim, who advocates microcosmic representation based on a modified lot, does not expect his suggestion to be put into practice within our lifetimes in any of the world's current democracies. The suggestions with a greater likelihood of being adopted add to existing electoral systems some component of microcosmic representation.[5]

In the far more frequent "selective" form of descriptive representation, institutional design gives selected groups greater descriptive representation than they would achieve in existing electoral systems in order to bring the proportions of those groups in the legislature closer to their percentages in the population. Selective forms of descriptive representation are necessary, if at all, only when some form of adverse selection operates within an existing system to reduce the proportions of certain groups below what they would achieve by chance. Otherwise, one would expect all the characteristics of the population to be duplicated, more or less, in the legislature in proportion to their occurrence in the population. Selective representation should thus be conceived as com-

[5] Mueller, Tollison, and Willett (1972), Barber (1984, 290–93), and Callenbach and Phillips (1985) have proposed election of officials by lot, but not with the expectation of having their suggestions widely adopted. Dahl (1970, 149; 1977, 17; 1985, 86–89; 1992, 54–57) has suggested adding a third assembly, chosen by lot from a nationwide population, to advise the United States Senate and House of Representatives. More recently Dahl has suggested creating smaller deliberative bodies, drawn by lot from a nationwide population, to consider specific issues, such as health care, in which the re-election incentives of politicians and the desire among the populace to benefit without paying costs combine to curtail appropriate deliberation (Dahl 1997). These bodies are similar to Nagel's (1992) "deliberative assembl[ies] on a random basis" (DARBs), Fishkin's (1991, 1995, 1996) "deliberative opinion polls," and Crosby's (1995, 1996) more local "citizen juries," the last two of which have already developed a notable track record in practice. None of these theorists advocating forms of microcosmic representation has, however, either used the terms "descriptive" or "mirror" representation, or evaluated their recommended microcosmic forms in explicit response to the literature critical of descriptive representation.

Should Blacks Represent Blacks and Women Represent Women?   633

pensating for the effects of some other process that interferes with an expected proportionality.

One version of the selective form of representation draws geographical district lines to encourage the election of representatives from proportionally underrepresented groups. In other versions of selective representation, parliaments and parties set aside a number of seats for members of specific descriptive groups, such as French speakers, Catholics, scheduled castes, or women. Other versions could seek to identify and mitigate or remove on a more universalist basis particular obstacles that now account for some of the underrepresentation of certain groups.

Representatives with selective descriptive characteristics need not be significantly less skilled or dedicated to the public good than representatives chosen for reasons that do not include descriptive characteristics. It is true that adding any criterion (e.g., that a representative have lived in a constituency five or more years, or be of a given gender or ethnicity) to a mix of criteria for selection will always dilute to some degree the impact of the other criteria for selection. The key question is, however, whether the reasons for the currently lower proportion of a given characteristic are functionally related to ability to perform the task of representation. Such lowered ability could be the reason that in the existing system those characteristics have been selected against (as in the case of "morons"). But if the reasons for lower proportions of the characteristic are not functionally related to the task, and if the descriptive characteristic on which one is selecting is widely shared, one would expect any decrement in talent from adding a descriptive criterion to the mix of criteria for selection to be almost infinitesimally small.[6]

The institutional tools that have recently been used to promote relevant descriptive representation (e.g., redrawing district lines in the United States or changing the composition of party lists in Europe) do not seem to have resulted in representatives with noticeably lesser skills or commitment to the public good. Although in microcosmic representation the costs in talent might be considerable, in selective representation those costs seem to be negligible.

The Costs of Selection: Which Groups, Why, and How Many from Each?

If microcosmic representation has the cost of some likelihood of lesser talent, at least it has no costs derived from having to choose some groups rather than others for descriptive representation. Selective representation presents exactly the opposite pattern. The cost in lesser talent is relatively low, but costs do arise

---

[6] If adding descriptive criteria in fact made a selection process dip significantly lower into the pool of potential reprentatives, polities could compensate for any expected descriptive decrement by reducing the negative impact of the other factors on selection (e.g., by instituting public funding for campaigns or increasing the salary of the legislators). The number of talented and dedicated individuals currently driven away from state and federal electoral politics by low salaries and the politically compromising activities of fund-raising is undoubtedly far higher than the number that would be overlooked if, say, ethnicity and gender played greater roles in the selection process.

in the process of group selection. Even here, however, the costs are far lower than is usually assumed.

In 1981, James Morone and Theodore Marmor criticized congressional legislation that required citizens on advisory boards to be "broadly representative of the social economic, linguistic and racial populations of the area"[7] by asking rhetorically what demographic characteristics ought to be represented:

> Common sense rebels against representing left-handers or redheads. What of Lithuanians? Italians? Jews? The uneducated? Mirror views provide few guidelines for selecting which social characteristics merit representation. (1981, 437)

Other commentators have similarly assumed that no principled guidelines could be enunciated to suggest what groups ought to be represented or when.[8] This criticism has so often been thought to be simply unanswerable that its mere statement has been taken as dispositive. We can answer it fairly easily, however, by examining both the deliberative and the aggregative functions of democracy.

The *deliberative* function of representative democracy aims at understanding which policies are good for the polity as a whole, which policies are good for a representative's constituents, and when the interests of various groups within the polity and constituency conflict. It also aims at transforming interests and creating commonality when that commonality can be genuinely good for all. In its deliberative function, a representative body should ideally include at least one representative who can speak for every group that might provide new information, perspectives, or ongoing insights relevant to the understanding that leads to a decision. It should not, however, simply reproduce all views in the polity. The process of choosing representatives should select to some degree against those views that are useless or harmful to the polity as a whole (Mansbridge 1998).

The *aggregative* function of democracy aims at producing some form of relatively legitimate decision in the context of fundamentally conflicting interests. In its aggregative function, the representative assembly should, in moments of conflict, ideally represent the interests of every group whose interests conflict with those of others, in proportion to the numbers of that group in the population. Proportionality with equally weighted votes in the legislature is the representative equivalent of the aggregative ideal of "one person, one vote" in direct democracy. The proportional representation of interests alone cannot create democratic legitimacy, but in combination with either cross-cutting interests or power

---

[7] 1981, 431, quoting the National Health Planning and Resources Development Act of 1974, which called for consumers of health care to sit on the boards of more than 200 Health Systems Agencies.

[8] Grofman writes, for example, "One difficulty with the mirror view is that it is not clear what characteristics of the electorate need to be mirrored to insure a fair sample" (1982, 98). See also Pitkin [1967] 1972, 87–88; Voet 1992, 395; Gutmann and Thompson 1996, 154.

Should Blacks Represent Blacks and Women Represent Women?   635

sharing, and with strong protections for minority rights, it comes sufficiently close.[9]

This analysis allows us to conclude that the perspectives and interests of left-handers should be represented in deliberation when their perspectives are relevant to a decision (e.g., in decisions regarding the design of surgical instruments) and in aggregation when their interests conflict with those of others. Similarly with redheads, Lithuanians, Italians, Jews, the uneducated, and all other groups.

In aggregation, interests are relatively easily represented by nondescriptive representatives. If a right-handed representative will suffer sufficiently in the next election from not voting for left-handers' interests, that incentive is by definition enough to make the representative cast the normatively appropriate vote. It is true that being a left-hander oneself helps produce internal commitment to the struggle, so that when the issue requires more than just casting a vote (e.g., when it requires preparing, proposing, and gathering support for legislation), left-handed representatives will usually be more likely to throw themselves into the fray. But on matters of pure aggregation, reelection incentives and other forms of accountability can make descriptive representation unnecessary. For aggregation alone, normative democratic theory demands only that power be exercised on behalf of particular interest bearers in proportion to their numbers in the population, not that this power be exercised by any particular mechanism.

In deliberation, perspectives are less easily represented by nondescriptive representatives. Through reading, conversation, and living with left-handers, right-handers can learn many of the perspectives of this group that would be relevant to a deliberation. As we will see, however, in the contexts of communicative mistrust and uncrystallized interests this vicarious portrayal of the experience of others by those who have not themselves had those experiences is often not enough to promote effective deliberation—either vertically between constituents and their representatives or horizontally among the representatives. Although a representative need not have shared personally the experiences of the represented to facilitate communication and bring subtlety to a deliberation, the open-ended quality of deliberation gives communicative

---

[9] The questions of which perspectives will contribute to understanding and which interests conflict will often be contested, as will the question of how close in any given case an issue comes to either common or conflicting interests. Moreover, the ideals of achieving understanding and settling conflict legitimately are always "regulative" ideals—that is, ideals at which one should aim but not expect fully to achieve (see Mansbridge 1996 on actual polities never achieving full democratic legitimacy). Giving any group veto power over issues deeply important to that group can be useful in a compromise instituting some form of cooperative self-rule when cooperation would otherwise not take place, but such vetoes favor the status quo in inegalitarian ways. Restricting such vetoes to disadvantaged groups (Young 1990) raises the thorny question of how to define which groups deserve such a veto (Kymlicka 1995, 145; Phillips 1992, 89; Williams 1998, 198).

and informational advantages to representatives who are existentially close to the issues.[10]

Do deliberations require the participation of representatives of relevant perspectives in proportion to the incidence of those perspectives in the population? In theory, deliberation seems to require only a single representative, or a "threshold" presence, in the deliberation to contribute to the larger understanding (Kymlicka 1993, 77–78, 1995, 146–47; Mansbridge 1981; Phillips 1995, 47, 67ff.; Pitkin [1967] 1972, 84). Getting the relevant facts, insights, and perspectives into the deliberation should be what counts, not how many people advance these facts, insights, and perspectives. In practice, however, disadvantaged groups often need the full representation that proportionality allows in order to achieve several goals: deliberative synergy, critical mass, dispersion of influence, and a range of views within the group.

First, deliberation is often synergistic. More representatives usually produce more, and sometimes better, information and insight, particularly when they may need to explore among themselves new ideas that counter the prevailing wisdom. Groups whose members will be affected by a decision might therefore legitimately demand, even under deliberative criteria, as many representatives as reflect their numbers in the population.

Second, representatives of disadvantaged groups may need a critical mass for their own members to become willing to enunciate minority positions. They may also need a critical mass to convince others—particularly members of dominant groups—that the perspectives or insights they are advancing are widely shared, genuinely felt, and deeply held within their own group.

Third, governing bodies usually include a variety of committees and subcommittees in whose deliberative spaces the most important features of policy are often hammered out. Having sufficient numbers of representatives to disperse into the relevant policy areas allows members of the disadvantaged group to influence decisions wherever those decisions would become better decisions by including these members' perspectives.

Finally and most importantly, because the content and range of any deliberation is often unpredictable, a variety of representatives is usually needed to represent the heterogeneous, varied inflections and internal oppositions that together constitute the complex and internally contested perspectives, opinions, and interests characteristic of any group. This range of views is not easily represented by only a few individuals.

This analysis suggests that African Americans in the United States are far more richly represented deliberatively by a Congress that includes William Gray III (a Black member of Congress who did not support the Congressional Black

---

[10] Pitkin's ([1967] 1972) condemnation of descriptive representation recognized its uses in deliberation, but set up what I believe to be a false dichotomy between "talking" and "actively governing" (63, 84), as well as sometimes seeming to restrict the deliberative function to simply "giving information" (63, 81, 83, 84, 88, 90).

Caucus's alternative budget because he was chairman of the Budget Committee in the House) and George Crockett (a Black member of Congress who condemned the State Department for refusing to grant Yasir Arafat an entry visa) than by a Congress that included only one of these two.[11] No matter how purely deliberative the assembly, reasons of synergy, critical mass, helpful dispersion and internal diversity insure that in practice each group will usually want to claim as many representatives on that body as is justified by proportionality.

The demand for proportionality is accentuated by the fact that in practice almost all democratic assemblies are aggregative as well as deliberative, and achieving the full normative legitimacy of the aggregative function requires that the members of the representative body cast votes for each affected conflicting interest in proportion to the numbers of such interest bearers in the population (see Mansbridge 1981, 1996, 1998 for a fuller exposition of these ideas).

"Essentialism" as a Cost of Selection

The greatest cost in selective descriptive representation is that of strengthening tendencies toward "essentialism," that is, the assumption that members of certain groups have an essential identity that all members of that group share and of which no others can partake. Insisting that women represent women or Blacks represent Blacks, for example, implies an essential quality of womanness or Blackness that all members of that group share. Insisting that others cannot adequately represent the members of a descriptive group also implies that members of that group cannot adequately represent others (Kymlicka 1993, 1995; Phillips 1992, 1995; Swain 1993; Young 1997).

This problem of essentialism haunts every group that hopes to organize politically around a facet of identity, including descriptive characteristics such as place of birth, gender, and race. Essentialism involves assuming a single or essential trait, or nature, that binds every member of a descriptive group together, giving them common interests that, in the most extreme versions of the idea, transcend the interests that divide them. Such an assumption leads not only to refusing to recognize major lines of cleavage in a group, but also to assimilating minority or subordinate interests in those of the dominant group without even recognizing their existence (Fuss 1989; Spelman 1988; see Young 1994, 1997 for ways of conceiving of group existence with a minimum of essentialist thinking). The problem is exacerbated when the facets of identity assumed to bind the

---

[11] See Swain 1993, 41, 49–71, for Gray and Crockett, and passim for the diversity in opinions and styles within the spectrum of African American representation in Congress in the 1980s and early 1990s. See Young 1997 for the concept of diversity of opinion within a single "perspective." For both deliberative and aggregative purposes, the full diversity within any larger perspective or interest should ideally be represented in proportion to numbers in the population, subject to the critical deliberative limitations of (1) threshold representation when a useful perspective would otherwise not be represented at all in a proportional distribution (Kymlicka 1995, 147) and (2) the winnowing out and reduction in salience of relatively harmful and useless ideas.

group together have biological markers, such as sexual organs or skin color, because such markers encourage seeing whatever commonalities are assumed central to the group as biological, not historical.

At its most basic, of course, the process of thought itself encodes a form of essentializing. Most of us cannot think "table" without unconsciously conjuring up a four-legged brown piece of furniture, thereby marginalizing in our considerations the many tables with more or fewer legs and different colors. The problem of simple categorization becomes much worse when, as is often the case in human affairs, one group is socially dominant and becomes the norm, setting expectations and structuring institutions so that those who do not conform to that norm are perceived as deviant or lesser beings, perceive themselves as deviant, and cannot function as well in the structures designed for the members of the dominant group.

Even political groups based on descriptive identity that challenge the hegemony of the dominant group cannot escape this internal dynamic. Feminist organizations that appeal to "sisterhood" have portrayed that sisterhood primarily in terms that reflected the concerns of the dominant (White middle-class) groups in the movement (cf., e.g., Harris 1990; Spelman 1988). Black feminist writers who have challenged that dominance within feminism have themselves portrayed Black women as having a singular "Afrocentric standpoint" (e.g., Collins 1990). Although human cognitive processes prevent our eliminating this tendency to assume homogeneity within a group, we can fight that tendency by cultivating avenues of dissent, opposition, and difference within our organizations, struggling to appreciate contradictions within a larger perceptual standpoint, and using plurals rather than singulars in our writing.

The advocacy of descriptive representation can emphasize the worst features of essentialism. When an extreme descriptivist writes, "it is impossible for men to represent women" (Boyle 1983, 797),[12] that statement implies the corollary, that it is impossible for women to represent men. It also implies that any woman representative represents all women (and all women equally), regardless of the women's political beliefs, race, ethnicity, or other differences.

The essentializing features of descriptive representation can be mitigated by stressing the nonessentialist and contingent reasons for selecting certain groups for descriptive representation. The entire argument in this article is an argument from contingency. Building on a more general argument for the proportional representation of interests, it highlights the historical contexts in which descriptive representation is likely to advance the substantive representation of interests. That descriptive representation most closely approaches normative ideals when it reflects the inner diversity of any descriptively denominated group.

---

[12] See also Phillips 1995, 52, quoting a group of Frenchwomen in 1789 ("a man, no matter how honest he may be, cannot represent a woman") and Williams 1998, 133, quoting the Reverend Antoinette L. Brown in 1852 ("Man cannot represent woman").

Should Blacks Represent Blacks and Women Represent Women?   639

One might also approach contingency from another angle, by asking first what features of the existing electoral process have resulted in lower proportions of certain descriptive groups in the legislature than in the population—a result that one would not expect by chance and that suggests the possibility that "certain voices are being silenced or suppressed" (Phillips 1992, 88; also 1995, 53, 63). The next screening question should be whether the members of that group consider themselves able adequately to represent themselves. If the answer is yes, the third question, bearing on normative responsibility, might be whether there is any evidence that dominant groups in the society have ever intentionally made it difficult or illegal for members of that group to represent themselves. A history of strong prejudice would provide such evidence. If the answer to this third question is also yes, the group appears to be a good candidate for affirmative selective representation. If a group has been in the past excluded by law from the vote, to take an extreme example, it seems likely that the social, political, and economic processes that allowed one group in the past legally to forbid the political participation of another may well have their sequelae in the present, working through informal social, political, and economic structures rather than through the law.[13]

A formulation like this points backward to contingent historical processes rather than inward to an essential nature. It also implies that when the systemic barriers to participation have been eliminated through reform and social evolution, the need for affirmative steps to insure descriptive representation will disappear. The institution of descriptive representation itself becomes contingent.

Other Costs of Descriptive Representation

Another potential cost of selective descriptive representation, related to that of essentialism, involves the way developing institutions that encourage citizens to see themselves as members of a subgroup may erode the ties of unity across a nation, a political party, or a political movement (see, e.g., Phillips 1995, 22ff.). This serious cost has greater or lesser weight depending on the precise institutional

---

[13] The intent of this argument is not to restrict groups designated for selective representation to those who have been legally deprived of the vote or other rights of citizenship, but to draw normative attention to this characteristic on the grounds of past societal responsibility. Such responsibility is also involved when a form of discrimination, such as that against gays and lesbians, has run so deep that it has not been necessary legally to forbid their political participation. Historical discrimination is also usually responsible for communication impaired by distrust, a social meaning of lesser citizenship, and impaired de facto legitimacy, three of the four contexts that in the central argument in the text mandate particular concern for descriptive representation. See Phillips 1992, 1995; Kymlicka 1993, 1995; and Williams 1998 on historical and systemic disadvantage; Guinier (1994, 140) points out, however, that her argument does not rely primarily on the historic context of group disenfranchisement. Political marginalization, our concern here, need not require economic inferiority (Aminzade n.d.).

arrangements. In some contexts, institutions that encourage subgroups tear deeply at the connected fabric of the whole. In other contexts, subgroups become the experiential anchors for participation that links the individual to the whole.[14] As work on "civil society" progresses, scholars may distinguish better than they have to date the characteristics and contexts that incline some institutions to the disintegrative, others to the integrative, function.

Yet another cost of selective descriptive representation applies specifically to a particular method for achieving this result—drawing electoral boundaries to create relatively homogeneous districts. This cost is the potential loss of influence in other districts. If, for example, White Democrats represent many substantive interests of Black voters much better than White Republicans, and if concentrating Black voters in Black districts produces a few more Black representatives at the cost of many more Republicans elected from other districts, then in some historical circumstances, such as when the percentages in a majority-rule legislature are almost tied between Republicans and Democrats, the substantive impact of losing those Democratic legislators will be high and the cost probably not worth paying (see, e.g., Swain 1993, 7–19, Lublin 1997).

A final cost of selective descriptive representation lies in the possibility of reduced accountability. The descriptive characteristics of a representative can lull voters into thinking their substantive interests are being represented even when this is not the case. As one Black representative to the U.S. Congress told Carol Swain, "One of the advantages, and disadvantages, of representing blacks is their shameless loyalty to their incumbents. You can almost get away with raping babies and be forgiven. You don't have *any* vigilance about your performance" (1993, 73).[15] One would expect this danger of blind loyalty to be eased as more descriptive representatives competed for and entered the representative assembly, allowing constituents to compare more easily the virtues of one descriptive representative against another. The appointment of Clarence Thomas to the Supreme Court of the United States may have served as a milestone in the evo-

[14] To draw an example from the organizational level, the American Psychological Association seems to have devolved into a series of separate subassociations after its sections acquired more power, whereas the American Political Science Association seems to have taken on greater vitality since the Organized Sections acquired a greater say in its governance. Arguments for and against strong state and local governance have also addressed these issues, but I know of no comparative studies designed to explore in what contexts strong subordinate governments weaken the superordinate government and in what contexts they strengthen the superordinate government.

[15] The representative's lack of vigilance derives in part from the fact that "Black representatives from historically black districts are essentially guaranteed reelection if they survive their primaries" (Swain 1993, 220), a condition that in turn derives partly from the almost uniform commitment of Black voters "to the party, faction, or individual candidate that is most supportive of racial reform" (Pinderhughes 1987, 113). See Guinier 1994, 35, 58–60, 82, and de la Garza and DeSipio 1993 on the importance of designing representative systems that increase political participation and attentiveness among the electorate, and the problems of majority-minority districts in this respect.

Should Blacks Represent Blacks and Women Represent Women? 641

lution of this process in the Black community, as some African American or-ganizations (e.g., the Congressional Black Caucus and the NAACP) opposed Thomas's nomination in spite of his descriptive characteristics (see Swain 1992; also Crenshaw 1992; West 1992). The decision of many women's groups not to support all women candidates for election represented a similar milestone among U.S. feminists (Mezey 1994, 261).

Against these costs, one must weigh the benefits for substantive representa-tion of enhanced deliberation through descriptive representation. These benefits, I argue, are greatest in contexts of communicative distrust and uncrystallized interests.

Contexts of Distrust: The Benefits of Enhanced Communication

The quality of the mutual communication between representative and con-stituent varies from group to group and era to era. Historical circumstances can interfere with adequate communication between members of one group and members of another, particularly if one group is historically dominant and the other historically subordinate. A history of dominance and subordination typi-cally breeds inattention, even arrogance, on the part of the dominant group and distrust on the part of the subordinate group.

In conditions of impaired communication, including impairment caused by inattention and distrust, the shared experience imperfectly captured by descrip-tive representation facilitates vertical communication between representatives and constituents. Representatives and voters who share some version of a set of common experiences and the outward signs of having lived through those expe-riences can often read one another's signals relatively easily and engage in relatively accurate forms of shorthand communication. Representatives and vot-ers who share membership in a subordinate group can also forge bonds of trust based specifically on the shared experience of subordination.

Claudine Gay's data, for example, indicate that African American con-stituents in districts represented by an African American legislator are more likely to contact their representative than African American constituents in districts represented by a White legislator (Gay 1996). As Representative Donald Payne, a Black member of Congress, commented to Carol Swain, "Black constituents feel comfortable with me, and see that I feel comfortable with them" (Swain 1993, 219). Groups that are disadvantaged in the electoral process differ, however, on this dimension. Replicating Gay's study but look-ing at women representatives, Elizabeth Haynes has shown that women in districts represented by a woman are *not* more likely to contact their repre-sentative than women in districts represented by a man (Haynes 1997). Problems in communication between men and women certainly exist, but the size of the male–female gaps in communication may well be smaller than the size of gaps in communication created by race, ethnicity, nationality, or class.[16]

In the United States, voters have many of their most vital interests represented through the "surrogate" representation of legislators elected from other districts. Advocates of particular political views who lose in one district, for example, can hope to be represented by advocates of those views elected in another district.[17] Surrogate representatives do not have to be descriptive representatives. But it is in this surrogate process that descriptive representation often plays its most useful role, allowing representatives who are themselves members of a subordinate group to circumvent the strong barriers to communication between dominant and subordinate groups. Black representatives, for example, are likely to be contacted by Blacks "throughout the region" and not just in their own districts. The district administrator for the late Mickey Leland, a Black Texas Democrat, told Carol Swain: "What people don't understand is that Mickey Leland must be the [Black] Congressman for the entire Southwest" (Swain 1993, 218).

One example will illustrate the communicative advantages of descriptive representation, even for women, whose barriers to communication with men are probably not as high as the barriers between Blacks and Whites. In 1970, before the current slight increase in the number of women representatives in the U.S. Senate, Birch Bayh was arguably the progressive senator most sympathetic to the Equal Rights Amendment (ERA). One of his roles was, therefore, to act as a surrogate representative for the women proponents of the ERA. Bayh served the ERA activists who consulted him both as mentor, through his commitments to progressive causes, and as gatekeeper, through his role as chair of the Judiciary Committee.

---

[16] See Williams 1998 on "trust," for the history of Blacks' justified mistrust of Whites in the United States. See Tannen 1994, 73, 188, for implied comparisons of gender and ethnicity differences. Only after Hyde's (1990) injunction to pay attention to size of difference as well as existence of difference have psychologists begun routinely to include measures of size of difference in their studies, particularly of gender difference. Many linguists have not yet adopted this strategy. In neither field is it standard to compare the size of gender differences to the size of other common differences—an omission that contributes to the common magnification of gender differences (Mansbridge 1993). I know of no studies on class differences in communicating with representatives (for suggestive data see Heilig and Mundt 1984, 85–91). Note that this analysis focuses on *communicative* distrust as it obstructs fruitful deliberation. On surveys taken in the United States women do not report having more generalized distrust of "the government" than men or Blacks than Whites (see Orren 1997, 86).

[17] Surrogate representation is in many ways similar to what Burke called "virtual representation" ([1792] 1871, 293). It differs in applying to the aggregative as well as the deliberative function of democracy, to will as well as wisdom, to changing preferences as well as relatively fixed and objective interests, and to negotiations among self-interested groups as well as the good of the nation as a whole (Pitkin [1967] 1972, 169–75; see Williams 1998, 33ff. for a nuanced discussion of Burke's concept of a "description" of people). Burke therefore did not address questions of proportionality, as does my concept of surrogate representation, Weissberg's (1978) similar "collective representation," and Jackson and King's (1989) "institutional" representation. For a fuller analysis of surrogate representation, see Mansbridge 1998.

Early in the constitutional amendment process, Senator Bayh suggested to the proponents an alternate wording for the ERA, based on the words of the existing Fourteenth Amendment to the constitution, which guaranteed equal rights based on race. The ERA proponents rejected Bayh's proposed wording as "weakening" the force of the Equal Rights Amendment. It is not clear in retrospect, however, that the alternate wording would have weakened the amendment. And the wording Bayh suggested would undoubtedly have greatly clarified the uncertainty that eventually became one main cause for the ERA's failure to be ratified in the states.

The history of the interaction between Birch Bayh and the ERA proponents reveals considerable distrust of Bayh among the proponents—a distrust greatly increased by the young male Ivy League staffer assigned to the project, who reportedly described the ERA proponents as "hysterical" women. Had the Senate at that time included a powerful progressive female legislator such as Patricia Schroeder, the ERA proponents would undoubtedly have chosen her as their mentor. The female legislator in turn would almost certainly not have assigned such an insensitive staff member to the project. A female legislative mentor might even have convinced the ERA supporters to adopt a wording parallel to the Fourteenth Amendment, which in turn would very probably have resulted in the ERA's being ratified in the states. This ratification would have induced the members of the Supreme Court to make gender a "suspect category" in their analyses, which it is not now. Alternatively the female legislator and the activists together might have decided, in a more thorough deliberative process, to retain the original wording even at the risk of failure in ratification.

The failure of Birch Bayh to communicate with the ERA proponents in an atmosphere of mutual trust exemplifies the importance of descriptive representation in the larger system of surrogate representation. It suggests the following rule: The deeper the communicative chasm between a dominant and a subordinate group, the more descriptive representation is needed to bridge that chasm.

Contexts of Uncrystallized Interests:
The Benefits of Experiential Deliberation

In certain historical moments, citizen interests on a given set of issues are relatively uncrystallized. The issues have not been on the political agenda long, candidates have not taken public positions on them, and political parties are not organized around them. In Eastern and Central Europe after the fall of communism, for example, many political interests were relatively uncrystallized, as hundreds of new political parties struggled to define themselves on the issue map. (One Polish party called itself "Party X," using a consciously contentless signifier; another defined itself, with almost as little content, as "slightly West of center.")

When interests are uncrystallized, the best way to have one's most important substantive interests represented is often to choose a representative whose descriptive characteristics match one's own on the issues one expects to emerge. One might want to elect a representative from one's own geographical territory, class, or ethnicity. Then, as issues arise unpredictably, a voter can expect the representative to react more or less the way the voter would have done, on the basis of descriptive similarity. The original geographic representation of voters in the United States was undoubtedly intended in part to capture this form of descriptive representation.

In political systems where many issues, such as those involving economic class, are relatively crystallized, other issues, such as those involving gender, are surfacing and evolving rapidly on the political agenda. When this is the case, individuals for whom these relatively uncrystallized interests are extremely important may get their best substantive representation from a descriptive representative.[18] Here, the important communication is not vertical, between representative and constituent, but horizontal, among deliberating legislators. In this horizontal communication, a descriptive representative can draw on elements of experiences shared with constituents to explore the uncharted ramifications of newly presented issues and also to speak on those issues with a voice carrying the authority of experience.

In the United States, where party discipline is weak and representatives consequently have considerable autonomy, legislators often vote by "introspective representation," acting on the basis of what they themselves have concluded is the right policy for their constituents and the nation. When this is the case, voters exercise power not by changing the behavior of the representatives, as suggested in traditional mechanisms of accountability, but by electoral selection.[19] In this process, the voters often use descriptive characteristics, as well as party identification and indicators of character, as cues by which to predict whether a particular candidate, if elected, will represent their interests, both crystallized and uncrystallized.

In 1981, for example, when the Illinois legislature was about to vote on the Equal Rights Amendment, I asked several legislators how they determined what their constituents thought about the amendment. One rural legislator explained that he knew what his constituents felt because they felt the way he did: "I come from my district, and they were brought up the same way that I am, or was, and

[18] Two of Anne Phillips's four "key arguments" for descriptive representation turn on this issue. One is "the need to tackle those exclusions that are inherent in the party-packaging of political ideas" and the other "the importance of a politics of transformation in opening up the full range of policy options" (1995, 25; see also 43–45, 50, 70, 151ff.). Her analysis, particularly of transformative politics, goes much further than I have the opportunity to do here. Holding other features of substantive representation equal, one might expect descriptive representatives in a field of uncrystallized interests to be most efficacious when dominant groups have kept key issues off the political agenda (see Bachrach and Baratz 1963).

[19] Mansbridge 1998. Others have called this process representation by "recruitment" (Kingdon 1981, 45), "initial selection" (Bernstein 1989), or "electoral replacement" (Stimson, MacKuen, and Erikson 1995).

worked the same way I always have" (Mansbridge 1986, 152).[20] As a descriptive representative of his constituents, he believed he could know their reactions to the ERA without the ERA having been on the political agenda when he was elected and without consulting his constituents subsequently. He took himself to be "one of them," and was presumably so taken by most of his constituents, by virtue of a cluster of descriptive characteristics, not one.

In the United States Congress, one Midwest Republican made a similar descriptive argument, assuming a similar homogeneity within another member's district:

> I could take you down the hall and introduce you to a member who just drips his district, from his shoes to his straw hat. You don't have to go to his district to know what it's like, you just have to look at him. . . . Congress represents its districts because each member comes from his district much more so than because he tries to adapt his personal philosophy [to what his constituents want]. (Bianco 1994, 39)

Focusing on what at first seems more like a single descriptive characteristic, a Black legislator told Richard Fenno, "When I vote my conscience as a black man, I necessarily represent the black community. I don't have any trouble knowing what the black community thinks or wants" (Fenno 1978, 115). Yet this legislator's stance of introspective representation derived from far more than the color of his skin. "His own identification with the black community," Fenno commented, "is obvious and total. Every expression he gives or gives off conveys the idea, 'I am one of you'" (ibid.). The representative assumed that he and his constituents shared a set of experiences that generated specific perspectives and interests requiring representation in the legislature. His constituents in turn used not only the visible characteristic of skin color but also his body language, choice of words, accent, and other external signals to predict the likelihood of a large body of experience shared with them and other African Americans.[21]

When unable to select a representative with reliable descriptive characteristics, voters often select for what I call "pseudo-description," mimicking descriptive behavior. Samuel Popkin recounts President Gerald Ford's adventures campaigning in Texas, as Ford tried unsuccessfully to eat a tamale in order to show Mexican American voters that he was "like them" to the extent of appreciating their food. Popkin comments that familiarity with a culture's food is "an obvious and easy

---

[20] Or, as a member of Congress put it to John Kingdon: "I grew up with these people and I guess I reflect their thinking" (1981, 45). Because of this almost complete attitudinal identity with a majority of their constituents, members of Congress will say and believe, "You'll find congressmen most of the time will want to vote according to their obligations and principles as they see them. The political considerations are less important" (ibid., 46). As one journalist summed up the relationship: "They [the members of Congress] just reflect where they came from" (ibid., 47). Such statements reflect assumptions of a relative homogeneity of interests and perspectives within the majority that elected the representative (Bianco 1994).

[21] Conversely, both the West Indian background of General Colin Powell and other signals in his language, deportment, and political identification led some African Americans not to see him as a descriptive representative whom they would expect to act "like them" in the legislature. See Williams 1998 for the centrality of shared experience to descriptive representation.

646 *Jane Mansbridge*

test of ability to relate to the problems and sensibilities of the ethnic group and to understand and care about them" (1994, 3). Later he confirms that

> [d]emographic facts provide a low-information shortcut to estimating a candidate's policy preferences. . . . Characteristics such as a candidate's race, ethnicity, religion, gender and local ties . . . are important cues because the voter observes the relationship between these traits and real-life behavior as part of his daily experience. When these characteristics are closely aligned with the interests of the voter, they provide a basis for reasonable, accessible, and economical estimates of candidate behavior. (1994, 63–65)

The accuracy of these cues, and the degree to which they predict "identification" (Fenno 1978, 58–59) or "common interests" (Bianco 1994), depends on the degree to which the descriptive characteristics are in fact aligned with the interests of the majority of voters in their districts, so that representatives engaged in introspective representation will reflect the policies their constituents would choose if they had greater knowledge and time for reflection.

In introspective representation both postelection communication and traditional accountability between the representative and the constituent can be nonexistent, and the relation still fulfill democratic norms. Because this is not a traditional principal–agent relation but rather a relation only of selection, democratic norms require that in the selection process communication be open, accurate, and likely to help participants achieve a better understanding of their interests. We can also judge the relationship normatively by making a third-person estimate of the interests of the constituents and the degree to which the representative actually promotes those interests effectively in the assembly (Mansbridge 1998).

When legislators are engaged primarily in introspective representation, descriptive representation will enhance that representation most when interests are relatively uncrystallized—that is, when party identification and campaign statements provide poor clues to a representative's future actions. On the many issues relating to gender, for example, where views are changing and policies developing in a relatively ad hoc way to meet a rapidly evolving situation, descriptive representatives are, other things equal, more likely than nondescriptive representatives to act as their descriptive constituents would like them to act.

Issues of race, which are somewhat more crystallized in the United States than issues of gender, also produce moments when a descriptive representative acts in a context of relatively uncrystallized interests. In 1993, when Carol Moseley-Braun was the only Black member of the U.S. Senate, only she was galvanized into action when Senator Jesse Helms attached to one piece of legislation an unrelated amendment renewing the design patent of the United Daughters of the Confederacy—a design that featured the confederate flag. Moseley-Braun argued vehemently against the Senate's legitimating the flag by granting this patent, and succeeded in persuading enough senators to reverse themselves to kill the measure.[22]

As an African American, Moseley-Braun was undoubtedly more likely than even the most progressive White representative to notice and feel it important to

---

[22] Adam Clymer, "Daughter of Slavery Hushes Senate," *New York Times*, 23 July, 1993. See also Gutmann and Thompson 1996, 135–36.

Should Blacks Represent Blacks and Women Represent Women?   647

condemn the use of the Confederate flag on the design patent of the United Daughters of the Confederacy. The flag issue had not previously appeared on the active political agenda of either the nation or the state of Illinois, Moseley-Braun's constituency. Moseley-Braun undoubtedly had never mentioned the issue in her election campaign. Nor could Moseley-Braun have feared reelection sanctions on this point, since without her intervention the amendment would have passed unnoticed. She did, it turns out, use the issue to consolidate her position with her Democratic constituency in the next election, but one can imagine a less dramatic issue in which this would not be the case. The most important reason for her action seems to have been the particular sensibility, created by experience, that led her to notice the Confederate flag and be offended by it. Her descriptive characteristics—going beyond skin color to her use of language and ties to her church—had earlier signaled that sensibility to her Black constituents. The visible characteristics were the outward signs of the shared experience that allowed her, as a representative, to react as most of her descriptive constituents would have liked.[23]

With respect to gender, many issues relating to sexual harassment and violence against women are politically salient but have not become sufficiently crystallized that the two main parties in the United States have developed distinctive and opposing positions in regard to them, or that candidates usually mention their positions on these issues in their campaigns. It is not surprising, then, that women legislators have usually been the ones to bring these issues to the legislative table. In Illinois, for example, the Commission on the Status of Women, a bipartisan legislative group including a few nonlegislators such as the antifeminist Phyllis Schlafly, suggested to the legislature a bill that, among other things, instituted the crime of rape in marriage. This pattern of distinctive attention has been repeated in legislature after legislature. Having more women in office unquestionably makes government policies more responsive to the interests of most women.[24] Proportional descriptive representation would undoubtedly reflect an even wider range of views among women, producing a more

[23] Her Experience as an African American also helped Moseley-Braun find words to describe the issue that would convince the other senators to change their minds. See Williams 1998 on "voice."

[24] Thomas (1994) summarizes the literature on gender differences among legislators and adds important data of her own. She and Mezey (1994) each point out that although on several feminist issues party affiliation predicts feminist position better than female gender, gender has its own independent effect. See also Berkman and O'Connor 1993; Skjeie 1991; Jonasdottir 1988; Strauss 1998. Representative diversity (and the critical mass of important subgroups within that diversity) in any descriptive group greatly increases the chances of diverse perspectives being represented in deliberation. For example, although there was one Black woman on the 16-member Illinois Commission on the Status of Women when it debated the Sexual Assault Act (which also changed the burden of proof in rape, requiring the alleged rapist rather than the victim to show that the victim had consented), it is not clear how deeply, if at all, the commission discussed the distinctive concerns of Black women on this issue. The differential conviction rates of African American and White men, the historical legacy of lynching, and the ongoing racism of most contemporary police forces complicate for Black women approval of any law such as this that shifts the burden of proof on consent in rape from the victim to the alleged rapist (see Crenshaw 1991; Gilmore 1996, chap. 3; Richie 1996; Walker 1981).

nuanced sensitivity to differences within that group. Reflecting internal group differences is a particularly important feature in deliberation when issues are uncrystallized and may be taking their first, and possibly defining, shape.

Disadvantaged groups also may need descriptive representation in order to get uncrystallized substantive interests represented with sufficient vigor (see Phillips 1995, 69 and passim, on the "degree of vigorous advocacy that people bring to their own concerns"). As Pamela Conover observed in a different context,

> [t]he way we think about social groups depends enormously on whether we are part of that group. Try as we might, the political sympathy that we feel for other groups is never quite the same as that which these groups feel for themselves or that which we feel for ourselves. (Conover 1988, 75)

In the case of Anita Hill versus Clarence Thomas, for example, an issue involving sexual harassment (which could not have been on the agenda of the members of the U.S. House of Representatives when they ran for election) emerged in the Senate hearings on the nomination of Thomas for the Supreme Court. It was the women in the House of Representatives, where the number of women had reached a critical mass, who took decisive action. The famous photograph of five women legislators from the House of Representatives charging up the Senate steps to demand a delay in the Thomas nomination captured for many women voters the need to have representatives of their own gender in the legislative body.

Particularly on issues that are uncrystalized or that many legislators have not fully thought through, the personal quality of being oneself a member of an affected group gives a legislator a certain moral force in making an argument or asking for a favorable vote on an issue important to the group.[25]

Beyond Substantive Representation

Two other benefits of descriptive representation do not enhance substantive representation, but nevertheless deserve consideration in any discussion of the costs and benefits of descriptive representation. These benefits arise from the representative assembly's role in constructing social meaning and de facto legitimacy.

The Construction of Social Meaning

In certain historical conditions, what it means to be a member of a particular social group includes some form of "second-class citizenship." Operationally, this is almost always the case when at some point in the polity's history the group has been legally excluded from the vote. In these conditions, the ascriptive character of one's membership in that group carries the historically embedded

---

[25] I take this point from Representative Barney Frank (personal communication, June 1998), who as an openly gay legislator in the U.S. Congress serves as a surrogate descriptive representative for many on gay and lesbian issues.

meaning, "Persons with these' characteristics do not rule," with the possible implication, "Persons with these characteristics are not able to (fit to) rule."[26]

Whenever this is the case, the presence or absence in the ruling assembly (and other ruling bodies, such as the executive and judiciary) of a proportional number of individuals carrying the group's ascriptive characteristics shapes the social meaning of those characteristics in a way that affects most bearers of those characteristics in the polity.

A parallel outside the polity may clarify the process of meaning construction. Before the Second Wave of the women's movement in the United States and the revolution in women's sports that it brought about, it was part of the definition of "female" to be nonathletic. The definition was not all encompassing: some women found ways of being female and athletic. But most women were expected, and expected themselves, to be poor athletes. Today, girls' and women's sports in schools and universities have begun to be funded, although not usually at levels comparable to those of boys' and men's sports. Women athletes are in the news—although again, not to the same degree as men. These social facts change the definition of being female in regard to athletics in a way that affects every female regardless of her own orientation and actions.

Similarly, when descriptive characteristics signal major status differences connected with citizenship, then a low percentage of a given descriptive group in the representational body creates social meanings attached to those characteristics that affect all holders of the characteristics. Low percentages of Black and women representatives, for example, create the meaning that Blacks and women cannot rule, or are not suitable for rule.

In 1981, Virginia Sapiro argued that increased descriptive representation of women in the legislatures would undermine the perception that politics is a "male domain" (1981, 712; see also Phillips 1995, 39, 79ff.). In 1976, Mack Jones reported that the growing number of Black elected officials in the South had changed that region's political culture: "The idea of Blacks as political participants rather than subjects is becoming the norm" (1976, 406). In 1989, a Black member of the Arkansas House of Representatives said he worked to help Blacks get elected in local races because he wanted to dispel "the myth that some white kids might have that blacks can't serve or shouldn't be serving at the courthouse" (cited in Guinier 1994, 54; see also 34, 36). If the women representatives are almost all White and the Black representatives are almost all men, however, the implicit message may be that Black women do not or should not rule. A similar message holds for gay men and lesbian women.

This is a historically specific and contextual dynamic. Normatively, making a claim for descriptive representation on these grounds requires historical grounding for the factual contention that the social meaning of membership in

---

[26] The concept has a word in German: *Regierungsfahig*, "fit to rule."

650   *Jane Mansbridge*

a given descriptive group incorporates a legacy of second-class citizenship. Such a claim could point, for confirmation, to a history of being legally deprived of the vote.

A major cost to this claim, in addition to the problem of essentialism discussed earlier, involves the way the very process of making a claim of historical disability to some degree undermines claims on other political tracks that members of the group have currently achieved the status of first-class citizens. As in any claim for justice based on disadvantage, signaling that disadvantage in public erodes the public presentation of the group as fully equal. This cost must be balanced against the benefit of creating new social meanings that include members of the group as truly "able to rule."

Claims like this one, based partly on the concept of reparations, do not in theory entail the cost of painting a group as disadvantaged, because—as in the restitution of property in the countries of the former Soviet bloc—claims for reparation can be and are made by political, economic, and social equals (or superiors). But claims for reparation do require both establishing a history of intentional injustice and arguing convincingly that a particular form of reparation (in this case establishing some form of selective descriptive representation) is the best way of redressing that injustice.[27]

The argument here for the creation of social meaning is an argument not for a right but for a social good. The argument is simply that if the costs are not too great, any measure is good that increases the degree to which the society as a whole sees all (or almost all) descriptive groups as equally capable of ruling.

De facto Legitimacy

A second benefit to descriptive representation comes in the increased empirical (or sociological, or de facto) legitimacy of the polity. Seeing proportional numbers of members of their group exercising the responsibility of ruling with full status in the legislature can enhance de facto legitimacy by making citizens, and particularly members of historically underrepresented groups, feel as if they themselves were present in the deliberations (Gosnell 1948, 131, cited in Pitkin [1967] 1972, 78; also Guinier 1994, 35, 39; Kymlicka 1993, 83; Minow 1991, 286 n. 69, 291; Phillips 1995). Seeing women from the U.S. House of Representatives storming the steps of the Senate, for example, made some women feel

---

[27] Distinguishing between minority "nationalities" and minority "ethnic groups" within a nation-state, Kymlicka (1995) makes a convincing case on the basis of reparations for nationalities having forms of representation separate from those of the majority population. Although Kymlicka does not espouse descriptive representation for minority ethnic groups or women, a similar historically based case could be made for temporary forms of selective descriptive representation. See Williams 1998 on "memory," suggesting for selective descriptive representation only the two criteria of contemporary inequality and a history of discrimination. Using only these criteria would generate as candidates for selective descriptive representation Asians, Latinos, 18- to 21-year-olds, and the propertyless, among other groups.

actively represented in ways that a photograph of male legislators could never have done.

To a great degree this benefit is a consequence of previous ones. Easier communication with one's representative, awareness that one's interests are being represented with sensitivity, and knowledge that certain features of one's identity do not mark one as less able to govern all contribute to making one feel more included in the polity. This feeling of inclusion in turn makes the polity democratically more legitimate in one's eyes. Having had a voice in the making of a particular policy, even if that voice is through one's representative and even when one's views did not prevail, also makes that policy more legitimate in one's eyes.[28]

These feelings are deeply intertwined with what has often been seen as the "psychological" benefits of descriptive surrogate representation for those voters who, because of selective bias against their characteristics, are less than proportionately represented in the legislature. The need for role models, for identification, and for what Charles Taylor (1992) has called "equal dignity" and "the politics of recognition" can be assimilated under this rubric. In many historical moments, these factors may be of great importance to a particular constituency.

I stress the creation of social meaning and de facto legitimacy rather than, say, the need for role models on the part of individuals in the descriptively underrepresented group precisely because points like these have often been presented as questions of individual psychology.[29] Instead, I want to point out that the social meaning exists outside the heads of the members of the descriptive group, and that de facto legitimacy has substantive consequences.

I agree that social relations among and between groups can have major effects on individual identity. It is important that members of a disadvantaged group not be given, in Taylor's words, "a demeaning picture of themselves" (1992, 65). From this perspective, if the costs are not too great, we should promote diversity in all positions of authority and excellence. Young people in particular need these kinds of role models. I have no quarrel with this point. Yet I consider of even greater importance the effects of social meaning on the perceptions and actions of members of the more advantaged groups. There are sometimes more of them, and they are more powerful. My aim, in short, is changing the psychology of the "haves" far more than the psychology of the "have-nots."

---

[28] Heilig and Mundt (1984) found that although moving from at-large to single-member district systems in the 1970s increased the number of Mexican American and Black members on city councils, the fiscal constraints of the cities were so great that even achieving a majority of the group on the council brought few results that greatly affected the citizens (see also Karnig and Welch 1980). At the same time, however, they found that council members from low-income districts were far more likely than at-large representatives to adopt an "ombudsman" role, helping constituents with personal problems and government services. Whatever the cause, the result seemed to be greater satisfaction among constituents after moving to a single-member district system (Heilig and Mundt 1984, 85, 152).

[29] On role models see, e.g., the interview with Representative Craig Washington in Swain 1993, 193. Preston (1978, 198) and particularly Cole (1976, 221–23) stress what I call social meaning.

Jane Mansbridge

For similar reasons I do not contrast "symbolic" and "substantive" representation. In political contexts the word "symbol" often bears the unspoken modifier "mere." Moreover, symbols are often perceived as being "only" in people's heads rather than "real." Psychological needs are intangible, and it is easy incorrectly to contrast the "intangible" with the "real" (as Swain 1993, 211, points out). In most writing on this subject, the structural consequences of descriptive representation have been deemphasized in favor of psychological ones in ways that I believe do not reflect their actual relative influence in contemporary political life.

Institutionalizing Fluid Forms of Descriptive Representation

Because there are always costs to privileging any one characteristic that enhances accurate substantive representation over others, voters and institutional designers alike must balance those benefits against the costs. And because I have argued that the benefits of descriptive representation vary greatly by context, it would be wise, in building descriptive representation into any given democratic institutional design, to make its role fluid, dynamic, and easily subject to change.

This analysis suggests that voters and the designers of representative institutions should accept some of the costs of descriptive representation in historical circumstances when (1) communication is impaired, often by distrust, (2) interests are relatively uncrystallized, (3) a group has once been considered unfit to rule, (4) de facto legitimacy is low within the group. The contextual character of this analysis suggests strongly that any institutionalization of descriptive representation is best kept fluid. Microcosmic forms of descriptive representation are best kept advisory and experimental for a good while, as they currently are. Selective forms are also best kept experimental. Permanent quotas are relatively undesirable because they are both static and highly essentializing. They assume, for example, that any woman can stand for all women, any Black for all Blacks. They do not respond well to constituents' many-sided and cross-cutting interests.

Drawing political boundaries to produce majority-minority districts is also both relatively static and essentializing. Cumulative voting in at-large districts (Guinier 1994) is far more fluid, as it allows individuals to choose whether they want to cast all their votes for a descriptive representative or divide their votes among different representatives, each of whom can represent one or another facet of the voters' interests. Such systems, however, have their own costs in party collusion to produce noncompeting candidates and the consequent voter demobilization.[30] Systems of proportional representation with party lists have well-known costs, but are still a relatively flexible way to introduce selective de-

---

[30] The state of Illinois practiced cumulative voting until the process was eliminated in 1982 in a cost-cutting effort that reduced the size of the assembly. The cumulative voting system produced greater proportional representation of Democrats and Republicans in the state legislature but not a great degree of voter choice, because for strategic reasons the two major parties often ran altogether only three candidates for the three seats available in each district (Sawyer and MacRae 1962; Adams 1996).

REPRESENTATION

Should Blacks Represent Blacks and Women Represent Women? 653

scriptive representation, as those lists can change easily in each election.[31] Similarly, experimental decisions by political parties to make a certain percentage of candidates descriptively representative of an underrepresented group are preferable to quotas imbedded in law or constitutions. Such ad hoc arrangements can be flexible over time.

Less obtrusive, although also undoubtedly less immediately successful, are other "enabling devices," such as schools for potential candidates (Phillips 1995, 57), and reforms aimed at reducing the barriers to representation, such as those studied by the Canadian Royal Commission on Electoral Reform: "caps on nomination campaign expenses; public funding of nomination campaign expenses . . . ; the establishing of formal search committees within each party to help identify and nominate potential candidates from disadvantages groups; and so on" (Kymlicka 1993, 62). Vouchers for day care or high-quality day care at the workplace of elected officials would reduce the barriers to political entry for parents of young children. Scholarships to law schools for members of historically disadvantaged and proportionally underrepresented groups would reduce another major barrier to entry.[32] This approach more generally aims at identifying and then reducing the specific structural barriers to formal political activity that serve to reduce the percentages in office of particular disadvantaged groups (see Table 1).

TABLE 1

Institutionalizing Fluid Forms of Descriptive Representation

LEAST FLUID
1. Quotas in constitutions
2. Quotas in law
3. Quotas in party constitutions
4. Majority-minority districts
5. Quotas as party decisions
6. Proportional representation and/or cumulative voting
7. "Enabling devices"
   a. schools and funding for potential candidates
   b. caps on nomination campaign expenses
   c. public funding of nomination campaign expenses
   d. establishing formal search committees within each party to help identify and nominate potential candidates from disadvantaged groups
   e. high-quality public day care for elected officials
   f. scholarships to law schools and public policy schools for members of historically disadvantaged and proportionally underrepresented groups

MOST FLUID

[31] See Zimmerman 1992, 1994 for the positive and negative features of cumulative voting and different forms of proportional representation.

[32] Directing attention to the eligible pool, Darcy, Welch, and Clark (1987, 101), indicate that the percentage of women in state legislatures rose from 1970 to 1984 in tandem with the percentage of women in the law.

654   *Jane Mansbridge*

This paper represents a plea for moving beyond a dichotomous approach to descriptive representation. It argues that descriptive representation is not always necessary, but rather that the best approach to descriptive representation is contextual, asking when the benefits of such representation might be most likely to exceed the costs. Representation is in part a deliberative process. Recognizing this deliberative function should alert us to contexts of communication impaired by distrust and contexts of relatively uncrystallized interests. In both of these contexts, descriptive representation usually furthers the substantive representation of interests by improving the quality of deliberation. Systems of representation also have externalities, beyond the process of representation itself, in the creation of political meaning and legitimacy. Recognizing these externalities should alert us to contexts of past denigration of a group's ability to rule and contexts of low current legitimacy. In both of these contexts, descriptive representation usually produces benefits that extend throughout the political system.

References

Adams, Greg D. 1996. "Legislative Effects of Single-Member Vs. Multi-Member Districts." *American Journal of Political Science* 40(1): 129–44.

Aminzade, Ronald. N.d. "Racial Formation, Citizenship, and Africanization." *Social Science History.* Forthcoming.

Bachrach, Peter, and Morton Baratz. 1963. "Decisions and Non-Decisions: An Analytical Framework." *American Political Science Review* 57(3): 632–42.

Barber, Benjamin R. 1984. *Strong Democracy: Participatory Politics for a New Age.* Berkeley: University of California Press.

Berkman, Michael B., and Robert E. O'Connor. 1993. "Do Women Legislators Matter?" *American Politics Quarterly* 21(1): 102–24.

Bernstein, Robert A. 1989. *Elections, Representation, and Congressional Voting Behavior.* Englewood Cliffs, NJ: Prentice Hall.

Bianco, William T. 1994. *Trust: Representatives and Constituents.* Ann Arbor: University of Michigan Press.

Birch, A. H. 1964. *Representative and Responsible Government.* London: Allen and Unwin.

Birch, A. H. 1993. *The Concepts and Theories of Modern Democracy.* London: Routledge.

Boyle, Christine. 1983. "Home Rule for Women: Power Sharing between Men and Women." *Dalhousie Law Journal* 7(3): 790–809.

Burke, Edmund. [1792] 1871. "Letter to Sir Hercules Langriche." In *The Works of the Right Honorable Edmund Burke,* vol. 4. Boston: Little, Brown.

Burnheim, John. 1985. *Is Democracy Possible?* Berkeley: University of California Press.

Callenbach, Ernest, and Michael Phillips. 1985. *A Citizen Legislature.* Berkeley: University of California Press.

Cole, Leonard A. 1976. *Blacks in Power: A Comparative Study of Black and White Officials.* Princeton: Princeton University Press.

Collins, Patricia Hill. 1990. *Black Feminist Thought.* London: Allen and Unwin.

Conover, Pamela Johnston. 1988. "The Role of Social Groups in Political Thinking." *British Journal of Political Science* 18(1): 51–76.

Crenshaw, Kimberlé. 1991. "'Mapping the Margins': Intersectionality, Identity Politics, and Violence against Women." *Stanford Law Review* 43(6): 1241–99.

Crenshaw, Kimberlé. 1992. "Whose Story Is It Anyway? Feminist and Antiracist Appropriations of Anita Hill." In *Race-ing Justice, En-Gendering Power: Essays on Anita Hill, Clarence Thomas, and the Construction of Social Reality*, ed. Toni Morrison. New York: Pantheon.

Crosby, Ned. 1995. "Citizen Juries: One Solution for Difficult Environmental Problems." In *Fairness and Competence in Citizen Participation*, ed. Ortwin Renn et al. Norwell, MA: Kluwer Academic Publishers.

Crosby, Ned. 1996. "Creating an Authentic Voice of the People." Presented at the annual meeting of the Midwest Political Science Association, Chicago.

Dahl, Robert A. 1957. "The Concept of Power." *Behavioral Science* 2: 201–15.

Dahl, Robert A. 1977. "On Removing Certain Impediments to Democracy in the United States." *Political Science Quarterly* 92(1): 1–20.

Dahl, Robert A. 1985. *Controlling Nuclear Weapons*. Syracuse: Syracuse University Press.

Dahl, Robert A. 1992. "The Problem of Civic Competence." *Journal of Democracy* 3(4): 45–59.

Dahl, Robert A. 1997. "On Deliberative Democracy." *Dissent* 44(3): 54–58.

Darcy, Robert, Susan Welch, and Janet Clark. 1987. *Women, Elections, and Representation*. New York: Longman.

de la Garza, Rodolfo O., and Louis DeSipio. 1993. "Save the Baby, Change the Bathwater, and Scrub the Tub: Latino Electoral Participation after Seventeen Years of Voting Rights Coverage." *Texas Law Review* 71(7): 1479–1539.

Diamond, Irene. 1977. *Sex Roles in the State House*. New Haven: Yale University Press.

Elster, Jon. [1987] 1989. "Taming Chance: Randomization in Individual and Social Decisions." In *Solomonic Judgements*. Cambridge: Cambridge University Press.

Fenno, Richard F., Jr. 1978. *Home Style: House Members in Their Districts*. Boston: Little, Brown.

Fishkin, James. 1991. *Democracy and Deliberation*. New Haven: Yale University Press.

Fishkin, James. 1995. *The Voice of the People*. New Haven: Yale University Press.

Fishkin, James. 1996. *The Dialogue of Justice*. New Haven: Yale University Press.

Fuss, Diana. 1989. *Essentially Speaking: Feminism, Nature, and Difference*. New York: Routledge.

Gay, Claudine. 1996. "The Impact of Black Congressional Representation on the Behavior of Constituents." Presented at the annual meeting of the Midwest Political Science Association, Chicago.

Gilmore, Glenda Elizabeth. 1996. *Gender and Jim Crow*. Chapel Hill: University of North Carolina Press.

Gosnell, Harold Foote. 1948. *Democracy: The Threshold of Freedom*. New York: Ronald Press.

Griffiths, A. Phillips, and Richard Wollheim. 1960. "How Can One Person Represent Another?" *Aristotelian Society*. Suppl. 34: 182–208.

Grofman, Bernard. 1982. "Should Representatives Be Typical of Their Constituents?" In *Representation and Redistricting Issues*, ed. Bernard Grofman et al. Lexington, MA: D. C. Heath.

Guinier, Lani. 1994. *The Tyranny of the Majority: Fundamental Fairness in Representative Democracy*. New York: Free Press.

Gutmann, Amy, and Dennis Thompson. 1996. *Democracy and Disagreement*. Cambridge: Harvard University Press.

Harris, Angela. 1990. "Race and Essentialism in Legal Theory." *Stanford Law Review* 42(3): 581–616.

Haynes, Elizabeth. 1997. "Women and Legislative Communication." Harvard University. Typescript.

Heilig, Peggy, and Robert J. Mundt. 1984. *Your Voice at City Hall: The Politics, Procedures, and Policies of District Representation*. Albany: State University of New York Press.

Hyde, Janet Shibley. 1990. "Meta-Analysis and the Psychology of Gender Differences." *Signs* 16(1): 5–73.

Jackson, John E., and David C. King. 1989. "Public Goods, Private Interests, and Representation." *American Political Science Review* 83(4): 1143–64.

Jane Mansbridge

Jonasdottir, Anna G. 1988. "On the Concept of Interest: Women's Interests and the Limitations of Interest Theory." In *The Political Interests of Gender*, ed. K. B. Jones and A. G. Jonasdottir. Beverly Hills: Sage.

Jones, Mack H. 1976. "Black Office-Holding and Political Development in the Rural South." *Review of Black Political Economy* 6(4): 375–407.

Karnig, Albert K., and Susan Welch. 1980. *Black Representation and Urban Policy*. Chicago: University of Chicago Press.

Kingdon, John W. 1981. *Congressmen's Voting Decisions*. New York: Harper and Row.

Kymlicka, Will. 1993. "Group Representation in Canadian Politics." In *Equity and Community: The Charter, Interest Advocacy, and Representation*, ed. F. L. Siedle. Montreal: Institute for Research on Public Policy.

Kymlicka, Will. 1995. *Multicultural Citizenship*. Oxford: Oxford University Press.

Lublin, David. 1997. *The Paradox of Representation: Racial Gerrymandering and Minority Interests in Congress*. Princeton: Princeton University Press.

Madison, James. [1788] 1987. "Federalist Ten." In *The Federalist Papers*, ed. Isaac Kramnick. New York: Penguin.

Manin, Bernard. [1995] 1997. *The Principles of Representative Government*. Cambridge: Cambridge University Press.

Mansbridge, Jane. [1980] 1983. *Beyond Adversary Democracy*. Chicago: University of Chicago Press.

Mansbridge, Jane. 1981. "Living with Conflict: Representation in the Theory of Adversary Democracy." *Ethics* 91(1): 466–76.

Mansbridge, Jane. 1986. *Why We Lost the ERA*. Chicago: University of Chicago Press.

Mansbridge, Jane. 1993. "Feminism and Democratic Community." In *Democratic Community: NOMOS XXXV*, ed. John W. Chapman and Ian Shapiro. New York: New York University Press.

Mansbridge, Jane. 1996. "Using Power/Fighting Power: The Polity." In *Democracy and Difference: Contesting the Boundaries of the Political*, ed. Seyla Benhabib. Princeton: Princeton University Press.

Mansbridge, Jane. 1998. "The Many Faces of Representation." Working Paper, John F. Kennedy School of Government, Harvard University.

Mezey, Susan Gluck. 1994. "Increasing the Number of Women in Office: Does It Matter?" In *The Year of the Woman: Myths and Realities*, ed. Elizabeth Adell Cook, Sue Thomas, and Clyde Wilcox. Boulder, CO: Westview Press.

Minow, Martha L. 1991. "From Class Actions to Miss Saigon." *Cleveland State Law Review* 39(3): 269–300.

Morone, James A. and Theodore R. Marmor. 1981. "Representing Consumer Institutions: The Case of American Health Planning." *Ethics* 91: 431–50.

Mueller, Dennis C., Robert D. Tollison, and Thomas D. Willett. 1972. "Representative Democracy via Random Selection." *Public Choice* 12: 57–68.

Nagel, Jack H. 1992. "Combining Deliberation and Fair Representation in Community Health Decisions." *University of Pennsylvania Law Review* 140(5): 2101–21.

Orren, Gary. 1997. "Fall from Grace: The Public's Loss of Faith in Government." In *Why People Don't Trust Government*, ed. Joseph S. Nye Jr., Philip D. Zelikow, and David C. King. Cambridge: Harvard University Press.

Pennock, J. Roland. 1979. *Democratic Political Theory*. Princeton: Princeton University Press.

Phillips, Anne. 1992. "Democracy and Difference." *Political Quarterly* 63(1): 79–90.

Phillips, Anne. 1995. *The Politics of Presence*. Oxford: Oxford University Press.

Pinderhughes, Dianne. 1987. *Race and Ethnicity in Chicago Politics*. Urbana: University of Illinois Press.

Pitkin, Hanna Fenichel. [1967] 1972. *The Concept of Representation*. Berkeley: University of California Press.

Popkin, Samuel L. 1994. *The Reasoning Voter*. Chicago: University of Chicago Press.

Preston, Michael. 1978. "Black Elected Officials and Public Policy: Symbolic and Substantive Representation." *Policy Studies Journal* 7(2): 196–201.

Richie, Beth. 1996. *Compelled to Crime: The Gender Entrapment of Battered Black Women*. New York: Routledge.

Sapiro, Virginia. 1981. "When Are Interests Interesting?" *American Political Science Review* 75(3): 701–16.

Sawyer, Jack, and Duncan MacRae. 1962. "Game Theory and Cumulative Voting in Illinois: 1902–1954." *American Political Science Review* 56: 936–46.

Schlozman, Kay, and Jane Mansbridge. 1979. Review of *Sex Roles in the State House* by Irene Diamond. *Harvard Educational Review* 49: 554–56.

Skjeie, Hege. 1991. "The Rhetoric of Difference: On Women's Inclusion into Political Elites." *Politics and Society* 19(2): 233–63.

Spelman, Elizabeth. 1988. *Inessential Woman: Problems of Exclusion in Feminist Thought*. Boston: Beacon Press.

Stimson, James A., Michael B. Mackuen, and Robert S. Erikson. 1995. "Dynamic Representation." *American Political Science Review* 89(3): 543–65.

Strauss, Julie Etta. 1998. "Women in Congress: The Difference They Make." Ph.D. dissertation, Northwestern University.

Swain, Carol M. 1992. "Double Standard, Double Bind: African-American Leadership after the Thomas Debacle." In *Race-ing Justice, En-Gendering Power: Essays on Anita Hill, Clarence Thomas, and the Construction of Social Reality*, ed. Toni Morrison. New York: Pantheon.

Swain, Carol M. 1993. *Black Faces, Black Interests: The Representation of African Americans in Congress*. Cambridge: Harvard University Press.

Tannen, Deborah. 1994. *Gender and Discourse*. New York: Oxford University Press.

Taylor, Charles. 1992. *Multiculturalism and the Politics of Recognition*. Princeton: Princeton University Press.

Thomas, Sue. 1994. *How Women Legislate*. New York: Oxford University Press.

Voet, Rian. 1992. "Gender Representation and Quotas." *Acta Politica* 4: 389–403.

Walker, Alice. 1981. "Advancing Luna—and Ida B. Wells." In *You Can't Keep a Good Woman Down*. New York: Harcourt Brace Jovanovich.

Weissberg, Robert. 1978. "Collective vs. Dyadic Representation in Congress." *American Political Science Review* 72(2): 535–47.

West, Cornell. 1992. "Black Leadership and the Pitfalls of Racial Reasoning." In *Race-ing Justice, En-Gendering Power: Essays on Anita Hill, Clarence Thomas, and the Construction of Social Reality*, ed. Toni Morrison. New York: Pantheon.

Williams, Melissa S. 1998. *Voice, Trust, and Memory: Marginalized Groups and the Failings of Liberal Representation*. Princeton: Princeton University Press.

Young, Iris Marion. 1990. *Justice and the Politics of Difference*. Princeton: Princeton University Press.

Young, Iris Marion. 1994. "Gender as Seriality: Thinking about Women as a Social Collective." *Signs* 19(3): 713–38.

Young, Iris Marion. 1997. "Deferring Group Representation." In *Ethnicity and Group Rights: NOMOS XXXIX*, ed. Ian Shapiro and Will Kymlicka. New York: New York University Press.

Zimmerman, Joseph F. 1992. "Fair Representation for Women and Minorities." In *United States Electoral Systems: Their Impact on Women and Minorities*, ed. Wilma Rule and Joseph F. Zimmerman. Westport, CT: Greenwood Press.

Zimmerman, Joseph F. 1994. "Alternative Voting Systems for Representative Democracy." *P.S.: Political Science and Politics* 27(4): 674–77.

12

American Political Science Review   Vol. 105, No. 3   August 2011

The Concepts of Representation
ANDREW REHFELD

In this reply to Jane Mansbridge's "Clarifying the Concept of Representation" in this issue (American Political Science Review 2011). I argue that our main disagreements are conceptual, and are traceable to the attempt to treat the concept of representation as a "single highly complex concept" as Hanna Pitkin once put it. Instead, I argue, it would be more useful to develop the various concepts that emphasize the underlying forms of representation. Against the view that empirical regularity should guide concept formation, I suggest that the failure to find instances of the cases I conceptualize is not itself a reason to reject them. Instead, I argue in favor of concepts that emphasize one side or other of a relationship, rather than treating both sides simultaneously, defending the view that "promissory" and "anticipatory" may usefully describe the activity of "representing" but ought to emphasize only one side of the representative–voter relationship. I also explain why adding substantive accounts of representation to any of Mansbridge's modifying concepts dilutes their practical value. I conclude by indicating the importance of developing concepts that stretch beyond the democratic contexts that feature prominently in her response.

I am grateful to Jane Mansbridge for her clarifying and generous response to my previous work. (Mansbridge 2011; Rehfeld 2009). I agree with her that political representation is complex and relational. I also agree that the traditional concepts that scholars have used are no longer adequate to the task. As she indicates in four of her five critiques, our disagreements are not so much about the nature of political representation per se as about the concepts we use to study it.[1] These disagreements center on three issues: (i) the standards we use to guide concept design; (ii) how concepts can best model the relational nature of the forms of political representation; and (iii) whether we must build substantive views of representation into the concepts we use to study it. On each of these questions, I argue that a more parsimonious approach to concept formation would yield more useful results.

I have benefited from the feedback of Co-editor Kirstie McClure, Jane Mansbridge and three anonymous reviewers for the *APSR*. For additional feedback I also thank Arash Abizadeh, Chad Flanders, Doug Hanes, Jacob Levy, Ian MacMullen, Nina Valiquette Moreau, Robert Sperling, Christina Tarnopolsky, and Ron Watson, along with participants in a graduate seminar at LUISS Guido Carli, Rome (November 2010), and the Groupe de Recherche Interuniversitaire en Philosophie Politique, Montreal (January 2011). Finally I am grateful for the generous support of Fulbright Canada, the Department of Political Science at McGill University, and its Research Group on Constitutional Studies.

[1] In summary, the four are, first, that the "'Burkean trustee" is an "inadequat[e] . . . analytical tool" (Mansbridge, 2011); second, that "conceptual tools should be chosen for their empirical utility" (ibid.); third, that I misconceived of "promissory and anticipatory representation" as characteristics of individual representatives rather than a relational concept (ibid.); fourth, that the concept of "'surrogate' representation . . combines deliberation and aggregation." (ibid.) The fifth critique (labeled number three in her introduction) takes up the relationship between the interests of the whole and the parts (ibid.), I will not have much to say about my oversight of Eulau and colleagues' 1959 intervention (Eulau et al. 1959). Although Mansbridge rather generously attributes it to the result of subfield specialization, I am inclined to view it as simply an error of scholarship on my part. In any case, I am grateful to Mansbridge for drawing attention to it and explaining the relationship of both of our views in contrast to theirs.

The conceptual disagreements between us speak to a larger issue that Henry Bertram Mayo prefigured 50 years ago when he suggested that the term "representation" had become so complex and shifting as to cease to be useful (Mayo 1960). I believe that he was correct and that the study of representation, particularly among normative scholars, has continued to suffer from the attempt, as Hanna Pitkin put it, to show that the term "does have an identifiable meaning" and that it is a "single, highly complex concept" (Pitkin 1967, 8). Rather than formulating these debates in terms of *one* concept of representation, let alone *the* concept of representation, as Pitkin put it, I believe it would be more useful to develop *concepts* of representation to study the broad array of phenomena that we often imprecisely classify as "representation." These concepts would usefully explore what a representative is and what activity we think is properly denoted by "representing," and separately explain what it means for one thing, or activity, to be "representative" of another. These concepts would further be developed by reference to a range of normative ideals of authority, accountability, consent, interests, responsiveness, recognition, sovereignty, and policy correspondence, to name just a few. There is simply no reason to presume that these very different ideas must share some common covering theme, or that the creation of a concept to do so would be of much use to normative and empirical scholarship, rather than serving merely to obfuscate and confuse. Indeed, the attempt to discern or create a single covering concept of representation has lead to some of the deepest confusions surrounding this topic since Pitkin's seminal work was first published over four decades ago.

Despite the titles of our original articles, and even Mansbridge's claim to be capturing the complexity of the concept itself, Mansbridge and I are not really attempting to "rethink representation." We are, rather, trying to understand the nature of one particular aspect of representation in a highly constrained arena: the relationship between those represented and their representatives in the activity of democratic law making, and democratic decision making more generally.

631

REPRESENTATION

The Concepts of Representation

This is why I think Mansbridge's work in this area is so potentially fruitful and illuminating: She is clarifying critical components of this relationship, even though I resist her own moves to combine them into more complex relational forms. One of the insights that came from my original analysis (Rehfeld 2009) is that the "trustee"/"delegate" distinction emerged from questions primarily about decision making rather than principal–agent questions that were thought to be at the heart of political representation itself. This was surprising, and although Mansbridge does not mention this view in her response, it was to me the most important contribution of the article.

In what follows I will take up a defense of conceptual clarity and disambiguation by responding to the particular substantive disagreements that appear in Mansbridge's response. In the second section, I argue against the view that empirical regularity should guide concept formation; in the third, I argue against building relational complexity into the concepts we use; in the fourth, I explain why including any substantive view of representation in "surrogate representation" minimizes its conceptual utility and also illustrate the disutility of including any notion of hierarchy in Mansbridge's otherwise helpful "selection model." I conclude by indicating the importance of developing concepts that stretch beyond the democratic contexts that feature prominently in her response.

WHY CONCEPTS SHOULD NOT BE (OVERLY) CONSTRAINED BY EMPIRICS

In my original article (Rehfeld 2009), I argued that the historic debate about the proper relationship between representatives and their constituents collapsed three kinds of decisions that representatives were making into the binary trustee/delegate framework. These three descriptive features of their decision-making process when they voted on laws were as follows:

(i) Representatives' *source of judgment*: Were they self-reliant, or did they depend upon their constituents' views about how to vote?
(ii) The *aims of legislation*: Were they promoting the good of all or the good of a part?
(iii) Representatives' own *responsiveness to sanction*: Were they more or less responsive to the prospect of re-election or other sanction?

With the alternatives framed in this way, a representative who acted as a trustee was usually described as (i) relying on his own judgment (ii) to promote the good of all (iii) in a manner that was relatively nonresponsive to electoral sanction. In contrast, a representative who acted as a delegate was usually described as (i) relying on his constituents' judgment (ii) to promote their more narrow good (iii) in a manner that was extremely responsive to electoral (or other) sanction. Once we separate out these three conceptual dyads we will develop eight underlying ideal types; when we force them into the trustee/delegate dyad alone we ignore six of these possibilities (Rehfeld 2009, Table 2).

Mansbridge objects to this typology because empirically two of its conceptually distinct features—responsiveness and source of judgment—tend to go hand in hand. Representatives who are more responsive to sanction tend to rely more on their constituents' judgment. And representatives who are less responsive to sanction tend to rely more on their own judgment instead. Because they are correlated empirically, Mansbridge believes it would be more useful to simply combine them in her concepts: A "gyroscopic representative," as she has described it, thus refer to a representative who is both nonresponsive to sanction *and* self-reliant as well. And because two of the cells in my original table describe unobserved phenomena there is little use in developing them: the nonresponsive representative who follows on her constituents' judgment and the responsive representative who nevertheless follows on her own judgment.

The first disagreement between Mansbridge's view and my own thus centers on our divergent views of how best to develop concepts for the study of social phenomena. As this example illustrates, Mansbridge claims that a concept is less useful if we cannot find many empirical instances (Mansbridge 2011, 629) of its logically independent features, and that our purpose is to choose concepts "for their empirical utility in particular contexts" (Mansbridge 2011, 621). By these standards, concepts should reflect fidelity to the world as it is, has been, or is likely to be, rather than the ways the world might be. As Mansbridge rightly argues, we do not usually see representatives who simultaneously are "nonresponsive to sanction *and* follow their constituents' judgment rather than their own. Nor do we often see its corollary, representatives who are "responsive to sanction" but who nevertheless follow their own judgment. Even though she concedes that my three distinctions are analytically precise and possibly useful in other contexts, she rejects their usefulness in studying democratic legislatures because, in those contexts, they produce empirically empty combinations.

By contrast, I do not think that concepts should be limited by their current or past utility in describing the empirical world, but rather by our theories about what might matter normatively or causally.[2] Because causal and normative theories often require us to

---

[2] I cannot hope to do justice to the multiplicity of views of conceptual analysis that span philosophical and social scientific literatures, but it is worth situating what follows in some of the main debates. Methodological and comparative political scientists have been most interested in developing concepts of use in quantitative and qualitative data analysis (Collier and Gerring 2008; Gerring 1999; Goertz 2006; Sartori 1971), and have offered accounts of concept formation not so far removed from those of the natural sciences with its emphasis on usefulness to understanding the world, their fidelity to nature, and their dependence on theory (Hempel 1966). Political theorists who attend to concepts have usually been more interested in the psychological, sociological, and political effects of the concepts we use, rather than in their epistemic value to come to know things about the world (Connolly 1974; Gallie 1956), going so far as to reject the view that there is even a world about which we might come to know things apart from our conceptualizations of it (see Boghossian 2006 for a pointed critique). For an exception to this view among political theorists, see Barry ([1965] 1990), whose views, along with those of Gerring, Goertz, and Sartori, I generally share. (For useful extensions

REPRESENTATION

American Political Science Review

imagine counterfactuals or mere possibilities as ideals or ideal types, we should develop concepts to cover entities beyond what we observe or are likely to observe. Limiting concepts to the empirically likely would also unjustifiably reify existing normative relationships and practices. As a way of illustration—though importantly not what Mansbridge had in mind for reasons I will explain in a moment—consider that if in 1850 we had to fashion a conceptual map of a "representative" in a way that reflected "many empirical instances" [or one in which we were required to "produce . . . examples . . . .of this sort" (Mansbridge 2011, 624)] we would have rejected the concept of the "female legislator," or worse, built "male" into the very concept of "legislator." Indeed, it is quite likely this is how people did conceive of "legislator" at that time. Yet it would have been a mistake to build "male" into the concept despite its fidelity to the observed cases of "legislator," because it would have then been difficult to ask whether or to what extent gender does or should affect a legislator's decisions, deliberations, etc.

The fact that concepts should not be limited by the way things are does not tell us how we *should* develop them. Nor does it explain why the distinctions I drew were useful in any way. Indeed, in my original article I merely asserted without any demonstration that the distinctions were "enough to provide a useful conceptual space . . . [providing] a rubric by which to assess the rest" (Rehfeld 2009, 225). Mansbridge is right to object, then, not because the distinctions I drew do not conform to empirical regularities but because they simply appear to be pointless. So let me turn to defend this view of concept formation, and then demonstrate the value of these particular distinctions in thinking about political representation.

Concepts express the underlying idea that variables seek to measure; they form the connective tissue between the variables we use and what we think is causally, descriptively, or normatively important. Consider, for example, that Americans who approve of the U.S. President are often found to think that the economy is doing well. If we wanted to explore this frequently observed correlation it would be unhelpful to have a concept and variable like "presconomy" whose meaning was "approve of the president *and* approve of the economy," because we want to test what the relationship between those two components is.[3] At still other times we will want to separate and then ignore other distinctions because we think they are irrelevant to the thing we want to study, again, for either normative or empirical reasons. To use an example from Plato close to my heart (or more precisely my head), we *could* develop a concept of "ruler" that collapsed a person's "fitness to rule" with "baldness," but such a distinction

would not be useful, because we have no good reason to think that these two features are causally related.

Turning to the particular examples under discussion, we first note, then, the empirical usefulness of keeping responsiveness and source of judgment as independent variables if we wish to test their causal relationship to one another. Mansbridge's own claim that "Nonresponsiveness to sanction and self-reliant judgment occur together in practice because they are *causally* linked" (Mansbridge 2011, 624) is impossible to make, let alone test, unless one separates responsiveness from source of judgment and lets each vary independent of the other. Does nonresponsiveness to sanction cause someone to rely on his or her own judgment, or the other way around? Or is there a prior cause for both (such as "arrogance and selfassuredness")? It thus must be possible for the variables to take on either of the values (or range between more or less of each, because they are continuous) for us to systematically study this relationship. This is why I still think it would be more useful for "gyroscopic representative" to denote only a representative's nonresponsiveness to sanction, allowing his or her source of judgment to vary independently. Indeed, it is only by separating these two variables, and thus these two concepts, that we can pursue the following question: Why does the activity of representation in democratic legislatures so often exclude some combinations of these components that are not null sets in other contexts? That returns us to the causal relationship between judgment and responsiveness that Mansbridge stipulates without argument, but that needs to be explored, and would require distinguishing judgment from responsiveness for analysis.

Let us turn, then, directly to the two seldom seen cases that Mansbridge raises in her objection and ask whether it is useful to combine them into separate ideal types. In the first, we find a representative who is responsive to sanction but still relies on his or her own judgment. Here I had put "Madisonian lawmaker" as one illustration (along with aiming at republican ends). Mansbridge was right that I had not fully developed the dynamics of Madison's view in my earlier work and that the citation I provided was incomplete; thus that I had not made my case that such a combination was useful. Indeed, in my book I claimed only that self-reliant representatives who used their own judgment to aim at the public good were more likely to be elected, without any indication of why or how this would come about.[4] The details are worth sketching out here, because they illustrate the usefulness of retaining this category to think about the highly responsive representative who relies on his or her own judgment, even if we cannot point to one today.

In my reading,[5] Madison presumed that most representatives would be very responsive to electoral

---

of Sartori and caution about over-thinking concepts see Mair 2008 and 2009, respectively.) Philosophers have attended to the underlying metaphysical and epistemic problems at the core of conceptual analysis, but have attended less to their practical application to social scientific problems per se. See Margolis and Laurence (1999) for a very helpful overview of this literature.

[3] The example of presconomy is indebted to Nelson Goodman's examples of "grue" and "bleen" (Goodman 1955).

[4] Later I added "As with Madison . . . [we can assume] that individual politicians want to be re-elected and will respond to incentives that emerge out of different electoral arrangements" (Rehfeld 2005, 212). The underlying dynamics being opaque, Mansbridge was right to object.

[5] The historical development of Madison's argument is presented in (Rehfeld 2005, 99–112). See also David Cannon and Melissa

278

REPRESENTATION

The Concepts of Representation   August 2011

sanction, leading him to endorse the extremely large and heterogeneous electoral constituency to incentivize representatives to rely on their own judgment. The Madisonian lawmaker, in my view, is someone who finds himself or herself in this situation, in a district with high heterogeneity of interests and great difficulty in having any one interest coalesce into a majority position. One town (or group) cares to keep butter prices low, another town wants road improvements, still another town wants to fight the creation of a national bank, and another wants a strong defense for the sake of the public good. Because the district is so large, Madison thought, each town would find it very difficult, if not impossible, to "communicate and coordinate" with others to build coalitions; candidates would discover that they could not do so either. In the face of this high heterogeneity of interests, where there is no singular "constituency judgment" to be had, candidates would quickly realize that promising to follow any one particular group's judgment about what to do would be a path to electoral defeat.

Why would these representatives then come to rely on their own judgment instead? Because voters would also come to realize that their preferred candidate (the one who would follow any subgroup's judgment about policy) would be unlikely to win election. So voters would opt for their second-best option: the man who would use his own good judgment to consider the best policy for all. (Madison also thought this dynamic would free up the candidate to be "republican"—aiming at the good of all—rather than "pluralist"—aiming at the good of the constituency or other subgroups.) Candidates would begin to campaign as if they were filled with republican virtue whether or not they actually were. They would begin to emphasize their qualities as men of good (self-reliant) judgment prone to act *as if* they cared about the public good, and not any partial view of it, even as they were highly motivated by sanction. What I took Madison's insight to be is *not* a defense of American-style pluralism but of what I called the Madisonian lawmaker: an individual motivated by sanction (future electoral success) who responds to the dynamics of the large, highly heterogeneous constituency by relying on his own judgment to pursue the common good.

Of course, Madison's plan did not work, because he failed to anticipate the rise of political parties, which made communication and coordination between subgroups much easier than he predicted. But the account illustrates the virtue of modeling the representative who is responsive to sanction, and self-reliant in judgment, because it gives us a view of the empirical and normative constraints we might face in trying to achieve it. The model might also inspire us to create the institutional conditions to realize Madison's vision for us today, perhaps by eliminating territorial districts and randomly assigning voters to permanent electoral constituencies instead. It is a plan I defend elsewhere (Rehfeld 2005, 2008) and would solve the perennial

problems of gerrymandering and local "pork" spending. Most importantly for this discussion, it provides an illustration of where these conceptual distinctions might usefully lead.

If I have demonstrated the usefulness of thinking about representatives who are self-reliant but responsive to sanction, and thus of the need to keep these features conceptually distinct, what of its fellow traveler, representatives who rely on their constituents' judgment instead of their own but are not responsive to sanction? We can see the usefulness of this dyad by imagining a "true" populist who enters politics dedicated to enacting the people's will, no matter what it is. Let us imagine a college professor—let us call him James "Jimmy" Chaplink—whose life work has been the study and promotion of participatory democracy. Chaplink cares more about the participatory process than election and re-election, and has always hated "begging for votes," as Plato once put it. So when some of his former students approach him to run for Congress to promote his ideas, he initially declines.

But then Chaplink reads an article about a different kind of representative who has not been seen before—someone who relies on the judgment of his constituents, but who is not motivated by the prospects of sanction (winning—or losing—an election). And then he realizes, "wait a minute, that's me, that's what I've stood for my whole life." After mulling over the possibilities, he realizes how this ideal type could bridge the gap between participatory and representational politics: If elected he would commit himself to cultivating participation among his constituents, educating them on the issues, bringing decisions to them as much as possible, and then relying on their judgments to cast his vote in Congress, whether or not he won re-election. He wants only to embody a pure "transmission belt" view of what a representative should do (Schwartz 1988)

Because Jimmy's academic expertise lies at the intersection between normative and empirical political science, he knows that simply asking his constituents for their views about policy is not what true democratic participation entails, nor is it likely to produce good answers. So he proposes to increase their opportunities for deliberative and educative participation, planning to hold daylong forums on public policy and legislation, his own "deliberation days" as it were (Ackerman and Fishkin 2004), and promises to do so as often as necessary and practicable. He will construct citizen juries (Warren 2008) and use his expense account and campaign funds to pay transportation costs and provide small stipends to make these sessions accessible to the less affluent.

Having made this his campaign platform, and in something of a fluke, Chaplink wins the election. He spends his next two years implementing his participatory program, running seminars, paying for public affairs shows to be broadcast via broadband Internet access in every one of his constituents' homes, getting people involved—in short, bringing the legislature to the people. And the initial results are promising. Chaplink's constituents are excited to participate in politics in this new way, treated as mature citizens whose

---

Williams' insightful critiques of it (Cannon 2008; Williams 2008) and my response (Rehfeld 2008, 259–61.)

634

REPRESENTATION

American Political Science Review — Vol. 105, No. 3

opinions matter by a representative *not* motivated by his prospects for re-election, but nevertheless reliant on their judgment.

But then reality sets in. The initial interest that surrounded Chaplink's seminars, workshops, and deliberative forums wanes, giving way to disinterest as people go back to leading their own lives. It seems that for all their initial enthusiasm, having tasted of the participatory fruit, voters no longer want such engagement and would now prefer to have someone who is less committed to those participatory values, but who generally shares their other values and motivations about policy, someone they might also set off on their own internal "gyroscope," as Chaplink had once put it, without the need for constant monitoring.

As poll numbers come in showing a precipitous decline in support, Chaplink remains undeterred. He keeps the faith even in the face of increasingly hostile letters from his constituents urging him to show some independent judgment and leadership. "If it isn't your function to use your own judgment," one of them angrily writes, "then what the hell is your function?"[6] Nevertheless, Chaplink continues to follow their judgment about how to vote and remains completely nonresponsive to their threat of sanction. Like most representatives who ignore all threat of constituent sanction, he loses office in the next election, becoming a one-term member of Congress, a mere footnote to history.

Despite being entirely reliant on his constituents' judgment about policy, Chaplink is the quintessential gyroscopic representative, but only if we limit the scope of that concept to Chaplink's nonresponsiveness to sanction: He tells the voters what he is going to do and sets about doing it, completely nonresponsive to their threat of sanction.[7] Further, as with Mansbridge's description of the selection model, voters originally chose this gyroscopic representative to pursue their own values of participatory democracy, but at the next election they chose a different gyroscopic representative when their values changed. Mansbridge is right that we do not see characters such as Chaplink often, or perhaps even at all in democratic politics. More realistically, as Mansbridge and I have both noted, people are more or less reliant and dependent upon their own or other people's judgment, so the extreme case presented here is simply an ideal type. But that really is the point: I would not want to preclude a character who moved in the direction that Chaplink represents simply because we have never seen him before, or because he is unlikely to be seen, and providing even a rough sketch helps us think about the underlying causal and normative relationships that we would want to study or promote. Chaplink is the example in the legislative sphere that illustrates what would be lost from ignoring these dis-

tinctions, and the value of conceptualizing the political world based on what could be, even though it never has been and likely never will be. This is why I think it would be more useful to limit Mansbridge's concept of "gyroscopic" only to describe nonresponsiveness to sanction and let it vary independent of the source of a representative's judgment. Of course sometimes categories will be empty and hard to imagine.[8] But it was precisely the formation of the conceptual category that, in this case, preceded and caused the imaginative exercise itself.

COMPLEXITY AND RELATIONAL ASPECTS OF REPRESENTATION

Our second point of disagreement arises because, as Mansbridge describes it, representation is a complex relational phenomenon; "representation" always entails one entity that represents, and another entity that is represented (Mansbridge 2011) Mansbridge wants concepts that reflect that relational complexity; thus she has embedded the relational structure of representation in the four kinds of representation she identified and developed—promissory, anticipatory, surrogate, and gyroscopic (Mansbridge 2003)—each of which is meant to describe the activities of representatives and their constituents simultaneously as they relate to each other. In contrast, Mansbridge claims that by focusing on a representative's "individual characteristics," I miss the relational quality of representation: Because "'surrogate' representation is a relationship, not a characteristic of an individual representative, it is missing from Rehfeld's analysis" (Mansbridge 2011, 621). Mansbridge's critique thus raises two distinct issues. The first concerns whether I have described characteristics of individual representatives or something else. The second, more important critique concerns how best to approach the relational nature of representation. I will take each in turn.

Mansbridge is right that my tripartite distinctions focused only on the representative's perspective as he or she made decisions. However, these distinctions were not meant to describe characteristics of the representatives but the kind of activity in which those representatives were engaged: making decisions about how to vote on laws. The difference between representatives and representation-as-activity presses on the noun and verb senses of representation, which, along with its adjectival form, I think are critical to distinguish for the purpose of normative and empirical analysis. They tend to be lost when scholars attempt, as both Pitkin and Mansbridge have, to form "single highly complex concepts" (Pitkin 1967, 8; quoted previously). And, as I said earlier, the failure to distinguish these parts into separate concepts has only contributed to the confusions and ambiguities that are at the heart of a good deal of scholarship on this topic.

Let us start by distinguishing the three different senses of representation that correspond to the noun,

---

[6] The quotation is taken from Fenno (1978, 170), as quoted by Mansbridge (2011), with its pronouns adapted to fit the example.

[7] Mansbridge allows that sometimes gyroscopic representatives will choose to seek their constituents' judgment on issues, but it is up to them to decide when to do so. Though I think this then contradicts her other descriptions, in the example I have used, the reliance on constituent judgment is the very value that voters gyroscopically set their representative to employ, thus illustrating the conflict.

---

[8] I thank an anonymous reviewer for making this point.

280 REPRESENTATION

verb, and adjective forms of the word. We can point to "representatives" (noun) as entities in the world: "Susan is my representative." We speak of "represent" (verb) as a kind of activity: "Susan represents me." Finally, we often describe two entities that share features with each other as "representative" (adjective) of the other—people who share the race, gender, or ideological commitments of other members of a group are sometimes said to be representative of them in this adjectival sense. Any theory of political representation, explanatory or normative, will have to account for the relations between these three forms, and that will require us to keep them conceptually distinct. For example, must one engage in the activity of representing[9] (verb) to be a representative (noun)? Does representing (verb) plus being a representative (noun) entail that one is representative (adjective) of a group? Probably not: A farmer of one ethnicity may be the representative (noun) of an urban constituency of another ethnicity, and represent (verb) them and their interests in Congress, without in any way actually being representative (adjective) of them.

Even if there is a minimal core shared sense that defines a Wittgensteinian family resemblance around concepts such as "representation," there is no reason to treat a concept's cognate forms—"represents," "representative," etc.—as referring to the same underlying idea. Consider, by analogy, H.L.A. Hart's *The Concept of Law*, in which Hart set forth the question, "What is Law?" (Hart 1961, 1). Had he asked instead "what is *legislation*?" he would have had to clarify first whether he meant its noun or verb forms, whether, that is, he wanted to inquire into the concept of law (as he did) or the concept of "legislate" that its verb form covers, and then to explain how those two related to each other. Although each may have been related to some overlapping idea (whether having to do with rules, as Hart believed, or fidelity to moral norms, as Fuller and Dworkin had thought) a concept of legislation that failed to clearly distinguish the linguistic forms of the concept, or attempted to conceptualize a "single, highly complex concept" of "legislation," would have been less useful, and perhaps doomed to failure.

The underlying concepts of "legislation" are easier to identify because we use distinct words to track them: law (noun), legislate (verb), and legal (adjective). In contrast, the related forms of "representation" [representative (noun), represent (verb), representative (adjective)] bear a far greater similarity to one another (its noun and adjective forms being identical). But the fact that history has given us words whose underlying forms are harder to distinguish does not tell us much about whether their forms bear a greater

or lesser similarity to one another than the forms of any other concept. Like "legislation," the word "representation" refers ambiguously to noun and verb forms. For example, "I did not receive representation in that case," might mean that I was not represented (verb) by anyone [whether or not by a representative (noun)], or it might mean that I had no representative (noun) in some context, without reference to the kind of activity in which that person engaged. This may explain in part why it is difficult to gain traction on some key issues of group representation, because it is not always clear whether that term is used to refer to a representative (noun) a group can control, being represented (verb) in a way that advances the group's interests, or a person who is representative (adjective) in the sense of "bearing some similarity" to the group in question. Each of these may in some sense be related to the other, and all of them might be important. (Phillips 1995) But they are certainly not the same set of issues, and treating them by reference to a singular concept of "group representation" cannot but confuse research into the topic.[10]

I certainly do not mean to decide these issues here. The point is only to demonstrate the value in keeping these forms distinct so that we may ask how each of the parts relate to one another and to further press the difficulty with attempting a conceptualization of a term such as "representation" that is supposed to span all these forms. With these distinctions in mind, my original article (Rehfeld 2009) meant to unpack what representing (verb) is often said to involve and was not meant to be speaking to characteristics of representatives (noun) per se, as Mansbridge has claimed.

This first point about separating the noun, verb, and adjective forms of representation is meant as clarification. Mansbridge's more important criticism was that I had failed to capture the relational nature of representation in my suggestion that our concepts should separate the activity of representatives (in terms of their expectations or judgments about voters) from the activity of voters (their expectations or judgments about their representatives). And here she is right in one sense: I am not considering directly the *relationship* between representatives and those whom they purportedly represent, but considering instead one side of that relationship at a time: the sources of representatives' judgment, their referent points, and the motivations that go into describing how they make decisions. However, I agree with her that representation is a relational concept, so that any of its forms (noun, verb, or adjective) always indicates two sides of a relation. Our disagreement thus centers on whether to design concepts that emphasize one side of the relationship at a time, as I prefer, or whether, as Mansbridge prefers, to design concepts to identify their simultaneous interactions.[11]

Let us start with our point of agreement and ask what it means to say that representation is a relational concept. Relational concepts are concepts that refer

---

[9] As Doug Hanes has pointed out to me, "representing" is a gerund and thus a noun form of the verb, rather than a verb itself. But because it is a form of the verb "represent," "representing" denotes activity in a way that the noun "representative" may or may not. It is an open question whether being a representative requires action, but one cannot be "representing" without being engaged in an activity. I use the gerund here only for facility of prose and the reader may substitute the verb "represent" instead for precision. I thank Hanes for his observation.

[10] The paragraph revises my earlier attempt to separate these strands in (Rehfeld 2010, 241–43)

[11] I thank an anonymous reviewer for suggesting this formulation.

REPRESENTATION 281

simultaneously to two entities that stand in relation to one another. So, for example, the relational concept of "parent" is impossible to understand without the concept "child" in hand, because one cannot be a parent without standing in relation to a child. Representation is the same way: One cannot be *a representative* (noun), or *represent* (verb) or be *representative* (adjective), without two entities being involved: an object of representation, and something else standing-in-for that object. The person or group represented may exist prior to being represented, but it is not formally a represented entity without a representative in-for-whom it stands. Thus, for example, an electoral constituency might exist prior to the election of their representative, but it is not an object of representation and cannot be until it is being represented (verb) or at the point where a representative (noun) of it exists.[12]

All relational concepts pose a particular challenge to concept formation, because there is no way to describe one side of the relationship without in some sense implicating the other. Non-relational concepts such as "table," "bus," or "pencil" have no such implications, for we can think of all these things on their own, as it were, without reference to other specific entities (even if they are related more generally to the world around them). In contrast, there is no way to conceive of one part of a relational concept without implicating the idea of its fellow traveler: Asking what a parent ought to do implicates the idea of "child," because one cannot *be* a parent or *act* in a parental way except in relation to a child. Even when we use the terms euphemistically, we imply both sides of the relation. For example, when we say, "The teacher acted parentally toward her students," we mean, "she treated them like children in some sense." Yet, as much as the concept "parent" implies the concept "child," the parent as an entity is conceptually distinct from the child; similarly, parenting as an activity is conceptually distinct from the child's activity, even if one side implicates the other. Emphasizing one part of the relationship never denies that it is somehow related to the other; it simply directs our focus to one side of that relationship at a time.

Returning to representation, the question before us is whether concepts that emphasize one side of the relationship, fixing values to the variables they identify, are more or less useful than concepts that emphasize and fix both sides of the relationship at once. Mansbridge insists that our concepts should emphasize not just the

representative's view of keeping promises, or anticipating voters, but also simultaneously the judgment of constituents who vote retrospectively or prospectively for keeping, or failing to keep, the promises they made. Though both perspectives are not always included in her definitions, they often are, as in this description of "promissory representation":

> Promissory representation works normatively through the explicit and implicit promises that the elected representative makes to the electorate. It works prudentially through the sanction the voter exercises at the next election. . . . (Mansbridge 2003, 516)

In her response, Mansbridge more forcefully explains that these concepts are meant to describe features of what both representatives and their constituents do, not just a description of a "representative's individual characteristics." Continuing, she explains,

> But the distinction has utility in an analysis of the relationship between voters and representatives. A focus on past promises conveys a different type of relationship from a focus on anticipating future voters desires. (Mansbridge 2011)

By this relational view, as we might call it, promissory representation would seem to apply only when the representative currently *and* the voter later looks back to past promises, whereas anticipatory representation would apply only when the voter and representative are both looking forward to what the representative or voters might do.

Yet if we used "promissory" and "anticipatory" to set both sides of the relation simultaneously, it would be incomplete, and leave us unable to classify cases where representatives acted in one way but voters acted another way. Consider the case of U.S. President George H.W. Bush's 1988 promise to raise "no new taxes," a promise he later broke. Let us presume for the sake of this example that Bush broke this promise anticipating that he could change voter minds in the subsequent election. So on his side of the relationship this is shaping up to be a case of anticipatory representation. Yet when he ran for re-election in 1992, many voters were firmly in the promissory camp; that is, they held him to account for having broken his promise. So according to Mansbridge, if we have to include both voter and representative perspectives simultaneously, when Bush signed a tax increase in 1990 it was *neither* a case of promissory representation (Bush broke his promise) nor a case of anticipatory representation (voters voted retrospectively). The named concepts are thus unhelpful precisely because they do not let each side of the relationship vary independent of (or more precisely, in reaction to) the other side.

Now consider how useful it would be to keep each side of the relationship independent of the other, one in which "honoring promises" and "anticipating future elections" were features that described different ways of representing (verbs), and, consistent with the existing literature, "prospective" and "retrospective" described different ways that constituents voted. Do or should representatives respect the promises they

---

[12] For an alternative view that representatives can create constituencies or interests to represent and thus exist prior to them, see Disch (2011) and Williams (1998). These arguments importantly emphasize representatives who often go out and become interest and constituency entrepreneurs, creating new interests and constituencies that they then can represent, often for their own partial good. But more precisely, these are cases in which a representative of one group creates another interest or constituency *and then* goes about representing it as well, for if an entity does not yet exist, then no one can represent it, or be its representative. By analogy, parents do not create children, even if in some cases parents of one child create a second human being, and thus become parents of that second child. That is the same idea here: no child, no parent; no object of representation, no representation at all. For a more precise characterization see Hayward (2010).

282 REPRESENTATION

made? Do or should they anticipate what they believe the voters will want at the time of the next election, and if so, do or should they actively attempt to change their constituents' views? And those questions concerning what representatives do would then stand in relation to voter judgment. Do or should voters vote prospectively based on what they believe their representative will do, or retrospectively based on sanctioning a representative for past performance? These questions require us to have concepts that emphasize one side of the relationship, rather than fixing both sides at once.

In fact, if we used these terms only to emphasize the representative's side of the relationship, and used the terms "retrospective" and "prospective" (already in wide use in many literatures of political science) to describe what voters do, we would move beyond the binary "promissory/anticipatory" space to one in which promissory and anticipatory *representing* (verb) vary along with prospective and retrospective *voting*:

- Promissory representing of prospective voters: A representative who keeps promises representing a constituency that votes based on its expectations of future performance. Arguably illustrated by the example of Jimmy Chaplink presented earlier, and described by Mansbridge's selection model (Mansbridge 2009).
- Promissory representing of retrospective voters: A representative who keeps promises representing a constituency that votes as a sanction or reward for past performance. Arguably what Mansbridge means by "promissory representation."
- Anticipatory representing of prospective voters: A representative who tries to anticipate what a constituency will want representing a constituency that votes based on its expectations of future performance. Arguably what Mansbridge means by "anticipatory representation."
- Anticipatory representing of retrospective voters: A representative who tries to anticipate what a constituency will want representing a constituency that votes as a sanction or reward for past performance. Arguably the case of George H.W. Bush's broken "no new taxes" promise.

Either way, if there is a relation of promising that involves looking back, and one of anticipating that involves looking forward, and we are emphasizing the relationship between constituents and representatives, we ought to let each of them be forward-looking or backward-looking independent of the other. And whatever we want to call them, these features of anticipation and promising are worth isolating from all the other features that Mansbridge suggests including in the terms.

SURROGATE/VIRTUAL REPRESENTATION AND ELITISM

Our last disagreement begins with a correction. In my original article, I described Mansbridge's "surrogate representation" as identical to Burke's "virtual representation"—each emphasizing the lack of an electoral connection between a represented group and their representative. I further claimed that the only reason Mansbridge resisted Burke's term was because she found his views elitist. This was a mistake. As Mansbridge (2011) has made clear, the term "surrogate" was meant to emphasize different substantive views of representation from Burke's, not merely the absence of an electoral connection. And Mansbridge's objection to Burke's elitism lead her away from Burke's term "trustee" in place of which her selection model "eschews such hierarchy" (623).

However, in defending these choices Mansbridge (2011) makes clear that her concepts are meant simultaneously to describe relational features *and* substantive views of representation, rather than keeping each distinct. "Surrogate representation" is meant to describe both a surrogate relationship between two parties *and* apply to aggregative and deliberative representing (verb) during that relationship. "Gyroscopic representation" and its corresponding "selection model" is meant to describe both an unmonitored relationship between two parties, *and* a relationship in which both sides eschew hierarchy. Our final disagreement then arises because I think these concepts would have far greater utility if they focused only on their relational features rather than building into them other substantive views. I take each in turn.

First, what exactly is the difference between Burke's view of virtual representation and Mansbridge's view of surrogate representation, and more generally what is the value of either modifying concept ("surrogate" or "virtual")? As I had written, "for Burke (and the many others who use the term), the critical point of 'virtual' was precisely, only, and no more than Mansbridge's own definition of the surrogate: 'representation by a representative with whom one has no electoral relationship'" (Rehfeld 2009, 221, note 17; quoting Mansbridge 2003, 522) The reason Mansbridge disagrees with that characterization is that she believes the use of "virtual" carries with it Burke's substantive view of representation, which the term modifies. As she described, "Edmund Burke had a version [of surrogate representation] he called 'virtual' representation, but Burke's concept focused on morally right answers, wisdom rather than will, relatively fixed and objective interests and the good of the whole" (Mansbridge 2003, 522). Furthermore, Mansbridge insists that surrogate representation involves aggregative and deliberative elements, whereas the virtual representation that Burke described "applies *only* to deliberation. Surrogate representation applies to *both* the aggregative and the deliberative functions of democracy" (Mansbridge 2011, 627). So although "surrogate" and "virtual" both capture the lack of an electoral connection between those represented and the representative, surrogate representation is meant to differ from Burke's views of virtual representation in that it includes a particular substantive account of representation that differs from Burke's substantive view of representation.

Note that the four qualities Mansbridge lists of Burkean representation ("morally right answers . . .

REPRESENTATION

283

American Political Science Review

Vol. 105, No. 3

wisdom . . . objective interests . . . and the good of the whole") are features of Burke's substantive view of good representation, but do not distinguish virtual or actual types. In other words, emphasizing those four qualities does not capture the work that "virtual" was meant to do in Burke's own theory. And if, as Mansbridge claims, deliberative and aggregative aspects of representation make surrogate representation different from Burke's virtual representation, it is unclear why she thinks that virtual representation was a version of surrogate representation at all[13] (Mansbridge 2003, 522).

What Burke really meant by "virtual" is of course something that Burke scholars may want to debate. And if Mansbridge or other scholars find it helpful to limit "surrogate representation" to those cases where representation-as-activity is both deliberative and aggregative, they should of course use the term in that way. But the substantive issue here is that it would not be particularly useful to adopt a concept of surrogate representation that covers lack of an electoral connection, *plus* deliberative and aggregative elements, *minus* morally right answers . . . wisdom . . . objective interests . . . and the good of the whole (i.e., Burke's key substantive views of representation). For if we were to employ such a concept, we would need many other concepts to cover cases of "lack of electoral connection" when paired with any number of alternative substantive views of representation, such as Urbinati's (2000) "representation as advocacy," Young's (2000) "representation as identity," or Stimson, Mackuen, and Erikson's (1995) "representation as policy correspondence." More importantly, it would be far more useful to have a concept that denotes the transformation of *whatever* substantive conception of representation-as-activity one uses to cases where the person acting has no electoral connection to those on behalf of whom he acts, for that would be the only way to treat the lack of an electoral connection as an independent variable for normative and empirical analysis. That is all that I believe Burke meant when he used the term "virtual"; that is the nub of what I believe is valuable from Mansbridge's idea of surrogate representation; and it allows us to investigate the very interesting causal questions of whether this transformation alone has other effects, and whether normatively it is worth pursuing.

As for Burke's elitism, Mansbridge (2011) objects to my use of "Burkean trustee" to illustrate the overlap of the republican, self-reliant, and nonresponsive representative. Having ignored Burke's elitist views, she argues, "this term does not and should not define that cell" (625). Though I had only used "Burkean trustee" as an *example* of the cell and explicitly not a definition (Rehfeld 2009, 223), Mansbridge is right that the three distinctions and the eight cells of my original table did not capture whether voters thought their representa-

tives were superior to them or not. Though I generally agree that Burke had what Mansbridge describes as elitist views of representatives (or, rather, dismissive views of voters) and I think it is of great importance to explore dimensions of political equality, I do not see the value of differentiating along these lines as part of the map of decision making I was trying to capture. Further, and consistent with the previous discussion, if we think it is useful to capture views of hierarchy between voters and representatives, we ought to differentiate clearly between the perspective of representatives toward their constituents ("swinish multitude") and the perspective of voters toward their representatives ("I want someone who's my equal"), a distinction that Mansbridge ignores.

However, the reason that Mansbridge believes we should prefer her selection model that "eschews such hierarchy" (Mansbridge 2011, 623) is again that it reflects one seemingly common regularity: the case where voters want representatives who are "like them." But even if this were the regular case, there will be greater value in having a concept of selection that allows perceptions of superiority to vary apart from the views either side has of the other. Is the utility of the selection model not chiefly, as Mansbridge described, that voters select representatives who "are internally motivated and have goals closely aligned with those of [the voters themselves]" (Mansbridge 2011, 622)? If so, it would be more useful to apply the model whenever voters select representatives who are internally motivated to seek those shared goals, no matter what hierarchical status voters attribute to their representatives or vice versa. Maybe, with Manin (1997), voters want or should want representatives who they believe are distinctive in many ways, so that those representatives are more likely to achieve those shared goals. Maybe voters want or should want representatives whom they perceive as equals because they want to feel a stronger personal connection to them. Or maybe they want or should want representatives whom they view as inferiors, because they want to feel powerful and in control. I see no utility in burdening her selection model—valuable as it is to describe "selection of gyroscopic representatives" by voters—with substantive dimensions of hierarchy or equality at all. It is another example of the value at the core of Mansbridge's concepts, but only when separated from the complexity that she wishes to build into them.

CONCLUSION

One final point of difference is worth emphasizing as I conclude. Although I think the conceptual parsimony I have defended will be useful whenever we want to understand the normative and empirical dynamics of political representation, Mansbridge's focus is squarely on developing concepts for use within democratic legislatures. Thus she repeatedly uses examples drawn only from that sphere, and acknowledges that my conceptualizations may be of greater use in other contexts. "The utility of distinction for democratic theorists and in other instances of representation remains to be

---

[13] It seems to me the reason that Burke's virtual representation is not merely a form of Mansbridge's surrogate representation but identical to it is that both signify lack of an electoral connection. Because that is what I had suggested, but what Mansbridge has objected to, I take that objection as the point of departure for my response.

284 REPRESENTATION

The Concepts of Representation

explored, and perhaps Rehfeld or others will take on this subject in future investigations" (Mansbridge 2011, 625). I want to emphasize the importance here of doing just that, of distinguishing the study of political representation from the study of representative government, a system of government that uses political representation to achieve an arguably democratic form. As I have argued elsewhere, we can point to many cases of political representation, particularly in international contexts, in which political representation appears to be going on (as it were) outside of the normal institutions of representative government (Rehfeld 2006). When, earlier this year, the Libyan delegation to the United Nations suddenly declared that the entity they represented had shifted from Kadaffi's regime to the people of Libya, something happened that cannot be explained by reference to elections or democratic authorization even if the shift was consistent with them. It seems to me to have great value to develop concepts that are fluid enough to get at the varied phenomena of representation whether within or without these democratic institutions.

I think that so long as we use concepts that import democratic ideals when we study these issues, we risk confusing our treatment of the forms of representation with the conditions that make them democratic, legitimate, or just (Rehfeld 2006). This view is reflected in a new wave of literature that conceptualizes representation in a way that can usefully study it in both democratic and nondemocratic contexts (Urbinati and Warren 2008) It is certainly not settled: Michael Saward's emphasis on "claim making" (Saward 2011),Jennifer Rubenstein's interest in surrogate accountability (Rubenstein 2007), Laura Montanaro's configuration of the legitimacy of self-appointed representatives (Montanaro 2010), are all motivated by the challenges that non-democratic contexts pose for representation; as is my own view that representation should be conceived in audience-centered ways entirely independent of democratic concerns such as elections, accountability, or responsive activity of any particular kind, and in which claim-making is neither necessary nor sufficient to institute any case (Rehfeld 2006).These interventions are not primarily about representative government as a form but about rethinking our basic understanding of what the forms of representation as social and political facts are, whatever their relationship to traditional democratic institutions may turn out to be.

To summarize, Jane Mansbridge and I agree that political representation is a complex relational concept. We also agree that representation at its broadest is systematic, in the sense of involving many different parts interacting with one another in interesting and complex ways. What we disagree about is the role conceptual analysis plays in understanding these complexities. The new contexts in which political representation is being employed provide an additional impetus to favor sparer, more precise concepts that isolate features of the social and political world we wish to investigate. Within her conceptual rethinking, Mansbridge has provided terrific insights that, when isolated, can provide

August 2011

more complete understandings of how representation operates, and ought to operate, in our social and political world.

REFERENCES

Ackerman, Bruce, and James Fishkin. 2004. *Deliberation Day*. New Haven, CT: Yale University Press.

Barry, Brian. [1965] 1990. *Political Argument: A Reissue with a New Introduction* (California Series on Social Choice and Political Economy). Berkeley: University of California Press.

Boghossian, Paul. 2006. *Fear of Knowledge: Against Relativism and Constructivism*. New York: Oxford University Press.

Cannon, David. 2008. "The Representational Consequences of a Random National Constituency." *Polity* 40 (2): 221–28.

Connolly, William E. 1974. *The Terms of Political Discourse*. Indianapolis, IN: Lexington.

Collier, David, and John Gerring, eds. 2008. *Concepts and Method in Social Science: The Tradition of Giovani Sartori*. New York: Routledge.

Disch, Lisa. 2011. "Toward a Mobilization Conception of Democratic Representation." *American Political Science Review* 105 (1): 100–14)

Eulau, Heinz, John C. Wahlke, William Buchanan, and Leroy C. Ferguson. 1959. "The Role of the Representative: Some Empirical Observations on the Theory of Edmund Burke." *American Political Science Review* 53 (3): 742–56.

Fenno, Richard F., Jr. 1978. *Home Style*. Boston: Little, Brown.

Gallie, W. B. 1956. "Essentially Contested Concepts." *Proceedings of the Aristotelian Society* 56: 167–98.

Gerring, John. 1999. "What Makes a Concept Good? An Integrated Framework for Understanding Concept Formation in the Social Sciences." *Polity* 31 (3): 357–93.

Goertz, Gary. 2006. *Social Science Concepts: A User's Guide*. Princeton, NJ: Princeton University Press.

Goodman, Nelson. 1955. *Fact, Fiction and Forecast*. Cambridge, MA: Harvard University Press.

Hart, H. L. A. 1961. *The Concept of Law*. Oxford: Oxford University Press.

Hayward, Clarissa. 2010. "Making Interest: On Representation and Democratic Legitimacy." In *Political Representation*, eds, Ian Shapiro, Susan C. Stokes, Elisabeth Jean Wood, and Alexander S. Kirshner. Cambridge: Cambridge University Press. 111–35.

Hempel, Carl. 1966. *Philosophy of Natural Science*. New York: Prentice Hall.

Mair, Peter. 2008. "Concepts and Concept Formation." In *Approaches and Methodologies in the Social Sciences*, eds. Donatella Della Porta and Michael Keating. Cambridge: Cambridge University Press.

Mair, Peter. 2009. "Guest Letter: Getting the Concepts Rights." *Newsletter of the Organized Section in Comparative Politics of the American Political Science Association* 20 (2): 1–4.

Manin, Bernard. 1997. *The Principles of Representative Government*. New York: Cambridge University Press.

Mansbridge, Jane. 2003. "Rethinking Representation." *American Political Science Review* 97 (4): 515–28.

Mansbridge, Jane. 2009. "A 'Selection Model' of Political Representation." *Journal of Political Philosophy* 17 (4): 369–98.

Mansbridge, Jane. 2011. "Clarifying the Concept of Representation." *American Political Science Review* 105 (3): 621–30.

Margolis, Eric, and Stephen Laurence, eds. 1999. *Concepts: Core Readings*. Cambridge, MA: MIT Press.

Mayo, Henry Bertram. 1960. *An Introduction to Democratic Theory*. New York: Oxford University Press.

Montanaro, Laura. 2011. "The Democratic Legitimacy of 'Self-Appointed' Representatives." University of British Columbia. Unpublished manuscript.

Phillips, Anne. 1995. *The Politics of Presence*. New York: Oxford University Press.

Pitkin, Hanna Fenichel. 1967. *The Concept of Representation*. Berkeley: University of California Press.

Rehfeld, Andrew. 2005. *The Concept of Constituency: Political Representation, Democratic Legitimacy and Institutional Design*. Cambridge: Cambridge University Press.

REPRESENTATION

Rehfeld, Andrew. 2006. "Towards a General Theory of Political Representation." *Journal of Politics* 68 (1): 1–21.

Rehfeld, Andrew. 2008. "Extremism in the Defense of Moderation: A Response to My Critics." *Polity* 40 (1): 254–71.

Rehfeld, Andrew. 2009. "Representation Rethought: On Trustees, Delegates, and Gyroscopes in the Study of Political Representation and Democracy." *American Political Science Review* 103 (2): 214–30.

Rehfeld, Andrew. 2010. "On Quotas and Qualifications for Office." In *Political Representation*, eds. Ian Shapiro, Susan C. Stokes, Elisabeth Jean Wood, and Alexander S. Kirshner. Cambridge: Cambridge University Press, 236–68.

Rubenstein, Jennifer. 2007. "Accountability in an Unequal World." *Journal of Politics* 69 (3): 616–32

Saward, Michael. 2010. *The Representative Claim*. Oxford: Oxford University Press.

Schwartz, Nancy. 1988. *The Blue Guitar: Political Representation and Community*. Chicago: University of Chicago Press.

Stimson, James A., Michael B. Mackuen, and Robert S. Erikson. 1995. "Dynamic Representation." *American Political Science Review* 89 (3): 543–56.

Urbinati, Nadia. 2000. "Representation as Advocacy: A Study of Democratic Deliberation." *Political Theory* 28 (6): 758–86.

Urbinati, Nadia, and Mark E. Warren. 2008. "The Concept of Representation in Contemporary Democratic Theory." *Annual Review of Political Science* 11: 387–412.

Warren, Mark E. 2008. "Citizen Representatives." In *Designing Deliberative Democracy: The British Columbia Citizens' Assembly*, eds. Mark E. Warren and Hilary Pearse. Cambridge: Cambridge University Press.

Williams, Melissa. 1998. *Voice, Trust, and Memory: Marginalized Groups and the Politics of Liberal Representation*. Princeton, NJ: Princeton University Press.

Williams, Melissa. 2008. "Rehfeld's Hyper-Madisonianism." *Polity* 40 (April): 238–45.

Young, Iris Marion. 2000. *Democracy and Inclusion*. Oxford: Oxford University Press.

13

Representation and Accountability: Communicating Tubes?

CHRISTOPHER LORD and JOHANNES POLLAK

Although representation and accountability require one another in modern democracy, there are many possible tensions between them. Democratic theories tend to combine the two but in ways that are not always obvious, and, depending on the institutional properties of a political system, varied ways of combining representation with accountability can amount to significant differences in the practice and quality of democracy. The authors review those effects through the lens of the British and American traditions of representative government, and they also make their own attempt to bring greater conceptual order to an understanding of the relationship between representation and accountability in democratic politics. They show how representation and accountability are 'unsaturated' concepts, whose relationship one to another can only be properly understood through several further stages of specification. These must at least include specification of what kind of representation is thought desirable, of the major choices that need to be made in the design of any democratic polity, and of social and international contexts. The last point is of special relevance to the transposition of representation–accountability relationships to the EU. ·

Although representation and accountability require one another in modern democracy, there are many possible tensions between them. Democratic theories tend to combine the two but in ways that are not always obvious, and, depending on the institutional properties of a political system, varied ways of combining representation with accountability can amount to significant differences in the practice and quality of democracy. We review those effects through the lens of the British and American traditions of representative government. But we also make our own attempt to bring greater conceptual order to an understanding of the relationship between representation and accountability in democratic politics. We do this by showing how representation and accountability are 'unsaturated' concepts, whose relationship one to another can only be properly understood through several further stages of specification. These must at least include specification of what kind of representation is thought desirable, of the major choices that need to be made in the design of any democratic polity, and of social and international contexts. The last point is of special relevance to the transposition of representation–accountability relationships to the EU.

Taking these various elements into account, we argue in the conclusion that the relationship between representation and accountability is subject to two contrary effects in contemporary politics that come together with special force in settings beyond the state such as the European Union. On the one hand new possibilities are being opened up by a 'governance revolution'. Yet that revolution leaves untouched, and possibly even aggravates, two difficulties that have long afflicted attempts to combine representation with accountability: namely, pluralities of values and indivisibilities of institutional design. The article proceeds as follows: first it defines varieties of representation and accountability. Then it explores their interdependence and their mutual tension. It discusses limits to institutional solutions and then considers contemporary developments. It concludes with an explanation of the theoretical challenges.

However, before exploring what is complex and variable, it is useful to set out what is simple and common in the relationship between representation and accountability. In so far as the large size of modern mass societies leave peoples with little alternative to ruling through representatives, publics are faced with a problem of how to ensure that their representatives remain representative of them. Whatever their concept of representation, it is likely that they will require representatives to account in some way for what they have done and for what they intend to do.

But citizens are likely to seek control *through* representatives and not just accountability *of* representatives. A combination of the two offers them improved public and private autonomy: public autonomy to the extent citizens can enjoy greater public control where, instead of attempting the task themselves, they can appoint accountable representatives who are, in turn, specialised and skilled in bringing other power-holders to account; private autonomy to the extent such an arrangement allows citizens to get on with the rest of their lives: to pursue individual life plans.

Certainly it is to render the burdens of citizenship manageable that representation typically functions as an organising framework for the other components of democracy, including accountability. As Richard Bellamy (2008: 1) puts it: 'in terms of democratic legitimacy, the system of representation offers a holistic framework within which to embed mechanisms of democratic authorization, control, and accountability'. Yet it should be noted that to identify representation as the more encompassing framework is to say nothing about the relative importance of representation and accountability. Indeed, we will discover there is huge variation here. In some polities representation may be little more than a passive transmission mechanism, whilst accountability contributes to a ferociously competitive process for the allocation of power. In others, representation entrusts huge discretion to representatives, whereas accountability is either fitful or formulaic. (See also Mansbridge's 2003 distinction between promissory, anticipatory and gyrascopic representation.)

970   *C. Lord and J. Pollak*

Varieties of Representation and Accountability

Before we can go on to examine ways in which the relationship between representation and accountability can be problematic, we need to make the more basic point that representation and accountability are individually difficult – or at least under-determined and highly context-dependent – concepts even before efforts are made to combine them. Both, as we will argue in this section, need some filling in.

Widely used definitions of representation are 'making present that which is absent', 'standing in for others' (Birch 1971; Pitkin 1967; Weale 1999: 112) or acting in the best interest of others (Eulau *et al.* 1959: 743; Pitkin 1967: 209; Przeworski *et al.* 1999: 2). But these are only bare bones definitions that do not get us very far. Once we attempt to put a bit of flesh on the bones, agreement dissolves. Should representatives resemble the represented in particular ways? Should they decide in ways the representatives would themselves have decided had they taken the decision themselves? Or should representatives see themselves more in the role of trustees, who are expected to use their own judgement, in a belief there is something special about representation and its place in the political division of labour, such as an ability to focus full-time on a certain set of problems, an ability to see the whole picture and transcend sectoral interests, an opportunity to participate in a deliberation with representatives of all others affected by the same system of rule, an ability to acquire specialist expertise and yet relate that expertise to the everyday needs and values of the citizen and so on?

The introduction of a normative dimension – the 'best' interest – only adds further questions to the puzzle: whose best interests should representatives devote themselves to representing? And at what time? Should representatives, first and foremost, be expected to discern the interest of all? This will often not be straightforward. Voters may lack clear and stable preferences (Goodin 1993: 234; Sunstein 1993: 197) and the 'common interest' may only be identifiable at such an abstract level as to leave unanswered the question of how to select between multiple 'best' and equally justifiable courses of action.

All these views and more have stirred controversy on how representation should work. Thus in her seminal work Hannah Pitkin (1967) characterises representation as a concept that only attains its full meaning through the way in which it is used in a specific context. The result is that use of the word 'representation' has come to be qualified by a dazzling variety of adjectives: from parliamentary to territorial, from anticipatory to promissory, and factual to sovereign, to name but a few (Pollak 2007a). Still, whatever the context, all theories as well as systems of democratic representation have to answer four sets of questions. How do we justify the authorisation of representatives? How do we select them? What room for discretion should representatives enjoy? And how can we make sure that representatives keep the common good in sight? Depending on how these questions are answered, different standards of accountability are appropriate.

Representation and Accountability 971

In liberal democracies there seems to be agreement that representatives should be selected, authorised and held to account by free and fair elections. An understanding of democracy as 'public control with equality' (Beetham 1994; Lord, 2008; Weale 1999) requires not only that citizens should be free to elect – and thus sanction and remove – their representatives but that they should enjoy that right on fair terms which acknowledge the equal moral worth of their opinions and values. Yet, as Ruth Grant and Robert Keohane (2005: 31) observe, it is by no means clear that representatives should only be internally accountable to those who appoint or authorise them as opposed to externally accountable to all those who are affected by their actions. We will return to this difficulty below.

Another way in which standards of accountability vary with concepts of representation follows from variation in the discretion those concepts allow representatives. We can distinguish three models historically: the first stems from pre-modern times and demands that representatives be a mirror of the represented; the second – the US model[1] – sees the direct dependence of the representative on the constituency as a precondition for effective representation[2] on the grounds that only dependence can ensure an identity of interest; the third – the British model – focuses on the independence of the representative who is expected to act as a trustee in the interest of the whole nation. It has to be emphasised though that no model developed independently, and without cross-fertilisation, especially in the American case where at the eve of revolution the understanding of representation mixed traditional ideas with modern practices (Rakove 1997: 213).

In pre-modern times, 'presence' was assumed to be the key criterion of representation. The aim of those demanding representation was literally to secure from Kings and Queens some 'presence' in the taking of decisions. The question of who should represent was largely based on Marsilius of Padua's idea of *repraesentatio identitatis* (Skinner 1978): in order to represent the represented in reality (Leibholz 1966: 27), i.e. to make the absent present, representative and represented need to share the same identity. Only if particular groups making up a political community were represented by members of their own group was it thought possible to talk about a 'politics of presence' (Gould 1996; Kymlicka 1996; Phillips 1995, 1997). Whether the groups in question were based on territory, religion, professional interests, or some mix of these and more besides, the overall quality of representation was thought to depend on assembling that collection of representatives which formed the most precise image possible of the political community. Hence its name: mirror, descriptive or statistical representation. Comte de Mirabeau described mirror representation as follows: 'Les Etats sont pour la Nation ce qu'est une carte réduite pour son étendue physique; & soit en petit, soit en grand, la copie doit toujours avoir les mêmes proportions que l'original' ['The Parliament should be to the nation as a map is to a geographical area; whether small or large the copy should always have the same proportions as the original'] (quoted in Schmitt 1969: 189).[3]

972   *C. Lord and J. Pollak*

The core assumption of mirror representation is that only socialisation within a social group can make it possible to understand and represent its demands. Some recent literature (Dovi 2002; Mansbridge 1999; Phillips 1995; Williams 1998) suggests that this form of representation is justified because it introduces the social perspective and experiences of disadvantaged groups into representative institutions. Yet several theorists have raised powerful objections to mirror representation (Griffiths and Wollheim 1960; Pennock 1979; Pitkin 1967). Its emphasis on representing the identity of the group can too easily lead to the exclusion of minorities. It can also slip into a kind of virtual representation based on little more than what representatives assume to be their common identity with the represented. Since representation does not refer to a pre-given social subject but rather creates political subjects, the key question is often how representatives evoke and create the represented.[4] Amongst other difficulties this presents, the representative's own imagined identity with the represented may become increasingly unreal as the advantages which normally come with a representative office, the quest for compromise and consensus, and the greater knowledge enjoyed by representatives, potentially lead to alienation, an estrangement from the electorate.

In contrast modern concepts do not emphasise identity, rather they expect representatives to 'act in the best interests of others'. But whose interests should be represented and how should those interests be understood? By the end of the eighteenth century, the British and American models emerged as different answers to this question (Pollak 2007b). Whilst the former – exemplified by Edmund Burke's famous letter to the electors of Bristol – assumed that representatives needed to be protected from the influence of local and sectional interests, the US Congress was conceived as an assembly of delegates for such interests. For the American Founding Fathers the multitude of interests represented in Congress was a safeguard against the emergence of a dominant political class. Together with frequent elections and a federal constitution, a balance between divergent interests was seen as a necessary ingredient of a republic. For Burke, the most noble and important task of 'the statesman' was the deliberation of informed elites, animated by enlightened consciousness and providence, and directed at the representation of the nation. Thus, where James Madison saw a multitude of interests of utmost importance, Burke only saw one nation unified by one interest.[5] Whilst these analytical models have obviously been further developed since the eighteenth century, the roles of delegate and representative intrinsically imply different forms of accountability.

Accountability raises rather different conceptual ambiguities to representation. Whereas disagreement on ends and means has resulted in competing models of representation, accountability consists more of broad categories – account-giving linked to punishments or rewards – which can be filled out in different ways without producing competing schools of thought. Mark Bovens (2006: 9–12) defines accountability as 'the obligation to explain and justify conduct'; or, to be more precise, as a relationship between an 'actor and a forum' in which the 'actor has an obligation to explain his or her conduct, the forum can pose questions and pass judgement, and the actor may face consequences'. Bovens is keen here to avoid the notion that accountability must involve sanctions, in order to hold open the possibility that it may be rewarding, and not just punitive (see also Manin *et al.* 1999: 10).

This point is well made. But it is worth emphasising that the indeterminacies of accountability relate not just to its consequences but to 'account-giving' itself. Thus James March and Johan Olsen (1995) argue that in a world of complex causation, complex actors, and obscurity of standards, account-giving often involves a misapprehension and even an injustice in its assumption that outcomes can always be neatly attributed to particular actions and particular authors. The result, they argue, is that representatives, and those they seek to bring to account, continuously attempt to renegotiate the terms of account-giving itself: to shift its standards and understandings of cause–effect relationships in ways which will make some behaviours more praiseworthy, others more reprehensible.

Moreover there is a second layer of indeterminacy. Complex polities and societies include several forums in which some actors are expected to account for their behaviour to others. Since these differ in their criteria and consequences it is important – whatever their interconnections – to distinguish them into qualitatively different kinds of accountability. Perhaps the main example is the all-important distinction between political and legal accountability (Harlow 2002). Although elections are the key element of political accountability, it would be naïve to ignore how far democracy, representation, and the electoral process themselves depend on account-ability to the courts and independent administrative bodies such as Ombudsmen, especially for protections against the grave misconduct of representatives. We will return to this theme in our discussion of how the relationship between representation and accountability changes when 'Governance' is substituted for 'Government'.

Interdependence

Representation often appears the more exotic and mysterious, and accountability the more dull and unglamorous of the two qualities. Be that as it may, a moment's reflection reveals their connection to democracy's core values and practices, as well as their dependence on one another. To understand this it helps to distinguish democracy as a method from democracy as an ideal (cf. Weale 1999). In its role as a decision-making method democracy assigns equal votes to all citizens and then stipulates that a majority of their representatives can make binding decisions. Whilst there are variations in how those majorities are calculated, and in the difficulties those majorities may need to overcome before they get their way, it is important to be clear that 'democracy as a method' is a harsh discipline for the out-voted. Its collective bindingness implies that it is better understood as a most unusual kind of coercive rule, rather than as a non-coercive system of government. John Dunn (2005: 19) puts the point thus:

> Like every modern state, the democracies of today demand obedience and insist on a very large measure of compulsory alienation of judgement on the part of their citizens. When they make that demand in their citizens' own name, however, they do not just add insult to injury ... they close the circle of civic subjection by setting out a framework of categories within which a population can reasonably think of itself over time as living together as equals, on terms and within a set of presumptions, which they could reasonably and freely choose.

Thus democracy is the one form of coercive rule which the people can be said to impose on themselves. Yet this observation is not quite enough on its own to reconcile 'democracy as an ideal' with 'democracy as a method', since, as Albert Weale (1999) points out, democracy is commonly justified not on the grounds that it allows a *whole* people to govern itself but on the grounds that it reconciles collective decision-making with the continued autonomy of *each* individual. Since voting is the very procedure by which democracy permits the collective to impose itself on the individual, democracy requires something more than voting if it is to be justifiable in terms of its own ideals of individual autonomy (Dewey 1927).

This is not the place to discuss in full what that 'something more' might be, save only to emphasise that the relationship between representation and accountability has a role to play in resolving the problem. As John Stuart Mill (1972 [1861]) noted, one way of ensuring that voting is not a mere 'act of will' is to establish a representative body in which those whose 'opinions are over-ruled feel satisfied that their opinion has been heard and set aside ... for what are thought to be better reasons' (239–40).

Majorities thus need to *account* to minorities for their decision to out-vote them. This can be seen as part of democracy's essential compact whereby losers accept being out-voted on the understanding that it should always be clear to them what procedures they would need to follow and what arguments they would need to answer if they are to form themselves into the majorities needed to reverse existing decisions. But a 'right to justification' (Forst 2007; Schmalz-Bruns 2007) also follows from a belief that it is meaningful in a democracy to see properly made decisions as those of each and every citizen, including those who profoundly disagree with them (see Miller 2007). If decisions are to have this aura, an account needs to be given that they have indeed been made in such a way that even dissenters are committed to them by their own belief in democracy. But who is to hear and sift such accounts? Limitations of time and expertise are likely to mean that citizens will prefer to appoint representatives, rather than undertake that task themselves.

Uneasy Twins

Yet the relationship between representation and accountability is anything but straightforward. If representatives are to be deliberating, judging or deciding actors in their own right, the lines of their own accountability to the electorate cannot be drawn too tightly. On the other hand, just trusting them to use their own judgement to the point at which they are accountable on a day-to-day basis to little more than their own sense of duty, may amount to a dangerous gamble on the virtue of representatives. While this danger can be reduced by the existence of regular elections (and the dubious existence of the rational voter) and the possibility to vote them out office, account-giving would no longer be based on the exchange of rational arguments since common criteria for the assessment of virtuous behaviour are extremely difficult to agree on.

Part of the answer may be to encourage representatives to account to one another in transparent ways that are likely to serve a wider public interest. Significantly the *caesura* noted above between British and American models of representative government reflected contrasting answers to the question of how representatives might be made to account to one another, and not just different understandings of representation itself. Following Burke's belief in the merits of face-to-face debate between representatives, the British model assumes that representatives should bring one another to account through the *deliberations* of a single representative body where, as Mill (1972 [1861]) would later put it, all views can be 'tested in adverse controversy against one another'. Following Madison's belief that 'ambition should counter ambition' – and that it is wise to design institutions on the assumption that individuals may behave badly in exercising their powers – the American model puts more confidence in *competition* between several mutually suspicious representative institutions and offices. We will return to this crucial difference below.

For the moment, though, we need to introduce another problem. It follows from our earlier observation that representative government simultaneously requires accountability *through* representatives and accountability *of* representatives that difficulties in the relationship of representatives to other power-holders may further complicate their relationship to the represented. Consider some problems raised by John Stuart Mill's classic argument for representative government. Mill insisted that all power-holders and all public decisions should be within the ultimate control of representative bodies. He wrote of the need for 'the representative body ... to be able to control everything in the last resort ... They must be masters, whenever they please, of all the operations of government' (Mill 1972 [1861]: 228–9).

976 *C. Lord and J. Pollak*

On the other hand, Mill also believed that representation and government should be two distinct activities. As he put it, 'there is a radical distinction between controlling the business of government and actually doing it'. Indeed, he believed that representative bodies should busy themselves with the detail of neither legislation nor administration. In contemporary parlance he was of the view that representatives should be restricted to yes/no choices over the passing of laws and the formation of administrations. Otherwise they should have only limited agenda-setting powers. Any form of government that allowed representatives to intervene in the detail – rather than the broad directions – would, in Mill's view (1972 [1861]: 229–32), allow 'inexperience to sit in judgement on experience, ignorance on knowledge'.

Yet, in the past 150 years representative government has evolved in ways very different to those Mill recommended. Representative bodies typically participate more than he thought desirable in the exercise of the detailed powers of democratic polities. They often have amendment powers – and not just veto rights – over policy and law, and their powers of appointment are usually understood as allowing them to penetrate, if need be, every nook and cranny of the public administration, all in the cause of accountability (Strøm 2003).

However, though representative bodies have secured more detailed powers of accountability and control than Mill thought desirable, it would be hard to argue that this has led, as he believed it would, to a threat to the professionalism of government. Rather, representative bodies have paradoxically struggled to secure their autonomy in the face of their own empowerment. The challenge has been one of how to give representatives powers to bring other branches of government to account without that conflating the generalist role of the representative with the expert role of the policy-expert, or without it, indeed, creating incentives for executives to seek to dominate the very representative bodies that are supposed to hold them to account, thus inverting relationships so that representatives become more a part of the polity than society – more interested in representing the polity to society, or in employing the powers and resources of the polity to improve their own standing in society than vice versa (Michels 1961 [1911]).

Not even the classics of political theory and science identify what is perhaps the fundamental logical difficulty: namely, that once a polity attempts to specify representation or accountability goals with any precision, it can only give priority to the one and not both. Consider two examples. Where the main goal is the authentic representation of individual identities, it is harder to hold representatives collectively accountable for how they combine together to exercise the overall powers of the polity. Thus consociational systems – which are perhaps the main modern survivors of 'mirror representation' in seeking to provide assured representation to particular cultural communities or social segments – do not easily support a strongly articulated shared politics of electoral accountability. Instead, electoral competition focuses on who is to pick up the guaranteed representation of the segments, since that guides the allocation of most other forms of representation, and, in any case, consociational systems often seek precisely to avoid mobilising attention around the affairs of the shared polity, either for fear of igniting tensions or in the hope of perpetuating an illusion of living apart – in culturally separate communities – whilst, in fact, enjoying the benefits of common institutions (Bogaards and Crepaz 2002; Lijphart 1979).

So what if the priority is reversed? Once elections cease to be simple means of selecting representatives – and are required first and foremost to serve as accountability tools – the attempt to combine the two tasks can be anything but straightforward. One obvious question concerns the extra knowledge citizens need if they are not merely to select representatives on the basis of some identity of interest or some feeling of trust but also to make some assessment of the performance of power-holders that can be used to decide which would-be representatives are to be sanctioned or rewarded. To be comfortable with this notion we have to be able to counter Joseph Schumpeter's (1942) profound scepticism about the knowledge requirements of democratic citizenship with the more reassuring observation that citizens may only need to have a very general political understanding: they

> [T]ypically have one comparatively hard bit of data: they know what life has been like during the incumbent's administration. They need *not* know the precise economic or foreign policies of the incumbent administration in order to see or feel the *results* of those policies ... In order to ascertain whether the incumbents have performed poorly or well, citizens need only calculate the changes in their own welfare. If jobs have been lost in a recession, something is wrong. If sons have died in foreign rice paddies, something is wrong. If thugs make neighbourhoods unsafe, something is wrong. If polluters foul food, water, or air, something is wrong. (Fiorina 1981: 5)[6]

But this argument moves too quickly. We can only really specify how much knowledge the citizen needs by asking 'Who exactly is supposed to be responsible for what?' 'To throw the scoundrels out' entails information about responsibilities and the relations between policies and output. If the political debate revolves around success or failure of policies, 'blame avoidance' and 'credit claiming' are the usual strategies. Opposition parties try to convince the public of the shortcomings of government strategies while governments present themselves as coping valiantly with unforeseen circumstances. Given the difficulty of identifying 'scoundrels' under these conditions, it is unsurprising that empirical studies confirm the often irrational character of sanctioning. Using a study of the political impact of

978 *C. Lord and J. Pollak*

flooding, drought and flu epidemics, Achen and Bartels (2002: 35; see also Fiorina 1981) question the

> customary fallback position ... that voters may know very little, but they can recognize good and bad government performance when they see them. In most recent scholarly accounts, retrospection is a natural and rational feature of democratic politics. In our view it is natural, but not so obviously rational.

A less bleak picture is suggested by studies of economic voting (e.g. Lewis-Beck 1988; Norpoth 1996). These confirm that in times of low growth, or high unemployment or inflation, voters really do hold politicians to account at the ballot box and that economic policies are, accordingly, a priority of all governments (van der Brug *et al.* 2001). Yet this finding may not be enough to rescue the retrospective model of accountability. Michael Lewis-Beck and Martin Paldam (2000) show that economic voting is highly unstable,[7] which would, in turn, suggest that voters find it difficult to use arrangements for the election of representatives to allocate responsibility (Powell and Whitten 1993; Taylor 2000). Knowledge and information 'even at the level of Kinsley or Will, let alone God' (Luskin 2002: 294) are of limited value if responsibility cannot be allocated.

Although space has only permitted us to consider two examples, it would not be hard to use others to generalise our conclusion that the exact nature of trade-offs between representation and accountability vary according to priorities that are given to the specific forms either quality can take. At one level this is no more than a technical constraint that is perhaps better understood in formal economics than in political science: namely, no two non-identical goals can ever be optimised simultaneously. But such constraints also have normative consequences, as we will demonstrate when we have completed our analysis of the institutional difficulties of combining representation with accountability.

Institutional Indivisibilities

Whilst the previous section doubted that a polity can optimise specific representation or accountability goals simultaneously, this section shows how the difficulty is aggravated by indivisibilities in the institutional design of democratic polities. Again, we discuss two examples that are sufficient to make our point: namely, any one polity can only choose one electoral system for any one office, and, second, it can only make a 'binary choice' between electing the executive and legislature together (parliamentary systems) or apart (presidential systems). We will show how these 'indivisible' choices close off, as much as much as they open up, options for how representation and accountability should relate to one another.

Representation and Accountability 979

Democracies use electoral systems to aggregate votes in different ways. Plurality systems turn votes into representation by dividing the polity into several districts and electing whoever gets the most votes in each district, no matter whether that person has an absolute majority of votes. In contrast, proportional systems relate representation to the overall number of votes received by competing parties at the level of the polity itself. If the aim is to fashion an electoral system that makes it easy for voters to 'throw the scoundrels out' and otherwise sanction poor performance, plurality systems have clear advantages. First, parties that lose a certain percentage of the people's vote are likely to lose a far higher proportion of the seats in the representative body. Second, it is more common in plurality systems for majorities in the representative body to change as a direct consequence of popular election, and not through the intermediation of coalition negotiations between parties. Yet plurality systems also have a major weakness. They often produce a huge mismatch between the number of votes cast for particular parties and the representation they receive. Not only do they over-represent some parties but they do not even guarantee that the party which comes first in the popular vote receives the most representation.

The conclusion is plain: one electoral system is better at institutionalising electoral accountability; the other is better at accurately matching representation to votes. A comparison of the Austrian and British systems illustrates how difficult it is to enjoy the strengths of the one arrangement without also suffering its weaknesses. Since electoral and coalition politics interact in such a way that Austrian governments are almost always formed by the same parties, even when those parties have been sanctioned by a loss of votes, it is often complained that the Austrian system makes it difficult to 'throw rascals out'. In contrast, all changes in British governments since the 1940s have come about as a direct result of change in popular vote. Moreover, where British voters choose to bring their governments to account, their electoral system provides a savage means of sanctioning failure. In 1997 a loss of 10 per cent in the sitting government's share of the popular vote translated into a 50 per cent loss of its parliamentary representation. Were we, however, to change the focus to the accuracy with which the two systems represent the popular vote, the Austrian system comes out much better than the British. The index of disproportionality – used by political scientists to calculate how far shares of parliamentary representation deviate from shares of the popular vote – is some 10 times higher in Britain than in Austria (Lord and Harris 2006: 48).

A second indivisibility in the institutional arrangements democratic polities typically use to relate representation to accountability follows from the distinction between parliamentary and presidential systems. As Kaare Strøm (2003) puts it, parliamentary systems amount to a long chain of singular principal–agent relationships. Each agent has just one principal in a chain that runs as follows: voters–parliament–cabinet–bureaucracy/agencies. Since, in contrast, presidential systems divide powers by electing the

980   *C. Lord and J. Pollak*

chief executive and legislature separately, 'agents' typically owe accounts to multiple principals. Once again both of these 'binary' choices have strengths and weaknesses that are the inverse of those of the other. The singularity of principal–agent relationships in the parliamentary case means that agents cannot play off multiple principals. On the other hand, the chain of delegation is often longer in parliamentary systems. For example, agencies may only answer to elected bodies through executives, whilst in division of powers systems they often find themselves having to answer directly to the representative body. Moreover, parliamentary systems forgo the advantage of dividing powers between mutually suspicious legislatures and executives whose members have every incentive to bring one another to account as part of their own competition for the people's vote.

The foregoing indivisibilities, however, do not just constrain what is institutionally possible in combining representation with accountability. They also amount to fundamental value choices. Given their effectiveness in delivering electoral accountability, plurality systems can be seen as giving priority to public control and hence to the value of autonomy contained in the idea of a people that can choose its own rulers with comparative ease. In contrast, proportional systems are better at securing the value of political equality, since they come closer than plurality systems to counting each vote equally in the apportionment of representation. For their part, parliamentary and presidential systems differ in what they imply for rights protection. The division of powers involved in holding executives and legislatives separately accountable to the electorate is often justified on the grounds that it offers better protection to any given set of rights. Yet it is, conversely, criticised precisely on the grounds that it privileges rights and values favoured by the status quo (Shapiro 1996). To the extent there is no reason to say that any of the value choices identified in this paragraph is inherently better or worse than the others, we arrive at last at a full understanding of why the different trade-offs that are possible in the organisation of democratic politics between representation and accountability pose such difficulties: none can prioritise all of a set of values, which would in Rawls' (1993) terms, appear 'equally reasonable'.

From Government to Governance

Modern politics has changed the face of political representation. Whilst in former times relations between representatives and represented were embedded in the framework of the nation-state, the increasing mobility of capital, people, services and goods has made state borders more permeable, eroding their role in demarcating separate systems for the articulation, organisation and representation of interests, and thus, more broadly, for the design of relationships between society and politics (Bartolini 1998, 1999). Moreover, the emergence of powerful transnational players and decision-making arenas which transcend the representative systems of territorially

Representation and Accountability 981

defined political communities has contributed to the dilution of representative politics (Warren and Castiglione 2004). Since political representation is of its nature a context-dependent activity, such changes are certain to have implications for relations between representatives and represented, and for our present concern with how representation and accountability interact in democratic theory and practice.

The hierarchical structure of policy-making that allowed the nation-state to provide such an effective answer to the question of how to relate representation with accountability is increasingly challenged by elements of heterarchy and polyarchy; or, in other words, by a growing number of semi-autonomous sites for decision-making within public institutions (heterarchy) and by a growing influence of informal semi-private non-state actors (polyarchy). Several collective decision-making areas and issues, at the national as well as the supranational level, are nowadays largely shaped by specialised and expert bodies. Moreover, policy-making differs substantially from policy area to policy area.

Often termed the 'governance revolution', these developments are hardly peculiar to the European Union. Yet an extensive literature has documented how the same factors that constrain the Union to be a 'government laggard' have made it a 'governance leader'. European integration can be seen as both contributing to and responding to the substitution of governance for government. It reflects attempts to reorganise politics in order to cope with societal transformation and transnational challenges. Yet, the technical complexity of policy-making in a political system characterised by different political traditions, discourses, and divergent economies and other circumstances has encouraged to two further trends: agencification and informalisation.

First, the Union has experienced an 'agency fever' (Christensen and Laegreid 2005: 15). In other words, authority has been delegated to non-majoritarian institutions which are not directly accountable to voters or their representatives (Majone 1999). The apparently technical nature of the agencies may, moreover, disguise the political character of their function (Pollak and Puntscher Riekmann 2008). Second, the Union has created informal structures and opportunities to influence decision-making which largely bypass parliamentary politics.

Scholars disagree on what the governance revolution implies for the topic of this paper: on whether it makes it easier or harder to combine representation with accountability. A common complaint is that the heterarchisation and polyarchisation of decision-making make it hard for citizens to identify the *locus* of politics and attribute responsibility. On the other hand, the rise of NGOs, civil society groups and wider use of consultation procedures may allow for new forms of stakeholder accountability. Thus in the case of the EU the Commission is forced to compensate for its own limited 'problem-solving capacity' (Bohman 1996: 240) by accounting to groups whose active cooperation it needs to deliver its

982   C. Lord and J. Pollak

objectives. Indeed the Commission itself has been eager to present its procedures for consulting citizens and civil society groups as potential forms of *ex ante* accountability (European Commission 2001).

Indeed, in terms of two distinctions discussed earlier – that between legal/administrative accountability and political accountability on the one hand and that between internal and external accountability on the other – the governance revolution is a potential source of innovation. As Giandomenico Majone (2005: 37) puts it, 'for many purposes expertise, professional discretion, policy consistency, fairness, or independence of judgement is considered more important than reliance upon direct democratic accountability. Whilst such values are, of their nature, most unlikely to be secured through accountability to actors who 'occupy particular points on the political spectrum', they may be secured where a wide range of political actors entrust some accountability to courts and to Ombudsmen. The governance revolution – and European integration in particular – arguably reinforce institutional technologies for legal and administrative accountability, precisely because both make it harder for any particular majority to get its way (Majone 1999). Turning to the distinction between internal and external accountability, Christian Joerges and Jürgen Neyer (1997a, 1997b) have used case studies to make the ingenious argument that comitology requires member states to account to one another for the external effects of their policies. As such, it mitigates the structural bias of representative systems to have more regard for those who elect representatives (internal accountability) than for all those affected by the behaviour of any one set of representatives (external accountability).

But are there limits to how far governance can ever substitute for representative government: to how far the foregoing innovations in external, legal/administrative or stakeholder accountability can substitute for elections and parliaments as means of securing accountability *of* and *through* representatives? Consider some problems of relying on stakeholder groups. (1) Who selects the groups which are entitled to represent? Article 10 para. 1 of the Lisbon Treaty starts off on a promising note: namely, every citizen of the Union shall have the right to participate in the democratic life of the Union. But already by the next article this right would seem to be whittled down to a requirement that Union institutions 'give citizens and representative associations the opportunity to make known and publicly exchange their views'. Participation is now understood as the right to make one's views known! Likewise, Article 11 promises an open, transparent and regular dialogue with representative associations and civil society with which especially the Commission shall carry out broad consultations. But it remains unclear on what criteria myriad groups will be singled out for access and consultation. Moreover, in the event that the claims of groups to representation collide, the Commission would be in a uniquely powerful position to decide who it is to listen to. (2) It is not always clear who consulted groups represent. Certainly not citizens at large, since they are only authorised by their members. Even large interest groups like the European Trade Union Confederation (ETUC), the European Centre of Employers and Enterprises Providing Public Services (CEEP) and the Union of Industrial and Employers' Confederations of Europe (UNICE) are not mandated by their national members to negotiate on their behalf at the supranational level.[8] (3) If the Commission, during the drafting of a legislative proposal, consults civil society groups and/or representative associations, the question is how the individual citizen can hold those groups to account. Even if s/he could know who did what in which phase of the policy-making process, there is hardly a way to hold them to account since the explanation of conduct is scattered over various audiences. (4) Groups are likely to be unequal in their ability to mobilise at transnational level. Mancur Olson's (1965) observation that not all groups in society that could possibly organise to influence any one polity – since only those for which the marginal cost exceeds the marginal return of organising will do so – is almost certainly aggravated by shifting decisions from national to transnational arenas.

The foregoing difficulties cannot be fully met by viewing governance mechanisms as somehow replicating the American model of representation of mutually suspicious interests, since, crucially, the latter is understood as mediated through classic institutions of representative government. There lies the rub. Governance may improve representation–accountability trade-offs in all the ways suggested, but it can surely only be said to meet minimum .democratic standards where it is regulated by institutions with precisely those features that have historically been associated with parliaments. That is not encouraging to the extent that the Union has struggled to develop a form of parliamentary politics that ties governance to such values as public control with political equality. In terms of the relationship between accountability and representation discussed in this article, European parliamentary elections are hard to view as providing accountability *of* representatives. Their second-order character means they are contested neither on *ex ante* screening of the promises (or political reputations) of would-be representatives nor on ex-post control of the performance of outgoing representatives. On the other hand, there are well-documented gaps in accountability *through* representatives, which include precisely those aspects of EU decision-making, such as comitology, which are most associated with claims that the Union is a new system of governance.

In sum, then, we need research which integrates governance into classic understandings of representative government. Another article would be needed to do that. However, we suspect the way forward is to follow Michael Saward's (2006) suggestion that instead of analysing representation as a more or less stable relationship between three defined components – the represented, representatives and a specified arena – we should also understand it as a constantly changing social dialogue in which various actors make representative claims to audiences which then discuss, reject, or amend them. Whilst this would still require us to take structures and

984   *C. Lord and J. Pollak*

institutions into account – by asking how free actors are to make claims and which claims have at any one time been constitutionally acknowledged and hard-wired into political systems – it is an approach that is well adapted to a time of flux in the practices and meanings of representation.

Conclusion

Democratic polities must combine representation with accountability. Political science and political theory have, however, long suggested a less than easy relationship between the two qualities. This article has attempted to make this basic intuition more systematic. It has argued that limits in how far any polity can optimise both representation and accountability goals are aggravated by indivisibilities in the design of democratic polities and made more perplexing by the nature of the value choices involved in preferring some of the limited solutions available to others. So does the governance revolution offer a way out? Whilst space has only permitted us to address this question peremptorily here, our hunch is the answer is 'yes' and 'no'. 'Yes' to the extent that governance introduces new possibilities for mutually suspicious clusters of actors to compete to hold one another to account, whilst opening up new possibilities for legal and administrative accountability, as well as external accountability. 'No' to the extent that the governance revolution rests on a proliferation of executive practices away from hierarchies that can, in turn, be held accountable to politically appointed actors and, through them, to representative bodies.

Notes

1. It seems fair to call it the US model since its theoretical content was mainly developed in the Federalist and Anti-federalist Papers and preceding discourses on the establishment of a new political order.
2. It is not surprising then that the principle of virtual representation is found in a number of European constitutions but not in any of the American constitutions. On the contrary, the constitutions e.g. of Massachusetts (1780), Pennsylvania (1776), North Carolina (1776), New Hampshire (1783), Vermont (1777) and Virginia (1776) explicitly allow for the imperative mandate.
3. The same definition can be found in John Adams (see Peek 1954: 68), Theophilus Parsons (see Handlin and Handlin 1966: 341), 'Brutus' in the Anti-Federalist Papers (Bailyn 1993: 320) and others.
4. Ankersmit (2002) and Saward (2003) see in the evocation of the represented an aesthetic moment.
5. Edmund Burke's insistence on the representation of the interests of the nation by the individual representatives is a reaction to George III's attempt to extend the royal prerogatives. In addition Burke was also carried by the wish to form England into 'one family, one body, one heart and soul' (Burke 1887: 21). And it is an expression of the Whig party's strategy to justify the narrow electoral base of the House of Commons.
6. For the assumption that citizens can arrive at rational decisions even under the condition of defective knowledge the ability to substitute through opinion leaders, parties etc. was introduced (Berelson *et al.* 1954; Downs 1957; see also Ferejohn and Kuklinski 1990; Lodge and McGraw 1995; Popkin 1991).

304   REPRESENTATION

Representation and Accountability   985

7. The more interesting question seems to be if voters would have decided otherwise under the condition of better information. Staffan Kumlin's (2004) excellent study deals with this question under the title of 'informed accountability'.

8. Consequently, possible negotiation results do not have to be implemented by the national members.

References

Achen, Chiristopher H., and Larry M. Bartels (2002). 'Blind Retrospection. Electoral Responses to Drought, Flu, and Shark Attacks'. Paper presented at the Annual Meeting of the American Political Science Association, Boston, 28 August–1 September.

Ankersmit, Franklin R. (2002). *Political Representation*. Stanford, CA: Stanford University Press.

Bailyn, Bernard (1993). *The Debate on the Constitution. Federalist and Antifederalist Speeches, Articles, and Letters During the Struggle over Ratification. Part One: September 1787 to February 1788*. New York: The Library of America.

Bartolini, Stefano (1998). 'Exit Options, Boundary Building, Political Structuring. Sketches of a Theory of Large-Scale Territorial and Membership "Retrenchment/Differentiation" versus "Expansion/Integration" (with Reference to the European Union)'. European University Institute Florence, SPS Working Paper No. 98/1.

Bartolini, Stefano (1999). 'Political Representation in Loosely Bounded Territories. Between Europe and the Nation-state'. Paper presented at the conference 'Multi-level Party Systems: Europeanisation and the Reshaping of National Political Representation', European University Institute, Florence.

Beetham, David, ed. (1994). *Defining and Measuring Democracy*. London: Sage/ECPR.

Bellamy, Richard (2008). 'No Delegation without Representation'. Paper presented at the international workshop 'A Re-assessment of Political Representation', University of Reading, 22 February.

Berelson, Bernard R., Paul F. Lazarsveld, and William N. McPhee (1954). *Voting: A Study of Opinion Formation in a Presidential Campaign*. Chicago: University of Chicago Press.

Birch, Anthony H. (1971). *Representation*. New York: Praeger.

Bogaards, Matthijs, and Markus Crepaz (2002). 'Consociational Interpretations of the European Union', *European Union Politics*, 3:3, 357–76.

Bohman, James (1996). *Public Deliberation. Pluralism, Complexity, and Democracy*. Cambridge, MA and London: MIT Press.

Bovens, Mark (2006). 'Analysing and Assessing Public Accountability. A Conceptual Framework'. European Governance Papers (EUROGOV), No. C-06-01, available at http://www.connex-network.org/eurogov/pdf/egp-connex-C-06-01.pdf (accessed 9 June 2010).

Burke, Edmund (1887). 'A Letter to Sir Hercules Langrishe on the Subject of the Roman Catholics in Ireland, and the Propriety of Admitting them to the Elective Franchise, Consistently with the Principles of the Constitution, as Established at the Revolution (1792)', in *The Works of the Right Honourable Edmund Burke*, Vol. IV. London: J. Dodsley 1899, 241–306.

Christensen, Tom, and Per Laegreid (2005). 'Agencification and Regulatory Reforms'. Paper prepared for the SCANCOR/SOG workshop on 'Autonomization of the State: From Integrated Administrative Models to Single Purpose Organizations', Stanford University, 1–2 April.

Dewey, John (1927). *The Public and its Problems*. London: George Allen and Unwin.

Dovi, Suzanne (2002). 'Preferable Descriptive Representatives: Will Just Any Women, Black or Latino Do?', *American Political Science Review*, 96, 729–43.

Downs, Anthony (1957). *An Economic Theory of Democracy*. New York: Harper & Row.

Dunn, John (2005). *Setting the People Free: The Story of Democracy*. London: Atlantic Books.

986   C. Lord and J. Pollak

Eulau, Heinz, John C. Wahlke, William Buchanan, and Leroy W. Ferguson (1959). 'The Role of the Representative: Some Empirical Observations on the Theory of Edmund Burke', *American Political Science Review*, 53, 742–56.

European Commission (2001). *European Governance, a White Paper*. Brussels: The Commission of the European Communities.

Ferejohn, John A., and James H. Kuklinski, eds. (1990). *Information and Democratic Processes*. Urbana: University of Illinois Press.

Fiorina, Morris P. (1981). *Retrospective Voting in American National Elections*. New Haven, CT: Yale University Press.

Forst, Rainer (2007). *Das Recht auf Rechtfertigung. Elemente eine konstruktivistischer Theorie der Gerechtigkeit*. Frankfurt am Main: Suhrkamp.

Goodin, Robert E. (1993). 'Democracy, Preferences and Paternalism', *Policy Sciences*, 26:3, 229–47.

Gould, Carol C. (1996). 'Diversity and Democracy: Representing Difference', in Seyla Benhabib (ed.), *Democracy and Difference*. Princeton, NJ: Princeton University Press, 171–86.

Grant, Ruth W., and Robert O. Keohane (2005). 'Accountability and Abuses of Power in World Politics', *American Political Science Review*, 99:1, 29–43.

Griffiths, Phillips A., and Richard Wollheim (1960). 'How Can One Person Represent Another?', *The Aristotelian Society*, 34, 182–208.

Handlin, Oscar, and Mary F. Handlin, eds. (1966). *Popular Sources of Political Authority*. Cambridge, MA: Belknap Press of Harvard University Press.

Harlow, Carol (2002). *Accountability in the European Union*. Oxford: Oxford University Press.

Joerges, C., and J. Neyer (1997a). 'From Intergovernmental Bargaining to Deliberative Political Processes: The Constitutionalization of Comitology', *European Law Journal*, 3:3, 273–99.

Joerges, Christian, and Jürgen Neyer (1997b). 'Transforming Strategic Interaction Into Deliberative Problem-Solving: European Comitology in the Foodstuff Sector', *Journal of European Public Policy*, 4:1, 609–25.

Kumlin, Staffan (2004). *The Personal and the Political. How Personal Welfare State Experiences Affect Political Trust and Ideology*. New York: Palgrave.

Kymlicka, Will (1996). 'Three Forms of Group-Differentiated Citizenship in Canada', in Seyla Benhabib (ed.), *Democracy and Difference*. Princeton, NJ: Princeton University Press, 153–70.

Leibholz, Gerhard (1966). *Das Wesen der Repräsentation und der Gestaltwandel der Demokratie im 20. Jahrhundert*, 3rd ed. Berlin: Walter de Gruyter.

Lewis-Beck, Michael S. (1988). *Economics and Elections. The Major Western Democracies*. Ann Arbor, MI: University of Michigan Press.

Lewis-Beck, Michael S., and Marrin Paldam (2000). 'Economic Voting: An Introduction', *Electoral Studies*, 19, 113–21.

Lijphart, Arend (1979). 'Consociational Democracy', *World Politics*, 32, 207–25.

Lodge, Milton, and Kathleen M. McGraw, eds. (1995). *Political Judgement: Structure and Process*. Ann Arbor: University of Michigan Press.

Lord, Christopher (2008). 'Some Indicators of the Democratic Performance of the European Union and How They Might Relate to the Recon Models', Recon Online Working Paper 2008/11. Oslo: Recon/ARENA.

Lord, Christopher, and Erika Harris (2006). *Democracy in the New Europe*. Basingstoke: Palgrave.

Luskin, Robert C. (2002). 'From Denial to Extenuation (and Finally Beyond): Political Sophistication and Citizen Performance', in James H. Kuklinski (ed.), *Thinking about Political Psychology*. Oxford: Oxford University Press, 281–305.

Majone, Giandomenico (1999). 'The Regulatory State and its Legitimacy Problems', *West European Politics*, 22:1, 1–24.

Majone, Giandomenico (2005). *Dilemmas of European Integration. The Ambiguities and Pitfall of Integration by Stealth*. Oxford: Oxford University Press.

Manin, Bernard, Adam Przeworski, and Susan A. Stokes (1999). 'Elections and Representation', in Adam Przeworski, Susan C. Stokes, and Bernard Manin (eds.), *Democracy, Accountability, and Representation*. Cambridge: Cambridge University Press, 29–54.

Mansbridge, Jane (1999). 'Should Blacks Represent Blacks and Women Represent Women? A Contingent "Yes"', *Journal of Politics*, 61, 628–57.

Mansbridge, Jane (2003). 'Rethinking Representation', *American Political Science Review*, 97, 515–28.

March, James G., and Johan P. Olsen (1995). *Democratic Governance*. New York: Free Press.

Michels, Robert (1961 [1911]). *Political Parties: A Sociological Study of the Oligarchical Tendencies of Modern Democracy*. New York: Free Press.

Mill, John S. (1972 [1861]). *Utilitarianism, On Liberty and Considerations on Representative Government*. London: Dent.

Miller, David (2007). *National Responsibility and Global Justice*. Oxford: Oxford University Press.

Norpoth, Helmut (1996). 'The Economy', in Lawrence LeDuc, Richard G. Niemi, and Pippa Norris (eds.), *Comparing Democracies. Elections and Voting in Comparative Perspective*. Thousands Oaks, CA: Sage, 299–318.

Olson, Mancur (1965). *The Logic of Collective Action: Public Goods and the Theory of Groups*. Cambridge, MA: Harvard University Press.

Peek, George A., ed. (1954). *The Political Writings of John Adams*. New York: Bobbs-Merrill.

Pennock, James R. (1979). *Democratic Political Theory*. Princeton, NJ: Princeton University Press.

Phillips, Anne (1995). *The Politics of Presence: Issues in Democracy and Group Representation*. Oxford: Oxford University Press.

Phillips, Anne (1997). 'Dealing with Difference: A Politics of Ideas or a Politics of Presence', in Robert Gooding and Philip Pettit (eds.), *Contemporary Political Philosophy. An Anthology*. Oxford: Blackwell, 174–84.

Pitkin, Hanna F. (1967). *The Concept of Political Representation*. Berkeley, Los Angeles and London: University of California Press.

Pollak, Johannes (2007a). 'Contested Meanings of Representation', *Journal for Comparative Politics*, 5:1, 87–103.

Pollak, Johannes (2007b). *Repräsentation ohne Demokratie. Kollidierende Modi der Repräsentation in der Europäischen Union*. Wien and New York: Springer.

Pollak, Johannes, and Sonja Puntscher Riekmann (2008). 'European Administration: Centralisation and Fragmentation as Means of Polity-Building?', *West European Politics*, 31:4, 771–88.

Popkin, Samuel L. (1991). *The Reasoning Voter: Communication and Persuasion in Presidential Campaigns*. Chicago: University of Chicago Press.

Powell, G. Bingham, and Guy D. Whitten (1993). 'A Cross-national Analysis of Economic Voting: Taking Account of Political Context', *American Journal of Political Science*, 37, 391–414.

Przeworski, Adam, Susan C. Stokes, and Bernard Manin, eds. (1999). *Democracy, Accountability, and Representation*. Cambridge: Cambridge University Press.

Rakove, Jack (1997). *Original Meanings. Politics and Ideas in the Making of the Constitution*. New York: Vintage.

Rawls, John (1993). *Political Liberalism*. New York: Columbia University Press.

Saward, M. (2003). 'Representing Nature and the Nature of Representation'. Paper presented at the 2nd European Consortium for Political Research Conference, Marburg, September.

Saward, Michael (2006). 'The Representative Claim', *Contemporary Political Theory*, 5, 297–318.

Schmalz-Bruns, Rainer (2007). 'The Euro-Polity in Perspective: Some Normative Lessons from Deliberative Democracy', in Beate Kohler-Koch and Berthold Rittberger (eds.), *Debating the Democratic Legitimacy of the European Union*. Lanham, MD: Rowman and Littlefield, 281–303.

988   C. Lord and J. Pollak

Schmitt, Eberhard (1969). *Repräsentation und Revolution. Eine Untersuchung zur Genesis der kontinentalen Theorie und Praxis parlamentarischer Repraesentation aus der Herrschaftspraxis des Ancien régime in Frankreich (1760–1789)*. München: Beck.

Schumpeter, Joseph A. (1942). *Capitalism, Socialism, and Democracy*. New York: Harper.

Shapiro, Ian (1996). *Democracy's Place*. Ithaca, NY: Cornell University Press.

Skinner, Quentin (1978). *The Foundations of Modern Political Thought*. Cambridge: Cambridge University Press.

Strøm, Kaare (2003). 'Parliamentary Democracy and Delegation', in Kaare Strøm, Wolfgang Müller, and Torbjörn Bergman (eds.), *Delegation and Accountability in Parliamentary Democracies*. Oxford: Oxford University Press, 55–106.

Sunstein, Cass R. (1993). 'Democracy and Shifting Preferences', in David Copp, Jean Hampton, and John E. Roemer (eds.), *The Idea of Democracy*. Cambridge: Cambridge University Press, 196–230.

Taylor, Michael A. (2000). 'Channeling Frustrations: Institutions, Economic Fluctuations, and Political Behaviour', *European Journal of Political Research*, 38, 95–134.

Van der Brug, Wouter, Cees van der Eijk, and Mark Franklin (2001). 'Small Effects, Large Consequences: Electoral Responses to Economic Conditions in 15 Countries, 1989–1999'. Paper presented at the ECPR General Conference, Canterbury, UK, September.

Warren, Mark, and Dario Castiglione (2004). 'The Transformation of Democratic Representation', *Democracy and Society*, 2:1, 5–22.

Weale, Albert (1999). *Democracy*. London: Macmillan.

Williams, Melissa S. (1998). *Voice, Trust, and Memory: Marginalized Groups and the Failings of Liberal Representation*. Princeton, NJ: Princeton University Press.

Toward a Mobilization Conception of Democratic Representation
LISA DISCH

This article analyzes what I term "the dilemma of democratic competence," which emerges when researchers find their expectations regarding democratic responsiveness to be in conflict with their findings regarding the context dependency of individual preferences. I attribute this dilemma to scholars' normative expectations, rather than to deficiencies of mass democratic politics. I propose a mobilization conception of political representation and develop a systemic understanding of reflexivity as the measure of its legitimacy. This article thus contributes to the emergent normative argument that political representation is intrinsic to democratic government, and links that claim to empirical research on political preference formation.

This article begins with an empirical finding: U.S. voters are more "competent" than research into opinion formation once took them to be (e.g., Carmines and Kuklinski 1990; Lupia 1992, 1994; Lupia and McCubbins 1998; Popkin 1991; Sniderman 2000; Sniderman, Brody, and Tetlock 1991).[1] They can form opinions and hold preferences that are coherent and stable enough to be represented. However, the reasoning process by which they form these preferences depends on communications put forward by political elites in their bids to forge a winning majority in an election or policy contest.[2] Elites educate constituents as they recruit them to positions that work to elites' own advantage in an interparty struggle for power, typically without avowing the dual motive (Gerber and Jackson 1993). Political learning takes place by means of communication that is at once explicitly oriented to constituents and silently enmeshed in a struggle for power.

This finding sits uneasily with two prominent democratic intuitions that belong to two different schools of democratic theory. First is the idea that representative

democracy is defined by the "continuing responsiveness of the government to the preferences of its citizens" (Dahl 1971, 1).[3] This idea, whose orientation toward preexisting preferences makes it one aspect of what Mansbridge (2003, 518) calls the "traditional model of promissory representation," not only makes responsiveness the signature feature of democratic representation, but also prescribes that it be unidirectional. Pitkin (1967, 140) captures this when she writes that, in democratic representation, the "representative must be responsive to [the constituent] rather than the other way around."

Pitkin expresses here what I term the "bedrock" norm, the common-sense notion that representatives in a democratic regime should take citizen preferences as the "bedrock for social choice" (Page and Shapiro 1992, 354; cf. Achen 1975, 1227; Bartels 2003, 62).[4] According to this norm, which configures the representation process as linear and dyadic, legitimacy turns on voters and representatives being oriented in the proper direction. As Mansbridge (2003, 518) aptly characterizes it, the "voter's power works forward" to hold representatives to the promises they made at election time, whereas the "representative's attention looks backward" to the previously expressed preferences of the constituency. Empirical findings about preference formation sit uneasily with this norm because they defy this static portrait of preferences together with this linear dyadic model of influence. They reveal, instead, that the representative process is dynamic and interactive. Representatives look backward to preferences that have been expressed, and orient themselves forward in a speculative mode toward what their constituency might want or be induced to want at the next election. In short, empirical research reveals political representation to be *constitutive*: legislators do not simply respond to constituent preferences but are "active ... in searching out and sometimes creating them" (Mansbridge 2003,

---

I am grateful to Mark Brown, Sam Chambers, Richard Flathman, Keith Gaddie, Jack Gunnell, Jonathan Havercroft, Clarissa Hayward, Jenny Mansbridge, Andrew Rehfeld, Mark Warren, and Justin Wert for their comments on various versions of this article. I thank the students who took my graduate seminars on political representation at the Universities of Minnesota and Michigan, colleagues at both of those institutions, and SABLE members Anne Carter, Anna Clark, Kirsten Fischer, Jeani O'Brien, Jennifer Peirce, and Gabriela Tsurutani. Final thanks go to anonymous reviewers for the *APSR* whose perceptive advice significantly improved this work, to the *APSR* coeditors, and to Coeditor Kirstie McClure, who supported this article with critical acuity and intellectual generosity.

[1] I define competence, after Lupia and McCubbins (1998, 2), as the capacity for "reasoned choice," which is nonarbitrary but distinct from "rational choice" in being exercised in the absence of full information and relying on the advice of others.

[2] I follow Zaller (1992, 6) in defining elites as "politicians, higher-level government officials, journalists, some activists, and many kinds of experts and policy specialists," as well as corporate elites. They influence preference formation primarily by means of the mass media, and secondarily through such organizations as lobbies, churches, and labor unions. The media serves them not as a platform from which to promulgate their views directly, but rather as means of framing issues and exercising agenda control (Althaus et al. 1996; Bennett 1990; Bennett and Manheim 1993).

---

[3] Garsten (2009), Hayward (2009), Warren and Castiglione (2006), and Williams (1990) join Mansbridge (2003) in calling "responsiveness" into question.

[4] The bedrock norm originated with the U.S. and French Revolutions whose most radical strands held the people to be the only "legitimate source of power" in a democracy and identified democratic legitimacy with the "idea of a mandate or delegation" (Rosanvallon 2008, 9, 236).

310   REPRESENTATION

American Political Science Review   Vol. 105, No. 1

518; cf. Manza and Cook 2002; Squires 2008; Williams 1990.

This research shows that responsiveness does, indeed, turn "the other way around." Does this inversion irredeemably compromise democratic ideals? For the most committed formal modelers and theorists of rational choice, the answer would have to be "yes" because preference endogeneity in itself troubles their model of the rational individual. In contrast, deliberative democratic theorists allow that political elites can shape constituent preferences as long as their interventions facilitate "mutual education, communication, and influence," rather than manipulation (Mansbridge 2003, 520). For them, the problem is not endogeneity per se but the opening it affords to what they deem strategic action by elites.

This belief that preferences, which are necessarily endogenous to politics, must be deliberatively formed is the second democratic intuition. It is even more at odds with the scholarship on opinion formation by virtue of its intellectual inheritance from discourse theories of democracy. Specifically, it derives from the Habermasian analytic separation of "communicative and strategic action," which aims to distinguish (counterfactually) social coordination that is achieved noncoercively, by the give and take of reasons among speakers oriented toward mutual understanding, from that which either results from the overt use of threats or bribes or occurs under conditions where a party conceals an orientation toward nonmutual advantage (Habermas 1990, 58; cf. Cohen 1989).[5] The discourse ideal casts suspicion on preferences that are formed in information contexts where power is at stake and where unstated motives exist—the very conditions of preference formation according to empirical scholarship.

Scholars who are influenced by this ideal propose to judge representation by a distinction between education and manipulation that, as Mansbridge (2003) acknowledges, is "not easy to operationalize." They define education as (1) lacking intent to deceive, (2) serving to clarify voters' "underlying interests and the policy implications of those interests," (3) leading voters to make choices in their interests, and (4) garnering support for changes that voters approve in retrospect (519; cf. Page and Shapiro 1992, 354; Zaller 1992, 313). One problem with these criteria is that they beg the question "what is and what is not in an individual's interests," another point that Mansbridge (2003, 519) acknowledges to be open to contest. Thus, identifying manipulation requires the analyst to posit the "counterfactual" of how voters would define their interests "under other, often ill-defined circumstances" (Druckman 2001a, 233). A second problem is that if one adheres to

these criteria, then one is bound to find manipulation everywhere.

This is not because deception is everywhere, although elites certainly engage in it (e.g., President Johnson's claims regarding North Vietnamese attacks in the Tonkin Gulf or President Bush's assertions regarding the existence of "weapons of mass destruction" in Iraq). Much of the time, political discourse is neither straightforwardly false nor intentionally misleading. It consists, rather, of what Jacobs and Shapiro (2000, 27) call "crafted talk"—messages that political elites systematically develop through the technologies of opinion polling and focus groups "in order to attract favorable press coverage and 'win' public support for what they desire." Such messages have a twofold motivation and a twofold effect: to declare a stand and to "shift ... the line of cleavage" in a bid for power (Schattschneider [1960] 1975, 61). Put simply, whereas elite discourse serves at once to inform potential voters and to recruit them into a winning majority, elites avow only the first of these goals. To disclose the second self-interested aim, as Habermasian deliberation requires, would make their speech acts less likely to succeed.[6]

Empirical research shows that in the "political environment," "communicative" and "strategic" action are linked inextricably.[7] Individuals form coherent and relatively stable preferences not in spite of but by means of messages that political elites deploy in pursuit of unavowed competitive goals. This sets up what I term the "dilemma of democratic competence": citizens' capacity to form preferences depends on the self-interested communications of elites. Research that aimed to vindicate representative democracy ends up provoking the discomfiting sense that "one form of incompetence simply replaces another. Specifically, while people who rely on party cues avoid basing their preferences on arbitrary information, they also expose themselves to the possibility of elite manipulation" (Druckman 2001a, 239). Thus, communication that discourse theory regards as manipulative turns out to be intrinsic to the learning process.

What are researchers to make of the fact that they can affirm citizens' capacity for preference formation only at the cost of revealing their susceptibility to the self-seeking rhetoric of competing elites? Must they

---

[5] This distinction gets its critical edge from Habermas' pejorative equation of strategy with instrumental action. If one defined "strategic" to mean simply "goal oriented," then the distinction would do very little critical work because all communication is oriented to some goal. Moreover, as Bohman (1988) argues, the idealization of communication and derogation of strategy works against Habermas' own project by discrediting the speech of the social critic who necessarily mixes the two.

[6] For example, in the early 1960s, when Democratic and Republican party elites radically altered their party's positions on the leading issues of the day (civil rights and the Vietnam War, respectively), they did so "to increase their likelihood of winning elections" but presented it as the right thing to do (Gerber and Jackson 1993, 639). Even if voters suspect (and they surely do) that most political discourse is partisan posturing, politicians would alienate voters by making that explicit. Voters prefer to imagine they are treated as principled decision makers, rather than as pawns in a bid to effect partisan realignment.

[7] Empirical researchers use the term "political environment" to designate the "totality of politically relevant information to which citizens are exposed" by various mediating institutions (Kuklinski et al. 2001, 411). It functions for them as a way to speak of what normative theorists would call the "public sphere," without crediting that environment with the virtues of equality, openness, reasonableness, etc.

REPRESENTATION

Toward a Mobilization Conception

despair of citizens' capacity to live up to democratic norms? Must they denounce the communications apparatus of mass democracy? Or is it time to call the norms themselves into question? I argue for the latter. To rest democratic representation either on the "bedrock" of citizen preferences or on a cognitivist model of deliberation is to misunderstand what preferences are and how they form. It is also to deprecate crucial features of democratic representation: figuration and mobilization.[8] Democratic political representation neither simply reflects nor transmits demands; it creates them as it actively recruits constituencies.[9]

The argument continues over four sections. I begin by specifying the challenge that empirical findings on opinion formation pose to preference-based conceptions of democratic representation. I turn next to the new wave of democratic theory and show how its allegiances to a vestige of foundationalism prevent it from answering this challenge. Following that, I make a brief return to Pitkin's (1967) classic text, which I argue both initiated a bolder move toward representation as mobilization than her successors have managed and opened the gap between normative expectations and empirical research. I build my conception of representation as mobilization out of Pitkin's most radical insights, bringing that conception within the compass of deliberative democracy by drawing on the work of scholars of "rhetorical deliberation" (Garsten 2006; cf. Bickford 1996). I propose "reflexivity" as the measure of its legitimacy. A term that I take up from Mansbridge (2003, 518), I elaborate "reflexivity" as a systemic capacity rather than an individual subjective one.

THE "CONSTRUCTIVIST TURN" IN OPINION FORMATION AND PREFERENCE-BASED DEMOCRACY

Beginning with Gamson and Modigliani (1989), research in public opinion and political psychology has taken what researchers call a "constructionist" or "constructivist" turn (Kinder and Nelson 2005, 103) from a rational individualist to an environmental or contextual account of preference formation. The former holds individuals to define their preferences according to needs, desires, and values that are fixed prior to political contests and relatively impervious to political influence. The latter contends that preferences are constituted in the communication that occurs during decision making, implying that choice is as much something that institutions effect as it is something that an individual makes. Insofar as this is a move from an individualist to an environmental account of preference formation, it might seem more appropriate to label this position "contextualist" rather than "constructivist." I contend that it can indeed be viewed as a "constructivist" turn by virtue of the commitment to the notion that opinion is not simply there to be "discovered or intuited" but must be built either by researchers or by the individual him- or herself (O'Neill 2002, 348).[10]

Findings regarding the context dependence of preferences have significant implications for the "bedrock" norm, which holds that democratic representation is necessarily preference based. For those who subscribe to this norm, preferences that fluctuate in response to politicians' and pollsters' "choice of language" lack the "nice properties of global coherence and consistency that would allow them to play the role of preferences" as "most liberal theorists of democracy (and their cousins, the economists)" have defined the term (Bartels 2003, 67, 56, 49). Their expectation is that citizens should hold "definite, preexisting preferences regarding the underlying issues [that] any reasonable choice of language might elicit ... equally well" (51, 67). I argue for a reframing of this expectation. Is it the case that preferences must display the constancy of bedrock to count as such? Must political representation take preferences as its starting place and ground in order to be democratically legitimate? Constructivist research in opinion formation says "no" to both.

As to the first expectation, Chong and Druckman (2007, 652) counter that the decisive question is not whether preferences change but whether they do so arbitrarily, in response to logically equivalent information.[11] In political discourse, opinion shifts in response to what Druckman (2001a, 235; 2004, 672) calls "issue" framing, instances where a speaker brings "a substantively different consideration ... to bear on the issue at hand." Such change, which is not necessarily arbitrary (although it may be so in some cases), is an ever-present feature of democratic politics, which "involves battles over how a campaign, a problem, or an issue should be understood" (Druckman 2001a, 235). Issue framing is one means of waging what Schattschneider ([1960] 1975, 64) termed the "conflict of conflicts."

---

[8] I specify "democratic" representation because I take mobilization to be specific to political representation following the eighteenth-century democratic revolutions. Before then, political representation entailed "direct adhesion" to social differences, with representatives acting primarily as delegates, as in the model of the French estates (Urbinati 2006, 49).

[9] The internecine struggles within parties, together with their efforts to navigate the riptides of third party or civil society forces (e.g., the Moral Majority or the Tea Party), show that recruitment goes on even when the constituency is formally defined as a legislative district or state population. Although I focus on that formal electoral context in this article because I chose to draw on empirical research conducted within that context, representation as mobilization is pertinent to the work of international nongovernmental organizations and other "self-appointed" (Montanaro 2010) or "unelected" (Saward 2010, ch. 4) representatives who act outside the bounds of citizenship and national elections.

[10] In fact, the term "constructivist turn" may strike some as a misnomer. These researchers exhibit neither a Kantian concern to justify ethical prescriptions nor a poststructuralist pleasure in relocating agency from conscious, willing individuals to the anonymous processes of meaning-making in language, but rather retain a humanist commitment to capacities of judgment and choice.

[11] Druckman (2004, 672) differentiates "equivalence" framing, which presents logically equivalent information with a different emphasis, from "issue" framing, which brings new considerations to light. Equivalence framing effects are not as pervasive in actual political debate as they have seemed to be in psychology experiments (Druckman 2001b).

312 REPRESENTATION

This sensitivity of preferences to contexts of conflict need not compromise their integrity as preferences, except to the methodological individualist who holds that preferences must have the "nice properties of global coherence and consistency" in and of themselves, that is, independent of or prior to political contests (Bartels 2003, 56). For Druckman and Lupia (2000), who have mustered the insights of cognitive science against rational individualist notions of rationality, preferences simply do not attain consistency in advance. As "comparative evaluation[s]" or "ranking[s] over a set of objects" that conflict brings into relationship with one another, they necessarily develop over the course of a political contest (2). This view of preferences takes the normative charge out of the distinction between preference "endogeneity" and "exogeneity" because it suggests that preferences are always endogenous to some context that is beyond an individual's control.

For these researchers, so-called endogenous preferences *are* preferences. Features of the environment such as cues and frames help individuals form preferences that are consistent and relatively stable. Such preferences can be represented; they cannot serve as a *basis* for responsiveness as the "bedrock" norm requires because they cannot have "independent causal import" (Manza and Cook 2002, 657). In sum, there is an emerging consensus that political representation need not and cannot take preferences as its starting place and ground. It remains in dispute whether—given the context dependence of preferences—representation can be democratically legitimate.

In exploring this question, it is noteworthy that researchers do not assess the rationality of voter preferences against the counterfactual of what their interests "really" are. They look at the interaction among messages, rather than at their content, focusing on the "external forces" that make it more likely for political learning to take place (Lupia and McCubbins 1998, ch. 2). Framing research, for example, has begun to study the competition among frames and between frames and cues (e.g., Druckman et al. 2010; Sniderman and Theriault 2004).[12] In effect, this research studies deliberation in the actual public sphere of electronically mediated, highly funded, two-party mass democracy.

Taking political communication as it is, neither oriented toward mutual understanding nor regulated by the principle of the unforced force of the better argument, but competitive, self-interested, and oriented toward winning elections, it asks: can competition prompt people to think twice about their preferences rather than absorbing them from elite propaganda? Studying frames, Chong and Druckman (2007) find three ways in which competition fosters political judgment in this sense. First, it can moderate ideological extremes. Second, exposure to multiple frames prompts people to consider which is the most applicable. Third, people make that judgment based on a frame's "relative strength," not merely on its frequency of repetition (639, 651).

That "strong" frames win out over loud and insistent ones is no guarantee of democratic legitimacy, however. For a frame to be "strong" means only that it is credible—that it is proposed by a respected source, taps familiar concerns, and applies to the matter at hand. A strong frame is not necessarily a strong—i.e., disciplined and well-reasoned—argument. It may derive that credibility "as much [from] its source and cultural values and symbols it invokes as [from] its causal logic" (Chong and Druckman 2007, 652).[13] It follows that competition among frames cannot satisfy the Habermasian counterfactual of producing a reasoned position that warrants the assent of all affected. Competition may raise the quality of public debate by improving the "odds that germane considerations will be publicized and discussed" (652). Druckman (2010) cautions, however, that a frame may prevail over its rivals by tapping insecurity and prejudice rather than by appealing to logic and fact. Some researchers who focus on cues rather than frames are more optimistic. Lupia and McCubbins (1998, 201) maintain that democratic institutions render people capable of drawing knowledge from the political environment that enables them to be "selective about whom they choose to believe."

Noteworthy here is researchers' turn from the bedrock of autonomous preference to the communication process. This shows, as Mansbridge (2003, 518) argues, that empirical research is newly open to the "deliberative side" of political representation. Yet, I argue that normative theory is not fully equipped to exploit this opening. There remains a mismatch between the constructivism of empirical research and the "deliberative theory of democracy," which Urbinati (2006, 118–19) rightly characterizes as "hesitant to face" the "ideological as rhetorical process of representation." This hesitancy is true of even the most politically astute defenders of deliberation insofar as they hold out for an ideal of independence from partisanship that puts their work out of synch with the findings on preference context dependency.

---

[12] In this article, I tend to generalize about elite communication. Note that I draw on results from two different research tracks: studies of informational "cues" (e.g., Carmines and Kuklinski 1990; Lupia 1992, 1994; Lupia and McCubbins 1998; Popkin 1991; Sniderman 2000; Sniderman, Brody, and Tetlock 1991), and studies of such argumentative strategies as "framing" and "priming" (e.g., Chong and Druckman 2007; Druckman 2001a, 2004; Gamson and Modigliani 1989; Kinder and Nelson 2005; Kinder and Sanders 1996; Sniderman and Theriault 2004). Although the lines of inquiry into heuristics and argumentation are distinct, the two phenomena overlap in practice because people can learn from frames and cues can be embedded in the frames proposed by political parties and interest groups (Druckman et al. 2010). A strong distinction between cues and frames does appear to hold with respect to the reasoning process. Framing is more powerful in its early stages and with "online processors," who rely on an initial judgment to screen subsequent information. Cues can provide information updates to those who take them in and will be more powerful with "memory-based processors" who make their decisions based on what they have most recently learned (Druckman et al. 2010).

---

[13] As a further cautionary note, some research suggests that only the moderately politically aware and well informed are actually open to new information and inclined to bring it to bear on an issue. If this is true, then the proportion of the populace that is open to persuasion and deliberation may be quite small (Druckman and Lupia 2000, 15).

THE DEMOCRATIC "REDISCOVERY" OF REPRESENTATION

Following the wave of academic theory that embraced "participatory" democracy in the wake of the Civil Rights, student, and antiwar movements (e.g., Barber 1984; Miller 1987; Pateman 1970), normative scholars have proclaimed a "democratic *rediscovery* of representation" (Urbinati 2006, 5; see Dovi 2002; Manin 1997; Mansbridge 1999, 2003; Plotke 1997; Schwartz 1988; Seitz 1995; Urbinati and Warren 2008; Young 1997, 2000). This rediscovery begins by questioning the assumption that democracy need have its origins in a constituency, as a democratic constituency exists "at best potentially" (Young 2000, 130). Being large, dispersed, and vaguely defined, it "rarely brings itself to affirm a common will," but requires "representative institutions and the process of authorization themselves [to] call its members into action" (130). In effect, then, as public opinion researchers have come to recognize the context dependency of preferences, theorists of political representation have taken a similar turn to conceive of the "people," democracy's political subject, as endogenous to the process of representation.

The rediscovery of representation alters the very valence of "representative democracy." This phrase that once struck participatory democrats as an "oxymoron" (Urbinati 2006, 4) for putting representatives in the place where the people should be, now strikes theorists of representation as "in fact a tautology" (Näsström 2006, 330). It is only *through* representation that a people comes to be as a political agent, one capable of putting forward a demand. Thus, representation cannot be regarded as either supplementary or compensatory; it is "the essence of democracy" (330).

This, too, is a constructivist turn, one motivated by a critical awakening to what Young (2000, 125) calls democratic political theory's "metaphysics of presence." Presence, a concept that Young borrows from Derrida ([1967] 1973), names the fantasy of a reality that is self-evident, unmediated by social processes, and sovereign so that it can be imagined to provide an origin and point of reference for assessing the accuracy and faithfulness of any attempt to represent it. To reject such a fantasy is precisely to refute the assumption that representation is a "descriptive and mimetic" process, one that merely transmits "something preexisting it, like for instance a single or collective sovereign that seeks pictorial representation through election" (Urbinati 2006, 46, 33). For proponents of the "rediscovery" of representation, "democratic politics is *constituted* partly through representation" (Plotke 1997, 31; emphasis added).

There remains a conceptual gap between normative and empirical bodies of work that opens at the most basic question of what is to be represented. Many normative theorists would agree with Plotke (1997, 32) that "interest representation" is the "starting point in a democratic view of representation." Plotke's choice of the term "interest" rather than "preference" marks something more than a semantic disagreement with empirical scholars. Mansbridge (2003, 519–20) affirms

a qualitative difference between the two, asserting that "questions regarding voters' interests, in contrast to their preferences, are not susceptible to certain resolution." Whereas Mansbridge (517, n. 6) regards preferences in behavioral terms, she takes pains to gloss "interest" as including "identity-constituting[,] ideal-regarding commitments as well as material needs." Mere preferences, she suggests, are unreflexive, but interests are "enlightened preferences," refined dialogically in light of not just "simple cognition" but "experience and emotional understanding" (517, n. 6). The question at stake between normative and empirical scholars is: would the context-dependent "preferences" theorized by Druckman, Lupia, and other such scholars count as what Plotke and Mansbridge term "interests" or "enlightened preferences"?

Not according to the most rationalist version of interest, which is modeled by Habermas' communicative action/strategic action distinction. Deliberative democrats have attempted to translate that ideal into politics by means of "citizens' juries," "mini-publics," and other such experiments that insulate "participants from the usual sources of information and persuasion and the usual conditions under which they respond to polls about their preferences" (Rosenblum 2008, 300).[14] Such experiments are at odds with empirical research on opinion formation because they juxtapose deliberation against "partisan contestation" (300). Not only do they participate in a long tradition of antipartisanship, as Rosenblum argues, but they also open a gulf between normative models of the way citizens *should* reason and empirical accounts of the way they *do* reason (300).

Even those deliberative democrats who have criticized the rationalism of the Habermasian model persist in an intersubjective model of dialogue and an attachment to independent interests as a point of departure for the representative relationship. Plotke (1997, 32) envisions a dialogic process in two stages where citizens first "aim to clarify their own preferences" among themselves, then "seek to select representatives who will try to produce suitable results." Young (2000, 132) also envisions a two-stage process, one that begins with "citizen participation" in a context of conflict to produce demands that are specific to that context, then seeks representatives to carry those demands forward. Even though Young describes demands emerging out of political conflict, she nonetheless insulates the process of their formation from party politics. Hers is a world where "citizens . . . form themselves into [constituencies]" and engage "in debate and struggle over the wisdom and implications of policy decisions" independently of elite cues and frames (131).[15]

---

[14] In a favorable review of the "macro-political impact of [such] micro-political innovations," Goodin and Dryzek (2006, 220) report that although they rarely have a direct influence on policy content, minipublics and other such forums can serve as a way to test-market policy proposals, promote legitimacy, and build a constituency for change.

[15] Forst (2001, 369) depicts a similar scenario of demands produced in "information networks of discussion" entering into the "center

314 REPRESENTATION

On such accounts, it is not elite communication but a "public sphere of discussion" that orients citizens in conflict by setting "an issue agenda and the main terms of dispute or struggle" (Young 2000, 130). To be sure, Young does not adhere strictly to the bedrock norm; she does not understand interests to be fixed, but rather conceives them to be arrived at dialogically. But she does preserve the temporal logic of bedrock, together with the requirement of unilateral responsiveness, by stipulating that it is only once citizens have "organize[d] and discuss[ed] the issues that are important to them" that they "call on candidates to respond to their interests" (130). As Squires (2008, 190) notes, the "process here flows from the constituents to the representatives." In sum, although both Young and Plotke recognize that interests are not fixed prior to politics, they make them endogenous to politics in an idealized way: they are formed by practices of public reason to secure the independence and autonomy of citizens' judgment against the opportunistic communications of elites.

These models of two-stage processes conflict with empirical accounts of context-dependent preferences in two ways. First, they hold onto an ideal of independence from partisan communication as a touchstone for democratic legitimacy, departing from liberal/economic models of politics by making interest (rather than preference) its site and dialogue (rather than preference exogeneity) its guarantor. This is effectively a deliberative rewriting of the bedrock norm. Second, they model deliberation out of the context of interparty conflict, as occurring first among citizens and then between citizens and their representatives. In contrast, as I argue, empirical research on preference context dependency shows preferences to evolve in the context of interparty competition and to be responsive to communications from representatives and other elites. These communications, although addressed to constituencies, are primarily oriented toward that competition. Put simply, citizens learn *from*, not *in spite of*, the frames and cues that political elites deploy to gain an edge in partisan contests. In short, empirical research recognizes political communication as twofold: addressed explicitly to constituencies and silently enmeshed in interparty struggle. What would happen to dialogic models if they had to confront this twofold character?

Mansbridge (2003, 515) grapples with precisely this question in a path-breaking article where she takes up the normative implications of empirical studies of "'retrospective voting,'" in which voters assess their representatives' performance based on priorities that they developed over the course of the term, rather than on those that they held at the moment of election. Mansbridge explains that retrospective voting effects a "shift in temporal emphasis" that gives rise to "unexpected normative changes" (518). In the traditional promissory model, the representative is bound by a

common-sense moral imperative "to do what he or she had promised the voters at [election time]" (515, 518). In retrospective voting, legislators act not only according to the "actual [past] preferences of the voter," but also according to their own "*beliefs*" about "the future preferences of the voter" at reelection time. When voting is retrospective, representation becomes "anticipatory," creating "a prudential, not a moral, relationship to those voters" (518). Whereas promissory representatives have only one course of action (to do as they said or to justify any deviation in terms of the principles they professed to hold), anticipatory representatives, who aim to please "future voters," have two. They attempt to gauge what a voting majority will want at the next election, turning to "public opinion polls, focus groups, and gossip about the 'mood of the nation'" so as to adapt themselves to the electorate's movement (517). They also make themselves agents of that change, attempting to shape public opinion so that voters "will be more likely to approve of the representative's actions" (517).

Mansbridge (2003) draws two important conclusions from this new landscape. First, anticipatory voting opens up the possibility that "voters can change their preferences after thinking about them" (517). In turn, because representatives will not merely follow those changes but will actively seek to influence them, it follows that anticipatory representation "encourages us to think of voters at [re-election time] as educable (or manipulable)" (517). Mansbridge insinuates into her text (by means of the parentheses) an all-too-familiar distinction. The question is: how does she propose to tell the difference between them?

This question brings Mansbridge (2003, 518) to her second important conclusion, that anticipatory representation is "in most instances interactive and more continually reflexive" than the promissory model allows. Consequently, the "appropriate normative criteria for judging [anticipatory and other] more recently identified forms of representation are systemic, in contrast to the dyadic criteria appropriate for promissory representation" (515). In other words, we can no longer assume that democratic representation is secured by the match (or "congruence") between constituent policy preferences and legislative votes. Nor can we emphasize, as Young and Plotke do, the quality of deliberation among constituents and between them and their legislators. Although Mansbridge notes that it is necessary to evaluate the "quality of mutual education between legislator and constituents," she cautions that this communication "depends only in small part on the dyadic efforts of the representative and constituent" (518–19). It is impersonal and systemic, relying on the "functioning of the entire representative process—including political parties, political challengers, the media, interest groups, hearings, opinion surveys, and all other processes of communication" (519).

Mansbridge (2003) moves much closer to the competitive political environment than either Plotke or Young is willing to venture. She recognizes that political reasoning is mediated by "opinion polls and

---

of decision-making processes" *by way of* "parliamentary debate and hearings," so that elected representatives do not craft demands but transmit them from below.

REPRESENTATION

Toward a Mobilization Conception

focus groups," as well as by "opposition candidates, political parties, and the media" (520). These need not be mere "tools of manipulation" but may contribute to a genuinely deliberative process of interest formation, one that need not be unidirectionally responsive (as in promissory representation) but would be "reflexive" (520). What would reflexivity entail? Despite her innovative moves beyond the foundationalist model of democratic representation, here Mansbridge falls back on a familiar communicative ideal, defining reflexivity subjectively as a property of an individual's judgment rather than as a systemic capacity. For Mansbridge, a reflexive "representative system [should contribute] to ongoing factually accurate and mutually educative communication" (519).

The difficulty is that what would count as education for Mansbridge rarely occurs in actual political discourse. Education, as Mansbridge (2003, 519; emphasis added) defines it, is a "form of influence" that meets two criteria: it "works through *arguments on the merits* and *is by definition in the recipients' interests*." Druckman's (2001a) arguments regarding issue framing—that politics involves conflicts over precisely what considerations should be brought to bear on a particular question—cast doubt on the feasibility of this first criterion. Although it is possible to identify deceitful, irrelevant, and misleading claims, there is often no neutral standpoint from which to resolve the question what is or is not on the merits of the case.[16] As to the second criterion, Mansbridge (2003, 519) herself has conceded that being "in the recipients' interests" is similarly contested. Once again, in a political environment where political elites never speak exclusively as educators of constituents but use political communication to gain an edge in interparty competition, education is not an orientation but a side effect of the battle.

Despite recognizing the need to give normative theory a "systemic" turn, Mansbridge's normative vision of political communication sets aside precisely what I take to be definitive of its systemic aspect—that representatives and opinion shapers are not only (or even primarily) in relationship to potential voters, but also in competition with each other. Her definition of education falls back on criteria better suited to assess an intersubjective relationship than a representative system. Why should this be so? The pervasiveness of the Habermasian paradigm of deliberation has something to do with it. Even those who, like Mansbridge, would not endorse Habermas' rationalism, nonetheless retain a vestige of his urge to separate "communicative" from "strategic" action. In addition, these scholars are following a path blazed by Hanna Pitkin who anticipated more of today's debates than she is credited with doing—both the insights and the impasses.

HANNA PITKIN'S "MOBILIZATION" CONCEPT OF REPRESENTATION

In 1967, Hanna Pitkin initiated a bolder break with the traditional dyadic model of representation than many of her successors managed. This claim might come as a surprise to the many scholars who would credit the most mainstream understanding of representative democracy to the summary definition that Pitkin (209) formulated: "representing here means acting in the interest of the represented, in a manner responsive to them."[17] As Rehfeld (2006, 3) notes, "few historical treatments have been so completely accepted as a standard account of a concept in all areas of political science" as Pitkin's. This "standard account" reduced Pitkin's central thesis to the nutshell formulation that "responsiveness is what representative government is all about" (Kuklinski and Segura 1995, 4). And this short phrase made Pitkin's work easy to assimilate to the empirical paradigm of the moment, which held "constituency influence" to be the hallmark of democratic political representation and made "congruence"—the literal match between a legislator's votes and the preferences of his or her constituents—its index (Miller and Stokes 1963).[18] That assimilation, in turn, covered over her intricately argued assault on a fundamental premise: that representation can be understood on the model of a principal–agent relation.

Pitkin refutes the principal–agent model by opposing the intuition, definitive for late twentieth-century liberalism, that citizen preferences are and ought to be the "principal force in a representative system" (Sunstein 1991, 6–7; Wahlke 1971, 272–73). She argues that legislators respond to too "great a complexity and plurality of determinants" for citizen preferences to be a driving force in legislative decisions (Pitkin 1967, 214 or 220). Such decisions are multidimensional; they cannot be reduced to a "one-to-one, person-to-person relationship" between a principal and an agent (221). Even if a legislator were to want to accord the constituency pride of place, constituents seldom hold articulate and well-formed preferences on the bills that actually come before Congress. When they do, the discrete preferences of the members of a district would not add up to a "single interest," and so lack the unity of a principal (221).[19]

Pitkin (1967) sets the dyadic model aside to propose that political representation should be conceived as

---

[16] Has anyone put this point better than E.E. Schattschneider ([1960] 1975, 66) who wrote: "political conflict is not like an intercollegiate debate in which the opponents agree in advance on a definition of the issues. As a matter of fact, *the definition of the alternatives is the supreme instrument of power*"?

---

[17] Kuklinski and Segura (1995, 4) claim that "this conception has motivated nearly all empirical work, often implicitly, from Miller and Stokes' classic study" to a range of recent work. Those who make it their take-away point include Eulau and Karps (1977, 237), Jewell (1983, 304), Peterson (1970, 493), Prewitt and Eulau (1969, 429), Rogowski (1981, 396), and Saward (2006, 300). Notable departures include Runciman (2007) and Näsström (2006), who aim to give Pitkin's "paradox" of representation its due.

[18] Miller and Stokes (1963) set out only to *measure* congruence between legislators and constituents; they emphasized that a "congruence" finding is *proof* of "constituency influence" only in a context of institutional arrangements that give citizen opinion leverage over official conduct.

[19] Pitkin's arguments on this point are at odds with Saward's (2006, 300) claim that Pitkin takes the represented as "unproblematically given."

316   REPRESENTATION

a "public, institutionalized arrangement," one where representation emerges not from "any single action by any one participant, but [from] the over-all structure and functioning of the system" (221–22). For representation to take place, there does not need to be a meeting of the minds between representative and constituency, or even so much as a meeting. Pitkin contends that legislators' "pursuit of the public interest and response to public opinion need not always be conscious and deliberate," and that "representation may emerge from a political system in which many individuals, both voters and legislators, are pursuing quite other goals" (224).

This is Pitkin's own constructivist turn. She effectively redefines democratic representation from an interpersonal relationship to a systemic process that is anonymous, impersonal, and not seated in intent.[20] The process will be judged representative so long as it "promot[es] the interests of the represented, in a context where the latter is conceived as capable of action and judgment, but in such a way that he does not object to what is done in his name" (Pitkin 1967, 155). As Runciman (2007, 95) insightfully argues, the measure of interest here is "negative." The representativity of the system turns not on the match between the opinions of the represented and the votes of the representative, but rather on what he terms Pitkin's "non-objection criterion": the "ability of individuals to object to what is done in his name" (95).

Pitkin's nonobjection criterion not only robs congruence of its substantive ground, but it also casts it under suspicion. She suggests that a congruence finding can be trusted as an indicator of democracy only when a constituency has the capacity to object. As provision for such a capacity, Pitkin calls for competitive elections, the guarantee that those who win genuinely have the power to govern, universal franchise, and the protection of opposition and its extension to all. I suggest that this list is inadequate, even on Pitkin's own terms, because it fails to make good on a significant clause of the nonobjection criterion: that the represented be "conceived as capable of action and judgment." This, which I call the "judgment" clause, is crucial because without it there is no trusting that citizens' objection or nonobjection has not simply been framed or primed out of the debate by habit, ignorance, or stereotype. As Druckman (2010) cautions, the most successful frames may not stimulate judgment but foreclose it by tapping exactly those features of the political environment (cf. Chong 2000, ch. 4). I come back to the question what it would take to satisfy the "judgment" clause at the end of this article.

A few of Pitkin's early readers picked up on the radicalism of her arguments. Registering this move to "understand representation as a systemic property," they warned that it could upset many "conventional assumptions" (Prewitt and Eulau 1969, 431; cf. Hansen 1975,

1186). Not least among these was the reigning wisdom that representative government is democratic because it realizes not majority rule but "*minorities* rule" (Dahl 1956, 132)—the representation of a plurality of groups, understood as "context-independent entities" (Lavaque-Manty 2006, 6). In contrast, Pitkin (1967, 215; emphasis added) holds democratic representation to involve acting for an "*unorganized*" group."[21] To the empirical democrats, who regarded self-organizing as prerequisite to political representation, an "unorganized" group would not only be an oxymoron, but its political representation would be next to impossible. Pitkin understands representing to participate in defining group identities. Speaking of the "national unity that gives localities an interest in the welfare of the whole," she insists that it is "not merely *presupposed* by representation [but] also continually re-created by the representatives' activities" (218; emphasis added). Her point is not that representation invents constituencies out of whole cloth but that it draws them together: it imputes to them a unity that they discover only through being represented. This makes representing an activity without a model, without certainty, and—in Pitkin's words—without "guarantee" (163).

At its most radical and unique, then, Pitkin's is what I term a "mobilization" conception of representation.[22] She holds the process of representation to participate in forming demands and social cleavages, not merely to reflect them. Thus, for Pitkin, as for Urbinati (2006, 37), political representation does "not simply allow the social to be translated into the political, but ... facilitates the formation of political groups and identities." It aims, then, not to *re*produce a state of affairs but to produce an effect: to call forth a constituency by depicting it as a collective with a shared aim.

A mobilization conception of representation is anticipatory, in Mansbridge's sense. It both seeks to attract potential constituencies and aims, prudentially, to please future voters. Pitkin (1967, 164) even sounds like Mansbridge when she writes, "legislators often pattern their actions not on what their constituents ought to want but on what they anticipate their constituents will want (in all their ignorance)." What neither Mansbridge nor Pitkin recognize is that this anticipatory aspect makes the mobilization conception of political representation analogous to aesthetic and literary models of representation that emphasize that representations are performative: representing is an activity

---

[20] Pitkin (2004, 340; cf. 1989) seems to retreat from this position in her later writings on representation, where she affirms the need for a "centralized, large-scale, necessarily abstract representative system [to be] based in a lively, participatory, concrete direct democracy at the local level."

[21] This notion made Pitkin a better interest group pluralist than those who claimed the title, being truer than they were to the "anti-foundationalism" of Bentley's (1908) conception of groups (Lavaque-Manty 2006, 10). Lavaque-Manty (2009, 109) writes that Bentley "conceived of interest as a relationship that depended on the context in which similarly situated individuals might find themselves," so that groups do not precede politics but "come into existence" in response to that context.

[22] Mobilization, as I use the term, applies to the work that images, narratives, and other mediated messages do in soliciting individuals to identify with a larger group or principle. This should not be confused with activities such as canvassing, phone banking, and other forms of direct contact that parties and other organizations use to get out the vote or turn members out to meetings (cf. Rosenstone and Hansen 1993).

REPRESENTATION

317

Toward a Mobilization Conception

February 2011

that produces ontological effects while seeming merely to follow from an existing state of affairs (cf. Butler 1995, 134).[23]

A mobilization conception of representation accords with "poststructuralist" or "post-Marxist" pluralist theories that have emphasized how political identities and demands do not emerge directly from social divisions, but rather that social differences and the politics they give rise are influenced by elite discourse (Laclau 1996; Laclau and Mouffe 1985; McClure 1992).[24] The idea is not that political elites create constituencies arbitrarily and in words alone.[25] Instead, the claim is that there is an inescapably figurative moment in the emergence of a democratic constituency.[26] Several theorists have proposed ways of characterizing this moment. Laclau (1996, 98; 2005, 155) writes of the "impurity" in political representation that "does not simply reproduce ... a fullness preceding it" but is primary "in the constitution of objectivity." Saward (2006, 300) proposes the concept "representative claim" to underscore that "at the heart of the act of representing is the depicting of a constituency as this or that, as requiring this or that, as having this or that set of interests." Ankersmit (2002, 115; emphasis added) explains that without representation, "we are without a *conception* of what political reality—the represented—is like."[27] Representing rouses a constituency to action by giving it a picture of itself that enables it to recognize itself in terms of a "generality"—a common enemy, shared problem, shared virtue—that is neither given nor self-evident but must be narrated into being (Rosanvallon 2008, 11).

---

[23] Saward (2006, 302), who also stresses the "performative side of political representation," tends to define the term theatrically as "performing" and "action by actors." I adopt the speech act theory conception of performativity in order to disrupt the imputation of cause to effect, a move that is significant to displacing the bedrock norm from its centrality in democratic representation.

[24] It is noteworthy that Urbinati and Warren (2008, 395) leave this work out of their account of the new wave, attributing the shift to "constitutive" representation, on the one hand, to scholarship on group-based inequalities and, on the other hand, to scholarship emphasizing the connections between political representation and political judgment.

[25] For a radically constructivist conception of political representation, see Bourdieu ([1981] 1991).

[26] Writing about the mobilization effects of political movements, Snow and Benford (1988, 198) argue that whereas movements "frame ... relevant events and conditions in ways that are intended to mobilize potential adherents and constituents, to garner bystander support, and to demobilize antagonists," activating (or suppressing) a constituency is no simple linear top-down initiative. It is a "dialectical" process, constrained by the belief system of the potential supporters, the range of concerns they consider to be relevant, and their assessment of the "utility of becoming active in the cause" (202, 204).

[27] It is important to underscore that representing creates the conception of reality, not the reality itself. Ankersmit (2002, 115; emphasis original) loses this subtlety in the very next sentence, writing that: "Without representation there is no represented—and without political representation there is no nation as a truly political entity." Nässtrom (2006, 331) criticizes Ankersmit for this radical constructivism, which assigns the creativity of political representation to the representative alone, thereby undercutting the democratic aspirations of his account.

To link Pitkin to this radical strand of contemporary democratic theory is to put her work at odds with the standard account of (unidirectional) responsiveness with which so many readers have associated it.[28] Are those readers simply wrong? No. Pitkin retreated from the most challenging implications of what I have termed her "constructivist turn."

The retreat begins at the end of the book, where Pitkin (1967) sums up her unconventional argument in these conventional terms: "representing here means acting in the interest of the represented, in a manner responsive to them" (208). Read out of context of her critique of the principal–agent model and endorsement of representation as a systemic process that is anonymous and impersonal, this could sound like (and was taken to be) a return to the standard dyad. Pitkin quickly counters this, however, writing that, as she understood it, responsiveness is not a "constant activity" but a "condition ... of potential readiness to respond" (233). This feature, that it "requires only potential responsiveness, access to power rather than its actual exercise," makes her conception of representation "perfectly compatible with leadership and with action to meet new or emergency situations" but "incompatible ... with manipulation or coercion of the public" (233).

Here is the language that so bedevils contemporary normative theories of democratic representation. Pitkin recognizes, as does Mansbridge, that as soon as representation becomes anticipatory (rather than merely responsive) it opens up the possibility for political elites to change voters' preferences. Pitkin, like Mansbridge, is inclined to parse this possibility in terms of what she presents as an opposition between "leadership" and "manipulation." Although Pitkin (1967, 223) acknowledges that the "line" between these two "is a tenuous one, and may be difficult to draw," she leaves no doubt that normative theory should find ways of doing so. As to just what this might entail, she does not say. Instead, Pitkin finishes by asserting, as if italics could make it so, "there undoubtedly *is* a difference, and this difference makes leadership compatible with representation while manipulation is not" (233; emphasis original).

Just what underlies Pitkin's italicized conviction? Nothing less that what she terms the "etymological origins" of the word representation, which she reads off its prefix: "*re-presentation*, a making present again" (Pitkin 1967, 8). That is, Pitkin invokes etymology to secure the distinction between democratic leadership and authoritarian manipulation. In a memorable passage, she writes: "as the 're' in 'representation' seems to suggest, and as I have argued in rejecting the fascist model of representation, the represented must be somehow logically prior; the representative must be responsive

---

[28] A notable exception is Garsten (2009, 91), who groups Pitkin together with Constant and Madison, thinkers who hold the "counterintuitive" position that the purpose of representative government is "to *oppose* popular sovereignty as it is usually understood"; it is not to aim for but to "undermine the idea that government can adequately represent the people."

REPRESENTATION

to him rather than the other way around" (140). Pitkin imposes here a stricture of unidirectionality that I term the "etymological protocol." This protocol is Pitkin's return to the bedrock norm. It ensures that there is a "one-way flow of influence from public opinion to policy" (Manza and Cook 2002, 639), establishing, as if it followed inevitably from the prefix to the word, that when responsiveness is functioning properly, it is properly democratic. Thus does Pitkin, by a linguistic sleight of hand, fuse representation to democracy in a way that turns one of her genuinely radical suggestions in reverse: she has moved from demonstrating that democracy is intrinsically representative to asserting that representation is intrinsically democratic (cf. Rehfeld 2006).

Scholars who came away from *Concept* with the common-sense notion that "responsiveness is what representative government is all about" at once got less from Pitkin's text than they might have and took on more than they bargained for. Whereas they missed her assault on the principal–agent model, they internalized the etymological protocol of unidirectionality. This protocol ensured that contemporary empirical findings, which leave no doubt that responsiveness has indeed turned "the other way around," would seem to betray a fundamental democratic norm. Furthermore, Pitkin left contemporary scholars with the urge to rehabilitate that norm by way of the leadership/manipulation difference. Yet, it is precisely this difference that proves so elusive in the face of current empirical findings about preference context dependency. First, as I argue, citizens learn from communication that recruits them to a side in interparty conflict. Second, there is no "bedrock"—unadulterated preference or enlightened interest—on which to ground a determination as to which of these has occurred. In short, by its fall back on unidirectional responsiveness and its normative orientation to a difference that proves difficult to discern, Pitkin's text left normative theory without a purchase over the empirical findings that have established elite cueing, framing, and other modes of influence as *preconditions* for democratic competence.

RETHINKING RE-PRESENTATION

I propose to change the terms of this debate by enlisting Derrida's ([1967] 1973) *Speech and Phenomena*, which, incidentally, was published in France in 1967, the same year that Pitkin's book appeared in the United States. This text, which demonstrates that the meaning of signs is not derived from the ideas that they are taken to represent but rather generated in their relations to other signs, casts suspicion on this habit of deriving governing protocols for re-presentation from its etymology. Against the presumption that a re-presentation must *follow* from something that has already been present ("primordial presentation"), Derrida proposes that it is from repetition that reality acquires the attribute of originality, the quality of seeming to be both logically and temporally prior to its repetition (45, fn. 4). As he puts it, "the presence-of-the-present is de-

rived from repetition and not the reverse" (52). On Derrida's account, representation is not a "reduplication that *befalls* a simple presence" (53). It is an activity that creates its own reference points and then affects, by "etymological" feint, to have done nothing at all.

I take Derrida's argument to call into question the etymological protocol of unidirectionality. Why assume that the "re" is a temporal "re," the "re" of return? It might just as well be an iterative "re," the "re" of repetition. When Pitkin defines representation as "*re-presentation*, a making present again," she puts both into play. One could follow the etymological protocol to emphasize making present *again*, the "re" of return (temporal and recapitulative). Yet, as I show, there is much in her text that violates this protocol and warrants a Derridean reading. Such a reading would put the emphasis on the *making* present, activating the "re" of repetition (iterative and active) and bringing out what I call its figurative and mobilizing aspects.

Derrida's account has the merits of explaining at once why violations of unidirectionality in responsiveness need not stir anxiety and why they will do so nonetheless. The very word representation perpetrates a ruse by the ambiguity that is built into its prefix. Representing is a making (the iterative "re") that affects fidelity to something prior (by the "re" of return). I suggest that the dilemma of democratic competence is, in part, an effect of this ruse. For to find politicians framing, cueing, and priming, and to find citizens forming preferences in response to that activity, is merely to find both exercising the practice of representation, understood in the iterative sense. At the same time, it is to find a breach of that practice insofar as the etymology of the word seems to promise not a *making* present but a making present *again*.

Understood as making present *again,* representing will inevitably give rise to a normative urge for fidelity to a popular mandate. If representing is a *making* present, as the mobilization conception would have it, then that mandate cannot be trusted; the risk will always be that it testifies not to the deliberative competence of the people but to the duplicity of the representative who seduced them into voicing a demand. This does not mean that a mobilization conception of representation cannot be democratically legitimate, only that it cannot be legitimate on the terms that the bedrock norm defines.

In fact, it is no simple matter to bring existing democratic norms to bear on representation as mobilization, which is at odds with the model of interest representation to which leading proponents of deliberative democracy subscribe. On the mobilization conception, representing is "not meant to make a pre-existing entity—i.e., the unity of the state or the people or the nation—visible" (Urbinati 2006, 24). Nor can it be regulated by the Habermasian distinction between communication and strategy. Representation as mobilization aims to persuade: its modus operandi is rhetorical and anticipatory. Urbinati (46; emphasis original) explains, representatives "prefigure courses of action and project their deliberation in the future, which is,

REPRESENTATION

Toward a Mobilization Conception

unavoidably, a dimension inhabited by *things* that have only a hypothetical or fictional nature."[29]

Representation as mobilization is at odds with deliberation on the Habermasian model, which aims to "legitimiz[e] one shared and authoritative perspective from which to judge all public controversies" (Garsten 2006, 190).[30] As Bohman (1988, 187) argues, this model denigrates rhetoric by "asserting the primacy of the literal use of language and often of the argumentative, if not logical, structure of discourse," requiring deliberators to argue their case in terms with which all reasonable people could agree.[31] In contrast, scholars who are building a model of "rhetorical deliberation" from Aristotle begin from the unabashed avowal that rhetoric aims to influence a particular audience. They argue that the constraints on the practice of rhetoric can only be immanent to its own orientation to success. Rhetors who want to persuade cannot invent frames out of whole cloth. They must engage the sympathies of a specific audience that holds particular value commitments at a particular place and time (Garsten 2006, 190). As Garsten explains, a good rhetorician targets an audience "where they stand" and seeks to bring them "to thoughts or intentions they might not otherwise have adopted" (3, 6). Rhetoric does not succeed without the active participation of the audience, who "*change their own* beliefs and desires in light of what has been said" (7; emphasis added). Bickford (1996, 42) adds that Aristotle's rhetoric is an art of attunement "whose function is 'to see the available means of persuasion in each case'" and thereby to identify what kinds of appeals are likely to set a particular audience thinking. This is the aim of deliberation on the Aristotelian model. Not to produce a justifiable general understanding but to "dra[w] out good judgment" in a time- and place-bound audience (Garsten 2006, 190).

In Aristotle's terms, the finding that citizen preferences respond to such rhetorical techniques as issue framing need not indicate a pathology. It simply confirms that persuasion has occurred. As Lupia and McCubbins (1998, 40) argue, "in settings where reasoned choice requires learning from others, *persuasion is [its] necessary condition*." If citizens are persuaded by a rhetor who respects their art as something that should provoke thinking rather than merely tap prejudice, the resulting preferences can be affirmed as reasoned choices. Yet, this notion of respecting the art brings us to the limit of this Aristotelian position. To establish, as

Aristotle does, that there is an art to rhetoric, hence that it is not in itself instrumental, is no guarantee that every rhetor will respect the constraints that are immanent to its practice as an art. In short, whereas these Aristotelian theorists of deliberation do make a place for representation as mobilization in deliberative democracy, they leave open the crucial normative question of how it is to be evaluated.

FROM RESPONSIVENESS TO REFLEXIVITY

To characterize representation as mobilizing is to call attention to its creative effects and, thereby, to alter expectations about what it ought to do. If democratic representation neither takes the social as its ground, nor relies on good reasons alone to recruit supporters, then it is not best assessed by its congruence with group interests because the very notion of congruence assumes that representatives do and should carry forward demands that "belong" to groups in a prefigured social field. In characterizing representation as mobilization, I emphasize how acts of representation work together with political practices to configure the social field and to frame the terms of conflict within which the pertinence and cogency of arguments are judged.

These claims suggest that representation as mobilization is not well suited to be judged by an ideal model of argumentation that forces a distinction between communication and strategy. For the democratic representative, as for the social critic, legitimate political communication can be simultaneously "oriented to understanding and oriented to success" (Bohman 1988, 195). Both the critic and the representative will recruit supporters as they educate them, employing rhetorical practices that aim to effect "changes in beliefs, desires, and attitudes" not by the unforced force of argumentation alone, but by appeal to identity, emotion, and bias (195). If elite communication is inescapably twofold, at once oriented toward constituents and enmeshed in interparty struggle, then does it follow that manipulation is inevitable? Is it no longer possible to tell the difference between a popular mobilization that uses its constituency as a pawn in elite partisan warfare and one that activates incipient concerns to stage a new and potentially transformative conflict?

Even without congruence, responsiveness, and other measures that rely on some version of bedrock, it should be possible to assess whether a democratic political system is more or less representative. But normative theory in the wake of the constructivist turn needs to break with typical assumptions about the relationship between democratic representation and popular sovereignty. It requires what Garsten (2009, 91) rightly identifies as "counterintuitive" thinking about what political representation is supposed to do. Its purpose, Garsten argues, drawing on liberal thinkers in eighteenth-century France and the United States, is not to respond to popular demands but to "*multiply and challenge governmental claims to represent the people*" (91). By his emphasis on contestation, I believe that Garsten gets closer to naming the conditions that

---

[29] Hawkesworth's (2003, 531) analysis of "racing-gendering" in the U.S. Congress shows how these rhetorical dynamics operate not only between elected representatives and their constituents, but also within the legislature itself, to produce "difference, political asymmetries, and social hierarchies."

[30] The core commitments of Habermasian deliberative democracy can be found in Habermas (1998, chs. 7 and 8) and Cohen (1986, 1989). Bohman (1996, 1–22) is an excellent overview.

[31] Garsten (2006, 6) clarifies that although such theories "do not call upon us to always reach consensus," they nonetheless presume "universal agreement" as setting the boundaries within which people disagree. This puts them in contrast to the "classical-humanist tradition of rhetoric, which assumed that people disagreed and asked how they could engage in controversy through speech rather than force" (6).

320   REPRESENTATION

would actualize Pitkin's "non-objection criterion" than she did herself.

I propose "reflexivity" as the normative standard for evaluating political representation understood in these (nonsovereign) terms. I elaborate this concept not primarily as a quality of individual judgment, but rather as a system capacity. As I use the term "reflexivity," it is not purely descriptive. It is not a synonym for feedback, the interference that occurs when authoritative predictions and pronouncements become an active force within the systems they are supposed merely to regulate or observe.[32] Nor is it normative in the strong sense, naming the mode of argumentation that produces warranted decisions, thereby securing the "moral right" of each individual "not to be subjected to certain actions or institutional norms that cannot be adequately justified to them" (Forst 2010, 712). It would not make sense to say of the design or outcomes of a representative system, as one might say of a principle of justice, that they are "right" in the sense of justifying the assent of all affected. Finally, reflexivity, as I use it, is not that consciousness of self in time or in relation to others that makes possible a modern sense of history or ethics, one ordered without reference to a transcendental principle (Koselleck [1979] 2004). It is, instead, the measure according to which a representation process can be judged as more or less democratic insofar as it does more or less to mobilize both express and implicit objections from the represented.

Building on Garsten, I try to imagine what it would mean to extend reflexivity not only to government institutions, but also to the representation process as a whole—"including political parties, political challengers, the media, interest groups, hearings, opinion surveys, and all other processes of communication" (Mansbridge 2003, 519). For a representation process to be reflexive, it would have to encourage contestation. First, no official or unofficial body could claim to speak for the people absolutely and definitively, so that dissent would be a norm rather than a betrayal. Second, the represented would enjoy both formal and informal means of communication and action to contest government and party initiatives and, equally important, to protest government and party inaction where initiative should be. Finally, the political communications of advocacy groups, mass media, and opinion shapers would be in competition with one another so as to mitigate passive absorption of elite communications.

For a system as for an individual, however, reflexivity means more than the mere fact of contestation. Official and unofficial representatives must have regular, structured ways of taking objections into account. In the case of official representatives (e.g., government or party), reflexivity would require provision for a formal response that at least registers (if not necessarily incorporates) popular challenges. In the case of unofficial or "self-appointed" representatives, reflexivity is difficult

to mandate but could be observed in the representative's response to challenges to his or her (or its) reputation or to a decrease in following or contributor base (Grant and Keohane 2005; Montanero 2010, ch. 5). As for the mass media and opinion shapers, it would be important to assess the degree to which audiences expose themselves to diverse sources or remain in discrete ideological "silos."

Although it is beyond the scope of this article to develop it in full, I draw an example of reflexivity from the constitutional design proposed by French revolutionary Condorcet, whom both Rosanvallon (2008) and Urbinati (2006) have rediscovered as a theorist of democratic representation. Condorcet's model of representation is reflexive because it is not "binary," premising democratic legitimacy on a link between the people and its representatives that is "zippered" by elections, but iterative, involving a dynamic movement between authoritative acts and opinion in process (176). Although Condorcet's model was never adopted and was limited to formal government institutions, it is nonetheless possible to extract principles from its features that could guide a more expansive democratically representative practice today.

The design begins with a system of primary assemblies. These were to be organized at the district level, composed of 450 to 900 members each, run by an elected bureau of 50 members, and federated—first into communes and then into the 85 departments that were represented in the National Assembly (Condorcet 1793, Title 7, Article 2). The primary assemblies were not sites of direct democracy, but rather entry points into representative government. In them, citizens would select nominees, vote on candidates, and, most important, set in motion the iterative process by which opinion and authoritative acts were made to engage each other (Title 8, Article 1). They would be the means by which, in Pitkin's terms, citizens object to government acts.

The objection process would begin with a motion to repeal a law, submitted by an individual citizen to the bureau of his or her primary assembly in the form of a petition signed by 50 members of his or her district (Title 8, Article 3). As long as the signatures were valid, the bureau would convene the District Assembly to hear the petition. Following a week's deliberation, Assembly members would be required to vote—yes or no—on whether the petition warranted consideration at the communal level. If a majority of its members voted yes, then the primary assemblies across the commune would be required to convene to decide whether to submit it to the consideration of the department as a whole. If majorities in a majority of the assemblies across the commune put it forward, then the departmental administration would have to order a general convocation, submitting the petition to the judgment of all assemblies in its communes.

I draw two principles from these aspects of Condorcet's design. First, reflexive institutions are interlocking so that a ruling by one triggers a review by another. Second, they are structured to incrementally broaden what Schattschneider ([1960] 1975, 3) terms

---

[32] Kaplan (2003) is a powerful analysis of the monumental effect that Federal Reserve chairman Alan Greenspan's speculative phrase, "irrational exuberance," had on global financial markets.

REPRESENTATION

the "scope of conflict." At the lowest levels of the structure, a commune simply heard what the majority in one district referred to it and decided whether the petition warranted further consideration, whereas a department would both hear and rule on the merits of a proposal that a majority of its communes deemed worthy of its attention (Condorcet 1793, Title 8, Article 10). In the move from the communal to the department level, then, there would be an expansion of the scope of conflict and an intensification of its stakes. At the departmental level, if voting majorities in a majority of the communes voted for repeal, then that judgment would extend the scope of conflict and raise its stakes once again, triggering reconsideration of the law by the National Assembly (Title 8, Article 13). In short, Condorcet's design would permit voting majorities of the Assemblies in just 1 of the 85 national departments to call the legitimacy of a national law into question.

Urbinati (2006, 196) argues that, by its "complex system of time delays" and multiplication of the "sites of debate," this structure increases the possibility of producing a judgment that "command[s] rational conviction" (Urbinati 2009, 196). This is, indeed, possible. But the more certain and, hence, striking feature of Condorcet's design is that it would steadily and automatically bring new participants into a conflict. It lends momentum to dissent. That Condorcet designed this momentum to build through deliberative public forums, rather than instantaneously (or "virally" by today's vehicle of blogs and 30-second advertising spots), *may* encourage greater rationality. Reflexivity is, however, a necessary but not a sufficient condition: although it protects against the spontaneous and immediate mobilization of citizen objections, it cannot guarantee that objections that make it through the process will be reasonable.

Finally, Condorcet ensured that no site would be privileged as the locus from which to express the popular will. As Urbinati (2006, 183) argues, Condorcet "set up political processes that presumed dissenting interpretations of the meaning of the 'common opinion,'" creating the means to put any statement of popular will—whether by majority vote, popular initiative, legislative action, or executive order—up for revision or even repeal. This is evident from the next step in the process, the ruling of the National Assembly, which would be required to happen within two weeks of a vote to repeal by the department (Condorcet 1793, Title 8, Article 13). The National Assembly would have the option to affirm the departmental repeal or oppose it and stand by its law. If it voted against repeal, then that ruling would not be final; on the contrary, it would perpetuate the conflict by occasioning a general convocation of every primary assembly in the 85 departments (Title 8, Article 20). The scope of conflict would expand again because, if the National Assembly stood by its law in the face of one department's challenge, the question of repeal would be referred to the citizenry as a whole.

Remarkably, that a majority joined in the opposition would still not suffice to repeal the law. For Condorcet, even a popular referendum is not synonymous with the voice of the people: it cannot make a substantive claim in the people's name. It can, however, set in motion what amounts to a recall of their representatives. If the general convocation results in a "yes" for repeal, then there would be new national elections in which members who stood by the law would be prohibited from competing. Once reconstituted, the National Assembly would take up the question of repeal again, with its decision subject to the same process of censure, beginning anew with a petition to the district (Condorcet 1793, Title 8, Articles 22 and 26). Condorcet's constitution makes it possible to call any statement of the popular will into question. Because no site is privileged for its expression, the process of its articulation is always open to amendment.

Condorcet's design exemplifies what reflexivity might look like as a capacity of formal government institutions. His account is limited by that focus and by the fact that it institutionalized deliberation by means of interlocking face-to-face arenas. Today, the principles of his design would have to be extended to the representative process as a whole, including opinion surveys, lobby groups, and other organized forces, and take account of the mediation of political communication by television, the Internet, and political advertising (together with the structure of its financing).[33] However, these principles—interlocking assemblies, systematically broadening the scope of conflict, and privileging no site as the locus of the popular will—foster the kind of competition that Chong and Druckman (2007) suggest may activate citizens' judgment. These principles, then, begin to fill in the details of what it would take to satisfy Pitkin's "non-objection criterion" together with its "judgment" clause. Expanding the scope of conflict mobilizes objections; competition among the sites aims to ensure (but cannot guarantee) that objections raised will be well reasoned. Insofar as it is reflexive, a representative process may be democratically legitimate in spite of the fact that it includes and even requires the participation of self-seeking elites.

CONCLUSION

This article opens with an apparent dilemma: the political environment that enables citizens to form representable preferences renders them susceptible to elite manipulation. This seems to be a pathology of mass-mediated democratic politics; however, I argue that it is not, or at least not entirely. What drives the sense of pathology is the bedrock norm, with its expectation of unidirectional responsiveness. In place of that norm, I propose a mobilization conception of democratic representation and put reflexivity forward as an alternative measure of its legitimacy. As a norm of representative democracy, reflexivity recasts the dilemma of citizen competence by taking the citizen-representative dyad out of its center. Rather than worry that elite communication affects citizen preference formation, and

---

[33] In their survey of the "incentive effects of democratic institutions," Lupia and McCubbins (1998, 206, ch. 10) find what I would term "reflexivity" internal to the legislative process in the U.S. House of Representatives and the bureaucracy.

322 REPRESENTATION

quest after criteria to determine when it is educative and when manipulative, reflexivity shifts the focus to the process that sets claims about preferences in play. There is no fixed standard against which to judge the representativity of such claims; it depends, instead, on having means to put them to the test, not by simple immediate refusal, but by a system of interlocking sites of opinion formation and decision making. Absent reflexivity, there is good reason for concern that context-dependent reasoning renders individuals susceptible to elite manipulation. Reflexivity is one condition (necessary but not sufficient) that enables them, instead, to be—in Pitkin's terms—"capable of action and judgment."

REFERENCES

Achen, Christopher H. 1975. "Mass Political Attitudes and the Survey Response." *American Political Science Review* 69 (4): 1218–31.

Althaus, Scott, Jill Edy, Robert Entman, and Patricia Phelen. 1996. "Revising the Indexing Hypothesis: Officials, Media and the Libya Crisis." *Political Communication* 13 (4): 407–21.

Ankersmit, F.R. 2002. *Political Representation*. Stanford, CA: Stanford University Press.

Barber, Benjamin, R. 1984. *Strong Democracy: Participatory Politics for a New Age*. Berkeley: University of California Press.

Bartels, Larry. 2003. "Democracy with Attitudes." In *Electoral Democracy*, eds. Michael B. McKuen and George Rabinowitz. Ann Arbor: University of Michigan Press, 48–82.

Bennett, W. Lance. 1990. "Toward a Theory of Press–State Relations." *Journal of Communication* 40 (2): 103–25.

Bennett, W. Lance, and Jarol B. Manheim. 1993. "Taking the Public by Storm: Information, Cueing, and the Democratic Process in the Gulf Conflict." *Political Communication* 10 (4): 331–52.

Bentley, Arthur F. 1908. *The Process of Government: A Study of Social Pressures*. Chicago: University of Chicago Press.

Bickford, Susan. 1996. *The Dissonance of Democracy*. Ithaca, NY: Cornell University Press.

Bohman, James. 1988. "Emancipation and Rhetoric: The Perlocutions and Illocutions of the Social Critic." *Philosophy and Rhetoric* 21 (3): 185–204.

Bohman, James. 1996. *Public Deliberation*. Cambridge, MA: MIT Press.

Bourdieu, Pierre. [1981] 1991. *Language and Symbolic Power*. Ed and intro. John B. Thompson. Trans. Gino Raymond and Matthew Adamson. Cambridge, MA: Harvard University Press.

Butler, Judith. 1995. "For a Careful Reading." In *Feminist Contentions*, eds. Seyla Benhabib, Judith Butler, Drucilla Cornell, and Nancy Fraser. New York: Routledge, 127–44.

Carmines, E., and J. Kuklinski. 1990. "Incentives, Opportunities and the Logic of Public Opinion in American Political Representation." In *Information and Democratic Processes*, eds. J. A. Ferejohn and J. Kuklinsky. Urbana: University of Illinois Press, 240–68.

Chong, Dennis. 2000. *Rational Lives: Norms and Values in Politics and Society*. Chicago: University of Chicago Press.

Chong, Dennis, and James Druckman. 2007. "Framing Public Opinion in Competitive Democracies." *American Political Science Review* 101 (4): 637–55.

Cohen, Joshua. 1986. "An Epistemic Conception of Democracy." *Ethics* 97: 26–38.

Cohen, Joshua. 1989. "Deliberation and Democratic Legitimacy." In *The Good Polity*, eds. A. Hamlin and P. Pettit. New York: Basil Blackwell, 17–34.

Condorcet, Marquis de. 1793. "Plan de Constitution, présenté à la Convention Nationale, les 15 & 16 fevrier 1793, l'an II de la République." http://mjp.univ-perp.fr/france/co1793pr.htm (accessed January 28, 2011).

Dahl, Robert. 1956. *A Preface to Democratic Theory*. Chicago: University of Chicago Press.

Dahl, Robert. 1971. *Polyarchy*. New Haven, CT: Yale University Press.

Derrida, Jacques. [1967] 1973. "Speech and Phenomena: Introduction to the Problem of Signs in Husserl's Phenomenology." In *Speech and Phenomena*, trans. David B. Allison. Evanston, IL: Northwestern University Press, 17–104.

Dovi, Suzanne. 2002. "Preferable Descriptive Representatives: Will Just Any Woman, Black or Latino Do?" *American Political Science Review* 96 (4): 729–43.

Druckman, James N. 2001a. "The Implications of Framing Effects for Citizen Competence." *Political Behavior* 23 (3): 225–56.

Druckman, James N. 2001b. "Evaluating Framing Effects." *Journal of Economic Psychology* 22: 91–101.

Druckman, James N. 2004. "Political Preference Formation: Competition, Deliberation, and the (Ir)relevance of Framing Effects." *American Political Science Review* 98 (4): 671–86.

Druckman, James N. 2010. "What's It All About? Framing in Political Science." In *Perspectives on Framing*, ed. Gideon Keren. New York: Psychology Press/Taylor and Francis, 279–302

Druckman, James N., Cari Lynn Hennessy, Kristi St. Charles, and Jonathan Webber. 2010. "Competing Rhetoric over Time: Frames vs. Cues." *Journal of Politics* 72 (1): 136–48.

Druckman, James N., and Arthur Lupia. 2000. "Preference Formation." *Annual Review of Political Science* 3: 1–24.

Eulau, Heinz, and Paul D. Karps. 1977. "The Puzzle of Representation: Specifying Components of Responsiveness." *Legislative Studies Quarterly* 2 (3): 241–47.

Forst, Rainer. 2001. "The Rule of Reasons: Three Models of Deliberative Democracy." *Ratio Juris* 14 (4): 345–78.

Forst, Rainer. 2010. "The Justification of Human Rights and the Basic Right to Justification: A Reflexive Approach." *Ethics* 120: 711–40.

Gamson, William A., and Andre Modigliani. 1989. "Media Discourse and Public Opinion on Nuclear Power: A Constructionist Approach." *American Journal of Sociology* 95 (1): 1–37.

Garsten, Bryan. 2006. *Saving Persuasion*. Cambridge, MA: Harvard University Press.

Garsten, Bryan. 2009. "Representative Government and Popular Sovereignty." In *Political Representation*, eds. Ian Shapiro, Susan C. Stokes, Elisabeth Jean Wood, and Alexander S. Kirshner. Cambridge: Cambridge University Press, 90–110.

Gerber, Elizabeth, and John E. Jackson. 1993. "Endogenous Preferences and the Study of Institutions." *American Political Science Review* 87 (3): 639–56.

Goodin, Robert E., and John S. Dryzek. 2006. "Deliberative Impacts: The Macro-political Uptake of Mini-publics." *Politics and Society* 34 (20): 219–44.

Grant, Ruth, and Robert O. Keohane. 2005. "Accountability and Abuses of Power in World Politics." *American Political Science Review* 99 (1): 29–44.

Habermas, Jürgen. 1988. *Between Facts and Norms*. Trans. William Rehg. Cambridge, MA: MIT Press.

Habermas, Jürgen. 1990. *Moral Consciousness and Communicative Action*. Trans. Christian Lenhardt and Shierry Weber Nicholsen. Cambridge, MA: MIT Press.

Hansen, S. B. 1975. "Participation, Political Structure, and Concurrence." *American Political Science Review* 69 (4): 1181–99.

Hawkesworth, Mary. 2003. "Congressional Enactments of Race-Gender: Toward a Theory of Raced-Gendered Institutions." *American Political Science Review* 97 (4): 529–50.

Hayward, Clarissa Rile. 2009. "Making Interest: On Representation and Democratic Legitimacy." In *Political Representation*, eds. Ian Shapiro, Susan C. Stokes, Elisabeth Jean Wood, and Alexander S. Kirshner. Cambridge: Cambridge University Press, 111–35.

Jacobs, Lawrence, and Robert J. Shapiro. 2000. *Politicians Don't Pander: Political Manipulation and the Loss of Democratic Responsiveness*. Chicago: University of Chicago Press.

Jewell, Malcolm. 1983. "Legislator–Constituency Relations and the Representative Process." *Legislative Studies Quarterly* 8 (3): 303–37.

Kaplan, Michael. 2003. "Iconomics: The Rhetoric of Speculation." *Public Culture* 15 (3): 477–93.

Kinder, Donald R., and Thomas E. Nelson. 2005. "Democratic Debate and Real Opinions." In *Framing American Politics*, eds. Karen J. Callaghan, Frauke Schnell, and Robert M. Entman. Pittsburgh: University of Pittsburgh Press, 103–22.

Kinder, Donald R., and Lynn Sanders. 1996. *Divided by Color*. Chicago: University of Chicago Press.

Koselleck, Reinhart. [1979] 2004. "History, Histories, and Formal Time Structures." In *Futures Past: On the Semantics of Historical Time*, trans and intro. Keith Tribe. Ithaca, NY: Cornell University Press, 93–104.

Kuklinski, James H., Paul J. Quirk, Jennifer Jerit, and Robert F. Rich. 2001. "The Political Environment and Citizen Competence." *American Journal of Political Science* 45 (20): 410–24.

Kuklinski, James H., and Gary M. Segura. 1995. "Endogeneity, Exogeneity, Time, and Space in Political Representation." *Legislative Studies Quarterly* 20 (1): 3–21.

Lavaque-Manty, Mika. 2006. "Bentley, Truman and the Study of Groups." *Annual Review of Political Science* 9: 1–18.

Lavaque-Manty, Mika. 2009. "Finding Theoretical Concepts in the Real World: The Case of the Precariat." In *New Waves in Political Philosophy*, eds. Boudewijn de Bruin and Christopher F. Zurn. Basingstoke, UK: Palgrave Macmillan, 105–24.

Laclau, Ernesto. 1996. *Emancipations*. New York: Verso.

Laclau, Ernesto. 2005. *On Populist Reason*. New York: Verso.

Laclau, Ernesto, and Chantal Mouffe. 1985. *Hegemony and Socialist Strategy*. New York: Verso.

Lupia, Arthur. 1992. "Busy Voters, Agenda Control, and the Power of Information." *American Political Science Review* 86 (2): 390–403.

Lupia, Arthur. 1994. "Shortcuts versus Encyclopedias: Information and Voting Behavior in California Insurance Reform Elections." *American Political Science Review* 88 (1): 63–76.

Lupia, Arthur, and Matthew McCubbins. 1998. *The Democratic Dilemma: Can Citizens Learn What They Need to Know?* New York: Cambridge University Press.

Manin, Bernard. 1997. *The Principles of Representative Government*. Cambridge: Cambridge University Press.

Mansbridge, Jane J. 1999. "Should Blacks Represent Blacks and Women Represent Women? A Contingent 'Yes'." *Journal of Politics* 61 (3): 628–57.

Mansbridge, Jane J. 2003. "Rethinking Representation." *American Political Science Review* 97 (4): 515–28.

Manza, Jeff, and Fay Lomax Cook. 2002. "A Democratic Polity? Three Views of Policy Responsiveness to Public Opinion in the United States." *American Politics Research* 30 (6): 630–67.

McClure, Kirstie. 1992. "On the Subject of Rights: Pluralism, Plurality and Political Identity." In *Dimensions of Radical Democracy*, ed. Chantal Mouffe. New York: Verso, 108–27.

Miller, James. 1987. *Democracy Is in the Streets: From Port Huron to the Siege of Chicago*. New York: Simon and Schuster.

Miller, Warren E., and Donald E. Stokes. 1963. "Constituency Influence in Congress." *American Political Science Review* 57 (1): 45–56.

Montanero, Laura. 2010. "The Democratic Legitimacy of 'Self-appointed' Representatives." Ph.D. dissertation, University of British Columbia.

Näsström, Sofia. 2006. "Representative Democracy as Tautology." *European Journal of Political Theory* 5 (3): 321–42.

O'Neill, Onora. 2002. "Constructivism in Rawls and Kant." In *The Cambridge Companion to Rawls*, ed. Samuel Freeman. Cambridge: Cambridge University Press, 347–67.

Page, Benjamin I., and Robert Y. Shapiro. 1992. *The Rational Public: Fifty Years of Trends in Americans' Policy Preferences*. Chicago: University of Chicago Press.

Pateman, Carole. 1970. *Participation and Democratic Theory*. Cambridge: Cambridge University Press.

Peterson, Paul. 1970. "Forms of Representation: Participation of the Poor in the Community Action Program." *American Political Science Review* 64 (2): 491–507.

Pitkin, Hanna. 1967. *The Concept of Representation*. Berkeley: University of California Press.

Pikin, Hanna. 1989. "Representation." In *Political Innovation and Conceptual Change*, eds. Terence Ball, James Farr, and Russell L. Hanson. Cambridge: Cambridge University Press, 132–41.

Pitkin, Hanna. 2004. "Representation and Democracy: Uneasy Alliance." *Scandinavian Political Studies* 27 (3): 335–42.

Plotke, David. 1997. "Representation is Democracy." *Constellations* 4 (1): 19–34.

Popkin, Samuel L. 1991. *The Reasoning Voter: Communication and Persuasion in Political Campaigns*. Chicago: University of Chicago Press.

Prewitt, Kenneth, and Heinz Eulau. 1969. "Political Matrix and Political Representation: Prolegomenon to a New Departure from an Old Problem." *American Political Science Review* 63 (2): 427–41.

Rehfeld, Andrew. 2006. "Towards a General Theory of Representation." *Journal of Politics* 68 (1): 1–21.

Rogowski, Ronald. 1981. "Representation in Political Theory and in Law." *Ethics* 91 (3): 395–430.

Rosanvallon, Pierre. 2008. *La Légitimité Démocratique: Impartialité, Réflexivité, Proximité*. Paris: Seuil.

Rosenblum, Nancy L. 2008. *On the Side of the Angels: An Appreciation of Parties and Partisanship*. Princeton, NJ: Princeton University Press.

Rosenstone, Steven J., and John Mark Hansen. 1993. *Mobilization, Participation, and Democracy in America*. New York: Macmillan.

Runciman, David. 2007. "The Paradox of Political Representation." *Journal of Political Philosophy* 15 (1): 93–114.

Saward, Michael. 2006. "The Representative Claim." *Contemporary Political Theory* 5: 297–318.

Saward, Michael. 2010. *The Representative Claim*. Oxford: Oxford University Press.

Schattschneider, Elmer Eric. [1960] 1975. *The Semisovereign People*. New York: Holt, Reinhart, and Winston.

Schwartz, Nancy L. 1988. *The Blue Guitar: Political Representation and Community*. Chicago: University of Chicago Press.

Seitz, Brian. 1995. *The Trace of Political Representation*. Albany: State University of New York Press.

Sniderman, Paul M. 2000. "Taking Sides: A Fixed Choice Theory of Political Reasoning." In *Elements of Reason: Cognition, Choice, and the Bounds of Rationality*, eds. Arthur Lupia, Mathew D. McCubbins, and Samuel L. Popkin. New York: Cambridge University Press, 67–84.

Sniderman, Paul M., Richard A. Brody, and Philip E. Tetlock. 1991. *Reasoning and Choice: Explorations in Political Psychology*. Cambridge: Cambridge University Press.

Sniderman, Paul M., and Matthew S. Levendusky. 2007. "An Institutional Theory of Political Choice." In *Oxford Handbook of Political Behavior*, eds. Russell J. Dalton and Hans-Dieter Klingemann. New York: Oxford University Press, 437–56.

Sniderman, Paul M., and Sean M. Theriault. 2004. "The Structure of Political Argument and the Logic of Issue Framing." In *Studies in Public Opinion*, eds. Willem E. Saris and Paul M. Sniderman. Princeton, NJ: Princeton University Press, 133–65.

Snow, David A., and Robert D. Benford. 1988. "Ideology, Frame Resonance, and Participant Mobilization." *International Social Movement Research* 1: 197–217.

Squires, Judith. 2008. "The Constitutive Representation of Gender: Extra-parliamentary Re-presentation of Gender Relations." *Representation* 44 (2): 187–204.

Sunstein, Cass. 1991. "Preferences and Politics." *Philosophy and Public Affairs* 20 (10): 3–34.

Urbinati, Nadia. 2006. *Representative Democracy: Principles and Genealogy*. Chicago: University of Chicago Press.

Urbinati, Nadia, and Mark E. Warren. 2008. "The Concept of Representation in Contemporary Democratic Theory." *Annual Review of Political Science* 11: 387–412.

Wahlke, John C. 1971. "Policy Demands and System Support: The Role of the Represented." *British Journal of Political Science* 1 (3): 271–90.

Warren, Mark E., and Dario Castiglione. N.d. "Rethinking Democratic Representation: Eight Theoretical Issues." Unpublished manuscript, University of British Columbia, Canada.

Williams, Melissa. 1990. *Voice, Trust, and Memory: Marginalized Groups and the Failings of Liberal Representation*. Princeton, NJ: Princeton University Press.

Young, Iris Marion. 1997. "Deferring Group Representation." In *NOMOS XXXIX, Ethnicity and Group Rights*, eds. Ian Shapiro and Will Kymlicka. New York: New York University Press, 349–76.

Young, Iris Marion. 2000. *Inclusion and Democracy*. Oxford: Oxford University Press.

Zaller, John R. 1992. *The Nature and Origins of Mass Opinion*. Cambridge: Cambridge University Press.

15

Representation and Democracy: Uneasy Alliance

Hanna Fenichel Pitkin

The concept of 'representation' is puzzling not because it lacks a central definition, but because that definition implies a paradox (being present and yet not present) and is too general to help reconcile the word's many senses with their sometimes conflicting implications.

Representation has a problematic relationship with democracy, with which it is often thoughtlessly equated. The two ideas have different, even conflicting, origins. Democracy came from ancient Greece and was won through struggle, from below. Greek democracy was participatory and bore no relationship to representation. Representation dates – at least as a political concept and practice – from the late medieval period, when it was imposed as a duty by the monarch. Only in the English Civil War and then in the eighteenth-century democratic revolutions did the two concepts become linked.

Democrats saw representation – with an extended suffrage – as making possible large-scale democracy. Conservatives instead saw it as a tool for staving off democracy. Rousseau also contrasted the two concepts, but favoured democratic self-government.

He was prescient in seeing representation as a threat to democracy. Representative government has become a new form of oligarchy, with ordinary people excluded from public life. This is not inevitable. Representation does make large-scale democracy possible, where it is based in participatory democratic politics at the local level.

Three obstacles block access to this possibility today: the scope of public problems and private power; money, or rather wealth; and ideas and their shaping, in an age of electronic media.

The idea of representation has been getting renewed attention lately, especially in Europe, where the effort to form some sort of regional institutions – less than a state but more than an alliance – has raised countless issues of both theoretical principle and political practicality, many of them involving representation. What institutions should there be, with what powers, and how should their offices be filled? Appointment? Elections? On what basis and by whom? Whom or what are these officials to represent? These European concerns also reflect the wider problems raised by our peculiar current combination of unchecked globalization with resurgent localism and ethnic separatism. What sort of political organization, what sort of representation can suit such conditions?

326 REPRESENTATION

Given the gravity, complexity, and urgency of such questions, together with the enormously technological outlook of our time, an audience attending a lecture on representation is almost bound to expect an expert, offering technical, institutional advice: unitary or district elections, winner-takes-all or proportional representation, majority rule or reserved quotas for minorities? Such issues do matter, but I am not such an expert. I fear that my remarks will disappoint you.

My own study of representation was not technically oriented but conceptual and theoretical (Pitkin 1967). True, it had its own kind of technicality, relying on the tools of 'ordinary-language' philosophy and semantic analysis. But it addressed none of the technical questions, offering at most an overview of this troubling concept's diversity.

The concept does have a central core of meaning: that somebody or something not literally present is nevertheless present in some non-literal sense. But that is not much help. First, the core itself contains an inescapable paradox: not present yet somehow present. And, second, the definition is too broadly vague to help in sorting out the many particular senses, often with incompatible implications or assumptions, that the word has developed over centuries of use.

The way a city or a mountain is 'made present' on a map differs totally from the way a litigant is 'made present' by an attorney. The way *Macbeth* is 'made present' on the stage differs from the way an ambassador represents a state, or the way one 'makes representations about' something, or what characterizes representational art or a representative sample. And all this is only in English. If one wants to know not just about the word, but about the actual phenomena of 'representation' in various times and cultures, things get much worse. Even in German – a language after all very close to English – representation in art or theatre has no conceptual connection with representation in court or in government (Pitkin 1989, 132).

That is as far as I got with the concept when I studied it some forty years ago. Since then I have pursued other interests, and in order to engage at least one of them, I want to talk about the relationship of representation to democracy, a topic never raised in my earlier study because at the time I took that relationship for granted as unproblematic. Like most people even today, I more or less equated democracy with representation, or at least with representative government. It seemed axiomatic that under modern conditions only representation can make democracy possible. That assumption is not exactly false, but it is profoundly misleading, in ways that remain hidden if one treats it as an axiom and asks only technical rather than fundamental theoretical questions.

The idea of 'democracy' is every bit as complex and troublesome as that of representation. Etymologically it means that the people (Greek *demos*) rule (*kratein*). But the meaning of *demos* is ambiguous. Is it that all the people jointly are to rule themselves, or that the common (demotic) people are to rule over the (former) aristocracy? And what criteria determine whether the people are in fact ruling? Words such as 'democracy' and 'representation' furthermore, like the vocabulary of human institutions more generally, have this peculiarity: their use ranges confusingly between expressing an idea or ideal, and designating uncritically the actual arrangements currently supposed to embody that idea (Pitkin 1967).

When I speak about democracy here today I mean to raise and acknowledge such difficulties rather than suppress them. Let us just say that by 'democracy' I mean popular self-government, what Abraham Lincoln spoke of – though John Wycliffe had used the expression some five centuries before – as 'government of the people, by the people, and for the people' (Lincoln 1980, 231). It is a matter of degree, an idea or ideal realized more or less well in various circumstances, conditions, and institutional arrangements. 'Fugitive', Sheldon Wolin calls it (Wolin 1996).

That the relationship between democracy so understood and representation is problematic is suggested already by the two concepts' disparate, even conflicting, histories. Democracy originated with the ancient Greeks. At least the concept did; the practice must surely have been lot older in some tribes and small settlements. Athenian democracy was won by political struggle, from below, and it was direct and participatory to an astonishing degree. It was also, by our standards, extremely constricted, unrelated to any notion of universal human rights. The Greeks thought of other peoples (barbarians) and of women as being generically incapable of politics. Their democracy also had nothing whatever to do with representation, an idea for which their language had no word.

Representation, at least as a political idea and practice, emerged only in the early modern period and had nothing at all to do with democracy. Take England, for example. The king, needing additional revenue beyond that from the royal estates and traditional feudal dues, required each shire and borough to send a delegate to commit the locality to special additional taxes. So representation was imposed as a duty from above, a matter of royal convenience and administrative control. As the practice was repeated, it gradually became institutionalized. Sometimes the delegates were sent with instructions from their communities; sometimes they were expected to report back on what had transpired. Gradually they began to make their consent conditional on redress of grievances, to think of themselves as members of a single, continuing body, and sometimes to join forces against the king. So representation slowly came to be considered a matter of right rather than a burden, though even then the selection of delegates was by no means democratic, often not even accomplished by election.

Only when these struggles between king and parliament culminated in civil war in England in the seventeenth century, and subsequently in the great democratic revolutions of the late eighteenth century, was the alliance between democracy and representation formed. The democrats challenged the twin medieval assumptions, that God assigned to each man at birth his station in a sacred hierarchy, and that the realm was the geographic land and so its affairs were the concern only of the king and landed aristocracy. Instead, the democrats held that everyone born and living in the land had a stake in public life: 'The poorest he that is in England hath a life to live, as the greatest he.' Each has a 'birthright' that includes a 'voice' in public affairs, and no one is bound to obey a government 'that he has not had a voice to put himself under' (Woodhouse 1951, 51, 69). The democrats held as 'self-evident' that 'all men are created equal' rather than situated in a hierarchy, 'that they are endowed by their Creator with certain inalienable rights', and that governments are legitimate only when they 'secure those rights' (Declaration of Independence of the United States of America). Far from consisting in the geographic land, the realm is a nation of citizens, all equally children of *la patrie*. The common people have no need of any special, anointed ruler or of any special class to govern them; we all are capable of participating in political life, and entitled to do so.

So democracy (re-)emerged in the modern world. But, since it emerged in large nation-states rather than small city-states, and since by then the practice of (undemocratic) representation was well established, the alliance seemed obvious. Extend the suffrage, and democracy would be enabled by representation. Since, as John Selden put it, 'the room will not hold all', the people would rule themselves vicariously, through their representatives (Arendt 1972, 238).

The democrats' conservative opponents, apart from a few die-hard monarchist absolutists, by this time accepted (undemocratic) representation as traditional. But far from equating it with democracy, they mobilized it as a tool for staving off the democratic impulse and controlling the unruly lower classes. In the debates accompanying the English Civil War, the conservatives said, once you start opening the traditional way of selecting members of parliament to the challenge of principle, 'you must fly ... to an absolute natural right', and then there is no limit; anyone can claim anything. There are five times as many in this realm without (landed) property as with, they said. 'If the master and servant shall be equal electors ... the majority may by law ... [enact] an equality of goods and estate.' Chaos will result (Woodhouse 1951, 53, 63, 57).

In America, similarly, James Madison in *The Federalist* contrasted representative government – which he called a 'republic' – to democracy, rather than linking the two. The 'pure' democracy of ancient Greece, he said, presupposed a small city-state, and it was marked by constant 'turbulence and contention', by hasty, passionate, and unwise decisions. A representative government as proposed in the new constitution, by contrast, not only would allow for a large and growing republic, but also would 'refine and

REPRESENTATION   329

enlarge' – that is, deflect or replace – the views of ordinary citizens by filtering them through a wise, responsible elite, better able to 'discern the true interests of their country' (Hamilton et al. 2003, 43–45).

But saying that the democrats conjoined representation with democracy while the conservatives contrasted the two ideas is too simple. There was also at least one idiosyncratic democratic voice that warned against representation: Jean-Jacques Rousseau. Now, Rousseau spoke not in terms of 'democracy', which he regarded merely as a form of executive, but of freedom in a legitimate state. Still, what he said was quintessentially democratic: freedom requires the active, personal participation of all, assembled together, jointly deciding public policy. It is therefore incompatible with representation. The English, Rousseau remarked, imagine themselves to be free, but actually they are free only at the moment of casting their ballots in an election; immediately afterwards they sink back into slavery, and cease to exist as a people (Rousseau 1968, 101–2, 110, 141).

Well, Rousseau was a romantic and a utopian, hopelessly impractical. By his account, freedom would be possible only in a very small community and among people who are heroically, self-sacrificingly public spirited. 'As soon as the public service ceases to be the main concern of the citizens', he wrote, or as citizens begin to say about the public good, 'What does it matter to me?', freedom disappears (Rousseau 1968, 140–41).

And yet, for all his romantic posturing, Rousseau was on to something about representation. The intervening centuries seem to have proved him right, at least in this respect. Despite repeated efforts to democratize the representative system, the predominant result has been that representation has supplanted democracy instead of serving it. Our governors have become a self-perpetuating elite that rules – or rather, administers – passive or privatized masses of people. The representatives act not as agents of the people but simply instead of them.

We send them to take care of public affairs like hired experts, and they are professionals, entrenched in office and in party structures. Immersed in a distinct culture of their own, surrounded by other specialists and insulated from the ordinary realities of their constituents' lives, they live not just physically but also mentally 'inside the beltway', as we say in America (that is, within the ring of freeways that encircle Washington, DC). Their constituents, accordingly, feel powerless and resentful. Having sent experts to tend to their public concerns, they give their own attention and energy to other matters, closer to home. Lacking political experience, they feel ignorant and incapable. ('The President has access to all sorts of classified information we don't have', I've heard repeatedly in recent months. 'He must know what he is doing.')

Not that people idolize their governors and believe all the official pronouncements. On the contrary, they are cynical and sulky, deeply alienated from what is done in their name and from those who do it. Yet in their conduct

339

330 REPRESENTATION

they continue to support – that is, to refrain from disrupting – the system. Most do not even bother to vote, let alone take any active responsibility for their nation's public life. Sporadically unruly, distrusting politicians and hating 'the government' even while they accept and pursue its largesse, they regard the resulting policies and conditions as if fated. It never occurs to them to think of the government as their shared instrument, or of the public as consisting simply of themselves collectively. (And why should it occur to them, given how things now work?)

Clearly, representation is not the only culprit in bringing about this lamentable state of affairs, but it is a culprit. The repeated widening of the suffrage and the many technical improvements in systems of representation have brought about neither the property redistribution and social chaos the conservatives feared nor the effective democracy the reformers expected. The arrangements we call 'representative democracy' have become a substitute for popular self-government, not its enactment. Calling them 'democracy' only adds insult to injury. The late Hannah Arendt, who wrote most eloquently and thoughtfully on these matters, says, 'Representative government has in fact become oligarchic government', in the sense that 'the age-old distinction between ruler and ruled which the [American and French] Revolution[s] had set out to abolish through the establishment of a republic has asserted itself again; once more, the people are not admitted to the public realm, once more the business of government has become the privilege of the few' (Arendt 1965, 273, 240).

Must we accept this as inevitable? Must we acquiesce in Rousseau's view, with its implication that in a globalized world, democracy is irrelevant? Arendt thought not. From her own study of modern revolutions and 'social movements' and from Alexis de Tocqueville's study of America in the 1830s, she concluded that the struggle for democracy is not yet lost. Genuinely democratic representation is possible, she held, where the centralized, large-scale, necessarily abstract representative system is based in a lively, participatory, concrete direct democracy at the local level.

Participating actively in local political life, people learn the real meaning of citizenship. They discover that (some of) their personal troubles are widely shared, and how their apparently private concerns are in fact implicated in public policy and public issues. Thus they discover a possibility based neither on private, competitive selfishness nor on heroic self-sacrifice, since they collectively *are* the public that benefits, yet disagree on what is to be done. In shared deliberation with others, the citizens revise their own understanding of both their individual self-interest and the public interest, and both together (Pitkin & Shumer 1982).

Having these experiences in a context of action and responsibility, seeing the actual results in the world, they also realize (that is, they both perfect and become aware of) their own capacities: for autonomous judgment, for deliberation, and for effective action. Seeing themselves in collective action, they observe their own powers and their shared power. People with this kind of face-to-face experience among their neighbours can then also be effective democratic citizens in relation to their more distant, national representatives. Local direct democracy undergirds national representative democracy.

Tocqueville claimed to have observed this in Jacksonian America. He saw a people passionately engaged with their public life, in a not at all self-sacrificing way. Take away politics from an American, he said, and it would be as if 'half his existence [had been] snatched from him; he would feel it as a vast void in his life and become incredibly unhappy' (Tocqueville 1969, 243).

As recently as the 1960s something like this kind of political engagement still seemed possible in many lands. Today the outlook is considerably more bleak; we democrats have reason to worry. I will conclude by just mentioning three big obstacles that stand in the way.

The first concerns the scope of public problems and private power. For local politics to be able to provide the experience of active citizenship, it must be real. Something that genuinely matters to people, some problem in their actual lives, must be at stake. A mere pretend politics, a simulacrum of public action without significant content or consequences, will not do. But in our world the conditions that trouble people's lives are – more and more – large scale. They are by-products of the activities of huge, undemocratic organizations, be they national mafias, transnational corporations, or even government bureaucracies and armies. If the local community's only water supply is owned by a transnational corporation with headquarters elsewhere (or, effectively, nowhere) and an annual budget larger than that of many states, then there may result local troubles of such overwhelming importance that nothing else matters by comparison, but which cannot be locally handled.

The second, related obstacle is money, or rather wealth. Not so much the corrupting role of money in elections which has been the focus of attention in America recently, but the more general, age-old tension between the power of wealth and 'people power', meaning the power of numbers and of commitment. (It is unfortunate that Marx is no longer read since the demise of the Soviet Union; for all their faults, his works are useful for thinking about these matters.)

The third obstacle is difficult to designate by a single apt name. It is about ideas and their shaping. Deception, propaganda, and indoctrination have always played a role in the rough and tumble of actual political life, but they take on new, disturbing dimensions in our age of electronic media and satellite surveillance, of 'hype', 'spin', and the 'infomercial', of 'image', 'credibility', and 'virtual reality'. Watching television from infancy, people not only acquire misinformation; they become habituated to the role of spectator. The line between fantasy and reality blurs (indeed, the line between television image and one's own fantasy blurs). As for those who set policy and shape the

332 REPRESENTATION

images, insulated from any reality check, they soon become captive to their own fictions. All this does not bode well for democracy, either.

Am I being too pessimistic? Perhaps things look more cheerful in other lands. I am painfully aware of the irony of writing today as an American on – of all things! – democracy and representation. I mean, where in the world has representative democracy had a better chance than in America, where its beginnings were so promising and the conditions so favourable? And look at it now! So maybe America distorts my vision. After all, the democratic impulse has proved amazingly resilient, and even the joint-stock limited-liability corporation is only a human invention, humanly changeable, not an inevitability.

Can democracy be saved? I am old; it is up to you.

REFERENCES

Arendt, H. 1965. *On Revolution.* New York: Viking Press.

Arendt, H. 1972. *Crises of the Republic.* New York: Harcourt Brace Jovanovich.

Arendt, H. 1974. *The Human Condition.* Chicago: University of Chicago Press.

Hamilton, A., Madison, J. & Jay, J. 2003. *The Federalist with the Letters of 'Brutus'*, ed. T. Ball. Cambridge: Cambridge University Press.

Lincoln, A. 1980. *Selected Writings and Speeches of Abraham Lincoln*, ed. T. H. Williams. Hendricks House.

Madison, J. 2003. 'Federalist paper no. 10', in Hamilton, A., Madison, J. & Jay, J. 2003. *The federalist with the Letters of Brutus'*, ed. T. Ball. Cambridge: Cambridge University Press.

Pitkin, H. F. 1967. *The Concept of Representation.* Berkeley: University of California Press.

Pitkin, H. F. 1989. 'Representation', in Ball, T., Farr, J. & Hanson, R. L., eds, *Political Innovation and Conceptual Change.* Cambridge: Cambridge University Press.

Pitkin, H. F. & Shumer, S. M. 1982. 'On Participation', *democracy* 2, 43–54.

Rousseau, J.-J. 1968. *The Social Contract*, trans. M. Cranston. Harmondsworth, England: Penguin.

Tocqueville, A. de. 1969. *Democracy in America*, ed. J. P. Mayer, trans. G. Lawrence. Garden City, NY: Doubleday.

Wolin, S. S. 1996. 'Fugitive Democracy', in Benhabib, S., ed., *Democracy and Difference: Contesting the Boundaries of the Political.* Princeton: Princeton University Press.

Woodhouse, A. S. P. 1951. *Puritanism and Liberty.* London: J. M. Dent.

16

A "Selection Model" of Political Representation*

JANE MANSBRIDGE

I. INTRODUCTION: SANCTIONS V. SELECTION

MANY political scientists, most economists, and almost all citizens who demand more "accountability" and "transparency" routinely rely on a *sanctions model* of principal-agent relations. In this model, the interests of the principals (in politics, the constituents) are assumed to conflict with the interests of their agent (the representative). The principals must therefore monitor the agent closely, rewarding the good behavior and punishing the bad.

This article elaborates a contrasting model of principal-agent relations, which I will call a *selection model*. This model works only when a potential agent already has self-motivated, exogenous reasons for doing what the principal wants. The principal and agent thus have similar objectives even in the absence of the principal's sanctions. As a general rule, the higher the *ex ante* probability that the objectives of principal and agent will be aligned, the more efficient it is for the principal to invest resources *ex ante* in selecting the required type rather than investing *ex post* in monitoring and sanctioning.

If we view democratic political representation as a principal-agent problem, a constituent can reasonably want to adopt a selection model and save on monitoring and sanctioning whenever the representative's established direction and policies are largely those the constituent desires and the representative also has a verifiable reputation for being both competent and honest.[1] In the selection model, the representative's accountability to the constituent will typically take

---

*I thank the Radcliffe Institute for Advanced Study for the fellowship year that allowed me to begin this work and the Austrian Political Science Association, the Oxford Political Thought Conference, the Centre for the Study of Democratic Institutions at the University of British Columbia, the Passmore Lecture series at the Australian National University, the E.U. Recon Workshop on Representation and Institutional Make-up in Brussels, and the Faculty Research Seminar at the Kennedy School of Government for the opportunity to present earlier versions of this article. I am grateful for the comments of participants in all of these events, especially Rainer Brauböck, Iris Bohnet, Geoffrey Brennan, Archon Fung, Christian Grose, Mark Warren, and Richard Zeckhauser.

[1] Some kinds of representation (e.g., surrogate representation, Mansbridge 2003) and representational claims (see Saward 2006) do not take a principal-agent form. This article will discuss representation only as a principal-agent problem. It will also concentrate largely on the U.S. case, which has generated most of the work promoting a sanctions model. In party list proportional representation systems and some other disciplined party systems, the party usually selects representatives primarily on party loyalty (including policy preference), competence and honesty. It then adapts its own platform to a greater or lesser degree in response to potential voter sanctions.

the form of *narrative* and even *deliberative* accountability rather than accountability based on monitoring and sanctions. In *narrative* and *deliberative accountability*, the representative explains the reasons for her actions and even (ideally) engages in two-way communication with constituents, particularly when deviating from the constituents' preferences.

In practice both selection and sanctions are always at work. Selection and sanctions map directly onto the two commonly cited motivations of representatives, the desire to make good public policy and the desire to be reelected. These two motivations are almost always mixed. The alignment of principals' and agents' objectives will also never be perfect. Thus constituents will always have some reason to monitor their representatives in order either to try to induce new behavior through the threat of sanction or simply to replace those representatives in the next election. Nor is the sanctions model ever pure. It is hard to imagine a representative with no intrinsic motivation to work for the policies he or she thinks good for the polity and hard to imagine any constituent voting for a representative whose preferences the constituent thought were always induced.

In democracies, elections are the main instrument for both selection and sanction. Yet tradeoffs exist, and the balance that any institution should strike between selection and sanction depends on contingency, that is, the costs and benefits of sanction and selection in a given context. The benefits of selection are high when agents will face unpredictable future situations, when agents must act speedily, creatively, flexibly, and adaptively, when they must dedicate their powers to an evolving goal and adopt different means as the need demands, when the goals are long-run rather than short-run, and when principals and agents prefer relationships based on mutual trust and common goals rather than instrumental relationships. Selection is also attractive when its costs are low—that is, in contexts where sufficient numbers of potential agents are self-motivated, where the probabilities of aligned objectives between principals and agents are high, where principals can fairly easily gather sufficient information about agents to make a reasonably accurate choice at the time of selection, and where agents can effectively self-sort into appropriate roles. Finally, selection is attractive when sanctions and monitoring are impractical or very costly.

Because both the sanction and the selection models are always mixed, it helps to think of the selection model as having selection at its core and sanctions at its periphery. In this core-periphery configuration, most of the congruence between the principals' desires and the agent's behavior is accomplished by the voters selecting a representative who is honest, competent, and already has policy goals much like the constituents'. The strongest and

---

Parties range from the most internally motivated or "gyroscopic" (responding largely to the members' principles and ideology) to the most externally motivated (responding largely to electoral inducements or sanctions).

most central mechanism for representing the constituent's views is selection, while sanction works at the edges of the system, disciplining the selected representative's tendencies to deviation only lightly and in the most important places. Political scientists should ask descriptively what the balance between core and periphery is in different contexts and normative theorists what that balance ought to be.

In normative theory, participatory democrats who cast a critical eye on all representative relations have been particularly suspicious of selection models, as subject to elitism, corruption, and failures in citizen control of the representative. These objections have little relevance in some specifiable contexts. Normative theorists have also not sufficiently considered either the possible efficiency gains of a selection model (gains that can perhaps be normatively discounted) or the quality of the constituent-representative relationship, which can be more humanly satisfying in a system that emphasizes selection.

In relatively uncorrupt democracies, the circumstances of political life frequently produce intrinsically motivated agents, the possibility of largely aligned objectives between voters and representatives, the capacity among voters to engage relatively easily in a reasonable selection process, and mechanisms by which potential representatives sort themselves into relatively well-aligned roles. In these contexts, the voter's efforts are efficiently concentrated on selection at the front end of the process and the electoral system can normatively reinforce a commitment to the public good and a warranted relationship of trust and goodwill between representative and constituent. In the political science literature, however, the selection model, advanced in the early 1960s as one of two paths to constituency control, was eclipsed by the sanctions model in the 1970s, despite, as we shall see, data suggesting that in many circumstances the selection model had greater predictive power. This eclipse may be coming to an end. My goal in this article is to restore the selection model to the status that it had in 1963, as an equal partner to the sanctions model both descriptively and normatively.

II. A STRUGGLING IDEA

Warren Miller and Donald Stokes first enunciated the selection model in 1963, when trust in government was at its peak in the United States. In their classic article on constituency influence in Congress, they specified two ways in which constituencies control their representatives. The first is "for the district to choose a Representative who so shares its views that in following his own convictions he does his constituents' will." This is the selection model. Their second is "for the Congressman to follow his (at least tolerably accurate) perceptions of district attitude in order to win re-election."[2] This is the sanctions model. Using data

---

[2]Miller and Stokes 1963, p. 50.

from the U.S. House of Representatives, Miller and Stokes concluded that the first (selection) path predominates in social welfare issues (because parties recruit candidates on the basis of the candidates' views on these issues and voters use party identification as a major signal in the selection process), while the second (sanction) path predominates in civil rights issues. These two paths formed the sides of their "well-known 'diamond model' of political representation," non-controversially assuming that selection played a co-equal role with sanctions.[3]

Ten years after Miller and Stokes, John Kingdon's classic *Congressmen's Voting Decisions* began discussing the mechanisms of constituency influence by stating, "The simplest mechanism through which constituents can influence a congressman is to select a person initially for office who agrees with their attitudes." Members of Congress "fully recognize the importance" of this "simple, elemental point," Kingdon wrote. "It often happens that a congressman never feels pressured by his constituency and in fact never even takes them into account, simply because he is 'their kind of people' anyway." Kingdon concluded from his interviews that "[a]pproximately three-quarters of the time . . . there was no conflict between the constituency position and the legislator's own attitude, at least in the congressman's mind."[4] In sum: "That the recruitment process [the selection model] affects congressmen's voting is an elemental, easy-to-understand proposition, but its profound importance cannot be emphasized too strongly."[5]

Yet only a year after Kingdon's book, his "simple," "elemental," "easy-to-understand" point of "profound importance" began to lose much of its traction in the profession, as a series of works on Congress, beginning with David Mayhew's *Congress: The Electoral Connection* and Morris Fiorina's *Representatives, Roll Calls, and Constituencies*, depicted a representative's prime motivation as the desire for reelection, with constituency control working through the sanctions made possible by this desire.[6]

Attempting to counter this trend, Robert Bernstein reported in *Elections, Representation, and Congressional Voting Behavior: The Myth of Constituency Control* that in his analysis of the House of Representatives he found "quite limited" evidence that "representatives may be influenced by reelection pressures." Instead, constituency influence over policy flowed primarily "from

---

[3]Erikson 2006. By 2006, Miller and Stokes (1963) had become the fifth most cited article in the *American Political Science Review* (Sigelman 2006, pp. 667–669), although not necessarily because of the two paths. In the top three journals for American politics (*APSR*, *AJPS*, and *JOP*), just over a third (34 percent) of the 125 articles citing this article referred to both paths, while 38 percent mentioned neither path, 27 percent mentioned the sanctions path alone, and less than one percent (one article) mentioned the selection path alone. I thank Philip Jones for this analysis.

[4]Kingdon 1973, pp. 44, 45; 1981, p. 46 (revised from first edition for clarity). Kingdon reports even less conflict in Northern Democratic, urban, and high majority districts. Presumably about a quarter of the legislative votes were induced (see "Electoral Consequences" later in the same chapter).

[5]Kingdon 1973, p. 46.

[6]Mayhew 1974. Fiorina 1974.

"SELECTION MODEL" OF POLITICAL REPRESENTATION   373

the constituencies' initial selections of who their representatives will be."[7] Bernstein's data and his analysis of the "myth" had no detectable effect on the prevalence of the sanctions model.

In 1994 William Bianco tried another tack, criticizing the now dominant sanctions model for its "unrealistic assumptions about the motives held by representatives and the beliefs that voters have about these motives." The standard principal-agent theory of representation generally assumed that "all incumbents prefer to shirk," that is, "act against constituent interests" with goals "antithetical" to those of the voters.[8] Bianco argued by contrast that in contemporary America by and large constituents generally "make good decisions" by applying "conditional trust," calculating roughly "the likelihood of a common interest" between them and the representatives and giving the representatives more or less leeway (engaging in different mixes of selection and sanction) depending on that calculation.[9]

At the same time that Bianco was suggesting selection as a significant counter to the then dominant sanctions model in rational choice theorizing, political scientists from the older tradition continued to use Miller and Stokes's two paths as received wisdom not even worth citing. In an important article on the way the representative system responded to public opinion change, for example, James Stimson, Michael MacKuen, and Robert Erikson assumed the two paths throughout and explicitly linked those paths to two different forms of representative motivation: "policy preferences" in the "electoral replacement" (selection) path and "expediency" in the "rational anticipation" (sanctions) path. They concluded that selection played the larger role in the Senate and presidency, while sanctions played the larger role in the House of Representatives.[10]

Thus while one group of political scientists continued uncontroversially to deploy Miller and Stokes's two paths, others saw themselves as making a contribution—perhaps even an embattled one—by stressing not only the analytic

---

[7]Bernstein 1989, p. 101. In his summary, "Constituency influence does not flow primarily from electoral threats against those in office, but rather from the initial selection of representatives. . . . The desire for reelection has only marginal impact in shifting members from ideological preferences should those preferences differ from the preferences of their constituencies" (pp. 104–5).

[8]Bianco 1994, pp. 26–27. For example, John Ferejohn (1986, p. 12, cited in Bianco 1994, p. 28) had designed his principal-agent game so that "the voter's problem is to police moral hazard [sanctions model] rather than to find and elect the more capable or benevolent officeholders [selection model]." Anthony Downs (1957, p. 28) had earlier argued that contestants for office "formulate policies in order to win elections [sanctions model], rather than winning elections in order to formulate policies [selection model]."

[9]Bianco 1994, pp. 87, 160. Bianco explicitly adopted the central procedural assumption in rational choice analysis that rational actors "evaluate the consequences of different actions in light of [their] goals" (p. 39) but contested the motivational assumption that "rational actors are invariably motivated by economic self-interest" (p. 40) and particularly that, in Terry Moe's words, legislators should be "assumed to be motivated by reelection. Their preferences over issues of policy and structure are induced" (1990, pp. 27–28, cited in Bianco 1994, p. 31).

[10]Stimson, MacKuen and Erikson 1995, p. 560; they did not discuss the differences between their findings and those of either Kingdon 1973 or Bernstein 1989. Although the article does not explicitly cite Miller and Stokes on the two paths, both Stimson (personal communication) and Erikson (2006, p. 674) were guided by that analysis.

power but the simple existence of the selection path. In 1999, for example, in a chapter for an influential volume on accountability that otherwise hewed to a straight sanctions model, James Fearon challenged that model with an account entitled, "Electoral Accountability and the Control of Politicians: Selecting Good Types versus Sanctioning Poor Performance." Although Fearon, like the volume's editors, defined accountability as requiring "powers to sanction or reward the agent," on the basis of this definition he then questioned "whether elections are best thought of in terms of accountability at all." His target was "an important tradition in democratic theory [that] understands elections . . . as a sanctioning device that induces elected officials to do what the voters want," in which "the anticipation of not being reelected in the future leads elected officials not to shirk their obligations to voters in the present."[11] Fearon argued that if voters instead "understand elections as opportunities to choose a 'good type' of political leader, one who would act on their behalf independent of reelection incentives" (the selection model), it "follows that electoral accountability is not necessary for elections to produce public policy that the principals (the voting public) want."[12] A selection model would also explain why voters dislike "office seekers," favor term limits, and put a high premium on principles and consistency even when their representative takes stands that they oppose, while a sanction model would wrongly predict the opposite. Fearon pointed out that selection and sanctioning "are by no means incompatible or mutually exclusive," but ultimately argued that in a game theoretic model, "Introduce *any* variation in politicians' attributes or propensities relevant to their performance in office, and it makes sense for the electorate to focus *completely* on choosing the best type when it comes time to vote."[13] The editors of the volume did not engage with or try to answer this strong challenge to their model, referring to it only in a brief summary in the introduction.

Meanwhile, economists had been developing their own line of thought on these matters. In 1985, in the first edited volume directly addressing the principal-agent problem, John Pratt and Richard Zeckhauser gave one page of their 35-page introduction to a pithy summary of the possibility of "alignment of objectives." When "productivity is the goal," they wrote,

> . . . principals and agents will seek situations in which purposes line up naturally. If we can get work that we like, we needn't worry about our boss's standing over us. Moreover, if we do not shirk, and there is no need for monitoring, we can share in the resulting cost savings.

They produced the examples of members of religious organizations and family businesses, student athletes working wholeheartedly at summer maintenance

[11]Fearon 1999, pp. 55, 56.
[12]Fearon 1999, p. 56. A "good type" has the characteristics of having policy preferences similar to those of the voter, being honest and principled, and being sufficiently skilled (Fearon 1999, pp. 59, 68).
[13]Fearon 1999, pp. 57, 77 (emphasis in original).

because they welcome the exercise, college presidents and corporate executives placing "like-minded managers in positions of responsibility," and politicians appointing people "who share their goals, who will make the choices regarding welfare or the environment that they would make." They concluded, "Those who share one's objectives tend to carry them out; monitoring and conflict are reduced, and such people may even make themselves available at a cheaper price." Thus, "alignment of objectives is beneficial to the performance of an agency relationship," and "both agent and principal have an incentive to make a good match."[14]

Two years later, another economist applied the selection model more fully to politics. In 1987 John Lott distinguished between guaranteeing quality through threat and knowing quality "prepurchase." In the second case (the selection model), "voters classify politicians by their 'pure ideological' beliefs. . . . Politicians are seen as directly consuming 'having done the right thing'. . . . If this altruistic consumption motive accurately describes political actions, cheating of constituency groups is effectively reduced or eliminated." After examining whether or not politicians' votes changed in the U.S. House of Representatives in their last term before retiring and finding that to an overwhelming degree they did not, Lott claimed empirical support for the prepurchase knowledge (selection) model.[15]

Almost a decade later, the economist Geoffrey Brennan again took aim at the "economic theory of politics," in which "common practice" assigns "uniformly self-interested motivations to all agents," relies on electoral competition for representatives' incentives to act in the interests of their constituents, and thus problematically "encourages institutional economists to overlook potentially important aspects of institutional design—those which depend on the operation of selection devices or 'screens' rather than on incentive devices or 'sanctions.' " He argued to the contrary that "selection is a potentially significant dimension of any institution's operation and that the methods of economic analysis tend to suppress that dimension." Rather than assuming "motivational homogeneity," he wrote,

> if one can identify the less knavish from the more knavish, one can locate the less knavish in those employments in which knavishness is most destructive. Put another

[14]Pratt and Zeckhauser 1985, p. 15.

[15]Lott 1987, p. 183. Looking at changes in voting patterns across retiring and non-retiring members of Congress between the 94th (1975–76) and 95th (1977–78) Congresses, Lott reported that "92 percent of the 216 regressions indicate that politicians in their last period do not behave any differently than other politicians" (1987, p. 19; see also literature review in Bender and Lott 1996). With a more precise methodology, however, Rothenberg and Sanders (2000) did show leavers changing their votes more than non-leavers in their last period in office (by .033 to .039 on a −1 to +1 liberal-conservative scale), although not to the degree predicted by sanctions theory and no more among retirees than among those going on to statewide office, some of whom a sanctions theory would predict to have an incentive to remain consistent. They conclude that even a member who moves her vote when leaving "is likely to agree with her constituents a large percentage of the time" (2000, p. 322), a result consistent with a "selection core, sanction periphery" hypothesis.

way, . . . such virtue as exists in society will be a positive resource for that society, and should be located in its highest valued use just like any other resource.[16]

For efficiency, if "virtue is a resource that commands a higher social value in these non-market institutions [e.g., politics, bureaucracy, and the judiciary], . . . the good functioning of society will depend on the extent to which the relatively virtuous are selected for non-market offices." Non-material rewards of different sorts would particularly encourage self-motivated agents to self-select into appropriate jobs.[17]

In a set of major works from 1997 to the present, Timothy Besley has recently posed the same contrast between a sanctions model and a selection model.[18] "At the core" of the method of "Public Choice,"[19] he writes, lies the assumption that, in James Buchanan's words, "Individuals must be modeled as seeking to further their own narrow self-interest, narrowly defined," with "no suggestion that improvement lies in the selection of some morally superior individuals who will use their powers in some 'public interest.' "[20] Besley counters: "But good government . . . also requires good leaders—persons of character and wisdom." While "first generation models" influenced by Public Choice adopt only a sanctions perspective with "elections as an incentive mechanism," "second generation models" such as his own look at "the implications of agents who differ in their type," with elections serving "two key roles: creating incentives and selecting the best type." "Fiduciary duty," a form.of intrinsic motivation that includes pursuing both honesty and "the interest of citizens at large," is an "important model of motivation in politics that has received less attention in modeling the behavior of politicians." Yet voters can and do select on this motivation.[21]

---

[16]Brennan 1996, pp. 257–9. He, quoting Alexander Hamilton: "The assumption of universal venality in human nature is little less an error in political reasoning than the assumption of universal rectitude" ([1788] 1961, p. 458, in Brennan 1996, p. 260).

[17]Brennan 1996, pp. 259–60, drawing in part on thoughts in *The Federalist Papers*. He also notes that "on at least some occasions, the same institutional device [e.g., elections] will perform both incentive and selection functions" (p. 262).

[18]Besley and Coate 1997. Besley and Ghatak 2005. Besley 2005; 2006.

[19]By "Public Choice" Besley (2006, p. 29) means "the work beginning in the Virginia School in the 1950s," which has "three distinctive features," of which the first is "the assumption of rational self-interest in the study of political interactions." (The second is the use of constitutions to constrain self-interest and the third the assumption of a state whose legitimacy is limited to the domain to which freely contracting agents would agree.) Besley (2006, p. 38) also associates the first assumption with "the Chicago approach to political economy".

[20]Buchanan 1989, pp. 18, 20. Quoted in Besley 2006, p. 29.

[21]Besley 2006, pp. 2, 106, 37, 40–41, citing Barro (1973) and Ferejohn (1986) *inter alia* as examples of "first generation" sanction models. For Besley, politicians are "congruent" (or simply "good") if for fidiciary or other reasons they "share voters' objectives exactly" (pp. 109, 176), and "dissonant" (or "bad") if they are less than fully competent and thus find it costly to do what voters want, if they are influenced by special interest groups to pursue directions contrary to those of the voters, if they have private agendas contrary to those of the voters (including ideological dispositions as well as rent-seeking desires), and even if they do constituency service that promotes their own reelection but distracts them from the public interest.

"SELECTION MODEL" OF POLITICAL REPRESENTATION

As Besley was developing his version of the selection model, other economists were coming around to this perspective. David Lee, Enrico Moretti and Matthew Butler, for example, summarized "two fundamentally different views of the role of elections in policy formation" as follows:

> In one view [the sanctions model], voters can affect candidates' policy choices: competition for votes induces politicians to move. . . . In the alternative view [the selection model], voters merely elect policies: politicians cannot make credible promises to moderate their policies, and elections are merely a means to decide which one of two opposing policy views will be implemented.[22]

They concluded that the selection model was empirically more predictive in the U.S. House of Representatives.

As economists, Brennan, Besley, and Lee, Moretti and Butler were unaware of the similar empirical conclusions drawn in political science by Miller and Stokes, Kingdon, Bernstein, Bianco, and Stimpson, McKuen and Erikson, all of whose data suggested that the selection model explained as much as, or more than, the sanctions model. Yet even in political science this line of thought had tended again and again to fade from view. Thus while Bernstein cited Kingdon, he did not cite Miller and Stokes on this point. Bianco cited neither Miller and Stokes, nor Kingdon, nor Bernstein. Fearon cited neither Miller and Stokes, nor Kingdon, nor Bernstein, nor Bianco. Each new David picking up the slingshot knew little or nothing of past stones that had bounced to the ground.[23]

It is not quite clear why the sanctions model had this Teflon effect for so long. Perhaps the selection model suffers from an intrinsic lack of intellectual interest, as Pratt and Zeckhauser speculated. Perhaps self-interest as a motivation is easier to model or is attractive for other reasons.[24] Perhaps self-motivated agents, particularly those inspired by the common good, are simply harder to explain than externally-motivated agents. Perhaps common interests are harder to explain than conflicting interests. But the greater efficiency of the selection model when it is feasible and its seemingly greater predictive power in the U.S. Presidency, Senate and even, in many studies, the U.S. House of Representatives make it a formidable empirical competitor to the sanctions model.

I turn now to the implications of the selection model's three necessary components: self-motivated agents, aligned objectives, and the selecting and sorting mechanisms that facilitate such alignment.

[22]Lee, Moretti and Butler 2004, p. 807.

[23]A clearer line of research had emerged in economics: Fearon (1999) cited Lott (1987) and primarily the economic literature; Besley (2004; 2006) similarly cited both earlier economists and Fearon. With the more recent works, the selection model can now be said to play in the economic analysis of political representation a role co-equal with that of sanctions, and economists are now turning their intelligences to the issues a selection model might raise (see, e.g., Kartik and McAffee 2007). In the rational choice subfield in political science, sophisticated scholars are also beginning automatically to add selection to sanctions (e.g., Ferejohn and Rosenbluth 2009, identifying the two models as the " 'moral hazard' and 'adverse selection' perspectives"). In political theory, Petitt has recently distinguished between "indicative" and "responsive" representation (2008; see also 2009).

[24]Mansbridge 1990.

III. SELF-MOTIVATED AGENTS

Since the work of Douglas McGregor in 1960, management theorists have often distinguished between what McGregor called "Theory X," appropriate to situations in which employees will avoid work if they can and do not care about organizational goals, and "Theory Y," appropriate to situations in which employees intrinsically enjoy their work, just as they enjoy play or leisure, and can be internally committed to the aims of the organization. Self-motivated employees, McGregor theorized, would be the more likely to exercise imagination, ingenuity, and creativity in their work.[25]

In Theory Y, the intrinsic motivation of an employee can be of any kind—a desire to solve puzzles, to exercise outdoors, or to keep things neat. In politics also, the intrinsic motivation of a representative can be of any kind. A representative might, in principle, promote lower taxes simply because he or she personally had a lot of property subject to tax. Certain occupations, however—including politics in relatively uncorrupt democracies—attract agents whose intrinsic motivations include what might be called public spirit, that is, concern with the common good and at least some willingness to make sacrifices in material interest for that good.[26] Although the mix of motivations in any given individual will almost always include some extrinsic motivation and will probably also include forms of intrinsic motivation not based on public spirit (such as the desires to feel efficacious, stand by one's comrades, or not be overruled), in non-corrupt democracies where politics does not produce great pecuniary rewards political office will tend to attract actors with some intrinsic public-spirited motivation.

Yet public spirit is vulnerable to being undermined by three factors associated with the sanctions model: extrinsic incentives, monitoring, and a culture that assumes self-interest as the primary motivation.

Psychological research has established that in many circumstances extrinsic motivation drives out intrinsic motivation, although extrinsic rewards framed as either inherent to the task or honoring the actor's intrinsic motivation do not have this negative effect. Extrinsic rewards can "crowd out" intrinsic rewards and motivation in real life as well as laboratory experiments, and such crowding

---

[25]The field of public administration the early 1940s also saw a "great debate" (Carr 1999, p. 4) between Carl Friedrich (1940) and Herbert Finer (1941) on the best way to secure responsible and ethical conduct among public officials. Friedrich argued for selecting self-motivated persons who sincerely wanted to work for the public interest and reinforcing those internal commitments, while Finer argued for external sanctions and controls. Neither argued for a contingency theory or core-periphery combination balanced to match the context; neither pointed out that when a context can support a selection model a sanctions model will be relatively inefficient; and neither argued normatively for cultivating common interests or good relationships between principals and agents.

[26]Besley and Ghatak (2005, p. 616) mention "doctors who are committed to saving lives, researchers to advancing knowledge, judges to promoting justice, and soldiers to defending their country in battle."

out will be most problematic when the agent has originally been selected for intrinsic motivation.[27]

Monitoring may also drive out intrinsic motivation, particularly when the subjects of the monitoring perceive it as expressing distrust. As Onora O'Neill puts it, "Plants don't flourish when we pull them up too often to check how their roots are growing." Thus the "audit explosion" in bureaucracy tends to undermine the "real work" of professionals. "Trust often invites reciprocal trust" in a virtuous spiral,[28] while "institutionalized suspicion undermines trust."[29] As for elected representatives, Richard Fenno quotes one member of Congress saying, "To me, representative government means you hire a guy to use his own judgment; and if you don't like what he does, you fire him. But you don't keep after him all the time. If it isn't my function to use my judgment, than what the hell is my function? And if that's not my function, I don't want the job."[30]

Even the act of describing most behavior in self-interested terms tends to undermine public-spirited motivation. The theory that self-interest is the major causal explanation for human behavior seems to play a role in its own confirmation. Citing several experiments supporting this phenomenon, Dale Miller suggests possible explanations. First, "The image of the human being as self-interested leads to the creation of the kinds of social institutions (e.g., workplaces, schools, governments) that transform the image into reality." Second, the implicit norm that one should act self-interestedly affects behavior because norms tend to change in the direction of the perceived majority's norms. Third, thinking of oneself as one of the few non-self-interested people in a group implies that one's altruistic behavior will have only a miniscule potential effect.[31]

For these reasons, although institutional designers have argued in the past that institutional arrangements based on self-interest will be the most impervious to destruction,[32] such arrangements also have the potential for crowding out public spirit. In democratic political systems, for example, the close races with little incumbency that are necessary to make the sanctions model work sometimes drive away the most public-spirited potential agents.

---

[27]See Deci, Koestner and Ryan 1999; Kruglanski et al. 1975; Deci and Ryan 1985; Frey 1997; Bohnet et al., 2001. I thank Iris Bohnet for this last suggestion.

[28]O'Neill 2002, pp. 19, 49, 25.

[29]Behn 2001, p. 83. See also: Philp 2004, p. 22; Anechiaro and Jacobs 1996, p. 202; and Goodin 1980; 1982 on moral incentives.

[30]Fenno 1978, p. 170.

[31]Miller 1999, p. 1053. On the prevalence of the norm of self-interest, Miller cites, among others, Alexis de Tocqueville in the mid-nineteenth century observing that "Americans . . . enjoy explaining almost every act of their lives on the principle of self-interest. . . . I think that in this they often do themselves less than justice, for sometimes in the United States, as elsewhere, one sees people carried away by the . . . spontaneous impulses natural to man. But the Americans are hardly prepared to admit that they do give way to emotions of this sort" ([1835]1969, p. 546, in Miller 1999, p. 1057). See also Eliasoph 1998.

[32]See Mansbridge 1990.

IV. ALIGNED OBJECTIVES

The selection model requires not only an internally motivated agent but also an alignment between the objectives of the principal and the self-motivated agent. Normatively, the closer representatives come to having common interests with their constituents, the less the constituents need to protect themselves against the greater power of the representatives. In the extreme, completely common interests could legitimate large inequalities of power, as long as—an important qualification—the less powerful could take back equal power when interests began to diverge and as long as the two other conditions of legitimately unequal power—the maintenance of equal respect and the opportunity for individual development—were fulfilled.[33] The alignment of objectives can take place not only on the high ground of similar understandings of what is best for the nation as a whole but also on what is best for particular individuals or communities, such as farmers, miners, or inner city residents.

Context affects the supply of aligned objectives. First, "good fits are most likely in homogeneous districts."[34] Second, context-specific norms and institutions encourage public spirit and discourage the more obvious forms of corruption[35]—as in the quite different interactions of culture and institutions in Sweden, in the English, German, and French civil service, and in the clergy of many religions. Third, widespread competence in potential representatives increases the supply of aligned potential agents, both because competence is required to further aligned objectives and because competence fosters internal motivation.

Context also affects the demand for aligned objectives. Recognizing that no principal and agent ever have perfectly aligned objectives, a "contingency" application of the selection model asks when it makes most sense for the principal to tolerate some divergence. Other things equal, a selection model is preferable when a principal needs an agent capable of flexible, adaptive, and creative performance, discretion in negotiation, and dedication to long-run aims, as well as when tools for adequate monitoring and sanctioning are absent or expensive.[36] In organizational theory, "high commitment" management practices, based implicitly on a selection model, are most effective in such contexts.[37] In politics, descriptive representation (by geography, occupation, religion, tribe, race, gender,

---

[33]Mansbridge 1980, 235–247.

[34]Fenno 1978, p. 125; see below, section VIII.

[35]By corruption here I mean only "behavior which deviates from the formal duties of a public role because of private-regarding (personal, close family, private clique) pecuniary or status gains; or violates rules against the exercise of certain types of private-regarding influence" (Nye 1967, p. 419).

[36]Sanctions models are not necessarily inflexible. "Anticipatory representation," in which the representative's behavior is induced by the prospect at the next election of the voters' retrospective judgments on the representative's past performance, is far more flexible than "promissory representation," in which the representative's behavior is induced by fear of retaliation if she does not keep promises made at the first election (Mansbridge 2003). Yet in a selection model voters usually give the representative even more leeway.

[37]Baron and Kreps 1999.

REPRESENTATION

"SELECTION MODEL" OF POLITICAL REPRESENTATION

or any other factor), one form of a selection model, is most in demand when interests are uncrystalized and the representative must exercise discretion[38] or when the standard forms of monitoring and sanctioning are either counterproductive or weak. Thus constitutional conventions, which have no subsequent elections, rely heavily for their legitimacy on selection models with a strong dose of descriptive representation.

V. SELECTION AND SORTING

The third necessary feature of an effective selection system involves accurate selection and sorting as well as the capacity to "de-select" easily when circumstances change. For accurate selection, the principal must have sufficiently good information at the time of selection about the potential agent's motivation (and thus the likelihood of aligned objectives). In appropriate conditions, agents also sort themselves into jobs and organizations whose aims match their own intrinsic motivation as closely as possible. In political representation, ease of de-selection usually depends on the capacities of ancillary institutions such as political parties and the media.

Voters often select not only on policy direction and competence but on intrinsic motivation, or "character." The less a voter knows about policies, the more rational it is to select on character.[39] Citizens may also want to choose "a good man" or "a good woman"[40] in part because they trust their own capacities, honed over a lifetime of social interaction, to choose well on this dimension. Finally, when voters find it hard to monitor their representatives, they may act like firms in a "low-enforcement environment," which "heavily invest in screening of potential employees, stressing that character is more important than the possession of specific skills."[41] When a collective action problem is voluntary, for example, both cooperators and defectors search for signals of a potential partner's character type, and if that evidence is relatively easy to collect, an efficient equilibrium will emerge, since cooperators will choose cooperators and defectors will be left without partners.[42] So too both principals and potential agents seeking a relationship based on aligned objectives will benefit if the agents can send a signal that is hard to manipulate.[43]

In countries with relatively corrupt systems or inexperienced voters, potential representatives find it hard to send accurate signals. Such countries can benefit

---

[38]Mansbridge 2003.

[39]In the United States, women, who are on the average less informed about politics than men (Delli Carpini and Keeter 1996) and also have had less political power (and may therefore rely less on sanctions), have traditionally been more likely than men to choose their representatives on the basis of character (Andersen and Shabad 1979). Popkin (1991) also stresses signs of character as one that voters use in selecting representatives.

[40]Miller and Stokes 1963. Fenno 1978.

[41]Bohnet et al. 2001, p. 132.

[42]Frank 1988.

[43]Bianco 1994, p. 56. Mansbridge 1999, p. 305.

from the side-effects of a war of independence, which allows some future leaders to give a costly signal of their willingness to give their lives for their country. The willingness of George Washington in the United States, Nkrumah in Ghana, Mandela in South Africa, Nehru in India, Tito in Yugoslavia, Mao in China, and others elsewhere to risk imprisonment or death in wars of independence earned them the trust of the citizens in contexts where more subtle forms of public spirit were hard to measure. As a result, wars of independence can (although they do not inevitably) generate the selection of genuinely public-spirited leaders for a time, before those leaders, not tempered by potential sanction, become ego-maniacal or corrupt. Once the generation from the wars of independence has died, voters have access to less reliable signals and the quality of the leadership is likely to decline.

Religious leaders too can send costly signals of non-self-interested motivation. In many forms of Judaism and Islam such a signal derives from devotion to a life of learning, when the cost of learning an ancient, non-vernacular language or memorizing large amounts of a foundational text may guarantee a meager living but have no clear payoff in significant wealth. In such cases, and in the absence of other reliable signals in the political world, it may be functional for people to select such religious leaders over secular leaders more likely to be motivated primarily by self-interest. Along the same lines, in the United States today citizens sometimes gauge public spirit from the willingness of the wealthy to invest their fortunes in their own political campaigns. In the absence of corruption (which insures a monetary payoff to taking office), the public may reasonably take such investments as evidence of public-spirited (if sometimes also wrong-headed or ego-driven) commitment to a cause. Voting against majority sentiment or against one's party sends another visible and costly signal of one's commitment and integrity.[44]

Repeated interaction is the most frequent basis for interpreting an actor's internal motivations.[45] In the absence of personal experience with a potential agent's past behavior, principals often rely on the agent's reputation within a network of individuals who have been better placed to observe those actions over time.[46] Professional networks—including the professional civil service in such countries as France, England, Germany, and Sweden—help create such reputations. Political parties play the same role for legislative candidates.

When both costly signals and reliable reputations are hard to come by, principals—including citizens choosing their representatives—often fall back on stereotypes, from which they infer both aligned objectives (shared interests) and the competence and honesty of the potential representative.[47] Although accuracy regarding any individual may be poor and a decision made by stereotype may be

---

[44]Fearon 1999, p. 63. Kartick and McAffee 2007.
[45]See Dixit (2002, p. 703): "repetition creates scope for building a reputation about one's type."
[46]Shapiro 2005, p. 276. Bianco 1994, p. 152.
[47]Bianco 1994, pp. 59, 120.

"SELECTION MODEL" OF POLITICAL REPRESENTATION

unjust to a given individual, if a stereotype is at all true of a group in general, that stereotype allows a principal to take the average characteristics of a group as a decisional cue to the density of a particular trait (e.g., cooperators vs. defectors) in the group.[48] For most citizens in large-scale advanced democracies, however, the party identification of a candidate serves as the most important indicator of policy alignment, and, for some, even of character.

De-selection (which Besley calls "ex post selection"[49]) generates an even worse information problem. Although the voter now has access to the public record of the representative's behavior in office, the representative also has an increased capacity to make her record look better than it is through easier access to the media and public events, the franking privilege, and the publicity attendant on constituency service. The selection model is not normatively tenable unless the citizenry retains sufficient capacity to remove representatives who have gotten out of touch with the prevailing objectives of the district's voters.[50] Thus party systems, other networks, and the media play a critical informational role, as does the internal competitiveness and vitality of the party system.

Self-selection among potential agents can also serve as an important sorting mechanism. Non-profit organizations often act differently from private firms because the managers, acting from more intrinsic motivations, "sort themselves, each gravitating to the types of organizations that he or she finds . . . most compatible."[51] Potential political representatives engage heavily in this sorting process. Those who might otherwise be interested in running for office refrain from the investment if their personal policy orientations do not sufficiently reflect the orientations of their potential constituents.[52] And when the orientations of their constituents change (through changed boundaries in the district, changing demographics, or the entry of new generational cohorts with new political views), many elected representatives retire and new candidates are drawn into politics. "If your conscience and your district disagree too often," members of Congress like to say, "you're in the wrong business."[53]

Low compensation plays two contradictory roles in this sorting process. The pay for mission-oriented agents must be high enough to facilitate a sorting that selects for competence, but low enough to facilitate a sorting that selects

[48]See Popkin 1991.
[49]Besley 2004.
[50]See below on incumbency.
[51]Weisbrod 1988, pp. 31–32. Besley and Ghatak (2005) thus advocate heterogeneity among missions, whether in the non-profit or other sectors (e.g., among different kinds of public schools), to make this sorting process most efficient. Different kinds of incentives attract different kinds of individuals (Brennan 1996; Bohnet and Oberholzer-Gee 2002), with the "currency" of reward helping in the sort. For example, when direct payments are low but certain consumption expenses high (research equipment for academics, religious edifices for clerics, well-trained clerks for judges), if these forms of compensation enhance desired output, they "cost" the principal less as well as improving the sort, being of greater value to individuals already motivated to produce the desired output (Brennan 1996).
[52]Fenno 1978. Lawless and Fox 2005.
[53]Fenno 1978, p. 142. Also Cox and Katz 2002.

for mission-orientation. The clergy and monks of the religions that demand celibacy or relative poverty have traditionally responded to these disincentives by sorting themselves on the dimension of mission-orientation. Low-paying "citizen legislatures" and public offices have generated the same self-sorting, with the same tension between sorting for competence and sorting for mission-orientation.

Self-sorting by low compensation is highly inegalitarian, as members of different groups bring greatly unequal resources to the sort. Unsalaried or uncompetitively compensated positions tend to attract individuals with additional resources to support themselves and their families, while sorting on "citizen duty" also disproportionately attracts members of the middle and professional classes, who have been socialized to value that form of duty.[54] Although religious, local, and ideological commitments sometimes cut across class in creating a mission-oriented motivation to run for office, the frequent class bias of those who take underpaid offices can make aligned objectives less likely and communication with working-class constituents more difficult. Low compensation also increases the risk of corruption.

VI. ACCOUNTABILITY AND TRANSPARENCY

In standard principal-agent theory, accountability means that a principal "has powers to sanction or reward the agent": *accountability as sanction*. In ordinary parlance sanctions are also often central to accountability: "When people seek to hold someone accountable, they are usually planning some kind of punishment."[55]

Yet an earlier understanding of accountability stresses "giving an account" (*rendre compte, Rechenschaft abgeben*).[56] When the principal and agent have largely aligned objectives, the focus of accountability shifts from monitoring and sanctioning to the agent's giving reasons for his or her acts, either through (one-way) *narrative accountability* or (two-way) *deliberative accountability*.[57]

Narrative and deliberative accountability work best when the principal, even if unhappy with the result, can see that the intrinsic motivation underlying the aligned objectives remains unchanged. Representatives can relatively easily explain changes in policy by new facts and circumstances, but changes in

---

[54]Prewitt (1970), criticizing a form of the selection model among Bay area councilmen.

[55]Fearon 1999, p. 55. Behn 2001, p. 4.

[56]The *Oxford English Dictionary* (2nd ed.) on "accountability" gives as a substantive definition only "liability to give an account of, and answer for, discharge of duties or conduct," touching on sanctions only through the implications of the phrase "answer for," which nevertheless has narrative overtones. On accountability as giving an account (showing, explaining, and justifying past actions), see Behn 2001, p. 4; Philp 2004, p. 12; and O'Neill 2002, p. 58.

[57]The opinions of the U.S. Supreme Court exemplify pure narrative accountability. In deliberative accountability principal and agent both ask questions and give answers, exploring whether or not they remain mutually aligned and whether the grounds of their alignment might have changed.

"SELECTION MODEL" OF POLITICAL REPRESENTATION

principles throw doubt on the consistency of their characters.[58] The selection model has the problem that narrative and deliberative accountability also work best when representatives can give full explanations in interaction with their constituents, an opportunity that few if any large-scale representative systems provide.[59]

No matter how selection-based, every system needs some monitoring of both elected officials and bureaucrats. Yet that monitoring need not be systematic and on-going. Matthew McCubbins and Thomas Schwartz contend that it is more efficient for individual citizens and interest groups to send in alarms when they come across wrongdoing ("fire alarm" oversight) rather than engage in continual monitoring ("police patrol" oversight).[60] Fire alarm oversight is particularly appropriate in high-commitment systems when intrinsic motivation on the part of the agent produces a high probability of honest, competent, and aligned behavior.

What organizational theorists call "network"—or "horizontal," or "professional"—accountability can also substitute effectively for the "vertical" accountability standard of the sanctions model.[61] If members of a network have a strong enough internal commitment to the norms of their profession, or even if the members have only a self-interested concern for the reputation of their network, they will have an incentive to monitor and sanction the behavior of others in that network to keep potential defectors up to network standards. Parties often play this role, particularly in disciplined party systems. These networks of horizontal accountability, along with recruitment systems and larger social norms, help produce honesty and competence outside any system of electoral sanctions. When these processes are functioning effectively, the amount of monitoring and sanctioning needed outside the network (e.g., through the electoral system) is only the minimum that experience shows is necessary to prevent the unraveling of a system based primarily on internal incentives and horizontal accountability. That is often not very much.

A similar analysis holds for transparency, that familiar cure for the ills of democracy advocated by both the public and many political scientists. Although some transparency is good, indeed necessary, for democracy, and many situations could benefit from more of it, more transparency is not always better. In contexts where the elected representatives are in general competent, honest, and well

[58] I thank Richard Zeckhauser for this suggestion.
[59] See Bianco 1994; Kingdon 1981, p. 48.
[60] McCubbins and Schwartz 1984. See also Aberbach (1990) on "alarm-based" vs. "constant-surveillance" models and Anechiaro and Jacobs (1996) on the counterproductive effects of monitoring and sanctions in New York City.
[61] See Goodin (2003) for network accountability in non-profit institutions, arguing that accountability based on "praising or shaming and shunning" (p. 12) will work most effectively among actors motivated by the public good. Yet networks can also function as "cozy cabals covering one another's incompetence"; thus the networks themselves often require some external monitoring and sanctions (p. 41). See also Keohane and Nye (2001) on network accountability in international organizations.

aligned with their constituents, each increase in efforts to produce transparency above an important minimum can create costs in efficiency and in motivation.[62] Many negotiations, great and small, are best conducted behind relatively closed doors. Negotiators need to show those with whom they are negotiating that they understand their positions. Accordingly, they need to be able to say things that some of their constituents might consider fraternizing with the enemy. They need to be able to explore avenues that, after exploration, they might repudiate. They need to able to act creatively and empathetically, without scrutinizing every word for how it will play in public.[63]

When transparency has such costs, we should favor not extreme *transparency in process* (for example making all committee meetings public), but instead *transparency in rationale*—in procedures, information, reasons, and the facts on which the reasons are based. In the Supreme Court of the United States the deliberations and the negotiations are secret, but the facts and reasons on which the decisions are based are public. When EU bureaucrats have been asked to be more "transparent," they have in most cases responded appropriately in this more communicative fashion—giving reasons, explanations and facts, and improving notification, rather than opening their processes to public monitoring.[64] A selection model of political representation, based on justified trust in the motivations and underlying orientation of the representative, makes transparency in the process less necessary.

VII. NON-HIERARCHICAL SELECTION

The selection model of representation should not be confused with either the "trustee" form derived from Edmund Burke or the elitism of Joseph Schumpeter. Trustee representation is only one instance of the selection model, and it is the least democratic kind. Both the word "trustee" itself and Burke's own stance suggest that the trustee is wiser and more far-seeing than his constituents, and for this reason more fit to rule. Linguistically, a trustee is "one to whom something is entrusted, one trusted to keep or administer something" or "one holding legal title to property which he must administer for the benefit of a beneficiary,"[65] with the strong implication that the trustee knows better what is good for the trust's beneficiaries than do the beneficiaries themselves. A financial trust is often created on the paternalistic assumption that it is better if the beneficiary never gets his

---

[62]See O'Neill (2002) against transparency.

[63]As Naurin (2004) points out, transparency impedes mutually-disclosive negotiations because often the most useful disclosures cannot be public. The costs are particularly great in potentially "integrative" or win-win solutions (Follett [1925] 1942; Fisher and Ury 1981). Examining transcripts of legislatures, Steiner et al. (2004) conclude that expressions of respect and understanding of others' positions are more frequent in closed sessions of the legislature than in public ones. On the deliberative costs and benefits of transparency, see Elster (1995; 1998) and Chambers (2004).

[64]Lodge 1994. Also see Keohane and Nye (2001, p. 230) and Magnette (2003, p. 151).

[65]*Webster's Third New International Dictionary, Unabridged* (1993), s.v. "trustee".

or her hands on the funds at all. Burke's stance was also elitist. Although in his speech to his constituents at Bristol he said only that a representative betrays his constituents if he sacrifices his judgment to their opinion, in his correspondence Burke made it clear that, like many of his class and time, he was skeptical about the capacities of "the people."[66] Bernard Manin makes a convincing case that in Burke's era electoral representation implied for many what Manin calls "the principle of distinction," that is, the idea that representatives "should rank higher than their constituents in wealth, talent, and virtue."[67]

Schumpeter too did not hide his disdain for the "typical citizen," whose "primitive impulses, infantilisms and criminal propensities" erupt in a crowd, whose "disillusioning" openness to subconscious messages makes him prey to false advertising, who pays scant attention to matters that do not engage his "immediate personal and pecuniary" interests, and who, in Schumpeter's most famous phrase, "drops down to a lower level of performance once he enters the political field."[68]

Yet the selection model of political representation need imply no more hierarchy than any representative process, whether based on sanctions or selection. The selection of a representative can rest purely on a division of labor, as the Abbé de Siéyès suggested years ago.[69] When the U.S. constitution was being debated in 1787-88, and the Federalists advanced their principle of distinction, the Anti-Federalists opposed that principle, arguing that representation required "likeness" and "resemblance" to constituents so that representatives could "possess their sentiments and feelings."[70] Both Federalists and Anti-Federalists assumed a model of representation based primarily on selection, but the criteria for selection were hierarchical in the one case and egalitarian in the other.

The selection model in developed democracies today has lost many of the hierarchical trappings associated with its "trustee" form. In Besely's formulation, for example, citizens select a "citizen-candidate" from among themselves—although in both sanction and selection models constituents generally choose representatives who are more highly educated and with more experience in politics than most of their supporters. Today when voters say they want to select a "good man" or "good woman" as a representative, they often seem to want someone like them, but with the interest, competence, and honesty to be a legislator. Edmund Burke did not present himself to his constituents as being "like them."

---

[66]Burke [1774] 1889; Burke to the Duke of Richmond, 26 September 1775, *Correspondence*, 3:218, quoted in Herzog 1998, p. 523 (also pp. 34, 504–27).

[67]Manin 1997, p. 94. By contrast, in modern societies principals may decide that they want to select agents more talented and virtuous than they, but this not entailed by the model.

[68]Schumpeter [1942] 1962, pp. 257, 258, 260, 262.

[69]See Manin, 1997, p. 3.

[70]Brutus 15 November 1787, in Storing (1981, vol. 2, p. 380), cited in Manin (1997, p. 110).

VIII. HOMOGENEITY AND EXTENDED INCUMBENCY—
HOW EVIL, REALLY?

The selection model is associated in practice with two features usually considered troubling for the quality of democracy: homogeneous districts and extended incumbency. As Fenno's "Congressman C" put it, "A congressman who comes from a homogeneous district like mine will vote the way his district wants most of the time because he's so much like them."[71] Once selected for overall direction and competence, a representative from a homogeneous district need only continue to be authentically herself, avoid corruption, and work hard.[72] If nothing changes—that is, the boundaries of the district do not change, younger voters maintain the same preferences and interests as their elders, new groups do not enter, the representative continues to be as constituency-centered, policy-congruent, honest, and competent as before, and no new challenger outshines the incumbent on these matters enough to outweigh the loss in experience—the same process that gave rise to selection can be expected to generate a long incumbency.

By contrast, heterogeneous districts encourage the threat of sanctions. With two or more groups trying to achieve different goals, a candidate for election or reelection must cobble together a majority by giving as many groups as possible as much as possible of what they want. These actions, at least, will be induced. Small shifts in the district's composition or the representative's actions can also cause an upset, making extended incumbency less likely.

The positive case for homogeneity is simple. The more homogeneous the district, the greater the proportion of voters who can be satisfied with their representative—a satisfaction that carries over, to a lesser degree, to the legislature as a whole.[73] If representation had only the goal of voter satisfaction, the ideal electoral district in a first-past-the-post single member system would always be one that included only constituents with exactly the same political preferences.[74] In a homogeneous district, communication between representatives and constituents is also easier. Representatives loosen up, feel relaxed, and communicate easily with their core constituencies. Constituents find it easier to

---

[71]Fenno 1978, p. 142.

[72]See Fenno (2007) on the importance of authenticity to both constituents and representatives. The association between selection and either homogeneity or incumbency is far from perfect. In a homogeneous district, a representative motivated only by the desire to hold office could give the constituents exactly the policies they want, never change the formula, and thus continue to be reelected. In a heterogeneous district, a representative motivated only by her convictions regarding the common good could offer the constituents an overarching vision and personal characteristics that they admire, never change that presentation, and thus continue to be reelected. Presidential candidates in the United States work largely on a selection model, particularly in their second term, but face a highly heterogeneous constituency.

[73]Brunell (2006), using ANES data to measure satisfaction; see Buchler 2005 for a model. On competitive versus homogeneous districts, see the debate between Issacharoff (2002a; 2002b) and Persily (2002).

[74]Brunell 2006, p. 80. Persily 2002, p. 668. In this case a single-member district system would begin to approximate multi-member proportional representation.

contact a representative whom they view as "like them." In the United States, for example, Black constituents are more likely to contact Black representatives and White constituents more likely to contact Whites.[75]

On the negative side, homogeneity is never total, and near-homogeneity lets a representative ignore the minority.[76] The more homogeneous districts are, therefore, the more critical it is to have institutions through which minorities in the district can both make connections with surrogate representatives in other districts and promote their needs and interests in associations that reach across district boundaries.

Homogeneity also risks increasing complacency and narrowmindedness. As more citizens move to districts where others share their core political values (as is happening between but perhaps not within states in the United States today),[77] they find it easier to select representatives who intrinsically share their views. Their political lives will become proximately more satisfactory as a result. But in these more homogeneous political spaces, neither voters nor representatives will have to pay the price of trying to communicate with others whom they do not immediately understand.[78] They may also not feel the need for compromises at the legislative level. Lack of diversity may foster extremism.[79] Short-run political satisfaction may be bought at the expense of long-run growth in understanding and capacity to compromise.

The positive case for incumbency is also simple and somewhat similar to that for homogeneity. In non-corrupt systems, long stretches of repeated reelection and the absence of opposition often signal a satisfied constituency. Incumbency also promotes communication between representative and constituent. The longer the selected representative remains in office, the better constituents will know the representative and her staff. Constituents will have had more chances to see the representative in person or to write and receive a reply. They will have built a relationship with the representative that, although necessarily distant, facilitates, at least in the best case, warranted trust and further communication.[80] Finally, with a good, internally motivated representative, incumbency increases voters' control over the legislature. The voters retain in office someone who has

---

[75]On relaxed communication, Fenno 1978; on contacting, Gay 2002.

[76]Guinier (1994, p. 135) argues, for example, that relatively homogeneous racial districts reduce the incentive to appeal across racial lines. List systems of proportional representation are vulnerable to a similar criticism (see e.g., Horowitz 2003).

[77]On increased sorting between states in the U.S., see Bishop (2008); on within-state sorting, see Rhode and Strumpf (2003). For evidence that geographical sorting has more effect than redistricting on incumbency, see Oppenheimer (2005). In the extreme, geographical sorting could eventually produce the territorially-based equivalent of proportional representation.

[78]See e.g., Mutz (2006) on citizens' distaste for discussing politics with others who disagree.

[79]See e.g., Sunstein 2003.

[80]Alice Wolf, currently my representative in the Massachusetts state legislature, exemplifies the incumbency feature of the selection model. She embodies the political stances of many of her constituents so well that she ran unopposed from her first election as a state representative in 1996 through 2004, when she had only token opposition. Her constituents judge her aligned objectives and internal motivation and the alignment of her motives with theirs on the basis primarily of a reputation established over time among informed activists and spread through informal networks.

learned the ropes, made the contacts, become expert on relevant policies, and, as a result of experience, has more impact on legislative outcomes than a newcomer could have.[81]

In a selection model, voters do not exercise control over the institutions of government by exercising control over the *representative*, getting the representative to do something the representative would otherwise not do through the threat of being voted out. In a pure selection model, voters would have zero control over the representative. Rather, voters get the *legislature* to do what it would otherwise not do by placing in it a representative who will pursue the policies that they favor. The voters' ultimate goal is not control over a particular representative but a fair share of control over the entire legislature. In a selection model, as we have seen, incumbency usually increases the voters' control over the legislature by making the instrument of their control, the representative, more effective.

The negative side to incumbency derives primarily from the difficulty of removing the representative. Normatively, the viability of the selection model depends not only on good information at the times of initial selection and potential de-selection but also on ease of removal when the selected representative is no longer aligned with the constituents' needs and desires. Yet in contrast to incumbency itself, certain advantages that come with incumbency lower "electoral control"[82] in both a sanctions and a selection model. Although necessarily facing fixed terms and the requirement of reelection, incumbents can draw, unlike challengers, on the renown that comes with their office as well as on gratitude for past policy work and constituency service. The franking privilege, staff, and travel allowances that let them communicate appropriately with their constituents are paid from government budgets, while challengers must pay for equivalent publicity from their pockets or by raising money from supporters. Thus if the legislator changes (becoming lazy, corrupt, legislature-centered, or simply tired of going out on the hustings) or if the constituency changes (through district boundary changes, generational or mobility replacement, or an exogenous policy shock), the very capacities for communication and trust-building that are normatively positive features of incumbency when representative and constituents are well aligned make it harder for challengers to get their credentials before the public when that alignment slips.

Incumbency, in short, can indicate either genuine constituent satisfaction or constituent disempowerment. Interrogating each incumbency requires first asking

---

[81]This pattern would hold even without institutional seniority advantages in the legislature. In the ideal, each citizen should have equal control over the legislature. It seems hard to produce this result, however, without forbidding the accumulation of experience among legislators, a course that has normative and practical costs.

[82]Ansolabehere and Snyder 2002, p. 329. Note that "incumbency *advantage*" is no more than "the increment to the vote margin that a candidate gains by virtue of being the incumbent" (Erikson and Wright 1993, p. 100); it does not include the underlying partisan advantage accruing from a relatively homogeneous political district (Alford and Brady 1989; Oppenheimer 2005, p. 137).

"SELECTION MODEL" OF POLITICAL REPRESENTATION

some questions with relatively easy answers: Does the representative by and large promote policies and a larger political direction that the majority of constituents approve? How satisfied are the majority and minority of constituents with their representative? It also requires questions that are harder to answer: Is satisfaction (or dissatisfaction) with the representative the result of ignorance or manipulation? Have scandals, indications of corruption, or other derelictions of duty affected the incumbent's majority? Will the existing media system publicize departures from citizen preferences or interests? Is there a lively set of interest groups that could bring attention to such departures and promote policies that would not otherwise be on the agenda? Are the citizens active in other forms of politics and therefore able to inform themselves easily and take action skillfully if their current representative no longer seems appropriate? Is the internal party system vital, self-policing, and continually infused with new activists and new ideas, or is it dormant, in the pocket of the incumbent, and relatively closed to newcomers? Although it is not easy to answer such questions, such an effort is required before we treat high rates of incumbency as evidence of democratic failure.

In addition to possibly signaling reduced voter control over democratic institutions due to incumbency advantage or corruption, extended incumbency may also exact a price in citizen activism. One would expect even positive, genuinely chosen, incumbency to undermine citizen political activity because once constituents have selected an honest and competent representative with approximately their own political views, they can turn to other matters, letting the representative get on with the business of politics. If representatives retain their constituents' loyalties and thus face few challenges at election time, the voters also will not have the stimulus of a close election to bring their attention back to politics. Yet the picture is not completely bleak. In some contexts, homogeneous districts with long-standing incumbents and satisfied constituents free up citizens for other forms of citizen activism.[83]

Nor would a theorist of common-interest politics like Rousseau value highly the forms of political participation that derive from either fascination with a close electoral race or fear of one's own side losing that race. Rousseau wanted citizens to "fly to the assemblies" in order to do their part in bringing a good polity into being, not because they feared that the other side might win.[84] A politics that produces turnout through enmity or conflicting material interests is not likely to cultivate attachment to the common interest. Thus while a selection model of

---

[83]E.g., with Alice Wolf in the Massachusetts legislature, turnout rates in her district drop, because only those who make a fetish of citizen duty bother to vote in an election for a representative who runs unopposed or with only token opposition. Yet that district (Cambridge, Massachusetts) is a relative hotbed of political activity despite having senators and representatives in the national and state governments whom the voters rarely replace. While far from typical, the city makes the point that competitive elections are not always necessary for citizen activism.

[84]Because Rousseau ([1762] 1997) opposed a representative conception of sovereignty, his views may not be thought relevant on this point. Yet he also painted a more compelling picture than any other theorist of the decline of a polity when its citizens fail to desire the common good.

political representation may reduce citizen activism, that result is far from necessary. And the close race that is the ideal of many a political scientist does not have indisputably positive normative qualities.

When a selection model of political representation is feasible, it may be better to look for incentives to citizen activism less in the process of electing representatives than in more direct forms of action. Citizen initiatives, now used only to initiate referenda, could trigger mandatory public hearings in which elected representatives or the bureaucrats responsible for an unpopular policy face questions and objections from the public and have to explain their reasons for these policies. Such citizen initiatives could also trigger representative citizens' assemblies composed of randomly selected citizens and modeled loosely on the ancient Greek system of the lot. Local, state, and national ombuds offices could accept individual and group petitions and class action cases. Citizen-directed vouchers allocating tax monies could fund associations to represent different political interests. Police beat meetings, participatory budgets and other empowered institutions in which citizens act directly could make or heavily influence policy at the local level.[85] Citizen action in these realms would not substitute for but could enhance the relationships citizens have with their representatives.

IX. CONCLUSION: THE NORMATIVE SIDE OF SELECTION

Ideally, politics should not be a market relationship. Voting for one candidate rather than another should not be like buying one toaster rather than another. At its best political representation demands a communicative relationship. In political representation, "we," plural, have many relationships with our representatives. We do not always agree with our representatives or one another, and we have conflicting interests with our representation and with one another. Accordingly, in any instance the representative-constituent relationship as well as the constituent-constituent relationship may be fraught with tension. In this tension, if the representative cares only about votes and the minorities in the constituency do not have enough votes, cannot get them, and cannot work in coalition, that ends the story. In a selection model much depends on the character of a representative's internal motivation. Normatively, such a representative should be open to persuasion. Even losing minorities should be able to respect the representative while making a deliberative case to both other citizens and their common representative that the representative's policy choice was wrong.

The characters of the representative and the constituents are also formed in the representative-constituent relation. A sanctions model, based on inducing a representative's preferences through the threat of electoral defeat replaces an

[85]See e.g., Warren and Pearse (2008); Schmitter (1995); essays in Fung and Wright (2003).

expectation of common interest between representative and constituent with an expectation that the representative will "shirk," ideologically or in other ways, and that sanctions are therefore necessary to bring her to heel. Such expectations are sometimes amply warranted. But they are not costless. They affect who will enter politics, what relationships they will attempt to establish with their constituents, and how those constituents will see the political system. A selection model, when feasible, will attract more internally-motivated candidates into politics. The character of these representatives and their approaches to politics will in turn affect how the constituents think of their polity and what they want from it.

Despite its disadvantages, in short, the selection model has several normatively satisfying features. It couples intrinsic motivation on the part of the representative with control (over the legislature, not the representative) on the part of the voter. Constituents will tend to get behavior that is more dedicated, more adaptive to long-run goals, and more flexible in the means from an honest, competent representative who intrinsically wants to pursue the same kinds of policies the constituents want than from a representative who, seeking only reelection, responds only to the promise of votes or the threat of withdrawing those votes. The harder it is to monitor and sanction, the more reason constituents have to distrust a representative who acts only for such extrinsic rewards.

Beyond efficiency, constituents can take some satisfaction from the quality of their relationship with an intrinsically motivated representative. A selection model privileges commitment to the common interest over the more self-interested motive of desiring reelection. Many constituents can also feel—correctly—that their representative is like them, at least in policy objectives and often in their overall approach to life. The constituent-representative relationship can be one of trust, even warmth. Although distant, it can partake of some of the characteristics of friendship, with an expectation of common interests. Without knowing each other personally, both partners in the relationship can wish the other well. Particularly in a country as populous as the United States, close communication between represented and representative is difficult on a national scale, making this kind of relationship hard to foster. A selection model both builds on and creates such relationships.

A "contingency" theory adapts the size of the selection core and sanction periphery to the empirical context. While monitoring should never be entirely absent and representatives should always be removable, a selection model works well in relatively uncorrupt polities where, by and large, representatives sort themselves into districts where they can present themselves as being what they are and internally want to be, and where constituents have sufficient information at the time of selection to make a reasonable choice. When feasible, a selection model will direct the attention of constituent and representative to the common interest and will foster that interest. It will also be more efficient than a model based on monitoring and sanctions. Thus whenever the ingredients of self-motivated agents, aligned objectives, and the appropriate selecting and sorting mechanisms are available, democracies that can base their representative systems primarily on selection will tend to succeed in competition with societies in which the political system has to operate primarily through sanctions.

REFERENCES

Aberbach, Joel. 1990. *Keeping a Watchful Eye: The Politics of Congressional Oversight.* Washington, DC: Brookings.

Alford, John R. and David W. Brady. 1989. Personal and partisan advantage in U.S. congressional elections, 1846–1986. In Lawrence C. Dodd and Bruce I. Oppenheimer (eds), *Congress Reconsidered,* 4th ed. Washington, DC: CQ Press.

Andersen, Kristi and Goldie Shabad. 1979. Candidate evaluation by men and women. *Public Opinion Quarterly,* 43, 18–35.

Anechiaro, Frank and James B. Jacobs. 1996. *The Pursuit of Absolute Integrity: How Corruption Control Makes Government Ineffective.* Chicago: University of Chicago Press.

Ansolabehere, Stephen and James M. Snyder. 2002. The incumbency advantage in U.S. elections: an analysis of state and federal offices, 1942–2000. *Election Law Journal,* 1, 315–38.

Baron, James N. and David Kreps. 1999. *Strategic Human Resources.* New York: Wiley.

Barro, Robert J. 1973. The control of politicians: an economic model. *Public Choice,* 14, 19–42.

Behn, Robert D. 2001. *Rethinking Democratic Accountability.* Washington, DC: Brookings Institution Press.

Bender, Bruce and John R. Lott, Jr. 1996. Legislator voting and shirking: a critical review of the literature. *Public Choice,* 87, 67–100.

Bernstein, Robert A. 1989. *Elections, Representation, and Congressional Voting Behavior: The Myth of Constituency Control.* Englewood Cliffs, N.J.: Prentice Hall.

Besley, Timothy. 2004. Paying politicians: theory and evidence. *Journal of the European Economic Association,* 2, 193–215.

Besley, Timothy. 2005. Political selection. *Journal of Economic Perspectives,* 19, 43–60.

Besley, Timothy. 2006. *Principled Agents? The Political Economy of Good Government.* Oxford: Oxford University Press.

Besley, Timothy and Stephen Coate. 1997. An economic model of representative democracy. *Quarterly Journal of Economics,* 112, 85–114.

Besley, Timothy and Maitreesh Ghatak. 2005. Competition and incentives with motivated agents. *American Economic Review,* 95, 616–36.

Bianco, William T. 1994. *Trust: Representatives and Constituents.* Ann Arbor: University of Michigan Press.

Bishop, Bill. 2008. *The Big Sort: Why the Clustering of America is Tearing Us Apart.* Boston: Houghton Mifflin.

Bohnet, Iris, Bruno S. Frey and Steffen Huck. 2001. More order with less law: on contract enforcement, trust, and crowding. *American Political Science Review,* 95, 131–44.

Bohnet, Iris and Felix Oberholzer-Gee. 2002. Pay for performance: motivation and selection effects. In Bruno S. Frey and Margit Osterloh (eds), *Successful Management by Motivation.* Berlin: Springer.

Brennan, Geoffrey. 1996. Selection and the currency of reward. In Robert E. Goodin (ed.), *The Theory of Institutional Design.* Cambridge: Cambridge University Press.

Brunell, Thomas L. 2006. Rethinking redistricting: how drawing uncompetitive districts eliminates gerrymanders, enhances representation, and improves attitudes toward Congress. *PS: Political Science & Politics*, 39, 77–85.

Buchanan, James. 1989. The public choice perspective. *Essays on the Political Economy*. Honolulu: University of Hawaii Press.

Buchler, Justin. 2005. Competition, representation and redistricting: the case against competitive Congressional districts. *Journal of Theoretical Politics*, 17, 431–63.

Burke, Edmund. [1774] 1889. Speech to the electors of Bristol. *The Works of the Right Honorable Edmund Burke, Vol. 2*. Boston: Little Brown.

Carr, Frank. 1999. The public service ethos: decline and renewal? *Public Policy and Administration*, 14, 1–16.

Chambers, Simone. 2004. Behind closed doors: publicity, secrecy, and the quality of deliberation. *Journal of Political Philosophy*, 12, 389–410.

Cox, Gary W. and Jonathan N. Katz. 2002. *Elbridge Gerry's Salamander: The Electoral Consequences of the Reapportionment Revolution*. Cambridge: Cambridge University Press.

Deci, Edward L., Richard Koestner, and Richard M. Ryan. 1999. A meta-analytic review of experiments examining the effects of extrinsic rewards on intrinsic motivation. *Psychological Bulletin*, 125, 627–68.

Deci, Edward L. and Richard M. Ryan. 1985. *Intrinsic Motivation and Self-determination in Human Behavior*. New York: Plenum.

Delli Carpini, Michael X. and Scott Keeter. 1996. *What Americans Know about Politics and Why it Matters*. New Haven, Conn.: Yale University Press.

Dixit, Avinash. 2002. Incentives and organizations in the public sector: an interpretative review. *Journal of Human Resources*, 37, 696–727.

Downs, Anthony. 1957. *An Economic Theory of Democracy*. New York: Harper and Row.

Eliasoph, Nina. 1998. *Avoiding Politics: How Americans Produce Apathy in Everyday Life*. Cambridge: Cambridge University Press.

Elster, Jon. 1995. Strategic uses of argument. In Kenneth Arrow et al. (eds), *Barriers to Conflict Resolution*. New York: Norton.

Elster, Jon. 1998. Deliberation and constitution making. In Jon Elster (ed.), *Deliberative Democracy*. Cambridge: Cambridge University Press.

Erikson, Robert S. 2006. Warren E. Miller and Donald E. Stokes, 1963. *American Political Science Review*, 100, 674.

Erikson, Robert and Gerald C. Wright. 1993. Voters, candidates, and issues in congressional elections. In Lawrence C. Dodd and Bruce I. Oppenheimer (eds), *Congress Reconsidered*, 5th ed. Washington, DC: CQ Press.

Fearon, James. 1999. Electoral accountability and the control of politicians: selecting good types versus sanctioning poor performance. In Adam Przeworski, Susan C. Stokes, and Bernard Manin (eds), *Democracy, Accountability, and Representation*. New York: Cambridge University Press.

Fenno, Richard F., Jr. 1978. *Home Style: Members in their Districts*. Boston: Little, Brown.

Fenno, Richard F., Jr. 2007. *Congressional Travels: Places, Connections, and Authenticity*. New York: Pearson/Longman.

Ferejohn, John. 1986. Incumbent performance and electoral control. *Public Choice*, 50, 5–25.

Ferejohn, John and Frances Rosenbluth. 2009. Electoral representation and the aristocratic thesis. In Ian Shapiro, Susan Stokes, Elisabeth Wood and Alexander Kirshner (eds), *Political Representation*. Cambridge: Cambridge University Press.

Finer, Herman. 1941. Administrative responsibility in democratic government. *Public Administration Review*, 1, 335–50.

Fiorina, Morris. 1974. *Representatives, Roll Calls, and Constituencies*. Lexington Mass.: Lexington Books, D. C. Heath.

Fisher Roger and William Ury. 1981. *Getting to Yes: Negotiating to Agreement without Giving In*. Boston: Houghton Mifflin.

Follett, Mary Parker. [1925] 1942. Constructive Conflict. In Henry C. Metcalf and L. Urwick (eds), *Dynamic Administration: The Collected Papers of Mary Parker Follett*. New York: Harper.

Frank, Robert H. 1988. *Passions within Reason: The Strategic Role of the Emotions*. New York: Norton.

Frey, Bruno S. 1997. A constitution for knaves crowds out civic virtues. *Economic Journal*, 107, 1043–53.

Friedrich, Carl J. 1940. Public policy and the nature of administrative responsibility. In Carl Friedrich and Edward S. Mason (eds), *Public Policy: A Yearbook of the Graduate School of Public Administration*. Cambridge, Mass.: Harvard University Press.

Fung, Archon and Eric Olin Wright, eds. 2003. *Deepening Democracy*. New York: Verso.

Gay, Claudine. 2002. Spirals of trust: the effect of descriptive representation on the relationship between citizens and their government. *American Journal of Political Science*, 46, 717–32.

Goodin, Robert E. 1980. Making moral incentives pay. *Policy Sciences*, 12, 131–45.

Goodin, Robert E. 1982. *Political Theory and Public Policy*. Chicago: University of Chicago Press.

Goodin, Robert E. 2003. Democratic accountability: the distinctiveness of the third sector. *European Journal of Sociology*, 44, 359–96.

Guinier, Lani. 1994. *The Tyranny of the Majority: Fundamental Fairness in Representative Democracy*. New York: Free Press.

Hamilton, Alexander. [1788] 1961. Federalist 76. *The Federalist Papers*. New York: New American Library.

Herzog, Don. 1998. *Poisoning the Minds of the Lower Orders*. Princeton, N.J.: Princeton University Press.

Horowitz, Donald R. 2003. Electoral systems: a primer for decision-makers. *Journal of Democracy*, 14, 115–27.

Issacharoff, Samuel. 2002a. Gerrymandering and political cartels. *Harvard Law Review*, 116, 593–648.

Issacharoff, Samuel. 2002b. Why elections? *Harvard Law Review*, 116, 684–695.

Kartik, Navin and R. Preston McAfee. 2007. Signaling character in electoral competition. *American Economic Review*, 97, 852–70.

Keohane, Robert O. and Joseph S. Nye. 2001. The club model of multilateral cooperation and problems of democratic legitimacy. In Roger B. Porter, Pierre Sauvé, Arvind Subramanian, and Americo Beviglia Zampetti (eds), *Efficiency, Equity, and Legitimacy: The Multilateral Trading System at the Millennium*. Washington, DC: Brookings Institution Press.

Kingdon, John W. 1973. *Congressmen's Voting Decisions*. New York: Harper & Row.

Kingdon, John W. 1981. *Congressmen's Voting Decisions*. 2nd ed, New York: Harper & Row.

Kruglanski, Arie W., Aviah Riter, Asher Amitai, Bath-Shevah Margolin, Leorah Shabtai, and Daliah Zaksh. 1975. Can money enhance intrinsic motivation? A test of the content-consequence hypothesis. *Journal of Personality and Social Psychology*, 31, 744–50.

Lawless, Jennifer L. and Richard L. Fox. 2005. *It Takes a Candidate: Why Women Don't Run for Office*. Cambridge: Cambridge University Press.

Lee, David S., Enrico Moretti, and Matthew J. Butler. 2004. Do voters affect or elect policies? Evidence from the U.S. House. *Quarterly Journal of Economics*, 119, 807–60.

Lodge, Juliet. 1994. Transparency and democratic legitimacy. *Journal of Common Market Studies*, 32, 343–68.

Lott, John R., Jr. 1987. Political cheating. *Public Choice*, 52, 169–186.

Magnette, Paul. 2003. European governance and civic participation: beyond elitist citizenship? *Political Studies*, 51, 144–60.

Manin, Bernard. 1997. *Principles of Representative Government*. Cambridge: Cambridge University Press.

Mansbridge, Jane. 1980. *Beyond Adversary Democracy*. New York: Basic Books.

Mansbridge, Jane. 1990. The rise and fall of self-interest. In Jane Mansbridge (ed.), *Beyond Self-Interest*. Chicago: University of Chicago Press.

Mansbridge, Jane. 1999. Altruistic trust. In Mark Warren (ed.), *Democracy and Trust*. Cambridge: Cambridge University Press.

Mansbridge, Jane. 2003. Rethinking representation. *American Political Science Review*, 97, 515–28.

Mayhew, David R. 1974. Congress: *The Electoral Connection*. New Haven, Conn.: Yale University Press.

McCubbins, Matthew S. and Thomas Schwartz. 1984. Congressional oversight overlooked. *American Journal of Political Science*, 28, 166–201.

McGregor, Douglas. 1960. *The Human Side of Enterprise*. New York: McGraw-Hill.

Miller, Dale T. 1999. The norm of self-interest. *American Psychologist*, 54, 1053–60.

Miller, Warren E. and Donald E. Stokes. 1963. Constituency influence in Congress. *American Political Science Review*, 51, 45–56.

Moe, Terry M. 1990. Political institutions: the neglected side of the story. *Journal of Law, Economics, and Organization*, 6, 213–53.

Mutz, Diana C. 2006. *Hearing the Other Side: Deliberative Versus Participatory Democracy*. Cambridge: Cambridge University Press.

Nye, Joseph S. 1967. Corruption and political development: a cost-benefit analysis. *American Political Science Review*, 61, 417–27.

Naurin, Daniel. 2004. Transparency and legitimacy. In Lynn Dobson and Andreas Follesdal (eds), *Political Theory and the European Constitution*. London: Routledge.

O'Neill, Onora. 2002. *A Question of Trust*. Cambridge: Cambridge University Press.

Oppenheimer, Bruce I. 2005. Deep red and blue congressional districts: the causes and consequences of declining party competitiveness. In Lawrence C. Dodd and Bruce I. Oppenheimer (eds.), *Congress Reconsidered*, 8th ed. Washington, DC: CQ Press.

Persily, Nathaniel. 2002. In defense of foxes guarding henhouses: the case for judicial acquiescence to incumbent-protecting gerrymanders. *Harvard Law Review*, 116, 684–95.

Pettit, Philip. 2008. Representation, responsive and indicative. Paper presented at the Workshop on Representation Beyond Elections, Princeton University, December 5–6.

Pettit, Philip. 2009. Varieties of public representation. In Ian Shapiro, Susan Stokes, Elisabeth Wood and Alexander Kirshner (eds), *Political Representation*. Cambridge: Cambridge University Press.

Philp, Mark. 2004. *Accountability and Democracy: A Millean View*. Unpublished mansucript.

Popkin, Samuel L. 1991. *The Reasoning Voter: Communication and Persuasion in Presidential Campaigns*. Chicago: University of Chicago Press.

Pratt, John W. and Richard J. Zeckhauser, eds. 1985. *Principals and Agents: The Structure of Business*. Boston: Harvard Business School Press.

Prewitt, Kenneth. 1970. Political ambitions, volunteerism, and electoral accountability. *American Political Science Review*, 64, 5–17.

Rhode, Paul W. and Koleman S. Strumpf. 2003. Assessing the importance of Tiebout sorting: local heterogeneity from 1850 to 1990. *American Economic Review*, 93, 1648–77.

Rothenberg, Lawrence S. and Mitchell S. Sanders. 2000. Severing the electoral connection: shirking in the contemporary congress. *American Journal of Political Science*, 44, 316–25.

Rousseau, Jean-Jacques. [1762] 1997. The social contract. In *The Second Contract and Other Later Political Writings*, trans. Victor Gourevitch. Cambridge: Cambrige University Press.

Saward, Michael. 2006. The representative claim. *Contemporary Political Theory*, 5, 297–318.

Schmitter, Philippe C. 1995. The irony of modern democracy and efforts to improve its practice. In Erik Olin Wright (ed.), *Associations and Democracy*. New York: Verso.

Schumpeter, Joseph. [1942] 1962. *Capitalism, Socialism, and Democracy*. New York: Harper and Row.

Shapiro, Susan P. 2005. Agency theory. *Annual Review of Sociology*, 31, 263–84.

Sigelman, Lee. 2006. The coevolution of American political science and the *American Political Science Review*. *American Political Science Review*, 100, 463–78.

Steiner, Jurg, André Bächtiger, Markus Spörndli, and Marco R. Steenbergen. 2004. *Deliberative Politics in Action: Analyzing Parliamentary Discourse*. Cambridge: Cambridge University Press.

Stimson, James A., Michael Mackuen and Robert Erikson. 1995. Dynamic representation. *American Political Science Review*, 89, 543–65.

Storing, Herbert J., ed. 1981. *The Complete Anti-Federalist*. Chicago: University of Chicago Press.

Sunstein, Cass R. 2003. *Why Societies Need Dissent*. Cambridge, Mass.: Harvard University Press.

Tocqueville, Alexis de. [1835] 1969. *Democracy in America*, trans. George Lawrence. Garden City, N.Y.: Anchor Press.

Warren, Mark and Hilary Pearse. 2008. *Designing Deliberative Democracy: The British Columbia Citizens' Assembly*. Cambridge: Cambridge University Press.

Weisbrod, Burton Allen. 1988. *The Nonprofit Economy*. Cambridge, Mass.: Harvard University Press.

17

Representation, Responsive and Indicative

Philip Pettit

Let us assume that one party, A, represents another, B, if and only if A, with B's authorization, purports to speak or act for B. B may authorize A directly, or may authorize the rules under which A is selected to speak or act, and in either event the authorization may consist in a positive endorsement or in a failure to exercise a capacity to disendorse. Building on this assumption about the nature of representation, let us assume in addition that there is some dimension in which the representing party is supposed to be faithful to the represented party so that, depending on the degree of fidelity displayed, the representer may perform better or worse in the representational role: the degree of fidelity provides a criterion for judging the quality of the representation.

These assumptions about the nature and quality of representation put important restrictions on the topic to be addressed here. Thus they mean that A may be statistically – or, more generally, descriptively[1] – representative of B without being a representer in our sense. And they mean that A may be an advocate for B without being a representer in that sense.[2] But they still leave a large number of issues open. The relationship envisaged may vary in three more or less familiar ways.

- It may be a relationship between one representer and one representee, or it may assume the form of one-many, many-many or, at the limit, many-one representation. The one-many representation is exemplified by the relationship of a member of parliament to a constituency; many-many by the relationship between congress and the people as a whole.[3]
- The dimension in which the representer is supposed to be faithful to the representee may be more or less constraining. The representer may just be expected to speak or act on the basis of her own best judgment; or, going to the other extreme, to act according to the preferences or judgments of the representee; or, in between, to act according to the representee's interests or values. The less constrained representer will count as a trustee, the more constrained as a delegate.[4]
- However fully authorized, the relationship may or may not give the representee a certain control over how faithful the representer is. Where there is representee-control, the factors that support it may include: a power of selection, a power of deselection, constraints on the process of representative action, constraints on the domain of representative action, and exposure to scrutiny and contestation.

In this essay, I want to introduce another respect in which the relationship of representation may vary. Representation may be responsive in character, as I put it, or rather, it may be indicative. This distinction has been unduly neglected, because theorists have focused mainly on the responsive variety of representation, and this essay is designed to help correct the balance.[5] The discussion is in three sections. In the first, I present the distinction in an abstract form. Then in the second, I describe some ways in which indicative representation has been recognized, side by side with responsive representation, in the tradition of political thought. And, finally, in the third section, I ask after the lessons that the recognition of indicative representation has for democratic politics today.

1. The Basic Distinction

Imagine that I am invited to take part in a committee – say, a University committee to inquire into how philosophy may be made as attractive to female students as to male. And suppose that I am unable to serve on the committee myself and am given the right to appoint a member in my stead. I accept the offer and think about who I should choose. Believing that the issue is important and trusting in my own values or interests, I want someone who serves in my place to reflect the same attitudes and to speak or act in a way that is faithful to those attitudes.

In this situation I might want to put someone on the committee who will be responsive to my wishes as to how the job should be done: someone who will serve as my deputy. In that case, I will look for a relationship in which I can make those wishes known and exercise some control, say by having the representer consult me. The wishes to which I want to make the representer responsive may be more or less constraining. I may just have a wish that the person should take time and trouble over the committee work, displaying suitable procedural interests or values in the committee's decision-making.[6] Or I might wish that the person should further certain substantive rather than procedural interests or values, supporting decisions of a particular character. Or I might wish, even more constrainingly, that the person implement my instructions on every vote and every decision.

But this is not the only way in which I might seek to be represented on the committee. Instead of seeking to install a responsive deputy, at whatever level of constraint, I might opt for having someone on the committee who shares my general attitudes, whether on procedural or substantive matters, and is likely to vote accordingly. I will not expect this person to be responsive to me. I may be happy that she does not know what my attitudes are or even know that I nominated her. I will choose her as a representer because her mentality is indicative of my own. Where she is led in her judgments and decisions, I would be likely to be led, if I were on the committee. Or so at any rate I believe.

This form of representation, like the other variety, would give me a certain control over the committee's reflections and decisions. The representer will not be a responsive deputy, ready to track what I think, whether on procedural or substantive matters. But, if I have chosen well, she will be a reliable indicator of my general attitudes and of where or how I would go on particular issues, were I a member of the committee. I exercise a certain control through her insofar as I chose her for the prospect that she will reflect my attitudes. We might describe her as an indicative proxy rather than a responsive deputy.

The control that I exercise in either of these cases might be increased, of course, with the help of other devices. The control I wield by courtesy of the responsive deputy or the indicative proxy will be increased if I have the power of de-selection as well as selection. And it also likely to be increased if the committee is constrained in a manner that guards against wayward influences. Thus the representative may be forced to make her decisions in a process of salutary interaction with certain other bodies or officials. Or she may be subjected to appropriate limits on the domain of committee action. Or she may be required to defend her decisions under public scrutiny and interrogation. And so on through a number of possibilities.

The essential difference between responsive and indicative representation is easily stated. In responsive representation, the fact that I am of a certain mind offers reason for expecting that my deputy will be of the same mind; after all, she will track what I think at the appropriate level. In indicative representation things are exactly the other way around. The fact that my proxy is of a certain mind offers reason for expecting that I will be of the same mind; that is what it means for her to serve as an indicator rather than a tracker. From the point of view of my being represented on the committee, having someone there who reflects my mind, it really does not matter whether the representer is a reliable tracker or indicator. This may not even matter from the point of view of my having some control over the committee. Given a power of selection and any of a number of other devices, I can exercise control via the presence of the deputy or the proxy. Either figure can give me a presence on the committee, as we say; either can re-present me.

The distinction between responsive and indicative representation is not my own invention, though it has not been explicitly invoked in the political domain and the terms in which I am drawing it are relatively novel. It parallels a distinction in epistemology between two ways in which my beliefs may be reliable: that is, reliable representers of the world they depict. They may be reliable trackers of facts about the world, so that if such and such is the case, then it is likely that I believe such and such. Or they may be reliable indicators of worldly facts, so that if I believe such and such then such and such is likely to be the case.[7]

Just as beliefs may relate in either way to the facts they purport to represent epistemically, so representers may relate in either way to the representees that they purport to represent in a political fashion. It may be the case that if a representee has such and such attitudes, at whatever level, then the representer may be expected, in response, to speak and act on those attitudes. Or it may be the case that if the representer speaks and acts on certain attitudes, at whatever level, then the representee may be assumed, given an indicative status, to hold those attitudes. In the first case the attitudes held by the representee are the causal source of the attitudes displayed by the representer; in the second, the attitudes displayed by the representer are a non-causal sign of the attitudes held by the representee. The faithful representer in the first scenario will be reliably responsive to the representee; the faithful representer in the second will be reliably indicative of the representee.

2. The Distinction in Political History

The staple examples of representation that are given countenance in political theory are almost all cases of responsive representation. Pride of place is given to the representation of a constituency by a member of congress or parliament, or the representation of a people by its legislature or executive, and both are responsive, electorally controlled relationships. Government is to be a government of responsive representers: that is, a government of individuals who are elected to track and respond to their constituencies. And at the same time, it is to be a responsively representative government: that is, a government whose electorally disciplined judgments and decisions are supposed to respond to the country as a whole, reflecting public values and opinions.

But where does the idea of indicative representation appear in politics? Where is it recognized in the tradition of political thought? And where does it have application in political institutions?

Three metaphors have dominated the political tradition of thinking about the meaning of representation. Quentin Skinner[8] has recently argued that two of these, associated respectively with the courts and the theater, provide an answer to the responsive idea of representation. As the attorney acts under the explicit or implicit direction of a client, so the idea is that political representers might act as delegated deputies, under the explicit or implicit direction of their representees. And as the actor constructively interprets the mind of a character, so the idea is that representers might serve as trustee deputies in interpreting and enacting the mind of representees. But the third metaphor identified by Skinner is drawn from representation in the pictorial arts, and it maps onto indicative representation. As the painting is indicative of how the subject of the painting looks, so on this image should representers be indicative of representees; they should be fitted to serve as proxies, not – or not just – as deputies.

The idea of indicative representation figures early in democratic theory, since it is the sort of representation that is achieved or is likely to be achieved under the lottery system favored by the Athenians and that also played an important part in later regimes like those of the Italian city-republics.[9] This lottery system might be taken as a version of the technique of random sampling but random sampling put to use in the service of advancing goals espoused by the people as a whole. While it may have been motivated by a desire to have a regular turnover in the representer body, the important thing from our viewpoint is that it would have ensured a degree of proportional and indicative representation.

The indicative idea also appears in the jury system, as that was developed in medieval Europe.[10] To be subjected to the judgment of one's peers, whether in determining that there is a legal case to answer, or that one is legally liable, is to be exposed, not to a random arbiter – a chance enemy, perhaps – but to a body that stands in for the community as a whole. The idea is that the jurors should represent a cross-section of the community or at least of the fully enfranchised members: in medieval Europe, the mainstream, propertied males.[11]

The indicative image of representation is particularly evident in those parliamentarian writers in England of the mid-seventeenth century who look for a "speaking likeness" of the people in those who rule them, "describing Parliament as a "representation" – a picture or portrait – of the body of the people."[12] And, perhaps as a result of that precedent, it became an established element in the thinking of those associated with the American war of independence and the French revolution.

Thus Melanchton Smith could write in 1788, in opposing the American constitution: "The idea that naturally suggests itself to our minds, when we speak of representatives is, that they resemble those they represent; they should be a true picture of the people."[13] Again, the idea was powerfully endorsed in a speech given by Mirabeau to the French Constituent Assembly in January 1789, though he used the image of a map rather than a picture to get it across. According to this version of the model, "a representative body is to the nation what a chart is for the physical configuration of its soil: in all its parts, and as a whole, the representative body should at all times present a reduced picture of the people – their opinions, aspirations, and wishes, and that presentation should bear the relative proportion to the original precisely as a map brings before us mountains and dales, rivers and lakes, forests and plains, cities and towns."[14]

With the growth of electoral machinery, the indicative idea was naturally applied to elections for the legislature, providing support for making the electoral system more and more proportional.[15] Is it also behind the practice of organizing the legislature around geographically dispersed districts? It is hard to believe that it did not play some role in justifying that practice but the evidence, according to Andrew Rehfield,[16] is against this hypothesis. Still, districting does induce a similarity – nowadays a fairly unimportant one – between the population as a whole and the legislature that represents it.

The indicative idea survives in the continuing enthusiasm for proportional representation and has been given new life in campaigns for supplementing electoral representation with novel, statistically representative bodies. It is there in the general policy of organizing citizens' juries that would review various policy issues.[17] And it is present in the notion of the deliberative opinion poll that is chosen as a random sample and then canvassed for its view on one or another issue at two separate times: first, before members of the sample

430   *Constellations Volume 17, Number 3, 2010*

make contact with one another, and second, after they come together to receive background information, to hear different points of view and to debate the right line to take on the issue under consideration.[18]

A particularly striking example of this general device appears in the Citizens' Assembly that was recently established in the Canadian province of British Columbia.[19] A more or less representative sample of 160 citizens was assembled and given the task, over much of 2004, of reviewing the existing electoral system in the light of various hearings and discussions, and making a recommendation on whether or not it should be amended. The group recommended a change that then went to referendum and won more than 50% support but fell short of the quota required to trigger a change.[20]

3. The Lessons for Contemporary Politics

As this review suggests, the main form of recognition that has been traditionally given to the distinction between the two forms of representation – and, in particular, to the role of indicative representation – is associated with the drive for proportionality in elected legislative bodies. John Stuart Mill, in particular, made this a centerpiece of his democratic philosophy and it continues to be a cause that is pushed in political theory.[21]

A first lesson of the discussion so far, however, suggests that this one area where there has been some emphasis on indicative representation is ill selected. Given the different bases of responsive and indicative representation, it is not at all clear that the two modes can be mixed usefully. And making an electoral, purportedly responsive body into a body that is also indicative of the population represented may prove to be a hopeless task.

In order to serve as an indicatively representative body, a legislature would have to meet two conditions. First, it would have to be statistically representative, embodying a range of attitudes that correspond distributively to those in the population at large. And second, its members would have to be disposed to act on those attitudes, reaching conclusions that we might expect the population as a whole to reach, could it operate in a single deliberative assembly. The problem with making an elected legislature proportional is that while proportionality would make for fulfillment of the first condition, the fact that the body is elected is likely to militate against its fulfillment of the second.

The reason for this possible failure is easy to see. The members of a body like the British Columbia Citizens' Assembly are likely to vote as their independently determined attitudes lead them, in light of their deliberation, to do so. They have no ulterior motives that would warp this pattern and it is for that very reason that we can have confidence in the body; we may think that as they are led to vote, so would the population as a whole have voted could they have assembled and deliberated appropriately. But this consideration is not going to apply with an elected body, at least if re-election is a possibility. For the members of such a body are likely to be moved, not just by the independently held attitudes that reflect the spread of attitudes in the community, but also by the desire to be re-elected – or for their party to be re-elected – and, more generally, by the desire to make a good impression on their supporters and on those who provide them with financial and other backing.

But while proportionality may not help to make an elected body indicatively representative, is it likely to help in other ways: say, in establishing a body with which people can generally identify as with a microcosm of their community. It may help in this way, but there is a countervailing consideration to consider as well: that as an elected body becomes more and more proportional, there is less and less likelihood that any one party or close alliance of parties, and so any one package of policies, will prevail. But that means in turn that with every policy to be implemented, there is likely to be a struggle between small groups, as the government seeks to buy off enough support to get a majority. The government in such a situation will certainly be a government of representatives – in Burke's image, it may operate like a "congress of ambassadors" – but it may not be a very representative government. It may put forward a patchwork of policies, each customized to get a suitable majority, that represents an outcome of crude interest-group bargaining. The package may not answer to the values of the community, not having to be defended, as a whole, in terms that all treat as relevant to collective decision-making.[22]

The first, tentative lesson of our discussion, then, is negative: making legislatures more and more proportional will not make them indicative and may have bad representative effects overall. But there are three other lessons that I am inclined to draw and they are more positive in character.

The first of these lessons is that there is very good reason why contemporary democracies might make more use of devices like the British Columbia Citizens' Assembly. Once we see that indicative representation is a bona fide mode of representation, subject to democratic control, the use of this sort of body comes to be very attractive. For clearly a government might make use of such bodies in a variety of contexts, taking their decisions, perhaps subject to approval in a referendum, as guides to legislation or even determinants of legislation. There are many very general issues that government faces where this mode of decision-making would be usefully informed and representative and would carry unassailable democratic credentials. Any objections that might be made to the use of such a device ought to be silenced in light of an appreciation of the possibility of indicative representation.

The second of the positive lessons that I am inclined to draw is less radical but, paradoxically, may be more controversial. It is that once we have the notion of indicative representation on hand, we can see familiar, unelected bodies and authorities as indicatively representative and so possessing, democratic credentials in their own right.

Consider the electoral commission or commissioner who is charged with establishing the boundaries of electoral districts. Or the auditor general who is given the job of reviewing the government's books. Or the bureau of statistics that has the task of making impartially derived statistics public. Or the ombudsman who provides an office for hearing and adjudicating various complaints about government administration. Or the central bank or federal reserve whose role it is to determine interest rates. Or indeed the judges whose brief is to interpret and apply the law impartially.

In standard ways of thinking, such figures – such statutory officers, to use a Westminster term – are authorized because of their mode of appointment by responsive, elected representatives. But authorized to do what? This is a problem for standard theory. The salient answer, that they are authorized like regular bureaucrats to act as agents of the elected representatives, does not fit with the independence they are given. But an alternative answer becomes available once we have the idea of indicative representation on hand. This is that they are authorized to act, in suitable domains, as indicative representers of the people.

In the areas where statutory authorities and bodies operate, it is fairly clear what the interest of the public is, by almost any criterion of public interest. And in these areas, the appointment of people with a professional investment in serving that interest – and, ideally, with a virtuous disposition to further it – promises to serve the public well. Their inclinations ought to conform in general to the requirements of the public interest, at least if they have the virtues of good statisticians, good auditors, good judges, and so on. And so in the relevant domain of public interest, they ought to be reliable, indicative representers of the people at large.

It may be said that giving representative power to statutory figures is a rash move, as it does not allow the people democratic control over their operation. But this is manifestly not so, for the virtue that would make them reliably indicative of the public interest can be strongly reinforced, even elicited, in a suitable institutional context. The individuals and bodies in question can be exposed to parliamentary, executive and popular contestation, constrained by rules for how and where they operate, dismissed for improper performance and subjected to a discipline of re-appointment. And in any case, they can be exposed to reputational constraints that give them a powerful personal interest in avoiding ignominy and winning esteem among their colleagues, and among the public in general.[23]

Can statutory authorities be seen, however, in a distinct, responsive light? Can they be depicted as representers who are responsive to the wishes of the people that they should conduct themselves in office according to a certain brief? This is not, in general, plausible, at least not with the sorts of statutory officers we are inclined to admire. Were they responsive representers of that stripe, then we should expect them to behave in this or that manner, depending on how the wishes of the people varied. But this is precisely what we would not expect of any statutory individual or body that we thought worthy of admiration.

The third positive lesson that I draw from this discussion is that it is not just proportional bodies or statutory appointees who can count as unelected representers of the people. With the category of indicative representation in hand, we also have to recognize the indicatively representative role of the whistle-blowers and complainants who expose abuses in public life or the private citizens who challenge and expose the unconstitutional character of certain laws. These are the "private attorneys general,"[24] so called, who serve the public well by challenging certain laws before the courts, or indeed administrative policies before appropriate tribunals or officials. The fact that the public or people give such complainants a license to use the courts and tribunals as they do – and the fact that they often provide protection against various forms of retaliation – means that these figures are authorized to act in their characteristic manner. When they act, they do so under conditions that are laid down in laws that the public accepts, and so they act under a suitable degree of public control. If their actions ceased to serve the public interest, perhaps creating an intolerable nuisance in the working of the system, then presumably those laws would be changed.

Private attorneys general serve the public well in the aggregate, acting on interests that converge with a manifest public interest. It may not be in the public interest that the law or policy challenged by such a figure is set aside or modified but it will certainly be in the public interest that there is the sort of interrogation of law and policy that private attorneys general trigger. Indeed, this is routinely recognized in the way in which complainants often claim to be acting in the name of the people. Their authorization by the public means that like formally appointed officials, they can be seen as representers who are allowed to play their particular part, because of the indicative relationship between their dispositions and the presumptive dispositions of the people as a whole.

These positive lessons should help to underscore the importance of recognizing that public representation may be indicative as well as responsive. Indicative representers may not be elected but they are nonetheless important for that. Their democratic legitimacy is ensured by the fact that they are still subject to a significant degree of public control. And their democratic utility – indeed their democratic indispensability – is manifested by the unique way in which they can serve the public. The citizen assembly can provide a fine indicator of how the people would go on a certain issue, were they well informed; certainly it may provide a better indicator in many domains than the consensus among elected representatives. Statutory officers can provide a reliable determination of how the public interest is best served

Representation, Responsive and Indicative: Phillip Pettit

in areas where the interests of elected representatives can induce a self-serving instability. And private attorneys general can hold all other representatives, elected and unelected, to standards and interests that have a constitutional or other hold in the community. Democracy is too important to be left to elected politicians alone.[25] We need indicative as well as responsive representation in public life.[26]

NOTES

1. Hanna Pitkin, *The Concept of Representation* (Berkeley: University of California Press, 1972).

2. Nadia Urbinati, "Representation as Advocacy: A Study of Democratic Deliberation," *Political Theory* 28 (2000).

3. Philip Pettit, "Three Varieties of Public Representation," *Representation and Popular Rule*, ed. Ian Shapiro, Susan Stokes, and E.J.Wood (Cambridge: Cambridge University Press, 2008).

4. Pitkin, *The Concept of Representation.*

5. I drafted this paper, and published another on similar lines (see Pettit, "Three Varieties of Public Representation") in ignorance of a wonderfully comprehensive article by Jane Mansbridge ("A "Selection Model" Of Political Representation," *Journal of Political Philosophy* 17 (2009)) that documents the history of a closely related distinction between a sanctions and a selection model of representation and establishes a range of points bearing on how the selection model may be developed. That article is broadly congenial to the viewpoint I defend here, though it is more sanguine about the possibility of combining responsive and indicative representation.

6. I am grateful to Kim Scheppele for making observations that alerted me to the need for recognizing the possibility that procedural considerations might play the same role in responsive representation as considerations of a more substantive kind.

7. Ernest Sosa, *A Virtue Epistemology* (Oxford: Oxford University Press, 2007).

8. Quentin Skinner, "Hobbes on Representation," *European Journal of Philosophy* 13 (2005).

9. Mogens Herman Hansen, *The Athenian Democracy in the Age of Demosthenes* (Oxford: Blackwell, 1991); Daniel Waley, *The Italian City-Republics, 3rd Ed* (London: Longman, 1988).

10. Jeffrey Abramson, *We, the Jury: The Jury System and the Ideal of Democracy* (New York: Basic Books, 1994).

11. It is significant that a supporter of the anti-federalist cause in 1787 could complain that in the enlarged United States there would not be a representative body in legislature or jury "which possesses the same interests, feelings, opinions, and views the people themselves would were they all assembled," Ralph Ketcham, ed., *The Anti-Federalist Papers* (New York: Signet Classic, 2003), 265.

12. Quinten Skinner, "Hobbes on Representation," *European Journal of Philosophy* 13 (2005): 155–184.

13. Ketcham, ed., *The Anti-Federalist Papers*, 342.

14. Hannah F. Pitkin, ed., *Representation* (New York: Atherton Press, 1969), 77.

15. John Stuart Mill, *Considerations on Representative Government* (London: Everyman Books, 1964).

16. Andrew Rehfield, *The Concept of Constituency: Poltical Representation, Democratic Legitimacy, and Institutional Design* (Cambridge: Cambridge University Press, 2005).

17. J. Stewart, E. Kendall, and A Coote, *Citizens' Juries* (London: Institute of Public Policy Researcg, 1994).

18. James S. Fishkin, *The Voice of the People: Public Opinion and Democracy* (New Haven, Conn.: Yale University Press, 1997).

19. Mark E. Warren and Hillary Pearse, eds., *Designing Deliberative Democracy* (Cambridge: Cambridge University Press, 2008).

20. Since everything is a perfect indicator of itself, a limit case of indicative representation is the participatory democracy where the whole population is present to vote, not just a sample. Far from being cast as the contrast point for indicative representation, the compulsory, participatory arrangement can be seen as a special case. The case is so special, however, and so infeasible, that I ignore it in this discussion.

21. Thomas Christiano, *The Rule of the Many: Fundamental Issues in Democratic Theory* (Boulder, Colorado: Westview Press, 1996).

22. See the appendix, written together with Rory Pettit, to Pettit, "Three Varieties of Public Representation." The argument there is that the presidential, Washington system can have the same effect of sacrificing representative government to government by representatives.

Constellations Volume 17, Number 3, 2010

23. Geoffrey Brennan and Philip Pettit, *The Economy of Esteem: An Essay on Civil and Political Society* (Oxford: Oxford University Press, 2004).

24. Jeremy A. Rabkin, "The Secret Life of the Private Attorney General," *Law and Contemporary Problems* 61 (1998).

25. Philip Pettit, "Depoliticizing Democracy," *Ratio Juris* 17 (2004).

26. I was aided greatly in developing this paper by discussion at a workshop on representation in Princeton, December 2008, organized by Nadia Urbinati, Mark Warren and Steve Macedo. I am particularly grateful to Annie Stilz, who was my commentator, and to Jenny Mansbridge and Mark Warren for later exchanges.

18

Feature Article: Theory and Practice

The Representative Claim

Michael Saward

Recent work on the idea of political representation has challenged effectively orthodox accounts of constituency and interests. However, discussions of representation need to focus more on its dynamics prior to further work on its forms. To that end, the idea of the representative claim is advanced and defended. Focusing on the representative claim helps us to: link aesthetic and cultural representation with political representation; grasp the importance of performance to representation; take non-electoral representation seriously; and to underline the contingency and contestability of all forms of representation. The article draws upon a range of sources and ideas to sketch a new, broader and more complex picture of the representative claim which — despite the complexity — helps us to reconnect representation theory to pressing real-world challenges.
Contemporary Political Theory (2006) **5**, 297–318. doi:10.1057/palgrave.cpt.9300234

The Representative Claim

In all fields, real progress sometimes depends on a basic shift in frame of reference. This is the case with the theory of political representation today — or so I shall argue.[1]

It is not that progress is undetectable. There is, of course, a good deal of recent empirical work which seeks to illuminate varied dilemmas of indigenous and minority representation, the representation of women, group representation, descriptive representation in deliberative forums, and the ambiguities of representatives' roles (see for example the essays in Sawer and Zappala, 2001; Saward, 2000; Laycock, 2004). There have been effective challenges to prevailing theoretical views too. Eckersley (2004), Dobson (1996) and Goodin (1996), for example, have sought to extend (in different ways) the notion of representation to encompass the interests of future generations and non-human nature through notions of stewardship and virtual representation. Held (1995) and Thompson (1999) have sought ways to have the interests of non-nationals represented, shaking up the notion of constituency in representative theory.

Phillips (1995) and Young (2000) have stressed the claims of groups to be represented, challenging individualism and the dominance of 'ideas' over 'presence'. Mansbridge (2003) has highlighted the theoretical importance of deliberative representation and surrogacy. Together, such efforts challenge aspects of notions such as election, individualism, fixed constituencies and human constituencies at the heart of the theory of representation.

However, there are limits to how far even this body of work can take us. For one thing, it largely retains a narrow legislature–constituency focus; it seeks to alter electoral and parliamentary systems to allow for more group representation (Phillips, Young), or for proxy representatives of interests other than present-generation human interests (Dobson), or for legislative representation by affected interests beyond national or constituency boundaries (Thompson), or to encourage more sophisticated approaches to the role of deliberative accountability over time in legislative representation (Mansbridge, 2003). Legislatures, constituencies and the institutions they support matter, of course. However, they are not all that matters to political representation. We need to separate analytically (a) what political representation is, and (b) this given (albeit important) institutional instance of it. I hope that move, among others, will enable us to examine representation as a creative process that spills beyond legislatures.

From a slightly different angle, many of the authors mentioned remain focused on *forms* of representation, and thus on expanding or altering existing typologies. In this article I advocate a significant shifting of our frame of reference in order to explore what is going on *in* representation — its dynamics, if you like — rather than what its (old or new) forms might be. Trustees, delegates, politicos, stewards, perspectival representatives — the shifting taxonomies are often illuminating, but they can distract us unduly from grasping what are the wellsprings of such roles. Reframing our efforts to ask directly what is going on in representation should help us to weave together varied disparate threads in recent theoretical and empirical writing, and as part of the same endeavour to question fundamental aspects of the theory of representation. Specifically, I will argue the benefits of refocusing our work on representation around what I call 'the representative claim' — seeing representation in terms of *claims to be representative* by a variety of political actors, rather than (as is normally the case) seeing it as an achieved, or potentially achievable, state of affairs as a result of election. We need to move away from the idea that representation is first and foremost a given, factual product of elections, rather than a precarious and curious sort of claim about a dynamic relationship.

Although my approach initially brackets normative as well as taxonomic concerns, challenging our received ideas about political representation matters.

Consider for example widespread arguments concerning the alleged remoteness of elected politicians in western countries from 'real issues' and core citizen concerns. If we conceive of representation as a zero-sum game (you are either elected, and therefore a representative, or you are not) and as institutionally locked-in (elections alone confer representativeness), then this widely felt remoteness and alienation naturally leads to condemnation of 'representative' government and politics. However, this is both too rigid and politically too conservative a view of representation; careful revisiting of the theory, based around the representative claim, can open our eyes to new and extra modes and styles of representation, electoral and non-electoral, which might in turn help varied actors to address the sense of remoteness and inadequacy.

Consider too new spaces and claims within politics, for example arguments and institutions that enact representation in territorial ways that are alternative to the nation-state (e.g. Held, 1995) — or indeed non-territorial bases of representation, including ones which seek to have non-human interests represented within human polities (Eckersley, 2004). Mainstream thinking about representation limits unduly creative thinking about who, or what, may be represented politically, and how this might be done. However, a conception of representation which stresses its dynamic, claim-based character, its performative aspects as well as its narrowly institutional ones, and its potential for radical extension, can open up new ways for us to think about political inclusion and a more pluralistic representative politics — going an important step further, I would argue, than even provocative work such as Held's or Eckersley's has taken us so far.

The deeper assumptions contained in existing theoretical baggage are best traced through a focused critique of Hannah Pitkin's contemporary classic, *The Concept of Representation* (1967), drawing out influential stipulations which (in my view) have unnecessarily restricted prevailing theoretical approaches to representation. To anticipate some of what is coming, my approach is distinctive in that it: (a) sees claim-making as the core of representation, (b) stresses the performative rather than the institutional side of representation, (c) starts with the micro and works out to the macro, and (d) creates space for creative normative work on radicalizing our notions of who, and what, may count as representative politically, though without setting out a normative stall in the first instance. I start with the critique of Pitkin, before secondly offering a detailed account of the basic currency of political representation, the representative claim. Third, I show how diverse and complex the representative claim can be by mapping key possibilities, and then by showing how aesthetic, cultural and political representation are necessarily bound together in representative claims. Finally, I draw out topics that conventional approaches to political representation often miss, such as the importance of identity to representation, and the constitution of constituency.

300

Hannah Pitkin and Paths not Taken

The thrust of Hannah Pitkin's, *The Concept of Representation* is to suggest that the best way to think of representation is as a 'substantive acting for others', not merely a formal authorization or accountability to others. Representing means 'acting in the interest of the represented, in a manner responsive to them' (1967, 209). Pitkin encourages us to ask: what is it about the representative that makes them representative? Is it something about their appearance, perhaps, or their actions, or more? Her focus is thus resolutely on the representative rather than on the represented; the latter is taken as unproblematically given. A key part of my argument will be that this unidirectional approach is unnecessarily but influentially limiting, in that it has encouraged theorists to underplay the subtle processes of constructing the represented, or that which needs to be represented.

Pitkin divides up the 'various views of the concept' of representation as follows:

(A) 'Authorization', 'accountability' and 'substantive acting for' are three modes of 'acting for' (a person)
(B) (1) descriptive, and (2) symbolic representation are modes of 'standing for' (a person or object)

Views of type A involve activity, 'acting for'. Views of type B are more passive — a person or a thing does not have to do anything in particular in order to 'stand for' something else. These categorizations look reasonable and innocent, but they are not, and it is important to see why. By this very process of categorization Pitkin denies the existence or legitimacy of a category of active symbolic or aesthetic representation. Politically, this involves screening out depictions of the represented by representatives and others. In other words, she screens out by definitional fiat the idea that representatives or their scriptwriters or sponsors are actively engaged in constituting certain ideas or images of their constituents, images which are inevitably partial and selective. And with this, she screens out the idea of 'representations' as depictions or portraits of the represented.[2] Any role in theories of political representation for the maker of representations is reduced by Pitkin to the mere giving of information, in the way a landscape painting might tell the viewer how many trees were in the field that day. For Pitkin, when it comes to symbolic and aesthetic representation, it is the inanimate object — the painting, the icon, the symbol, the map — that represents. The intentions of the maker of the symbol, etc. are either ignored or reduced to merely informational impulses.

Thus denuded of power and interest for politics, Pitkin can write that: 'When this view of representation is applied to the political realm, the implication is that in politics, too, the function of representative institutions is to supply information, in this case about the people or the nation'. 'It is not an "acting for" but a giving of information about, a making of representations about ...' (1967, 83–84). In one deft move, Pitkin sidelines the maker of representations and puts her preferred (highly limited) vision of the politician centre-stage, the politician who acts for others and only secondarily (and less interestingly) offers him or herself as standing for something in a distinctive and selective manner. The represented is transparent; to Pitkin's way of thinking; 'information' can be 'given' about it because it is a known or knowable quantity. The mere transfer of 'information' is enough — information whose ready availability and truthful status Pitkin does not question.[3] In this way, Pitkin defines away what I will argue is a central aspect of political representation — the active making (creating, offering) of symbols or images of what is to be represented.

Part of my goal is to place at centre-stage the necessary figure of the maker of representative claims about themselves and about their audiences. Just as representation is not a mere fact that 'just is', so representations (depictions, portrayals, encapsulations) of self and others in politics do not just happen. People construct them, put them forward, make claims for them — *make* them. More specifically, political figures (or political parties or other groups, for example) make representations of their constituencies, their countries, themselves. Crucially, these representations are an unavoidable part of a 'substantive acting for', and any theory of political representation must take them on board.

Seeing political figures as the makers of representative claims forces us to see in a new light more traditional views of the representative; for example, we need to move well beyond the mandate–independence, delegate–trustee frame for discussing political representation. Both of these perspectives *assume* a fixed, knowable set of interests for the represented: the capacity to be a 'delegate' or a 'trustee' is built precisely upon the more or less transparent knowability of the interests of the represented. However, constituencies can be 'read', inevitably, in various ways. At the heart of the act of representing is the depicting of a constituency *as* this or that, as requiring this or that, as having this or that set of interests. The character of the represented cannot be placed unproblematically to one side. I now set out the basic currency of analysis that can help us to do just that — the representative claim.

The Representative Claim

I have suggested, *contra* Pitkin, that representation in politics is at least a two-way street: the represented play a role in choosing representatives, and representatives 'choose' their constituents in the sense of portraying them or

302

framing them in particular, contestable ways. If I allege that you, a potential constituent of mine, possess key characteristic X, and if I can get you to accept this, I can then present myself as possessing capacity or attribute Y that enables me to represent you — by virtue of a certain resonance between X and Y. In other words, would-be political representatives, in this process of portrayal or representation of constituencies, *make claims* about themselves and their constituents and the links between the two; they argue or imply that they are the best representatives of the constituency *so understood*. Political figures (and their scriptwriters and spin doctors and party supporters, etc.) are in this sense creative actors. They may well be 'agents', as representatives are conventionally understood, but equally or more importantly they are 'actors', makers of claims. The world of political representation is a world of claim-making rather than fact-adducing. Note that, seen in this light, no would-be representative can fully achieve 'representation', or be fully representative. Facts may be facts, but claims are contestable and contested; there is no claim to be representative of a certain group that does not leave space for its contestation or rejection by the would-be audience or constituency, or by other political actors. To argue in this way is to stress the performative side of political representation. Representing is performing, is action by actors, and the performance contains or adds up to a claim that someone is or can be 'representative'. To an important extent, representation is not something external to its performance, but is something generated by the making, the performing, of claims to be representative. To stress the performative is not to downgrade material or institutional aspects of political representation (such as specific electoral systems). I will say more about that below. However, first, let's look at what exactly is going on when representative claims are made. We can map out the broader form of the representative claim, I suggest, in the following way:

A **maker** of representations (**M**) puts forward a **subject** (S) which stands for an **object** (O) which is related to a **referent** (**R**) and is offered to an **audience** (A).

Representation is often seen as triangular in conception — subject, object, referent.[4] However, representation does not just happen as the result of a process or by the functioning of familiar (e.g. electoral) institutions; it is claimed as the key part of someone making it happen[5] through the deployment or exploitation of a wide variety of formal and informal institutions. Subjects (or signifiers) and objects (or signifieds) are not just 'out there', in a certain number and of a certain type. There are 'makers' — spin doctors are a clear enough political example but there are many more — of claims about them, claims which generate and enervate specific senses of subject and object (and which generate and focus upon specific would-be 'audiences'). The makers of representative claims (and the depictions or portrayals of themselves and others that are bound up in those claims), it should be noted, are not necessarily good, or successful, at it. The Conservative Party leader in the UK

REPRESENTATION 379

at the 2005 general election, Michael Howard, and his advisers, made representative claims depicting the British people as deeply concerned by the issue of 'immigration', but the claim was not substantially borne out in the actual vote (a large part of the audience didn't buy the claim at the heart of the performance). Makers of representative claims could be makers of bad, or unacceptable, or unaccepted claims; they could also be makers of compelling, resonant claims about themselves and would-be constituents.

Nor are the makers of representative claims magicians. They cannot simply conjure claims out of the air (or if they do they are highly unlikely to succeed). Representative claims that are compelling, or which resonate among relevant audiences, will be made from 'ready mades', existing terms and understandings which the would-be audience will recognize (see my comments on the cultural aspects of representation below). The style, timing and content of a representative claim must tap into familiar contextual frameworks. Claims must repeat the familiar as well as (indeed, in order to) create something new; must iterate features of political culture to cross a threshold of potential acceptability.[6]

In addition, representative claims only work, or even exist, if 'audiences' acknowledge them in some way, and are able to absorb or reject or accept them or otherwise engage with them. As I have indicated, a representative claim is a double claim: about an aptitude or capacity of a would-be representative, and also about relevant characteristics of a would-be audience (nee constituency). There is little political point in a claim that does not seek to address a specified (national, local, ethnic, religious, linguistic, class or other) audience, and more to the point, to bring a potential audience to a self-conscious notion of itself *as* an audience as the result of claim-making. Representation is produced by processes of claim-making and consequent acceptance or rejection by audiences or parts of audiences. Indeed, we can pinpoint three characteristics and potential effects that are crucial to the power dynamics of the representative claim: audience-creation, reading-back and silencing.

Makers of representative claims attempt to evoke an audience that will receive the claim, and (hopefully, from the maker's point of view) receive it in a certain, desired way. Makers of representative claims suggest to the potential audience: (1) you are/are part of this audience, (2) you should accept this view, this construction — this representation — of yourself, and (3) you should accept me as speaking and acting for you. The aim of the maker of the claim in such cases can be said to be to avoid disputatious 'reading back', or contestation of their claims, by would-be audience members.

However, avoiding 'reading back' by audience members is difficult for claim-makers. It is true that politicians are not like many contemporary artists who create works that are deliberately set up to provoke engagement and even contestation. Political makers of representations tend to foreclose or fix the meanings of themselves and their actions. Nevertheless, there is no representative claim that cannot be 'read back' or contested or disputed by observers or audiences. The maker of a representative claim may intend that the audience invoked by the claim sees it as he wishes, but they are always to some extent free to reinterpret the claim, to turn it back against the maker: 'who are you to tell me what I want?' In the same way that postmodern literary theorists posited the 'death of the author' — readers become authors in that they actively recreate the story through reading — we might say that there is no representative claim without its being open to a counter-claim or a denial from part of the very audience that the claim invokes. This is a point which runs directly counter to what I called above the undue 'unidirectionality' of Pitkin's account of political representation. So for example a claim along the following lines ...

> The MP (maker) offers himself or herself (subject) as the embodiment of constituency interests (object) to that constituency (audience).
> .... may provoke a constituent 'receiving' the representative claim to read it back, dispute it, seek to unmask it by revealing its coded character, etc.

Exploring the effects of representative claims might also include the need to examine the possibility that they include a series of interlinked silencing effects. Claims can by their nature silence the constituencies or people or groups which they constitute by evoking; reinforce, or bring about, or claim the necessity of the absence of the represented from the political arena; appropriate the voice of the represented by the very process of evoking into being a represented with a voice; and become privileged weapons in the hands of elite minorities with privileged access to technologies and institutions of claim-making.

These possibilities — all too often actualities — look at the potential dark side of the processes of representative claim-making. However, in principle the representative claim is neither good nor bad. Representative claims can activate and empower recipients or observers, even if that is not the intention of the makers. Recipients or audiences are 'on the map' by being invoked in representative claims, even if an initial effect of a claim is a silencing one. One needs an identity as *a prior condition* of being silenced by a claim to represent one. Once established, that very identity can be a basis of dissent. This can empower those on the receiving end of claims, for example, to 'read back' the nature of the claim.

For these reasons, then, I have added *makers* and *audiences* to conventional triangular conceptions of representation, which focus in a less political and dynamic, and in a rather bloodless, manner on the subject–object–referent relation only. It is vital to take on board these extra aspects of representation as claim-making. As Louis Marin wrote: '... to represent signifies to present

REPRESENTATION   381

oneself as representing something, and every representation, every sign or representation process, includes a dual dimension — a reflexive dimension, presenting oneself; a transitive dimension, representing something — and a dual effect — the subject effect, and the object effect' (2001, 256). Elsewhere, Marin notes that representations at once signify and show that they signify (2001, 204). Here, Marin makes two crucial points. First, there is no representation without a *claim* that I or you or it represents — maps, paintings, politicians and terrorists are *presented* as representing something or someone, implicitly or explicitly; subject and object are the effects of an act of claim-making. Marin prompts us to take on board the importance of what I am calling the maker of the representative claim. He also usefully separates the maker from the subject (though the two may be the same person). And second, Marin suggests that subject and object are refined and clarified in the process of representation. By making representative claims, the maker-subject constructs a new view of itself. And by presenting the object in a certain way, he or she also constructs a new view of the object. Translated into more directly political terms, an elected politician, for example, makes a claim to be adequately representative of a constituency or their nation each time she speaks for or about it. And each time she does so, she offers a construction or portrayal of herself and of her object (constituency or nation).

So, a representative claim is a claim to represent or to know what represents the interests of someone or something. To use those words is to give it a certain spin, so it is important to note that the claim could be expressed in a variety of .ways. For example, I as a maker of representative claims could ...

Claim to represent	the interests	of a person
Claim to embody	the needs	of a group of people
Claim to stand for	the desires	of a country or region
Claim to know	the wants	of animals
Claim to symbolise	the preferences	of sentient nature
Claim to project	the true character	of non-sentient nature

... to an observer or intended audience. The terms in the three columns can be mixed and matched, within limits (non-sentient nature could not be said to have preferences for example).

My overall argument is that exploring the representative claim can provide us with a rich range of insights and hypotheses about the dynamics of political representation that conventional, and even more recent innovative, views miss, by and large. Not least among these insights are ones about how power relationships are created and exploited through representation. Again, the potential of this broader perspective derives largely from the way in which focusing on representative claims leads us to look at representation as a claim, not as a fact or as the given outcome of a process (electoral or other). The consequent need to examine the evaluation, contestation and legitimacy of representative claims leads us in turn to break through many barriers set up by orthodox thinking on representation. For example (I am only being indicative here), first, the representative claim can come from electoral candidates, party leaders, interest group or NGO figures, local figures, rock stars, celebrities and so on (see Street, 2004). Even innovative studies tend to confine authentic representation to elected figures, whether under existing or new and imaginative electoral and legislative arrangements. Second, the representative claim can never be fully redeemed, always contains ambiguities and instabilities. As such, 'representation' can be said from this perspective not to exist; what exists are *claims* and their receptions. This, I suggest, is a new and liberating perspective which does not privilege particular actors by virtue of their institutional positioning. Third, more than existing literatures this theoretical focus on the claim and its performance forces us to look at representation in its cultural contexts, in a way that chimes, for example with the work of Jean-Pascal Daloz (2003), which shows the great differences in the ways would-be representatives need to disport themselves in different contexts (Nigeria, France and Sweden in his study). Fourth, the claim-based focus opens up what is often taken for granted — the character of constituency and the stability and ready knowability of its interests. Claims play a key role in *constituting* constituencies (or audiences).

I turn now to explicating the representative claim further, focusing on key lines of variation.

Key Lines of Variation of Representative Claims

Highlighting representation as an economy of claims is a way to show how much representation is going on, politically. It happens — claims are made, offered, disputed, and accepted — often and in greatly varied ways, well beyond narrow confines of electoral politics (important though that domain is). I shall now discuss key lines of variation of the representative claim as a way of mapping some of its main features. Under this heading I discuss briefly four axes along which representative claims vary: singular–multiple, particular–general, implicit–explicit and internal–external. The enormous range and scope of the representative claim through these variations is vital to explore; it radically enriches our grasp of the diversity and texture of political representation, bringing together micro-psychological concerns and macro-structural ones within a dynamic framework of representation as claim-making.

REPRESENTATION 383

307

Singular–multiple

There is near-endless scope for variation of a seemingly single claim. Consider how one claim can admit multiple variations.

The MP (maker) offers himself or herself (subject) as the embodiment of constituency interests (object) to that constituency (audience).

The maker could become the party, or the constituency organization, or a wing of the party. The subject could encompass the politician by enveloping him in a wing or faction of the party, for example. Constituency interests could be recast as majority or significant minority interests, or functional group interests or even national interests, or a combination. The audience could be the politician himself, or the party itself, or the government.

These claims come 'all at once'; or one suggests the others; or one is intended but another 'comes across' to audiences ... or observers/potential audiences interpret claims differently from makers or other observers. Mixing and matching, appealing to multiple audiences in economical ways, 'buy one get one free' claims, strategic fomenting of a confusion of claims: all are possible and all happen. Who is represented to whom? Is it more effective to attempt to fabricate multiple audiences within one claim? Why do political figures wish to signal their representativeness to different audiences in different ways, even through the same verbal claim? These are some of the empirical questions that are prompted by attention to the singular–multiple dimension of the representative claim.

Particular–general

The degrees of generality of political representations could crudely enough be divided into two. First, at the most general level, we have claims which concern the basic constitutive character of a political system. One might, for example set out a claim like this:

The founding fathers (makers) deployed the elected offices and assembly (subject) to stand for the nation (object) in the eyes of its people and other watchers (audience).

One could call this a 'framing' claim, one that delimits and defines the contours of the basic system and constitutionalizes or 'encodes' it. I shall say more about coding in the context of the cultural aspect of representation in a moment. Clearly, in modern democracies the coding of representative claims into varied electoral systems is deep and powerful.

Within this frame, we might locate 'strategic' representative claims. For example, these might take the shape of claims which take advantage of the constitutional frame or code of the system. Thus for example a claim might look like this:

The Conservative Party (maker) offers itself (subject) as standing for the interests of 'family' (object) to the electorate (audience).

However, of course representative claims of different levels of generality need not be (and very often are not) about or within electoral politics. Consider for example:

Marx (maker) offered the working class (subject) as the symbol of a revolutionary political future (object) to the would-be members of that class (audience).

If that is a claim at a high level of generality, then it enables more specific claims which (in this case) would-be socialist politicians can call upon for more strategic purposes: for example, 'Marx's theory created the lens through which the politician could see the constituency as standing for united class interests'.

Why does attending to this dimension matter? For example, electoral representative claims do not happen in isolation. They can rely on a background of larger, often deeply institutionalized, claims, and themselves provide a further context for specific claim-making. Representative claims form a complex weave at different levels of generality, a point that conventional views often overlook.

Implicit–explicit

Some representative claims are made openly and outright. Others are perhaps barely recognizable as representative claims, so implicit are they in familiar institutions, actions and rhetoric. A particularly explicit claim might be:

Genoa anti-globalization demonstrators (makers) set up themselves and their movements (subjects) as representatives of the oppressed and down-trodden (object) to western governments (audience)

A much more implicit claim might be:

The MP (maker) offers himself or herself (subject) as the embodiment of constituency interests (object) to that constituency (audience).

I suggest as a hypothesis that explicit claims will most often be made where the claim is new or controversial or unfamiliar, or cuts across conventional codes and categories of representations. Implicit claims will most often be made where the style or the focus of the claim is familiar, and invokes or rests upon accepted representational, often framing or constitutional, codes or institutions. It is worth noting that we are dealing with shades of grey here: a representative claim is never wholly unprecedented, never *entirely* drawing on established or highly familiar codes. However, it matters hugely for us to acknowledge and understand which claims we accept unthinkingly, and which ones strike us as new or troubling. Our cultural and temporal situatedness is a key part of what we need to analyse, since it is that which conditions what sorts

REPRESENTATION 385

of representative claims will be familiar and comfortable, unfamiliar and unsettling.

Internal–external

Two variants of the representative claim are: (1) where the maker and the subject are one and the same person, and (2) where the maker and subject are not the same person. Examples of the first variant include 'I represent ... ' claims. Examples of the second variant include 'She represents', 'They represent', and also 'It represents'. With regard to the first variant, in a nutshell: one cannot present oneself as representing without making representations in the sense of claiming to symbolize something (being a subject); and, one cannot make representations without presenting oneself as someone who can make them.

Note in this context that some representative claims can be almost entirely mental or infra-individual. For example:

I (maker) can think of myself (subject) as representing the interests of my students (object) to myself (audience).

This claim can all happen in my head — behaviour consequent on the representative claim may be evident socially, but the claim itself is wholly internal. This is an example of a highly self-referential representative claim. Rodney Barker (2001), in the related context of legitimation, writes of the importance of this sort of 'legitimation of rulers, by rulers, for rulers' (2001, 45): 'The public, though they may be an audience, have never been the principal audience in the theatre of endogenous legitimation' (2001, 54). A more-or-less endogenous representative claim would consist of largely different components, for example:

I (maker) claim that Bono (subject) symbolizes the needs of debt-ridden societies (object) to western politicians (audience).

Politics displays all shades of representative claims. Private, infra-individual representative claims are ones we have little access to but which may prove to be politically significant. Public, open ones may be more available to contestation on the one hand, and more effective and transforming on the other.

Political Representation: Electoral, Aesthetic *and* Cultural

Conventional views of political representation are concerned with how electoral mechanisms do or do not induce responsive behaviour in elected representatives; whether accountability works prospectively or retrospectively; and what is the appropriate role for the representative to play (see for example

310

Przeworski, Stokes and Manin, 1999). I have argued that such approaches are one-sided and limited — they tend to ignore other political senses of an extraordinarily rich word and set of practices.

The approach recommended here differs, for a start, in that it is more interpretive than normative — it is a conception intended to aid analysis and understanding rather than to support prescription. In this light, a key goal is to graft together insights with respect to aesthetic representation and cultural representation along with electoral representation. There are aesthetic, cultural and (sometimes) electoral moments in political representation. Much of what I have said so far supports this view, but let me say a word about each of these moments explicitly and briefly here.

Representative claims, as we have seen, take place all the time, in local and larger contexts, against a huge variety of backgrounds. The ones that *are* electoral in some sense include the claims that competing candidates make in the course of election campaigns, the claims that others make on their behalf, and the claims of the victor to be representing his or her constituency after the election. However, business and labour organizations, new social movements, individual public figures like Arundhati Roy or Bob Geldof, claim (or are claimed) also to represent politically. Political life in its larger sense consists of myriad, competing, multi-layered and diverse representative claims, pressed and contested in electoral contexts, to be sure, but in many others too.

There is an indispensable *aesthetic* moment in political representation because the represented is never just given, unambiguous, transparent. A representative — or someone making a representative claim — has necessarily to be creative. He or she has to mould, shape, and in one sense create that which is to be represented. She has to be an artist — though, as I have commented above, not necessarily a good one — to operate aesthetically, to evoke the represented. Consider in the above schema the separation between signifier (S), signified or object (O), and referent (R). If an electoral district or constituency's interests were transparent, patently evident, singular and obvious, to most people, then a representative could simply 'read off' those interests and act on them. However, the signified, or the object, is not the same as the thing or district itself (the referent). It is a picture, a portrait, an image of that electorate, not the thing itself. It is no closer to *being* the thing itself than a Rembrandt self-portrait was to Rembrandt himself. Competing significations are precisely what political debate and dispute is all about. The 'interests' of a constituency have to be 'read in' more than 'read off'; it is an active, creative process, not the passive process of receiving clear signals from below. Political figures, parties, lobby groups, social movements — as makers of representative claims, their business is aesthetic *because* it is political.

And political representation is necessarily *cultural* in the sense that there are cultural limits to the types of subject–object links that can plausibly be made in a given context. I have mentioned that representative claims need to be built out of 'ready-mades', even if they are re-interpreted and re-presented in new ways; ready-made tropes like 'I am one of you', 'you can trust me with your futures because I'm straight and honest', 'he's an expert and he understands what's going to work for you and what isn't', tap into existing understandings of what might make for a successful (i.e. accepted) representative claim in a given context. In Stuart Hall's terms, cultural representation is about shared meanings by sharing 'codes': 'Codes fix the relationship between concepts and signs [subject and object in my terms]. They stabilize meaning within different languages and cultures' (Hall, 1997, 21). If the aesthetic moment in political representation is unavoidable — representation cannot function without claims, portrayals of self and other, and the performance of the same — then it is the cultural moment which sets the limits or parameters for the aesthetic possibilities. It centres upon cultural codes which carry meanings in characteristic, more-or-less local ways. These are codes which would-be political representatives can exploit. One way of looking at this is to see 'audiences' as sharing meanings which make them variously receptive or resistant to certain styles of representing, or to certain types of representative claim.

It may seem odd to include formal institutions, including electoral institutions, in this 'cultural' frame but that is a further key dimension. Electoral laws dictating the frequency of elections, vote-counting procedures, the number of representatives to be elected from constituencies, and so on, are settled codes within countries (and states, regions and localities, and within a variety of public and semi-public organizations). These codes, congealed into laws and associated procedures, become familiar and accepted parts of national and other political landscapes. They are critical in helping to constrain and even determine how 'representation' is produced in particular places. However, I would resist confronting the 'institutional' with the 'performative'. Electoral and other institutions, of course, condition the styles of representative claims. However, those institutions are themselves 'performed' or enacted. They are pieces of crucial institutional and constitutional culture.

Every making of a representative claim involves challenging, reinforcing or modifying a certain code, including electoral ones. Cultural codes do not render representative-claim-making a static or predictable affair. Constraint and enablement of the politically feasible in representative politics means that cultural codes are inevitably present, but *no one code* is inevitably present (including sole understandings of electoral laws and the incentive effects they establish for different claims). Let me give an example. We might say that in a

312

political system in which clientelism and patronage — 'providing for your own' — is the key 'code' of electoral politics, then the style of representative claims that electoral candidates and parties offer to voters will be cast accordingly. Within this patronage-driven code there will still be room for varied claims, and for pushing the boundaries of the claim. Coding may be narrow, parochial and highly constraining politically; or it might be open, cosmopolitan and pluralistic. Clearly the range of independent media outlets in a polity, among other factors, will have an impact on cultural codes and their evolution. Cultural codes provide for a delimited but shifting set of exploitable meanings.

Why are codes so important, and culture so important to political representation? Bear in mind the fact that a representation, a political claim, is nothing if it is not heard, seen, or read by its intended audience, those whom it is meant to attract and convince. A voter in an election, for example, may or may not recognize the depiction of himself as 'really me' or 'really my interests'; to accept it and be influenced by it, he needs to decode meanings and accept them, and to recognize the legal or institutional context in which claims are advanced. As Hall puts it, in terms immediately analogous of our political context, 'The reader [audience] is as important as the writer [claim-maker, or politician] in the production of meaning. Every signifier given as encoded with meaning has to be meaningfully interpreted or decoded by the receiver' (1997, 31).

Making Representations: Identity, Constituency, and Partiality

These observations lead directly on to the ways in which representation, understood primarily through processes of claim-making, leads us to focus further on the constitution of subjects, the making of identities, and the partiality of each of these processes. I have commented in passing on each of these aspects above, and now extend those observations further. Characterizing identity and constituency are largely what the aesthetic and cultural aspects of political representation boil down to.

Identity

In politics, portrayals of constituencies or the nation or voters' interests are just that: portrayals (Spivak, 1988, 276). There is no self-presenting subject whose essential character and desires and interests are transparent, beyond representation, evident enough to be 'read off' their appearance or their behaviour. Politicians often *claim* to be able to read off constituency and national interests, to have a unique hotline to voters' real wants and needs.

REPRESENTATION

389

313

However, the fact is that they can only do so after first deploying an interpretative frame containing selective representations of their constituents. In the terms of Spivak in her dense and challenging essay *'Can the Subaltern Speak?'* (1988), how one is represented aesthetically will condition how one can be, or wishes to be, represented politically. The subaltern can be produced, positioned and silenced through a process of representation. To speak for others — as elected representatives do, of course — is to make representations which render those others visible and readable. Linda Alcoff puts the point well: 'In both the practice of speaking for as well as the practice of speaking about others, I am engaging in the act of representing the other's needs, goals, situation, and in fact, *who they are*. I am representing them *as* such and such ... I am participating in the construction of their subject-positions. This act of representation cannot be understood as founded on an act of discovery wherein I discover their true selves and then simply relate my discovery' (Alcoff, 1991, 9).

The identity issue leads us to question any suggestions that groups, individuals or constituencies have a single, undisputed, *authentic* identity that can merely be received by a political representative as if the flow of meaning was all in one direction. In this sense the theory of political representation I am putting forward is resolutely opposed to the approach associated with Carl Schmitt, who thought that true representation 'is only ever an expressive realization of the unity of an authentic community' (Barnett, 2004: 517). Claims to authentic or 'true' representation remain just that — claims. A claim may be compelling, largely accepted, motivating or prompting self-conscious awareness among members of an invoked community, and so forth, but even so to accept it as 'authentic' is to try to foreclose the unforecloseable play of politics.

Constituting constituency

The painter Paul Klee took the view that painting did not mimic or copy, or even in the first instance interpret, its referent. What it did, first and foremost, was 'make visible' the referent.[7] By analogy, elected politicians construct verbal and visual images of their constituencies and their countries (among other things). Constituencies are 'hard-working', 'good honest folk', 'family-oriented', 'patriots', 'concerned' or 'worried' or 'angry'. Constituencies, like communities, have to be 'imagined', in Benedict Anderson's sense (Anderson, 1991). The equivalent of Klee's painting is required in order to make it imaginable, to make it visible.

Politics is, in the words of Latour, 'a work of composition' (2003, 158). In one sense, of course people and groups exist prior to evocation or constitution in politics. There is always a *referent*. However, the real political work lies in the active constitution of constituencies — the making of representations. Pierre Bourdieu argues a strong version of this line: 'in *appearance* the group creates the man who speaks in its place — to put it that way is to think in terms of delegation — whereas in *reality* it is more or less just as true to say that it is the spokesperson who creates the group. It is because the representative exists, because he represents (symbolic action), that the group that is represented and symbolized exists and that in return it gives existence to its representative as the representative of a group' (Bourdieu, 1991, 204). Recognizing a dark side to political representation in these respects, he writes also of 'a sort of embezzlement' tied to delegation, and even of a 'usurpatory ventriloquism' involved in being authorized to speak for (or represent) others. Whether the represented, the imagined and constructed see *themselves* as they are seen or portrayed is of course another matter.

Incidentally, this view might lead us to turn on its head the orthodox modelling of the constituent–representative relationship as one of principal-agent. Perhaps the constituency is the agent, and the representative the principal? Looked at from this angle, the constituency must enact or reveal what the representative wants of it, must conform to the representative's images or depictions or representations of it. At least, one might want to insist on the 'mutual constitution' of representative and constituents (cf Young, 2000). Both are, in Seitz's words, 'the effect of a practice', the practice of representation itself: 'Representation fills in the blank spaces of possibility reserved for representatives, but it also fills in what gets represented' (Seitz, 1995, 144;134).[8] From a slightly different angle, note Ankersmit's comment that: ' ... without political representation we are without a conception of what political reality — the represented — is like; without it, political reality has neither face nor contours. Without representation there is no represented ...' (2002, 115).

We need to pay attention to the political strategies that actors employ in the depiction/construction of constituencies. Special attention may need to be paid in instances where there is an effort to hide the constructedness of the construction, to hide the aesthetic moment in representation in order to mask the constituted nature of constituency.

Partiality

Representative claims which make constituencies politically visible are partial (Becker, 1986, 125). They are always one version among plausible others of what could render the object 'visible', of dealing with 'the problem of identity' (Cohen, 1968). In this respect they are necessarily selective, proposing that 'we see the world from a certain perspective and that we arrange what can be seen in a specific way. As a landscape cannot determine from what perspective it is seen, so the representation always contains an element that is essential to its representationality and that can never be reduced to aspects of the world *itself* and to what is true or false' (Ankersmit, 1996, 39).

This partiality raises significant questions about the status of 'true' representations — and, indeed, the place of 'truth' in political argument. Representations, selective depictions, draw on a referent, a materially existing group or entity, and they partake of cultural codes that carry meaning and truth within specific social contexts. In these respects truth is a core part of political representation. Alongside this, however, alternative representative claims (e.g. about voters' interests) can be no less efficacious, recognized and accepted than the currently prevailing ones. Creating and using alternative representative claims is, again, perhaps the core ingredient of political activity in general terms. To ask too much of these claims using a strong criterion of truth is, in an important sense, to misunderstand politics, to demand of it something it precisely cannot deliver. (Whether non-political contexts like scientific processes can get closer to satisfying strong truth criteria is a whole other story). As Latour writes, if 'faithful representation' is the political holy grail, then politics will always be disappointing, based on unrealistic assumptions about immediacy and authenticity, as if a sort of 'double-click communication' can bypass representatives' necessarily interpretative work. Latour writes that we expect too much of political representation if we 'expect it to provide a form of fidelity, exactitude or truth that is totally impossible' (2003, 143).

Conclusion

Political representation is a significantly broader topic than even relatively radical and innovative recent approaches would suggest. One upshot of placing the representative claim at the centre of our concerns is that a good deal of traditional scepticism about representation is helpfully displaced. For one thing, it is difficult to conceive of a regime of direct democracy — the radical hope of many trenchant critics of representative politics — which is not shot through with representative roles and practices (Budge, 1996; Saward, 1998). For another, loosening up categories of what can count as a representative claim, and what can count as a constituency, renders representation a newly radicalized notion which can be adapted and extended across geographical and even species boundaries, as Eckersley (2004) goes some way towards demonstrating. In other words, 'radical' critiques of representation in favour of different ways of organizing politics or democracy often miss the point: representation is more ubiquitous than the critique may suggest, and is an idea

316

containing far more radical potential than is commonly acknowledged. Nothing I have said suggests that 'representative democracy' is legitimate where other conceptions of democracy are not. Rather, I suggest that we should not too easily fetishize 'models' of democracy, as if they really do describe separable political visions. The question of the legitimacy of representation requires radical and prior recasting in line with the fundamental currency of representation as a practice — the representative claim — which operates in regimes of 'direct democracy' no less than in regimes of 'representative democracy'.

We need, I am suggesting, to adopt an approach that takes the aesthetic and cultural moments in political representation to be as important as electoral ones. We need to bring these and other perspectives to bear on our analyses by shifting our frame of reference, focusing on representation as a dynamic and differentiated process of claim-making, extraordinary in its variations and potentialities. In this way we can cast a new light on familiar issues, and (I trust) gain a greater understanding of what is happening when political representation is evoked as fact and as a concept.

Notes

1 I would like to thank Andrew Dobson, Raia Prokhovnik, Grahame Thompson and two anonymous referees for their helpful comments. An early version of this article was presented at the ECPR Joint Sessions workshop on Political Representation at Edinburgh in 2003, and I also thank participants for their feedback.

2 Pitkin discussed relevant aspects of symbolic and artistic representations, but only to diminish their political relevance in the end. See Pitkin (1967, 12;54;69;72–73).

3 Others have dismissed the activity of making symbolic or aesthetic representations from the topic of political representation even more forthrightly. See for example Pennock (1968, 6, fn9) and Diggs (1968, 35).

4 In Mitchell's formulation: 'representation is always of something, or someone, by something or someone, to someone' (1990, 12). On triangular conceptions see also Slezak (2002), Prendergast (2000) and Barthes (1985).

5 The idea of a 'performative', in the concept's journey from Searle's discussion of speech acts to Butler's notion of gender as a product of performance, centres upon the way in which performatives 'organize the world rather than simply representing what is', a formulation that Culler (2000, 511) associates particularly with Paul de Man.

6 The notions of iterability and repetition, for example, form key parts of Derrida's and Butler's renditions of the performative (see Culler, 2000).

7 Klee wrote that 'Art does not reproduce the visible but makes visible'. As Riley comments on this, 'In painting the thing seen is, at best, a factor that gives rise to both the actual perception and to the sensation that places it within our experience' (Riley, 2002, 18).

REPRESENTATION   393

8 Young writes that: ' ... in most situations the specific constituency exists at best potentially; the representative institutions and the process of authorisation themselves call its members into action' (2000, 130).

References

Alcoff, L. (1991) 'The problem of speaking for others', in *Cultural Critique*, Winter. Vol. 17.
Anderson, B. (1991) *Imagined Communities*, London: Verso.
Ankersmit, F.R. (1996) *Aesthetic Politics*, Stanford: Stanford University Press.
Ankersmit, F.R. (2002) *Political Representation*, Stanford: Stanford University Press.
Barker, R. (2001) *Legitimating Identities*, Cambridge: Cambridge University Press.
Barnett, C. (2004) 'Deconstructing radical democracy: articulation, representation and being-with-others', *Political Geography* 23: 503–528.
Barthes, R. (1985) *The Responsibility of Forms*, Berkeley and Los Angeles: University of California Press (trans. by R. Howard).
Becker, H.S. (1986) 'Telling About Society', *Doing Things Together*, Evanston, IL: Northwestern University Press.
Bourdieu, P. (1991) *Language and Symbolic Power*, Cambridge: Harvard University Press (trans. by J.B. Thompson).
Budge, I. (1996) *The New Challenge of Direct Democracy*, Cambridge: Polity.
Cohen, J. (1968) 'Commentary: representation and the problem of identity', in J.R. Pennock and J.W. Chapman (eds.) *Nomos X: Representation*, New York: Atherton Press.
Culler, J. (2000) 'Philosophy and literature: the fortunes of the performative', *Poetics Today* 21: 3.
Daloz, J.-P. (2003) 'Political representation and the distinction between symbols of distinction and symbols of likeness', paper presented to the workshop on Political Representation, ECPR Joint Sessions, Edinburgh.
Diggs, B.J. (1968) 'Practical Representation', in J.R. Pennock and J.W. Chapman (eds.) *Nomos X: Representation*, New York: Atherton Press.
Dobson, A. (1996) 'Representative Democracy and the Environment', in W.M. Lafferty and J. Meadowcroft (eds.) *Democracy and the Environment*, Cheltenham: Edward Elgar.
Eckersley, R. (2004) *The Green State*, Cambridge, MA and London: The MIT Press.
Goodin, R.E. (1996) 'Enfranchising the earth, and its alternatives', *Political Studies* 44: 5.
Hall, S. (1997) 'The Work of Representation', in S. Hall (ed.) *Representation: Cultural Representations and Signifying Practices*, London: Sage and The Open University.
Held, D. (1995) *Democracy and the Global Order*, Cambridge: Polity.
Latour, B. (2003) 'What if we talked politics a little?' *Contemporary Political Theory* 2: 2.
Laycock, D. (2004) *Representation and Democratic Theory*, University of British Columbia Press.
Mansbridge, J.J. (2003) 'Rethinking Representation', *American Political Science Review* 97: 4.
Marin, L. (2001) *On Representation*, Stanford: Stanford University Press (trans. by C. Porter).
Mitchell, W.J.T. (1990) 'Representation', in F. Lentricchia and T. McLaughlin (eds.) *Critical Terms for Literary Study*, Chicago and London: University of Chicago Press.
Pennock, J.R. (1968) 'Political Representation: an overview', in J.R. Pennock and J.W. Chapman (eds.) *Nomos X: Representation*, New York: Atherton Press.
Phillips, A (1995) *The Politics of Presence*, Oxford: Oxford University Press.
Pitkin, H.F. (1967) *The Concept of Representation*, Berkeley and Los Angeles: University of California Press.
Prendergast, C. (2000) *The Triangle of Representation*, New York: Columbia University Press.
Przeworski, A., Stokes, S.C. and Manin, B. (1999) *Democracy, Accountability, and Representation*, Cambridge: Cambridge University Press.

318

Riley, B. (2002) 'Making Visible', in R. Kudielka (ed.) *Paul Klee: the nature of creation*, London: Hayward Gallery.

Saward, M. (1998) *The Terms of Democracy*, Cambridge: Polity.

Saward, M. (ed.) (2000) *Democratic Innovation: Deliberation, Representation and Association*, London: Routledge.

Sawer, M and Zappala, G (2001) *Speaking for the People*, Melbourne: Melbourne University Press.

Seitz, B. (1995) *The Trace of Political Representation*, New York: SUNY Press.

Slezak, P. (2002) 'The tripartite model of representation', *Philosophical Psychology* 15: 3.

Spivak, G.C. (1988) 'Can the Subaltern Speak?', in C. Nelson and L. Grossberg (eds.) *Marxism and the Interpretation of Culture*, London: Macmillan.

Street, J. (2004) 'Celebrity politicians: popular culture and political representation', *British Journal of Politics and International Relations* 6: 4.

Thompson, D. (1999) 'Democratic Theory and Global Society', *The Journal of Political Philosophy* 7: 111–125.

Young, I.M. (2000) *Inclusion and Democracy*, Oxford: Oxford University Press.

19

ARTICLE

The Pitfalls of Representation as Claims-Making in the European Union[1]

CHRISTOPHER LORD* & JOHANNES POLLAK**

ABSTRACT   Standard accounts assume that representatives are authorised and held accountable through elections in territorially defined constituencies. In contrast, claims-making approaches hold that representation does not always depend on an electoral connection. This paper argues that the claims-making approach addresses some of the difficulties in the standard account, but remains itself theoretically underspecified. This becomes especially clear when applied to systems with exceptional institutional complexity like the EU. As an alternative to both those other approaches, the paper proposes a revised claims-making approach in which rights claims are used to specify representative claims. It then shows how rights claims do, indeed, play an important role in the representative claims that are made in the European Union arena, and how that, in turn, allows the Union to deal with some of the problems of applying standard forms of representation to its decision-making.

Introduction

European integration poses considerable theoretical and practical challenges to political representation. Variously depicted as a multi-level system of governance, as politics without a polity, as a non-state political system, as a federal polity in the making and so on, the Union often appear to take much of what is simple in political representation and turn it into a series of complex practices. That political representation is simple

518 *Christopher Lord & Johannes Pollak*

is in many ways a standard view (Castiglione and Warren 2006; Rehfeld 2006) that can be summarised as follows. Regular elections – in which a clearly defined citizenry casts votes in one or several territorially organised constituencies – provide a mechanism for citizens to select their officials and entrust them with the running of public affairs. Representatives then 'stand for' or 'act for' the citizens, reflecting (representing) their interests, values and opinions in the normal business of government. The mandate is then renewed or revoked at regular intervals. Representation is understood as a more or less smooth transmission belt: politicians read the demands and wishes of their constituency and since they want to be re-elected they care for the proper implementation of those demands into policies. Since this simple model is itself the product of the capacity of the state to simplify and demarcate citizenship, territory, political orders and arrangements for political competition, it is unsurprising that many of its ingredients often appear to be missing from the European Union: (1) EU decisions lack the kind of distinct audience we find at the national level. (2) The electoral bond between decision-makers and constituency is blurred at best. (3) Accountability structures, namely the clear allocation of political responsibilities to the myriad of decision-making bodies, are fuzzy. (4) The representative process which should ideally allow any one view to be justified or challenged in relation to any other (Mill 1972 [1861]), suffers from the distance between the only directly elected body, the European Parliament, and its voters' perception of its political powers as well as from a serious attention deficit. (5) Intermediate institutions like political parties, responsible for the aggregation of preferences and interests are only developed rudimentarily.

If, however, this is a standard critique of representation in the European Union (EU) that itself follows from a standard view of how political representation works in general, it may need to be rethought, given that recent developments in the literature have called the standard account of representation into question. This paper contributes to that goal by considering implications for representation in the EU of an adjusted version of Michael Saward's claims-making approach. Section 2 briefly reviews criticisms of the standard account of representation. The following section 3 sketches our own version of the claims-making approach, which, we term, 'claims-making 2'. Section 4 considers implications for representation in the EU, with the help of some examples of some very large claims that have been made about the ability of some people to represent others in the European arena. Section 5 concludes. Summarised simply we use 'claims-making 2' to argue that institutional complexity need not be an obstacle to representation in the European arena. The problem has more to do with ways in which elements of institutional complexity are compounded together within processes of claims-making than institutional complexity itself.

Standard Theories of Representation and the Claims-Making Approach

Standard theories of representation usually start with the assumptions that representation means to 'make present what is absent' (Pitkin 1967; Birch 1971) or to 'act in the best interest of the represented' (Eulau et al. 1959,

The Pitfalls of Representation 519

743; Pitkin 1967, 209; Przeworski et al. 1999, 2). Since many people purport to know what is best for the rest, liberal democracies use universal adult suffrage for the selection and authorisation of those representatives citizens want to be ruled by. Today's concept of citizenship makes clear who is entitled to cast his or her vote and who is not, namely it constitutes a polity. In order for this selection process to bring about a proper acting in the best interest of the people three conditions have to be satisfied. Even if we could agree on what this best interest is we might still differ in how to achieve it. Thus, in order to decide between the different paths leading to this best public and transparent competition during electoral campaigns is needed *and* so is an institutionalised, transparent form of competition between different standpoints and opinions. To ensure agency loss is kept at bay various forms of democratic oversight and accountability are employed. Those forms range from a carefully grafted balance between political institutions meant to check on each other to an independent judiciary and a free press.

We discern three major problems with the standard accounts in general (see also Pollak 2007): (1) Standard accounts assume the existence and unity of an object, a constituency or its parts. It is the absent which needs to be made present. And since the representative enjoys a certain independence from the represented, he or she is also free to invent, create, constitute the absent. Thus, it is not about the mere aggregation of interests as we find it for example. in James Madison's account. It is about making the object of representation and making it visible to all the members of the constituency. (2) It is obvious that political representation includes some sort of social relationship. In standard accounts this relationship is supposed to be direct. Let us assume the principal is defined by citizenship rights of a political community whose territorial borders are clearly demarcated. Those citizens cast their votes and authorise representatives. Given the size of modern assemblies it is obvious that without assumptions about the relatively homogeneity of the demands, wishes, preferences and needs of the constituency standard accounts cannot work in large communities. Thus, the relationship between represented and representative is mediated by a series of intermediate institutions, most importantly by political parties. (3) In order to enable a collective to act and decide, to select potential representatives and hold them to account, elections play a crucial role in standard accounts. It is clear that different electoral systems have different impacts on the independence and performance of the representative and that they influence the relationship between representative and represented significantly. What is important is the core assumption of standard theories that citizens are only represented by formally elected officials and mainly by the legislative assembly. Instead, modern liberal democracies are characterised by a co-existence of formal and non-formal representatives, the difference referring mainly to who is entitled to authorise the respective representatives and the scope/reach of the decisions made (see Lord and Pollak 2010).

Applying the standard model to the case of the EU quickly shows that we find a compound form of representation (Lord and Pollak 2009)

520 *Christopher Lord & Johannes Pollak*

comprising different modes of representation in addition to the traditional mode of parliamentary representation: executive and administrative representation, representation by civil society groups and NGOs as well as transnational industrial actors crisscrossed by functional, territorial and institutional forms of organisation. It is as of yet not sure whether this system works to the advantage or to the detriment of the European citizens, whether these different modes collide or collude (Lord and Pollak 2010). It is a system in which the representatives are selected according to different procedures, based on different grounds with widely different mandates and tasks leading to different representative styles and modes of responsiveness as well different forms of accountability. These important differences lead to a vast array of representative rights (and not just claims) potentially cancelling each other out, blocking the policy process and leading to suboptimal results in terms of responsive politics. In the resulting complex and compounded representative system of the EU comprising different levels it is often unclear who represents what and whom and how this representation feeds into the policy-making process.

The constructivist turn in representation theory takes off where the standard theories end. Or rather, it identifies the considerable gaps the standard theories have glossed over and fills them with a highly flexible and dynamic but also 'elusive' (Saward 2010, 1) concept of claims-making. Michael Saward, the main proponent of the claims-making approach, convincingly suggests focusing on what representation does and not what it is.[2] Instead of focusing on representation as an institutional fact resulting from elections, Saward sees it as constitutive activity or an event (Saward 2010: 14, 43). It is suggested to understand the relation between represented and representatives as an ongoing, constant, tripartite dialogue between representatives, their representative claims they put forward to an audience of potentially represented, and the ones who are subject to the decisions by the representatives (Saward 2003, 2006, 2010; see also Lord and Pollak 2010). Its general form is expressed as: 'The maker of representations puts forward a subject which stands for an object that is related to the referent and is offered to an audience' (2010, 36). Saward (2010, 37) offers some examples specifying the general form: 'An MP (maker) offers herself (subject) as the embodiment of constituency interests (object) to that constituency (audience). The reference is the actual, flesh-and-blood people of the constituency. The object involves a selective portrayal of constituency interests.' Of course, the MP is more than just the embodiment of the referent, and of course, the constituency is more than the creatively constructed version the MP offers in his claim.[3] In addition to subject, object and referent which we also find as elements in the standard account of representation, Saward introduces the 'maker' and the 'audience' thereby providing a more complex account. Audience and referent may be the same but this is not always and not necessarily the case. The same holds true for maker and subject. The maker of a representative claim can put forward a different entity embodying the referent. And indeed, there are competing interpretations of the referent by different makers, of the object by the audience, of the referent by the maker, and of

The Pitfalls of Representation 521

the audience by the referent (and vice versa). Representation becomes a fluid and endogenously defined standard in which some actors – be they parliamentarians, NGOs, interest groups civil society associations, etc. – make claims to represent others which are, in turn, accepted, amended, or rejected by various, sometimes overlapping, social groups or audiences. Thus, political representation is not confined to those citizens vote into offices which allow them to make binding decisions (i.e. formal representatives) but also includes social groups which are increasingly part and parcel of modern governance systems. This approach permits going beyond the sterile differentiation between participation and representation because the former is a pre-condition of the latter. While standard theories of representation intend to make the object of representation visible, the claims-making approach is about the creation of such an object and its maker. The represented does not exist per se, it is not about representing a selection of preferences out of a wide range of possibilities, it is about the actual creation of the represented. Saward defines representation as an event or constitutive activity, 'one that involves offering constructions or images of constituents to constituents and audiences' 2010:14). Representative, represented and audience are constituted in the event of representation. Thus, the problems of the standard account are circumvented: (1) The object of representation is not pre-existing to the practice of representation. The claims-maker shapes an object of which he orshe thinks it is appealing, accurate, vote-winning, empowering etc. (and is thereby shaped his/herself). This object is not bound to territorial borders, social classes or even time. It is up to the audience to accept such a claim or to reject it. (2) Between the ever shifting units of represented and representative stands the claim. It does not matter in what form or what medium this claim is made. (3) Representative claims can be made by everyone about everything (Saward 2010, 46). There is no need to differentiate between formal and informal representatives because it is about the claims and not the claims-maker. While standard theories do not exclude the possibility of claims-making (without granting it a constitutive power) elections are a defining element deciding about the question who is entitled to make decisions on behalf of the citizenry. Of course, elected representatives continue to make claims during their terms of office but they are to a certain extent exempt from the daily grind of claims-making. The constructivist approach on the other hand equates claims-making with the political process as such, it purports the 'ubiquity of claims-making' (Saward 2010, 163). Representation becomes a systemic phenomenon.

There is no doubt an enormous amount of theoretical innovation and intellectual appeal to the constructivist interpretation of representation. It opens, however, a range of indeterminacies: (1) How can we differentiate between legitimate and preposterous claims? Is it merely left to the constituency to decide about the legitimacy of claims? (2) How to appeal to multiple audiences without reverting to 'dog-whistle politics' and who are they? (3) How to assess what 'good representation' is? (4) How to determine whether they are claims to represent at all, contrary to mere claims? Implicit in the last two indeterminacies is the question what are the a

522 *Christopher Lord & Johannes Pollak*

priori criteria for determining what representation is. Without such criteria we are committed to taking all statements of a kind 'I represent you' as a representative claim however absurd. Contrariwise we are committing to NOT classifying as representation a good deal of behaviour that does allot of things that many people would count as representation just because the representative function is left implicit and it is not accompanied by any claim in the form 'I represent you'. We hold that while these indeterminacies are applying to the traditional framework of representation, that is. the nation-state, the dynamics of a multi-level system of policies without politics are not prone to enhance the democratic credentials of political representation.

The Pitfalls of Claims-Making and 'Claims-Making 2'

Taken on its own, all the claims-making approach says is that a successful claim to represent is just a claim that is recognised as such. Such a radical form of constructivism plainly avoids the residual essentialism of standard theories of representation, including, for example, their assumption that representation must always contain some notion of constituency. Yet the claims-making approach brings indeterminacies of its own. An obvious criticism is that it is loose, vague, open-ended, and under-specified. Can this difficulty be avoided without collapsing back into the *a prioristic* assumptions about the nature of representation to which the claimsmaking approach is supposed to be an antidote?

One way forward may be to ask: is there 'something special' that people must be able to do when they make claims to represent others that is in and of itself likely to make those claims *self*-limiting and *self*-specifying? The 'something special' might then be enough to counter the objection that holding the acceptance of claims to represent to be sufficient to establish representation may be empty and tautologous. The self-limiting and self-specifying nature of that 'special something' could be enough to provide determinate understandings of representation that rest exclusively on how real people make and accept representative claims, without any need for the study of representation to rely on its own arbitrary and *a prioristic* assumptions about the nature of good representation.

Our suggestion here is that the claims of some people to represent others are, indeed, likely to be self-limiting and self-specifying in one special way. People usually distinguish between types of representative claims according to the rights and obligations they believe would-be representatives are capable of assuming. Consider an example from Michael Saward's work that has probably been as much discussed as his claims-making approach itself. 'Amid the Make Poverty History' campaign in 2004, the U2 singer and political activist Bono said "I represent a lot of people [in Africa] who have no voice at all...They haven't asked me to represent them. It's cheeky but I hope that they are glad I do"' (quoted in Saward 2010, 82).

One response to this example is to agree that Bono is, indeed, well placed to represent the views of others on poverty. But he would be in no

The Pitfalls of Representation 523

position to represent others in making democratically binding laws on poverty. That would not just be cheeky. It would not even be a claim that he could meaningfully make – or probably want to make – under certain commonly held criteria of legitimate law-making. The claim to have a right to represent someone else's opinion is redeemed by just saying something to which they can agree. In contrast, a claim to have a right to represent someone else in a democratic process of law-making may require election by equally entitled citizens and an ability to assume a series of correlative obligations such as a willingness to take part in a process of public debate and justification with other elected representatives. To paraphrase Nancy Fraser there just is a difference between claiming to represent the views of others in 'discourse' aimed at forming 'public opinion' and claiming to represent others in discourse aimed at 'binding, sovereign decisions authorizing the use of state power' (Fraser 1990, 75).

So, it appears that we often interpret, categorise, accept or reject representative claims on the basis of alternative understandings of the rights and obligations that we think are involved in making representative claims successfully. Even if the original claim does little to say why one actor has a right to represent another or to spell out any obligations that would follow from representing that other person, those rights and obligations are likely to be deliberated and tested over any process of accepting, rejecting or ignoring the claim in a manner that contributes to the specification of the claim. Hence, our tentative suggestion that the analysis of representation could benefit from a kind of 'claims-making 2'. Instead of analysing how the claims of some people to represent others are accepted, rejected or ignored (claims-making 1) we should study what rights and obligations to represent others can be inferred from the manner in which claims of some people to represent others are accepted, rejected or ignored (claims-making 2).

All this, of course, begs the following questions. Do views about rights and obligations really play the role we suspect they might in assessing and judging different representative claims? And is it possible to study that role empirically? To consider these questions we now look briefly at two of the most important attempts in recent years to make claims to represent others within the institutions of the European Union. Our intuition here is that the European Union is a hard case. The claims of some actors to represent others are presumably most likely to be tested in demanding ways where polities have certain unifying features, including, first, an intense process of political competition in which actors have strong incentives to contest one another's claims and, second, a public sphere that is at least integrated enough to ensure that most claims are sufficiently scrutinised somewhere in the process of public debate, even where it would be hopelessly utopian to assume that everyone follows the entirety of public debate on all matters at all times.

'Claims-Making 2' in the European Union

In contrast to considerations such as these, it is less than self-evident that the complexity of the Union's institutional order lends itself to the testing

524   *Christopher Lord & Johannes Pollak*

of representative claims in political competition and public debate. Policy-making in the EU is a dynamic process which demands that formal and informal representatives from different levels collaborate and compete to secure the outcomes they desire. In place of any single policy-making process, decision rules and policy styles vary across policy areas, often reflecting the historical particularities of the moment in the Union's development when they were originally agreed (Warleigh 2001). The possibility of a central form of democratic representation seems to be ruled out by the evolving and non-hierarchical network character of the EU. Since, moreover, the EU is a 'fused' (Wessels 1997) polity – which merges rather than replaces – the instruments and structures of the member states, any role of formal representatives in scrutinising Union decisions has to be shared out between the regional, national and supranational levels. Even then formal representatives do not have a monopoly either on policy itself or on representative roles. Instead, various formal actors – the Commission, the Council, the EP, the European Economic and Social Committee (EESC), the Committee of Regions (CoR), national parliaments – and various informal actors NGOs and interest groups, etc. claim to represent not just distinct constituencies, but sometimes overlapping, and sometimes even identical ones. Indeed, there is no systematic and principled basis for including informal representatives in Union decision-making. Rather they are included for ad hoc reasons of convenience or necessity. Depending on the policy, or even the individual decision, they might be included as representatives of a body of expertise; as representatives of a group of actors whose active cooperation is needed in the delivery of a policy; or as representatives of opinions that policy-makers find convenient to mobilise into the European arena to unsettle the status quo. Thus both the formal and informal dimensions of representation in the EU would seem to be segmented by institutions, levels and purposes of representation.

Thus in the remainder of the paper we do not just sketch two recent examples of representative claims- making in the EU. We also discuss whether those examples really produced a *process* in which claims were specified and tested, in spite of institutional complexity. Only then do we discuss how far arguments about rights and obligations played a part in making, accepting, rejecting, limiting and specifying claims in the two examples, as would be required for our revised form of claims-making analysis – claims-making 2 – to work.

Our first example is highly significant in so far as it consists of the first attempt to agree and set out in the Treaties an overall account of how representation does and should work in the European Union. Thus, in effect, it amounts to an authorised representative claim. As the Lisbon Treaty puts it '"Member States are represented in the European Council by their Heads of State or Government and in the Council by their Governments, themselves democratically accountable either to their national Parliaments or their citizens' (TEU art. 10). On top of that, the Treaty claims that 'political parties at the European level contribute to European political awareness' and Union institutions maintain an 'open transparent and

The Pitfalls of Representation 525

regular dialogue with representative associations and civil society' (TEU art. 8) in which 'citizens and representative associations' have 'the opportunity to make known and exchange their views in all areas' (TEU art. 10).

In effect, then, the view of representation set out in the Lisbon Treaty suggests that representation in the Union is not just hybrid. It is also hybrid in different ways. It is hybrid between member states, non-state actors and sub-state actors. It is hybrid between actors who busy themselves with what passes for the executive and legislative 'branches' of government at Union level. It is hybrid between actors who are directly elected, indirectly elected or not elected at all. It is hybrid between actors who have some formally authorised role in the Union polity and those who organise themselves spontaneously and informally in the hope of representing views to the Union. It is hybrid between public and private actors, and so on.

Yet, even the 'Lisbon claim' under-states the fragmentation and dispersion of the Union's institutional order and representative practices. All of the categories that have just been mentioned are further fragmented and cross-cut by processes that have been variously conceptualised as networks, policy communities and epistemic communities. This brings us on to a second, very different attempt, to develop a set of claims of how actors should represent others in Union decisions. The claims we have in mind are those set out in the Commission's White Paper on Governance as preceded by a series of more interesting studies, including two from what was then its Forward Studies Unit (FSU). Like the Lisbon Treaty these studies saw the challenge as one of representing others under conditions of great complexity. However its understanding of that complexity and of the representative practices it claimed would best respond to complexity that could hardly have been more different from the Lisbon Treaty. The FSU studies argue that parliaments – which obviously play a central role in the view of representation set out in Lisbon – are inadequate on their own 'for legitimate rule production'. Given the practical complexity and normative pluralism of modern society, the FSU questions arrangements in which elected representatives 'formulate broad policies in legislative chambers, oversee their detailed implementation by bureaucratic departments' and 'impose a particular understanding of the problem and the means to resolve it'. In contrast, the FSU argues that Union institutions should encourage the self-representation of all affected interests in stakeholder networks, intervening only to ensure the following conditions of fairness: inclusiveness of representation of all those affected by a rule; compensation for inequalities in cognitive resources; and substitution of public reason for purely sectional patterns of preference formation. The public authority should thus retreat from attempting to represent views at the Union level to a role of moderating how the directly-affected represent their own views. Actors, the study urges, should be asked to 'clarify the presuppositions they bring to a particular issue, to reflect on the contingency of their models', and to 'demonstrate the coherence of their constructions, not only in terms of their initial positions but in terms of

526   *Christopher Lord & Johannes Pollak*

positions of others as they have evolved during a process of collective learning' (European Commission 1997).

Now that we have set out two different attempts to make representative claims that acknowledge the complexity of Union institutions and deci-sions, we can discuss whether those examples really produced a *process* in which claims were specified and tested, in spite of institutional complexity. Here it is useful to distinguish three possibilities. Institutional complexity can presumably be a problem for: (a) claims-makers (b) their audiences and (c) connecting the two so that the audience test, or even notice, the representative claims. We now consider each of these in turn.

(a) *Institutional Complexity as a Problem for Claims Maker?*
It might be expected that the diffuse and fragmented nature of Union deci-sion-making would leave individual actors with little incentive or ability to make representative claims on behalf of the system as a whole. Yet, it is by no means obvious that this has been a difficulty in the case of the Union. As seen, the Lisbon Treaty does make a representative claim that has been made on behalf of the system as a whole. Elsewhere we have argued that this may well be based on a 'fallacy of composition' to the extent that it assumes that lumping together multiple channels of represen-tation will add up to 'good' representation or even to a system of repre-sentation (Lord and Pollak 2010). Still, this is a criticism of the coherence with which actors are combining their representative claims in the Euro-pean arena. To make the criticism at all is already to accept that actors would appear to be motivated to relate their representative claims to one another in some way.

There are two possible explanations for this that do not make demand-ing assumptions about the extent of engagement of public audiences with Union matters. The first might be termed the insufficiency of representative claims based on the kind of 'Governance' perspective set out in the Com-mission's White Paper. For all the benefits of using informal and decentred forms of representation, decisions need to 'pass at some point' (Habermas 1996) through representative processes that are formally structured to meet basic standards of liberal democracy such as public control, political equality and public justification (ibid). Thus actors who make representa-tive claims based on governance perspectives usually end up – sooner or later – going in search of government. That, indeed, was precisely why the representative claims made in the Commission's White Paper were eventu-ally absorbed into the discussions that led to the view of representation set out in the Lisbon Treaty. A second possibility is that the complex and dis-persed nature of Union decision-making actually has the effect of requiring elite actors to acknowledge one another's representative claims and thus synthesise them into an overall view of representation at the level of the polity itself. We will come back to this in a moment.

(b) *Institutional Complexity as a Problem for Audiences?*
One obvious audience to whom actors might want to make representative claims is the public itself. However, it is widely supposed that public attention is only intermittently mobilised around Union matters. Assuming

The Pitfalls of Representation 527

that the media either shapes public attention or responds to it, extensive academic research demonstrates that Union matters are only sparsely and fitfully covered in ways that have massive selection biases to stories that can be framed nationally, around personalities or specific sectoral interests in European integration. Likewise it might be supposed that the willingness of the public to respond to the full range of representative claims that emanate from the European arena presupposes two factors that are largely absent: namely civic capabilities that are sufficiently developed in relation to the Union arena, and, as Majone puts it, publics that are interested in associating together at the Union level on a basis of political community (Majone 2005). Thus it would seem likely that publics would respond to representative claims in what is the least helpful way from the point of view of testing them: that is to say, in Saward's terms, by 'ignoring' them rather than 'accepting' or 'rejecting' them, or, in other words, taking a 'yes/no' position on them.

Yet, a public audience is not the only one that may be relevant to testing representative claims. The same conditions of complexity and consensus which weaken vertical accountability to publics may encourage horizontal accountability between decision-makers. The dispersed nature of Union decision-making may itself create a highly demanding environment for the mutual justification of representative claims between elite actors. Union decisions often require the active cooperation of a large and heterogeneous range of actor types, who are often constrained to act by consensus, with few means of achieving that consensus other than mutual persuasion within a policy process which, for practical purposes, relies heavily on segmenting decision-making by areas of expertise. A classic statement of what may be involved is provided by Adrienne Héritier: 'Because decision-making involves a consensus among different actors who monitor one another suspiciously, every step in policy development implies a high degree of mutual control among knowledgeable actors' (Héritier 1997, 180).

(c) *Institutional Complexity as a Problem of Connecting Claims-Mmakers to Audiences?*
There are at least three ways of connecting claims-makers to audiences in ways that are likely to test alternative understandings of what rights and duties may be needed to establish a claim to represent others in the European arena: through Treaty ratifications, through elections and through day-to-day debate in the public sphere. All of these have well-known limitations. The public sphere is limited on European matters by problems of media coverage that have already been noted. Treaty ratifications may only allow claims to be tested by limited and somewhat controlled audiences in so far as they are entrusted to national parliaments. Where, however, they are put to referendum voting behaviour is often heavily influenced by domestic politics. It is thus hard to discern how far it reflects views on Union matters at all, let alone acceptance or rejection of alternative claims about desirable forms of representation in the Union arena. Likewise, the Union has yet to develop a form of electoral political and electoral competition relevant to its own arena. Neither in national nor even in European elections are Union issues salient. Political competition

528 Christopher Lord & Johannes Pollak

is mainly structured in both arenas around left–right issues, rather than a pro-anti integration dimension which would be more likely to motivate would-be representatives to respond to them in their voting behaviour. In any case, the dependence of Union decisions on high levels of consensus between multiple actor types may leave little room for political and electoral competition.

However, the foregoing arguments that voter choices and public attention are insufficiently structured around Union issues for the public to get opportunities to test different claims as to who should represent them and how in the European arena tend to assume that would-be representatives only make salient those issues on which they are likely to be sanctioned or rewarded by a process of political competition. Yet, it is conceivable that even in the absence of a direct focus of electoral competition on European issues, representative claims in the European arena could be tested by other means. In the case of the EU, claims to represent others may work through what Jane Mansbridge (2010) calls a 'selection' model of representation. That is to say, claims to represent others in the European arena may be accepted when some people are selected as representatives, not on the basis of any competition, knowledge or attention to EU matters, but on the basis of other known beliefs that make it likely that they will behave in certain ways on European matters. Hermann Schmitt and Jacques Thomassen's (2000) analysis of European elections fits exactly this pattern. Even if there is little competition on European matters, it does not follow that voters select representatives in a manner altogether irrelevant to the exercise of political power in the European arena. To the contrary, they select between candidates on the basis of their left–right views. That is broadly consistent with the left–right character of the powers of the institution in which those candidates claim to be able to represent voters.

Now that we have mapped the Union's institutional complexity and questioned how far it need be an obstacle to the making, accepting and rejecting of representative claims, we can better understand the role that rights and obligations played in specifying understandings of representative claims in our two examples. Perhaps two patterns stand out. In the case of the complex reprsesentative claims laid out in the Lisbon Treaty, member states do not even pretend to a monopoly *right* to represent their own citizens, as would, arguably, be normal in an international body. To the contrary, they fall over themselves to claim that the Union is legitimated by multiple channels of representation that compound together the contributions of (1) national governments responsible to their own national parliaments and publics, (2) a directly elected European Parliament with party groups of its own (3) arrangements for the representation of sub-state regions, and (4) a complex representation of non-state civil society actors, both formal and informal, both value-based and interest-based. In the case of the White Paper on Governance, the Commission began by implying that those affected by legislation had a right to properly structured forms of stakeholder representation. That at least is what seems to follow from its claim that legislative chambers are inadequate 'for *legitimate* rule production'. However, the European Parliament, perhaps

The Pitfalls of Representation 529

predictably, countered with a very different set of representative claims that, as it were, re-asserted a right to parliamentary representation as a right that guides other rights to representation: 'organised civil society, while important is inevitably sectoral and cannot be regarded as having its own legitimacy, given that representatives are not elected by the people and therefore cannot be voted out by the people...consultation of interested parties can only ever supplement and never replace the procedures and decisions of legislative procedures which possess democratic legitimacy' (European Parliament 2001). Thus it would appear that – even in complex institutional settings where decision-making is often dispersed and segmented and politics are weakly aggregated into overall processes of political competition or public debate – views about rights and obligations play an important part in specifying how representative claims are made, accepted or rejected.

Conclusions

If, following Saward (2006), we are to understand representation as a social relation which is enacted in a constant dialogue, we can expect this dialogue to comprise different actors (MPs, MEPs, civil society, NGOs), taking place in different frameworks (legislative, economic, political), in different institutional contexts (parliamentary, executive, administrative), in different locations (regional, local, national supranational, international), to be of varying extent (size of the audience) and scope (validity) as well as having different content. Institutions in the broadest sense – be they parties, social groups, organisations, or networks – shape these dimensions of dialogue. Given a system that has gained in complexity since its inception by a series of treaty reforms not only deepening and widening integration but also adding various new institutions and fora, we can expect a bewildering array of claims. Thus, in the EU a representative system has emerged which comprises the following, partly overlapping fora of representation: parliamentary representation in the EP, the various committees in national parliaments dealing with EU affairs and the Conference of Parliamentary Committees for Union Affairs of Parliaments of the European Union (COSAC); nation-state and regional representation in the European Council, the Council of the EU and the Committee of the Regions; Bureaucratic representation embodied in the European Commission; and finally informal representation via lobby groups, NGOs and the Economic and Social Committee.

The resulting institutional complexity partly neutralizes the advantages of representation as claims-making. Instead of a democratisation of representation we see hybridisation. Moreover, audiences and claims-makers are difficult to identify so that the necessary connection between the two is substantially weakened – unless elements of the standard approach are included. Thus it seems to us that the most promising avenue for democratic and accountable representation in the EU still lies with a combination of national and supranational legislative fora in which claims can be discussed after they have been legitimised by electoral procedures.

530   *Christopher Lord & Johannes Pollak*

Notes

1. We are grateful to Sandra Kröger, Richard Bellamy and the anonymous reviewer for their very helpful comments and suggestions. The usual disclaimer applies.
2. Pitkin (1967) also aims at the representatives' activities but does so rather through the lenses of several seminal authors in the history of political thought without constructing an abstract model.
3. Saward makes it clear that '[t]he "interests" of a constituency have to be "read in" more than "read off"; it is an active, creative process. Political figures, parties, lobby groups, social movements – as makers of representative claims, their business is aesthetic *because* it is political.' (2010, 74).

References

Birch, A.H. 1971. *Representation*. New York: Praeger.

Castiglione, D., and M. Warren. 2006. Rethinking democratic representation: eight theoretical issues. Vancouver: University of British Columbia.

Eulau, H., J. Wahlke, W. Buchanan, and L. Ferguson. 1959. The role of the representative: some empirical observations on the theory of Edmund Burke. *American Political Science Review* 53: 742–56.

European Commission. 1997. *Evolution in governance: what lessons for the commission? A first assessment*. Brussels: The European Commission.

European Parliament. 2001. *Resolution on the Commission white paper on European governance*. Brussels: European Parliament.

Fraser, N. 1990. 'Rethinking the public sphere: a contribution to the critique of actually existing democracy'. *Social Text* 25, no. 26: 56–80.

Habermas, J. 1996. *Between facts and norms*. Cambridge: Polity.

Héritier, A. 1997. Policy-making by subterfuge: interest accommodation, innovation and substitute democracy legitimation in Europe: perspectives from distinctive policy arenas'. *Journal of European Public Policy* 4, no. 2: 171–89.

Lord, C., and J. Pollak. 2009. The EU's many representative modes: colluding? Cohering? *Journal of European Public Policy* 17, no. 1: 117–36.

Lord, C., and J. Pollak. 2010. Representation and accountability: communicating tubes? *West European Politics* 33, no. 5: 968–88.

Majone, G. 2005. *Dilemmas of European integration: the ambiguities and pitfalls of integration by stealth*. Oxford: Oxford University Press.

Mansbridge, J. 2010. A selection model of political representation. *Journal of Political Philosophy* 18, no. 1: 64–100.

Mill, J.S. 1972 [1861]. *Utilitarianism, on liberty and considerations on representative government*. London: Dent.

Pitkin, H. 1967. *The concept of political representation*. Berkeley/Los Angeles/London: University of California Press.

Pollak, J. 2007. *Repräsentation ohne Demokratie?* Vienna/New York: Springer.

Przeworski, A., S.C. Stokes, and B. Manin, eds. 1999. *Democracy, accountability, and representation*. Cambridge: Cambridge University Press.

Rehfeld, A. 2006. Towards a general theory of political representation. *Journal of Politics* 68, no. 1: 1–26.

Saward, M. 2003. Representing nature and the nature of representation, paper presented at the 2nd European Consortium for Political Research Conference, Marburg, Germany, September 2003.

Saward, M. 2006. The representative claim. *Contemporary Political Theory* 5: 297–318.

Saward, M. 2010. *The representative claim*. Oxford: Oxford University Press.

Schmitt, H., and J.A. Thomassen. 2000. Dynamic representation: the case of European integration. *European Union Politics* 1, no. 3: 318–39.

Warleigh, A. 2001. Europeanising civil society: NGOs as agents of political socialisation. *Journal of Common Market Studies* 39, no. 4: 619–39.

Wessels, W. 1997. An ever closer fusion? A dynamic macropolitical view on integration processes. *Journal of Common Market Studies* 35, no. 2: 267–99.

20

Discursive Representation
JOHN S. DRYZEK and SIMON NIEMEYER

*D*emocracy can entail the representation of discourses as well as persons or groups. We explain and advocate discursive representation; explore its justifications, advantages, and problems; and show how it can be accomplished in practice. This practice can involve the selection of discursive representatives to a formal Chamber of Discourses and more informal processes grounded in the broader public sphere. Discursive representation supports many aspects of deliberative democracy and is especially applicable to settings such as the international system lacking a well-defined demos.

In his recent survey of the legitimacy claims of unelected representatives, Saward (2008) opens with a quote from Bono, and so shall we[1]:

> I represent a lot of people [in Africa] who have no voice at all.... They haven't asked me to represent them.

Nobody elected Bono, he is not formally accountable to anybody, and most of the people he claims to represent have no idea who he is or what he proposes. Nevertheless, his representation claim makes some sense. It makes most sense not in terms of representing African people, nor in terms of representing a place called Africa, but rather in terms of representing a discourse of Africa. "Africa" as constructed in this discourse may bear some relation to people and places, but more important is that it constructs them in a particular kind of way: as victims of an unjust world and the caprice of nature, lacking much in the way of agency themselves, with claims on the conscience of the wealthy.[2] These claims stop at a better deal within the existing world system, falling short of structural transformation. A cynic might also see a place for celebrity and conspicuous charity in the discourse. This discourse is transnational, may be only weakly present in Africa itself, and is generally only one among several or many discourses that particular individuals who engage it (be it at G8 meetings or live8 concerts) subscribe to.

Discursive representation does, then, already happen, although as our invocation of Bono suggests, it is not necessarily done without controversy. Bono himself might insist he is representing real people, not a discourse. His critics might accept that he is indeed representing a discourse, but not one that actually benefits people in Africa. In this article we make the case for representing discourses as an integral aspect of democracy, especially deliberative or discursive democracy. We link discursive representation to theories of deliberative democracy that emphasize the engagement of discourses in existing institutions of government and the broader public sphere, and those that ponder the design of deliberative institutions as part of the architecture of government. Discursive representation is one way to redeem the promise of deliberative democracy when the deliberative participation of all affected by a collective decision is infeasible. We show how to organize representation in a Chamber of Discourses and how to evaluate representation practices in the more informal interplay of discourses in the public sphere. We draw contrasts with more conventional notions about representing individuals and groups, and identify discursive counterparts to concepts of authorization and accountability that figure in most accounts of representation. Representation is conventionally defined as "substantive acting for others," in Pitkin's (1967) terms; "others" may be captured in terms of the discourses to which they subscribe. Whether discourses are represented *by* particular persons is an open question. We show not only how to designate discursive representatives, but also demonstrate less tangible ways in which discourses can find representation. We do not claim that representation of discourses is always preferable to that of individuals, just that it is different, sometimes feasible when the representation of persons is not so feasible (especially in transnational settings lacking a well-defined demos), and, on some criteria and in some settings, may do better.[3]

A discourse can be understood as a set of categories and concepts embodying specific assumptions, judgments, contentions, dispositions, and capabilities. It enables the mind to process sensory inputs into coherent accounts, which can then be shared in intersubjectively meaningful fashion. At a basic level, any political discourse will normally feature an ontology of entities recognized as existing or relevant. Among these entities, some (e.g., individuals, social classes, groups, or states) will be ascribed agency, the capacity to act, while in competing discourses the same entities will be

---

Versions of this article were presented to the Conference on Rethinking Democratic Representation, University of British Columbia, 2006; Department of Political Science, University of Stockholm, 2007; Symposium on Representation and Democracy, University of Birmingham, 2007; and the 2007 conference of the American Political Science Association. For comments, we thank Katherine Curchin, Carolyn Hendriks, Alnoor Ibrahim, John Keane, Gerry Mackie, Eric McGilvray, Ricardo Mendonça, and Michael Saward. This research was supported by Australian Research Council Discovery Grant DP0558573.

[1] Sophisticated and wide ranging, Saward's paper remains wedded to the representation of people rather than discourses.

[2] On social constructions of Africa, see Ferguson (2006).

[3] We believe the term "discursive representation" was first used by Keck (2003) for whom in international politics it means representing perspectives or positions, not discourses as we define them.

REPRESENTATION

denied agency (e.g., liberal individualists deny the agency of classes). For those entities recognized as agents, some motives will be recognized, others denied. So, for example, administrative discourses recognize the agency of managers motivated by public interest values, whereas market liberal discourses ascribe to administrators only rational egoism. Any discourse will also contain an account of the relationships taken to prevail between agents and others. So, economistic discourses see competition as natural, whereas feminist discourses would see the possibility of cooperation while recognizing pervasive patriarchy. Finally, discourses rely on metaphors and other rhetorical devices. So, a "spaceship earth" metaphor is central to some environmental discourses, whereas horror stories about "welfare queens" and the like are central to individualistic conservative discourses on social policy (Alker and Sylvan 1994; Dryzek and Berejikian 1993).

Discourses enable as well as constrain thought, speech, and action.[4] Any discourse embodies some conception of common sense and acceptable knowledge; it may embody power by recognizing some interests as valid while repressing others. However, discourses are not just a surface manifestation of interests because discourses help constitute identities and their associated interests. The relevant array of discourses depends on the issue at hand (although some discourses can apply to a number of different issues) and can evolve with time. For example, when it comes to economic issues, relevant discourses might include market liberalism, antiglobalization, social democracy, and sustainable development. When it comes to international security, pervasive discourses might include realism, counterterror, Islamic radicalism, and neoconservatism. Discourses do not constitute the entirety of nonindividual political phenomena that may demand representation. In particular, discourses should not be confused with groups defined by ascriptive characteristics such as race, class, or gender; coalitions of actors who may favor a policy for different reasons; interests, which although they may be constituted by discourses, can also exist independent of discourse; interest groups, which have a tangible organization that discourses lack; or opinions on particular issues, which may be embedded in particular discourses, but need not be.

WHY REPRESENT DISCOURSES

Given that other modes of representation already exist, why might discursive representation be attractive? We begin our argument through reference to the rationality of systematically involving multiple discourses in collective decision. We then turn to an ontological justification of the priority of discourses, grounded in the discursive psychology of a world of fractured individual commitments. This account enables an ethical argument that even the individual autonomy prized by liberals can be promoted by representing the multiple discourses each individual inhabits. We then show

that discursive representation is especially appropriate when a well-bounded demos is hard to locate, and helps realize the promise of contemporary theories of deliberative democracy.

Rationality

In a long tradition encompassing, among others, J.S. Mill, John Dewey, Karl Popper (1966), and Charles Lindblom (1965), democracy is seen as more rational in the production of collective outcomes than its alternatives. It provides opportunities for policy proposals to be criticized from a variety of directions, both before and after their implementation, thus providing the ideal setting for systematic trial and error in policy making. Democracy is, in Mill's terms, a "Congress of Opinions." The key consideration here is that all the vantage points for criticizing policy get represented — *not* that these vantage points get represented in proportion to the number of people who subscribe to them. When it comes to representing arguments, proportionality may actually be undesirable because it can pave the way to groupthink and the silencing of uncomfortable voices from the margins or across divides. Sunstein's (2000) deployment of social psychological findings on group polarization show that if members of a group (e.g., a jury) start with an inclination in one direction, deliberation will have the effect of moving the average position in the group toward an extreme version of that inclination. If a substantial majority of the population lean in one direction, proportionality in their representation in the forum may produce this movement to an extreme. Thus, it is important from the point of view of responsiveness to the initial distribution of positions, let alone collective rationality, to have countervailing discourses well represented in the forum at the outset to check this polarizing effect.

For policy-making rationality, then, all relevant discourses should get represented, regardless of how many people subscribe to each. Rationality may even benefit from the presence of a vantage point to which *nobody* subscribes; such was presumably the rationale for the use of a "Devil's Advocate" when evaluating cases for sainthood in the Catholic Church (which is, of course, not a paragon of democracy in any other sense).[5]

Now, it is one thing to ask that for the sake of rationality all vantage points, perspectives, or viewpoints get represented more or less equally in a forum, but quite another to ask that all relevant *discourses* get represented. Our justification here is that discourses have a solidity that perspectives do not. Furthermore, discourses can be measured and described (we explore methods later), whereas perspectives can be more elusive. In contemplating the representation of perspectives, Young (2000, 143–44) solves this elusiveness problem by assuming that "to the extent that persons are positioned similarly in those [social] structures, then they have similar perspectives," such that

---

[4] In like fashion, Anthony Giddens' structuration theory treats social structures as simultaneously enabling and constraining.

[5] The Devil's Advocate was abolished by Pope John Paul II, leading to a proliferation of saints.

REPRESENTATION

analysis of social structure can guide the selection of representatives. In contrast, we are open to discourses having a force independent of, and possibly prior to, social structure. Discursive representation is a conceptually simpler matter than the complex representations of perspectives, interests, opinions, and groups that are the ingredients of what Young calls "communicative democracy."

An Ontological Justification

What are the key entities that populate the political world and merit representation? In the liberal tradition, the answer would be "individuals." However, as Castiglione and Warren (2006, 13) point out,

> ...from the perspective of those who are represented, what is represented are not persons as such, but some of the interests, identities, and values that persons have or hold. Representative relationships select for specific aspects of persons, by framing wants, desires, discontents, values and judgments in ways that they become publicly visible, articulated in language and symbols, and thus politically salient.

Thus, the whole person cannot be represented (see also Young 2000, 133). Which "aspects of persons" merit representation, and what happens when they point in different directions? This question has received a number of analytical treatments. Sagoff (1988) distinguished between the "consumer" and "citizen" preferences of individuals; so (to use one of his examples), the same individuals who would as consumers love to use a ski resort will as citizens oppose its construction in a wilderness area. Sagoff resolves the problem by asserting the superiority of politics and citizen preferences over markets and consumer preferences; economists wedded to contingent valuation would disagree, as would market liberals. Goodin (1986) speaks of "laundering preferences" before they are ready to be put into collective choice processes. When it comes to elections, Brennan and Lomasky (1993) argue that the very fact that any one person's vote is almost always inconsequential releases voters' "expressive preferences" as opposed to their material self-interest in deciding whom to vote for. Thus, in choosing whether to emphasize voting systems or markets, we also choose the relative weight of individuals' expressive preferences and their material interests. Expressive preferences might involve ethics or identity politics.

We prefer a less analytical and more empirical treatment of what Elster (1986) calls the "multiple self." Speaking in terms of preferences is unduly restrictive, for aspects of the multiple self may not be reducible to preferences (and the instrumental form of rationality it implies). This question can be illuminated by discursive psychology (Edwards and Potter 1992). Discursive psychology takes seriously the Wittgensteinian notion of language games as the framework in which cognition is possible. The mind itself lies at the intersection of such games: "I inhabit many different discourses each of which has its own cluster of significations" (Harré and Gillett 1994, 25). Subjectivity is, then, multifaceted:

"most of us will fashion a complex subjectivity from participation in many different discourses" (25). This is not a matter of an autonomous self picking and choosing across discourses because the multifaceted self is constituted by discourses; we cannot think outside discourses because they also enter and help constitute the mind. However, the very fact that each individual engages multiple discourses provides some freedom for maneuver, such that "fluid positionings instead of fixed roles" are possible (36), which is crucial when it comes to the possibilities for the reflection that is central to deliberative and democratic interaction. Thus, persons are not simply bundles of discourses; autonomous individuals can reflect across the discourses they engage, even as they can never fully escape their constraints.

The individual selves prized by liberals can, then, be quite fractured by the discourses that the individual engages. Group representation is no less problematic in this light. Group representation, where "blacks represent blacks and women represent women," as Mansbridge (1999) puts it. There may be more than one discourse relevant to black interests or women's interests, which a unitary framing of that group's interests will not capture. Some of its advocates recognize the need to "pluralize group representation," but then face indeterminacy in how far to go in representing different subgroups (Dovi 2002, 741). This indeterminacy can be ameliorated (although not eliminated) if we can show how the range of relevant discourses can be described.

Ethics

The liberal argument for the representation of individuals has an ethical as well as an ontological aspect, on the grounds that individuals are capable of self-government, and the repositories of moral worth. There are nonliberal arguments in which groups, social classes, and communities have similar moral standing, but what about discourses? There is actually no need to give discourses any moral standing that is not reducible to that of the individuals who subscribe to them. Yet, there is still a moral (as opposed to ontological) argument for discursive representation. Once we accept the insight from discursive psychology that any individual may engage multiple discourses, it is important that all these discourses get represented. Otherwise, the individual in his or her entirety is not represented. Discursive representation may, then do a morally superior because more comprehensive job of representing persons than do theories that treat individuals as unproblematic wholes. Liberals might reply that each individual should manage the demands of competing discourses him- or herself prior to seeking representation because an autonomous person is one who chooses not just among options, but also among reasons for that choice (Watson 1975). Yet, demanding this management prior to representation may paradoxically disrespect individual autonomy, if it requires the individual to repress some aspect of his- or herself. For example, a government employee may choose to vote

412   REPRESENTATION

Discursive Representation   November 2008

for party X because he or she fears that party Y, whose platform he or she otherwise prefers on moral grounds, will undertake budget cuts that endanger his or her job. Their moral preferences are repressed in their voting choice. Discursive representation would ensure both aspects of the self of this government employee get represented in subsequent deliberations.

The Decline of the Demos

Rationality, ontology, and ethics can justify discursive representation in any time or place. We now introduce some developments in contemporary politics that reinforce the case. Democratic theory has traditionally been tied closely to the idea of a well-bounded demos: no demos, no democracy. Correspondingly, in Pitkin's (1967) classic statement about representation, the definition of the people is logically prior to contemplation of their representation. Representative democracy in this light requires a precisely bounded citizenry, normally defined by membership of a political unit organized on a territorial basis, which then elects representatives. However, today's world is increasingly unlike this. Authority increasingly escapes the sovereign state, to be located in, or diffused throughout, the global system. Sometimes authority is transferred to an international governmental organization such as the World Trade Organization (W T O). When a tangible organization such as the WTO exists, it is possible to imagine global elections to its board, but impossible to institute them in any feasible future. The most that can be hoped for is the representation of states, which entails representation of peoples at one very considerable remove (and, of course, not all states are internally democratic). Currently, the WTO runs according to a single discourse, that of market-oriented neoliberalism. A more democratic WTO would be responsive to a broader range of discourses, such as the counterdiscourses constructed by antiglobalization activists.

Political authority is also increasingly diffused into informal networks made up of governmental and nongovernmental actors, be they businesses, professional associations, unions, nongovernmental organizations (NGOs), social movements, or individual activists (Rhodes 1997). Networked governance is almost impossible to render accountable in standard democratic terms because there is often no unique demos associated with a network. This is especially true when networks cross national boundaries. If networks cannot be held formally accountable to any well-defined demos, we have to look in other directions to render them accountable. One way of doing this is to try to ensure that a network is not dominated by a single discourse whose terms are accepted uncritically by all involved actors in a way that marginalizes other discourses that could claim relevance. For example, the international networks of finance and capital described by Castells (1997) have generally been dominated by economistic discourses to the exclusion of social justice discourses. International environmental networks have often been dominated by a moderate discourse of sustainable development that by the lights of more radical green discourses is too easily accommodated to economic growth rather than effective environmental conservation.

If the demos is in decline, then Ankersmit's (2002) contention that the process of representation itself constitutes any "people" gains in plausibility. This kind of indeterminacy can be embraced by discursive representation, under which different discourses can constitute the relevant people in different ways. So, for example, in a cosmopolitan discourse, "the people" is global; in a nationalist discourse, it is always more particular.

Discourses in Theories of Deliberative Democracy

Deliberative democracy ought to be less wedded to conventional notions of representing persons than is the aggregative kind of democracy to which it is often contrasted because it puts talk and communication at the center of democracy (Chambers 2003, 308). From the viewpoint of the discursive self in deliberative democracy, it may then be more important for the quality of deliberation that all relevant discourses get represented, rather than that all individuals get represented. As Mansbridge (2003, 524) points out, in deliberative democracy there is no requirement that perspectives get "presented by a number of legislators proportional to the numbers of citizens who hold those perspectives." Weaver et al. (2007) show experimentally that the "weight" of a message in the forum depends more on the frequency with which it is repeated than on the number of people who present it, a finding that further undermines any argument for proportionality in representation in communicative settings.

The account of deliberative democracy presented by Dryzek (2000) highlights the generation and engagement of discourses in the public sphere. Public opinion is then defined as the provisional outcome of the contestation of discourses as transmitted to the state or other public authority. This feature fits nicely with discursive psychology because the reflective agents who populate a deliberative democracy can be seen as negotiating the field of discourses in which they necessarily participate, with more or less competence. This conceptualization of deliberative democracy is compatible with, but more precisely connected to discourses, and so their representation, than the formulations of Habermas (1996) concerning diffuse "subjectless communication" that produces public opinion and of Benhabib (1996, 74) concerning an "anonymous public conversation" in "interlocking and overlapping networks and associations of deliberation, contestation, and argumentation." Benhabib, Dryzek, and Habermas all assign the public sphere a central place in the architecture of deliberative democracy. Spaces in the public sphere have proliferated along with new communications media. Democratic legitimacy is generated in the extent to which collective decisions are consistent with the constellation of discourses existing within the public sphere, in the degree to which this

REPRESENTATION

balance is itself under the decentralized control of reflective, competent, and informed actors (Dryzek 2001). This is not the place to debate the pros and cons of these approaches; suffice it to say that there are versions of deliberative democracy for which discourses and their contestation or engagement are a central feature, begging the question of how they might be represented. There are also versions of deliberative democracy that have moved beyond the idea that effective deliberation requires a demos with a well-specified set of actors united by bonds of social solidarity. Indeed, it is in such settings that key features of deliberative democracy are now being tested (Scheuerman 2006).

In Joshua Cohen's classic statement, deliberative legitimacy is to be found in all those subject to a decision participating in deliberation about its content (Cohen 1989). However, given the impossibility of organizing participation by *all* those affected, another solution needs to be found in order that communication from those not in the deliberative forum itself be somehow represented inside the forum when the deliberation of all yields to the deliberation of some (Manin 1987). Critics of deliberative democracy (Shapiro 1999; Walzer 1999) have pointed out that effective face-to-face deliberation can only ever involve a handful of people. Thus, seeking democratic legitimacy via participation in deliberation by all those affected looks futile. Conventional electoral representation to reduce the number of deliberators is one solution, but elections themselves are not necessarily deliberative affairs (and proposals to make them more deliberative rarely involve anything like the deliberation of *all*). Furthermore, the number of legislators in a general purpose legislature is still generally too large for them all to deliberate together.

Discursive representation offers a solution to this key problem of scale that confronts deliberative democracy. The number of discourses that need representing on any issue is generally much smaller than the number of representatives in general-purpose legislatures, so it ought to be possible to constitute a small issue-specific deliberating group that contains representatives of all relevant discourses. We now ask how such small groups might be constituted formally in order to combine effective deliberation with discursive representation. Then we turn to more informal ways of securing discursive representation that resonate with accounts of deliberative democracy emphasizing engagement of discourses in a broad public sphere.

FORMALLY CONSTITUTING THE CHAMBER OF DISCOURSES

It is possible to imagine a Chamber of Discourses corresponding to more familiar assemblies based on the representation of individuals. Existing parliamentary chambers do of course feature discourses, but only unsystematically, as a by-product of electoral representation.

We have already argued that there is no need for proportionality in discursive representation. Epistemic

justifications for deliberation (Estlund 1997) also suggest that the composition of the deliberative forum need not mirror that of the population at large. However, it is important to ensure that each relevant discourse gets articulate representation, and we should be wary of the "lottery of talent" introducing inequalities across discursive representatives. Having multiple representatives for each discourse ought to ameliorate at least chance factors. It may also be true that the nature of a discourse is associated with the capacity of its adherents to articulate its content. Here, deliberative democrats would stress the need for forum design to bring out the "communicative competence" of representatives. Experience with deliberative "minipublics" shows that ordinary citizens can become capable deliberators.

In thinking about the Chamber of Discourses, we must allow that in deliberation individuals reflect on the discourses they engage and can change their minds. Mansbridge (2003, 524) suggests that when "deliberative mechanisms work well" they should select against "the least informed political positions in the polity." It is entirely possible that particular discourses initially identified for representation in the forum will not survive deliberation unscathed, but that may not be so bad if the transformation renders the constellation of discourses more publicly defensible. Niemeyer (2004) demonstrates this process empirically. On an environmental issue deliberated in a citizen's jury, he shows that a discourse that tried to assuage anxieties on both sides of the issue was transformed for its adherents toward a more clearly preservationist discourse. The possibility that discourses get transformed once represented does mean that discursive representation is inconsistent with a "delegate" model of representation.

We should also recognize that discourses can be transformed, or even constituted, by the very fact of their representation. Representing a previously marginalized discourse may mean that a particular category of people gets constituted as agents within the discourse. For example, the fact that the discourse of environmental justice became heard in policy-making processes in the United States in the late 1980s validated the agency in environmental affairs of low-income ethnic minority victims of pollution. The discourse of Africa associated with Bono perhaps exists mainly in the fact of its representation at high-profile international events. However, this last feature is by no means unique to discourses. As Ankersmit (2002, 115) puts it, perhaps overstating the point, "without political representation we are without a conception of what reality—the represented—is like; without it, political reality has neither face nor contours. Without representation there is no represented."

To constitute formally a Chamber of Discourses would require to begin a way of identifying and describing the array of relevant discourses on an issue. We would then need a way to designate representatives of each discourse (or of positions in the array of discourses). Members of the Chamber of Discourses could not be elected because then they would represent constituencies of individuals. Another option would be

414

REPRESENTATION

through random selection—as advocated, for example, in Leib's (2004) proposal for a fourth "popular" branch of government in the United States. The problem with random selection is that large numbers are needed to guard against the possibility that a relevant discourse might be missed. However, the larger the number of representatives, the harder it becomes for them to deliberate together. This is why large-scale processes such as deliberative opinion polls and citizens' assemblies subdivide their participants into smaller deliberative groups of no more than 20 or so each. Thus, we need a procedure better than random chance to ensure that all discourses are effectively represented in each group.

A more economical alternative would involve constituting a deliberative minipublic of around 15 to 20 citizens, the kind of number now used extensively in institutions such as citizens' juries, consensus conferences, and planning cells. The standard procedure is to begin with an initial random sample of citizens, and then target individuals with particular social characteristics—age, education, place of residence, income, ethnicity, and so forth. This is essentially a "politics of presence" kind of approach to representation (Phillips 1995). However, discursive representation involves (in Phillips' terms) a "politics of ideas." There is no guarantee or even strong likelihood that people with different social characteristics will in fact represent different discourses, or that a reasonably full range of social characteristics will guarantee a reasonably full range of discourses is present in the forum. Discursive representation can improve the deliberative capacities of institutional designs featuring random selection by ensuring that a comprehensive range of discourses is present. Fortunately, there are methods available to both (a) map the constellation of discourses relevant to an issue and (b) determine which individuals best represent each discourse. We now describe some methods. These methods illustrate what is possible. Our basic argument for discursive representation does not depend on commitment to any or all of them.

SYSTEMATIC SELECTION OF DISCURSIVE REPRESENTATIVES

Davies, Sherlock, and Rauschmayer (2005) show how Q methodology can be used to recruit individuals who best represent particular arguments to deliberative mini-publics. Q methodology involves measuring an individual's subjective orientation to an issue area in terms of his or her ranking of a set of 35 to 60 statements about the issue in a "Q sort." These statements can be keyed to the five features of discourses listed previously: ontology, agency, motives of agents, relationships, and metaphors (although this is not done by Davies, Sherlock, and Rauschmayer). For example, in a study of discourses surrounding local sustainability issues in the United Kingdom, Barry and Proops (1999, 342) deploy 36 statements. One of their statements about ontology is "LETS [local employment and trading systems] is a new type of economy in which sustainability is a key aspect." A statement referring

to agency is "We all have to take responsibility for environmental problems." A statement on motives is "People are taking a short-term view: they're not thinking about the long term." One about relationships is "You can't look at one part of the planet, because all the parts interact."[6]

The ranking process is itself reflective, so consistent with the notion that discourses can be transformed and winnowed in the process of their representation. Individuals from the subject population are asked to order the statements into a manageable number of categories from "most agree" to "most disagree." The subject population could be several hundred individuals selected at random (Q methodologists are happy working with much smaller numbers of subjects, but the link we are trying to make here to representation means that a larger number might be required to help us find particularly good representatives of each discourse). The Q sorts so produced can then be factor analyzed; factor analysis is essentially a summary procedure that produces a manageable number of (in this case) discourses. We can compute a loading (correlation coefficient) between each discourse and each individual. Those individuals loading highest on a particular discourse will make particularly good discursive representatives—at least in the sense that they are characteristic of the discourse in question, although, of course, they can vary in how articulate they are when it comes to deliberation itself. However, there may be circumstances in which it is desirable to select more complex individuals who load on more than one discourse (as we see later).

To take an example, consider the study of political discourses in Russia in the late 1990s reported in Dryzek and Holmes (2002, 92–113). This study identified three discourses. The first, chastened democracy, remained committed to democracy despite current political disasters. The second, reactionary antiliberalism, regretted the demise of the Soviet Union and opposed the postcommunist status quo. The third, authoritarian

---

[6] Although Barry and Proops do not have a "metaphors" category, an example of a relevant metaphor statement about sustainability is "If we continue with activities which destroy our environment and undermine the conditions for our survival, such as a virus" (speech by UK Environment Minister Michael Meacher, Newcastle University, 14 February 2003). Many (but not all) Q methodologists describe what they do as a form of discourse analysis. The justification for using principles of political discourse analysis to select the statements that are the grist for the Q analysis (Q sample) is established by Dryzek and Berejikian (1993). We can begin by generating several hundred statements relevant to an issue (which can be done by holding discussion groups and transcribing what is said, or surveying sources such as newspaper letters columns, talkback radio, political speeches, weblogs, etc.). We then apply a sampling frame to select around 35 to 60 statements for the Q sort itself. The frame can be based on the five categories we introduced previously in defining the concept of discourse: ontology (entities whose existence is affirmed or denied), agency (who or what has the capacity to act, and who or what does not), motives ascribed to agents, relationships (e.g., hierarchies on the basis of expertise, age, wealth, or gender; or their corresponding equalities), and metaphors and other rhetorical devices. Once the statements are classified, the required numbers of statements can be selected from each category. Dryzek and Berejikian and Barry and Proops also use a second dimension for statement categorization based on the kind of claim made in the statement (definitive, designative, evaluative, advocative).

REPRESENTATION

development, disapproves of both the Soviet Union and the postcommunist present, seeking a better economic future under a disciplined autocracy. Among the Russians interviewed, the person with the highest loading on chastened democracy (70, where 100 would indicate perfect agreement) is a public relations manager who describes herself as a liberal. The person with the highest loading (59) on reactionary antiliberalism is a teacher who describes himself as a Russian nationalist. The two people with the equal highest loading (60) on authoritarian development are a student who describes herself as a nonpartisan atheist and a construction worker who claims not to care about politics. Assuming they are articulate, these individuals would on the face of it make particularly good representatives for any forum in which representation of the discourse in question is required—within Russia, or even internationally. (At meetings of international economic organizations, it could be instructive to have somebody representing authoritarian development.)

Most Q studies seek only to map discourses present. Davies, Sherlock, and Rauschmayer (2005) use Q to select participants for deliberative forums. We can designate those participants as representatives of discourses. In most theories of representation, those represented somehow authorize the representation. The method we have described seems to substitute social science for political process, with the risk of empowering an unaccountable social scientific elite. We address procedures for countering this hazard in the "Authorization and Accountability" section, but one check might be to expand the range of methods used, to which we now turn.

OTHER METHODS FOR SELECTING DISCURSIVE REPRESENTATIVES

Although we have discussed Q methodology as a particularly systematic way to identify relevant discourses and choose discursive representatives, there are other ways. When it comes to discourse identification, there exist in many issue areas enumerations of relevant discourses based on historical analysis. So, for example, for U.S. environmental politics, Brulle (2000) enumerates seven discourses on the environmental side: wildlife management, conservation, preservation, reform environmentalism, deep ecology, environmental justice, and ecofeminism, along with an antienvironmental discourse of "manifest destiny." In criminal justice policy area, at least four discourses can be enumerated. One stresses the psychopathology of criminals, a second treats crime as a matter of rational choice, a third emphasizes the social causes of crime, and a fourth the social dislocation of individual offenders. Each discourse comes with a range of treatments: respectively, retribution, deterrence, social policy, and restorative justice. In the criminal justice policy area, one could imagine constituting a chamber with representatives from these different discourses. In these environmental and criminal justice examples, it is not difficult to identify individual activists, publicists, or politicians associated with each discourse, who could serve as discursive representatives.

Q is an interpretive methodology that happens to be quantitative, but other interpretive methods for discourse analysis are qualitative or ethnographic. Both in-depth interviews with individuals and focus groups could be used to map relevant discourses in an issue area. Hochschild (1981) analyzes 28 in-depth interviews of rich and poor Americans in order to map different beliefs about distributive justice and the sorts of distributive rules that should be applied to different policy areas. Despite considerable ambiguity and inconsistency among her subjects, Hochschild's analysis could be mined for discourses and their representatives. Notably, Hochschild finds six kinds of distributive rule applied by her subjects, although their application is issue-area specific. However, for example, when it comes to policy for financing schools, it would be possible to identify using her analysis an individual who subscribes to a discourse of need, one that stresses performance, and so forth. An ethnographic study that began with the intent of identifying discourses and their representatives would enable a much sharper focus.

Opinion surveys could also inform the identification of relevant discourses, although their lack of interpretive depth may mean that they have to be supplemented by other sorts of analysis. So, for example, Kempton, Boster, and Hartley (1995) combine surveys and semistructured interviews. They find a vernacular environmental discourse that appears to be shared by most ordinary people in the United States (including categories of people they targeted for explicit antienvironmental sentiments), although for some individuals in-depth interviews reveal that it is overridden by discourses that stress either employment and social justice or cynicism about the way environmental values get deployed (215). Discursive representation here would mean identifying individuals who prioritized the latter two discourses, as well as those who did not.

There are then a number of methods that could be deployed to select discursive representatives. Different methods might yield different representations, just as different electoral systems produce different configurations of political parties. Triangulation across different methods might increase our confidence in the validity of any particular representation, although it would be of little help should representations differ. However, in the latter case, there would be no problem in using different methods to pick different discursive representatives. One method might simply pick up on a discourse that another method missed. For example, opinion surveys would miss subjugated or marginal discourses that were not preconceived by the survey designer; it might take in-depth interviews or Q methodology to reveal these. We should also allow that particular discourses may only crystallize in the process of selection of their representatives. In-depth interviews might well have such an effect, especially if they have the salutary effects that psychotherapists claim.

Among alternative methods for the selection of discursive representatives, Q methodology or in-depth interviews should be used when the content and configuration of relevant discourses is weakly understood. In-depth interviews should be used to tease out discourses that have yet to crystallize fully in the understandings of any actor. Opinion surveys can be used when the content of relevant discourses is well understood and/or financial constraints suggest a low-cost method. Historical methods are appropriate when conducting interviews is impossible, too expensive, or the population from which one might select discursive representatives is highly dispersed (as in transnational affairs).

DIFFERENT SORTS OF DISCURSIVE REPRESENTATIVES

Choosing as representatives for participation in deliberation only those individuals who are strongly identified with particular discourses is not necessarily the most defensible procedure. Discursive psychology suggests that the typical individual actually has access to more than one discourse. In this light, choosing individuals who identify strongly with a single discourse might look a bit like selecting for extremism. One solution here might be to constitute two deliberating subchambers, one made up of individuals initially identifying strongly with single discourses, the other made up of individuals identified with two or more discourses. The first group might then be best at opening up the relevant range of issues, whereas the second might be better at reaching reflective judgment across discourses. Alternatively, we might decide what we actually want the deliberating group to do, and select for extremism and moderation accordingly. If the deliberating forum is akin to a jury delivering a verdict (say, a health care committee deciding whether an expensive lifesaving treatment is warranted in a particular case), we might want to select for moderation across discourses. If we want the forum to generate ideas (e.g., on a novel policy problem), we might want to select for extremism in discursive representation.[7] However, in light of the possibility of deliberation-induced change in individuals' commitments to particular discourses, and even the content of discourses, these suggestions remain speculative. Designing empirical studies to test the effects of different forum compositions along these lines would actually be quite straightforward.

It might even be useful to have a Chamber of Extremism and a Chamber of Moderation sitting in parallel. This would be analogous to the way lower and upper houses currently operate in bicameral parliaments, with the upper house expected to be a moderate house of review controlling the partisan excesses of the lower house. In practice, lower houses are themselves vulnerable to excessive moderation as parties converge on the median voter in elections, so an explicit Chamber of Extremism might actually improve the quality of debate by sharpening differences.

Another possible institutional design might involve a Chamber of Moderation adjudicating the presenta-

tions made to it by individuals strongly associated with particular discourses. Such a design would resemble the way mini-publics such as citizens' juries and consensus conferences already operate, although citizen-adjudicators in these forums are currently selected on the basis of their lack of any prior partisanship, rather than sympathy with multiple discourses.

In thinking about discursive representation, it is important to stress that discourses are not necessarily reducible to the opinions of a well-defined set of subscribers. Discursive psychology accepts, and Q methodological studies typically confirm, that any given individual may subscribe partially to several different, perhaps competing, discourses, each of which resonates with a particular aspect of the "self." For this individual, different situations may then invoke different discourses. Discursive representation then involves representing discourses, not selves, even when we need to identify individuals to articulate the discourse in question. It is even possible that a particular discourse may find no complete resonance with any individual, although partial resonance with many, attracting minor aspects of a number of "divided selves." How exactly might the representation of any such discourse be organized? One solution might be to find the individual or set of individuals loading most highly on this discourse, even if they load more highly on another discourse. The likelihood of any such fugitive discourse on any issue is an empirical question. However, such a discourse could conceivably represent a new understanding currently at the margins of public opinion, with the potential to become more significant in the future. It might, of course, also represent an understanding on the way out, or one that is destined to remain marginal. However, from the point of view of problem-solving rationality discussed previously, marginal discourses may still be important. Representation of marginal discourses is especially important from the point of view of democratic equality to the degree dominant discourses embody privilege and power.

DECISION AND POWER

How should decisions be reached in any formal Chamber of Discourses? A theory of representation is not a full theory of democracy, so one can imagine a variety of decision mechanisms, including voting. Consensus may be a plausible rule if the chamber is composed of a small number of individuals, each of whom can be associated with more than one discourse (so featuring moderation as defined previously), although undesirable conformity pressures may accompany small size. Consensus is less plausible as numbers increase, or to the degree each participant is strongly associated with a particular discourse, although even here we should not assume that discourses are necessarily incommensurable.[8] "Working agreements" may still be

---

[7] Discursive representatives could reflexively help constitute the "we" here.

[8] Metaconsensus that structures communication and decision may in fact be more defensible than simple consensus as the goal of deliberation (Dryzek and Niemeyer 2006).

REPRESENTATION

possible in which participants agree on a course of action for different reasons, but understand as morally legitimate the reasons of others (Eriksen 2006). Even if they cannot agree on major issues, participants might still practice the "economy of moral disagreement" advocated by Gutmann and Thompson (1996), what we could style an economy of discourse disagreement, searching for aspects of issues representatives can agree on. There is no justification for giving discursive representatives veto power over decisions that affect their discourse, of the sort that Young (1990) believes should be possessed by representatives of oppressed groups.

How much power should any Chamber of Discourses possess in relation to other sorts of representative institutions, such as legislatures? Again, a theory of representation is not a complete theory of democracy, and so the idea of discursive representation cannot itself adjudicate across any competing representative claims. Discursive representation might complement the work of familiar institutions, rather than replace them. A formal Chamber of Discourses could take its place in existing institutional architecture in a variety of ways. Mini-publics deployed so far have generally been issue specific, authorized by legislatures or political executives, constituted for one occasion, and then dissolved immediately afterward. This is the normal procedure when it comes to consensus conferences, planning cells, citizens' juries, and the citizens' assemblies used to frame referendum questions on constitutional reform in British Columbia, Ontario, and the Netherlands. If (in contrast to the Canadian Citizens' Assemblies, which had a specified role in decision making) the Chamber of Discourses is advisory, then it needs an audience, which may be found in the broader public sphere, as well as in the legislature. Taking the idea of a Chamber of Discourses very literally would suggest that it could begin with several hundred citizens serving a term as members of the upper house of a bicameral legislature (a proposal of this sort was made by the Demos think tank in the context of debates about reform of the House of Lords in the UK). Subsets of the house could then be chosen along the lines we have specified to deliberate particular issues. Alternatively, these citizens could constitute Leib's (2004) proposed fourth "popular" branch of government, reviewing policy proposals generated in executive or legislative branches, or generating proposals for review by the other three branches. In nonstate and transnational contexts, it is easier to imagine granting more substantial and perhaps even final authority to a Chamber of Discourses, if other sorts of representative institutions are not available. Within more familiar governmental contexts, legislative mandates for public consultation and participation present opportunities for experimentation, especially in cases where established forms of consultation are recognized as ineffective. Liberal democratic governments are occasionally willing to experiment, as for example in UK Prime Minister Gordon Brown's 2007 "big idea" for citizens' juries on major policy issues, plus a Citizens' Summit to deliberate basic national values.

AUTHORIZATION AND ACCOUNTABILITY

Theories of representation from Pitkin (1967) to Young (1990, 128–33) require not only the selection of representatives, but also their authorization by and accountability to those represented. Issues concerning authorization and accountability become pressing to the degree a Chamber of Discourses has an explicit share in decision-making authority. Authorization is, on the face of it, problematic in the methods we have described for the selection of discursive representatives, which would involve social science rather than political process. Such use of social science is already practiced when it comes to the constitution of familiar mini-publics such as deliberative polls, citizens' juries, consensus conferences, and citizens' assemblies. Random selection itself is a social scientific technique that often makes little sense to those not versed in social science. The use of social characteristics to narrow down an initial random sample into a smaller deliberating group is again soaked in social science theories about what individual characteristics matter, as well as assumed links between social characteristics and points of view. Furthermore, when it comes to the engineering of electoral systems, social scientific theories inform the selection of alternative systems (Reilly 2001) (although as the British Columbia Citizens' Assembly shows, such theories can be made intelligible to lay citizens). Yet, the authorization problem remains.

There are several ways to ameliorate this problem. To begin, the social science itself can be done as democratically as possible. In the case of Q methodology, this principle would entail using only statements that appear in ordinary political language, not ones contrived by the analyst. The initial set of statements should be as comprehensive as possible in capturing the variety of things that could be said about the issue at hand, so as to enable capture of the extant variety of discourses. For all methods, data should be analyzed in ways that minimize the observer's discretion in interpreting results. Multiple methods can be used to ensure no discourse is missed. Once results are produced, they can be presented in plain language for validation by citizen participants. In Q methodology, it is easy to summarize an identified discourse in narrative form (Dryzek and Holmes 2002), and those designated as representatives of a discourse can be asked if the narrative really does describe them.

Once we have identified a set of individuals loading highly on a discourse, we could ask them to select a representative. This would require informing this set about both the content of the discourse and the way it was delineated. Furthermore, it may be possible to involve citizens themselves in doing the social science. Social scientists could still be technical consultants, but defer to citizens when it comes to judgments about (say) the items to be included in a Q sort or survey, or the interpretation of in-depth interview transcripts. Whatever use is made of social science, it is important to make it transparent to nonexperts involved in the forum in question. Analysts could then be accountable before hearings, just as executive officials can be

418

REPRESENTATION

Discursive Representation

November 2008

called before hearings of nonexpert representatives in an elected legislature. However, those conducting the hearings could not be discursive representatives because they would have been selected by the procedure they are assessing. Instead, they could be drawn from the larger pool from which discursive representatives are selected. As a final check, validation of the configuration of discursive representatives could be sought from actors in the broader public sphere by inviting their comments on forum composition.

Accountability cannot in discursive representation be induced by the representative's fear of sanction because there is no subsequent election at which the representative might be punished. Discursive accountability must be understood instead in communicative fashion. To be accountable to the discourse (or discourses) they represent, representatives must continue to communicate in terms that make sense within that discourse (or discourses), even as they encounter different others in the Chamber of Discourses, and even as they reflect and change their minds in such encounters. If, in the limiting case, representatives seem to be abandoning their discourse and adopting another (as happened in the environmental citizens' jury we discussed previously), then discursive accountability requires that any shift make sense in the terms established by the original discourse.[9] This requirement is not necessarily met when, for example, social justice advocates get drawn into the language of stability, security, and efficiency; when environmentalists abandon the language of intrinsic value in nature, and start speaking in terms of how preserving nature has economic benefits; or when advocates of an ethical foreign policy slip into the language of realism. Discursive accountability can be facilitated by publicity, such that representatives are always mindful of how what they say will be received in the terms of the discourse(s) that validate their representation. Discursive representatives do not have to be "delegates" of discourses, unable to reflect and change their minds. However, if they do change their minds, they must justify the change in terms set by the discourse(s) they represent.

A MORE INFORMAL CHAMBER OF DISCOURSES

We noted at the outset that discourses currently get represented in mostly informal fashion (e.g., by high-profile activists such as Bono). Contemporary democratic theory can welcome this kind of activity, especially in conceptualizations of deliberative democracy that emphasize the engagement of discourses in a broad public sphere (see the "Discourses in Theories of Deliberative Democracy" section). Discourses are generated within and populate the public sphere,

and so a more informal Chamber of Discourses could be grounded in this public sphere. Historically, new discourses have been brought onto the democratic agenda from oppositional public spheres, outside the formal institutions of the state. Think, for example, of how environmentalism and feminism arrived in the 1960s. In some cases, these discourses were brought very quickly into governing processes—environmentalism in the United States in 1970, and feminism in Scandinavian countries around the same time. (However, the result in these countries was rapid attenuation of any radical critique associated with the discourse.) This informal chamber could coexist with the formal chamber we have described, and they could be linked as elements in what Hendriks (2006, 499–502) calls an "integrated deliberative system." Within that system, representatives in the informal chamber could present discourses for validation in the formal chamber. These informal representatives could also exercise critical oversight over the constellation of discourses identified for the formal chamber (as indicated in our previous discussion of discursive accountability).

If we think of a Chamber of Discourses in these informal terms, then it would seem at first sight that all that needs to be done is to leave it alone. In Habermas' terms, the public sphere is a "wild" zone that can be protected by, for example, a standard range of liberal rights to free belief, expression, assembly, and association. Beyond that, critics might need to expose and counter agents of distortion in the public sphere, such as the influence exercised by large media corporations, lack of material resources meaning that some sorts of voices do not get heard, hegemonic discourses that serve the interests of the powerful, and so forth.

In this light, discourses get represented by the normal array of actors present in the public sphere. However, the idea of discursive representation enables and provides criteria for reevaluation of some standard normative treatments of civil society. Putnam (2000) disparages "checkbook" groups such as the Sierra Club that demand nothing more than money from their members and that have little in the way of internal participation of the sort that might help build social capital in the larger society in which the Sierra Club operates. In light of discursive representation, Putnam's criticism misses the point. Checkbook groups may build discursive capital (in the sense of facilitating the articulation of discourses), if not social capital. The Sierra Club exists to represent a particular discourse of environmental preservation, and contributors to the Sierra Club express solidarity with that discourse. Discursive accountability can be sought by these leaders continuing to communicate in terms that make sense within the discourse of preservation (even as they engage other discourses). If leaders could not justify their actions in these terms, contributors can back other groups instead.

Discourses engaging in the broad public sphere get represented to more authoritative political structures (e.g., states) through a variety of mechanisms. Public opinion defined in the engagement of discourses can reach the state or other public authority, and so find

---

[9] This requirement was in fact met in the citizens' jury. The two discourses were not mutually exclusive (orthogonal), enabling those who shifted to reason their way from the original discourse on which they loaded to a more exclusive association with preservationism in a way that could make sense to those outside the jury who subscribed to the original discourse.

490

REPRESENTATION

American Political Science Review

representation. In his "two-track" model of deliberation in the public sphere influencing deliberation in the legislature, Habermas (1996) (very conventionally) eventually stresses elections. In this light, we might evaluate electoral systems by how well they represent discourses. For example, preferential voting as practiced in Australia almost guarantees a two-party system in parliament. However, minor discourses get represented even when nobody in parliament is formally associated with them because the two major parties need to cultivate minor parties in order to receive their voters' second preferences, so preferential voting may at least be better than first-past-the post plurality voting in representing discourses. However, elections are not the only transmission mechanisms. Others include the use of rhetoric by activists, influence on the terms of political discussion that can change the understandings of government actors, and arguments that are heard by public officials (Dryzek 2000). Conceptualizing such transmission mechanisms as forms of discursive representation drives home the need to subject them to critical scrutiny. Rhetoric, in particular, is often treated with suspicion by democratic theorists, on the grounds of its capacity for emotional manipulation and coercion (e.g., Chambers 1996, 151). However, rhetoric may be vital in representing a discourse to those in positions of political authority not initially subscribing to it. The solution here would be to hold rhetoric to standards such as noncoerciveness and the need to connect particular interests to general principles. The latter could, for example, curb the racist or ethnic nationalist rhetoric of demagogues.

In addition, all forms of transmission need to be held to the discursive accountability standard introduced previously. People claiming to represent a discourse or discourses should always communicate in terms that make sense within the discourse or discourses in question, even when they contemplate shifting in relation to the constellation of discourses they subsequently encounter. This standard is probably met more easily to the degree representatives keep their distance from explicit participation in collective decision making in, for example, corporatist arrangements.

In the case of networked governance, discursive accountability could be facilitated by specifying that a network does not require as the price of entry that participants commit to the hegemonic discourse of the network and renounce other relevant discourses. This kind of accountability would be hard to secure in transnational financial networks, which currently exclude discourses of sustainability and social justice.

Informal discursive representation may currently be found directed toward familiar and conventional authority structures (e.g., states and international organizations). However, this informal representation could also mesh with any formal Chamber of Discourses in this context, public sphere activism could provide a check on the degree to which the formal chamber features a comprehensive and accurate set of the relevant discourses, and promote discursive accountability by calling changes of language in the formal chamber to account.

TRANSNATIONAL DISCURSIVE REPRESENTATION

Representing discourses in transnational political action is actually more straightforward than representing persons (especially in the absence of elections). Indeed, it is already happening. In recent years, even economistic global institutions such as the World Bank and (begrudgingly) the International Monetary Fund (IMF) have begun a program of outreach to global civil society, meaning accountability no longer runs strictly to states. Who elects the NGOs? Nobody. Is there an identifiable constituency or category of people with which each NGO is associated and to which it is accountable? Not usually. International relations scholars have started to think about accountability (Grant and Keohane 2005), albeit mainly in terms of how sanctions can be levied on advocates, rather than discursive accountability as we have characterized it. However, NGOs pushing for human rights, fair trade, sustainable development, demilitarization, transparency, and so forth, may best be thought of as representatives of particular discourses in international politics. Is the world any more democratic for their activities? Clearly, yes, the international governmental institutions they target now have to justify their activities in light of a variety of discourses, whereas previously they either felt no need to justify at all, or did so in narrowly economistic and administrative terms. Thus, the idea of discursive representation provides democratic validation for the activities of NGOs and other transnational activists.

This kind of transnational discursive representation is currently informal in character, but more formal representation can be imagined. Thompson (1999) suggests that cross-border policy impacts can be brought into democratic accountability by the device of a "tribune for non-citizens." Such a tribune could not easily be elected —the appropriate electorate would be dispersed and extraordinarily hard to organize. However, for particular policy issues, it would be possible to identify relevant extranational or transnational discourses, and identify a good representative for them. For example, there exists a very well-defined transnational discourse of sustainable development. Perhaps global sustainability tribunes could be identified to represent this discourse in particular national governments. The problem, of course, is that those representatives would be least welcome where they were needed most. One can imagine them being welcomed by countries that are exemplary international citizens (Sweden), but resisted by countries that are poor international citizens, those that subscribe to hard-line notions of sovereignty, superpowers, and rogue states.

For most states, transnational discursive representation will probably have to be informal in any foreseeable future, constituted mostly by NGOs and networks of political activists in transnational public spheres exerting pressure. It is easier to envisage more formal Chambers of Discourses established in association with international organizations. Organizations such as the WTO, IMF, and World Bank have (as we have noted) accepted the need to legitimate their activities beyond

420

REPRESENTATION

Discursive Representation

the states that are their members, funders, or clients. Constituting formal Chambers of Discourses would be one very public way of discharging this obligation.

CONCLUSION

Once the basic idea of discursive representation is accepted, choices need to be made on several dimensions. Should discursive representation be formal, informal, or an integrated combination of both? Discursive representation could be formalized, especially in connection with growing enthusiasm for the constitution of mini-publics to deliberate complex and controversial policy issues, and as a way for governments to meet mandated requirements for public consultation. If discursive representation is formal, what method should we use to select representatives? How much authority should any Chamber of Discourses possess in relation to other representative institutions? There is no universal answer to any of these questions, although we have provided guidance about how each might be answered in particular contexts.

We have argued that discursive representation already occurs, although it is not always recognized as such. Whether formal, informal, or an integrated mix of both, discursive representation can help render policy making more rational, respect individual autonomy by more fully representing diverse aspects of the self, assist in realizing the promise of deliberative democracy, and make democratic theory more applicable to a world where the consequences of decisions are felt across national boundaries.

REFERENCES

Alker, Hayward, and David Sylvan. 1994. "Some Contributions of Discourse Analysis to Political Science." *Kosmopolis* 24 (3): 5–25.

Ankersmit, Frank R. 2002. *Political Representation*. Stanford, CA: Stanford University Press.

Barry, John, and John Proops. 1999. "Seeking Sustainability Discourses with Q Methodology." *Ecological Economics* 28: 337–45.

Benhabib, Seyla. 1996. "Toward a Deliberative Model of Democratic Legitimacy." In *Democracy and Difference: Contesting the Boundaries of the Political*, ed. S. Benhabib. Princeton, NJ: Princeton University Press, 67–94.

Brennan, Geoffrey, and Loren Lomasky. 1993. *Democracy and Decision*. Cambridge, UK: Cambridge University Press.

Brulle, Robert J. 2000. *Agency, Democracy, and Nature: The U.S. Environmental Movement from a Critical Theory Perspective*. Cambridge, MA: MIT Press.

Castells, Manuel. 1997. *The Rise of the Network Society*. Oxford, UK: Basil Blackwell.

Castiglione, Dario, and Mark E. Warren. 2006. "Rethinking Representation: Eight Theoretical Issues." Presented at the Conference on Rethinking Democratic Representation, University of British Columbia, Vancouver.

Chambers, Simone. 1996. *Reasonable Democracy: Jürgen Habermas and the Politics of Discourse*. Ithaca, NY: Cornell University Press.

Chambers, Simone. 2003. "Deliberative Democratic Theory." *Annual Review of Political Science* 6: 307–26.

Cohen, Joshua. 1989. "Deliberation and Democratic Legitimacy." In *The Good Polity*, ed. A. Hamlin and P. Pettit. Oxford, UK: Basil Blackwell, 17–34.

Davies, B. B., K. Sherlock, and F. Rauschmayer. 2005. "Recruitment', 'composition', and 'mandate' issues in deliberative processes: should we focus on arguments rather than individuals?"

Environment and Planning C-Government and Policy 23 (4): 599–615.

Dovi, Suzanne. 2002. "Preferable Descriptive Representatives: Will Just any Woman, Black, or Latino Do?" *American Political Science Review* 96 (4): 729–43.

Dryzek, John S. 2000. *Deliberative Democracy and Beyond: Liberals, Critics, Contestations*. Oxford, UK: Oxford University Press.

Dryzek, John S. 2001. "Legitimacy and Economy in Deliberative Democracy." *Political Theory* 29 (5): 651–69.

Dryzek, John S., and Jeffrey Berejikian. 1993. "Reconstructive Democratic Theory." *American Political Science Review* 87 (1): 48–60.

Dryzek, John S., and Leslie T. Holmes. 2002. *Post-Communist Democratization: Political Discourses Across Thirteen Countries*. Cambridge, UK: Cambridge University Press.

Dryzek, John S., and Simon John Niemeyer. 2006. "Reconciling Pluralism and Consensus as Political Ideals." *American Journal of Political Science* 50 (3): 634–49.

Edwards, Derek, and Jonathan Potter. 1992. *Discursive Psychology*. London: Sage.

Elster, Jon, ed. 1986. *The Multiple Self*. Cambridge, UK: Cambridge University Press.

Eriksen, Erik O. 2006. "Democratic Legitimacy: Working Agreement or Rational Consensus?" Centre for the Study of the Professions, Oslo University College, Oslo, Norway.

Estlund, David. 1997. "Beyond Fairness of Deliberation: The Epistemic Dimension of Democratic Authority." In *Deliberative Democracy: Essays on Reason and Politics*, ed. J. Bohman and W. Rehg. Cambridge, MA: MIT Press.

Ferguson, James. 2006. *Africa in the Neoliberal World*. Durham, NC: Duke University Press.

Goodin, Robert. 1986. "Laundering Preferences." In *Foundations of Social Choice Theory*, ed. J. Elster and A. Hylland. Cambridge: Cambridge University Press, 75–102.

Grant, Ruth W., and Robert O. Keohane. 2005. "Accountability and the Abuse of Power in World Politics." *American Political Science Review* 99: 29–44.

Gutmann, A., and D. Thompson. 1996. *Democracy and Disagreement*. Cambridge, MA: Belknap Press.

Habermas, Jürgen. 1996. *Between Facts and Norms: Contributions to a Discourse Theory of Law and Democracy*. Cambridge, MA: MIT Press.

Harré, Rom, and Grant Gillett. 1994. *The Discursive Mind*. Thousand Oaks, Ca: Sage.

Hendriks, Carolyn M. 2006. "Integrated Deliberation: Reconciling Civil Society's Dual Role in Deliberative Democracy." *Political Studies* 54: 486–508.

Hochschild, Jennifer L. 1981. *What's Fair? American Beliefs About Distributive Justice*. Cambridge, MA: Harvard University Press.

Keck, Margaret. 2003. "Governance Regimes and the Politics of Discursive Representation." In *Transnational Activism in Asia*, ed. N. Piper and A. Uhlin. London: Routledge, 43–60.

Kempton, Willett, James S. Boster, and Jennifer A. Hartley. 1995. *Environmental Values in American Culture*. Cambridge, MA: MIT Press.

Leib, Ethan J. 2004. *Deliberative Democracy in America: A Proposal for a Popular Branch of Government*. University Park: Pennsylvania State University Press.

Lindblom, Charles E. 1965. *The Intelligence of Democracy: Decision Making Through Mutual Adjustment*. New York: Free Press.

Manin, Bernard. 1987. "On Legitimacy and Political Deliberation." *Political Theory* 15 (3): 338–68.

Mansbridge, Jane J. 1999. "Should Blacks Represent Blacks and Women Represent Women? A Contingent 'Yes'." *Journal of Politics* 61 (3): 628–57.

Mansbridge, Jane J. 2003. "Rethinking Representation." *American Political Science Review* 97 (4): 515–28.

Niemeyer, Simon John. 2004. "Deliberation in the Wilderness: Displacing Symbolic Politics." *Environmental Politics* 13 (2): 347–72.

Phillips, Anne. 1995. *The Politics of Presence*. Oxford, UK: Clarendon Press.

Pitkin, Hannah F. 1967. *The Concept of Representation*. Berkeley: University of California Press.

Popper, Karl R. 1966. *The Open Society and Its Enemies*. London: Routledge and Kegan Paul.

Putnam, Robert. 2000. *Bowling Alone: The Collapse and Revival of American Community.* New York: Simon and Schuster.

Reilly, Benjamin. 2001. *Democracy in Divided Societies: Electoral Engineering for Conflict Management.* Cambridge, UK: Cambridge University Press.

Rhodes, R. A. W. 1997. *Understanding Governance: Policy Networks, Governance, Reflexivity, and Accountability.* Buckingham, UK: Open University Press.

Sagoff, Mark. 1988. *The Economy of the Earth: Philosophy, Law and the Environment.* Cambridge, UK: Cambridge University Press.

Saward, Michael. 2008. "Authorisation and Authenticity: Representation and the Unelected." *Journal of Political Philosophy* forthcoming.

Scheuerman, William. 2006. "Critical Theory Beyond Habermas." In *The Oxford Handbook of Political Theory,* ed. J. S. Dryzek, B. Honig, and A. Phillips, Oxford, UK: Oxford University Press, 85–105.

Shapiro, Ian. 1999. "Enough of Deliberation: Politics is About Interests and Power." In *Deliberative Politics,* ed. S. Macedo. Oxford, UK: Oxford University Press, 28–38.

Sunstein, Cass R. 2000. "Deliberative Trouble? Why Groups Go to Extremes." *Yale Law Journal* 110 (1): 71–119.

Thompson, Dennis. 1999. "Democratic Theory and Global Society." *Journal of Political Philosophy* 7: 111–25.

Walzer, Michael. 1999. "Deliberation, and What Else?" In *Deliberative Politics: Essays on Democracy and Disagreement,* ed. S. Macedo. Oxford, UK: Oxford University Press, 58–69.

Watson, Gary. 1975. "Free Agency." *Journal of Philosophy* 62 (8): 205–20.

Weaver, Kimberlee, Stephen M. Garcia, Norbert Schwarz, and Dale T. Miller. 2007. "Inferring the Popularity of an Opinion from Its Familiarity: A Repetitive Voice Can Sound Like a Chorus." *Journal of Personality and Social Psychology* 92: 821–33.

Young, Iris Marion. 1990. *Justice and the Politics of Difference.* Princeton, NJ: Princeton University Press.

Young, Iris Marion. 2000. *Inclusion and Democracy.* Oxford, UK: Oxford University Press.

21

Representation in the deliberative system

JAMES BOHMAN

Democracy has historically taken many different forms. The recognition that there are limits on the scope of democracy as an organizational principle has been equally variable. For the purposes of this discussion, I will take democracy in its most minimal sense to be some ideal of *self rule*, whatever institutional form it takes. Given the wide variety of circumstances of politics, this form can be quite variable, from Greek assemblies to modern nation states and contemporary transnational polities. We cannot simply assume that there is some single best conception of democracy for all the different types of polities and political units, nor can we assume for that matter that there is some particular feature common to all democracies, such as territoriality or a unified demos, or that the subjects of the laws are also its authors. Indeed, new, plural forms of democratic self rule have emerged, including the European Union (EU), which, in Weiler's (1999: 268) terms, is 'a People of others', so that there is a lack of fit between much of traditional democratic theory based on nation states and new kinds of entities such as the EU. Once we abandon the idea that a polity is a democracy only if it accords with some single democratic principle or set of such principles, we must also change how we regard many of the familiar features of democratic institutions, many of which have undergone fundamental transformations in recent years.

When concerned about improving democratic practice, deliberative democrats have focused on the idea of an ideal deliberative forum and thus sought to improve deliberation and overall legitimacy based on such an ideal. No single forum, however ideally constituted, could possess sufficient deliberative capacity to legitimate various decisions and policies. A different approach would be more institutional. Instead of focusing on ideal

72

conditions, it would be better to look at deliberative, democratic practices as a whole with interacting and interdependent parts. Here I do not wish to engage in discussing the idea of a deliberative system itself, but rather use such a conception normatively to evaluate one of the more important institutions in democratic practice that is undergoing significant transformation: the democratic practice of representation. Recent criticisms of representative democracy might be thought to suggest that new emerging forms cannot be understood on the common electoral model, such as when they argue for descriptive forms of representation they are concerned not so much with the lack of meaningful participation, but with exclusion due to a lack of a basic political status. Representation is not just a necessity imposed by the size of modern polities, but is rather an important means by which the legitimacy of the demos can be expressed, challenged, and transformed. As Urbinati and Warren (2008: 402) put it, representation is not desirable as some second best, practical alternative but 'an intrinsically modern way of intertwining participation, political judgment' and, most importantly, 'the constitution of *demoi* capable of self rule'. How these tasks are to be fulfilled no longer depends on either electoral forms of representation, or the normative significance of a single legislature that is the authoritative voice of the People, where representation depends on a pre-existing and bounded demos.

This analysis will not pursue these more standard forms of analysis, but rather show how representation does indeed constitute 'an intrinsically modern way of intertwining participation and political judgment'. But it does so because it plays an important role in modern deliberative systems. A system designates a relation among interdependent parts. As a part of a deliberative system, it is important to see representation as promoting deliberation in both general and particular settings. Deliberation is not usually located in only one institution or forum, but involves many different feasible institutions and forums. My purpose here is to show how a systems approach makes it possible to see the range of different institutional roles that representation plays in a deliberative system (which could be either national or transnational). Indeed, the idea of a system captures the complex interrelationships among various institutions in any complex modern polity and as such it is a powerful tool for the normative appraisal of institutional norms and practice. But it also suggests a constructive principle for improving democratic practice without looking for some optimal design or blueprint. The focus on representation in modern democracies, both national and transnational, allows us to engage in both types of analysis of deliberative systems. While the first half of my argument is primarily evaluative of practices of representation, the second and more practical half employs the conception of the deliberative system in order to construct and improve democratic deliberative systems.

My discussion of the role of representations in modern deliberative systems has three steps. First, I discuss the importance of the idea of a deliberative system as a way of understanding profound changes in the current organization of democratic institutions and use the idea of a deliberative system to test the capacities of such forms of democracy. Using an example of debates about health care reform in the UK, I want to show that the resolution that was reached can best be illuminated by a deliberative system approach. With this account in mind, I turn to the functional role of representation within this and other deliberative systems: that is, to how representation makes the emergence of communicative freedom and communicative power possible through practices of inclusion. Third, I want to show that under conditions of wide pluralism, electoral and other common forms of representation fail to fulfil this role by themselves. However, it is still possible for communicative power to be distributed throughout the deliberative system as a whole and across its various levels.

With this discussion the use of the idea of a deliberative system can be made more practical. But the accompanying distributed conception of communicative power requires considerable innovation: new forms of representation, new sorts of deliberative institutions, and new ways in which citizens act as representatives for other citizens. Here, too, the standard accounts fail to see the interaction among representatives and the represented within various institutions and publics. Rather than employing standard models of these relations between representatives and the represented, a multilevel modern polity develops new locations in which representation can be distributed. In order to convert communicative freedom into communicative power successfully, citizen bodies and assemblies must begin to act as intermediaries within the deliberative system. These include different types of citizen representatives who convert communicative freedom into communicative power in two distinct forms: indirectly in minipublics and directly in minidemoi. Thus, a deliberative system approach shows the need for a variety of forms of citizen representation, if the system is to intertwine judgment and participation in a distinctly modern way at a variety of levels of scale.

Democracy and deliberative systems

Given that changes in the global order mean that long-held assumptions about democracy and representation can no longer be taken for granted, we must find an alternative to one of the most common solutions to the problem of identifying what is distinctively democratic. As Bruce Ackerman

(1991: 181) puts it, it is tempting to resort to a 'naïve synecdoche' that identifies some part, such as the legislature or parliament, for the whole. Instead, it is only because each part together with all the others makes up a democratic system that legislatures have their functions and roles. This potential can be shown when they are thought of in terms of their contribution to the whole, even with their weaknesses taken singly. Thus, on the deliberative systems approach representation can more clearly show that some of the functions of representation are no longer tied to the standard legislative model, particularly in the wider public role in opinion formation and in creating the access to political influence against powerful interests. Every deliberative system at whatever scale must find a variety of ways to fulfil this functional role and to secure the two great achievements of modern democracy: it must link free and open communication in the public sphere to empowered participation by citizens in decision-making. Every deliberative system must be able to generate communicative power out of the different spaces for communicative freedom opened by the deliberative system as a whole. Of course, this function is not achieved by representation alone. In this way, a deliberative system ought to be structured so as to promote political interaction across various levels and types of institutions so as to achieve the possibility for self rule.

An example of employing representation in a deliberative system in use may be helpful. John Parkinson has analysed a case of deliberative public involvement in health policies in the UK through a citizens' jury, an issue which he describes as 'a tough testing ground of the ability of any deliberative process to handle legitimacy deficits' (Parkinson 2006a: 44). He argues that focusing on the citizens' jury as a single deliberative forum is misleading, since the deliberative process involved a complex deliberative system with interacting parts. In the case of health care policy, a whole set of actors and institutions contributed to the achievement of a deliberatively legitimate public policy, including public hearings, activism, expert testimony, administrative consultation, designed forums, the media, referendums, and more. Not only that, the issue could only be resolved if the solution takes into account the myriad ways in which such problems cut across a variety of levels, from the local and regional to the national. Parkinson shows that it matters a great deal which groups commission various 'micro-deliberative' forums; it also matters a great deal at what level of the hierarchy the different deliberative procedures are used. Citizen representatives and other such experimental forums 'tend to be used lower down in the hierarchy because their legitimation needs are stronger and because of the pressure on them to be responsive' (Parkinson 2006a: 64). In a deliberative system, the differentiation among actors at various levels opens up the possibility that citizens' forums are not necessarily the best way to organize health care reform. As Parkinson notes, we have to understand interactions and interconnections among the parts of the system: 'the citizens' jury was not the entire deliberative process, but just its focal point' (Parkinson 2006a: 177). In taking a deliberative system approach, the analysis sees the citizens' jury in relation to the various networks and the larger deliberative system that allows us to see its democratic weaknesses.

There is a clear sense in which any deliberative system cannot do without appropriate claims to representativeness. In any particular deliberation, it is impossible for all to deliberate and hence those who do so are acting as representatives for those who are not participating. In general, the experience of people in deliberation in which some deliberate for others (such as the British Columbia Citizens' Assembly) is that these citizens are competent and representative, acting on behalf of everyone else. Thus, given the limits on number of participants, real-world deliberation is inherently representative. At the normative level, one central role of representation in most of its modern forms is to provide a means by which actors are able to introduce communicative freedom into the deliberative system; as such, it has to also be a location in which issues of political exclusion are thematized and worked out. If it can do so, then the system possesses sufficient deliberative capacity to be consequential and thus able to transform communicative freedom into communicative power. Dryzek (2010a: 10–11) offers three important features that must be present in a deliberative system. Such a system possesses deliberative capacity 'to the degree that its structures are able to accommodate deliberation that is authentic, inclusive and consequential'. But it can do so only if the system's deliberative capacity is able to generate communicative freedom and communicative power (Urbinati and Warren 2008: 403–4). However, when thinking of representation as part of a deliberative system, it is, as van Gunsteren (1998: 34) argues, important to see that in both of these respects 'a definition of plurality only in terms of social groups will omit a great many phenomena for which we do not yet have an established conceptual category'. In these contexts inclusivity is a function of spaces for the exercise of communicative freedom. The role of representation in parliamentary contexts is primarily deliberative and decisional; the laws are made for the people by the representatives that they authorize and empower to act on their behalf; but it is in generating communicative power that such a system is consequential. This role of representation is in the first instance to generate decision-making authority; but even in the parliamentary element of the deliberative system, representation is often also clearly deliberative; even if it does not aim at an authoritative decision, it is nonetheless often democratizing by the achievement of communicative power that can receive uptake at other modes and locations within the system.

With this deliberative context in mind, the second task is to determine which among the many possibilities is to be represented within various formal and informal deliberative bodies: groups, interests, opinions, discourse, and so on. Discourses fail to be authentic, primarily because they are constructed prior to deliberation. Discourses also fail to realize communicative freedom to the extent that such freedom requires a continual openness to new perspectives. While this approach is a feasible alternative to electoral representation at the global level, just how discourses are selected to be part of 'the Chamber of Discourses' (Dryzek and Niemeyer 2008) is also insufficiently democratic, since selection seems to be left to social scientists. Thus for the purposes of determining the deliberative purpose of representation it seems that perspectives are fundamental to the possibility of achieving new policies or institutions. For this reason, such a political form is 'multiperspectival' precisely because it does not seek to transform 'citizens' heterogeneity into an assembled People' (Ruggie 2000: 186), but rather seeks to transform heterogeneity into creative new possibilities through the exercise of communicative freedom. While Ruggie is here discussing transnational democratic forms, the same applies within porous, contemporary states. Such an account embraces institutional pluralism, especially when it is put in the context of a deliberative system that would include a variety of modes of representation. It may be difficult to tell in advance why one part of the system may be more responsive to public opinion and function to be better able to represent certain interests and perspectives within political judgment. Indeed, as Dryzek himself points out, the greater the differentiation among actors and forums the more the system as a whole is able to engage in good deliberation and achieve overall legitimacy (Dryzek 2010a: 8).

While representatives do not mirror their constituents, it is still the case that deliberation can function formally and informally to assemble the People. Using the EU as a model, two sorts of institutions are crucial for the functioning of the deliberative system as modes of distributing representation in discursive interaction and formal decision-making, which I call minipublics and minidemoi (Bohman 2007). These particular institutions are not only important features of the deliberative system; they are also locations for the generation of communicative power. While minipublics play an important deliberative role, minidemoi offer a form of representation in which deliberative decision-making is sufficient to transform communicative freedom into communicative power, to the extent that they become authorized to make binding decisions. With these distinctions in mind, the deliberative systems approach can help determine what role non-elective representation plays in the generation of communicative power.

From communicative freedom to communicative power

In the modern state, a self-ruling people consists of all those and *only* those who are both authors *and* subjects of the law. In this sense, the People are a supreme sovereign, as it is often expressed in constitutions. But this standard view neglects the fundamental tensions between universality and particularity built into the constitutions of most democratic states, especially those aspects that concern universal human political rights on the one hand and the rights of citizens on the other. As Habermas (2001: 63) puts it, the form of natural law theory espoused by most founders of modern constitutional orders requires that the political community as a whole (and not just its electoral jurisdictions) must consist of *a determinate group of persons*, 'united by the decision to grant to each other precisely those rights that are necessary for the legitimate ordering of their collective existence by means of positive law'. Thus, the fundamental distinction is between the status of being a citizen *within* a political community and the often negative status of being merely a non-citizen bearer of human rights with claims *against* the political community. The body of citizens cannot really directly decide what is to be done, and for this reason Thomas Christiano (Chapter 2, this volume) sees the citizens as only determining the ends of the polity and not its means, where public officials may act as their trustees. Thus, there is an unavoidable gap between the ideal of self rule and the requirements of representation, so that, in their role as citizens at least, the people do not actually transform communicative freedom into communicative power. Discursive forms of representation in fact gain their appeal through the lack of a well defined people at certain levels of complexity and scale.

At the very least this suggests that having only one form of representation, electoral or otherwise, is insufficient for the task of self rule under conditions of large scale and wide diversity. A variety of devices must be used to connect delegates and agents to their principals, and representatives to their constituents. These ties may become more tenuous as the community grows larger and multilevelled, and generally the legitimacy of international institutions is often thought to come entirely through the executive function of national governments, over which citizens have little democratic control. Such institutions have in fact developed to the point that they are neither deliberative nor easily influenced by electoral control except in the long run, so that they may often be sources of domination. Are there forms of representation that might preserve the possibility of self rule in a large-scale and plural form of democracy? From a deliberative systems perspective, other institutions may take over some of the functions of representation, as when a vibrant public sphere transmits citizens' claims and successfully mediates between the free and open public sphere and the decision-makers, often without being concerned with issues of constituency. This signals the importance of communicative freedom in a deliberative system.

Habermas's (1996) idea of the public sphere as a 'transmission belt' leads to new possibilities of public rather than political representation. Electoral representation can fail to capture the relevant dimensions of the diverse public, and it may also lack the institutional capability to exercise communicative power through various forms of accountability. For this very reason, Dahl (1999) and others are sceptical of the idea of any form of democracy in which the chains of delegation expand, because the accountability of officials to citizens becomes more difficult to achieve. Rather than thinking of assemblies and legislatures as deliberative in the usual sense, there may also be cases in which citizens act as representatives for others, either formally or informally, in various kinds of minipublics, so that communicative freedom and communicative power emerge through a subset of the people who act as representatives of others. In multilevel polities, parliaments or legislatures must transfer their decision-making powers to some other subset of citizens who are better able to make some particular authoritative decision. Thus, we might say that legislatures are themselves minipublics; constructed out of the public at large, they act in such a way as to use their deliberation to acquire some testable and public decisional authority through the common exercise of communicative freedom. Indeed, as Saward has pointed out, elections can undermine communicative freedom by restricting the nature and range of representative perspectives and voices (Saward 2010: ch. 1).

Nonetheless, it is important to recognize that *any* such group of citizens acting to represent others, however constituted, may always fall short descriptively and normatively and fail to be inclusive and consequential. How might representation nonetheless be legitimate? Here we might think of what a jury does when it acts as a fully empowered public capable of deciding guilt or innocence of the accused under the appropriate legal constraints. This empowerment of the public fits the description of what we have been looking for: a form of representation in an institution that transforms the communicative freedom of citizens into communicative power (subject to the revisions by other citizens doing the same). What is distinctive is that they do so not by directly consulting the opinions of their fellow citizens, but rather, in Mark Warren's (2008) apt phrase, by acting as 'citizen representatives', and thus to that extent citizens in these contexts represent themselves in their role as citizens. At the same time, they are citizens who represent other citizens, in which a few actively deliberate and decide for the sake of all other citizens. The important difference is, then, that citizens not only represent other citizens, but that the decision-making power of the body of citizens is no longer only tied to a single form and mechanism for representation. This has in fact been the role of various kinds of minipublics.

Whatever the role that officials play in making and executing proposals, the difference is that citizens deliberate by handing over their powers of citizenship to other citizens who act independently and on their behalf. But because they are citizen representatives, they cannot claim that they form a demos, even as they may claim to represent many demoi. In the deliberative system, properly selected citizen representatives can for particular issues represent other citizens precisely because their decision-making can be justified in deliberative terms. Given that this use of representation is open to being scaled up, representation is primarily a matter of inclusion and thus can be distributed across institutional levels. As part of a deliberative system, the state has important problem-solving functions that make it difficult to see how citizen representation could function without this or some similar capacity to help in resisting the domination of powerful private actors. Thus far, no other institutions have such capacity, even if it is now expected to be exercised more broadly in a multilevel deliberative system, even as states are now finding their problem-solving capacities diminished in the face of transnational issues.

Citizenship as a multilevel status: perspectives or opinions?

In existing democracies, citizenship and representation are statuses tied to territory in a variety of ways. Once an institution that generalized statuses beyond locales, territorial citizenship has now become a status that cannot assure that all those affected will be able to have a say on issues and problems that affect them. In current conditions, many non-citizens should be counted among those affected by many issues within the territorially delimited community. The EU has established rights of local participation that are based on residence alone. Even so, interdependence extends affectedness to many of those who are outside of the delimited community, and the same is true of even large territorially defined political communities. If citizenship and representation are so delimited, then they may not be sufficient for the purpose of avoiding domination even by democratic polities themselves. One goal of democratic representation should be precisely to avoid both of these forms of domination internal to the practice of democracy itself. Under such circumstances, the tasks of representation are at the very least twofold: to secure self rule and freedom from domination. Many constitutional democracies identify universal statuses, including the rights of citizens to *habeas corpus* and other minimal conditions of justice (Bohman 2009). Dennis Thompson (1999) has argued for a special form of representation for the unrepresented within legislative deliberative bodies, so that at the very least the generalizable claims of those outside the polity (and of future generations) could be heard. Thus, he argues for a 'tribune' whose task it is to monitor the effects of policies upon the interests of such unrepresented groups and exercise a veto in cases when their interests are ignored. The *desiderata* of good representation could also help identify at least counterfactually the range of concerns that result from the exclusion of those who lack standing on territorial grounds or access to influence over decision-making because they are dominated. Various institutional and non-institutional locations for such pre-emptive and inclusive deliberation have been proposed and debated, as has their feasibility.[1] It is important that any such mechanism cannot be based directly upon electoral mechanisms.

Properly generalized to include statuses, Thompson's (1999) solution has the advantage of organizing deliberation so that people outside the polity will be less likely to be dominated or have costs externalized to them. The issue is indeed one of expanding deliberation by rethinking the role of representation in transnational issues. We might think that such a possibility functions as an ideal, on the basis of which all such arrangements are subject to revision. Addams's (1902: 11–12) idea that the legislature 'should be an exact portrait, in miniature, of the people at large' offers a fully extended descriptive account of representation or what that might mean. Nonetheless, it provides no guidance as to the relevant features of inclusion. Stratified sampling appears to be successful in making even small groups statistically representative, thus achieving Addams's aim of a portrait in miniature according to some specific criteria, whatever they are. Here deliberative accounts could serve to narrow the range of considerations, since in any particular case the criteria cannot achieve some perfectly proportioned miniature. Richardson (2002), for example, shows that deliberative approaches reject preference- or interest-based accounts, since these would presuppose an independent fixity of individuals' positions. Thus, it is not these qualities of citizens that ought to be fairly represented, but rather 'their political views' (Richardson 2002: 23). Hence, proportional representation through voting, for example, wrongly distributes communicative power according to just such considerations. However, by Richardson's own criteria, this unduly makes citizens' views rather than perspectives the basis for representation. Opinions seem too fluid to be the basis of representation, even if they may be the marker of something else more fundamental. These issues become salient when deliberation

---

[1] For discussions of the varieties of theories of deliberative democracy, see, among others, Bohman (1998); Chambers (2003); and from a Rawlsian perspective, Freeman (2000).

operates through the selection of citizens in a minipublic that must in some sense be a 'public in miniature' to achieve legitimacy sufficient for the exercise of communicative power.

The aspects of diversity among citizens can be defined along cultural, social, and epistemic axes. Furthermore, each aspect of diversity can be measured along various deliberative dimensions: in terms of values, opinions, and perspectives. These roughly correspond to the main aspects of diversity, and thus provide the basis for thinking about what it is that should be represented. They can all be taken into consideration, even if they are often at cross purposes. In order to avoid such conflicts, those who see the importance of diversity favour one aspect over others. Like Richardson, Mill (1975) and others celebrate diversity of opinion as important to deliberation. This is certainly true so long as deliberators can isolate disagreements along this dimension, and difficulties arise when issues include not just basic beliefs, but also beliefs about the way in which beliefs are justified. Values in this sense include basic moral norms, various cultural conceptions of the good, religion, and important political norms (including conceptions of the common good). The complexity and pluralism across multiple criteria create many different social positions, whose differences in perspective primarily emerge from the range and type of experience.[2]

Instead of the selection process, one alternative to deal with possible error is to impose *ex ante* limits on possible reasons or *ex post* constraints on outcomes. This way of constructing empowered minipublics points in the right direction. However, such policies on their own fail to promote sufficient diversity to avoid bias and other cognitive errors. Goodin argues that representative inclusion is limited by the conditions of effective participation in a deliberative forum, since it 'proves to be impossible to represent the particulars of diversity within the assembly'.[3] Goodin argues that there are strict limits on 'presence' and thus that there is no viable solution to 'the sheer fact of diversity'. Alternatively, we might, with David Estlund, adopt a policy that it would be best to maximize the quantity of available reasons, since judgments of quality might suggest 'individious comparisons' that adversely affect the chances of the least influential to participate effectively in deliberation.[4] There are, however, many possible versions of this

---

[2] For a fuller development of the argument for toleration aimed at perspectives, see Bohman (2003).

[3] See Goodin (2008: 247). Instead of seeking maximal, but impossible, inclusion, Goodin believes that it is possible for representatives to act in such a way as to deliberate without the pretension of maximal inclusion and thus internalize their fundamental fallibility in overcoming the 'sheer fact of diversity'.

[4] On 'the epistemic value of quantity', see Estlund (2000: 144); this leads to his 'epistemic difference principle' as formulated to emphasize quantity (Estlund 2000: 147). However,

'epistemic difference principle', to use Estlund's term. Any such difference principle must identify the appropriate *maximandum* that would achieve this end. Otherwise, the policy suggested by a difference principle might be self-defeating. Maximizing all possible inputs, for example, may also increase opportunities for manipulation. But within a deliberative system maximization at every level is not necessarily desirable, and looking at representation in terms of specific deliberative mechanisms rather than as a system leads to a mistaken focus of the epistemic difference principle on reasons rather than perspectives.

Goodin (2008: 11–38) and Estlund (2002: 78) point to limitations in linking the use of minipublics to the ideal of descriptive representation. Goodin comes close to a feasible version of such deliberation when he recognizes that in any political order deliberation cannot be concentrated in a few institutions, but rather must be 'distributed'. However, he fails to see that inclusion via representation is also a distributed property of the *deliberative system* as a whole, whatever criteria of selection or deliberative norms we use in order to maximize the pool of available reasons. The epistemic motivation for selecting a particular formulation of the difference principle is better served by looking at the use of various kinds of representative publics. In light of the democratic aims of the deliberative system as a whole, any deliberative system should not seek to optimize the outcomes of each and every deliberative institution as much as seek to avoid bad ones. This is because the relevant aspect of diversity that is necessary for improving the process of deliberation is not the pool of *reasons* as such but the availability of the *perspectives* that inform these reasons and give them their cogency. Mill (1975: 188) argued that the 'workingman's view' was excluded from deliberation. Richardson (2002: 201–2) argues that in certain contexts perspectives are significant because they 'orient the ways in which political views would be articulated and adapted to face new challenges' and thus 'deserve independent attention'. These arguments, however, do not go far enough, even as they suggest that the inclusion of perspectives is an important corrective. Given the variety of topics of deliberation, it is not possible to decide in advance which among the potential candidate perspectives ought to be included, as Young (2000: ch. 3) does when she argues that it is social perspectives defined by 'objective structural positions' in a society that are

> maximizing input is not intrinsically valuable from the participants' perspective unless it increases the possibility of each perspective being heard. Increasing input could be democratically justified to the worst off only if it increases the number of perspectives in discussion. In order that the worst off (here the least effective in deliberation) may accept the epistemic difference principle, the relevant value is the diversity of perspectives rather than quantity of input.

worthy of inclusion for their distinctive contribution to the reduction of bias overall. Thus, a systems approach suggests that the reduction of bias overall is the proper goal for the system as a whole, and this is best achieved by inclusion of perspectives.

But the benefits of such inclusion in avoiding bad outcomes are quite real and depend on previously excluded groups acquiring representative status. For example, Argarwal (2001) has studied the effects of the exclusion of the perspective of women from deliberation on community forestry groups in India and Nepal. Because women had primary responsibility for wood gathering in their search for cooking fuel, they possessed greater knowledge of what sort of gathering was sustainable and about where trees were that needed protection. Mixed groups of participants were in this case much more effective in achieving the goals of enforcement. In such cases, the improvement of practices depended upon achievement of representative status, by which women's available reasons came to have the decisional authority that they previously lacked. This is not just the status needed to be heard in deliberation, but the status to have one's perspective become representative of the group as a whole. The difference is not simply in having one's interests considered by others, but that such interests are now the interests of the group and thus inform one of the perspectives in terms of which a decision may be framed. In these cases, communicative freedom can be transformed into communicative power, from discussion and persuasion to playing a part in self rule. It is also important to see that institutions that generate the joint exercise of communicative freedom and power create the deliberative capacity to address domination within and across borders. Deliberation, representation, and non-domination are key features of democratization. In the next sections, I use the deliberative system approach constructively to improve practices of representation with various forms of deliberation.

From minipublics to minidemoi

Democratization has two main dimensions: first, it requires institutions, publics, and associations in which communicative freedom is realized; and second, that this communicative freedom also be exercised in institutions that link such freedom to the exercise of normatively generated communicative power. As I have argued, communicative freedom is the exercise of a *communicative status*, the status of being recognized as a member of a public. It is a societal and thus a universal property, which can be attained for each only if all have it. But communicative freedom is transformed into communicative power only when it is incorporated into institutionalized processes of decision-making. Communicative power is thus exercised by those who possess a *decisional status* within an institution in which one's perspective is taken to be representative of those who exercise communicative freedom. Under these conditions, the communicative freedom to initiate deliberation becomes the communicative power to place an item on an institutional agenda and then further to have the status to influence decisions made about items on that agenda. But whatever else characterizes these forms of decision-making, these bodies will inevitably consist of some subset of participants and citizens taken as a whole. For this reason, such bodies must be able to plausibly claim that they are representing others at one or many different levels.

This description focuses on the process of democratization as a whole. An adequate account must capture complex interrelationships of civil society, the public sphere, and formal democratic institutions, all of which are required as conditions for democratization as I have described it. As the deliberative systems approach suggests, rather than look for a single axis on which to connect emerging publics to decision-making processes to various institutions, it will be more useful to consider how a variety of connections can be made between communicative status and decisional status. In considering possible institutional designs that enhance and democratize deliberation, it is necessary to see that different institutional arrangements can function best at different levels and scales, and distribute decisional authority across the local, the national, the regional, and the transnational levels.

This systems approach will require different forms of representation at various levels, with different modes of constituency and legitimacy. Such an account checks the tendency to see only one sort of representative body as distinctively democratic or closer to some particular democratic ideal. Or, as Dryzek (2010a) argues, we might see interactive effects, where weaknesses in one part of the deliberative system are compensated for by developments in another part, say the informal public sphere compensating for poor deliberation in formal bodies such as legislatures. These interactive effects of the deliberative system might at times lead to bad consequences, as when the presence of well functioning deliberative institutions like a constitutional court could permit the legislature to propose bad laws simply to appeal to voters, expecting them to be struck down. Currently, different forms of democracy are often discussed, such as corporatist or consociational democracy, and we might see such variety within deliberative systems. This suggests that we do not need to idealize deliberation in each dimension (or that a particular part must be maximally deliberative according to its type), but rather test the deliberative system as a whole and how it functions overall according to a basic list of democratic functions, including representation.

Here we might think of the EU as an example of a deliberative system in which certain functions are weak or even missing, such as a transnational public sphere for the EU as a whole. The EU decision-making practices claim to be deliberative, and some organize empowered deliberation across various levels in practices such as the open method of coordination. A clear advantage of a deliberative system is that it permits not just various interacting and interconnected sites for deliberation, but also relations across various levels and types of deliberation. Here I want to focus on the different ways in which deliberative representation becomes as significant as non-electoral forms. In keeping with the distinction between communicative freedom and communicative power, I want to look at two distinct types of deliberative institutions: minipublics and minidemoi. Minipublics take many forms from citizen juries, to deliberative polls, to citizens' assemblies that are authorized to supplement rather than replace other forms of representation. Random selection provides a kind of legitimacy to their deliberation, not because they will somehow mirror the public as a whole, but because they promote political equality and better deliberation (Parkinson 2006a: 74ff). A reason to adopt such innovations in the transnational context is that the relatively small groups of deliberators that make up minipublics can lay claim to various kinds of representativeness. They also may have various claims to legitimacy, often tied to the procedures of selection (such as random selection) or to the forms of non-partisan deliberation they engage in (Fung 2003). However participants are selected and whatever the norms governing their deliberation, the members of minipublics act as representatives in two ways: first, as mutually recognized members of a public stand-in for the deliberation of the many (whose agreement is revocable); and second, in their deliberative standing they may have some kind of decisional power, however weak. In the case of the British Columbia Citizens' Assembly, the task of the minipublic was to deliberate about and propose electoral reforms to be voted upon by all citizens. The use of this procedure was clearly motivated by having the decision about electoral reform exhibit 'representativeness', that is, the randomness of the selection procedure was supplemented with broader recruitment of citizens, so that the decision was made by 'citizens like us'. Even so, the Citizens' Assembly only made recommendations to be approved (or not as in this case) by a referendum.

Such representative publics then fall between weak and strong publics. Unlike weak publics, they do not merely spontaneously engage in discourses within the broader public sphere, thereby introducing arguments that may flow in various ways into the formal political system, as when environmental groups introduce a discourse of sustainability. At the same time they are also not strong publics in the full sense, since many such publics lack full decisional authority. Rather, whatever decisional power they have, they have in virtue of being authorized by some body or authority within the formal political system, usually by legislatures of various kinds. But this is not sufficient; while minipublics may improve deliberation and even political equality, they need not improve democracy. What is needed here is a combination of both: a public with the representativeness of minipublics and the decisional authority of existing democratic institutions. However complex the deliberative system becomes, it is possible for constructed publics to achieve decisional status, often on the background of the absence of effective territorial institutions for dealing with pressing problems of international society. The lack of effective and empowered global deliberation has meant that crosscutting issues of common concern, such as climate change, have not been easily made subject to binding deliberative agreement.

Minipublics are different from many other representative bodies to the extent that their selection procedures are constructed precisely to validate their claim to be representative for the citizenry as a whole, at least sufficiently to raise the legitimacy conferred by political equality. In terms of the representation of interests, minipublics are often more diverse than most empowered institutions such as legislative bodies. But the importance of inclusion becomes most pressing in the case of deliberation that aims at an authoritative decision. When, in addition to their shared communicative status, such strong but small-scale publics also possess a decisional status, their members have ceased to be minipublics and have become minidemoi. As a minidemos, citizens have all the structural features of an inclusive public, but so as to provide opportunities for the exercise of communicative power through participating in deliberation aimed at making a determinate decision, where groups of citizens, rather than experts or office holders, have the communicative freedom to deliberate and form opinions as well as the communicative power to make recommendations or actual decisions (as they do on juries who decide the facts of law and citizen juries who often make recommendations). The deliberative advantage is that such minidemoi are able to deliberate within specific institutional, functional, and temporal constraints in ways that the public at large cannot (except over the long term, as in the case of the abolition of the slave trade). Rather than being simply a form of consultation or of recommendation, this form of deliberation would require that institutions jointly transfer some of their authority to the minidemos whose deliberation they empower, opening up a directly deliberative process within the institution which includes as many perspectives as possible. The use of randomly selected citizens for empowered deliberation is useful not only for democratization at the transnational level, but it can also serve to enhance the quality of deliberation. Such empowered publics with decision-making powers for particular issues or sets of issues would likely be authorized by the wider set of institutions in which communicative power is exercised; and while the minidemos is concerned with making some decision, this issue and process would still be debated and tested in the relevant public spheres. Decision-making competence can thus be distributed among various types of publics, which then become minidemoi to the extent that they are formed to make authoritative decisions. As minidemoi, publics are empowered to decide as strong publics; their use is of course rare within states, given their monopoly powers. Even so, officials of the World Trade Organization (WTO) represent state interests with powers transferred to authorized experts that act as their agents. A strong minidemos would not act as an agent to some principal; instead it would be an instance of an empowered form of citizen representation, where citizens are empowered to deliberate in the place of other citizens in a more direct form of deliberation, analogous to the strong decisional power of juries rather than weaker consultative bodies.

The advantage of this form of deliberative representation is that it can develop different forms of representation across various overlapping demoi. The fundamental justification here is republican: democracy at any level is better served by overall institutional pluralism, in which there is a variety of overlapping and mutually checking procedures, each formulated according to its contribution to the division of decision-making and epistemic labour within the deliberative system as a whole. Thus, given the variety of forums and decision-making bodies, inclusive representation does not limit empowered decision-making to territorial bodies alone. Indeed, territorial bodies oversimplify the task of representativeness, and in doing so cannot take available perspectives into account. Unlike other, more broadly distributed, forms of representation they are more likely to be able to ensure non-domination. A robust public sphere may often be more effective in ensuring non-domination due to its capacities to mobilize and contest dominating forms of decision-making whose constituencies are fixed too narrowly or are too restrictive in identifying available perspectives.

According to this approach, constituencies are variable depending on a diagnostic use of the all affected principle. Even if constituencies remain variable, it would be possible for citizen members of a minidemos to develop forms of citizen involvement and accountability that can also be exercised within the wider deliberative system and compensate for the lack of strong publics and consequential forms of representation. Experts will sometimes exert some influence over such decisions and improve their epistemic quality, particularly when certain types of issues are at stake. The normative basis of the legitimacy of these representatives can thus develop over time and in interaction with citizens whom they represent. New forms of representation are particularly important when the deliberative system expands and is in need of greater legitimacy in the use of communicative power.

This lack of democratic legitimacy has been an important impetus for change in emerging and incompletely multiperspectival polities, such as the EU, in which the deliberative system still lacks capacity for deliberation to be sufficiently diverse, inclusive, and consequential (Dryzek 2010a: 10). In making such judgments about such a deliberative system, it is important to distinguish between the deliberative capacities distributed throughout all the macro-level institutions in the system as a whole from the capacities of any particular micro-level deliberation in a given public or demos. Institutionalization at the macro-level is important to democratization to the extent that interacting with such institutions helps to shape the diversity of perspectives according to the goals that they have and the means of representation that they make available. In this way, institutions can bring out latent perspectives, perhaps even bring them about in terms of the various sorts of legitimate decision-making powers that they have. Given that institutions play an important role in shaping how perspectives get taken up in deliberation, no single institution such as parliaments or legislatures could fully express the decision-making capacities of the various demoi. When perspectives are integrated into the deliberative system, empowered minidemoi and not merely authorized minipublics can emerge. In a multiperspectival, transnational polity, minidemoi of empowered and diverse citizens can shape deliberative outcomes so as to incorporate the overlapping perspectives of citizens, who in constituting themselves as a representative minidemos transform their communicative freedom into communicative power. While the concept of a strong public is the more typical way of discussing this kind of institutional possibility, it is misleading to the extent that any strong public is so only in virtue of its having become a demos. In this way, democratization aims at transforming publics into demoi through deliberation. The exercise conception of representation through demoi makes democracy the achievement of self rule through the deliberative system as a whole. This achievement is that citizens can represent other citizens not in their beliefs or any other descriptive features, but in their active capacity *qua* citizens.

Representing transnational demoi: citizen representation and the EU

Addams's well-known portrait conception of representation (see Pitkin 1967: 60–8) has plausibility only if we presuppose that there is a determinate and delimited demos to be portrayed, with the goal of complete representation within a legislative assembly. When structured by the assumption that democracy is such because it entails such a demos, citizen representation may not go far enough for cases in which many different possible demoi exist so that the difficulties of any mirror conception of representation proliferate. But what sort of representation could there be when it is not the constituent parts of the demos that is to be represented? In this respect, Cohen and Sabel (1998) are correct that there is both a certain directness and diversity involved in a 'directly deliberative polyarchy'. Nonetheless, such a polyarchy that is also deliberative involves some form of representation or another. A polyarchy is in the first instance direct only in the sense that the representatives are *citizens*, acting in their representative capacity. Thus, we might think of direct citizen representation in terms of an 'exercise conception' of deliberative representation (Maliks 2009). Citizens represent other citizens in their active capacity within an institutional division of deliberative labour, so that a polyarchy of demoi gain political agency and exercise their political freedom through their representatives exercising their same powers. The exercise conception thus serves to emphasize the agency of both the represented and the representative in the deliberative process, precisely because communicative power is generated from communicative freedom in the deliberative system as a whole. Minidemoi represent via specific achievements, such as the emergence of an overlapping consensus on specific recurring issues, rather than a once and for all comprehensive constitutional settlement.

Given size, scale, and complexity, citizens cannot have influence if they only act for themselves in deliberation, but rather become influential by distributing the decisional status through representation to others. Thus, citizen representatives are such only by having such powers distributed into a variety of roles and institutions, rather than by having some more unitary conception of self rule in a collective assembly. When acting in a variety of ways through others, we make manifest that the minidemoi are plural, that we do not, to paraphrase Rousseau (1987: 116), obey only ourselves when we act through the decisional status of others. Even if Habermas (1996: 327) is correct that publics as such do not rule, they act through their representatives who participate in empowered processes of deliberation that are so empowered by other citizens, not simply by some legal mechanism or other. Thus, having the role of representative even as one is represented is rather open ended, since it does not necessarily map on to other, non-deliberative aspects of citizenship. An undocumented worker could act in a representative capacity so long as they are able to jointly realize communicative freedom and communicative power in some recognized deliberative process and thus act in a representative capacity for citizens and non-citizens. Here representatives are performing a complex function of bringing together distributed participation and inclusive deliberation, and in so doing constitute demoi capable of self rule, as Urbinati and Warren (2008) have put it. It is time to consider how transnational representation might be possible as a special case of deliberative representation.

For citizen representatives in a deliberative system, this way of exercising representation does not necessarily depend on electoral authorization. Were citizen representatives to depend on this form of authorization, they would simply represent other representatives and thus form another parliamentary body. But in this case, they cease to be citizens who are acting as the representatives of other citizens. This problem is manageable once we see that there is no single source of such authorization. Instead, the authority to empower citizens to represent other citizens must be distributed across many different institutional locations from the informal to the executive, judicial, and legislative branches, each of which is able to distribute the tasks of citizen representatives, often when the formal and official structures suffer from democratic deficits. If the EU were based on citizen representation, its authorization as a minipublic or minidemos would often best be done by a representative European Parliament, whose function would be to act as an intermediary and to set procedures and monitor the democratic character of the deliberations and outcomes. We might think that one central function of the EU parliament is to act as a kind of Ministry of Minipublics and Minidemoi, when its authorization includes not only procedural specifications such as selection criteria, but also the basic task about which citizens are supposed to act as representatives. Here we have to go beyond current EU practices, although perhaps some, such as the much discussed open method of coordination, provide structural analogues to the representation of demoi. One might think that in contrast to a minipublic, a minidemos would be self authorizing, to the extent that it realizes both by exercising jointly held communicative freedom and communicative power. Even such directly deliberative and polyarchical processes cannot do without some institutional intermediaries at both the deliberative and the implementation phase.

Besides the epistemic benefits that representation across different groups would bring, inclusive decision-making of this sort also promotes democracy through the joint exercise of self rule. Such a process can also benefit from informal intermediaries that seek to transform a weak public into a strong public. In this regard, the history of the Women's International League for Peace and Freedom (WILPF) illustrates how communicative status can be transformed into decisional status at the international level (Cochran 2008). The WILPF saw their task as twofold: they sought not only to form public opinion by bringing women's perspectives to bear, but also attempted to shape the decision of extant international institutions, the League of Nations in particular. Their communicative freedom was effectively transformed in a campaign to influence the League of Nations to do something about the many stateless women and children who continued to be held in Turkey after World War I. It was a self-consciously formed public that sought to legitimate its influence on such decisional processes as representatives of women and humanity as a whole. The WILPF did not just influence specific decisions but interacted with the League of Nations so as to reshape and direct this institution away from its initial orientation that gave priority to member states and towards emerging strong international publics who were at the time concerned about creating the conditions for peace through publicity.

The example of the WILPF also shows that transnational representation does not always require explicit and formal authorization. Given how dispersed global governance institutions are, it is not surprising that this role is occupied by a wide variety of organizations and groups, many of which attempt to influence a particular domain or policy issue. Apart from the sort of structure found in the EU, current transnational publics are weak, in the sense that they exert influence only through changing discourses and general public opinion without the benefits of institutionalized deliberation. We might consider such non-authorized forms of representation as primarily discursive, as when Dryzek insists that 'deliberative and democratic global politics can most fruitfully be sought in the more informal realm of international public spheres'.[5] As in the case of the abolition of the slave trade in the early nineteenth century through transnational networks of advocates, such discourses can influence important informal norms, and may become representative without any formal electoral or institutional authorization. Global publics and social movements have contributed not only towards instituting conditions of communicative freedom, but also attempt to achieve what Dryzek calls discursive representation so that international institutions are not dominated by one kind of perspective, as has been the case with neoliberalism in global

---

[5] Dryzek (2006: vii). In *Foundations and Frontiers of Deliberative Governance* (Dryzek 2010a), Dryzek has now changed his view, allowing not only for discursive representation but also for ways in which deliberative decision-making is distributed and secured in a transnational deliberative system. This view is similar to the one I endorse here and in Bohman (2007: ch. 1).

Conclusion: democracy, representation, and non-domination

I have used intentionally broad terms in describing citizen representation in deliberation; it is both a means to achieve greater democratic legitimacy, but also for democratization, as the union of communicative freedom and communicative power, of the communicative and decisional status of publics. It is also broad because there does not seem to be a royal road to democracy, and democratization has to be possible even without fully democratic institutions. Many democratically minded cosmopolitans have turned to the informal realm of civil society and social movement in order to talk about discursive democracy or democracy from below. However important transnational associations and movements have been to many social struggles, they provide only one dimension of the processes of democratization. As political communities become more transnational, pluralistic, and complex, democratization requires both various formal and informal intermediaries, emerging publics to generate communicative power across borders, and transnational institutions in which publics can elaborate constituencies with decisional statuses.

These same considerations of size and complexity also suggest that informal democratization works best with formal democratization, when the communicative freedom of publics becomes linked to decisional status within a larger deliberative system. In this context, representation of some sort is not only inevitable for reasons of scale and complexity, but also promotes democratization. I have argued for a conception of citizen representation in deliberation in which citizens *qua* representative have some sort of decisional status, however weak or strong that might be. In this case, it is not only possible to represent demoi, but also to form them so as to enable the exercise of a distributed form of self rule across an inclusive deliberative system aimed at distributing decisions and statuses to all those affected. The mark of the achievement of such a deliberative system would be the prevalence of the exercise of communicative power, especially through the authorization of a variety of minipublics and minidemoi. The absence of an effective deliberative system that is genuinely representative at the international level is an obstacle to important achievements of political equality in the international system (including the recognition of increased global inclusion), resulting in the recognition of the costs of problems with highly uneven consequences, such as global climate change.

22

REPRESENTATION AS ADVOCACY
A Study of Democratic Deliberation

NADIA URBINATI

INDIRECTNESS IN POLITICS has never enjoyed much fortune in democratic theory. Direct ruling had generally been seen as paradigmatic of democracy because it entails a fusion of "talking" and "doing" in political action, and the full participation of all citizens in the process of decision making.[1] The modern "discovery" of representation has left the normative value of this paradigm unchallenged. Too often, representation has been given merely an instrumental justification and has been seen as a pragmatic expedient to cope with large territorial states, or a useful "fiction" by means of which the method of division of labor has been adapted to the function of government.[2]

Particularly since the French Revolution, democracy has come to denote, like Athens, a state of perfection that the moderns admire and long for all the while knowing it is unattainable to them: "Today, in politics, democracy is the *name* of what we cannot have—yet cannot cease to want."[3] While, therefore, for thinkers such as George W. F. Hegel and Benjamin Constant "classical" democracy was the name of something the moderns could no longer have, for contemporary democrats it has become the name of a good society we can still have, provided we interpret it as a ceaseless process of political education in citizenship. The former explained (and rationalized) the indirectness of sovereign action through representation as a destiny the moderns could not escape.[4] The latter turned their attention away from representation and looked

---

AUTHOR'S NOTE: Previous versions of this essay were presented at the 1998 annual meeting of the American Political Science Association in Boston, the New School Political Theory Colloquium, the Columbia Colloquium in Political Theory, and the Political Theory Workshop at the University of Chicago. I would like to thank the participants of these discussions, especially Jean L. Cohen, Sankar Muthu, David Plotke, Jon Elster, Jack Snyder, Bernard Manin, Andreas Kalyvas, Charles Larmore, and Andrew Rehfeld, for their very helpful comments. I owe particular thanks to Jane J. Mansbridge, whose suggestions helped me in the final revision of this essay. The Grant of Humanities and Social Sciences Council of the Faculty Development Committee of Columbia University is gratefully acknowledged.

for some reminder of directness within civil society.[5] In either case, representation has been associated with the weakening of self-government. For democrats in particular, it has held little appeal, first because it is seen as justifying a vertical relation between the citizens and the state, and second because it is seen as promoting a passive citizenry.[6] Even the attempt to make it more consistent with the democratic principle of equality, for instance by making it proportional, has been considered not only useless but also insincere. It is useless because proportionality cannot fill the gap between the citizens and their representatives. It is insincere because proportional representation can actually become a way of using minorities' representation to legitimize the majority's decisions. Proportional and descriptive accuracy in representation, Hannah Pitkin has argued in her seminal book, takes away with its left hand what it gives with its right: it meticulously reflects the social topography but, at the same time, makes the assembly into a "talking rather than acting, de- liberating rather than governing" body.[7] Finally, in a proportional electoral system the costs—governmental instability and fragmentation of the electorate—outweigh the benefits. In sum, there is no way of making representation be what it cannot be: a valid substitute for direct democracy.

My intention is not to put into question the normative value of direct participation but to argue for the relevance of representation. I think this is not only necessary but also worthy, particularly if we value the deliberative character of democratic politics. When we express our dissatisfaction with the way in which we are represented, we implicitly allude to some ideal of representation. As for the character of democratic politics, focus on deliberation allows us to perceive participation and representation not as two alternative forms of democracy but as related forms constituting the *continuum* of political action in modern democracies. Seen from this angle, the distinction between direct and indirect politics is a promising path of interpretation: it frames the institutional and sociocultural space within which the various components of political action—from opinions and will formation to decision making—take shape.

Contemporary democratic theory encourages the revision I am proposing. Indeed, while until recently the defense of representative democracy has generally been endorsed by the neo-Schumpeterian theorists of electoral democracy against the proponents of "participatory democracy,"[8] now representation attracts the interest of democratic scholars in a more direct way. In his *Inner Ocean*, George Kateb writes that the institution of representation is the source of the "moral distinctiveness" of modern democracy, and the sign of its superiority to direct democracy.[9] Even more radically, David Plotke states that in a representative democracy, "the opposite of representation is not participation" but exclusion, while Iris Marion Young argues that "the elevation of direct democracy to the apex," as the only "real" democracy, "is mistaken"; in fact, "political representation is both necessary and desirable."[10]

I find the 'rediscovery' of representation both interesting and compelling.[11] However, a systematic and comprehensive defense of the normative core of representative democracy is still missing. In writing this essay, I have been inspired by three main ideas. First, public discourse is one of the main features that characterize and give value to democratic politics. Second, indirectness (and representation, which is a type of indirectness) plays a key role in forging the discursive democratic character of politics. Third, representation highlights the *idealizing* and *judgmental* nature of politics (its reflexivity, in contemporary terminology), an art by which individuals transcend the immediateness of their experience and interests, and "educate" their political judgment on their own and others' opinions.[12] Representation—and the electoral trial that is a necessary part of democratic representation—projects citizens into a future-oriented perspective, and thus confers politics an ideological dimension.[13] In this sense, it gives ideas full residence in the house of politics. Representation is a comprehensive filtering, refining, and mediating process of political will formation and expression. It shapes the object, style, and procedures of political competition. Finally, it helps to depersonalize claims and opinions, and in this way makes them a vehicle for the mingling and associating of citizens. Representation can never be truly 'descriptive' of society because of its unavoidable inclination to transcend the 'here' and 'now' and to project instead a "would-be" or "ought-to-be" perspective. Hegel captured extremely well the idealizing function of representation when he pointed out its power of unifying the "fluctuating" "atomic units" of civil society.[14]

Furthermore, representative democracy, particularly when it is combined with a proportional electoral system, is well suited to address issues of control (and thus security) and more consistent with political equality and participation. My argument, which follows three steps, builds on John Stuart Mill's attempt to link representative government, proportional representation, and the agonistic character of the assembly. I am aware that Mill interpreted Thomas Hare's device as a tool for making sure that good intellectuals were selected. However, I think that the work of interpretation should try to apprise ideas from the perspective of their theoretical and practical development; that it should enable us to capture those principles and visions that transcended their historical context. Hence, despite Mill's own 'elitist' use of proportionality, his theoretical argument carries within itself democratic implications that are undeniably relevant to our own time. Remarkably, his ideas lucidly anticipate the main themes in contemporary deliberative theory of democracy and offer some cogent arguments that are today employed to defend proportional representation. However, I further develop Mill's insights by introducing into his theoretical framework the idea of deliberation as advocacy, which remained only suggestive in Mill's writings.

In part I, I argue that indirectness (and speech as a form of indirectness) makes room for deliberation. Indirectness, a constitutive mark of representative democracy, encourages the distinction between "deliberating" and "voting." A deliberative form of politics favors representation; it fosters a relationship between the assembly and the people that enables the demos to reflect upon itself and judge its laws, institutions, and leaders. The spatial and temporal gap opened by representation buttresses trust, control, and accountability if it is filled with speech (an articulated public sphere). Representation can also encourage political participation insofar as its deliberative character expands politics beyond the narrow limits of decision and administration. The agora model is the device I will employ to articulate these views, with Jean-Jacques Rousseau and Mill as my alternative points of orientation.

In part II, I claim that, theoretically, proportional representation fulfills the democratic principles of equal political opportunity and control better than a majoritarian electoral system (single-member territorial constituency). As some of its earliest theorists argued, proportional representation better safeguards those principles because it resists the misleading identification of the "right of representation" with the "right of decision" that the majoritarian system implies.[15] Whereas the majority retains the latter, the whole citizenry should not be deprived of the former. Democratic deliberation requires us "to search for systems of representation that will enhance deliberation for all citizens."[16] Proportional representation, one of its contemporary critics acknowledges, better fits this requirement insofar as it "would enforce a broad scope for public debate and would encourage the development of judgmental competence among the electorate."[17]

Finally, in part III, I introduce and discuss the category of advocacy. Advocacy avoids the rationalistic and cognitivist assumption underlying some recent models of deliberative democracy and withstands the conventional critique of proportionality as a descriptive "mirror" that simply reproduces existing social segmentations. While capturing the complex character of representation—its commitment to as well as its detachment from a cause—the analogy between the advocate and the representative can be an interesting attempt to transcend the two extremes of partiality and an objectivist vision of the general interest that have been crossing modern representative democracy since its inception. Moreover, it helps to highlight the two main political functions of representation, as a means both for expressing individual opinions and choices and therefore exercising self-government and for resisting exclusion and therefore achieving security.

I. THE SALIENCE OF INDIRECTNESS

Because democracy has acquired its value from, and generally goes along with, direct political action, we need first to understand how "directness" is to be interpreted, and what citizens need to perform directly in order to enjoy democratic status. To answer these questions, I will refer to the ancient republics and the way the moderns have judged them. Indeed, only in the ancient polis was political autonomy fulfilled through a direct and physical presence of the citizens in the places where public decisions were to be made—the *ekklesia* and the *dikasteries*.

Following Robert Dahl, Young has maintained that even "in assemblies of a few hundred people, most people will be passive participants who listen to a few people speak for a few positions, then think and vote."[18] Indeed, the "direct" political presence of all citizens did not prevent the Athenian ekklesia from being an assembly in which the large majority abstained from *active* participation. Periclean and post-Periclean reforms were intended to discourage absence, not silence. It is true that the basic principle of Athenian democracy was *isegoria*—the individual right to speak in the assembly. Nevertheless, adult male citizens were paid for attending, not for speaking: "There was no law requiring anybody to appear in the role of *ho boulomenos* [any one who wanted to speak], and the orators found no fault with the fact that many Athenians never addressed their fellow citizens."[19]

Attendance and speech are the structural forms of democratic participation. They are prior to, and the precondition for, any democratic decision. They entail both passivity and activity while denoting the plastic dimension of speech that actually presumes both outward expressiveness and inward reflection, talking and listening.[20] They highlight the difference between isolation and solitude, and between mere presence and a deliberative kind of presence.[21]

In any event, directness does not mean that all talk. A "direct" presence does not necessarily entail a vocal presence. This was even more so in Sparta (which until the end of the eighteenth century was taken to be a model of direct government and the good republic[22]), where the physical presence of citizens in the assembly meant standing and listening passively, and finally resolving (by shouting) without any explicit articulation of either consent or dissent. Historians believe that the rule that "anyone who wished" could address the ekklesia remained only an ideal in Athens too where direct democracy still produced an elite: "A minority came to dominate the field of politics and the majority of citizens never trod the speakers' platform."[23]

Mogens Herman Hansen lists three kinds of citizens in Athens: "the *passive* ones" who did not go to the assembly; the "*standing* participants" who went to the assembly, but listened and voted, and "did not raise their voice in discussion"; and the *"wholly active* citizens" (a "small group of initiative-takers, who spoke and proposed motions").[24] Hansen challenges the myth that all Athenian citizens could gather together in the ekklesia and deliberate, since the gathering place, the Pnyx, could hold only about 6,000 people, and in fifth- and fourth-century Athens there were many more citizens.[25] If we compare Athens to contemporary democracy, we can say that our right to vote corresponds to Athenian standing participation, to abstain from voting corresponds to passive citizenship, and representation corresponds to wholly active citizenship. Perhaps Mill had these parallels in mind when he argued that voting is a "public function" or *duty*, not a right to be performed at will, and when he advanced proposals to fund electoral campaigns with public money and to make the ballot free and accessible to all.[26] Pericles paid Athenians a day salary to discourage passivity in dikasteries; similarly, Mill wanted to remove all obstacles to voting. Pericles tried to make standing participation convenient; Mill wanted to make it not *in*convenient.

However, what is most important to consider in order to understand what democratic directness meant in Athens' deliberating institutions is the role played by wholly active citizens. Did the absence of representation make Athenian citizens speak their minds directly?[27] There are two models of directness that ancient history has bequeathed to us: that of Sparta and that of Athens. Rousseau, who advocated isolated individual reasoning and silent voting, regarded Sparta, not Athens, as the best republic. By contrast, Mill (and before him, Madison), who advocated public discussion and deliberative process, judged Athens superior.

Rousseau believed that in a well-ordered republic, each citizen should make up his mind alone, without entering into a dialogue with his fellow citizens. He interpreted solitude as isolation and, not unlike Plato, saw Reason (the general will) as a force able to speak equally to all as long as external influences, such as passions and opinions, did not interfere. Rousseau had so little confidence in individual disinterestedness that he was unwilling to leave individual citizens to the mercy of their own or others' impulses. His admiration for the virtues of the ancients was as deep as his disdain for the weakness of the moderns. But instead of choosing, like Montesquieu and Madison, the constitutional stratagem of a mechanical balance of opposing forces, he adopted an obstructionist strategy. He disassociated citizens from one another in order to keep them safe from the risk of partiality and thus to avoid imposing the general will upon them through coercion. Hence, he rejected delegation because it entailed citizens' relying on others' judgment and misjudgment, and the assembly becoming a stage for demagogues.

Rousseau related directness to reasoning and the will and related indirectness to action that could be performed by chosen magistrates.[28] Because reasoning had to avoid collective deliberation, direct political action meant only voting, not debating. It is truly striking that *The Social Contract* stresses the communal moment of political participation without contemplating public speech. This means that for Rousseau, the deadly risk to political autonomy came from citizens' interaction with one another rather than from their passivity. Thus, in his republic, *all* were standing participants, but *none* was a wholly active participant—citizens were neither speakers, nor activists of parties and movements, nor opinion makers or receivers. Rousseau's well-ordered society lacked the intermediary sphere of public opinion. It was a society of silence. It should come as no surprise, then, that he dismissed both Athenian democracy and representative democracy. In his mind, the most negative aspect of representation was that in making public deliberation necessary, it violated the basic principle of judgmental individual autonomy. Athens had the same defect in his eyes. Indeed, even if its citizens did not delegate their sovereign power, they nevertheless practiced some form of *mediated* participation insofar as their assembly was actually run by the orators.

Rousseau's perception was far from inaccurate. In the Athenian ekklesia, the speakers did not speak *on behalf of*, *for*, or *in the place of* someone who was de jure physically absent, and in this sense they were neither trustees nor delegates. However, one should not be too quick to conclude that the orators did not represent anybody or anything. Indeed, they were masters of the art of rhetoric. Despite the contemporary myth of the polis as the place of a disinterested and dialogic exercise of public reason, private and class interests did not in fact remain outside the ekklesia. Moses I. Finley has deemed "commonplace" the idea that Athenian citizens divorced "personalities from issues," participation from interests. For them, too, "politics were instrumental." Although they did not have "structured political parties," they did have corporate and antagonistic interests.[29] Aristotle depicted Athenian political life as a theater of an endless struggle between the oligarchs (who never disappeared) and the demos.

Given these premises, it is not entirely correct to say that the orators spoke their own minds. They spoke their minds to promote some interests, and in this sense they spoke *for* someone or something, even if nobody gave them any mandate. Moreover, we know that the great orators used to deliver their speeches only on important or exceptional occasions. In ordinary times, and on ordinary policy, they used "to speak" *through* "their identifiable expert-lieutenants" who 'represented' their opinions and acted in their place.[30] In Athens, direct democracy produced an elite despite the fact that it did not elect representatives. And even if in the ekklesia anyone who wished could "make a denunciation," a petition, or a law proposal, nevertheless political leaders shaped citizens' opinions.

It should come as no surprise, then, that Rousseau dismissed both Athenian democracy and representative democracy. Despite their manifest differences, they shared the quality of indirectness. Public discussion characterized the kind of mediated politics that Rousseau attributed, correctly, to both and motivated his rejection. Deliberation in the assembly involves a kind of dissension that goes well beyond conflicting opinions for him. Speech promotes the fragmentation of the general will and makes it hard for citizens to escape the interference of passions and interests.[31] Eloquence, particular interests, and disagreement on the interpretation of the general will go hand in hand.

Rousseau's perception was correct. Public deliberation, not simply voting, characterizes democracy, which does not regard the sovereign body as a homogeneous collective unity. In a democracy, a plurality of opinions makes speech the main instrument for reaching decisions. Taking Rousseau seriously, we can say that representative democracy is a living confutation of a rationalist vision of politics. Its assembly, Mill understood, generates consent that is always provisional.

What makes modern democracy secure and lasting is the sense of endlessness that the debating character of the decision-making process transmits to citizens, the voters as well as the representatives. Disagreement (and thus plurality of political opinions) and free speech were the two elements that made Athens so different from Sparta, and that, in Rousseau's view, characterized representative democracy. It is not by chance that although Athens lacked representation, theorists of representative democracy such as Mill chose it as their model. Athens and modern democracy are similar insofar as both involve an indirect form of political action. That form is public speech.

Speech is a means of mediation that belongs to all citizens, linking and separating them at the same time. Speech interjects individual ability into politics and lifts the veil of unanimity and sameness. It gives meaning to voting, which presumes evaluation and discrimination among articulated options. As Mark A. Kinshansky has perceptively remarked, the distinctiveness of the Spartan assembly rested in the lack of individuation of its resolving procedure. Shouting served to expressed assent, not public judgment: "The shout was a ritual of affirmation and celebration. As a process, it was both anonymous and unanimous. It was the very opposite of voting."[32]

Thus, it is not indirectness per se that distinguishes representative democracy from direct democracy. Rather, what makes the former truly different is the character and broadness of its mediated politics. Representative democracy lacks *simultaneity* in political deliberation and decision making. Recalling Hansen's division, one can say that "standing participants" and "wholly active citizens" do not operate in the same time and space dimension. Simultaneous standing, deliberating, and deciding is achieved only by the representatives. The assembly is the only place where the kind of political indirectness belonging to the ancient ekklesia exists. Contrary to direct democracy, the attendance of "standing participant" citizens (the voters) in a representative democracy is *wholly* mediated: not only speech, but time and space as well are mediating factors. The particular relation between electors and their representatives consists of the lack of coextensiveness and the time elapsing be- tween the speaking/hearing moment and the rectifying/voting moment.

Quite appropriately, thus, representative democracy has been described as *deferred* democracy.[33] Here, petitions and legislative proposals are not discussed and acted on one by one by standing citizens when orators bring them up. The vote of standing citizens is split into two moments: one is future oriented (the package of promises and proposals made by candidates) and one is retrospective or past oriented (the actual outcome achieved by the elected representatives).[34] In both Athens and a modern democracy, the "standing participants" limit themselves to listening and voting. But in contrast to Athens, judgment and resolution in a modern democracy take place at separate times. The deferred dimension of modern democracy makes it necessary to develop an articulated public sphere capable of creating symbolic simultaneity: citizens must feel *as if* they are standing, deliberating, and deciding *simultaneously* in the assembly. Accordingly, as Stephen Holmes has pointed out, Mill maintained that freedom of speech is not only a negative right of the individual, but the precondition for representative government to function legitimately.[35]

Unique to modern democracy is the intermediary network of communication that fills the gap between speaking/hearing and rectifying/voting. Such communication can reunite the *actual* dimension (parliament) and the *deferred* dimension (voters) so that representative democracy might enjoy what made Athenian democracy exceptional—the simultaneity of "standing" and "acting": "The newspapers and the railroads are solving the problem of bringing the democracy of England to vote, like that of Athens, simultaneously in one *agora*."[36] A deferred agora requires participation to supplement representation. Periodic participation in electoral campaigns, "free and public conferences" between representatives and their constituencies, and regular participation in local government are crucial for helping citizens exercise control over "wholly active citizens." Thus, all citizens can become "wholly active citizens."[37]

These devices conform to the fact that representation is—and needs to be—on a continuum with participation. A representative can be an advocate who turns the whole nation, not merely the assembly, into a public forum. The representative is an intermediary who can expand the space for political discussion beyond governmental institutions and at the same time bring political decisions to the people's attention for scrutiny. The representative takes the claims and ideas of the people to the assembly so debate there expands and is enriched. Yet, for this to happen, society cannot be a silent place. Advocacy in parliament both requires and stimulates advocacy in society.[38]

Although scholars still read Mill as a pre-Schumpeterian and hardly a democrat, he would never have subscribed to the idea that voters "must understand that, once they have elected an individual, political action is his business and not theirs."[39] In fact, his agora paradigm assumes representation as a complex institution that encompasses several layers of political action that fill "the interval between one parliamentary election and another"; and they replace a spatial agora that no longer exists with a temporal one.[40] Representation is a "course of action" rather than a "simple act"—a practice of political interaction among citizens that goes well beyond voting.[41]

Thus, the difference between direct and indirect democracy does not lie merely in the fact that only the former presumes a wholly active participation on the part of all citizens. More interesting, it lies in the way the form of standing participation—which is common to both—is performed. Only in a representative democracy does popular voting have the character of a credit and great role is assigned to trust. Trust, control, and accountability are more or less effective depending on the degree to which citizens can be *like* the "standing participants" in the Athenian ekklesia.[42]

I would say, then, that in relation to the legislative process, the difference between direct and representative democracy pertains to the form of indirectness attained: synchronic in the one case and diachronic in the other. This difference is evident once we consider the way citizens perform as "standing participants." Whereas in Athens the citizens' *visibility* was immediate and needed no particular effort on their part, save to go to the Pnyx, in a representative democracy their *standing* itself is symbolic and needs to be constructed and nurtured. Thus, speech acquires a broader significance because it is a kind of medium that in order to do its mediating work, it has to give body and configuration to the "standing participants." One can say that in a representative democracy, words 'give life' because citizens (with their variety of claims and opinions) need to make themselves heard if they want to make themselves visible and to communicate with the wholly active citizens sitting in the assembly.

This is an extremely important conceptualization because it entails that representation is more than merely instrumental. One of the most frequent criticisms ancient philosophers and historians made was that in Athens, citizens attending the assembly were at the mercy of the orators. The destiny of the city was in the hands of skillful rhetoricians, the impact of whose character was even more important than the decision-making power of the people. As Thucydides wrote of Pericles's Athens, "The democracy existed in name, but in fact the first citizen ruled."[43] Public discourse, it has recently been observed, easily turned the orator into a demagogue, while the people had practically no chance to shield themselves from the power of speech.[44]

Representation allows citizens to shield themselves from speech. It gives them the chance to reflect by themselves, to step back from factual immediacy and to defer their judgment.[45] Representation creates distance between the moments of speech and decision and, in this sense, enables a critical scrutiny while shielding the citizens from the harassment of words and passions that politics engenders. This is what gives representation a "moral distinctiveness," what makes it not simply prudentially necessary but also valuable in itself.[46]

II. THE AGORA MODEL AND PROPORTIONAL REPRESENTATION

The acknowledgment of a structural relationship between representation and deliberation brought Mill to maintain that in a "good" democracy, the assembly needs to be like an agora in which citizens' "voices" are represented proportionally. Mill derived the justification of proportional representation from the two powers he assigned to the assembly—control and discussion. Concerning control, the assembly could check the executive by shedding "the light of publicity" on its acts, compelling their "full exposition and justification" and, if needed, by censuring and dismissing politicians from office. The representative agora had to be "an organ of popular demands," a place in which "adverse discussion" on "public matters" could "produce itself in full light." The power of control aimed at securing "the liberty of the nation."[47] Mill cautioned that this power would decrease in proportion to the assembly's increased identification with the majority that supported the executive. To preserve its power of control, the assembly had to function as the public forum of the whole country where "not only the general opinion of the nation" but "every interest and shade of interest" had its say and causes were "passionately pleaded" so as to compel others to listen and to produce justifications. Through proportional representation, Mill translated the democratic principle of equality into an argument for political liberty. He thus advanced a notion of democracy that was quite original in his time, when democracy was generally identified with equality or, in de Tocqueville's words, with a regime dominated by the blind "passion of equality."

The antityrannical argument of liberty as "security for good government" was the weapon Mill used against a majoritarian interpretation of democracy—whether in the form of "pure" or direct democracy (Rousseau's model) or representative democracy "by a mere majority of the people" (James Mill's model).[48] The core of his theoretical justification for representative democracy lies in his objections to these two models. His principled insight has not lost its value.

Mill aimed his first and more radical criticism at the deductivist structure of Rousseau's system and at his father's, systems that presumed an axiomatic identification between political liberty and the unity of the body politic. While naturally in agreement with direct democracy, that axiom had a devastating effect on James Mill's strategy for defending representative government.

According to James Mill's theorem, the interest of a democratic government coincided necessarily with the general interest; the general interest was identical to the interest of the majority because the "laborious many" were less likely to misuse political power than were the few (in any event, their misgovernment would result from ignorance, not "sinister interests"); and, as a consequence, each could represent the interests of others without neglecting, abusing, or exploiting them.[49] The theory of representation as a "mirror" fits James Mill's model perfectly. In his vision, the parliament should accurately reflect a uniform citizenry that chooses a "certain number of themselves to be the actors *in their stead.*"[50] The benefits of representation would vanish "in all cases in which the interests of the choosing body [were] not the same with those of the community."[51] Representation did not represent claims or ideas but, rather, what people held in common, that is, their potential to pursue their well-being. It worked as a *simplifier* of interests and an *assimilator* of subjects because the more industrious were assumed to promote the interests of others by promoting their own. This 'Chinese box' model worked particularly well with dependent people: women's interests were included within their husbands' and fathers' interests; workers' interests within their employers'. Voting was a means for protecting the majority, not for promoting political equality. Finally, no one could act as an "advocate" for anyone else because "the laborious people" could allow no segmentation if "sinister interests" were to be avoided. Despite his defense of representative government, James Mill ended up restating Rousseau's theory with this crucial difference: now the sovereign people were the majority.[52]

James Mill's model undermined representation by defining it as aggregate interests instead of individuals' ideas and claims and by linking it to objective truth instead of opinions. His assembly was a place where the representatives of the "laborious people" arrived at an objective estimation of their interests. A difference of opinion could arise only if the representatives lacked knowledge or defended "sinister interests."[53] In James Mill's assembly, causes "passionately pleaded," as well as disagreement, were out of place. A defense of the assembly as an agora required instead exactly the idea that majoritarianism obfuscated: that representation is personal, that its task involves more than producing a majority, and that the representative is an "advocate."

John Stuart Mill countered his father's doctrine with a more individualistic foundation for democracy. For him, democracy does not mean that people are involved as bearers of interests that differ only in quantity and thus can be aggregated but that people are involved as individuals holding ideas and opinions on their interests and their position in relation to the society and the demos. Mill's conception of representative government comprised both the principle of equality and the principle of individual expressiveness, that is, liberty. It revived Aristotle's idea that the basis of democracy "is that each citizen should be in a position of equality," which means the "position" of *each citizen* needs to be considered, not what aggregates the citizens.[54] The normative distinctiveness of democracy is not that the majority—"a flock of sheep innocently nibbling the grass side by side"—rules but that each citizen consciously shares in the life of the country. The institutional power of control in a democracy is vested in a collective body that (through its representatives) ought ideally to profit from the voice of "every citizen."[55]

The individual nature of the vote makes debate in the assembly inevitable. It also strengthens the argument that proportional representation, *ideally*, ensures that *every voice* will be heard. Proportional representation, for Mill, is not a political calculation that generates an accurate mathematical average of social interests. Whereas universal suffrage guarantees that all citizens are treated equally, proportional representation tries to make sure that the specific condition of the individual citizen is not ignored. The former needs to be blind to differences; the latter is conscious of them.

Yet, proportional representation is not a form of differential treatment because it does not distribute political voice unequally to unequals. Its regulative principles are equality and the intensity of individual preferences. Proportional representation supports minorities not because it favors them. Indeed, it does not give a minority *more* than its numerical due. Rather, it guarantees that all have the same chance to choose representatives. It does not follow a "compensatory" logic because compensation presumes that the stronger will remain stronger and treats the weaker with benevolent charity.[56] It is therefore misleading to think that proportional representation implements the Aristotelian principle of proportional equality.[57] Instead, proportional representation takes seriously the principle underlying universal suffrage: that every individual has the right to an equal vote (or voice). Proportional representation also recognizes pluralism in the first instance, whereas majoritarianism first recognizes the majority and then tries to deal with the reality of pluralism through "compensatory" treatment. Proportional representation reflects a philosophy that takes equal opportunity seriously.

Mill's important intuition was that the legitimacy of majority decision rests on the stipulation that people have the chance to express themselves in order, potentially, to influence and eventually reverse legislation.[58] By making themselves heard, minorities remind the majority that it is just one possible majority. Thus, proportionality provides an equal opportunity to participate in the race and an equal opportunity to be represented. Indeed, we can say that a proportional electoral system does not make losers. More than a race it is a form of participation in creating the representative body. It is a means by which electors 'send candidate to the assembly'. The distinction between "the right of representation" and "the right of decision" is captured well here because the equal prospect of success should refer first to the possibility of acquiring representation.[59]

Thus, Mill's agora model requires proportional representation because it presumes democracy as a system whose political process must be judged from the point of view of "all"—those who are in the majority and those who are in the minority—and because it presumes a final decision is achieved through a debate whose participants present the "whole" of "every opinion which exists in the constituencies" and "obtains its *fair share of voices*."[60] In criticizing the majoritarian model, Mill spoke openly of the "slavery of the majority," and, despite his 'elitist' aim, his conclusions captured the link between democracy and proportional representation. A majoritarian democracy is a "government of privilege" and, as such, contradicts the democratic principle of equality.[61] In a government where the majority "alone possess practically any voice in the State," the *political* counting of voices is deemed identical with the *arithmetical* counting of votes—which means that only the majority counts.[62]

Arithmetical democracy pays most attention to the role of the majority because it stresses the moment of decision rather than the entire deliberative process. Mill did not deny that "the minority must yield to the majority, the smaller number to the greater" when decisions are taken. But he forcefully opposed the idea that counting should mean that only the majority is counted. When the representative body vote, "the minority must of course be overruled."[63] But, as I have already shown, the assembly does not limit itself to voting, and debate cannot occur without a plurality of opinions. Representation is not only a tool for "accommodating" interests and forming majorities. Control and public judgment are no less important than effective government.[64] As Jane Mansbridge has observed, "The more a democracy approaches the 'unitary' state of common interests, the less it requires political equality."[65] In a pluralist and, even more so, in an inegalitarian society, opportunity to participate particularly matters to participants.

The conception of the assembly as a deliberative body rather than a silent congregation that simply votes is one of the main contributions to modern democratic thought made by eighteenth- and nineteenth-century theories of representative government.[66] It is also one of the central themes of *Considerations on Representative Government*. Mill helped to revise an old tradition that cut across ideological lines and enjoyed a solid reputation in modern political thought. Disdain for rhetoric and admiration for the Spartan assembly went along with the decline of the humanist tradition. Speech and the art of disputation were esteemed in Machiavelli's time, but not in the time of Descartes and Hobbes. Sparta, with its laconic assembly, was a model for James Harrington and for Rousseau, but not for Machiavelli (or Mill).[67]

The dichotomy between a deliberative republicanism and a rationalist republicanism bore fruit in the post–French Revolution era, when the conceptualization of representative government was perfected. In Mill's time, the English conservatives who opposed a democratic transformation of the state referred explicitly to the rationalist tradition. In spite of his antirepublican stance, for instance, the "reactionary" Willian Mitford relied on Rousseau and Harrington to support his antidemocratic ideas.[68] Mill contributed in reviving the deliberative tradition of republicanism. Furthermore, he suggested that representative democracy should not be defined as a system in which people govern indirectly, but as a system in which political action has to pass public scrutiny and control. While the majority makes the laws, debate and judgment give the majority moral legitimacy and make people feel secure because they see that both the majority and the minority can contribute to the legislative process. As Bernard Manin has recently argued, discussion and disagreement for theorists of representative government were the consistent outcomes of an egalitarian premise: discord among opinions should not terminate "through the intervention of one will that is superior to the others."[69] Thanks to deliberation, the common good can be seen as a cooperative construction of the whole community and as the outcome of ongoing persuasion and compromise that never ends in a permanent verdict.

We can now fully grasp the relevance of linking a talking assembly to the two main principles of democracy: control (which provides security) and equality. Control implies the anti-Platonic notions that no one possesses the "right" solution in political matters and that human knowledge is fallible.[70] Fallibility implies the recognition of various opinions and equality of opportunity. As Anne Phillips has recently argued, popular control is not simply a matter of prudence (self-protection from the monopoly of power), it is also a value in itself because it presumes equality.[71]

Control and equality imply that every citizen should be able to count on "a *point d'appui*, for individual resistance to the tendencies of the ruling power; a protection, a rallying point, for opinions and interests which the ascendant public opinion views with disfavor."[72] In this sense, one can argue that political exclusion in representative democracy would take the form of *silence*, of not being heard or represented. The task of resisting against this modern form of exclusion is what makes representation not simply instrumental: "Including those previously excluded matters *even if* it proves to have no discernible consequences for the policies that may be adopted."[73]

III. ADVOCACY AND DELIBERATION

As a point d'appui, representation acquires the feature of "advocacy." Advocacy has two components: the representative's "passionate" link to the electors' cause and the representative's relative autonomy of judgment. On one hand, advocacy gives representatives firm convictions and thus nurtures a spirit of controversy. (Mill spoke of sympathy joining "friends" and "partisans" against their "opponents."[74]) On the other hand, it steers partisan convictions down the path of deliberation and, ultimately, toward decision. Advocacy testifies to the structural tension of democratic deliberation: diverse (and seldom rival) interests, subjective visions, and aspirations compete in an open political space with the goal of reaching a decision that is not supposed to serve partisan interests or end deliberation.

Different interpretations of democracy result mainly from the different ways theorists view consent. Rousseau's model of direct democracy entails gradually overcoming the sources of disagreement because a diversity of interests obstructs the general good. The representative model stresses discussion and maintains that antagonistic interests and opinions do not impede policies that are in the general interest.

The contemporary debate on deliberative democracy centers more or less on the same division. Some theorists propose a conception of deliberation that is reminiscent of a Platonic dialogue, since interlocutors are allowed to hold 'incorrect' ideas provided they give up the passions that would impede the attainment of truth. (Thrasymachus had no alternative but to leave the stage.) They see deliberation in terms of the outcome expected to reduce differences by correcting "distorted" interpretations of the public good.[75] I would call this a consensus model of deliberative democracy. Other theorists are not troubled by the persistence of differences because they see them as necessary for deliberation to occur. They avoid the rationalist "vice" by rejecting the "dichotomy between reason and desire." They emphasize the critical moment, or the process, more than rational consensus on a final definition of general good.[76] I would call this an agonistic model of deliberative democracy.

Mill's theory of representative democracy belongs to the latter model. It anticipates some of the main themes of contemporary democratic theory, in particular the agonistic component and antirationalistic notion of deliberation.[77] Mill shared a sincere aspiration for the general good, but he also interpreted it as a regulative principle. With respect to the "identification of interest between the rulers and the ruled," he assumed that such an identification could hardly exist; in fact, it did not. If it did, representation, and perhaps government itself, would be unnecessary.[78] In this sense, we could say that the general interest does not lie before public debate. The general interest does not have a definitive location precisely because it cannot be defined once and for all.[79] It is the "direction" toward "the interest of the people. Not that vague abstraction, the good of the country, but the actual, positive well-being of the living human creatures who compose the population."[80]

In his parliamentary speeches, Mill restated Tocqueville's idea that while democracies are "perpetually making mistakes, they are perpetually correcting them too, and that the evil, such as it is, is far outweighed by the salutary effects of the general tendency of their legislation."[81] The advantage of democratic deliberation consists of the habit of self-revision and self-learning that it fosters and the energy it produces.[82] It does not claim to yield better results than other decision-making procedures. Rather, by leaving the door open to emendation, it imbues politics with a healthy sense of possibility. This acknowledgment of fallibility makes democracy the most reasonable regime and the one most consistent with the human condition: "It is not one of the faults of democracy to be obstinate in error. . . . The better way of persuading possessors of power to give up a part of it [is] by reminding them of what they are aware of—their own fallibility."[83]

Although there is no alchemic transformation of 'plurality into unity', the world of deliberation does not simply lead people to change their minds for instrumental reasons.[84] It also transforms people's disposition toward the object of deliberation and the ideas of others. Deliberation enriches knowledge, disposes the individual mind to make public use of reason, refines citizens' "powers of intelligence and combination," and encourages citizens to pursue their claims through friendly rivalry.[85]

From a theoretical point of view, the tension between commitment to the electors' cause and a representative's autonomous judgment, which animates advocacy, exemplifies the character of representative democracy. Democratic "advocacy" requires steadfast commitment to agreed-upon procedures; it does not favor outcomes that are "true" or "definitive" so much as congruent with the shared principles of political equality that deliberation presumes. The constitutive character of these principles limits advocacy, whose rationale is that no decision is sheltered from disagreement. Making the interpretation of general interest mutable in order to make it more consistent with the democratic principles binds it to a cooperative searching process.

This seems to be a plausible answer to the question of how agonism can generate policies that serve the general interest. In objecting to Mill's theory of advocacy, Melissa S. Williams notes that conflict "produces nothing of itself"; therefore, it can hardly transform people's opinions.[86] Yet, accustoming people to seek solutions through open discussion strengthens their loyalty to democratic procedures because these procedures are responsible for the rivalry that people come to value. As Albert Hirschman has persuasively remarked, democratic debate and antagonism play an unseen and unplanned unifying role in that they "produce themselves the valuable ties that hold modern democratic societies together and provide them with the strength and cohesion they need."[87]

This reasoning makes sense of Mill's belief that an increased number of voices in the assembly would actually produce reconciliation and also better laws. For every group to further its ideas when there is no strong majority party, each must compromise with the others, thus attenuating its partisan claims and giving its positions broader scope.[88] On the other hand, a two-party system seems prime to favor politics that reflect partisan interests in a less compromising way.

The theory of representation as "advocacy" acquires its relevance within this agonistic model. It is deceptive to oppose advocacy to deliberation (as if passionate commitments prevent debaters from being open to changing their ideas and compromising their claims in response to others' arguments). Nor would it help to depict the political arena as containing a split between advocacy and deliberation.[89] What we learn from Mill is that such readings rely on an incorrect premise: the assumption that the role of the advocate and deliberation are mutually exclusive.

In defining representatives as advocates, we have to see them not merely as partisans but as deliberators. Even though representatives do not deliberate when acting as advocates (one could say that representatives are advocates and deliberators in turn), nevertheless they consciously speak with deliberation in mind. Without deliberation, there would be no reason for advocacy. Advocacy is not blind partisanship; advocates are expected to be passionate and intelligent defenders. An advocate who is exclusively a partisan is not an advocate. And deliberators who are exclusively rationalizers are not deliberators—even if they produce rational justifications. A good representative democracy needs neither fanatical (or bureaucratic) representatives nor philosopher kings but, rather, deliberators who judge and in turn plead causes "passionately" in accordance with the principles and procedures of democratic government.

Thus, an "advocate" is not asked to be impartial like a judge, or to reason in solitude like a philosopher. Unlike a judge, advocates have ties to their 'clients'; their job is not to apply the rule but to define how the facts fit or contradict the rule or to decide whether the existing rule conforms to principles that society shares or a "good" government should adopt. Unlike a philosopher (and like the politician), advocates have "to conform to the wishes of an electorate in order to win." The philosopher owes a justification only to his principles. He is not seeking external consensus: "A philosophical justification cannot refer to the interests and passions of a particular group"; it "must be rational, or at least reasonable."[90] On the contrary, the relationship between candidate and electors does "not require the electors to consent to be represented by one who intends to govern them in opposition to their fundamental conviction."[91]

Far from transcending the specific situation of citizens, deliberative reasoning rests on the premise that specificity needs to be known and acknowledged. Therefore, "understanding" and "seeing" are the faculties at work in deliberative speech just as they are in forensic speech. They express the complex nature of advocacy, which should adhere to its cause but not be driven by it. Good advocates believe in their cause but understand the reasoning of others to the point of being able to reconstruct it in their minds. They must "feel" the force of others' arguments in order to envision the path toward the best possible outcome.[92]

Advocacy relies heavily on personal ability and character. So although every citizen can become a representative in theory and de jure, citizens select those whom they judge to be better advocates. They do not choose randomly or feel it is enough that the candidate belongs to their group (they, in fact, discriminate within their own group). So proportional representation excludes an organic conception of representation that would be representation as a transcription of a pre- or nonpolitical identity.[93] Proportionality also excludes a vision of society as a corporate federation of groups that it would work to preserve.[94]

Advocacy, like election, entails a selection because we seek to get the best defendant, not a copy of ourselves.[95] It is not people's identity *as such* that seeks for representation, but their ideas and claims as citizens who suffer, or are liable to suffer, injustice *because of* their identity. In Mill's time, for example, "laborers" were not looking for "mirrors" in the assembly. They wanted advocates because they did not enjoy equal consideration as citizens as a result, in part, of their social and economic condition. They looked for representatives who were *sympathetic* to their cause, who "felt," whether directly or indirectly, their actual experience of subjection. If "the question of strike" was ignored by parliament—we read in *Representative Government*—it was because workers did not have representatives who shared their views and could effectively advocate their cause. "The leading members of the House" might have been qualified to understand workers' claims, but since they did not *share the workers' conviction*, they did not understand effectively and consequently were not able to attract the attention of the assembly.[96]

Electors, one might say, do not seek an existential identification with their representatives; they seek an identity of ideals and projects.[97] This is even more so with minorities, which want an advocate, not a rubber stamp, because their goal is "resistance to the tendencies of the ruling power" to refuse their claims and equal consideration. This confirms what I mentioned at the beginning—representation is future oriented; it is not a mere registration of a given social configuration. Its *political* and *idealizing* function frames the character of advocacy that entails, on one hand, representatives needing to share the visions and ideals of their constituencies but also needing to enjoy a certain degree of autonomy.[98]

Advocacy can be seen as an alternative to the dichotomy of representative as delegate or representative as trustee. Mill's strongest argument against the representative as delegate had to do with corruption. Delegation would lead to corruption because it would transform the main political function of the state—legislating—into an instrument for advancing corporate interests, thus jeopardizing political liberty and equality.[99] Proportional representation was consistent with the two anticorruption measures. Ideally, the whole nation could be made into a single district so that votes would not be wasted and the national perspective not obfuscated. It also gave representatives a "certain discretion to choose a course of action" within the limits of the main claims and ideas they were elected to represent.[100] This, however, was a relative, not an absolute, autonomy.

The idea of advocacy made Mill a spurious Burkean. Given the actual cleavages of class interests, Mill reasoned, filling the assembly with disinterested representatives would not guarantee minorities a voice. As for Burke, the representative (a trustee) ought to be responsible to the whole nation regardless of the pluralism that constituted the nation itself. Unlike Burke's trustee, however, Mill's representatives fulfilled their responsibility if they regarded their service as an opportunity for "substantial" groups to have their claims expressed by an advocate who *interpreted* the public interest from the point of view of those in disadvantaged conditions, and in order to redress them:[101] "In some cases, too, it may be necessary that the representative should have his hands tied, to keep him true to their interest, or rather to the public interest as they conceive it."[102] Representatives function as advocates insofar as they can judge the condition of their constituency from the point of view of the "'real' interest" of the whole country. In this sense, they are asked "to subordinate to reason, justice, and the good of the whole" the claims of their constituency.[103]

The figure of the representative-advocate is peculiar to a democracy whose civil society does not fully embody democratic principles. Thus, representation encompasses two perspectives. On one hand, it is defensive and transformative insofar as it considers social inequality in order to counter and redress it. On the other hand, it aims at independence from material and social circumstances and refers to qualities that are representative of the democratic community. The former ensures that disadvantaged groups and citizens are not penalized and excluded from the deliberative process. The latter projects an egalitarian notion of political community in which representation would finally depend on individual citizens' free choice.[104] On one hand, representation is pragmatic; on the other hand, representation is a regulative ideal.[105]

Thus, the theory of representation as advocacy entails a notion of citizenship that is egalitarian in principle but still takes power relations into account. Because its normative principle is political equality, it aims to give voice also to positions of subordination. This theory rests on a conception of citizenship that unifies the two basic equalities that have characterized democracy since the classical age: *isopsephia* (equality of voting that gives all citizens the right to equal participation) and *isegoria* (the equal chance to speak that gives all citizens the opportunity to express their opinions publicly and to be heard [or represented] equally).[106] While the former implies a simple conception of equality (one citizen, one vote), the latter does not exclude the use of diverse devices. One might say that thanks to the equality of voice, difference gives substance to equality. Proportional representation is a "special manner" by which citizens try to resist an imbalance in political power (which is a form of domination no matter how large the dominant class is). But proportional representation also expresses different visions for molding democratic society. It is this understanding that gives salience to the recognition that democratic deliberation is a form of democratic advocacy.

NOTES

1. Jane J. Mansbridge, *Beyond Adversarial Democracy*, with a revised preface. (Chicago: University of Chicago Press, 1983), 279-81. Mansbridge questioned the accuracy of the idea that direct democracy allows for more participation and more control than indirect democracy: "Small size does increase the average individual's power within his or her own group, but it also reduces the group's power vis-á-vis the rest of the world. But direct analysis of outcomes suggests that the interests of the poor are better protected in larger units."

2. See, respectively, Hanna Fenichel Pitkin, *The Concept of Representation* (Berkeley: University of California Press, 1967), 86, and Hans Kelsen, *General Theory of Law and State*, trans. Anders Wedberg (Union, NJ: Lawbook Exchange, 1999), 289.

3. John Dunn, *Western Political Theory in the Face of the Future* (Cambridge: Cambridge University Press, 1993), 28.

4. Nostalgia may foster resignation, but it may also encourage a realistic disenchantment toward what is actual. This was the accomplishment of Hegel's task of ideological normalization: he situated the ancient republics at the height of an uncontaminated perfection to make them innocuous and their ideal meaning powerless. Constant adopted a similar strategy, although his militant anti-Jacobean passion led him to declare ancient democracy undesirable instead of simply unattainable, old instead of simply ideally eternal.

5. As an example, recall the 1960s and 1970s theory of industrial democracy, a revival of the nineteenth-century ideal of cooperation combined with the early twentieth-century experience of factory councils. Radical democrats thought it possible to reconcile capitalist ownership with worker control of the factory by applying to the sphere of the economic the logic of the political sphere where all are entitled to a vote regardless of their unequal social status and property holding; for example, see Carole Pateman, *Participation and Democratic Theory* (1970; reprint, Cambridge: Cambridge University Press, 1997).

6. "Representation is incompatible with freedom because it delegates and thus alienates political will at the cost of genuine self-government and autonomy." Benjamin Barber, *Strong Democracy: Participatory Politics for a New Age* (Berkeley: University of California Press, 1984), 145.

7. Pitkin, *The Concept of Representation*, 84.

8. For a lucid defense of the realist school, see Giovanni Sartori, *The Theory of Democracy Revisited* (1962; reprint, Chathman, NJ: Chathman House, 1987), 102-15.

9. George Kateb, *The Inner Ocean: Individualism and Democratic Culture* (Ithaca, NY: Cornell University Press, 1992), 36-56.

10. David Plotke, "Representation Is Democracy," *Constellations*, 4 (1997): 19, and Iris Marion Young, "Deferring Group Representation," in *Nomos XXXIX, Ethnicity and Group Rights*, ed. Ian Shapiro and Will Kymlicka (New York: New York University Press, 1997), 352.

11. In fact, the idea of a moral distinctiveness of representation is not new (e.g., see *Federalist 10*), but it has mostly been lost to contemporary democratic theory.

12. See Adam Przeworski, *Democracy and the Market: Political and Economic Reforms in Eastern Europe and Latin America* (Cambridge: Cambridge University Press, 1991), 18.

13. Mark Kishlansky, *Parliamentary Selection: Social and Political Choice in Early Modern England* (Cambridge: Cambridge University Press, 1986), 225-30. In his fascinating reconstruction of the transition from "selection" to "election" in seventeenth-century England, Kishlansky shows that the institutionalization of the electoral form of selection brought ideology

into politics thus engendering a process of identification between the candidate and his constituency: "Unity now meant the agreement of the like-minded."

14. George W. F. Hegel, *Philosophy of Rights*, ed. and trans. T. M. Knox (London: Oxford University Press, 1967), 200-1. Hegel's definition, however, referred to corporate representation, not individual ("democratic") representation.

15. Simon Sterne, *On Representative Government and Personal Representation* (Philadelphia: Lippincott, 1871), 25, 50, and John Stuart Mill, "De Tocqueville on Democracy in America [II]," in *Collected Works*, vol. 18, *Essays on Politics and Society*, ed. John M. Robson (Toronto: University of Toronto Press, 1977), 165.

16. Amy Gutmann and Dennis Thompson, *Democracy and Disagreement* (Cambridge, MA: Belknap Press, 1996), 154.

17. Charles R. Beitz, *Political Equality* (Princeton, NJ: Princeton University Press, 1989), 137.

18. Young, "Deferring Group Representation," 352-53. Young refers to Robert Dahl, *Democracy and Its Critics* (New Haven, CT: Yale University Press, 1989), 225-31.

19. Mogens Herman Hansen, *The Athenian Democracy in the Age of Demosthenes*, trans. J. A. Crook (Oxford: Blackwell, 1993), 267, 150, and Aristotle, "The Constitution of Athens," in *Aristotle and Xenophon on Democracy and Oligarchy*, ed. J. M. Moore (Berkeley: University of California Press, 1986), 41.3.

20. I would not hesitate to view these as a universal form of human communication, peculiar to our relations to others as well as to ourselves. Socratic dialogues and Petrarca's lyrics are among the most exquisite examples of the phenomenology of the discursive life as an act of reciprocation, of giving and taking words.

21. Hannah Arendt, *The Life of the Mind* (San Diego, CA: Harcourt Brace Jovanovich, 1978), 1:184-85. Distinguishing solitude from isolation, Hannah Arendt identifies the former with the act of thinking itself. She sees it as a condition in relation to which "soundlessness" means intimacy, not, however, "speechlessness."

22. Elizabeth Rawson, *The Spartan Tradition in European Thought* (Oxford: Clarendon Press, 1969), 220-67.

23. Hansen, *The Athenian Democracy*, 267.

24. Ibid., 268 (emphsis added).

25. Ibid., 130-32.

26. Mill, *Considerations on Representative Government*, in *On Liberty and Other Essays*, ed. John Gray (Oxford: Oxford University Press, 1991), chap. 10. Mill opposed the use of private money in electoral campaigns because it encouraged passive citizenship and made representatives into mere delegates or agents.

27. Bernard Manin, *The Principles of Representative Government* (Cambridge: Cambridge University Press, 1997), 8-41. It should be noted that the absence of representation did not entail absence of elections—but in Athens, elections served to fill administrative, not legislative, functions.

28. Rousseau did not reject elections; in fact, the magistrates of his ideal republic were elected. What he rejected was the delegation of sovereign power. His rationale rested on his distinction between *action* and *will*. The former amounted to instrumental doing and therefore could be delegated; the latter amounted to the intention that leads to and shapes the doing and cannot be delegated without undermining citizens' intentional power over the action. To use a trivial example, it makes sense for me to delegate you to buy an ice cream for me, but it would be odd to let you decide whether I want an ice cream.

29. Moses I. Finley, *Democracy Ancient and Modern* (New Brunswick, NJ: Rutgers University Press, 1985), 97-98, 75.

30. Ibid., 79.

31. Jean-Jacques Rousseau, *The Social Contract*, in *The Basic Political Writings*, ed. Donald A. Cress (Indianapolis, IN: Hackett, 1987), 4.2. "But long debates, dissension, and tumult betoken the ascendance of private interests and the decline of the state."

32. Kishlansky, *Parliamentary Selection*, 10-11.

33. Young, "Deferring Group Representation," 355-57.

34. On the relationship between future-present-past in elections, see Manin, *The Principles of Representative Government*, 178-79.

35. Mill, *Considerations on Representative Government*, 241-42, 247-48. "Popular sovereignty is meaningless without rules organizing and protecting public debate." Stephen Holmes, "Precommitment and the Paradox of Democracy," in *Constitutionalism and Democracy*, ed. Jon Elster and Rune Slagstad (Cambridge: Cambridge University Press, 1988), 233. Holmes correctly remarks that in Mill's representative government, the institutional arrangements are not simply "depressants" but also "stimulants" because they guarantee the opposition's ability to express itself freely (p. 232).

36. Mill, "De Tocqueville on Democracy," 165. Finley stressed the 'absurdity' of this parallel because the agora cannot be symbolic, and was not in Athens. For him, this was "a false analogy" between the modern public sphere and the ancient ekklesia put forward by Mill. *Democracy Ancient and Modern*, 36.

37. Mill, *Considerations on Representative Government*, 370.

38. For instance, Mill was convinced that women's claim for suffrage could win a political consideration in the chamber only if the social movement for universal suffrage was in place. He sought outside support for advocacy in the parliament.

39. Joseph A. Schumpeter, *Capitalism, Socialism, and Democracy*, 3d ed. (New York: Harper Torchbooks, 1950), 295.

40. Mill, *Considerations on Representative Government*, 413.

41. Ibid., 370. A similar point was made by Young, "Deferring Group Representation," 357-58.

42. On the role of trust, control, and accountability, see Holmes, "Precommitment and the Paradox of Democracy," 195-240; Anne Phillips, *The Politics of Presence* (Oxford: Clarendon Press, 1995), 155-58; and Manin, *The Principles of Representative Government*, 203-4.

43. Thucydides, *The Peloponnesian War*, ed. Moses I. Finley (London: Penguin Classics, 1972), 2.65.11-13.

44. Harvey Yunis, *Taming Democracy: Models of Political Rhetoric in Classical Athens* (Ithaca, NY: Cornell University Press, 1996), 43-46.

45. The need to safeguard the electors' autonomous judgment induced some contemporary democratic constitutions to look for a further shield besides representation. For instance, the Italian constitution states that electoral campaigns must stop two days before elections take place. This suspension applies both to parties and to the media. Beneath this procedure of silence, there is Rousseau's idea that popular sovereignty entails the sovereignty of each citizen's judgment (I owe to Jon Elster the suggestion of looking for the "shielding" strategy of silence in contemporary constitutional democracies).

46. Kateb, *The Inner Ocean*, 36-56. Sartori adds an important corollary: through its *intermediary* role, representation "reduces power to *less* power" because "nobody is in a position to exercise an absolute (i.e., limitless) power" in a representative democracy. *The Theory of Democracy Revisited*, 71.

47. Mill, *Considerations on Representative Government*, 282.

48. Ibid., 302.

782   POLITICAL THEORY / December 2000

49. James Mill, "On Government," in *Political Writings*, ed. Terence Ball (Cambridge: Cambridge University Press, 1992), 7.

50. Ibid., 8 (emphasis added), and Pitkin, *The Concept of Representation*, 60-91.

51. James Mill, "On Government," 27.

52. James Mill, *Analysis of the Phenomena of the Human Mind*, 2 vols., ed. Alexander Bain, Andrew Findlater, George Grote, and John Stuart Mill (London: Longmans, Green, 1878), 2:187. "The People, that is, the Mass of the community, are sometimes called a class; but that is only to distinguish them, like the term Lower Order, from the aristocratic class. In the proper meaning of the term class, it is not applicable to the People. No interest is in common to them, which is not in common to the rest of the community." See also Joseph Hamburger, *Intellectuals in Politics: John Stuart Mill and the Philosophic Radicals* (New Haven, CT: Yale University Press, 1965), 45-63.

53. Carl Schmitt, *The Crisis of Parliamentary Democracy*, trans. Ellen Kennedy (Cambridge: MIT Press, 1994), 2-6. Schmitt's observation that the theorists of "government by discussion" saw free discussion as an instrument for discovering "the truth" is pertinent to James Mill or Bentham, not John Stuart Mill.

54. Aristotle, *The Politics*, ed. and trans. Ernest Barker (Oxford: Oxford University Press, 1994), 6.1317a49-50.

55. Mill, *Considerations on Representative Government*, 244.

56. Beitz, *Political Equality*, 157. It is puzzling that contemporary majoritarians prefer plural voting (which Mill used to protect intellectual minorities) to "favor the members" of "minority" groups rather than proportionality. In doing so, they miss the fact that "number" needs to be considered equally—for the majority as well as for the minority. "Double" or plural voting for the weak means accepting as a given an unfair electoral system and then proposing "compensation." Would it not be better to address the cause of electoral injustice rather than "compensating" its unjust outcome? In Mill's scheme, which is egalitarian, minorities do not ask for compensation but, rather, for equal treatment.

57. Beitz, *Political Equality*, 156. Beitz writes that whereas "the aim of quantitative fairness is to give public recognition to the equal political status of democratic citizens, the aim of qualitative fairness is the promotion of equitable treatment of interests." Hence, a system of plural voting is better than a proportional system. It seems to me that Beitz's argument rests on the fact that he relates proportional representation to the Aristotelian notion of proportional justice. But their logic is different. Proportional equality seems to justify plural voting rather then proportional representation. As Mill showed, the logic of proportional representation takes seriously the "quantitative fairness" of the "equal political status of democratic citizens." If we do not give citizens more than two choices, we cannot reasonably say that the winner represents a majority of various opinions, since citizens have been forced to adapt their opinions to fit either A or B. This is a violation of "quantitative fairness," since we aggregate preferences that would distribute themselves differently within a proportional counting. In Mill's words, proportional representation "secures a representation, in proportion to number, of every division of the electoral body: not two great parties alone." *Considerations on Representative Government*, 310.

58. Mill's "expressive" interpretation of political representation has been stressed recently by Melissa S. Williams, *Voice, Trust, and Memory: Marginalized Groups and the Failing of Liberal Representation* (Princeton, NJ: Princeton University Press, 1998), 47.

59. For a critique of this principle see Beitz, *Political Equality*, 135.

60. Mill, *Considerations on Representative Government*, 305 (emphasis added).

61. Ibid., 303.

62. Ibid., 302, 304.

63. Ibid., 303.

64. Mill's distinction between "talking" and "doing" answers the criticism that proportional representation is not of great advantage because "while proportionality allows all voices to be heard, it does not guarantee that all interests will be proportionally accommodated." Bernard Manin, Adam Przeworsky, and Susan C. Stokes, "Elections and Representation," in *Democracy, Accountability and Representation*, ed. Adam Przeworsky, Susan C. Stokes, and Bernard Manin (Cambridge: Cambridge University Press, 1999), 32n. 5. Disagreement on electoral systems makes sense precisely because the task of representation is not simply to implement policies, even if that is its final goal. A good policy does not compensate for a bad system of representation any more than a good paternalism can compensate for a lack of liberty.

65. Jane L. Mansbridge, "Living with Conflict: Representation in the Theory of Adversary Democracy," *Ethics* 91 (1981): 469. See also Brian Barry, "Is Democracy Special?" in *Philosophy, Politics and Society*, 5th ser., ed. Peter Laslett and James Fishkin (New Haven, CT: Yale University Press, 1979), 162.

66. Manin, *The Principles of Representative Government*, 183-92. James Madison and Emmanuel-Joseph Siéyès played a crucial role in conceptualizing modern political representation.

67. On Harrington's rationalist republicanism, see Jonathan Scott, "The Rapture of Motion: James Harrington's Republicanism," in *Political Discourse in Early Modern Britain*, ed. Nicholas Phillipson and Quentin Skinner (Cambridge: Cambridge University Press, 1993), 148-60.

68. Rousseau, *The Social Contract*, 4.2. When a new law is proposed, if it is a just law, there is no need for discussion because it expresses what "every body has already felt; and there is no question of either intrigues or eloquence to secure the passage into law of what each has already resolved to do." See also William Mitford, *History of Greece* (London: Cadell, 1829), 1:272-75.

69. Manin, *The Principles of Representative Government*, 188-90.

70. Mill, *On Liberty*, in *On Liberty and Other Essays*, 22. Mill's vision of the assembly as an agora is a theme that relates *Representative Government* to *On Liberty*. Indeed, it entails both the Socratic assumption that knowledge is a searching enterprise without an ultimate end and the conviction that consent gives legitimacy to obedience. "To refuse a hearing to an opinion, because they are sure that it is false, is to assume that *their* certainty is the same as *absolute* certainty. All silencing of discussion is an assumption of infallibility."

71. Phillips, *The Politics of Presence*, 27-28.

72. Mill, *Considerations on Representative Government*, 316.

73. Phillips, *The Politics of Presence*, 40.

74. Mill, *Considerations on Representative Government*, 282.

75. Joshua Cohen, "Democracy and Liberty," in *Deliberative Democracy*, ed. Jon Elster (Cambridge: Cambridge University Press, 1998), 199. "Not that the *aim* of such deliberation is to change citizen preferences by reducing their diversity: the aim is to make collective decisions. Still, one thought behind a deliberative conception is that public *reasoning* itself can help to reduce the diversity of politically relevant preferences because such preferences are shaped and even formed in the process of public reasoning itself. And if it does help to reduce that diversity, then it mitigates tendencies toward distortion even in strategic communication."

76. Manin, "On Legitimacy and Political Deliberation," *Political Theory* 15 (1987): 338-68; Iris Marion Young, *Justice and the Politics of Difference* (Princeton, NJ: Princeton University Press, 1990), 102-11; and Nancy Fraser, "Rethinking the Public Sphere: A Contribution to the Critique of Actually Existing Democracy," in *Habermas and the Public Sphere*, ed. Craig Calhoun (Cambridge: MIT Press, 1997), 121-30.

77. For example, see Cass R. Sunstein, *Legal Reasoning and Political Conflict* (New York: Oxford University Press, 1996), 58-59.

78. Mill, "Rationale of Representation," in *Collected Works*, vol. 18, *Essays on Politics and Society*, 22-23. "Identification of interest between the rulers and the ruled, being, therefore, in a literal sense, impossible to be realized, must not be spoken of as a condition which a government must absolutely fulfill; but as an end to be incessantly aimed at, and approximated to as nearly as circumstances render possible, and as is compatible with the regard due to other ends."

79. Arendt, *On Revolution* (1963; reprint, London: Penguin Books, 1977), 191-94. Arendt made a very similar comparison between truth that "needs no agreement" and thus no persuasion, and truth that requires argument and persuasion; she located the former in the nonpolitical and "despotic power" and the latter in the political life of the polis. This amounts to saying that rationality that aims not at demonstration but at deliberation is not, properly speaking, cognitive reason, but "practical" or pragmatic. See Chaim Perelman, *Justice, Law, and Argument: Essays on Moral and Legal Reasoning* (Dordrecht: Reidel, 1980), 59.

80. Mill, "Representation of the People [II]," in *Collected Works*, vol. 28, *Public and Parliamentary Speeches*, pt. 1, *November 1850-November 1868*, ed. John M. Robson (Toronto: University of Toronto Press, 1988), 67.

81. Ibid., 66.

82. Jon Elster, "The Market and the Forum: Three Varieties of Political Theory," in *Deliberative Democracy: Essays on Reason and Politics*, ed. James Bohman and William Rehg (Cambridge: MIT Press, 1997), 21-22.

83. Mill, "Representation of the People [II]," 64.

84. Elster, "Deliberation and Constitution Making," in *Deliberative Democracy*, 104. Elster has outlined the "hypocritical" strategy set up by the deliberative setting: because opinions become public, "speakers have to justify their proposal by public interest" arguments. Yet, in the end, the speaker cannot be purely hypocritical because "if all appeals to the common interest were hypocritical and were known to be so, they could not persuade anyone and nobody would bother to make them." In sum, 'hypocrisy' is a point of departure, not an end point.

85. John Rawls, "The Idea of Public Reason Revisited," in *Collected Papers*, ed. Samuel Freeman (Cambridge, MA: Harvard University Press, 1999), 378-79. Rawls ascribes to these characteristics of deliberative democracy the capacity to foster "civic friendship."

86. Williams, *Voice, Trust, and Memory*, 47.

87. Albert O. Hirschman, "Social Conflicts as Pillars of Democratic Market Society," *Political Theory* 22 (1994): 206. Bonnie Honig developed a similar argument in her interpretation of Arendt's agonal perspective as one that "involves us in relation not only 'with' but also always simultaneously 'against' others." "Toward an Agonistic Feminism: Hannah Arendt and the Politics of Identity," in *Feminist Interpretations of Hannah Arendt*, ed. Bonnie Honig (University Park: Pennsylvania State University Press, 1995), 160.

88. Jennifer Hart, *Proportional Representation: Critics of the British Electoral System 1820-1945* (Oxford: Clarendon Press, 1992), 33. In the case of Italy, the most progressive laws were passed when there was proportional representation.

89. Phillips, *The Politics of Presence*, 161-63. This is Phillips's view, which proposes a compromise between advocacy and deliberation.

90. Perelman, *Justice, Law, and Argument*, 59, 66.

91. Mill, *Considerations on Representative Government*, 382.

92. Mill, *Autobiography*, in *Collected Works*, vol. 1, *Autobiography and Literary Essays*, ed. John M. Robson (Toronto: University of Toronto Press, 1981), 21-27. Mill acknowledged Aristotle's *The Art of Rhetoric*, Quintilian's *De Institutione Oratoria*, and Cicero's *Orators* as among the most important texts of his intellectual formation.

93. Pitkin, *The Concept of Representation*, 90. If proportional representation is interpreted as map making, then the criticism that it depersonalizes both the voters and the elected is justified

It would banish both authorization and accountability. Will Kymlicka, *Multicultural Citizenship* (Oxford: Clarendon Press, 1995), 134, and Young, "Deferring Group Representation," 358-61.

94. Hegel produced the most consistent theory of corporate versus individual representation in *Philosophy of Rights*, 199-203. Mill engaged in a never-ending polemic against the conservative idea that "not the people, but all the various *classes* or *interests* among the people" should be represented. "Rationale of Representation," 43.

95. Ronald Dworkin, "What Is Equality? 4. What Is Political Equality?" *University of San Francisco Law Review* 22 (1988): 5. As Dworkin puts it, the very moment we claim an equal political say for all citizens, we are also forced to admit that people are different in how they perform politically. Some have more ability or more passion than others and, thus, more chance to pursue their preferences. The link between election and choice is effectively discussed by Manin, *The Principles of Representative Government*, 132-42.

96. Mill, *Considerations on Representative Government*, 246-47.

97. Phillips, *The Politics of Presence*, 133. "But the notion that shared experience *guarantees* shared beliefs or goals has neither theoretical nor empirical plausibility."

98. Ibid., 56, 156. As Phillips acknowledges, in a proportional system, the representative has more autonomy than in a majoritarian one; for advocates to be deliberators, they "have to be freed from stricter forms of political accountability."

99. Mill, "Thoughts on Parliamentary Reform," in *Collected Works*, vol. 19, *Essays on Politics and Society*, edited by John M. Robson (Toronto: University of Toronto Press, 1977), 318-20. Mill thus regarded "the function of a member of the Parliament" as a "duty to be discharged" rather than a "personal favor to be solicited." Against that "evil," he devised two solutions: the proposition that large districts be established so that "local influences of families and corporations would then have more chance of neutralizing one another," and the proposition that the state pay election expenses.

100. Thomas Christiano, *The Rule of the Many: Fundamental Issues in Democratic Theory* (Boulder, CO: Westview Press, 1996), 213-14.

101. On the ambiguous relationship between Mill's and Burke's view on representation, see Williams, *Voice, Trust, and Memory*, 45-53.

102. Mill, *Considerations on Representative Government*, 377.

103. Ibid., 295, 300, 323.

104. Ibid., 246-47, 309-11. These two perspectives prove that, contrary to what contemporary theorists of multiculturalism seem to suggest, Mill did not identify group representation with proportional representation. The former was a strategic answer to a highly exclusionary and divided society; the latter embodied the normative ideal of representative democracy. Proportional representation was based on the individual, not the group. Group representation (e.g., such as the case of the workers) was a device to counter domination. Proportional representation was true self-government because it presupposed that opinions and ideas ought not to be narrowly determined by the prepolitical constraints of group membership, such as economic status or gender. It assumed individuals could make free use of their reason and did not have to identify with a group in order to express themselves. Mill's model of good democracy was Athens because in Athens, he thought, the assembly was an arena in which individual character and ability truly counted, and agonism was truly in place.

105. Jurgen Habermas, *Moral Consciousness and Communicative Action*, trans. Christian Lenhardt and Shierry Weber Nicholsen (Cambridge: MIT Press, 1993), 70-76. Advocacy can amend Habermas's procedural normativism because it encompasses the two levels of democratic deliberation: resisting or neutralizing imbalances of power and justifying this resistance with arguments that appeal to the community's shared political values.

786   POLITICAL THEORY / December 2000

106. As I clarified at the beginning, this does not imply that they should count equally in the moment a decision is taken. The claim that all should have the chance to be heard makes sense if deliberation (discussion) is not identified with decision (voting). See Dunn, *Western Political Theory*, 17-19.

23

Democratic Representation Beyond Election[1]

Sofia Näsström

Introduction

What, if anything, makes representation democratic? For a long time, the answer to this question was taken to be self-evident. Representation is democratic if it makes political decisions responsive to the will of the people, and responsiveness is accomplished by the simple yet powerful rule of "one person, one vote."[2] In the last decades, however, the growing mismatch between the formal rule of political equality and its actual achievement has created a loss of confidence in election as the embodiment of popular will. It is argued that while election is an important element of democracy, the reduction of representation to electoral competition can in fact work to restrict the range of voices, issues and interests able to be heard.[3]

In the wake of this critique, recent years have witnessed a constructivist turn in the debate on representation.[4] Many theorists stress that in order to open up a new chapter in the history of democracy one must distinguish representation from election, and acknowledge that numerical representation rests on a more general and performative role of representation. The central thrust of the argument is that representation is constitutive of popular power, rather than the other way around. When representatives speak in the name of the people they are not merely responding to the will of a pre-existent people, but they are in fact rendering present the people they claim to represent. They make what Michael Saward calls a "representative claim."[5] Still, while the constructivist approach has the merit of calling attention to the role of representation as a creative force in the enactment of popular power, it also gives rise to a critical question. For without recourse to election as a source of legitimacy, how do we know that such representation is democratic?

Today this question has moved into the center of political theoretical concerns. Both domestic and global politics harbor a number of non-governmental organizations, popular movements, advocacy groups and celebrities professing to act on behalf of the people. At the same time, these actors are not elected by the people they claim to represent, nor are they equal in resource, status and power. Taken together, this state of affairs raises doubts about their democratic legitimacy. The worry is that while the decoupling of representation from election has the merit of bringing new and marginalized voices to the attention of the public, it may also pave the way for a scheme of representation in which

representatives "act not as agents of the people but simply instead of them."[6] The challenge for the constructivist view is therefore to say what is democratic about representation, once it is decoupled from election. Otherwise it runs the risk of being co-opted by forces using the constructivist turn as a way of displacing, rather than enacting, the power of the people.

The purpose of this article is to assume this challenge, and work out a framework for thinking about democratic representation beyond election. This framework will be developed in two steps. The first point I will make is that in order to say what is democratic about representation beyond election it is necessary to revitalize the classical question about forms of governments, and ask what is *unique* about the modern form of democracy.[7] This argument will be developed through an engagement with Claude Lefort, whose work is central to this debate.[8] Inviting us to return to the democratic revolution, Lefort famously argues that when the people take the place of the king the locus of power becomes an "empty place." If the body of the king served as the natural anchor of the monarchical regime, the people are bodiless. To Lefort, this lack of a clear definition of the people is ultimately what guarantees the continuity of the democratic struggle. It signals that in a democracy no one (not God, the nation, the party, the leader) can put an end to the conflict on who has the right to instantiate the power of the people. Popular power belongs, literally, to nobody. It follows that to act on behalf of the people without electoral backup — as many organizations, movements, groups and actors do today — is not foreign to modern democracy, but integral to its very operation.[9]

At the same time, not all claims to act on behalf of the people are necessarily democratic. They may work to subdue the democratic struggle, or in other ways foster allegiance to more authoritarian forms of government. In order to tell what is democratic about representation beyond election it is therefore necessary to *qualify* what it means to act in the name of the people. In this second step of the argument I will confront Lefort's account of democracy with Montesquieu's study of the spirit of laws. Montesquieu is perhaps best known for his theory of the separation of powers. However, in *The Spirit of Laws* he argues that there are three forms of governments, and that each form of government has its own nature and principle. The "nature" of a government refers to its constitutional makeup: the king in a monarchy, the people in a republic, and the despot in a despotic government. The "principle" refers to the public commitment needed to sustain the government in question: honor in a monarchy, virtue in a republic and fear in a despotic government.[10]

Drawing on this basic insight, I will argue that while Lefort has successfully demonstrated that modern democracy is a *sui generis* form of government characterized by the absence of a concrete power-holder, his account remains within the purview of what Montesquieu calls the nature of government. It does not specify the public commitment or principle needed for setting it in motion. The result is that it becomes difficult to judge "which group, which assembly, which meeting, which consensus is the trustee of the people's word."[11] By re-examining the shift from the king to the people, I will demonstrate that democracy harbors its own immanent principle for making such judgments. What happens in the democratic revolution is that human beings can no longer appeal to a natural or divine authority in solving political disagreement. They become their own source of authority in political affairs. This removal of an external limitation on political affairs creates a sense of absolute freedom, but also a sense of absolute responsibility. It is only by sharing this burden that human beings can take it on, and this is precisely what the modern form of democracy does. It limits the burden by dividing it equally. Accordingly, to act in the name of the people does not in itself qualify as a democratic form of representation. What is required is that the act is committed to the principle of equality: it unburdens human beings from the excess of responsibility that comes with the removal of an external authority in political affairs by sharing and dividing it equally.

The article falls into four parts. I begin by examining the merits of Lefort's account of modern democracy as a unique form of government built on representative claims. To come to terms with its limits, I next recapitulate Montesquieu's distinction between the nature and principle of governments, only then to retrieve the principle of equality behind Lefort's account. I conclude by exploring the significance of this framework for the crisis of electoral democracy. I do so by contrasting it with Pierre Rosanvallon's interpretation of the crisis, an interpretation which, I argue, corrupts the principle of equality and therefore ought to be regarded as a non-democratic form of representation.

The Nature of Modern Democracy

Modern democracy is often described as a government in which the people rule indirectly by the election of representatives. Still, what this description leaves out is that modern democracy is characterized by a unique

dynamic of change. As John Dunn points out, the word democracy was in Athens a noun designating a system of rule. It is only in the late eighteenth century that democracy turns into a noun of agency (a *democrat*), an adjective (*democratic*) and a verb (to *democratize*). Ever since, human beings have associated democracy with the activity of democratizing the societies in which they live.[12] This association of democracy with activity, mobilization, and change seems closely related to the fact that modern democracy is a representative form of government. In the words of Dunn, it apparently "shifted it from one of history's hopeless losers to one of its more insistent winners."[13] Why is that?

One common answer to this question asserts that what makes modern democracy into a winner is that it strikes a historical compromise between the common people and the elite. Unlike in a direct democracy, people do not rule themselves in modern democracies. They choose representatives to do it for them. What is specific for modern democracy is therefore that it combines the power of the ruling classes with that of the common people. By making popular rule indirect rather than direct it becomes less threatening to those in power, and at the same time acceptable to those without power. It becomes a compromise both groups are willing to accept. For, although election gives the people a right to have a say in political affairs it also, by the same token, prevents them from actually intervening in the rule of society.[14]

However compelling, there is something limited about this description. To argue that modern democracy is a compromise between the people and the elite does not capture its propensity for change. From the time of its birth in the American and the French revolutions, modern democracy has been able to constantly revitalize itself in response to new political crises. It has activated demands to include historically marginalized groups into politics, such as workers, women, and immigrants, and it has developed new rights, from civil to political, and social rights. This development suggests that modern democracy is something more than a mere compromise between the people and the elite. It is a form of government able to *compromise with itself.* An alternative interpretation to the longevity of modern democracy takes this latter aspect into account. It holds that the winning side of modern democracy must be traced back to its lack of a natural power holder, and the process of contestation it opens up in society about who has the right to rule.

This view is most thoroughly defended by Lefort. As he argues, it is from within the matrix of the political-theological logic of monarchical rule that one must begin if one wants to understand the singularity of modern democracy. The democratic revolution did not only overthrow the power of the monarchy. Taking over its power, it also took over and remoulded some of its defining characteristics, of which the most important is the notion of power incarnated in a body. In the monarchy, the place of power was occupied by the king, and the king in fact had two bodies that together sustained his exercise of power.[15] On the one hand, he had a natural body that secured distinction and rank in society by means of heritage and birth. On the other, he had an immortal body that incorporated the entirety of the body politic. In this way, the body of the king assigned everyone to their proper place in the natural order, and at the same time kept society together in a single polity under the auspices that the distinction between orders and ranks incarnated the mystical authority of God on earth.[16]

If the king's body occupied the place of power, and thereby gave society a form in which everyone knew their place in the natural and divine order of things, Lefort shows that the democratic revolution signals a mutation of this symbolic order. What happens when the people take the place of the king, is that the reference to a natural body disappears. For unlike the king, the people have no material body. It cannot be seen or touched. Moreover, if the king had a mystical body that pointed towards an unconditional pole, the people have no such authority attached to them. When the people take the place of the king they become their own authority in political affairs. To Lefort, the fact that the revolution deprives society of both a natural and a mystical body reveals the unprecedented nature of modern democracy. What is born in the democratic revolution is a form of government "instituted and sustained by the *dissolution of the markers of certainty*."[17] The locus of power becomes linked to an empty place, by which is meant that who it is that has power, and therefore counts as the appropriate incarnation of the people, now turns into the very *question* of democracy.[18]

According to Lefort, this association of modern democracy with an empty place of power is an important factor behind its historical success. It means that it "combines two contradictory principles: on the one hand, power emanates from the people; on the other, it is the power of nobody," and instead of creating a political stalemate, "democracy thrives on this contradiction."[19] The reason is that with this form of popular power no individual or group in society can claim to instantiate its authority, or possess the prerogative to establish its boundaries. Since who "we, the people" are is the very question of democracy anyone may act and speak in its name.[20] Modern democracy is "born from the collectively shared discovery that power does not belong to anyone, that those who exercise it do not incarnate it, that they are only the temporary trustees of public authority, that the law of God or nature is not vested in them, that they do not hold the final knowledge of the

world and social orders, and that they are not capable of deciding what everyone has the right to do, think, say and understand."[21]

But, granted that modern democracy lacks a concrete foundation, and as such cannot be confiscated by any particular individual or group, how does it exercise its power? How does "nobody" rule? According to Lefort, the fact that popular power cannot be naturalized means that it requires an institutional mechanism that allows for continual contestation on who "we, the people" are. Since the American and French revolutions, this mechanism has been manifested in the institutional pillars of universal suffrage and human rights, and together they have served to mobilize the power of the people:

First, since no one can be consubstantial with the people, democracy makes the exercise of power "subject to procedures of periodical redistributions."[22] Through the institutional apparatus of universal suffrage it structures society around a conflict as to who should have the power to speak in the name of the people, and in this way it prevents specific individuals or groups from monopolizing power or wielding it to further their own ends.[23] Second, in this conflict no one can be the supreme judge. Since the identity of the people is open to question the moment of judgment dissolves into the public itself. Through human rights to freedom of speech, opinion, assembly and demonstration it is now "founded upon the legitimacy of a *debate* as to what is legitimate and what is illegitimate — a debate which is necessarily without any guarantor and without any end."[24]

At the same time, modern democracy is not progressive by nature. On the contrary, it is a form of government characterized by "institutionalized uncertainty," and this uncertainty has two sides.[25] On the one hand, the difficulty of locating the authority of the people in society can be destructive of democracy. If the empty place of power has the potential to mobilize human beings to democratize the societies in which they live, it also harbors a risk of degenerating into less attractive forms of rule. The most extreme example is totalitarianism, which is what originally brought Lefort to formulate his theory of the empty place of power. In times of crisis, the discovery that power belongs to no one may be disconcerting. It may prompt a desire to "banish the indetermination that haunts the democratic experience," and restore the certainty associated with monarchical rule.[26] The result is not increased certainty, however, but a new form of despotism in the image of the people-as-one.

On the other hand, the fact that the authority of the people is difficult to locate in society also means that it harbors a potential for change. Not being tied to a specific group of people, it may adapt and remold to fit new political realities. When Olympe de Gouges during the French revolution contests the exclusion of women from political life she is drawing on an authority which, in Lefort's terminology, "eludes all power which could claim to take hold of it — whether religious or mythical, monarchical or popular."[27] With this in mind, the contemporary disillusionment about election as the embodiment of popular will, and the widespread preoccupation in both domestic and global politics with questions of inclusion and exclusion, are not necessarily bad news. Rather than being a signal of democratic decline, they may indicate that the contemporary conflict on who "we, the people" are has outgrown its current institutional form. The power of the people can no longer be expressed through a scheme of national electoral competition. It has become a democratic straightjacket. What is called for is a new institutional outlet in which human beings may debate and decide who has the right to instantiate the power of the people.

This uncertainty about the direction of modern democracy, whether it leads to the destructive image of the people-as-one or to a new mobilization of popular power raises an intriguing question.[28] For, granted that there is nothing deterministic about the progress of democracy — and this is a central assumption from a constructivist point of view — what does it take for this form of government to channel the experience of uncertainty in an emancipatory direction? This is the point where one reaches the limits of Lefort's interpretation. The problem is that while Lefort elucidates the *sui generis* nature of modern democracy as a government built on an empty place of power, he does not tell us how this form of government emanates in an institution that gives everyone equal power of decision and judgment. To borrow Hans Lindahl's term, the *positive* meaning of democracy's logic of negation — the absence of a natural power-holder — is not elaborated on.[29] What makes the fact that nobody rules into a form of government characterized by equal rule?

The question is motivated. The most conspicuous example of how the absence of a natural power-holder may contribute to a non-democratic form of government is presented by Hobbes. What he shares with Lefort is precisely the idea that there can be no people prior to the act of representation. As he famously points out, the people only exist as an entity through the act of a representative, which is why one needs Leviathan to act in its place: "For it is the unity of the Representer, not the Unity of the Represented, that maketh the Person One."[30] If one wants to take representation beyond election, and do so in a way that fosters a *democratic* form of government it is therefore not enough to emphasize the lack of a natural power-holder in politics, or to point to the role of representation as a constitutive force in the construction of popular power. One has to show that such representation entails a commitment to equality, or else there is no way to tell the difference between the kind of representation that displaces democracy and the one that enacts it.

At this point, it might be objected that such commitment forecloses the radical openness of democracy. The negativity of the empty place of power is all that is needed to guarantee the continuity of the democratic struggle, and this operation of negativity is precisely what distinguishes Lefort from Hobbes. For while Hobbes fills the empty place of power with the mortal god of Leviathan, Lefort leaves it open. But this objection is deceiving. For how can one be so sure that claims to represent the people do not obliterate the radical openness of democracy? Arguably, the only reason as to why someone would leave this question hanging is because one is already committed to a much *stronger* thesis than the one advanced in this article, namely that there is some kind of progressive logic involved in the empty place of power. From a constructivist point of view, however, history is not a history foretold. It is relational and contingent, which means that popular power does not have an existence independent of the actions of human beings. It must be continually enacted and performed if it is to sustain over time.[31]

In the rest of the article, I will take issue with this limitation of Lefort's interpretation of modern democracy by confronting it with Montesquieu's insight about the principles of government. What Montesquieu allows us to see is that different forms of government are enacted by different kinds of public commitments. The intention of the following discussion is thus to retrieve the commitment needed for the empty place of power to remain in force, and then ask what bearing it has on the present crisis of electoral democracy. Let us begin, however, by looking more generally into the role of the principle in the enactment of government.

The Principle as a Source of Action and Judgment

In *The Spirit of Laws*, Montesquieu argues that there are three forms of governments; republics, monarchies and despotic ones, and that each form of government has its own nature and principle. By the nature of government, Montesquieu means its constitutional make up, or "that by which it is constituted."[32] Accordingly, the nature of a republic is one in which "the body of the people" governs.[33] The people so conceived have the final authority to govern everything within their reach, and in case there are questions that exceed their ability they choose ministers who conduct the tasks for them. By contrast, the nature of a monarchy consists of the fact that one person alone governs. What is characteristic of a monarchy is that the person who governs does so by means of fixed and established laws, and with the intermediate power of the nobility. The nature of a despotic government, finally, is one in which a single person governs without laws, rules or intermediaries. This person directs everything by their own will and caprice, and does so by nominating a vizier to execute their will and desire at any particular point in time.[34]

However, government is not merely a constitutional form. These governments would not exist without someone giving life to them by adhering to and enacting their respective power. According to Montesquieu, this means that there has to be a specific commitment in society for these kinds of government to persist, and it is this commitment he calls the principle. It is "that by which it is made to act."[35] The commitment that sets a republic in motion is virtue, or "love of the laws and the country."[36] The republic requires a disposition of the people to sacrifice their own private will to the common good. Only in this way can the republic be sustained as a form of government. In a monarchy, it is the principle of honor that gives life to the government. Accordingly, if a republican government requires that "we should love our country, not so much on our own account, as out of regard to the community," a monarchical government is sustained by a commitment to distinction, to the idea of each having to differentiate themselves from the rest and promoting their own interests without regard to the community as a whole.[37] Finally, it is the principle of fear that keeps a despotic government alive, for by fearing the despot the subjects do not rise up against the despot's whims and impulses. On the contrary, they are themselves slaves to the same passions as the despot in the form of instinct, compliance, and punishment.[38]

As Louis Althusser points out, Montesquieu's distinction between the nature and principle of government in this way responds to two different questions. The nature of a government provides an answer to the question, "Who holds power, and how does the holder of power exercise that power?" The principle answers a different question, namely. "On what condition can there be a government which gives power to a people, a monarch or a despot, and make it exercise that power?" By introducing this distinction Montesquieu shows that government is not merely a legal order, but a political form "engaged in its own life, in its own conditions of existence and survival." To understand how a government works as it does it is therefore not enough to focus on its formal rules. One has to be attentive to its condition of possibility. The point is that different governments are guided by different principles, and that one cannot have one without the other. Just as some motors will only go on petrol, different governments have different drives that set them in motion.[39]

What, then, is the role of the principle in this schema? As a public commitment, the principle has a dual role to play. It is at once a principle of action and a principle of judgment.[40] First of all, it is important to distinguish Montesquieu's account of the principle from human motivation in general. As human beings we act out of a number of sensations in the form of love, fear, compassion, and anger. What makes Montesquieu's account unique is that, while he works with common sensations such as fear, virtue and honor, he does not take them to be equally important for all societies. On the contrary, each principle dominates a certain form of government, and as such allows us to say that the government in question is "republican," "despotic," or "monarchical." This is not to say that there is no fear in republics, or no virtue in monarchies. The point made by Montesquieu is that while governments are sustained by a mixture of principles, each form of government is guided by a principle that spurs the others in a direction favorable to the nature of that government:

In a word, honor is found in a republic, though its spring be political virtue; and political virtue is found in a monarchical government, though it be actuated by honor.[41]

Montesquieu's principles are in this respect not individual human motivations. They are relational. Bound up with particular forms of governments, they refer to the public commitment that makes each of them tick.[42]

Principles are enacted by human beings, but they are also fostered by laws and governmental policies, and it is by turning to society itself — in its historical variety — that Montesquieu develops his hypothesis about the difference between forms of governments. Investigating the role of education, the constitution, sumptuary laws, civil and criminal law, as well as practices of luxury and the question of women, he identifies the principles that guide monarchies, republics and despotic governments. Education is of particular importance. A monarchy exists only on the condition that the commitment to honor and distinction permeates the educational system, just as a republic exists only as long as it keeps nurturing a sense of public virtue among its subjects. The moment the commitment to distinction fades, or people cease to care for their common political life, the monarchy and the republic are deprived of their enabling conditions. The point is that a monarchy and a republic "ought to be directed by these principles, otherwise the government is imperfect," that is, otherwise it will cease to exist as a particular form of government.[43]

The principles of virtue, honor and fear are not merely what set a certain form of government in motion. They also guide our judgment insofar as we evaluate the government in question from their perspective. They provide what Hannah Arendt calls "standards of right and wrong."[44] In a republic, for example, political action is evaluated on the basis of how well it protects public virtue against private corruption, and in a monarchy it is evaluated on the basis of how well it guards honor against baseness and disgrace. In democratic theory, one usually thinks of evaluation as a matter of what ought to be, as opposed to what is. What Montesquieu discovers, however, is a principle of judgment immanent to a certain form of government. The point of introducing the principle is not to say that we ought to embrace virtue, honor or fear. The argument is that these principles constitute the condition of possibility for a certain form of government. Standing at the intersection between the institutional and the societal level, they provide an immanent basis from which to judge political action.[45]

The legacy of Montesquieu is controversial, and scholars debate whether his thinking offers a defence of liberal, republican or monarchical government, as well as how these forms of government come together in contemporary political life.[46] However one characterizes his legacy, it is clear that Montesquieu is a child of his time. Although his thinking has served as an important source of inspiration in the birth of modern democracy, he did not himself live to see the radical overturning of society that took place in the American and the French revolutions. When he refers to the republic as a democratic form of government he has the popular rule of Athens and Rome in mind, and when he refers to the mixed government it is the English Constitution that stands as a model. Modern democracy, which Lefort describes as a form of government based on an empty place of power, is not part of his investigation. It is to this form of government that we shall now turn. What kind of public commitment is needed for this particularly modern form of democracy to be sustained over time?

The Principle of Equality

In the scheme offered by Montesquieu, the nature of a government refers to the one who holds power, and how this power is exercised. In this respect, Lefort reveals the uniqueness of modern democracy. He demonstrates that, unlike other forms of government based in the king, the people or the despot, modern democracy is based on the *absence* of a power-holder. Instead of making reference to a natural authority, it refers to a government "in which the people will be said to be sovereign, of course, but whose identity will constantly be open to question."[47] Moreover, he shows that the implication of this view for the exercise of popular power is a continual process of conflict and critique about who has the right to rule; a process which, since the late eighteenth century, is materialized in the institution of universal suffrage and human rights. Still, if the democratic revolution engenders a shift in the nature of government, it also carries with it a *revolution in principle*. This side of the democratic revolution has not been examined

by Lefort. In what follows, I will therefore seek to complement his account of modern democracy by retrieving its principle.[48]

As Lefort points out, revolutions are to a great extent shaped by the kind of governments that they seek to overthrow. By replacing the order that comes before them, they have to fill up the gap opened up by the revolutionary act.[49] In this respect, the democratic revolution harbors both change and continuity. For, although it replaces the power of the king with that of the people, the terms of power as incarnated in a body — however emptied out of its content — still remain. The same logic of the revolution as at once giving rise to something entirely new and taking over the characteristics of what preceded it can be applied to the accompanying shift from divine right to popular right, and it is here that the principle of equality comes into view.[50]

To rule by divine right means that the king rules with an omnipotent and infallible authority behind his back. This authority gives him a considerable amount of power insofar as he now manifests on earth, in his own person, a higher and more perfect order. However, it also limits his power. It signals that although the king stands above positive law he has to adhere to a higher law that is not of his own making. As Edmund Morgan points out, divinity may be an omnipotent and infallible authority, but when assumed by humans it becomes most constrictive. It raises the king to a height "where he could scarcely move without fracturing his divinity."[51] This divine limitation on monarchical rule is well-known, and Lefort calls attention to it. The fact that power was embodied in the person of the king "does not mean that he held unlimited power."[52] On the contrary, the king "was supposed to obey a superior power."[53] However, what is not mentioned is that this limitation on monarchical rule is not merely a limitation in the sense of being an obstacle the king would strive to overcome. It is also a relief. It stands to reason that without the notion of divine right the king would be as absolute as God himself. He would be an unlimited power, absolutely free but therefore also absolutely responsible. Nothing would stand between him and his will. He would be powerful, but alone.

Taking this into consideration, divine right is not merely an impediment to the pursuit of power. It is also a kind of freedom. It releases the king from what is perceived as an absolute and therefore also inhuman form of power. On the one hand, it unburdens him from a responsibility suited to God rather than humans, and as such impossible to carry for a single person. On the other, it frees him from the charge of blasphemy since his taking the place of God would be intolerable in the eyes of his subjects. Politically speaking, divine right is therefore not so much an obstacle as a blessing to the king. It means that the power of the king "pointed towards an unconditional, other-worldly pole, while at the same time he was, in his own person, the guarantor and representative of the unity of the kingdom."[54] The result is that whatever the king decides, he can always hold the divine authority equally responsible for it. He is not alone on the throne.

When divine right is replaced by popular right, this notion of a divine limitation on political power disappears. The democratic revolution consists precisely in the dismissal of any such external constraint. Popular sovereignty means that "people must perform operations which allow them to be their own midwives," or in more classical terms, that they must be at once authors and addressees of law.[55] Nevertheless, if the democratic revolution nullifies the divine limitation on political power it does not remain unaffected by its removal. Revolting against the divine right of the king means that people have to fill up the gap opened up in its wake. Unlike the king, in other words, they must take the place of God. In the conflict on who should have the right to govern — and this conflict is the paramount theme of the revolution — they cannot appeal to a higher law. Gone is the external limitation on power, and the relief that goes with it. What is left is the place once occupied by God, and seizing it exposes human beings to a difficult task. The task is to assume this position without either being overburdened by a power too heavy for humans to shoulder, or being accused of blasphemy.

It is against this background that one ought to understand the principle of equality. The democratic revolution is at once liberating and demanding. It is liberating since people are unchained from the order of divine and natural right associated with monarchical rule, and its division of society into orders and ranks. It is demanding since they now have to assume the task that comes with its overthrow; that of being the ultimate guarantor of right. This position has hitherto been reserved for an omnipotent and infallible authority, and occupying its place means that human beings become absolutely free, but also absolutely responsible. From now on nothing happens, be it right or wrong, that falls outside the realm of their power. However, if omnipotence and infallibility without much effort can be projected onto God, it becomes most burdensome when put on the shoulders of humans, and the attempt to respond to this absolute sense of responsibility — or this summoning of humanity unto itself — is the momentum of modern democracy. The problem is that, since finding relief by appealing to an external authority is no longer a valid option in the adjudication of political conflict, the only way to limit the responsibility that arises in the shift from divine to popular right is to share and divide it between equals.

According to this interpretation, modern democracy is a form of government set in motion by a principle of equality. The principle of equality makes it possible for human beings to replace God as the final guarantor in politics, and to do so without either being overburdened by an inhuman form of power or being accused of blasphemy. The reason is that, by setting in motion a process of equalization in society, no one has the last word. What is born in the democratic revolution is a divided form of power characterized by human fallibility. Everyone has an equal say in political affairs, yet no one has the final say. But why divide the power of decision and judgment equally? What is most puzzling about the democratic revolution is not the fact that it gives rise to a system of popular control over government, for this idea had a long republican prehistory. The puzzle is rather how revolutionaries come to the conclusion that the exercise of public control should be divided equally. At the time of the revolution, human beings are perceived to be highly unequal in terms of status, wealth, power, and skills. It would therefore seem more natural to reject the idea of equality in favor of a division of power based on status and rank.

To understand how the principle of equality is able to take hold of the public imagination it is important to recall that revolutions harbor both change and continuity. Taking over the power that comes before them, they have to fill the gap opened up by the revolutionary act. This logic of the revolution puts a constraint on the formation of popular power. It means that the sharing of power cannot be carried out in just any way. Since God is one, and everyone is perceived to be equal under the one, the former division of society into order and ranks no longer counts as a valid marker for the distribution of power. God, as we know, "did not have much to say about the rights of gentlemen."[56] In this way, and no matter what the intentions of the revolutionaries are, the reoccupation of divine right compels them to speak in universals. The sharing of power must be conducted on terms that do not favor some human beings at the expense of others. This is precisely what the modern form of democracy does. Through the institution of universal suffrage and human rights it makes everyone equally responsible for deciding and judging what is right and wrong, and thereby it also makes everyone equally free: no one has more say than anyone else in authorizing the direction and content of political affairs.

In Montesquieu's scheme, the principle does not only set a certain form of government in motion. It also serves as an immanent standpoint from which to judge it. A republic, for example, is both enacted by the principle of virtue and evaluated on its terms. It follows that in this form of government, the protection of private interest over public virtue will be judged as harmful. By not committing itself to country and law, it fails to uphold the public sentiment needed for the republic to be sustained as a form of government.[57] In a similar vein, it should be acknowledged that modern democracy is both enacted by the principle of equality and evaluated on its terms. In this form of government, as Lefort writes, "power does not belong to anybody in particular." The result is that any attempt to shove the power of judgment and decision onto particular individuals will be detrimental to democracy. Instead of securing equality in society, it bestows these individuals with a burden of responsibility that, if not publicly shared and divided between equals, soon turns into a liability they are inclined to project onto external forces, be it God, nature or the inevitable forces of history.

The upshot is that while Lefort offers a convincing account of the unprecedented nature of modern democracy vis-à-vis the republican, monarchical and despotic forms of government described by Montesquieu, he gives us only half the story. The democratic revolution contains not one, but two symbolic moments that together make up the distinct form of modern democracy. It engenders a shift in both the nature and the principle of government. Just as the revolution against the king means that the people takes over his characteristic of power as incarnated in a body, yet empties it of content, the overthrow of divine right harbors both change and continuity. The people take over the unlimited authority of God, yet limit the burden it generates by dividing it equally. The principle of equality can in this way be interpreted as the positive meaning of democracy's logic of negation. It is what conditions its power or, in Montesquieu's terms, "that by which it is made to act."[58]

Reinterpreting the Crisis of Electoral Democracy

Today it is generally acknowledged that electoral democracy suffers from crisis. Coming back to the topic of representation forty years after the publication of her seminal work on the issue, Hanna Pitkin expresses deep concerns about the representative system. As she argues, "the arrangements we call 'representative democracy' have become a substitute for popular self-government, not its enactment."[59] In a similar vein, Sheldon Wolin warns against a managed form of democracy in which governments "are legitimated by elections which they have learned to control," and Colin Crouch argues that contemporary democratic societies are moving towards a condition of "post-democracy."[60]

It is not evident what to make of these judgments. On the one hand, the realistic tone of these authors is justified. For while the demand for inclusion and extension of rights has marked the development of modern democracy, many politicians are today preoccupied with justifying exclusion rather than inclusion, and instead of a steady progression of rights we witness their rolling back in many developed democracies. Any naive belief in the progress of democracy is therefore misplaced. On the other hand, to think that democracy will stop short before this political reality seems unrealistic as well. Today we see protests and movements calling for a reclaiming of democracy, and the birth of new international organizations and agencies that speak in its name. Considering this, the suggestion that democracy is on the decline looks more doubtful. Are we to believe that the political struggles that took off during the revolutions in the late eighteenth century, and that have led to an ever-renewed demand for democratization, have now come to an end?

One influential attempt to answer this question is offered by Pierre Rosanvallon. According to Rosanvallon, the crisis of electoral democracy is at bottom a crisis of understanding. By identifying representation with election one fails to acknowledge that election is but "an empirical convention" in the history of democracy.[61] Rosanvallon's interpretation of the crisis differs from the one advanced in this article, and I will therefore conclude by briefly contrasting the two. The aim is to show that if one wants to take representation beyond election, and do so in a way that fosters a democratic form of government one must enact the principle of equality in two ways: both as a source of judgment in the analysis of wherein the crisis consists, and as a source of action for redirecting society in a democratic direction. Rosanvallon does neither. Accordingly, while his account of representation may be expedient and legitimate, it is not democratic on the interpretation offered in this article.

When Rosanvallon argues that election must be understood as an empirical convention in the history of democracy he draws on work undertaken over many years on the historicity of democracy. The central point he makes is that the crisis we experience in the form of widespread distrust in electoral politics is not exceptional. It is a constitutive feature of democracy. Civic distrust is "an original political form," yet one that tends to be overlooked due to an overly institutional and electoral emphasis in democratic theory.[62] By widening the horizon from the political institutions of the state to those of civil society he wants to show that disbelief in electoral politics is not *all* that has happened in the last decades. This distrust has gone hand in hand with an increased civic activity, and it is by turning to these civic activities of distrust that Rosanvallon finds a new form of democratic representation. As he argues, these activities "reflect a range of procedures and institutions that preceded the advent of universal suffrage" such as regulatory instances and constitutional courts, and together they offer a new way of making political leaders accountable to those over whom they wield power.[63]

The last decades have indeed witnessed an explosion of civil society activity, both domestically and internationally. This activity is often prompted by the conviction that while electoral politics limits the range of voices, issues and interests able to be heard, civil society actors have the capacity to step in and do what elected representatives no longer are prepared or able to do; namely, to "make present" the people they claim to represent. However, to understand wherein the crisis of electoral democracy lies one cannot be too quick in moving from the institutional to the societal level. The problem is that since the principle of equality is what animates the institution of election, the relationship between representation and election is more complex than Rosanvallon's analysis suggests. Election is not merely an empirical convention in the history of democracy. It has harbored a sense that goes beyond numerical equality: the public unburdening of responsibility. The result is that when democracies fail to live up to the task of guaranteeing political equality through electoral competition, it does not only create distrust. It also creates a sense of burden.

What is striking in this context is that the crisis of electoral democracy is accompanied by intensified "responsibility talk." This responsibility talk now dominates the entire spectrum of representative politics. Not only should already elected politicians "take responsibility" for their decisions, and be subject to naming and shaming if they do not; civil society actors such as non-governmental organizations, private companies and celebrities should too. Rather than being perceived as interest groups or public opinion makers, they are asked to be accountable to the people they speak up for. "Who Elected Oxfam?" is asked in an article in *The Economist*, and under the name of "corporate social responsibility" companies are expected to behave in a responsible manner vis-à-vis their shareholders and stakeholders.[64] In addition, celebrities who speak in favor of a certain issue, group or action — like Al Gore for the environment, Bono for people in Africa and Russell Brand for the revolution — are required to act in a responsible manner in relation to those affected by their claims. Most important of all, citizens are expected to be responsible; they should hold political leaders, companies and non-governmental organizations to account for their actions and decisions in everyday life, be it as choice-makers, consumers or contributors. Citizenship is itself associated with an increased individualization of responsibility, and this individualization of responsibility goes hand in hand with a sense of burden that in recent years has even mobilized a new social class: "the precariat."[65]

The central point of this article is that a democratic form of representation is committed to the principle of equality. This principle is engendered by an unlimited form of responsibility that overtaxes the capacity of human beings, and which for this reason must be levelled out and shared between equals. This interpretation suggests that the increased talk of responsibility is not merely the manifestation of a new form of distrust against "the politics of politicians," or a signal that political leaders should be more accountable to those over whom they wield power.[66] It should rather be understood in a symptomatic way; it resurfaces when political institutions fail to uphold equality in society. The fact that the crisis of electoral democracy is associated with a call for increased responsibility on the side of citizens and their representatives testifies to a problem of *rising inequality* in society. It indicates that the public unburdening of responsibility accomplished by the institution of election gradually has been corrupted. In short, the more talk of responsibility in the debate on representation, the less democratic it is.[67]

This is not to say that electoral reform is the only or most appropriate answer to the crisis. Rosanvallon is right in that one has to distinguish democracy from its institutional incarnation in the form of election. The reason is that while election is an integral part of modern democracy it is not itself the source of its legitimacy. As we have seen in this article, the order is in fact reversed. What distinguishes modern democracy from other forms of governments is that it is structured around the absence of a concrete power holder, and it is precisely this absence that calls for a periodic redistribution of power. It requires an ongoing competition on who ought to instantiate the power of the people. The worry among democratic theorists should therefore not merely be with election *per se*, but with how to uphold the principle of equality once the institution of election is no longer able to fulfill the task. Here the emphasis on forms of governments becomes important. It draws attention to the fact that there are other institutions in society besides election with a great impact on the action-orientations of human beings, such as laws and policies related to education, work, ownership, rights, gender and citizenship. In times of electoral crisis, one would do well to ask what principles animate *these* institutions, and how they may foster or hinder confidence in democracy.[68]

This leads up to the second point, which is how to find a remedy to the crisis of electoral democracy. In *Democratic Legitimacy*, Rosanvallon argues that in order to foster commitment to democracy one should not cling to the institution of election. Instead one must build on the new sources of legitimacy that emerge in domestic and global civil society. What they offer is a new democratic ideal, what he calls "democracy of appropriation." This ideal includes three central aspects, and together they serve to correct the weaknesses associated with electoral democracy. First, it involves counter-democratic practices of civic distrust in the form of oversight, impeachment and judgment. Second, it involves agencies of indirect democracy such as regulatory agencies and constitutional courts. Third, and consequently, it involves "an insistence that leaders conduct themselves democratically."[69]

Seen as a strategy by which to combat the abuse of popular power, or as a form of rule by which to hold powerful leaders to account, the democracy of appropriation offers an important contribution to democratic theory. Seen as an ideal of democracy, however, it suffers from a major problem. A democratic form of representation does not merely require popular control of government. It requires that such activity of popular control is conducted on equal terms.[70] This element of equality is lacking in the democracy of appropriation. The trouble is that, by bestowing citizens and their representatives with a responsibility that is expected to be shared and divided between equals, this ideal runs the risk of playing into the hands of forces that seek to redirect the confidence invested in democracy in the direction of more authoritarian forms of rule. The reason is that, without guaranteeing equality in the enactment of popular control, it renders democracy into a realm of burden rather than a realm of freedom. The responsibility talk in society tells us that democracy needs the very opposite of what Rosanvallon suggests: a new institutionalization of the principle of equality in the form of public unburdening of responsibility.

Conclusion

In this article I have proposed a framework for thinking about democratic representation beyond election. At a time of widespread disillusionment about electoral competition as the embodiment of popular will, this framework has both a critical and constructive purpose.

First, it means that one can tell what is democratic about representation once it is decoupled from election. This is essential to assess the democratic legitimacy of non-electoral claims to represent the people, and thereby to be clear what can and cannot be claimed in its name. The relevant question to ask is whether the claim is committed to the principle of equality: does it foster a scheme of representation that unburdens human beings from the excess of responsibility that comes with the removal of an external authority in political affairs by sharing and dividing it equally?[71] Second, and more constructively, it means that one has an immanent democratic basis for discussing and proposing institutional reforms. By distinguishing between the principle and nature of a democratic form of government, it becomes possible to take a step back and ask whether existing institutions of democracy encourage commitment in its support. In addition, one can experiment with new representative arrangements within, across and beyond

existing constituencies, and at the same time ensure that whatever constitutional make up such a scheme of representation may take it will be a compromise that enacts rather than displaces the power of the people.

NOTES

1. Previous versions of this article have been presented at various workshops and university seminars, and the author wishes to thank the participants for many helpful comments. Particular thanks to Hans Agné, Dario Castiglione, Lisa Disch, Raf Geenens, Magnus Hagevi, Hans Lindahl, Anthoula Malkopoulou, Kari Palonen, Johannes Pollak, Stefan Rummens, David Runciman, Michael Saward and Rainer Schmalz-Bruns.

2. Hanna Pitkin, *The Concept of Representation* (Berkeley: University of California Press, 1967), 140.

3. See, among others, Colin Crouch, *Post-Democracy* (Cambridge: Polity Press, 2004); Robert Dahl, *On Political Equality* (New Haven and London: Yale University Press, 2006); James Bohman, *Democracy Across Borders* (Cambridge, MIT Press, 2007); Sheldon Wolin, *Democracy Incorporated. Managed Democracy and the Specter of Inverted Totalitarianism* (Princeton: Princeton University Press, 2008); Nancy Fraser, *Scales of Justice* (New York: Columbia University Press 2009).

4. Lisa Disch, "Toward a Mobilization Conception of Democratic Representation," *American Political Science Review* 105 (2011): 100–14.

5. Michael Saward, *The Representative Claim* (Oxford: Oxford University Press, 2006). For different variants of the constructivist approach, see Frank Ankersmit, *Aesthetic Politics: Political Philosophy Beyond Fact and Value* (Stanford: Stanford University Press, 1997); Nadia Urbinati, *Representative Democracy. Principles and Genealogy* (Chicago and London: Chicago University Press 2006); Pierre Rosanvallon, *Democracy Past and Future*, ed. S. Moyn (New York: Columbia University Press, 2006); Pierre Rosanvallon, *Counter-Democracy. Politics in an Age of Distrust* (Cambridge: Cambridge University Press, 2008); Mónica Brito Vieira and David Runciman, *Representation* (London: Polity Press, 2008); Bryan Garsten, "Representative Government and Popular Sovereignty," in *Political Representation*, edited by I. Shaprio, S. Stokes, S. Wood, and E.J. Kirschner (New York: Cambridge University Press, 2009); Clarissa Hayward, "Making Interest: On Representation and Democratic Legitimacy," in *Political Representation* edited by Shapiro, Stokes, Wood, Kirschner; Miguel Abensour, "Savage Democracy and the Principle of Anarchy," in *Democracy Against the State* (Cambridge: Polity Press, 2011); Lisa Disch, "Democratic Representation and the Constituency Paradox," *Perspectives on Politics* 10, no. 3 (2012): 599–616.

6. Hanna Pitkin, "Representation and democracy: an uneasy alliance," *Scandinavian Political Studies* 27, no. 3 (2004): 335–42, at 339. See also Nadia Urbinati, "Unpolitical Democracy," *Political Theory* 38, no. 2 (2010): 65–92; Sofia Näsström, "Where is the Representative Turn Going?" *European Journal of Political Theory* 10, no. 4 (2011): 501–10.

7. This focus on forms of government must be distinguished from other recent attempts to develop criteria for democratic representation, such as those developed with regard to democratic systems, democratic procedures and acceptance by affected constituencies. See Jane Mansbridge and John Parkinson eds. *Deliberative Systems. Deliberative Democracy at the Large Scale* (Cambridge: Cambridge University Press,

2012); Nadia Urbinati and Maria Paula Saffon, "Procedural Democracy, the Bulwark of Equal Liberty," *Political Theory* 41 (2013): 441–81; Saward, *The Representative Claim*; Laura Montanaro, "The Democratic Legitimacy of Self-Appointed Representatives," *Journal of Politics* 74, no. 4 (2012): 1094–107.

8. Claude Lefort, *The Political Forms of Modern Society. Bureaucracy, Democracy, Totalitarianism*, ed. J.B. Thompson (Cambridge, Mass.: MIT Press, 1986); Claude Lefort, *Democracy and Political Theory*, trans. D. Macey (Cambridge: Polity Press, 1988); Claude Lefort, *Complications. Communism and the Dilemmas of Democracy*, trans. J. Bourg (New York: Columbia University Press, 1999).

9. For Lefort's view of representation, see among others Chantal Mouffe and Ernesto Laclau, *Hegemony and Socialist Strategy* (London, New York: Verso 1985); Hans Lindahl, "Democracy and the Symbolic Constitution of Society," *Ratio Juris* 11, no. 1 (1998): 12–37; Alan Keenan, *Democracy in Question. Democratic Openness in a Time of Political Closure* (Stanford: Stanford University Press, 2003); Wim Weymans, "Freedom through Political Representation," *European Journal of Political Theory* 4, no. 3 (2005): 263–82; Sofia Näsström, "Representative Democracy as Tautology," *European Journal of Political Theory* 5, no. 3 (2006): 321–42; special issue ed. Brian Singer on Claude Lefort in *Thesis Eleven* (2006), 97, 1; Raf Geenens, "Democracy, Human Rights and History: Reading Lefort," *European Journal of Political Theory* 7, no. 3 (2008): 269–86; Miguel Vatter, "The Quarrel between Populism and Republicanism: Machiavelli and the Antinomies of Plebeian Politics," *Contemporary Political Theory* 11, (2012): 242–63; Jeremy Valentine, "Lefort and the Fate of Radical Democracy," in M. Plot ed. *Claude Lefort* (London: Palgrave MacMillan, 2013); Benjamin Arditi, "The People as Representation and Event," in *The Promise and Perils of Populism. Global Perspectives*, edited by Carlos de la Torre (Lexington, KY: University of Kentucky Press, forthcoming).

10. Montesquieu, *The Spirit of Laws* [1748] (New York: Prometheus Books, 2002), 19.

11. Lefort here repeats Furet's question. See Lefort, *Democracy*, 107.

12. John Dunn, *Setting the People Free. The Story of Democracy* (London: Atlantic Books, 2005), 16.

13. Ibid., 20.

14. Representation here means that when we choose our "better selves," those we deem superior in character, wisdom and judgment. See Edmund Burke, "Speech at Mr. Burke's Arrival in Bristol," in *The Portable Edmund Burke* edited by I. Kramnick (London: Penguin, 1999); James Madison, "Federalist 10," in *The Federalist Papers*, A. Hamilton, J. Madison and J. Jay ed. C. Rossiter (New York: Penguin, 1961); Bernard Manin, *The Principles of Representative Government* (Cambridge: Cambridge University Press, 1997).

15. Ernst Kantorowicz, *The King's Two Bodies. A Study in Mediaeval Political Theology* (Princeton: Princeton University Press, 1997).

16. Lefort, *Democracy*, 17–20.

17. Ibid., 19.

18. How to read Lefort on this point, whether he means that modern democracy entails a radical break with the political-theological matrix of monarchy or whether there is a permanent dimension of transcendence in politics, is a question open to debate. See Lefort *Democracy*, chap. 11; Bernard Flynn, *The Philosophy of Claude Lefort. Interpreting the Political* (Evanston: Northwestern University Press, 2005), chap. 3–5. For the more general debate on modernity and secularization, see Karl Löwith, *Meaning in History* (Chicago and London: University of Chicago Press, 1949); Hans Blumenberg, *The Le-*

gitimacy of the Modern Age, trans. R.M. Wallace (Cambridge: MIT, 1983); Carl Schmitt, *Political Theology*, tr. G. Schwab (Chicago and London: University of Chicago Press, 2005).

19. Lefort, *The Political Forms*, 279.

20. For "we, the people" as object rather than source of democracy, see Margaret Canovan, *The People* (Cambridge: Polity, 2005); Sofia Näsström, "The Legitimacy of the People," *Political Theory* 35, no. 5 (2007): 624–58; Andreas Kalyvas, *Democracy and the Politics of the Extraordinary. Max Weber, Carl Schmitt and Hannah Arendt* (Cambridge: Cambridge University Press 2008; Bonnie Honig, *Emergency Politics: Paradox, Law, Democracy* (Princeton: Princeton University Press, 2009); Jason Frank, *Constituent Moments. Enacting the People in Postrevolutionary America* (Durham and London: Duke University Press, 2010); Paulina Ochoa Espejo, *The Time of Popular Sovereignty* (Pennsylvania: Pennsylvania State University Press, 2011); Hans Lindahl, *Fault Lines of Globalization. Legal Order and the Politics of A-Legality* (Oxford: Oxford University Press, 2013).

21. Lefort, *Complications*, 114.

22. Lefort, *Democracy*, 17.

23. On this point, see also Urbinati, *Representative Democracy*; Pierre Rosanvallon, *Democratic Legitimacy. Impartiality, Reflexivity, Proximity.* (Princeton and Oxford: Princeton University Press, 2011).

24. Lefort, *Democracy*, 39. See also Samuel Moyn, "The Politics of Individual Rights: Marcel Gauchet and Claude Lefort," in *French Liberalism from Montesquieu to the Present Day*, edited by R. Geenens and H. Rosenblatt (Cambridge: Cambridge University Press, 2012), 291–310.

25. Jan Werner Müller, *Contesting Democracy* (New Haven, London: Yale University Press), 242.

26. Lefort, *The Political Forms*, 305.

27. Lefort, *The Political Forms*, 258.

28. On the relationship between populism and modern democracy, see Ernesto Laclau, *On Populist Reason* (London, New York: Verso, 2005); Benjamin Arditi, "Populism as a Spectre of Democracy: Response to Canovan," *Political Studies* 52 (2004): 135–43; Koen Abts and Stefan Rummens, "Populism versus Democracy," *Political Studies* 55, no. 2 (2007): 405–24; Cristobal Rovira Kaltwasser, "The Responses of Populism to Dahl's Democratic Dilemmas," *Political Studies* 62 (2013): 470–87; Andrew Arato, "Political Theology and Populism," *Social Research* 80, no. 1 (2013): 143–72.

29. Lindahl, *Democracy*, 23–26. For the problem of commitment in Lefort, see Raf Geenens, "When I was Young and Politically Engaged . . .: Lefort on the Problem of Political Commitment," *Thesis Eleven* 87, no. 1 (2006): 19–32.

30. Thomas Hobbes, *Leviathan* [1651] ed. R. Tuck. (Cambridge: Cambridge University Press, 2005), 114.

31. For the argument that the historical success of democracy may lead to a "confidence trap," see David Runciman, *The Confidence Trap. A History of Democracy in Crisis from World War I to the Present* (Princeton: Princeton University Press, 2013).

32. Montesquieu, *The Spirit*, 19.

33. Ibid., 8.

34. Ibid., 8–18.

35. Ibid., 19.

36. Ibid., 34.

37. Ibid., 6.

38. Ibid, 26–28.

39. Louis Althusser, *Politics and History. Montesquieu, Rousseau, Marx*, trans. B. Brewster (London, New York: Verso, 2007), 45–60.

40. Hannah Arendt, *Essays in Understanding 1930–1954*, ed. J. Kohn (New York: Schocken Books, 1994), 328–38.

41. Montesquieu, *The Spirit*, xv.

42. Hannah Arendt, *Between Past and Future* (New York: Penguin, 1993), 152ff.

43. Montesquieu, *The Spirit*, 28.

44. Arendt, *Essays*, 335.

45. Arendt, *Essays*, 331–2; Althusser, *Politics and History*, 46–50.

46. See, among others, Thomas Pangle, *Montesquieu's Philosophy of Liberalism* (Chicago and London: University of Chicago Press, 1979), Sharon Krause, *Liberalism with Honor* (Harvard: Harvard University Press, 2002); Michael Sonenscher, *Before the Deluge: Public Debt, Inequality and the Intellectual Origins of the French Revolution* (Princeton: Princeton University Press, 2007); Paul Rahe, *Soft Despotism, Democracy's Drift. Montesquieu, Rousseau, Tocqueville, and the Modern Prospect* (New Haven and London: Yale University Press, 2009); Annelien de Dijn, "On Political Liberty: Montesquieu's Missing Manuscript," *Political Theory* 39, no. 2 (2011): 181–204; Celine Spector, "Was Montesquieu Liberal?" in *French Liberalism from Montesquieu to the Present Day*, edited by Greenens and Rosenblatt (Cambridge: Cambridge University Press, 2012), 57–72; Marco Goldoni, "Montesquieu and the French Model of Separation of Powers," *Jurisprudence* 4, no. 1 (2013): 20–47.

47. Lefort, *The Political Forms*, 303–4.

48. Although there is a clear sociological and historical dimension to this question, the interpretation offered in this article is of a more philosophical kind. Extrapolating from the revolutionary shift, it seeks to retrieve the public commitment needed for a specific *form* of government to sustain. At issue is therefore not the history of modern democracy, or its sociological preconditions, but its principle. In the spirit of Montesquieu, yet also unlike him insofar as the principle is derived through philosophical interpretation rather than historical investigation, the attempt is "to go back from appearances to principles, from the diversity of empirical shapes to the forming forces." Ernst Cassirer, *The Philosophy of Enlightenment*. Trans. F. C. A. Koelln and J. P. Pettegrove (Princeton and Oxford: Princeton University Press, 2009), 210.

49. For a similar point about revolutions being "channeled into concepts which had just been vacated" and the turn to modernity as "the reoccupation of answer positions that had become vacant," see Arendt, *On Revolution* (New York: Penguin, 1963), 155 and Blumenberg, *The Legitimacy*, 65.

50. The political-theological aspects of this mutation, such as how it changes the relationship between immanence and transcendence, as well as the role of religion in the enactment of the principle of equality are both important questions in this context. However, they will not be addressed in this article.

51. Edmund S. Morgan, *Inventing the People: The Rise of Popular Sovereignty in England and America* (New York, London: W.W. Norton & Company, 1988), 21.

52. Lefort, *Democracy*, 17.

53. Lefort, *The Political Forms*, 306.

54. Lefort, *Democracy*, 17.

55. Lefort, *Democracy*, 107. Jürgen Habermas, *Between Facts and Norms* trans. W. Rehg (Cambridge: Polity Press, 1996), 33. See also Stefan Rummens, "Deliberation Interrupted: Confronting Jürgen Habermas with Claude Lefort," *Philosophy and Social Criticism* (2008) 34, 2: 383–408.2008.

56. Morgan, *Inventing the People*, 24.

57. Montesquieu, *The Spirit*, 21, 20, 109.

58. On the face of it, the principle of equality may seem close to the republican principle of virtue. Both make equality into an essential aspect of society, something that must be sustained by public action and nurtured by laws and institutions. However, the principles are radically different in orientation, and it is therefore important to set them apart. The central difference is that in a democratic form of government, the principle of equality trumps commitment to country and law. Unlike the republican principle of virtue, the democratic principle of equality does not require that we love our fellow citizens, or that we endorse the laws under which we live. What it requires is that when resolving conflicts *about* country and law — such as who has the right to instantiate the power of the people in times of crisis — we do not support institutions that grant some human beings more responsibility than others in deciding and judging what is right and wrong. It is this commitment that renders modern democracy into a form of government able to constantly revitalize itself in response to new political demands, even when they, as they often do, go against what country and law require of us. Or as Furet puts it, in a quote by Lefort: "The French revolution is not only the Republic. It is also an unlimited promise of equality, and a special form of change." Lefort, *Democracy*, 94.

59. Pitkin, "Representation and Democracy," 340.

60. Sheldon Wolin, *Democracy Incorporated*, 47; Colin Crouch, *Post-Democracy*.

61. Pierre Rosanvallon, "The Metamorphoses of Democratic Legitimacy: Impartiality, Reflexivity, Proximity," *Constellations* 18, no. 2 (2011): 114–23, at 122.

62. Rosanvallon, *Democracy Past and Future*, 243.

63. Rosanvallon, *Democratic Legitimacy*, 224.

64. Jennifer Rubenstein, "The Misuse of Power, not Bad Representation: Why it is beside the point that no one elected Oxfam," *The Journal of Political Philosophy* 22, no. 2 (2014): 204–30; Magdalena Bexell, *Exploring Responsibility: Public and Private in Human Rights Protection* (Lund: Department of Political Science, 2005).

65. Guy Standing, *The Precariat. A New Dangerous Class.* (London, New York: Bloomsbury, 2011). See also Ulrich Beck and Elisabeth Beck-Gernsheim, *Individualization* (London: Sage, 2002).

66. Rosanvallon, *Democratic Legitimacy*, 222–24.

67. For the argument that we today witness the rise of "monitory democracy," which includes a number of new mechanisms by which to render political actors responsible and on their toes, see John Keane, "Monitory Democracy?" in S. Alonso, J. Keane and W. Merkel, *The Future of Representative Democracy* (Cambridge: Cambridge University Press, 2011), 212–36.

68. For such an undertaking, see Sofia Näsström and Sara Kalm "A Democratic Critique of Precarity," manuscript.

69. Rosanvallon, *Democratic Legitimacy*, 220–21.

70. Urbinati, "Unpolitical Democracy."

71. To assess whether a particular claim to speak in the name of the people lives up to the principle of equality one needs to operationalize the principle. Although an important step in bringing the framework developed in this article closer to political practice, this is not something that I have done here.

24

The Democratic Legitimacy of Self-Appointed Representatives

Laura Montanaro

How should we theorize and normatively assess those individual and collective actors who claim to represent others for political purposes, but do so without the electoral authorization and accountability usually thought to be at the heart of democratic representation? In this article, I offer conceptual tools for assessing the democratic legitimacy of such "self-appointed" representatives. I argue that these kinds of political actors bring two constituencies into being: the authorizing—that group empowered by the claim to exercise authorization and demand accountability—and the affected—that group affected, or potentially affected, by collective decisions. Self-appointed representation provides democratically legitimate representation when it provides political presence for affected constituencies and is authorized by and held accountable to them. I develop the critical tools to assess the democratic credentials of self-appointed representatives by identifying nonelectoral mechanisms of authorization and accountability that may empower affected constituencies to exercise authorization and demand accountability.

Democratic representation is usually the authorization of a representative by a constituency through election, combined with the capacity of a constituency to hold the representative accountable for their performance in subsequent elections. Yet an increasing number of individual and collective actors "self-appoint": they make claims to represent others outside of electoral institutions or offices and apart from state authority. To take one well-known example, the musician Bono claims to represent the interests of Africans on the issues of AIDS, debt, and trade. As Bono himself pointed out, he has not been elected by any Africans. Likewise, the nongovernmental organization, Oxfam, presses decision makers and governments for fair trade rules on behalf of the world's poor. What entitles these kinds of political actors to speak and act for the poor? As *The Economist* asked, "Who elected Oxfam?"

On most standard accounts of representation, the absence of electoral authorization and accountability renders the claims and activities of actors such as Bono and Oxfam nondemocratic, regardless of any good they might achieve. *The Economist*'s question was rhetorical: it assumed that "No one elected Oxfam" is both the answer to their question and also the last word about Oxfam's democratic credentials. Yet, as I shall argue, the case for an actor's

credentials as a democratic representative can and should be developed out of a basic normative intuition that lies at the heart of most contemporary democratic theories: those potentially affected by a collective decision should have opportunities and capacities to influence that decision (proportional to the extent to which they are affected). This is the "affected interests standard," sometimes called the "all affected interests principle" (Goodin 2007). From this perspective, actors whose claims to represent rely on self-appointment may play an important role in democracy, particularly in a complex and globalizing world, where electoral constituencies fail to coincide with those affected by collective decisions.

Self-appointed representatives are particularly useful politically when they provide representation for peoples whose interests are affected by policies but who are not situated within electoral constituencies that can determine those policies (Hirst 1994). Nation-state policies, for example, often affect individuals beyond its borders. Bono met with leaders of the G8 countries, who in turn promised to cancel debt for some of the world's poorest countries. The World Bank has also included nongovernmental organizations such as Oxfam in their multilateral debt relief discussions. Such self-appointed representatives can make these kinds of constituencies politically present—visible and audible *as* affected constituencies—providing a *prima facie* case for their importance to the depth and breadth of democracy and representation. I argue here that not only does self-appointed representation supplement democratic theory and practice by providing representation for affected constituencies within and across borders, but it also recasts some core premises of democratic theory and practice. It does so *precisely because* it functions as a mechanism of constituency formation. Under some circumstances, I shall suggest, self-appointed representatives call forth constituencies in ways that are democratically legitimate—addressing a problem often considered irresolvable within democratic theory. If the alternative to self-appointed representation is the political exclusion of individuals from the opportunity to influence decisions that affect them, then we shall need to rethink our received understandings of democratic representation.

The above examples demonstrate, however, that although in the current political landscape decision makers often receive actors who self-appoint as representatives of groups that are otherwise poorly represented, for the most part we do not understand what it means for groups and individuals to function as democratic representatives outside electoral institutions. We lack adequate theoretical frameworks for identifying what these actors do when they make representative claims and criteria for assessing the legitimacy of those claims. Generally speaking, democratic representation is clearly recognizable when based on elections. Over the years, democracies have articulated criteria by which to judge the legitimacy of such representatives. Free and fair elections are conventionally taken as establishing legitimate representative relationships and doing so in a way that is clear, identifiable, and effective in establishing relationships of authorization and accountability between representatives and their constituencies. The legitimacy of the claims of self-appointed representatives is far more difficult to determine. I argue here, however, that if we view representative relationships generically, as occurring not only within but also beyond governmental institutions, we can develop a set of distinctions that will enable us both to conceptualize self-appointed representation as an important domain within political representation and also to distinguish its different kinds as more or less democratically legitimate.

I develop this argument by outlining the concept of self-appointed representation and arguing that a self-appointed representative, if successful in his or her claims, brings two kinds of constituencies into being: the authorizing—those empowered to exercise authorization and demand accountability—and the affected—those whose interests are affected or potentially affected by collective decisions. Conceptualizing a dual constituency highlights both the democratic potential and danger to democracy posed by self-appointed representatives: they may represent (and empower) an affected constituency, but they may also empower an authorizing constituency, while claiming to represent those who are affected but remain disempowered. Second, I outline the contemporary problems that limit the critical purchase of standard/ electoral accounts of democratic representation. Third, I discuss the potential of the self-appointed representative to call forth constituencies on the basis of the affected interests standard. Fourth, I outline the powers of the self-appointed representatives in order to determine mechanisms of nonelectoral authorization and accountability appropriate to their powers and functions. I then distinguish mechanisms of nonelectoral authorization and accountability that empower authorizing constituencies from those that empower affected constituencies. Fifth, I illustrate the critical capacities of the approach with several examples. I conclude by noting that if these arguments are successful, we should view self-appointed representatives as having the potential to address conditions in which the institutions of representative democracy are underdeveloped, inadequate, or entirely absent. In the final analysis, my strategy for determining democratic legitimacy is relatively straightforward. I consider self-appointed representation "nondemocratic" if the constituency empowered to authorize and demand accountability is different from the constituency whose interests the representative claims affect. The authorizing constituency could be, for example, a group that is already powerful and well represented, so reinforcing and perhaps exacerbating existing inequalities and cleavages. By contrast, I consider self-appointed representation "democratic" if the affected constituency is empowered to authorize and demand accountability of the self-appointed representative. Thus self-appointed representatives are democratically legitimate only to the degree that the affected are empowered to authorize and hold accountable the self-appointed representative.[1]

---

[1]Democratic legitimacy in the self-appointed context does not mean the legitimate use of state monopoly of force, but other informal forms of power.

The Concept of Self-Appointed Representation

"Self-appointed representation," as I develop the concept here, is a subset of nonelectoral political representation that occurs primarily in civil society and the public sphere and is disconnected from the coercive political authority of the state, whether or not that authority is organized through electoral democracy. Grassroots actors often fulfill the functions of a self-appointed representative: a constituent who initiates a movement on behalf of others, speaks with individuals on the street, gathers signatures for petitions, and so on, is a self-appointed representative. Such constituents embody the Tocquevillian norm of participation in local associations as a key mechanism for a healthy democracy. Yet self-appointed representation may also be a top-down activity in which an elite actor claims to represent others for political purposes. Here I am interested in both types of actors, and particularly in their ability to form—to call into being through their claims—a constituency that would not otherwise have political presence, and in a context apart from elections or other institutionalized processes.

In conceptualizing self-appointed representation, I adopt Saward's (2006, 2010) framework of the "representative claim," which considers representation "in terms of *claims to be representative* by a variety of political actors, rather than (as is normally the case) seeing it as an achieved, or potentially achievable, state of affairs as a result of elections" (2006, 5). Saward's framework is especially suggestive for developing the notion of a self-appointed representative since it focuses on the function of claiming both in identifying, calling forth, and organizing latent interests in the form of a (represented) political constituency and also in identifying sources of authority outside of representative institutions.

Suppose that an individual, a nongovernmental organization, or a foundation offers a claim of representation and, in so doing, effectively appoints themselves to a representative role. In the example of Bono, an interviewer from the *London Evening Standard* suggested to Bono that he represented the 18–30 year olds who listen to his music. Bono famously responded: "Outside of that I represent a lot of people who have no voice at all . . . They are the 6,500 people who are dying of AIDS in Africa every day for no good reason. They haven't asked me to represent them. It's cheeky but I hope they're glad I do" (Iley 2005).

A self-appointed claim of representation, that is, a claim of representation that occurs apart from electoral and other forms of state-centric representation, consists of four elements.[2] First, an actor self-identifies as one who aims to provide political presence for a constituency to an audience. Second, the claim identifies a constituency potentially affected if the claim and the actions pursuant to it were successful, such as certain Africans who need medicine to prevent and treat HIV/AIDS. Third, the claim identifies a constituency that is empowered by the claim to authorize the representative and demand accountability, such as "first-world donors." And fourth, the representative claim identifies a group whose recognition is required in order for the self-appointed actor to function as a representative (the audience), such as leaders of the G8 countries.

It follows from this analysis that a representative claim maker is potentially constituting two constituencies: one that is empowered by the claim to exercise authorization and demand accountability—the authorizing constituency—and the other whose interests are affected or potentially affected by collective decisions—the affected constituency. This dual constituency is not unique to self-appointed representation. In electoral contexts, individuals outside the district are often affected without being able to demand direct accountability (for example, if they live in another district or even country). The concept of a dual constituency allows us to see that although electoral representatives always act formally on behalf of their electoral constituency, their acts can have effects on others beyond electoral boundaries, producing, as it were, other constituencies of those affected. Similarly, self-appointed representatives can act on behalf of their empowered constituency, but affect others who are not empowered by the claim.

It also follows from this analysis that a claim of self-appointment is not sufficient to establishing the political authority required to function as a representative. Put simply, it is only a *claim* until recognized by an audience (Rehfeld 2006).[3] The authority of an elected representative follows from election to a representative office, already constituted apart from the election of any particular representative. The

---

[2]See Saward (2010) for a more detailed conceptualization of the representative claim.

[3]Because the claim depends on the recognition of the audience to function as representation, the term "self-appointed" is connotative rather than precisely correct. The term, however, captures the independence of the claim maker from the generally institutionalized and predictable sources of authority and legitimacy found in formal representative institutions.

authority of self-appointed representatives, however, is not pregiven by institutional function. Rehfeld (2006) helpfully notes that political authority is derived from a relevant audience—that group of people whose recognition a representative requires to take on the function of representation. On Rehfeld's account, though both Bono and Bob Geldof self-appoint, it is Bono who is a representative of certain Africans because the relevant audience identified by the claim (e.g., leaders of the G8 countries) accepts his claim. That audience accepts Bono as a representative from its perspective, conferring political authority on the basis of whatever rules it uses to recognize a claimant as a representative (Rehfeld 2006). Its acceptance holds in practice even if the affected and authorizing constituencies enacted by Bono's claim do not accept him as a representative. The audience has the power to recognize and accept a claimant as a representative because Bono requires its recognition in order to act as a representative.

Less explicit claims of self-appointment may still function as representation because of the recognition of the audience. Oxfam does not explicitly claim, "We represent the poor," or "We represent donors concerned for the poor." Yet Oxfam claims to "seek to influence the powerful to ensure that poor people can improve their lives and livelihoods and have a say in decisions that affect them," and to "press decision makers to change policies and practices that reinforce poverty and injustice" (Oxfam 2011). With this claim, Oxfam constructs itself as an actor aiming to make the poor visible and audible as an affected constituency to the World Bank, so identifying the relevant audience, and also to members/donors concerned for the poor, so constituting an authorizing constituency. Importantly, the World Bank includes Oxfam in its debt-relief discussions, enabling Oxfam to provide political presence for the poor, and to function as their representative.

Conceptualizing political authority as derived from a relevant audience provides a conceptual distinction between political representation and democratic representation. This distinction enables the recognition of nonelectoral representation *as* political representation irrespective of its legitimacy. Self-appointed representation is an example of representation that "really does happen" (Rehfeld 2006, 4) but that does not fit standard accounts of representation. By itself, however, considering representation from the perspective of the audience does not provide us with the grounds to make normative judgments about nonelected relationships of representation—nor does representation as claim making. We still

require the conceptual tools, therefore, to assess if, and when, self-appointed representation can be democratically legitimate.

The Standard Account of Democratic Representation and its Limits

We can now compare the concept of self-appointed representation to more common accounts. Standard accounts of representation equate democratic representation with electoral democracy (Huntington 1991; Pitkin 1967; Schumpeter 1947). The result is a "standard account" of political representation (Rehfeld 2006; Urbinati and Warren 2008), in which elections are seen as the defining institutional feature of democratic representation, justified by the standard of self-determination with respect to affected interests, though narrowly defined, often based in residence.

It has been widely noted, at least within democratic theory, that the standard account of representative democracy narrows the question of inclusion in the *demos* almost exclusively to a question of the relationship between citizens and their state, almost always interpreted as a relationship between citizens and their elected representatives, and almost always assuming that constituencies are defined by residence (Dovi 2011; MacDonald 2008; Rehfeld 2006; Saward 2010; Urbinati and Warren 2008; Young 2000). The authority of a democratic state is rendered legitimate by including in the *demos* those who reside within the territorial boundaries of that state and/or who share nationality, providing those individuals with equal political status, expressed in the equal right to vote. The standard account of political representation thus narrows the domain of representation to issues and interests that can be organized through electoral constituencies and which can be signaled and enforced through electoral systems.

The key normative limitation of the standard account, then, is that it ties the democratic legitimacy of representation to (territorially based) electoral democracy rather than to the basic normative question: who is affected by collective decisions (Goodin 2007)? Even with the universal franchise, elected representation is relatively unresponsive to large classes of the (potentially) affected in two ways. First, the affected are not always included in the electorate. Many problems of the standard account involve the complexity of constituency in issues such as global warming, disease, and trade, where people are affected by laws and policies to which they are subject but have little capacity to influence. When the affected do not form a geographically bound electoral constituency, or a people bound by shared citizenship, the assumption that electoral membership ensures inclusion of the relevant constituency may result in marginalizing or excluding many who are affected—sometimes the most affected—by collective decisions.

Second, even when the affected are formally included in the electorate, they may still go relatively underrepresented because of the aggregating character of electoral representation. When elected representatives combine many different issues to present a platform, that process of aggregation sometimes "includes" while failing to represent fully many interests with legitimate claims to representation, that is, interests affected by the relevant issues. In the United States, for example, the Democratic Party has long been accused of "taking Blacks for granted." The votes of African Americans have often failed to produce adequate representation because they are aggregated with so many others in the course of producing an electoral majority. In the course of such aggregation, a citizen has a voice only if her interests happen to be prioritized in the winning platform (Warren 2008, 58).

Self-appointed representatives have their greatest value when they fill the gaps in electoral representation, narrowing the difference between formal voting equality and what is normatively required by the affected interests standard (Hirst 1994). Postnational, transnational, and regional bodies, informal bodies in both formal and nonformal settings, and individuals, some self-appointed, have stepped in to fill the gaps in electoral representation. For example, the National Association for the Advancement of Colored People supplements electoral representation in the United States, providing representation for minorities who are not always well served by their elected representatives. A standard account that collapses democratic representation into elections makes it impossible to conceptualize or judge the democratic potentials of these actors. As Rehfeld puts it, "By wedding representation with the conditions that render it legitimate, the standard account is doing double duty: not only does it tell us when a representative is legitimate or democratic, it also purportedly tells us when a person is a political representative at all" (2006, 3). Put differently, the standard account conflates the fact that a representative is elected with democratic legitimacy.

Of course, self-appointed representatives do not necessarily include everyone in a manner that promotes egalitarianism of the kind indicated by the affected interests standard. They often empower the already privileged. Consider, for example, the dominance of business interests represented by K Street lobby firms in Washington who can buy representation simply because they have the resources. These kinds of cases notwithstanding, self-appointed representatives have the *potential* to represent those who *need* representation: those whose interests are not well served by existing structures of power. We need to develop distinctions that distinguish these differential effects, and I begin this work in the next section of this article. Here, however, I simply note that self-appointed representation can fill in democratic deficits common in electoral representation, either because of the design of electoral systems, or because electoral representation does not reach democratically relevant interests at all.

The Affected Interests Standard

In order to identify what counts as democratically legitimate representation without relying on the fact of election—indeed, without any presuppositions about institutional location—we require a norm to apply to representative claims. I have suggested that the "affected interests standard" may serve this function. That is, if a representative claim functions to give political presence to those whose interests are affected, or potentially affected, by collective decisions, and empowers them to exercise authorization and demand accountability, then we can say that it has democratic legitimacy.

To conceptualize the domain of "affected interests" in a way that is democratically relevant, I use a definition of "interests" borrowed primarily from the work of Young (2000). As Young develops the concept, interests are defined as "what affects or is important to the life prospects of individuals" (134). They differ from ideas, standards, and values, which help define the ends a person sets for herself, in that interests define the means for achieving those ends (134). On Young's view, the key interests that need representation in a democracy are interests in self-development and self-determination. Self-development pertains to both the distribution of the material resources that allow people to survive and flourish and also "the institutional organization of power, status, and communication" (32; see also Sen 1990, 1992; Young 1990). Self-determination involves "participation in making the collective regulations designed to prevent domination" (Young 2000, 33; see also Pettit 1997).

The point of conceiving of representation in terms of the affected interests standard is to expand the range of democratically relevant voices in such a way that the boundaries of contestation and public deliberation expand to include those who would otherwise be excluded from decision making by the boundaries of electoral constituencies or other relations of power. What is required to justify such expansion is a standard that would allow us to identify normatively the boundaries of representation that would include those whose interests are organized out of political processes by residence-based constituencies and/or other social structures or relations of power. Electoral constituencies may be the right unit with respect to certain laws and policies. But, from the perspective of democratic theory, the unit needs to be justified. Once the question is posed, it is clear that in many important instances, the democratic justifications for electoral constituencies fail. The affected interests standard should identify the normative importance of providing political presence to those affected by collective decisions, while acknowledging greater and lesser claims to representation depending upon the degree to which a constituency's interests are affected.

Self-Appointed Representatives and Reflexive Constituency Formation

If the concept of representation is detached from territorial constituency and electoral institutions, however, we shall need to reconceive the notion of "constituency." As suggested above, to do so, we shall need to look more closely at what is accomplished by the act of claiming. The representative claim is constitutive: it calls forth the authorizing constituency and the affected constituency. These constituencies are not "constituted" in the sense that they did not exist prior to the claim of the self-appointed representative. In Bono's case, 18–30 year olds existed prior to his representative claim, but it is the claim that identified and constituted them *as* an authorizing constituency, and so empowered them to authorize him and hold him accountable for his claims. Similarly, Africans affected by AIDS, debt, and trade policy existed before Bono's representative claim, but it is the claim that made them visible and audible *as* an affected constituency to the leaders of the G8 countries (the relevant audience), to the authorizing constituency, and perhaps also to themselves.

As Laclau puts it, "The represented depends on the representative for the constitution of his or her own identity" (2007, 158).

Once the claim is made, the affected constituency has a point of identification around which they might coalesce as a "people" or *demos* defined along some dimensions of common interest, for example, problems, feelings, and experiences of injustice. When a representative makes a claim, the claim might function to raise consciousness, identify latent injustices, and/or provoke a discursive process. These functions may work to not only bring a constituency together as a collective with a shared interest, but also to develop the autonomy of those whom the representative claims to represent, helping to develop the very capacities necessary for them to hold their representative to account. In this way, the representative claim may transform a latent constituency into a self-conscious and effective one.

The relationship between (self-appointed) representation and democracy is this: (self-appointed) representation not only renders constituencies politically present in decision-making processes where they might otherwise be excluded, it also renders the constituency (Disch 2011; Laclau 1996, 2007; Laclau and Mouffe 1985; McClure 1992; Rosanvallon 2008; Saward 2010). In so doing, self-appointed representatives not only aim to make constituencies visible and audible as affected, but they also potentially empower a constituency to authorize the claim together with the power to demand accountability. In this way, representation has constitutive force in a manner still consistent with democratic norms of autonomy. If a constituency is empowered to exercise authorization and demand accountability, it can then accept or decline and/or refine the claim that identifies it *as* an affected constituency, so exercising self-determination. Self-determination in democracy requires a reflexive form of self-constitution in which, as Bohman puts it, "the terms and boundaries of democracy are made by citizens themselves and not others" (2007, 2). Non-electoral constituencies cannot always give themselves law through an elected legislature, but through authorizing (or not) the claims of civil society representatives, they can define the boundaries of their own *demos* or *demoi*.

The Powers of Self-Appointed Representatives

Locating their fundamentally discursive and reflexive nature points to an ambivalent potential: self-appointed representatives can either support or undermine the standard of affected interests. If they empower constituencies affected by collective decisions, otherwise without capacities to influence those decisions, self-appointed representatives serve the standard of affected interests. But if they empower constituencies which are not affected, or not the most affected, by a given issue, self-appointed representatives may create or aggravate inequality, and so undermine the standard of affected interests. This tension of the dual constituency and its impact for the democratic standard of affected interests highlights the importance of holding self-appointed representatives accountable to standards of democratic representation.

Although both individual and organizational self-appointed representatives operate mostly within civil society and the public sphere, and lack the coercive powers of legislators and administrators, the claim of self-appointed representatives to legitimacy requires some accountability of the sort that can grant or withhold the conditions for the power of the self-appointed representative—the power to make constituencies visible and audible. The powers of self-appointed representatives are *discursive*, and their capacities to affect people—to call forth constituencies—work primarily through publicity, advocacy, and persuasion. Thus, the thresholds of accountability for self-appointed representatives are and should be different from those for representatives who wield coercive power—particularly power that includes the state's monopoly of violence. It is also the case that, unlike state powers, discursive power is not subject to monopoly control. Self-appointed representatives do not have monopolies over certain publics or issues: more than one actor can represent the same constituency, interest, or issue. It is for this reason that discursive power works only through agreement or consent. Because a self-appointed representative makes claims for which she seeks to gain authorization, she relies on the response of the public to her claims.

Important to determining the legitimacy of self-appointed claims of representation, then, is *publicity*: the claim must be made public—seen and heard (Arendt 1958)—in order to be authorized (or not) and to establish accountability—to be justified/ justifiable (Habermas 1996). For the purposes of democratic legitimation, a representative claim must be made known not only to the audience and to the authorizing constituency, but to those whom it affects. Publicity provides a constituency with the opportunity to demand reasons, to assess the claim in question—an assessment then registered by its authorization, refusal, and/or amendment of the claim. There is a reflexive element to the publicity: the claim is offered and the constituency then authorizes the claim that, in part, identifies a constituency *as* an affected constituency. In this way, publicity is also part of the process through which affected people are constituted (and self-constitute) as a constituency, even a *demos*, by the claim. The role of publicity must be to mobilize objections from the affected, which then enables us to make judgments about the representative's response to such challenges (Disch 2011).

Publicity also invokes a less critical "seen and heard," in the sense of public relations, as something that is amplified, often by the power of money and/or celebrity, or staged, aided by mass media. Amplification may have benefits—if it makes visible and audible a constituency as affected—but it may serve to undermine a constituency's capacity to discern the claim of the representative (Mansbridge 2011). Publicity, in this sense, may influence the authorizing constituency to recognize Bono as a representative solely because of his celebrity and charisma. Or publicity may enable the overrepresentation of authorizing constituencies, who can use their relatively larger access to resources (as compared to affected constituencies) to amplify their demands for representation. Indeed, such examples underscore the importance of conceptualizing criteria by which to assess such claims. Specifying legitimacy in relation to the affected interests standard, and conceptualizing the dual constituency, begins the work of identifying and assessing the relationships claimed by the representative. We can identify whether a constituency (and which constituency) is empowered by the claim to register objections to the representative and judge the response of the representative to such objections.

Nonelectoral Sources of Authorization

With these specifications of the concept of self-appointed representation and the dual constituency it may establish, we can now examine those constituencies' capacities to authorize the claim and then hold the representative to account. Authorization poses an obvious conceptual difficulty. Because (as I have been arguing) self-appointed representatives bring constituencies into being, the temporal sequencing we associate with voting—that authorization is prospective—does not apply in the same way. The claim of representation is made *before* authorization and is then affirmed or refused. Any claim of representation, whether electoral or self-appointed, receives authorization *retrospectively*. Even electoral representatives offer their claim when they run for office, arguing that they can and should be our representative—and then receive a plurality or majority vote, or not. Sometimes that authorization is granted on the basis of promises made in advance (Mansbridge 2003), but the authorization takes place after the claim making. Once a self-appointed representative brings a constituency into being, it can retrospectively authorize, as it were, building legitimacy around the claim.

Authorizing constituencies derive their capacity to authorize from the resources—as examples, money and status—they can offer the self-appointed representative. These resources may produce, reproduce, and even exacerbate inequalities between the authorizing constituency and the affected constituency who likely do not have the same access to resources or, at least, not to the same degree. Some of these resources are funneled through *organizational authorization* (e.g., Grant and Keohane 2005), which may take one or more of the following forms: (1) organizations can recognize as representative those who claim to represent by self-appointment in a formal or informal mission statement (e.g., Bono's 18-30 year olds provide visible instances of membership or followership); (2) organizations can give self-appointed representatives financial contributions to pursue their work (e.g., donors); and (3) voting within organizations can formally authorize self-appointed representatives. Members can elect such representatives to formal positions of power in an organization, and boards of trustees can support or undermine such representatives through their votes on issues of policy such as grant making, geographic focus, spending, investment, and management.

Discursive authorization (e.g., Dryzek and Niemeyer 2008) takes the form of public agreement. An authorizing constituency offers not only its money but also its allegiance and public approbation, expressed in actions and in words. When a self-appointed representative of the poor makes a public speech, the size and enthusiasm of the appreciative crowd creates a greater or lesser authorization. Public agreement is also expressed through support of protests, boycotts, letter writing, and petitions, among others, all of which contributes to an actor's public reputation.

Affected constituencies may also have some power to authorize, depending upon the extent of their marginalization, dispersion, and other conditions that affect their opportunities and capacities to exercise authorization. They can use their comparatively small resources of money and time to signal their authorization through organizational means, such as membership or followership, attendance at meetings, participation in programs, and so on. Discursively, members of affected constituencies may express public agreement with the self-appointed representative or even acclaim that individual or organization as a representative. Participation in and approbation of organizations signal their authorization. Conversely, members of affected constituencies may publicly and vocally denounce any authorization. As those members take such actions of either authorization or deauthorization, of course, they themselves are acting as self-appointed representatives.

Nonelectoral Sources of Accountability

Just as we can ask about sources of authorization beyond the vote, we can also ask about nonelectoral sources of accountability. In the case of self-appointed representatives, I refer to two categories of accountability: organizational and discursive. The sources of sanction that the authorizing constituency can wield to hold the self-appointed representative to account are much the same as the resources that signal their authorization: money and organizational capacities, including memberships. That is, authorizing constituencies derive their capacities to hold self-appointed representatives accountable, at least in part, from withholding, or threatening to withhold, resources. As I noted with sources of authorization, affected constituencies may employ different mechanisms than authorizing constituencies to demand accountability, or employ the same mechanisms but to a lesser degree, because resources of money and organizational capacity may be more readily available to authorizing constituencies.

Although authorization and accountability are analytically distinct, a particular mechanism sometimes serves both, as does the vote (Mansbridge 2009). Similarly, membership will serve both authorization and accountability: through joining (authorization) and through exit or anticipation of exit (accountability). The mechanisms of organizational accountability wielded by authorizing constituencies correspond to organizational authorization provided by memberships, donations, and voting within organizations: voice and exit.

Following Hirschman, voice is "any attempt at all to change, rather than to escape from, an objectionable state of affairs" (1970, 30). According to Hirschman, a firm's customers or an organization's members employ *voice accountability* when they express their dissatisfaction to those in charge who, in turn, "search for the causes and possible cures of customers' and members' dissatisfaction" (1970, 4). Voice accountability is supported by the threat of exit. *Exit accountability* derives from market-based consequences of members joining and leaving organizations, paying or not paying membership dues, and of following calls to rally or failing to show up. Self-appointed representatives such as NGOs often occupy a competitive market for both funding and members. They will usually be attentive to their members because of the threat of exit.

Other forms of organizational accountability often wielded by authorizing constituencies include hierarchical, supervisory, fiscal, and legal. Leaders of organizations wield *hierarchical accountability* over their subordinate officials: subordinates' tasks are constrained, and/or financial compensation is adjusted, or they are removed from office altogether. Hierarchical accountability "applies to relationships within organizations, including multilateral organizations such as the United Nations or the World Bank" (Grant and Keohane 2005, 36). Similarly, states wield *supervisory accountability* over multilateral organizations. Supervisory accountability "refers to relations between organizations where one organization acts as principal with respect to specified agents," as when, for example, the World Bank is held accountable by states (Grant and Keohane 2005, 36). Funding agencies wield *fiscal accountability* when they, for example, "demand reports from, and ultimately sanction, agencies that are recipients of funding," such as the United Nations (Grant and Keohane 2005, 36). And courts wield *legal accountability* over an individual official or agency. Legal accountability "refers to the requirement that agents abide by formal rules and be prepared to justify their actions in those terms, in courts or quasi-judicial arenas" (Grant and Keohane 2005, 36). These four mechanisms of accountability are examples of what Grant and Keohane call a "delegation model of accountability," in which "performance is evaluated by those entrusting them with powers" (2005, 31). That is, these mechanisms are not primarily wielded by those affected.

Turning to discursive accountability, the basis of the power of self-appointed representatives is important: because their power to call forth constituencies depends upon publicity, advocacy, and persuasion, the discursive (or deliberative) basis of their authority also functions as a means of accountability. Accountability involves both deliberation (to give an account, to explain and justify one's behavior to others), and the possibility of control (to be held accountable, to be sanctioned in some way) (Savage and Weal 2009, 69). Mansbridge terms the former narrative or deliberative accountability, which differs from accountability based on monitoring and sanctions. As she describes, "In narrative and deliberative accountability, the representative explains the reasons for her actions and even (ideally) engages in two-way communication with constituents, particularly when deviating from the constituents' preferences" (2009, 370). Traditionally, such public reasoning occurs between elected representatives and their constituents, in which they "seek to justify to one another their preferences for alternative forms of public policy" (Savage and Weal 2009, 70). This simple registering of preferences, however, does not fully capture the creative elements of the discursive activity of the self-appointed representative. Through public reasoning, justification, and explanation, affected constituencies may be formed. Thus, when considered as a part of constituency formation, discursive accountability is in itself constitutive. Accountability is not simply or primarily "a summons of compliance but rather provides understanding, as Shotter (1989) argues, of how we constitute the sense we have of ourselves (our identities) as well as shared ways of constructing the meanings that inform our social orders" (Ranson 2003, 461). Viewed through the lens of representation, discursive accountability is constitutive, the medium through which latent constituencies become—to borrow loosely from Marx—constituencies in and for themselves.

These considerations bring into view a number of discourse-based accountability mechanisms. If public agreement is a key authorizing mechanism, public *dis*agreement can serve as an accountability mechanism. Authorizing constituencies express public disapprobation of self-appointed representatives in actions and in words, effectively sanctioning self-appointed representatives by undermining their public reputations. *Public reputational accountability* derives also from exit and discursive exit accountability. "[S]uperiors, supervisory boards, courts, fiscal watchdogs, markets, and peers all take the reputations of agents into account. Indeed, reputation is a form of 'soft power,' defined as 'the ability to shape the preferences of others'" (Grant and Keohane 2005, 37, citing Nye 2004, 5). Self-appointed representatives will often try to develop their reputations *as representatives* by investing their time and resources in a cause, manifesting consistency of purpose, and attending to the continuity of their "brand" as standing for those affected by the cause, in order to prevent either exit or discursive exit. The ensuing public reputational accountability is an important mechanism of accountability for individual self-appointed representatives, who are unlikely to be subject to more formal forms of accountability (Grant and Keohane 2005, 37). Al Gore, for example, has established a reputation as an environmental activist and is now a self-appointed representative of those concerned about global warming. He thus has an interest in monitoring the integrity of that representative relationship. In an example of public reputational accountability, Gore's private consumption of energy resources became a subject of criticism after his film, *An Inconvenient Truth*, was released. This criticism prompted Gore to explain that he purchases carbon offsets and undertook renovations to include solar panels as an energy source for his home. Gore was held accountable: he was made to explain, to give an account, to justify his behavior to the public.

Like authorizing constituencies, affected constituencies derive their capacities to hold self-appointed representatives accountable from withholding, or threatening to withhold, resources. Affected constituencies wield voice accountability within organizations when they articulate their opinions to leaders, explaining why they prefer change, and threaten exit. Accordingly, affected constituencies wield exit when they cancel memberships, donations, and cease participation in meetings, programs, and the like. "Exit" may be in a sense less democratic than "voice," but the two are often structurally related; as Hirschman argues, "the *effectiveness* of the voice mechanism is strengthened by the possibility of exit" (1970, 83).

When affected constituencies are unable to pay the dues required of member organizations, they can still wield forms of voice and exit. Outside of organizations, affected constituencies can articulate their opinions in an attempt to change their circumstances, when a self-appointed representative actually speaks to those people the self-appointed representative hopes to affect—and of course, not only speaks to them, but listens to them and responds to them. Just as voice within organizations is supported by the threat of exit, voice outside of organizations is also supported by what I call *discursive exit*, following the suggestion above that the powers of self-appointed representatives have a fundamentally discursive nature.

Discursive exit occurs when a member, or members, of the affected constituency actively refuse the grounds of a representation claim (and instead authorizes an alternative claim). Unlike voice, in which constituents articulate their opinions in an attempt to change the content of the representative claim, discursive exit refuses the representation claim altogether. Some black Americans, for example, exercised discursive exit when they argumentatively refused Dr. King's claims and instead supported the claims of Malcolm X (and vice versa). Discursive exit may communicate information, such as the reason for exit, and so has the potential to inform the broader public about the reasons for exit. Like exit *tout court*, discursive exit is especially effective as a mechanism of accountability when alternatives exist to which the constituency can exit. Discursive exit-based accountability has three desirable attributes: first, the cost of exit is low; second, entrance and exit is voluntary, unlike citizenship; and third, provided that there are other choices available, exit can occur at any time the member chooses, unlike periodic elections.

This list of mechanisms is not necessarily exhaustive. It does, however, begin to identify the places in which we might look for mechanisms of non-electoral accountability that are appropriate to the discursive power of self-appointed representatives. Although self-appointed representatives are not elected and not subject to electoral accountability, their constituents can nevertheless provide authorization and demand accountability for their representative claims. Their constituents can grant or withhold the conditions for the power of the self-appointed representative—the *power to* make their constituencies visible and audible.

Applying the Theory: Kinds of Self-Appointed Representatives

As I have argued, to assess the self-appointed representative as democratically legitimate or not, we must consider the relationship of the representative to the authorizing constituency and the affected constituency, and so to the standard of affected interests. In order to be considered a *democratic representative*, the self-appointed representative must both provide political presence for an affected constituency *and* be authorized by and held accountable to them. In theory, we should be able to apply these criteria to examples of self-appointed representatives to judge their contributions to democracy. If we do, we are

REPRESENTATION

likely to find that self-appointed representatives fall into four ideal-types with respect to democratic criteria, as illustrated in Table 1.

If the self-appointed representative succeeds on neither of these dimensions—that is, the self-appointed representative does not provide political presence for an affected constituency and is not authorized by or held accountable to them—the representation simply *fails*. This category is not mutually exclusive of *skewed representation*, in which the self-appointed representative provides disproportionate political presence for, and disproportionately empowers, authorizing constituencies over affected constituencies.[4] If the self-appointed representative provides political presence for an affected constituency but does not empower them, I refer to *surrogate representation*. Finally, if a self-appointed representative both provides political presence for an affected constituency and empowers them, I term this representation *democratic*. Conceptualizing these relationships in this manner clarifies where self-appointed representatives work to democratic effect and in democratic ways and also where they do not work to democratic effect and in nondemocratic ways.

The Pro-Femmes/Twese Hamwe organization provides an example of democratic self-appointed representation. This organization works toward "the eradication of all forms of discrimination toward women and promotion of their socioeconomic political and legal status" (Pro-Femmes/Twese Hamwe 2011). Pro-Femmes is an umbrella organization for 52 member associations, concerned to rid society of all forms of gender-related discrimination. Pro-Femmes represented Rwandan women to their government for the purpose of increasing women's representation in the new constitution and is recognized as "having had a major influence on policies such as the revision of inheritance laws" (USAID 2002, 37). Pro-Femmes made Rwandan women visible and audible as an affected constituency and receives their authorization and is subject to their demands for accountability both through their member organizations and also through the consultations they conduct with the women they claim to represent. These women *organizationally authorize* Pro-Femmes, if indirectly, through their participation in its member organizations. They *discursively authorize* Pro-Femmes by speaking out in support of its goals

and programs. Pro-Femmes is also subject to both *exit* and *voice accountability*: Rwandan women can express their dissatisfaction to Pro-Femmes by exiting its organizations and by expressing dissatisfaction in its consultations. The constituents also enjoy *discursive exit*. Rwandan women can refuse the claim of representation made by Pro-Femmes by not participating in its programs and provide reasons for their disaffection. Finally, the affected constituency can employ *public reputational accountability*, which overlaps with the other mechanisms, and holds Pro-Femmes accountable through publicity and its attendant benefits.

Surrogate representation occurs when the self-appointed representative provides political presence for an affected constituency but without empowering them to exercise authorization and demand accountability. Rather, the surrogate representative receives authorization from and is accountable to an authorizing constituency, for example, a set of donors. The affected constituency is called into being—made visible and audible *as* affected—but not empowered, perhaps because the constituency is dispersed or marginalized to such a degree that empowerment is difficult or impossible. In these cases, there is (nondemocratic) legitimacy derived from providing political presence for a group affected by a decision that would otherwise be excluded from (consideration in) decision making (Mansbridge 2003; Rubenstein 2007). I call this "constitutive legitimacy." Surrogate representation anticipates a moment when the affected *will* be active and agentic (Alcoff 1991–92). It is a form of predemocratic representation if the representative helps to identify issues of injustice, so provoking a discursive process, and/or may spark the organization of more democratic alternatives that are still not formal and electoral. It is therefore preferable to no representation, but it is not democratic.

Oxfam, like Bono, is an example of a surrogate self-appointed representative. Although the organization makes the poor visible and audible as affected, and so can be judged to be constitutively legitimate, it does so without their authorization and accountability. Instead, Oxfam is authorized by and accountable to a sympathetic, proxy constituency. *The Economist's* challenge, "Who elected Oxfam" and "Who holds the activists accountable?" is answerable. The relatively privileged in the developed world authorize Oxfam to pursue its work and hold Oxfam accountable through nonelectoral mechanisms of authorization and accountability such as membership, donations, exit, and public reputation. Oxfam is also

---

[4]Quadrant I is empty to indicate conceptual impossibility. It seems unlikely that a self-appointed representative would be authorized by and accountable to the affected constituency, while not also providing political presence.

500 REPRESENTATION

TABLE 1 Dimensions of Democratically Legitimate Self-Appointed Representation

		Empowerment of Affected Constituency (powers of authorization and accountability)	
		−	+
Political Presence of Affected Constituency	−	Failed/skewed representation	—
	+	Surrogate representation	Democratic representation

subject to discursive authorization and accountability, exemplified by *The Economist*'s challenge. For Oxfam to be a democratic representative, its claim must empower the affected to exercise authorization and demand accountability; instead, Oxfam is authorized and held accountable by its members and donors. Perhaps Oxfam trades off democratic legitimacy for the purposes of efficiency and reach of assistance. Whatever Oxfam's motivation, identifying the representative claim, the constituencies involved, and nonelectoral mechanisms of authorization and accountability, provides the criteria by which we can conceptualize and judge its legitimacy as a representative.

Skewed representation occurs when the self-appointed representative disproportionately represents the already powerful. This self-appointed representative advances the claims of more powerful interests, effectively crowding out affected constituencies. The skewed self-appointed representative thereby contributes to the overrepresentation of powerful interests and undermines the affected constituency by providing the privileged with yet another forum of representation. Consider the number of organizations representing business and professional interests that are wealthier, more powerful, and more numerous than those representing, as examples, women and African Americans (Baumgartner and Leech 1998; Gray and Lowery 1996; Schlozman and Tierney 1986; Strolovitch 2007; Tichenor and Harris 2005).

The term "skewed representation" calls attention to a problem identified by Dara Strolovitch: "advocacy organizations are much more active on policy issues affecting a majority of their constituents than they are on issues that affect subgroups within their constituencies" (2007, 8). Strolovitch explains that issues affecting "advantaged subgroups," such as affirmative action for women in higher education, are given disproportionately high levels of attention compared to issues affecting "disadvantaged subgroups," such as welfare reform for women. The latter issue affects "intersectionally disadvantaged"

women—women who are affected both by their interests as a woman and also by poverty. When they do claim to speak for disadvantaged subgroups, self-appointed representatives will, ideally, be held to account for these claims, either by an authorizing constituency or by the affected themselves. The claims made on behalf of disadvantaged subgroups enter into common discourse, generating accountability. This may help to create the conditions under which the authorizing constituency might speak for the affected and/or, eventually, the affected might speak for themselves.

If a self-appointed representative neither provides political presence for an affected constituency, nor empowers them to exercise authorization and demand accountability, the representation simply *fails*. The role of churches that not only supported the Canadian government but "led the way" (Royal Commission on Aboriginal Peoples 1996) in establishing residential schools for Aboriginal children is an example of such failed representation. Education was seen as instrumental to solving the "Indian problem," intended to move Aboriginal peoples "from their helpless 'savage' state to one of self-reliant 'civilization' and thus to make in Canada one community—a non-Aboriginal, Christian one" (Royal Commission on Aboriginal Peoples 1996). The result of the residential school system was instead "profound cultural damage and pain" (Arneil 2006, 30). The assumed inferiority and imposed wardship that inhibited the self-development and self-determination of Aboriginal peoples demonstrates both a lack of political presence for an affected constituency, as well as an abuse of power made possible by a lack of authorization and accountability.

All of this is to suggest that this theory provides criteria by which to analyze such representative relationships. Most organizations and movements are complicated entities with identities that stretch over time and space and that will continue to evolve. In an ideal world, in response to representative claims that are surrogate, skewed or fail, self-appointed

REPRESENTATION

501

representatives would evolve to generate representative claims that are democratically legitimate.

Conclusion

In a globalizing era, nonelected actors increasingly offer claims of representation. They make these claims in response to representative deficits produced by the institutions of electoral politics and by disparities in political weight and efficacy. We therefore require a theory of democratic representation that will provide the conceptual tools to assess if, and when, nonelectoral forms of representation can be democratically legitimate. Self-appointed representatives are important to democracy because they have the potential to form constituencies on the basis of the affected interests standard. Some groups that I have called constituencies, like donors, can be empowered to exercise authorization and demand accountability, even when they are not the affected constituency. But when the affected constituency is made visible and audible as affected *and* has powers of authorization and accountability, that is what I call a democratically legitimate relationship of self-appointed representation.

Acknowledgments

Earlier versions of this article were presented at the annual meeting of the American Political Science Association, the Rockefeller Foundation Bellagio Study and Conference Center working group on *Rethinking Representation*, and the workshop *Beyond Elections* at Princeton University. The work benefited greatly from these audiences and from the comments and criticisms of Mark Warren, Jane Mansbridge, Laura Janara, Bruce Baum, Lisa Disch, Michael Saward, Andrew Rehfeld, Kirstie McClure, Margaret Keck, and John McCormick, as well as the anonymous reviewers for and editors of *The Journal of Politics*.

References

Alcoff, Linda. 1991–92. "The Problem of Speaking for Others." *Cultural Critique* 20: 5–32.

Arendt, Hanna. 1958. *The Human Condition*. Chicago: University of Chicago Press.

Arneil, Barbara. 2006. *Diverse Communities: The Problem with Social Capital*. Cambridge: Cambridge University Press.

Baumgartner, Frank R. and Beth Leech. 1998. *Basic Interests: The Importance of Groups in Politics and Political Science*. Princeton, NJ: Princeton University Press.

Bohman, James. 2007. *Democracy Across Borders*. Cambridge, MA: MIT Press.

Disch, Lisa. 2011. "Toward a Mobilization Conception of Democratic Representation." *American Political Science Review* 105 (1): 100–14.

Dovi, Suzanne. 2011. "Political Representation." In *The Stanford Encyclopedia of Philosophy* (Fall ed.), ed. Edward N. Zalta. http://plato.stanford.edu/archives/fall2011/entries/political-representation (accessed October 14, 2011).

Dryzek, John S., and Simon Niemeyer. 2008. "Discursive Representation." *American Political Science Review* 102 (4): 481–93.

Goodin, Robert E. 2007. "Enfranchising All Affected Interests, and Its Alternatives." *Philosophy & Public Affairs* 35 (1): 40–68.

Grant, Ruth and Robert O. Keohane. 2005. "Accountability and Abuses of Power in World Politics." *American Political Science Review* 99 (1): 29–44.

Gray, Virginia, and David Lowery. 1996. *The Population Ecology of Interest Representation*. Ann Arbor: University of Michigan Press.

Habermas, Jürgen. 1996. *Between Facts and Norms*. Cambridge, MA: MIT Press.

Hirschman, Albert O. 1970. *Exit, Voice, and Loyalty: Responses to Decline in Firms, Organizations, and States*. Cambridge, MA: Harvard University Press.

Hirst, Paul. 1994. *Associative Democracy: New Forms of Economic and Social Governance*. Amherst: University of Massachusetts Press.

Huntington, Samuel. 1991. *The Third Wave: Democratization in the Late Twentieth Century*. Norman: University of Oklahoma Press.

Iley, Chrissy. 2005. "Why Africa Needs U2." *London Evening Standard*, June 28.

Laclau, Ernesto. 1996. *Emancipations*. New York: Verso.

Laclau, Ernesto. 2007. *On Populist Reason*. London: Verso.

Laclau, Ernesto, and Chantalle Mouffe. 1985. *Hegemony and Socialist Strategy*. New York: Verso.

Macdonald, Terry. 2008. *Global Stakeholder Democracy*. Oxford, UK: Oxford University Press.

Mansbridge, Jane. 2003. "Rethinking Representation." *American Political Science Review* 97 (4): 515–28.

Mansbridge, Jane. 2009. "The 'Selection Model' of Political Representation." *Journal of Political Philosophy* 17 (4): 369–98.

Mansbridge, Jane. 2011. "Clarifying the Concept of Representation." *American Political Science Review* 105 (3): 621–30.

McClure, Kirstie. 1992. "On the Subject of Rights: Pluralism, Plurality and Political Identity." In *Dimensions of Radical Democracy*, ed. Chantal Mouffe. New York: Verso, 108–27.

Nye, Joseph S. 2004. *Soft Power: The Means to Success in World Politics*. New York: Public Affairs Press.

Oxfam International. 2011. "What We Do." http://www.oxfam.org/en/about/what (accessed July 2, 2011).

Pettit, Philip. 1997. *Republicanism*. Oxford, UK: Oxford University Press.

Pitkin, Hanna. 1967. *The Concept of Representation*. Berkeley: University of California.

Pro-Femmes/Twese Hamwe. 2011. "Mission." http://www.profemme.org.rw/index2.html (accessed September 21, 2011).

Ranson, Stewart. 2003. "Public Accountability in the Age of Neoliberal Governance." *Journal of Education Policy* 18: 455–80.

Rehfeld, Andrew. 2006. "Towards a General Theory of Political Representation." *The Journal of Politics* 68 (1): 1–21.

Rosanvallon, Pierre. 2008. *La Légitimité Démocratique: Impartialité, Réflexivité, Proximité*. Paris: Seuil.

Royal Commission on Aboriginal Peoples. 1996. Report of the Royal Commission on Aboriginal Peoples. *Government of Canada*, Ottawa: Collections Canada.

Rubenstein, Jennifer. 2007. "Accountability in an Unequal World." *Journal of Politics* 69 (3): 616–632.

Savage, Deborah, and Albert Weale. 2009. "Political Representation and the Normative Logic of Two-level Games." *European Political Science Review* 1: 63–81.

Saward, Michael. 2006. "The Representative Claim." *Contemporary Political Theory* 5: 297–318.

Saward, Michael. 2010. *The Representative Claim*. Oxford, UK: Oxford University Press.

Schlozman, Kay Lehman, and John T. Tierney. 1986. *Organized Interests and American Democracy*. New York: Harper & Row.

Schumpeter, Joseph. 1947. *Capitalism, Socialism, and Democracy*. New York: Harper.

Sen, Amartya. 1990. Justice: Means versus Freedoms. *Philosophy and Public Affairs* 19: 111–21.

Sen, Amartya. 1992. *Inequality Reexamined*. Cambridge, MA: Harvard University Press.

Shotter, John. 1989. "Social Accountability and the Social Construction of 'You.'" In *Texts of Identity*, ed. John Shotter and K. Green. London: Sage, 133–51.

Strolovitch, Dara. 2007. *Affirmative Advocacy: Race, Class, and Gender in Interest Group Politics*. Chicago: The University of Chicago Press.

Tichenor, Daniel J. and Richard A. Harris. 2005. "The Development of Interest Group Politics in America." *Annual Review of Political Science* 8: 251–70.

Urbinati, Nadia and Mark Warren. 2008. "The Concept of Representation in Contemporary Democratic Theory." *Annual Review of Political Science* 11: 387–412.

USAID Office of Democracy and Governance (2002). *Rwanda Democracy and Governance Assessment*. Washington, DC: Management Systems International, Inc.

Warren, Mark E. 2008. "Citizen Representatives." In *Designing Deliberative Democracy: The British Columbia Citizens Assembly*, ed. Mark E. Warren and Hilary Pearse. Cambridge: Cambridge University Press.

Young, Iris Marion. 1990. *Justice and the Politics of Difference*. Princeton, NJ: Princeton University Press.

Young, Iris Marion. 2000. *Inclusion and Democracy*. Oxford, UK: Oxford University Press.

25

Citizen representatives

Mark E. Warren

Democratic theorists commonly distinguish between *direct* democracy and *representative* democracy.[1] In a direct democracy, citizens rule themselves, while in a representative democracy they elect representatives to rule on their behalf. Today's democracies are all representative in structure – a form dictated by scale and complexity – with some direct elements such as initiatives and referenda, as well as some forms of citizen engagement. The concept of *participatory democracy* usually refers to these latter two elements: direct decision-making as well as citizen involvement in decision-making within representative structures. If, however, we consider these two forms of participation from the perspective of representation, the first involves citizen participation in government or other formalized decision-making, on the assumption that citizens *represent themselves* within these processes. The second involves citizens themselves serving in *representative capacities*: lay citizens represent other citizens. I shall refer to these roles as *citizen representatives* – a form of representation that is increasingly common in practice, but almost untheorized in democratic theory.[2]

To be sure, the idea that citizens are best represented by other lay citizens serving as representatives is an old democratic ideal. It justified early notions that elected representatives should be salaried so as to enable ordinary citizens – not just the rich – to serve in public office, as well as the more

---

[1] I am indebted to Lisa Disch, David Laycock, Hilary Pearse, Dennis Thompson, and members of the British Columbia Citizens' Assembly workshops at the University of British Columbia for their comments and criticisms. I am grateful to Menaka Philips and Hilary Pearse for research assistance.

[2] The two exceptions are Stephan (2004) and Brown (2006).

CITIZEN REPRESENTATIVES

recent idea that term limits will prevent elected representatives from becoming professional political elites. These and other devices are based on the presumption that when citizens represent other citizens, the representative relationship is secured through common experience. The presumption is not a good one, however. Common experience usually gives way to the realities of running for and holding office, which subjects lay citizens and professional politicians alike to the same constraints of campaigning, brokering, and responding to interest group pressures, and leads to very similar behaviors (Fisher and Herrick 2003). Moreover, as Max Weber noted almost a century ago, governing complex societies provides little room for amateurs and dilettantes, who are at best ineffective and at worst more easily manipulated by interest groups and bureaucrats than are professional politicians.

Over the last few decades, however, new forms of citizen representation have been rapidly evolving (Brown 2006; Fiorino 1990; Row and Frewer 2000; Warren 2003). These forms involve non-professionals who are selected or self-selected rather than elected for representative purposes. The oldest form of citizen representative is the legal jury, which represents the considered judgment of peers within courtroom proceedings. We can now add to this limited form more recent experiments with citizen juries and panels, advisory councils, stakeholder meetings, lay members of professional review boards, representations at public hearings, public submissions, citizen surveys, deliberative polling, deliberative forums, focus groups, and advocacy group representations (Fiorino 1990; Fung 2006b; Rowe and Frewer 2000). Citizen representatives typically function not as alternatives but rather as supplements to elected representative bodies or administrative bodies in areas of weakness, usually having to do with limitations of communication, deliberation, legitimacy, governability, or attentiveness to public norms and common goods (Brown 2006).

Although it has been common to refer to these forms of political activity under the category of "participatory democracy," the term fails to identify what is perhaps their most important feature: each involves a form of representation that depends upon the *active participation of a relatively few citizens who function as representatives of other citizens*. Thus, whereas the notion of *participatory* democracy suggests that most citizens participate in self-rule – a worthy ideal – what is most important about these new forms is their *representative* qualities. Accordingly, they should not be measured by *how many* citizens are enabled to participate through these forms (although this remains a valid measure of democracy), but rather by the *nature and quality of democratic representation* achieved through these forms. Theories of participatory democracy are not equipped to guide these judgments (Urbinati 2006).

This theoretical deficit is highlighted by the case of the British Columbia Citizens' Assembly (CA), precisely because it was constructed as a body of non-professional citizens who would represent other citizens in the fundamental constitutional matter of assessing and designing an electoral system. In this chapter, I address this theoretical gap first by highlighting deficits in democratic representation through elected legislative bodies. Second, I suggest that strategies for increasing citizen participation often frame the democratic deficit problem in ways that are unlikely to be successful. At the same time, the lens of participatory democracy tends to obscure the increasingly important concept of representative relationships among citizens – usually, between the active few and the passive many. Third, if we approach citizen-based political venues through the framework of representation, we can ask about how well emerging forms of citizen participation measure up as *citizen representatives*: who authorizes citizen representatives? How egalitarian are their effects? How are they held accountable? Using these criteria, I assess the CA model as a *citizen representative body*. Considered as a representative body, the CA shows strengths in areas where both elected legislatures and other kinds of citizen representative bodies tend to be weak. Finally, I conclude that owing to certain weaknesses of CA-style citizen representative bodies – particularly with respect to accountability to constituencies – they should be viewed as supplements to, rather than replacements for, other forms of representation.

Representation deficits

Most conceptions of democratic electoral representation share certain formal features, which in turn indicate criteria in terms of which the quality of representation might be judged (Mansbridge 2003; Pitkin 1967; Warren and Castiglione 2004). The most recognized of these features is the role of elections in *authorizing* representatives to represent those who inhabit geographic constituencies. Electoral representation is held to be *egalitarian and inclusive* owing to the universal franchise. Every member of an electoral unit, excluding those unfit or not yet fit to exercise the responsibilities of citizenship, is entitled to one vote. Subsequent elections function to hold representatives *accountable* for their performance while in office.

As is well-known, democratic linkages between citizens and representatives can and do break down in numerous ways (see, e.g., Fung 2006a). Citizens may have unstable preferences that are neither adequately formed by the electoral process, nor communicated by the blunt instrument of the vote. Voting may not serve as a sufficiently strong incentive to hold representatives accountable, especially when voters are inattentive, information is incomplete, and other forms of power permeate the system, including actors that can provide or withhold economic resources, or administrative officials who have knowledge that representatives cannot match. Electoral mechanisms such as single member plurality systems may function to disadvantage or exclude minorities. Where there are descriptive differences between representatives and their constituents, distinctive group experiences and disadvantages may not be represented at all (James, Chapter 5, this volume). And because pressure groups tend to represent those with the resources to organize and who care intensely about a single issue, constituency communication may systematically disadvantage public will formation around common goods. Finally, citizens may demand contradictory things from government, such as first-rate health care and schools combined with low taxes. Each of these possibilities are, of course, common in the developed democracies.

The concept of an *institutional* representation deficit is poorly developed in theories of electoral democracy, in part because the very notion of representative institutions serving as collective representatives of the people is poorly developed, with the exception, of course, of political parties. However, people tend to expect legislatures to do their work – deliver decisions – in ways that are responsive, competent, and fair. And there is a sense in which the kind of accountability that attaches to these expectations is quite different than the expectations leveled at individual representatives. Voters are quite willing, as the 2006 mid-term elections in the United States demonstrated, to use their vote for individual representatives to hold the institution to account *as an institution*.

Theoretically, there are at least two distinct senses of accountability at the institutional level. The first is, simply, whether the institution can "do its job" – delivery legislation. And its capacity for accountability in this sense will depend upon its institutional capacity to handle conflict by avoiding stalemate, as well as its capacity to handle the high levels of complexity that come with many legislative decisions. The second sense of accountability has to do with whether the institution can provide *public justifications* for its decisions. No doubt there are trade-offs between these dimensions of institutional accountability: the ability of a legislative body to broker complex agreements, for example, may mean that its capacity to justify its decisions *as a body* to the public is quite low.

Certainly citizens are increasingly likely to *believe* that representative linkages are not working well. Nor, to judge by the American case, do they believe that legislative institutions are doing a good job of representing the public interest. Approval of Congress, for example, rarely ranges above 50 percent, and is typically in the 30–40 percent range (National Election Studies 2007). As Dalton (2004), Norris (1999), and others have argued, the developed democracies now contain a new group of "critical citizens," who tend to be educated and have post-material values and high democratic expectations. These citizens appear to be on the leading edge of political disengagement and distrust, and are more likely to view the gap between politicians, government, and citizens as wider than ever. Citizens' expectations are increasingly difficult to meet, it appears, the more complex and politicized the governing environment. In Dalton's view, "contemporary democracies do not suffer from a surfeit of interest articulation, but from a lack of institutions and processes that can aggregate and balance divergent interests into a coherent policy program that participants can accept" (2004: 205).

It seems, then, that the traditional and recognizable forms of democratic representation – elected officials convened in representative assemblies such as legislatures, parliaments, and councils – are no longer sufficient to carry out the functions of democratic representation, at least not as stand-alone institutions. Many of the problems are probably intrinsic to the *electoral* form of representative democracy under contemporary conditions, and include the following:

- Owing to the electoral context, representative institutions respond better to intense and well-organized special interests than to latent interests, unorganized interests, and public goods.
- Because representatives function within a context that combines public visibility and adversarial relations, they must weigh the strategic and symbolic impact of speech. Thus, representative institutions have limited capacities for deliberation, which requires a suspension of the strategic impact of communication in favor of persuasion and argument.
- Because of electoral cycles, representative institutions have limited capacity to develop and improve public policies over a long period of time.
- Because representatives must attend to vested interests, representative institutions are have limited capacities for innovation and experimentation.

The nature of the electoral system will affect the degree to which each of these limits holds. Indeed, this is what the CA was charged with investigating. Its recommended single transferable vote (STV; see page 000) electoral system might very well lead to improvements in the first three of these areas. However, even the best electoral institutions will remain limited by the electoral form of accountability – which, even when it serves accountability, produces a structural bias toward aggregative accountability at the expense of deliberative accountability. I hasten to add two points.

First, it is not the initial authorization, but the subsequent electoral form of accountability – the *serial* nature of elections – that produces these tendencies. Second, for key aspects of democratic government, there are no good alternatives to elected representation. The questions are, therefore: (a) How might we reform the electoral systems to provide for better representation? This was the mandate for the CA, but not the topic of this chapter. (b) How might we supplement the electoral form of representation with other forms of representation so as to produce a system in which institutions complement one another according to their strengths and weaknesses? This is the question I am addressing here.

Democratic deficits in the participation response

These observations are not new. What is new is that decision-makers have increasingly identified "democratic deficits" as an issue in all of the consolidated democracies. We have thus seen a number of initiatives aimed at increasing governability – initiatives which aim, varyingly, at more trust in government, more legitimacy, more efficiency, and less political gridlock. These initiatives often include increasing "citizen participation," "citizen involvement," and/or "citizen engagement" as ways of closing the gap between what citizens want and what government provides. It is surely interesting that the initiatives have come mostly from the administrative/policy arenas rather than from representative institutions – with the CA a notable exception.[3] Perhaps the administrative sources of these initiatives are to be expected: the first concern of elected representatives is to be re-elected – not to govern. Those who do govern – administrators – must square legislated goals with resource constraints, personnel, organizational structures, and then fit these with citizen expectations and, often, the resistance of organized interests.

So perhaps it is also not surprising that, as governance strategies, citizen "participation" and "engagement" tend *not* to be understood as *political* processes of representation and decision-making (the exceptions, perhaps, being democratic corporatism based on functional constituencies in Sweden, Norway, Austria, and Germany). In most democracies, "politics" has been understood as a legislative matter, with legislative results turned over to administrators to execute. Administrators typically understand "participation" as a strategy for gaining advice, coopting pressures, and improving services, in this way seeking to increase the legitimacy of their policies (Brown 2006). They are looking for citizen "engagement" and "involvement" – not citizen decision-making. There is,

---

[3] The 1989 Oregon Health Reform Plan is another exception.

no doubt, often much professionalism and little ill-will toward citizens. But the frameworks remain administrative rather than political, and citizen participation is viewed as a matter of advice-giving rather than empowered participation.

But because the new experiments *are* political, it is not surprising that the conceptions of "participation," "involvement," and "engagement" prove insufficient, so much so that we can now see a number of democratic deficits in what was thought to be the most democratic of activities. At the system level, expanding opportunities for participation can actually exacerbate deficits in democratic representation. Many kinds of new opportunities, for example, are based on self-selection, and therefore tend to favor those who are better educated and wealthier. On a system-wide level, more participation may increase the overrepresentation of those who are already well represented, generating the paradox that increasing citizen opportunities for participation may increase political inequality (Dalton, Cain and Scarrow 2003).

At the institutional level, unmediated participation tends to suffer from a number of defects. Because participants often self-select, the most intense interests and loudest voices often dominate, leading to under-representation of those who are less organized, less educated, and have fewer resources (Mansbridge 1980). Participatory venues can increase the neglect of public goods or increase the unjust distribution of their burdens by empowering local resistance by well-organized groups. Forms of participation that merely aggregate existing opinion (e.g. public submissions and hearings) contribute little to the deliberative formation of preferences and policy. And participation without power can lead to more disaffection, as citizens go through the exercise of engaging, only to have decisions taken elsewhere and for other reasons (Abelson and Eyles 2002: 8ff, 16; Irvin and Stansbury 2004: 58–60).

Citizen representatives

Owing in large part to the lens of participatory democracy, it has largely escaped notice that *with respect to most citizens* the functions of these participatory institutions are less *participatory* than they are *representative* (cf. Stephan 2004; Brown 2006). Most participatory institutions are, in fact, designed in such a way that some citizens represent others, either directly, or – more often – through claims to represent perspectives, considered opinions, goods, interests, and values of those who are not present in the process (Fishkin 1995; Hanley *et al.* 2001; Lenaghan 1999; Parkinson 2003; Smith and Wales 2000; Ward *et al.* 2003). Because most citizens do not participate through these institutions – subject, as they are, to the same constraints of scale and complexity as other institutions – we should be conceiving of them as *citizen representatives*.

The defining criterion of a "citizen representative body" is that members are *selected or self-selected, or authorized through initial election alone* – rather than functioning as professional elected representatives. In this way, members are freed, as it were, from the imperatives of the election cycle that produce representative deficits. At the same time, *precisely because of this freedom from electoral accountability*, the kinds of questions that apply to elected representative bodies are more urgent, especially if citizen representatives have influence or power, as was the case with the CA. Thus, it makes sense to apply criteria of democratic representation, looking for the functional equivalents of the representative functions of legislative bodies with respect to authorization, egalitarian inclusiveness, and accountability.

Authorization

Elected representatives and bodies benefit from the clear authorization of the electoral process. In contrast, the initial authorization of citizen representatives is often ambiguous. For most non-governmental (civil society) associations and forums, there are no authorization procedures beyond self-selection. Groups initially *claim* to represent (in the sense of "speak for") citizens or issues, and these claims are "authorized" only retrospectively, usually as a consequence of a representative claim attracting a following. Formal advisory processes are explicitly authorized, often with a representative mandate to include, for example, "community representation" or some other term of art. In part because such terms are vague, in practice authorization can be arbitrary.

In contrast, the CA was a body legislated into existence by an elected government. Authorization was explicit, coming in the form of enabling legislation that specified the manner in which CA members would be chosen, the task, and the timetable for completion. With respect to formal authorization, the CA is more comparable to citizen juries than to other kinds of citizen representatives.

It is another question as to whether the citizens of BC perceived the Legislative Assembly's formal authorization of the CA as representative authorization. In the CA case, the level of trust – a key indication of authorization – expressed by citizens far exceeded the level of trust they typically place in politicians and legislative bodies. Theoretically, trust in the CA might be based on (a) perceptions of convergent interests, and/or (b) descriptive similarities between the body and the citizenry (James, this volume). Survey findings presented in this volume (Cutler and Johnston,

58   MARK E. WARREN

Chapter 8) suggest that most citizens viewed the CA and its members as "ordinary citizens" who had the public interest in view in their deliberations and decision-making. Two mechanisms seem important to this result. First, the near random selection produced a large number of "ordinary citizens" with no apparent vested interests. And the screen against organized political interests and professional politicians assured that the body would not incorporate those with immediate stakes in the outcomes. While cases of designed democratic corporatism in Europe suggest that a screen against politicians and organized interests is not generally necessary for legitimacy, the case of electoral reform is distinct, since politicians and closely identified interests would be in a clear conflict of interest (Thompson, Chapter 1, this volume). The CA experience suggests that near-random selection performs at least as well as elections to authorize representatives, and in some ways better.

Egalitarian inclusiveness

If a representative body is "democratic," then it will include ways and means of representing all affected interests. One way of including affected interests is through descriptive representation – and this was the key mechanism of inclusion in the CA (Gibson 2002). The egalitarian inclusiveness of citizen representatives is often suspect, since most are constituted through self-selection, thus favoring the intensely interested and those with political resources – particularly education, but also time, experience, and income (Verba, Schlozman and Brady 1995). In the case of some public hearings, public submissions, and single-issue advocacy groups, self-selection combines with the natural exclusions that follow from the issue. In most cases, egalitarian inclusiveness is not even an aim of representatives: their interests are in other citizens with similar or convergent interests. This *aggregative* pattern of citizen representation achieves egalitarian inclusion only when the range of representatives in public domain is sufficient to include the interests of every citizen. In practice, these conditions are rarely if ever met.

But it is possible for citizen representative bodies to be constituted in such a way that they are egalitarian and inclusive of all affected interests, either through random selection or initial stratification. These techniques are used to constitute legal juries, citizen juries and deliberative polls. The CA used both: geography and sex were used in such a way that each riding was represented by a man and a woman. Other descriptive categories such as race and ethnicity, religion, income, education, and age were left to the process of random selection, though the Chair was empowered to add members of groups under-represented in the sample – a power he exercised in adding two Aboriginal members who had agreed to serve, but were not among the final 158 who were drawn at random.

Several features of the process introduced some bias. First, the voter rolls were used as the basis for random invitations to serve. Second, those who received letters had to respond affirmatively if they were interested in serving. Third, fluency in English was a requirement of service. These features no doubt produced the overrepresentation of people with more education, more income, and more time (e.g. retired people), and an under-representation of less educated, lower-income, younger, and recently arrived citizens, which in turn produced an under-representation of visible minorities. These likely biases were known and justified in advance: Gibson argued that they were necessary to produce a group of capable people sufficiently committed to the process (Gibson 2002: 12–13, cf. James, Chapter 5, this volume). The direct effects of income inequality, however, were mitigated with modest pay for service and reimbursement for expenses.

While the CA might have been more inclusive and egalitarian (see James, Chapter 5, this volume), when compared to two other alternatives it looks very inclusive indeed. Elected representation tends to produces bodies with highly biased demographic characteristics, while those forms of citizen representation that rely on self-selection magnify the biases of education, income, time, and ethnicity.

Accountability

Taken at face value, the democratic accountability of the CA appears to be problematic. On the one hand, the CA lacked the formal accountability mechanisms of re-election or removal from office. On the other hand, these forms of accountability would seem to be *more* important in the case of the CA than with other citizen bodies for two reasons. First, the CA was *involuntary* from the perspective of the citizens it represented. Thus, the market-like accountability mechanisms at work in the case of advocacy group representation – members "vote with their feet" by exiting if they feel they are misrepresented – could not function in this case. Citizens of BC could opt out of being represented by the CA only by moving from the province. Second, with the exception of legal juries, the CA was unique among citizen representative bodies in being *empowered* to set the agenda for electoral reform. To be sure, the CA's recommendation went to a referendum (and will do so again in 2009), allowing citizens to exercise a check over the CA's power. But the CA was empowered to set the agenda, which is a nice bit of power indeed. Under democratic expectations, when representation is involuntary and empowered (as with states), the normative requirements for democratic accountability increase – and this is what makes the lack of formal accountability mechanisms apparently troubling.

At the same time, what it means for a representative or representative institution to be "accountable" is multifaceted. It is a peculiar strength (or so I shall argue) of the CA model that it includes forms of democratic accountability that do not depend on election of representatives, and would be undermined by electoral accountability. To see this, we need look no farther than the conflicting features of accountability within elected legislatures, which will both identify the senses in which the CA was accountable, and identify the ways in which the CA model might complement electoral accountability.

Elected representatives are accountable not only to the constituents who elected them, but also to the public purposes of the legislative bodies in which they serve – a complexity that has been covered, inadequately, by the distinction between the delegate and trustee roles of representatives (Pitkin 1967; Mansbridge 2003). In addition, there is an accountability that attaches to the institutions themselves: people expect legislatures to do their work with effectiveness and fairness. They will use their votes for individual representatives against the institution if they perceive that it is not performing, or is performing in ways that are unfair or corrupt.

To develop these dimensions of accountability sufficiently to assess the CA, I shall combine a distinction borrowed from theories of deliberative democracy between the *aggregation* and *deliberation* of interests and values (e.g. Habermas 1994), with the observation that the *individual representatives* and the *legislative institution* each define distinct loci of accountability. Although not commonly discussed in theories of electoral democracy, individuals should not only be able to have their interests, values, and positions formulated and represented by members of representative bodies, but also formed into decisions by those same bodies, in a way that citizens can recognize the outputs as representing either their aggregated and negotiated interests and values, or a public will (Urbinati 2006). So for their part, legislative bodies may be accountable for *brokering agreements* among the interests represented by representatives, or for forming *public wills* through deliberation. From the point of view of process, the distinction between the accountability of representatives and the accountability of institutions is roughly parallel to a distinction now common in discussions of the European Union between "input legitimacy" based on democratic inputs and "output legitimacy" based on institutional performance, so we might also speak of "input accountability" through representatives, and "output" accountability of the institution. Combining these distinctions, we can speak of four kinds of accountability, two of which are attached to

CITIZEN REPRESENTATIVES

Table 2.1. *Forms of accountability*

	Aggregative	Deliberative
Member (input) accountability	(A1) Accountability for interest and value representation	(A2) Discursive accountability to constituents
Institutional (output) accountability	(A3) Accountability for decision-making (institutional capacity to deal with conflict and complexity)	(A4) Public accountability (institutional capacity to justify decisions)

individual representatives, and two of which attach to representative institutions, as summarized in Table 2.1.

Thus, (A1) *accountability for interest and value representation* identifies the relationship between the representative and her constituents' interests and values. In this role, the representative articulates her constituents' interests as she best understands them, and votes accordingly. (A2) *Discursive accountability to constituents* identifies the representative's role in representing positions and arguments both within legislatures, and before constituents. In this role, the representative engages in persuasion, serving as a pivot between the public arguments and positions of constituents, and the processes of argumentative persuasion within legislatures. (A3) *Accountability for decision-making* identifies the institutional responsibility for aggregating interests sufficiently to produce compromises and brokered agreements, based on inputs of constituents' interests and values as articulated by representatives. This responsibility depends on institutional capacities to not only to manage conflict, but also to manage complex decisions. (A4) *Public accountability* identifies an institutional responsibility as a public forum, for producing agreements that reflect considered public opinion refined through processes of debate. Ideally, all four modes of accountability are present and empowered in democratic institutions, varying, of course, by the nature of the issue, levels of interest definition, mobilization, polarization, and citizen interest and involvement.

So how does the CA measure up in each of these four modes of accountability?

(A1) Member accountability: accountability for interest and value representation Precisely because of the lack of constituency-based electoral accountability, we should expect accountability to the values and interests of defined constituencies to be minimal. But it was not absent:

although no *member* of the CA was subject to electoral recall or removal from office, the *product* of the CA was subject to the stricture that it had to be approved not just by a 60 percent majority, but also in 60 percent of the ridings, thus introducing an element of accountability to interests of geographically defined constituencies – evidenced, for example, in the emergence of "the North" as an interest group within the CA (see Pearse, Chapter 3, this volume). Still, the CA was designed in large part to sever these ties: not only were there no formal constituent accountability mechanisms, but ties to specific constituencies were weakened by the exclusion of organized interests and politicians. These exclusions together with the demographic inclusiveness of the Assembly, the internal deliberative structure, and the explicit and narrowly defined mandate from the Legislative Assembly, were all factors that limited members' accountability to specific constituencies, while focusing their attention on the CA and its task.

Member accountability for the representing the interests and values of constituents is best achieved by other means of representation. Electoral representation, for example, is responsive to constituencies with the power to elect or remove from office. And for issue-specific representation, civil society groups are likely to be superior, unconstrained as they are by mandates or timetables, and under no particular pressure to deliberate or otherwise compromise the full range of interests and values within society. At the same time, from a normative perspective we should not be too worried about low accountability to specific constituencies, in part because this kind of accountability often trades off against *public* accountability. If one of the aims of the CA design was to avoid the weaknesses of legislative bodies in this respect, then weak accountability to specific constituencies was both necessary and appropriate.

(A2) Member accountability: discursive accountability In the dimension of discursive accountability, the CA fares better. In contrast to representation that reflects the values and interests of specific constituencies, the CA structure provided incentives for members to develop and represent discursive arguments and positions. This particular representative role was not explicitly defined for members. But it was, as it were, "discovered" as members sought to make sense of their tasks and responsibilities (see Pearse, Chapter 3, this volume). During the first stage, members learned about electoral systems. There were no distinct accountability issues in this stage, simply because it was unclear to most members what the impacts of their potential decisions would be. In second stage, members engaged in public hearings in their ridings, and the CA office collected public submissions. During this stage, members were faced with the question of what, exactly, their representative roles required (Pearse, Chapter 3, this volume). Some simply saw their task as one of learning from others and then making informed decisions as individuals – much as would a professional public official who holds a "public trust" and acts as a trustee. Others saw their tasks in more complex, "political" ways: they actively organized public hearings and created, as it were, constituencies for electoral reform that they would later represent within Assembly deliberations. In such cases, representation was about discovering the common good through learning and deliberation. Finally – and perhaps most interesting – in the deliberation phase members were careful to create an atmosphere of deliberation. Most chose not to show their hand, presumably so they would not contribute to the formation of interest blocs within the Assembly. Importantly, the effect was to maintain a representative relationship between the CA and the public considered as a whole rather than as an aggregate of constituencies. The only apparent compromise with a partial constituency involved the rural areas of BC – "the North" – for whom the STV recommendation was altered to provide for closer geographic proximity of elected Members of the Legislative Assembly.

(A3) Institutional accountability: delivering the decision In what ways was the CA accountable as an *institution* responsible for delivering a specific outcome? From a legal perspective, this dimension of accountability is quite clear. The legislation that created the CA provided it with a specific performance mandate: to return to the people of BC a judgment about the suitability of the current electoral system, and, if necessary, a proposal for change. Had the CA not met this mandate, presumably its accountability to the legislature would have been breached. In this sense, the CA *as a body* was accountable to the Legislative Assembly for a specific performance, within a specific period of time. Behind this form of accountability, however, is the question of institutional capacity to deliver on a formal mandate. Of particular relevance to representative political institutions are their capacities to handle *conflict* and *complexity*, which are necessary conditions of accountability.

With respect to *conflict*, voluntary organizations tend to externalize conflict through exit. In contrast, involuntary organizations must develop ways and means of handling the conflict that cannot be externalized (Warren 2001: 96–109). The CA falls on the "involuntary" side of the spectrum, in the sense that although members chose to serve, they did not choose to be grouped with others who were chosen, and those others represented a broad range of interests and values in the province. For this reason, the CA developed rules of conflict management as its first agenda item, which included norms of civility and rules of discourse. No doubt possible and legitimate conflicts were dampened by these rules (Lang, Chapter 4, this volume). Nonetheless, the CA managed conflict sufficiently to produce a near-consensus decision on schedule.

With respect to complexity, the CA's mandate was not as complex as, say, most areas of health-care policy. But neither was it simple, as the design of electoral systems has aspects that are relatively technical. The fact that the CA was structured with a learning period was crucial to its ability to render a decision, and, indeed, the decision was a learned and sophisticated one. Most members transformed themselves from lay citizens with little knowledge of electoral systems into experts over a period of several months, a process assisted by the generous staffing of the CA office (Pearse, Chapter 3, this volume; Blais, Carty and Fournier, Chapter 6, this volume).

That the CA was designed to have high capacities to handle conflict and complexity was no doubt essential to the fact that it was able to deliver its product – a referendum item – on time and within budget, replete with reports and other materials to showcase the process and back up its reasoning. It is not clear that these capacities would translate into other issue areas: the CA benefited from the fact that few members had specific preferences about electoral reform prior to serving in the CA. No doubt matters would have been different with higher-profile, more volatile issues such as health care. At the same time, experiments with citizen juries and deliberative polling suggest that citizen representatives might be constituted in ways that may be successful in these kinds of arenas as well (Fishkin 1995; Smith and Wales 2000).

(A4) Institutional accountability: forming the public will Perhaps the highest threshold for accountability is "public" in nature: does the output of the representative body represent a formation of the public will? Was the CA able to *give a public account* of its reasoning and decisions? Did it seek to motivate the public by providing reasons and justifications?

From one perspective, the CA was, perhaps, not successful in forming a public will: by the time of the referendum, only slightly more than half of the BC electorate was aware of the CA and its work, leading to an important gap between the mini-public of the CA, and the public at large (Cutler and Johnston, Chapter 8; Ratner, Chapter 7, this volume). The last word is not yet in, however, as the Province of British Columbia will fund advocacy aimed at forming public opinion with respect to CA results in the period prior to the 2009 referendum.

From the perspective of institutional design, however, the CA seemed optimally structured for public accountability. Its mandate was to provide an assessment and proposal in the interests of "the people of BC," as was certainly appropriate for a fundamental issue of constitutional change. And the members sought to represent the justifications for the collective decision of the CA to the people of BC. The motivations, capacities, and incentives for public accountability were part of the CA design. With respect to motivations, two design factors were especially important: organized interests were screened out, while self-selection into the pool of potential CA members biased the Assembly toward public-spirited individuals (Warrea and Pearse, Introduction, this volume). These factors created a strong likelihood that members of the Assembly would understand themselves as accountable to the people of BC as a whole rather than to particular constituencies.

From the perspective of the CA's capacities for public accountability, broad inclusions of interests and values combined with a deliberative structure provided necessary material and opportunity for discerning the public interest. In addition, the CA sought several forms of public input, including public hearings and internet submissions. These circumstances meant that members of the CA had to create representative roles for themselves that would bridge, as it were, input from particular constituencies with the common good. But because of the lack of any particular constituency-based accountability mechanisms, the members were free to translate particular representations into a common position. Viewed in this way, the lack of formal, constituency-based accountability may be a condition of public accountability (see, e.g., Mansbridge 2004).

A further design factor provided a powerful incentive for the public orientation of the CA: the body did not have power over the *outcome*, but rather over the *agenda*. As a body, the CA naturally developed a strategic interest in their (close to consensus) recommendation. But because the CA did not have power over the outcome, its sole means of influence was to explain and justify its proposal to the public – that is, engage in discursive public will-formation. In this way, the design of the process introduced a relationship of accountability between the CA and the public, based on public argumentation and justification. This relationship between the mini-public of the CA and the BC public was not well supported in the period before the referendum. But it is precisely this relationship that the province will fund in the period before the 2009 referendum.

With respect to democratic accountability, then, the combination of initial constitution, deliberative structure and mission, produced a kind of citizen representative with weak accountability of members to individual constituents, but strong discursive accountability of members to the public, as well as strong institutional accountability for forming and delivering a publicly justifiable decision.

Assessing the Citizens' Assembly model within the ecology of representative institutions

The theoretical frame of *citizen representative*, I am arguing, highlights the novelty of the CA, which was designed at the outset as a new kind of *representative* institution focused on electoral reform, much as if it was a special single-issue legislature constituted by lay citizens. Considered as a representative institution, should it be put to other uses? This question is, in part, now answered: the CA model can carry out some kinds of democratic representation, and it may even carry these out better than other kinds of institutions. Yet because the CA model is a non-elected, purpose-built institution, it cannot cover all the representative requirements of a democratic system. But then neither can any other institution. So we should think about the CA as a complementary form of representation, best aimed at two kinds of problems: (1) those that are so intractable or so important that they require broad public deliberation and consensus; or (2) those that pose a clear conflict of interest for elected bodies, as is the case with electoral reform. This claim, however, depends on a more systematic comparison of the CA model to other representative venues, in terms of which we could identify its niche role in democratic systems.

While a full comparison is beyond the scope of this chapter, Table 2.2 is indicative of what a comparison might look like.

The table combines a set of structural and functional distinctions across the top, with the normative criteria of representation listed in the left-hand column. The theoretical claim is that the structural and functional distinctions across the top have an impact on the kind of representative functions a venue might serve within a democratic system. The cells represent the expectations, with a summary reason for the expectation.

The most obvious distinction is between bodies that are elected and regularized, and the bodies and venues that serve as citizen representatives. Within the class of citizen representatives, we can distinguish between formal and informal venues. *Formal* representatives are constituted by governments, and serve as complements to the formal political, administrative, and judicial systems. *Informal* representatives are non-government, including non-governmental organizations (NGOs), associations, and devices such as deliberative polls. The importance of this distinction is that, on average, formal venues will be more successful at integrating public interests and opinion into policy, just because they are designed for particular kinds of governmental purposes. Informal venues will be more sensitive to emerging issues and existing exclusions and injustices, just because they do not need to reflect government purposes.

Table 2.2. *Assessing the Citizens' Assembly model within the ecology of representative institution*

	Elected representative bodies	Forms of representation				
		Citizen representatives				
		Formal empowered	Formal advisory		Informal (non-governmental bodies)	
		Deliberative	Deliberative	Aggregative	Deliberative	Aggregative
Criteria of democratic representation	Elected legislatures, councils, boards	*Citizens' Assembly*, legal juries	Citizen juries, advisory councils, stakeholder meetings	Public hearings, public submissions, citizen surveys	Deliberative polling, deliberative forums	Single issue advocacy, interest group brokering
Authorization	**High** (voting)	**High** (explicit authorization procedures)	Mixed (explicit authorization; often vague directives for representation)	Low (no authorization procedures)	Mixed to Low (ambiguous or "market" authorization)	Low ("market-style" authorization)
Egalitarian inclusiveness	Mixed to Low (universal franchise limited by SMP majoritarianism and responsiveness to organized interests)	**High** (selection often random, subject to screens)	Mixed to Low (selection by elites and self-selection does not assure inclusiveness)	Mixed (low where self-selection produces exclusion, high for random sampling)	**High** (selection often random, subject to screens)	Low (self-selection produces exclusion)
Member accountability (interests)	Mixed (responsive to organized interests)	Low (externally-fixed agendas)	Mixed to Low (externally-fixed agendas)	**High** (low institutional threshold for voice)	Mixed (lay sensitivities limited by elite agendas)	**High** (low institutional threshold for voice)

Table 2.2. (*cont.*)

	Forms of representation					
			Citizen representatives			
	Elected representative bodies	Formal empowered	Formal advisory		Informal (non-governmental bodies)	
Criteria of democratic representation	Deliberative	Deliberative	Deliberative	Aggregative	Deliberative	Aggregative
	Elected legislatures, councils, boards	*Citizens' Assembly*, legal juries	Citizen juries, advisory councils, stakeholder meetings	Public hearings, public submissions, citizen surveys	Deliberative polling, deliberative forums	Single issue advocacy, interest group brokering
Member accountability (discursive)	Mixed (responsiveness to organized interest competes with public justifications)	**High** (deliberative influences dominate decision processes)	**High** (deliberative influences dominate decision processes)	Low (expressions of revealed preferences rather than reasons)	**High** (deliberative influences dominate process)	Mixed (advocacy stimulates public debate)
Institutional accountability (capacity for deliver decision)	**High** (specialized for conflict; handles complexity though internal divisions of labor)	**Mixed to High** (rules for interaction limit conflict; high capacity to deal with complexity though learning)	**Mixed to High** (rules for interaction limit conflict; high capacity to deal with complexity though learning)	Low (no mechanisms for deliberating conflicting positions; no context or incentives for learning)	**Mixed to High** (rules for interaction limit conflict; high capacity to deal with complexity though learning)	Low (conflict leads to exit; no context or incentives for learning or deliberation)
Institutional accountability (public will formation)	Mixed (deliberative structure limited by responsive to organized interests and electoral exigencies)	**High** (deliberative structure without organized interests)	**High** (deliberative structure)	Low (expression of segmented and partial preferences)	**High** (deliberative structures responsive to common goods)	Mixed (advocacy stimulates public debate)

In addition, we should distinguish between *empowered* and *non-empowered* venues. Empowered venues, such as legal juries and the CA, are more immediately consequential, and for this reason must be more carefully designed to ensure democratic authorization and inclusion. Venues that are not empowered – and this includes most citizen representative bodies and venues – are freer to reflect particular interests, as well as to engage in broader public deliberation and debate because they are less constrained by the constraints of agendas, timetables, and processes.

Finally, it is important to distinguish *deliberative* from *aggregative* venues. Aggregative venues such as public hearings and surveys collect existing preferences. Deliberative venues, such as juries and deliberative polls, form, inform, and solidify preferences, a condition for producing stable and legitimate collective decisions.

We can then ask about the representative capacities of each kind of venue, using the dimensions of accountability applied to the CA in the discussion above, and make some rough judgments as to what we might expect of each kind. The judgments in Table 2.2 are only indicative – their purpose is to suggest that we understand the CA as a potential part of the ecology of democratic institutions, and then judge its contributions to democratic representation in terms of its relative strengths and weakness. Nonetheless, by combining a number of expectations about representative functions into a single table, it is easy to see that the CA model ranks higher on most dimensions than other forms of representation, while ranking much lower in one dimension. The CA form is particularly weak in constituency accountability, which implies that it must be externally constituted by bodies that are inherently responsive to emerging issues – legislatures under pressure from civil society groups, for example. But importantly, once constituted, the CA form is likely to have representative strengths where legislatures, advisory groups, and civil society groups are weak – or so the expectations represented in Table 2.2 would suggest.

In sum, if the judgments in the Table 2.2 are credible, then we should see the CA as a uniquely powerful form of democratic representation. But we should also understand the CA model as a potential supplement to, rather than replacement for, other democratic institutions and practices within a broader ecology of democratic institutions and practices.

26

NOTES FOR A THEORY OF NONDEMOCRATIC REPRESENTATION

DAVID E. APTER

INTRODUCTION

These notes are preliminary to a theory of nondemocratic representation. Need for such a theory has been apparent for some time, particularly in relation to the processes of development, which is a different context from that in which we are accustomed to consider representative institutions and their functions. In my view, most (although not all) nondemocratic representation is better seen as "predemocratic," rather than as alternative or hostile to it. Such representation is also functionally varied, depending for its relevance on the stage of development and the prevailing type of political system. Indeed, different political systems stress forms of political

This essay was written under the auspices of the Politics of Modernization Project of the Institute of International Studies, University of California, Berkeley.

Notes for a Theory of Nondemocratic Representation   279

participation relevant to the immediate context of their social situations. Because a political type is a means to solve problems, each type of system has its advantages and disadvantages. None is permanent any more than the context of social life is permanent. Representation is a variable thing, and its forms and consequences are different in each type of political system. I offer these remarks to challenge the more commonly accepted view which evaluates all representation as it approximates our own Western experience or some ideal type of it.

The analysis begins with an effort to describe the changing character of social life by focusing on the special relation between government and society formed through some form of representation. Three main types of representation are emphasized: *popular,* as associated with "one-man, one-vote," and a conciliar form of decision-making; *interest,* as with special corporate groupings seeking special and parochial attention; and *functional,* as with technicians, planners, civil servants, and so on. Each type represents a moral claim, so to speak. Popular representation is based on the rights of *citizenship.*[1] Interest representation is based on some presumed social significance or contribution to society from a particular type of group, primarily *occupational*—for example, trade unions or business or professional organizations. Functional representation is based on presumed or recognized expertise useful to society, primarily *professional.*[2]

This framework implies some main lines for research: (a) a

[1] Although an elaborate numbers game can be played with representation, particularly the form known as electoral geometry, we incorporate in this notion two main types of popular representation, which may or may not involve electoral machinery. In the first, direct representation, citizenship becomes a shared condition or a common property of the members of a community with defined obligations and rights requiring direct participation on a Rousseauean standard. In the second, because of size, numbers, and complexity, direct democracy is impossible; citizens cannot participate directly in the decision-making process, and some "representative" must do the job. Representation in this sense requires a manageable elite speaking on behalf of a wider public. This form of popular representation is most common, and is our primary concern.

[2] Functional representation derives from the more technical aspects of social life, opening up special access to decision-making on the basis of a particular utility. Administrators and civil servants, governors and soldiers, specialists of various kinds in public works, such as irrigation, public health, and even religious or ideological matters, gain key access in proportion to the need for their skills by government. See Harold Wilensky, *Organizational Intelligence* (New York: Basic Books, 1967), pp. 94–129.

developmental social context imposing conditions within which representation occurs; (b) a set of political types, each of which emphasizes alternative modes of representation; (c) a competitive relation between each type of representation—popular, interest, and functional—in terms of a set of functions which we call the functions of representation; and (d) the functions themselves, which are *goal specification, institutional coherence,* and *central control.* (We assume that representation has these three functions as a significant minimum.) Hence two models emerge. The first, a general one, specifies the relation between society and government in terms of stratification and political systems-type variables. The second, a model of representation, is based on types of claim to access and functions of a representational elite. This representational model is an intervening variable in the general model.

Although the concepts employed can be applied to any concrete system, our concern here is to elaborate them in the special context of predemocratic, developmental polities. Illustrations of their use will be suggested in a series of short synoptic descriptions. These are intended to be suggestive of some possible future lines of application. Although these illustrations are purely descriptive and impressionistic, it is possible to operationalize the entire approach by identifying the main groupings of social actors (clustered in the present stratification categories) and determining empirically and over time their type of claim to representation (popular, interest, and functional), the "weight" of that claim, and the elite functions they perform (goal specification, central control, and institutional coherence).[3]

THE ROLE OF REPRESENTATION

As already indicated, these comments are designed to refer to predemocratic, rather than "anti-" democratic, systems. Special attention is warranted because the association of representation with democracy is so close that to speak of nondemocratic forms of representation seems somehow a travesty. Certainly there is an "incompleteness" about predemocratic representation, as if somehow it waits for "fulfillment." Our Western conception of government

[3] Empirical work of this kind on Argentina, Chile, and Peru is presently under way in collaboration with Torcuato di Tella under the auspices of the Politics of Modernization Project of the Institute of International Studies, Berkeley, California.

Notes for a Theory of Nondemocratic Representation   281

implies an integrated political system in which needs (motives), access (participation), and goals (purposes) are balanced through representatives popularly elected and brought together in a conciliar decision-making body.

But, predemocratic systems of government are not simply imperfect forms of democracy. They imply a different pattern of integration, perhaps a more coercive one, in which needs are more arbitrarily defined, access is restricted, and goal priorities are realized within a public context. Public and private tend to be the same. But, representation exists here too, as we shall see. Discussion of it, however, requires us to assess both the political form of government and the general underlying complexity and structural characteristics of society by identifying groups which demand government recognition in many ways: expressing needs, demanding access, and identifying goals, which governments may or may not acknowledge.

In general we can say that representation implies a permanent relation between a government and its society. The limits of authority each can impose on the other change, however. Because these limits are in some measure determined by "social capabilities," they are best evaluated in a context of development and modernization. Analysis of the evolving bases of social life leads to identification of the particular representational claims that form the tension between society and government common in all systems, which is ultimately manifested in a changing equilibrium between discipline and freedom as follows:

a. Concretely, in order to identify the group representational basis of society in a developmental context, I use certain stratification categories that seem to correspond to a particular developmental stage. These categories are pre-class, e.g., caste and ethnicity; class in the sense of the formation of occupationally based classes; class in the sense of the emergence of multibonded forms of class; and finally, postclass, e.g., the growth of specialized functional status groupings. Generalizing, we obtain a picture of the developmental process in which multiple and overlapping claims to representation result from a mixture of traditional social clusters and contemporary innovative ones introduced from industrialized systems.[4]

---

[4] Interesting combinations of roles result, which affect permissible behavior, such as a Latin American economist (functional status membership)

282   DAVID E. APTER

b. Analytically, the relationship between discipline and freedom provides a more directly political concern. It makes a difference if society is the independent variable and government is dependent, or if government is the independent variable and society is dependent. In the first instance, the claims of the society become the boundaries within which a government needs to act; while in the second, society is to be molded and changed by governmental decision. To handle this set of political problems we have developed four types of political systems: two in which government is the independent variable, *mobilization systems* and *bureaucratic systems;* and two in which society is the independent variable, *theocratic* and *reconciliation systems.* None of these systems needs to be "democratic" in the sense of Western representative government, which is excluded from this discussion.[5]

It should be clear from the discussion so far that the representational variables that link stratification to political system are central for this analysis. We are able to treat the relations between society and government in terms of those elite formations that compete for priority performance of three main functions: *goal specification, central control,* and *institutional coherence.* The general proposition emerges that, where society is the dependent variable and government the independent one, these three functions are more likely to be performed by government-sponsored elite formations, such as party leaders in a single-party system. In contrast, where society is the independent variable, competition between private and public bodies for the performance of these functions is likely. In both cases, however, the ability of particular groups to take a priority position vis-à-vis these functions will be seen to depend upon the stage of development in terms of the prevailing group structure. How these elite functions are distributed determines the participant basis of the society. Today, when these functions are seen in the context of modernization and development, we describe the result as a "participation explosion." This "explosion" includes greater access to roles in the modernized sectors of society as well as the spread of

---

living in an upper middle-class community (multibonded class) descended from an aristocratic family of landowners (caste origin changed into occupational class). Such a role is likely to be linked with planners and economists from the United Nations and other international bodies, yet it is associated in a reasonably comfortable manner with all other social groups in the system.

[5] For a more detailed discussion of these types, see my *The Politics of Modernization* (Chicago: The University of Chicago Press, 1965).

Notes for a Theory of Nondemocratic Representation

such roles in the society itself. Hence the wheel comes full circle. Greater proliferation in the modernized role sector means more modernization. This, in turn, changes the pattern of prevailing needs in the system.

THE DEVELOPMENT PROCESS AND
THE GENESIS OF NEEDS

So far we have referred to the concept of *need* derivatively in terms of modernization and made visible in the form of political demands. It is obvious that needs in traditional societies will differ in many important respects from those in industrial societies. During modernization, however, old needs will continue long after new ones appear. Need seen in developmental terms becomes progressively more complex. It has two aspects: concrete demands and the mechanisms by which these demands are represented. The first is a series of events of a day-to-day sort. The second is a set of institutional arrangements. This latter aspect concerns us at the moment.

Representative institutions are based on claims to representation by interest, functional utility, or equality of right. They derive their complexity from the overlapping qualities of traditionalism, modernism, and industrialism.[6] We can describe the systemic aspects of development in terms of the continuum shown in Figure 1.[7]

Each general stage of development corresponds to a particular cluster of defined needs arising from social displacement and the formation of new tasks and objectives in the society, in combination with an overlay of "obsolete" ones. The result is cumulative and

[6] The contrast between modernizing and industrializing in social terms is that modernization is a process in which roles appropriate to (integrated with) an industrial society are established in the absence of an industrial infrastructure. Industrialization, on the other hand, means that the economy has passed beyond the stage where resources are used directly to produce technically simple products for export or direct consumption and has reached a stage of complex application of resources and technology—all within "a pattern of inter-sectoral flows involving capital and intermediate products." See R. H. Green's review of Szereszewski's "Structural Changes in the Economy of Ghana, 1891–1911," *The Journal of Modern African Studies,* 4: 1 (May 1966), 126.

[7] The continuum is a common one. It is often used in comparing modernizing countries. There are some special problems here, however. If we set the continuum on an axis, we find that, while traditionalism can give way to modernization, it is a contradiction in terms to say that modernization gives way to industrialization. The point is that modernization does not end in industrialization but is, rather, continuously defined by it.

determines which roles are appropriate. However, a set appropriate to one developmental stage is never completely abandoned. It continues to remain significant in the next stage—sometimes serving a useful purpose and sometimes producing negative consequences. More important, the combination of need with role creates an integrative problem of the greatest importance, both in terms of the stratification system as well as effective decision-making. If the institutional arrangements for linking them are seen in the particular combination of representational claims prevailing in the society in question, then the opportunities these provide for competitive elites to perform elite functions become a central empirical concern, be-

	Traditionalism	Modernization	Industrialization
	interest	interest	interest
Claims to Representation	function	function	function
	right	right	right

FIGURE I: *Developmental Continuum and Representation*

cause such competition creates information for government and, more generally, results in participation in decision-making precisely in the most sensitive areas of developmental change—for example, the alteration in the hierarchy of power and prestige in a system. We can now turn from the concept of need to the analysis of stratification.

THE STRATIFICATION CATEGORIES

Each stage of development has been described in terms of social mobility. The most limited pre-class case is caste (or caste-like), in which portions of a population are separated into distinct and separate groupings (whether religious, ethnic, or racial). Boundaries here emphasize primordial attachments or an exclusivism which goes beyond ordinary prejudice.[8]

[8] Such exclusivism extends this concept well beyond its ordinary usage in India to include ethnic and all other exclusivist boundaries difficult to penetrate except through kinship. Hence intratribal relationships in Africa, even in the same contemporary political framework, can be regarded as a form of

Notes for a Theory of Nondemocratic Representation 285

More complex stages of development enlarge *class* access. Mobility is greater than with caste but still clearly bounded (as in a Marxian sense). It includes a subjective awareness of membership in a semipermeable group, the life chances of whose members are similar and primarily determined by occupation. This notion (similar also to the one held by Weber) makes class dependent on the relation to the means of production. Much less restrictive than caste, it is not "primordial" in identification, although it tends to transform its class interests into general values for a whole society. Its boundaries are fixed when opportunities for occupational mobility are limited. With this type of class one can also speak of the formation of class "consciousness." Demands for class representation here include seeking redress for grievances arising from limited access to mobility. We refer to this as class *A*.

At a more advanced stage of development, class is a more multibonded affair and attributes of membership derive from many factors: religion, occupation, income, residence, family background, style of leisure, and so on. Class in this more Marshallian sense, which we refer to as type *B*, puts forward claims which, also based on interests, *transform issues of value into negotiable interests.* The result is opposite to class type *A*. It breaks up rather than creates solidarity.[9]

Finally, we have postclass status differentiation based on types of status clusters, particularly those associated with industrial skills and embodying a degree of professionality. These create claims for functional representation and include private as well as public bureaucratic status groups and technocratic groups. The latter are specially characteristic of highly industrialized countries.

We can restate the argument so far by combining the developmental and stratification variables in the structural model shown in Figure 2.

During industrialization the multibonded class type (class *B*) comes to predominate, as do the new types of status elites based on a functional role in industrialization or its related activities. These

---

caste relationship as the term is employed here. Caste may, of course, vary independently of hierarchy. See Clifford Geertz, "The Integrative Revolution," *Old Societies and New States* (New York: The Free Press of Glencoe, 1963) for a discussion of "primordial" attachments.

[9] See T. H. Marshall, *Class, Citizenship, and Social Development* (New York: Doubleday, 1964), pp. 138–143. See also S. Ossowski, *Class Structure in the Social Consciousness* (London: Routledge & Kegan Paul, 1963), Part 2.

groups form an organizational elite. Using highly germane functional criteria (education, training, professional skill), such groups represent an intellectual "class" in the limited sense that they create information and knowledge which becomes the basis for innovation within industrial societies. Innovating status groups are found not only in industrialized societies, where they occupy central power and prestige roles, but also, more derivatively, in late-stage modernizing societies. Indeed, such groups are part of the modernizing process linked, too, to their counterparts in industrial systems.

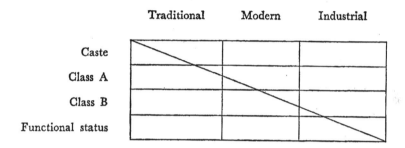

FIGURE 2: *Development Sequence*

Hence, while we speak of development as a process along a continuum from traditionalism to industrialization (from left to right), in practice modernization is a process which moves from right to left—that is, from roles originating in an industrial society, which we recreated in a nonindustrial setting. The consequence of this "reverse" overlapping of roles leads to the "embourgeoisement" hypothesis.

THE "EMBOURGEOISEMENT" HYPOTHESIS

If this analysis is correct, this reverse formation of roles (reverse in a historical sense) describes both a process and a tendency, which at the most general level can be called the "production of pluralism"—that is, the proliferation of roles and role sets organized around primarily instrumental ends. Class *B* and status relations are thus common even in early stages of modernization. This has the effect of converting conflicts over values into conflicts over interests. It allows us to suggest that the behavioral consequence of the growth of functional representation is the instrumentalization of need, which results in preferences for immediate gains rather than postponed gratifications. This consequence produces a predicament in nondemocratic systems precisely because, in varying degrees, they operate on the basis of a higher component of "postponed" satisfactions than do representative democratic systems. Modernization, then, produces "embourgeoisement," which in turn creates a plurality of instrumental ends, located unevenly in the stratification system and creating a tug-of-war among popular, interest, and functional claims.

This leads to a central proposition underlying the present analysis. We have already suggested that the greater the degree of modernization, the more the modernized roles in the society gain predominance, proliferate, and expand. These roles are predominantly instrumentalist in consequence. In the absence of an industrial infrastructure, however, such roles are not integrated around some central allocating focus; hence they create a severe "management" problem for government. The reason follows from the explanation suggested above: while representation on the basis of modernized roles may take the form of demands for popular representation, remnants of traditional roles may outnumber them. Popular representation then leads to a struggle for power. Those leading demands for a genuine popular representational system are the traditionals or near-traditionals, while the modernized section supports a doctrine of the "weightier part." More often, "populism" is the result, with popular participation channeled into purely formal conciliar bodies lacking functional substance, as in most "single-party" systems. Claims may be made on the basis of interest groups formed in the modern sector. Also functional claims may arise. Whatever the form of representational need, however, the proliferation of modernized roles creates such ambiguity, coalitional possibilities, and competition between principles of representation by various elites that not only does the management problem become great but also the possibilities both of conflict and of stagnation tend to grow. The greater the problem of such role conflict, the likelier is a drastic nondemocratic political solution. *Hence, the greater the degree of modernization, the greater the possibility of multiple claims to representation, and the greater the possibility of restrictive and authoritarian political solutions.* We can explore this proposition a bit more fully.

REPRESENTATION

In the period of traditionalism (despite the variation in political types), the relations between systems were both horizontal and vertical caste, or caste-like (ethnic), involving a high degree of exclusiveness. In Africa, Europeans were virtually a caste group at first (cultural, racial, and religious primacy), imposed vertically on hitherto horizontally related ethnic caste groups (tribes). Subsequently, in most territories, the Europeans became a class group. In Latin America, vertical caste-caste relationships tended to harden in terms of Spaniards and Indians. In the African case, the dominant caste-status group was expatriate; in Latin America, it was first Spanish, then creole, and eventually aristocratic and nationalistic. The typical form it took in the latter case was the patron-client relationship to sustain rural power. (Conflicts over federal or unitarian rule commonly erupted with this relationship.) Methods of cutting across such exclusiveness could also be found. Empire was one practical way whereby a dominant ethnic group could create political links and, by imposing hegemony, change caste into status —slave, warrior, and so on. Perhaps the most common links, which in varying degrees reflected traditional social organization, were based on kinship.[10]

In the early stage of the transition from traditionalism to modernization these caste-class or caste-status relations change. Caste tends to remain primarily in rural areas (especially in the form of patron-client relations, as with the *haciendados* and *campesinos* in Peru or Chile), while in urban areas a "middle class" of the *A* type emerges, sandwiched between the caste or caste-like status groups. (Such a middle class also represents the commercial and mercantile development characteristic of modernization.)

This second-stage phenomenon shows similar characteristics in many parts of the world. In Africa it included occupational groups, such as clerks, teachers, and others related particularly to commercial life. At this point political factions representing class interests arise. Caste and status groups may also form into factions with restrictive but primordial ideologies of primitive nationalism. (In Africa the former were usually concerned with widening the possibilities of representation in local and, more particularly, municipal councils.)

[10] Tribal or ethnic-ethnic forms of caste, as in precontact Africa, can be described as horizontal linkages. Caste in terms of political and culturally defined groups can be described as a form of vertical linkage.

Notes for a Theory of Nondemocratic Representation 289

At a still more advanced stage of development, status groups may survive as a sector of an aristocratic class. The most rapidly growing group is a middle class of the multibonded type, lacking class consciousness, but aware of the self-rewarding characteristics of modernization, and very much preoccupied with social mobility.[11] During the transition to industrialization, this multibonded class begins to draw in both upper and lower class groups of the *A* type (as when *campesinos* move toward and into *barriadas* to become lower-middle-class groups).[12] Toward the end of the modernization period the *A* type class disappears. Modernization thus favors a class structure similar to urban middle-class life in industrial societies, the characteristics of which are increasingly accessible to all. In addition, because modernization today takes place through links with highly industrialized societies, the transposition of key roles creates salient points for the spread of "middle-classness." Hence modernization brings about the "embourgeoisement" of developing societies.

This "embourgeoisement" accounts for the fact that even under conditions of high modernization with extreme inequality, as in Latin America, radical working class activity of the class *A* variety is slight. Even peasant movements succumb to the lure of the cities. The multibonded notion of class does not lead to polarization of groups into ideological extremes showing ideological propensities. Instead, issues of values are translated into issues of interest. Issues of interest result in demands for representation on the basis of corporate groupings, including well-entrenched interest groups which can function best within the context of the formal pattern of "one-man, one-vote" while using special advantages to rig elections and sustain group representation. True, frustrations of some of the middle class of the type *B* variety, especially the intellectuals, may take the form of a radicalization, especially among youth or university students; but it is the middle class which shows these radical

---

[11] This is essentially what has already happened in Latin America. The broad public remained a residual caste (for example, Indians in Peru) or a peasant class. In Africa, on the other hand, in few areas has an aristocracy emerged. The old caste (ethnic) groupings have been rendered increasingly obsolete. No status elite has emerged aristocratic in quality, but rather a new type of elite, based on universalistic criteria: civil servant, technocrat, i.e., professional, trained abroad, but with strong middle-class associations.

[12] The aristocratic class becomes obsolete, some of its members becoming members of the technocratic elite, others gradually becoming submerged in the elite section of the middle class.

offshoots, not the working class.[13] Indeed, when a country reaches the final stage of advanced industrialization, it is characterized by such a proliferation of multibonded class roles that it is difficult to speak about class at all; and it is preferable to refer to interest groups and competing (popular and functional) status roles.

The point is that if one sees development in structural terms, one can define a functional pattern of increasing need differentiation. The "embourgeoisement" phenomenon changes the demand for access from collective caste or class claims to personal status advantages by means of multiple organizational groupings. Thus conditions are created for competitive elites, which cater to increasingly fractionalized interests.

As suggested earlier, each stratification category—caste, class A, class B, and functional status—indicates a type of need and demand. We have emphasized that these needs and demands will overlap and reinforce each other, just as the different stratification groups themselves will overlap. Hence the "symposium of needs" and the coalitional linkages possible in the society, which become more complex and differentiated as a society moves from a more traditional to a more industrial footing, create the "pluralistic" problem for government. The key question about representation with nondemocratic governments is how they will confront and manage this problem.

TYPES OF POLITICAL SYSTEMS
AND THE FORMS OF ACCESS

Public need has been discussed in terms of developmental patterns of stratification. Before going on to a discussion of representation itself, we must first examine the problem of *access*. Access is a function of the political system. The political system as used here is formed as the result of a relation between the norms of a society and the prevailing patterns of authority. On the first axis, norms may be expressed symbolically in ideological or religious terms, in ethical precepts, or in terms of concrete goals of society.

---

[13] Some of the late-stage countries in Latin America have more in common with the highest stage of industrialized countries than with early-stage industrializing ones, with the exception that many of the former tend to have the atmosphere of industrial societies during depression. Of primary concern in both is distribution in the face of frustrated production.

Notes for a Theory of Nondemocratic Representation 291

The most effective political systems combine in a linked system both intermediate and ultimate ends with powerful motivational results, such as Calvinism in the seventeenth and eighteenth centuries or socialism in modern China. By "authority," the second axis of the relation defining a political system, we refer to the degree of accountability of leaders to those led. *In theory, perfect accountability exists where there is perfect representation*. The two sets of variables define four possible political types, each involving different types of access. Systems emphasizing ethical (consummatory) values and hierarchical authority result in "mobilization" systems. Those emphasizing concrete (instrumental) values and pyramidal authority are "reconciliation" systems. Systems with instrumental values and hierarchical authority can be called "bureaucratic" systems. Those with consummatory values and pyramidal authority can be called "theocratic" systems. We can diagram these as shown in Figure 3.

Concrete applications of each type are:

1. *Mobilization systems*, such as Communist China, have a universalizing political ideology in which issues of interest are concerted into issues of value. A command system of control comes closest to the pure type.[14]

2. *Reconciliation systems* are not necessarily democratic, although they are representative. Examples include democratic countries, as we know them, as well as "single-party" states, such as Senegal and some socialist countries, such as Yugoslavia. Consummatory values exist; but they are essentially privatized, inhering in the individual. Public behavior is seen in instrumental ends.[15]

---

[14] Mobilization systems do not need to be of the "left." They may be of any political persuasion. Peron's Argentina began with an effort to create a mobilization system combining both "left" and "right" characteristics. It failed, especially in the second half of its tenure. Guinea, Ghana, and Mali attempted to establish mobilization systems around a universalized political ethic (African socialism); but they had limited developmental capacities. Characteristics include a charismatic or prophetic leader, looking outward and employing a proselytizing ideology. The main problem, as Weber first pointed out in terms of charismatic authority, is the ritualization of leadership and decline in belief leading to self-interest rather than community interest, which proves inimical to the latter.

[15] The problem is that the instrumental ends are in danger of becoming completely separated from consummatory ones so that the latter are randomized. The resulting conflicts strain the legal framework or mechanism of bargaining by affecting the sanctity of their rules. A high degree of self-restraint

292   DAVID E. APTER

3. *Bureaucratic systems* tend to result from a change from one of the other systems. For example, the military subtype of the bureaucratic system would be of a "Kemalist" or possibly "Nasserist"

Authority

		Hierarchical	Pyramidal
Consummatory Values		Mobilization Systems	Theocratic Systems
Instrumental Values		Bureaucratic Systems	Reconciliation Systems

Norms

FIGURE 3: *Political System-Types*

type in which the main problem would be the accessibility of the elite. Here the danger of institutional formalism would arise in the fashion described by Crozier. The advantage of this type of system is that it sustains specialized instruments of political control in order to maintain integration. Examples include Egypt, Argentina, and post-Nkrumah Ghana. Subtypes other than the military form are also common.[16]

4. *Theocratic systems* were seen classically in feudalism, when, by virtue of the local pattern of government based on proprietary and memorial rights as well as local and reciprocal allegiances, they were held together through lines of unstable kinship. The whole system was infused by devotional extremism and a religious ideology. The problem was that the system's stability depended heavily on ideological or religious unity; this dependence contradicted the realities of local power with consequent conflicts over the proper roles of church and state. However, more stable theocracies have existed, as in the small New England religious communities.[17]

---

in behavior is required. The emphasis on instrumental ends tends to erode this self-restraint, and a loss of generalized meaning ensues.

[16] One we have called the "neo-mercantilist" subtype, with civilian bureaucratic control; the other a modernizing autocracy, which (like Afghanistan, Thailand, or Morocco) employs monarchical leadership and components of a military, party, or army bureaucracy for political rule.

[17] To reject the publicly defined consummatory norms would normally

Notes for a Theory of Nondemocratic Representation

It should be pointed out that these types of political systems are not real or concrete in the sense of a membership group; but instead, they must be seen as analytical and applied as ideal types (although they are not ideal types in the Weberian sense). More important, each system tends to give priority access to different kinds of claims to representation.[18] Mobilization systems, although as suggested earlier they may be populist in character, tend to favor functional claims to representation. Such functional claims, however, may not be restricted to purely development functions, but may also include catering to party organization. Bureaucratic systems will tend to favor claims to representation based on interest and regulate these according to recognized and institutionalized standards. Theocratic systems (and here we have in mind only historical, not contemporary, cases) tended to favor popular claims to representation in the context of a widespread religious reform or messianic movement, yet allowed scope for interest claims by means of which the more instrumental qualities of social life were realized. In reconciliation systems all three claims to representation—popular, interest, and functional—tend to compete with industrial subtypes showing considerable conflict between the first and third. We can diagram these propositions as shown in Figure 4.

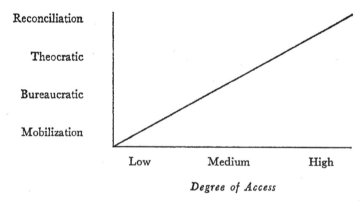

FIGURE 4: *Representational Access by System-Type*

---

mean expulsion from the community, or constitute grounds for terminating any meaningful participation. Control in the system is in the hands of those claiming a special quality of religious or devotional inspiration.

[18] It must be pointed out that the variable of access and type of claim is a function not merely of the type of political system which prevails but also

SOME PROPOSITIONS

1. Mobilization systems respond to pluralism and "embourgeoisement" by restructuring society along political lines in which popular representation becomes a symbolic gesture of unity; interest group representation is made public; and functional representation is bureaucratized.

2. Reconciliation systems respond to pluralism and "embourgeoisement" by oligarchical manipulations, corruption, and the use of economic advantage to restrict popular representation and expand interest group representation with subordinate functional representation.

3. Theocratic systems respond to pluralism and "embourgeoisement," ensuring a good fit between consummatory religious values and popular belief, by allowing popular representation, interest representation, and functional representation to occur as long as none threatens the sanctity of the religious values.

4. Bureaucratic systems respond to pluralism and "embourgeoisement" by manipulating interest group representation and functional representation and restricting popular representation.

To translate these propositions into more operational terms would require ranking the type of claim and the degree of significance within that claim of various concrete groupings in the system. Hence we could rank representative groupings from the various sectors of the stratification system in terms of their significant access on the basis of right, function, and interest. A number of interesting hypotheses would emerge almost immediately. For example, in the case of Argentina it is possible to show over time how various groups, such as landowners or trade unionists, shifted from popular representational significance to interest representational significance as the system of government changed from one type to another, when the bureaucratic government of Peron changed, eventually becoming a reconciliation system under Frondizi. Hence differential

---

of the degree of development. Hence early-stage reconciliation systems may show some popular representation, but this tends to be limited to "citizens" who represent only a small part of a total population, excluding slaves and other categories of "noncitizens" from participation, as in the Greek city-states.

access on the basis of claims, although it may occur for a variety of reasons, needs to be seen in the context of changing patterns of stratification on the one hand and alternative model types of government on the other. As we have already suggested, both "systems" are linked by representation.

The result is a sequence of differentiation reflecting the proliferation of need and the instrumentalization of ends embodied in the development process as it moves from a state of traditionalism to industrialism. Each stage of the process presents a problem for each type of government; namely, its response, by virtue of its own "systems-properties," to the problem of managing and controlling pluralism and "embourgeoisement." To summarize, the variables can be arrayed in diagrammatic form as shown in Figure 5.

Stage of Development	Stratification Relationships	Nondemocratic Political System-Types			
		Theo-cratic	Bureau-cratic	Mobili-zation	Reconcil-iation
Industrial	Class B Functional Status Residual Class A	Representational Claims (popular, interest, and functional)			
Modern	Class A Class B Residual caste	Representational Claims			
Traditional	Caste Ethnic	Representational Claims			

FIGURE 5: *The Developmental Typology as a General Model and Representational Claims*

FUNCTIONS OF ELITE REPRESENTATION AND THE GENERAL MODEL

So far, we have concentrated on the evolving relations between changes in stratification resulting from development and government according to system-type. These have been linked by representational access on the basis of access claims. The precise nature of these claims and the rights and proprieties they imply form an important part of the normative dimension of politics. Moreover, they define what kind of information government should have at its disposal by recognizing the legitimacy of the claims implied. Much political struggle has been precisely over the degree of access each type of representation can be allowed in a political system.

However, this analysis says nothing about the various types of participation in decision-making by virtue of these claims. For this we must turn to the analysis of elites and the competition among them. Elites, as used here, constitute a set of variables intervening between society and government, which have their own significant subsystem properties. Representational elites are those with special access to power and prestige by virtue of the wider grouping they represent in society or the functional significance of the roles they perform for some object of government.[19]

We can now define the functions themselves:

1. *Central control:* the ordered maintenance of discipline in a political system on a day-to-day basis.

2. *Goal specification:* the identification and priority ranking of policies; hence, a sharing in policy formulation on the basis of a longer term.

3. *Institutional coherence:* the continuous review, reformulation, and adaptation of the fit between boundaries of subsystems, including both the regulation of overlapping jurisdictions and ideological adjustment.

With such a formulation it is possible to determine in each case whether the concrete organizational elites are specialized vis-à-vis

[19] By organizational elites we include a wide variety of roles, including administrators, chiefs, army officers, civil servants, priests, businessmen, etc., behind which stand particular organizational groupings, administrative bodies, clans or castes, armies, bureaucracies, churches, and industrial enterprises. How elite functions are distributed is the key not only to nondemocratic representation; it is in conflicts over which groups shall monopolize these functions that the case of nondemocratic policies can be isolated. In bureaucratic systems (with government the independent variable) priority is given to functional elites relating to discipline and administration, i.e., armies and civil servants. In mobilization systems (where government is the independent variable) popular representation cannot be expected to be restricted only within a single-party framework (in which party serves to distribute the elite functions and allocate access at the request of government); it is also nonfunctional. In theocratic systems (where society is the independent variable) popular representation needs to be managed by religiously organized functional elites, who thereby restrict and shape government policy.

Notes for a Theory of Nondemocratic Representation 297

these functions or whether they are engaged in a constant conflict to extend their degree of access.[20]

By combining these categories with those already employed we obtain the diagram in Figure 6.

. Just as it was possible to operationalize the access claim of various groups in terms of their claim to representation, so it is possible to evaluate the significance of the elite in terms of its degree of access in decision-making by functional significance. Particular elites, such as landowners, members of government, civil servants, businessmen and merchants, trade union officials, and the like, can be seen in the context of their access to decision-making by means of their ability to perform functions of central control, goal specification, and institutional coherence. For example, it is quite possible for businessmen in the United States, with claims to access based on interests, to take part in goal specification and institutional coherence to a very high degree. Their degree of access, however, will be limited by competing claims based on popular and functional claims from other elite representatives of the system. Since the United States is a democratic subtype of a reconciliation system, the general pattern of competition is built into the political system and quite acceptable. In a quite different situation, as in a mobilization system such as Guinea's, not only would the claim to representation from the same group (whether public or private) be far less acceptable; but even if it were accepted, the group's share in functional access to decision-making would still be smaller than it would be in a democratic reconciliation system.

Assuming we could find numerical values for these rankings, what would we be able to identify as significant but derived theories from the data? One answer is that we should be able to account for many specific structural relations within society and between society and government. Moreover, since this is a predominantly structural model, we should be able to determine the major sources and gains and losses of information in a system. This has far-reaching theoretical significance, because the general efficiency of a type of political system can be related to various levels of development. If the

---

In reconciliation systems, the manipulation of popular, interest, and functional elites is a basis of political bargaining and negotiation.

[20] In the first instance, the claim to legitimate access is likely to be on the basis of functional expertise. In the latter instance, functional expertise and representation by virtue of public participation are likely to be employed.

Stage of Development	Types of Stratification and "Embourgeoisement"	Types of Political Systems											
		Theocratic			Reconciliation			Bureaucratic			Mobilization		
		Functions of Elite			Functions of Elite			Functions of Elite			Functions of Elite		
		C.C.	G.S.	I.C.	C.C.	G.S.	I.C.	C.C.	G.S.	I.C.	C.C.	G.S.	I.C.
Industrializing	Class B Functional Status Residual Class A				▨	▨	▨				▨	▨	▨
Modernizing	Class A Class B Residual Caste				▨	▨	▨				▨	▨	▨
Traditional	Caste Ethnic	▨	▨	▨	▨	▨	▨	▨	▨	▨	▨	▨	▨

FIGURE 6: *The General Structural Model and Representational Functions*

(Shaded boxes refer to illustrative cases discussed previously.)

Notes for a Theory of Nondemocratic Representation

theory is correct, we should be able to make some predictions about the capacity of different political systems to handle integrative and developmental tasks at different stages of development—a useful object in its own right, which also sets the stage for further studies concentrating on behavior within the structural context.

We can now review the dimensions of this model:

1. The traditional-industrializing continuum is a statement of the growth in complexity of social need leading to demands.

2. The differentiation in stratification indicates the group basis of competitive claims to access—popular, interest, and functional—which arise from social need.

3. The degree of hierarchy in a system indicates the differential pattern of access which government will allow in terms of the functions of the elite.

4. The degree to which ends are consummatory and nonempirical, or instrumental and empirical, will determine the quality of political response.[21]

We can now restate the central proposition: *The greater the degree of hierarchy, the narrower the participation in central control, goal specification, and institutional coherence.* To which we can add *"the lower will be the supply of information available to government."* In other words, we use the functions of the organizational elite to indicate how much information the government is able to obtain. This leads to another proposition: *Where the amount of information available to government is small, coercion will be applied in order to maintain the balance between government and society. Coercion is a substitute for uncertainty.*[22]

Coercion, which we define as the application of violence or the threat of violence by the state, in turn causes a loss of information. It does so by using the organization elites as a coordinating and punitive arm of government. Hence the following proposition: The more advanced the system in developmental terms and the greater the degree of hierarchy, the more the organizational elites will be used to *control* the sectors of society. The greater the degree of

---

[21] These four propositions suggest a relation in which empirical patterns emerge from the analysis of real or concrete units through developmental-time and between types of systems. It is thus possible to use them for heuristic comparative purposes.

[22] On the variables of coercion and information, see the discussion in *The Politics of Modernization,* p. 40.

development, but the less the degree of hierarchy, the more the organizational elites will be used to *coordinate* the sectors of society. The first implies coercion through the elites. The second implies a sharing in power through the application of information.

The main points should now be clear. When representation is viewed as the link between social need and government decision-making, it defines the relation of public need to access in government. The pattern of representation will vary with system-type, in terms of both participation and function.[23]

In mobilization systems, where government is the independent variable and society the dependent variable, representation is therefore a control device "representing" government to society through the organizational elites. Minimum information and maximum coercion are the results. In a reconciliation system, where society is the independent variable and government dependent, the organizational elites share in power, provide information to government, and help coordinate society through participation in decision-making. Information is at a maximum, coercion at a minimum. In both cases the intervening variable is representation. Thus, by determining how well social need combines with political effectiveness, representation is the most sensitive general indicator of structural balance in a system.

THE REPRESENTATIONAL MODEL

We have attempted a development approach using stratification to indicate the formation of group needs and interests by means of which representative elites can be identified in a general model and organized separately in a representational model. Such needs have been seen to produce three types of representation: popular, interest, and functional. Access has been defined in terms of legitimate claims (popular, interest and functional), operating within each governmental type: mobilization, reconciliation, theocratic, and bureaucratic. The role function of the representative

---

[23] It would be possible to devise a scale of participation and a scale of functional access in each general type of political system at each stage of development (including the variable access between those who claim technical knowledge, i.e., technocrats, and those who claim information about public needs). We can ask how effective is the role of the expert in monopolizing the functions of the elite, and how competitive with popular representation.

Notes for a Theory of Nondemocratic Representation 301

elites varies in each. These functions are: central control, goal specification, and institutional coherence. Since we have treated representation as an intervening variable, the three types of representation and the three functions will result in very different consequences and purposes of representation in each political system as well as in each stage of development. Operationalizing representation in these terms thus emphasizes its multiple purposes, its many different aspects, rather than the habitual, although often implicit, one of assuming that a particular combination of representational forms or functions leads to a particular political type of pattern of balance.

My emphasis has been entirely conceptual, and it is so primarily so as to enable us to develop a true theory of representation. To do this we should be able, first, to correlate certain types of representation with certain functions; second, to universalize the correlations; and third, to find a generalized explanation of why the correlations appear. It would then be possible to make representation the independent variable with political system and developmental stage as intervening or dependent. Hence, my object has been to specify the conditions under which a theory of representation is possible, even though this is perhaps only the first step; namely, the establishment of the matrix for empirical correlations, as seen in Figure 7.

Types of Representational Access Claims	*Functions of a Representational Elite*		
	Central Control	Goal Specification	Institutional Coherence
Popular			
Interest			
Functional			

FIGURE 7: *A Matrix for a Theory of Representation*

At the present stage, however, we can see only the variable consequences of each "box" in Figure 6, rather than correlations or syndromes. These remain entirely problematical. Still, the possibili-

A PRELIMINARY APPLICATION
OF THE TWO MODELS

Applying so many variables represents severe problems of language. Not only is it difficult to handle the simultaneous relations involved without distortions imposed by our ordinary notions of sequences, but we are dealing with two "sets." In one, society seen from the standpoint of the development process is the independent variable. The functions of the elite and government are intervening variables, with "political balance" or the stable relations between rulers and ruled as the dependent variable. Here we want to know how, in the absence of freely representative relations in a political system, governments manage the growing complexity of need and provide suitable satisfactions to the members of a society. In the second "set," government is the independent variable. The functions of the representative elite are intervening. The development process is the dependent variable. In the first "set" we find concrete systems which fall predominantly in the pattern of theocratic and reconciliation system. In the second are those which fall mainly in the pattern of bureaucratic and mobilization systems.

Using these differences as our guide, we can now discuss the dimensions of the model employed in terms of its implications for non-democratic representation as well as different stages of development. We will not discuss all the possible types but use several for illustrative purposes.

A Traditional Theocratic System and Change to a Traditional Bureaucratic Type. Stratification in traditional theocratic systems was based on caste relations determined by kinship, i.e., tribal ethnicity. Such systems tend to link kinship with ancestors; in which case, ancestral obligation is a form of shared central control between the living and the dead. Conflicts between ethnic groups define the central poltical problem; elites emerge from kin groups. Institutional coherence derives from priests and others, such as elders, to ensure the propriety of religious beliefs. Representation thus combines lineage and

Notes for a Theory of Nondemocratic Representation 303

kin or clan leaders with ancestors in the form of kin "interest" and client "function." Government is not separate or distinct from the kinship elites; but rather, the central figure. Indeed, priest, king, and lineage merge. The combination results in the performance of the central control function by government.

What keeps the balance of the system is stability in the stratification sphere and the harmonization of social relations with sustained belief in imminent practices by a kinship elite with popular links through clans or other familial units. Emphasis on functional representation is at a minimum. Popular forms of pluralism are managed on the basis of reciprocal kinship or ethnic relations. This arrangement is accepted as a divine expression. The problem of control is, therefore, to sustain the relation between consummatory and instrumental values. Kinship representation combined with priestly authority is the general method employed.

We have chosen the case of the Arab caliphate as an illustration, because it was in our terms "traditional" in its developmental stage; i.e., organized on caste-ethnic lines (Semitic tribes), which originated in a theocracy (founded by the Prophet), and transformed itself first into an expansionist mobilization system (the Arab conquest), and then into a bureaucratic system (the Arab Empire). Our primary purpose here is to use the typology first in a dramatic, historical way to illustrate some of the categories suggested above. The Arab caliphate was organized for war in order to spread the faith. Its first phase was purely religious. After the death of Mohammed a military organization developed that represented hierarchical authority but with instrumental values subordinate to religious ones. This combination has frequently been a compelling force in history. Ibn Khaldūn notes that "religious propaganda gives a dynasty at its beginning another power in addition to that of the group feeling it possessed as the result of the number of its [supporters]."[24] (The quotation notes the temporary quality of this form of religious power.) Bernard Lewis, commenting on the caliphate after the death of the Prophet, suggests that those who elected Khalifa (the deputy of the Prophet) "can have had no idea of the later functions and development of the office. At the time they made no attempt to delimit his duties or powers. The sole condition of his appointment was the maintenance intact of the heritage of

[24] See Ibn Khaldūn, *The Muqaddimah*, trans. Franz Rosenthal (New York: Pantheon Books, 1958), Vol. 1, p. 320.

the Prophet."[25] So established, the Arabs, organized along military lines, began the twin tasks of conversion and conquest.[26] If the early caliphate was hierarchical in its system of authority, its very imperial successes meant that military commanders and governors could exercise increasing autonomy and control. The principle of election to the caliphate by powerful governors was followed. In theory at any rate, the Muslim community as such was represented.

The forms of representation during the early expansion period of the Arab Empire were extremely limited. Important family dynasties exercised influence in court. Administrators, tax collectors, and other officials associated with the organization of public lands and rents occupied central decision-making positions. The key to representation was military, administrative, or familial power, with each serving as a claim to wealth. In Mecca a wealthy class of patricians dominated the elections to the caliphate. Their representation, based on political skill supported by great wealth, quickly turned them into an oligarchy, which in turn led to a decline in religious commitment. Conflicts arose between civil administrators and the oligarchy. Competition for support from non-Arab converts to Islam, who were anxious to obtain advantages as well as the financial success of the empire, shifted the priority away from consummatory and toward instrumental values. "The assumptions of this system were the identity of Arab and Muslim and the maintenance of the religious prestige by which the Caliph exercised his authority. Its breakdown became inevitable when these assumptions ceased to be valid."[27] The result was a growth in oligarchical corruption, nepotism, and eventually civil war.

"The administration of the Empire was decentralized and in disorder and the resurgence of nomad anarchism and indiscipline, no longer restrained by a religious or moral tie, led to general instability and lack of unity. The theocratic bond which had held together the early caliphate had been irrevocably destroyed by the murder of 'Uthman, the civil war that followed it, and the removal of the capital from Medina. The oligarchy in Mecca was defeated and discredited. Mu'awiya's problem was to find a new basis for the cohesion of the Empire. His answer was to start the transformation

[25] Bernard Lewis, *The Arabs in History* (New York: Harper & Row, 1960), p. 51.
[26] *Ibid.*, p. 52.
[27] *Ibid.*, p. 59.

Notes for a Theory of Nondemocratic Representation 305

from the theoretical Islamic theocracy to an Arab secular state, based on the dominant Arab caste."[28]

What were the dominant groupings to be represented? They were first organized around war and administration by means of appointed chiefs who came to have territorial jurisdictions. Their importance to the caliphate was so critical that they formed a "court" in which intrigue was a key characteristic, particularly against the Mecca castes. Functional "representation" based on administration was thus arrayed against group "representation" based upon caste. The former prevailed and the secular, bureaucratic Arab state resulted.

The case emphasizes forces that tend to limit the effectiveness of a mobilization system and lead to its demise. Its success is likely to produce limited accountability but many claimants to power. Representation as such barely exists and is more likely to result in intrigue than in responsible actions. The reason there is virtually no representation is that the leader personifies the total community, and any publicly defined pattern of accountability is seen by him as a division in that community. Harmony and devotion, not division and conflict, are the aims. When the consummatory values associated with such devotion begin to decline, then de facto representation leads to civil war between rival chieftains and the rise, first, of a bureaucratic system.

A Traditional Reconciliation System and Its Consequences. Traditional reconciliation systems are organized in stratification terms around kinship. Kin groupings clustered into caste-like relations are entered by marriage, adoption, or co-optation. Coalitions of caste relations hover somewhere between caste and class *A* and are characteristic of ancient European reconciliation systems about which we have some knowledge, such as Athens, the Roman Republic, or the Florentine city-state. In each of these cases and within the general category of caste-type relations, a dynastic pattern of stratification could be found. However, such general characteristics hold for more than antique European protoypes and would even include those age-grade segmentary systems in Africa, in which entry is based on generation. Central control in such reconciliation systems is normally through a king in council dominated by senior castes, coalitions of castes, or age-grades. These may vary in type

---

[28] *Ibid.*, p. 64.

from dynastic familial organizations and other groups which maintain stewardship over land and possess other property rights not easily attainable by the ordinary public. Goal specification consists primarily in special protection for the major economic and ethnic groupings. Institutional coherence rests with the consultative and conciliar procedures, including courts and councils, magistrates and priests, and shared participation of overlapping caste-like groupings in the reconciliation of conflicting interests. The traditional reconciliation system thus emphasizes representation on the basis of familial seniority. To illustrate this more fully we can analyze the case of the Roman Republic.

The Arab case demonstrates how systems change from theocracy to mobilization to bureaucratic representation. Another case of a traditional system is better known because historically it is closer to the European experience; namely, the traditional reconciliation system of the Roman Republic, particularly during the attempted reforms of the Gracchi. Government had been primarily aristocratic with the domination of the burgesses by the old senatorial families. During the expansionist phase of the Roman Empire this worked reasonably well. But, at the height of Rome's glory, as Mommsen suggests: "The government of the aristocracy was in full train to destroy its own work. Not that the sons and grandsons of the vanquished at Cannae and of the victors at Zama had so utterly degenerated from their fathers and grandfathers; the difference was not so much in the men who now sat in the senate, as in the times. Where a limited number of old families of established wealth and hereditary political importance conducts the government it will display in seasons of danger an incomparable tenacity of purpose and power of heroic self-sacrifice, just as in seasons of tranquility it will be short-sighted, selfish, and negligent—the germs of both results are essentially involved in its hereditary and collegiate character."[29] The Roman case would indicate a shift from claims to popular representation on the basis of a narrowly limited definition of citizenship to rural interest representation on the basis of clanship estates. Struggles over access to decision-making resulted in a corresponding decline in institutional coherence (and the formation of a religious vacuum that prepared the ground for the successful entry

[29] Theodore Mommsen, *The History of Rome* (New York: The Free Press, n.d.), Vol. III, pp. 297–98.

Notes for a Theory of Nondemocratic Representation 307

of Christianity at a later stage), leading to struggles over central control and goal specification among various clans, and, as well, to the development of different classes.

Attempts to prevent the senate aristocrats from plundering the system and to recognize the needs of the public gave rise to conflict between "optimates," who wished the rule of the best, and "populares," who favored the will of the community. The result was conflict over and struggles between rival "classes" as well as between "estates." Attempts to create major reforms, first by Tiberius and subsequently Gaius Gracchus ended, in each case, with their deaths.

The Roman illustration is interesting because it demonstrates the difficulties as well as the typical problems of reconciliation systems that are not democratic; i.e., they exclude part of the community from effective representation. The Roman case excluded slaves, foreign burgesses, and effectively the urban poor; yet, nevertheless, considered them part of the society. The civic community was thus only a part of the whole. The magistrates were chosen from a relatively small number of families. Nevertheless, the citizens could record a vote on important issues. Politicians, in order to be elected, needed to have a faction behind them. The basis of faction was in the *gens*, the family. Hence, family connection and political marriage was extremely important.

In addition to family, personal obligation and the resulting patron-client stratification system was important. Faction, intrigue, personal connection are all characteristics of representation in reconciliation systems that provide for accountability in conciliar bodies representing the "weightier part" of the community but not necessarily the most functionally significant. What H. H. Soullard suggests for Rome is certainly true of reconciliation systems more generally. "It is this far-reaching nexus of personal and family relationships and obligations that underlies the basis of Roman public life, a fact which the nobles themselves may have sought to obscure. Its form naturally will have varied at different periods of Rome's history. Thus in the early days the tie of the clan was probably the predominant factor; families would group themselves around such leading patrician clans as the Fabii, Aemilii, and Claudii."[30] The Roman case merely illustrates in a historically familiar context a general phenomenon found in many modernizing societies today. If

[30] H. H. Soullard, *Roman Politics 220–150* B.C. (Oxford; The Clarendon Press, 1951), p. 3.

we take the same characteristics, the separation of society from effective civic community, and put them in the context of modernizing nations—whether old ones, as in Latin America, or new ones, as in Africa—we see many of the same problems. In the Latin American case the result has been the growth of class A conflict and class B coalitions, thereby providing manipulative control over representative organs by various oligarchies. Representation has been on the basis of family. Although such representation was originally based primarily on rural landowning wealth, it has expanded latterly in the form of controlling dynastic commercial and industrial oligarchies. Hence, overrepresentation of a "weightier part" has developed and the patron-client relationship has extended into every aspect of political life. Precisely to change this system, many of the modern "democrats" in Latin America, such as Frei in Chile, have turned their attention and have attempted to create a theocratic modernizing society by means of land reform and more effective representation.

The Modernizing Reconciliation System. Modernizing reconciliation systems are likely to be extremely unstable in the primary stages of modernization because of the survival of many traditional practices. Overlapping caste, class A, and class B relations provide the basis of competing coalitions. Interest representation predominates; central control is weak and bureaucratic; goal specification of the developmental variety is manipulated by politicians with only marginal participation by technocrats; and institutional coherence is based on corruption, mobility, and payoff. If popular representation occurs, it militates against developmental planning. Uneven access to power accentuates inequality and social discrimination. Many Latin American countries fall in this category.

In later stages of modernization, with the growth of class of the B type and its intermediary status clusters between class A structures, central control tends to become more organized around a bureaucracy; goal specification is shared by competing class and status groupings; while institutional coherence is sustained through multiple and overlapping institutional groupings. The pattern is likely to lead to organized plunder, with repeated interventions by the military. The combination of political and economic stagnation, popular representation in voting, and functional representation through the bureaucracy, army, and developmental agencies creates

Notes for a Theory of Nondemocratic Representation 309

conflict between popular and functional principles of representation.

As we have suggested, reconciliation systems are not necessarily democratic in the Western sense of the term. Caste, class *A*, and class *B* relations are linked to familial and personalistic ties. Such overlapping role sets combine within a single community elements of caste opportunism and class conflicts (as in *campesino* movements), so that the development of multibonded class and status relations uses the structure of representative government as an umbrella to protect its interests from demands produced by caste and class *A* types of conflict. Moreover, when such conflict gets out of hand, representing a management problem for the class *B* elites, the latter tend to favor military intervention leading to a new constitutional framework.[31] Such efforts attempt to link, by political means, the structure of social relations and roles established in each sector of the stratification system with government on the basis of interest representation. A new round of corruption occurs as well as a new tendency to plunder the system in the absence of more positive representational links and associations. The crisis in central control soon repeats itself; hence the predicament. Sharing power through popular representation by means of the proliferation of voluntary associations, committees, local governments, and general participation in assemblies and councils throughout the structure of pyramidal authority only intensifies the conflict between popular and interest claims to representation. But in the exercise of their functions, the elites emphasize distribution rather than development. This exaggerates a "plunder" psychology with few possibilities for managed and enforced savings in the community. Representational access in terms of any organized interest—whether based on class or function—becomes dominant at the expense of the others.

The problem of the nondemocratic reconciliation system is thus accountability without constraint and political participation for short-term gains. The result is likely to be political and social stalemate, punctuated by periods of conflict.

An Industrializing Reconciliation System. The third type of reconciliation system, that occurring in industrialized countries,

---

[31] See the interesting theory of military intervention advanced by José Nun in "América Latina: La crisis hegemónica y el golpe militar," *Desarrollo Económico*, 6 (July-December 1966), 22–23.

DAVID E. APTER

represents the most acute stage of the "crisis of meaning"—inherent in the model itself. Class conflicts have given way to status coalitions, each supporting popular representation and interest representation in competition with functional representation. Central control has become a function of conflict among bureaucrats, technocrats, and politicians. Goal specification is a tug-of-war between interest and functional representation. Institutional coherence is based upon popular representation. Here lie many of the familiar problems confronting pseudo-democratic societies, including the inadequacy of representative mechanisms and restricted access. Yugoslavia and Poland might serve as examples of industrialized reconciliation systems, with even the USSR moving in that direction. A few Latin American countries, such as Brazil and Argentina, might also fall into that category, despite their military regimes, but for the fact that they are not yet sufficiently industrialized. In any case, representation is much the same as in the modernizing society, except that either a party, a bureaucracy, or a military group is responsible for both central control and goal specification, while institutional coherence is left to whatever class and associational groupings are found available, perhaps surviving from the previous system. In other words, nondemocratic reconciliation systems in industrial societies tend to be "tolerant" of the social system and to allow institutional coherence to be handled locally by the community itself, while functional access is increasingly prominent.

Modernizing Mobilization Systems. Characteristic cases of modernizing mobilization systems would include Guinea, Ghana, and Mali immediately after their independence. The stratification relations of modernizing systems are of both the caste and the class A types. One finds a typical traditional caste/colonial, or expatriate, caste stratification system alongside of a "middle class" conscious of its position and performing modern tasks.[32] A mobilization system tries to eliminate the colonial caste, root and branch, and to integrate class and remaining traditional caste relations around new political clusters—a political "class" of the A type which embodies the community, such as attempted by the Parti Démocratique de Guinée, the Union Soudannaise in Mali, or the Convention People's Party in

[32] In this usage I would reject the notion advanced by those who claimed that there was no "class" in Africa. Vertical caste (European/African) was followed by class A/caste (African elites versus tribal groups) and class A/class B relationships relatively quickly.

Notes for a Theory of Nondemocratic Representation 311

Ghana, while manipulating populism as a substitute for popular representation. Party organization creates representative clusters and attempts to define participation in functional terms: the socialization function (youth movements); the production function (trade unions and corporations); the rural innovation function (cooperatives and farmers associations); and the ideological function (ideological institutes). Interest representation is likely to be suspect and regarded as "neo-colonialist" or imperialist. Attempts to alter caste relations are made by changing the principles of representation and by modifying sources of mobility—both politically, through a "single party," and by bureaucratic co-optation. Central control is likely to be in the hands of a party-government coalition in which the key posts in each are occupied by the same individuals. Goal specification is in terms of planning based on a combination of ideological and technical goals, in which technocrats, engineers, economists, statisticians, and the like, play a large part, normally in some conflict with political leaders. Institutional coherence is based on increasing bureaucratization, again with a high ideological component. Two characteristic conflicts of principle exist between government-sponsored elites and the remnants of traditional elites, and between ideological specialists in the party and civil servants and technocrats. Here we find representation on the basis of function ideologically linked with relevant groupings in the society. Counter-elites are excluded; but even these may not necessarily be restricted in terms of social mobility within the system.

The main differences between traditional and modern forms of mobilization systems are (1) that populism is used to support functional representation in the modern forms; and (2) that populism requires a consultative base, while functional representation requires a special access to functional elites. Populist and functional elites contend with each other for power. Popular representation is limited to being of the testimonial variety of populism. Access to central control and goal specification is restricted to those concerned with development or maintenance of support. The institutional coherence function is restricted to programmatic ideology, with organizations modified according to the degree to which they fit the ideological pattern.[33]

In general, we can say that, even where popular representation

[33] See Aristide R. Zolberg, *Creating Political Order* (Chicago: Rand McNally, 1966), pp. 93–125.

is minimal, growing competition between populist and functional elites for access to central control and goal specification produces considerable accountability. Even the functional elites seek to expand their competitive access by broadening their recruitment base in society. The tendency is to move downward through the restratification of the public into corporate functional groupings relevant to development and systems-maintenance. Not class, but *corporate* grouping is characteristic; hence, a kind of "corporate representation" in primary stage modernizing mobilization systems is seen as the means of reconciling populism with functional expertise.

The solution just mentioned is rarely achieved, however, because of the appearance of the "embourgeoisement" phenomenon, which breaks up the stratification pattern into too many complex coalitional multiples for restratification along corporate-functional lines. Moreover, even caste elements prove difficult to eradicate, not to speak of class *A* type groupings. The middle class of the type *B,* growing as modernization proceeds, makes demands based on wider needs. Thus, central control needs to be even more tightly organized in a military or paramilitary type of formation. The result is government versus the elites. Goal specification then relies more heavily on systems-maintenance than on development. Institutional coherence tends to be a combination of ideological orthodoxy and coercion. Government-monopolized central control is allocated on an appointive basis to administrators. Goal specification is toward a future objective. An elite of ideological specialists is required both to create such goals and to ensure their status as consummatory values. Institutional coherence is handled by administrative magistrates or tribunals dedicated to the preservation of ideological uniformity. The functions of an elite are joined within a narrow circle, closely associated with government and hostile to other groupings, particularly other caste groupings in the system. When there is weakness or failure in the performance of any of the elite functions, government is likely to apply coercion. Hence, "embourgeoisement" creates the conditions for mobilization and also prevents the mobilization system from working.[34] Under such paradoxical conditions, popular representation, in the form of a party elite, would collide with the governmental functionaries or technocrats over an increasingly restricted access to elite functions.

[34] *Ibid.,* p. 127.

Notes for a Theory of Nondemocratic Representation 313

The Industrializing Mobilization Systems. During industrialization the problem of the decline of consummatory values in combination with the primacy of instrumental ones tends to fit directly with a structural pattern of differentiation, in which class conflict gives way to multibonded class with coalitions and groups forming on the basis of functional significance. Party leaders and technocratic elite are likely to compete for central control, as in the modernizing case; but party leaders and bureaucrats are likely to handle goal specification by means of consultative instruments; while institutional coherence is similarly dealt with by party leaders and plant managers. The industrial system injects new and mutually opposing elements into the picture: on the one hand, the need for decentralization of command units (as the complexity of the system grows); and on the other, the increasing bureaucratization occasioned by the effort to retain command over a decentralized decision system. Representation is thus likely to be functional on the basis of the productive system and consultative on the basis of the hierarchy. We can call the resulting subtype *consultative* (as distinct from popular) representation, as exemplified in China by the direct contact between cadres and the masses.[35] Even in China, however, the emerging stratification pattern creates an interesting problem; namely, the "embourgeoisement" phenomenon, which breaks up society into competitive status groupings, making it difficult to treat the population in terms of any given class or corporate interest, but rather as representative of elaborately distributed needs.

Breaking up the class pattern into multibonded class emphasizes competitive claims to popular representation under the guise of consumer interests. If new technocratic elites, crucial to the developmental process, gain supremacy over the party elite, central control would be shared by administrators, civil servants, and managers. Goal specification would be decentralized with a corresponding depoliticization of many aspects of social life. Institutional coherence would be provided by the shared and overlapping organizational pluralism associated not only with production and distribution but also with local government. At this point consultative representation may be transformed into popular representation. If that should occur, then the political system could become democratic.

[35] James K. Townsend, *Political Participation in Communist China* (Berkeley and Los Angeles: The University of California Press, 1967), *passim.*

314   DAVID E. APTER

The industrializing mobilization system is of great importance because it seems to produce a contradiction between political and economic needs. In highly industrialized societies the multibonded pattern of class spreads throughout the system. It becomes virtually meaningless to speak of classes in the Marxist or Weberian sense.[36] The new types of status groupings, each with special claims to representation and power, are competitive in terms of the function of the elite and their type of claim to representation. Most important is the role of the new technocrats, whose functional value is based upon knowledge or innovation. They are opposed by the bureaucrats, whose claim is based upon continuity and efficiency; and by the politicians, whose claim is based on instrumental or consummatory values of a populist variety. This conflict arises because of the role of information. The modernizing society has a model and a goal—industrialization. It can afford to be imitative. The main difference between modernization and industrialization is that the latter creates a revolution in innovation and technique. In industrial systems it is necessary to reconcile representation of interests and function with new knowledge (innovation). Each of these types of representation involves a form of information which govermnent requires during industrialization. Hence the effect of high industrialization is to diversify need as a basis of information, setting up the following causal chain: *The need of information results in more diverse representation on the basis of complex interests. This emphasizes instrumental values. As consummatory values decline and the need for information grows, the mobilizing industrial system will move toward a reconciliation system.*

SOME TENTATIVE GENERALIZATIONS

By putting so much emphasis on development, we have related system-type to representation in terms of changing needs and information. Our formulation does not deal with democratic systems, but it could include them. In modern predemocratic developing societies, and in some industrial ones as well, democracy is a goal based on developmental priorities rather than an independent normative aim, based on a prior, if implicit, agreement on popular

---

[36] The concept of false consciousness seems merely a presumptuous convenience, adopted by messianic intellectuals as a warrant of superiority in a world which otherwise largely ignores them.

Notes for a Theory of Nondemocratic Representation 315

representation. The maintenance of representative government in democracies is partly a function of an ability to convert potential conflicts over values into conflicts over interests *without, nevertheless, allowing interest representation to become dominant. This implies an effective blend of consummatory and instrumental values and high accountability on the basis of popular representation, both of which imply agreement over the balance of representational claims with regulated competition of functional access by elites.* Such a system is subtle, complex, and delicate.

In a mobilization system, on the other hand, consummatory values clearly dominate. Overt challenges to hierarchical authority are uncommon and popular representation is minimal. Indeed, pluralism is the enemy. The corporate community is, at least formally, highly unified; and dissidents are silent. However, a tendency toward functional representation manifests itself. During the early stages of development, particularly in premodern systems, these functional representatives include military and administrative figures in bureaucratic roles.[37] In mobilization systems at the highest stage of development, industrialization, these roles tend to become more specialized around those most germane to generating information and technique; and the clusters of functional roles facilitates central control and goal specification.

We conclude with the following propositions:

1. Both mobilization and bureaucratic polities are limited accountability systems, with government the independent variable and society dependent. Emphasis in the former is on functional representation. In the latter, functional representation is mixed with various forms of patron-client interest relationships.

2. Both reconciliation and theocratic polities are high accountability systems in which society is the independent variable and government dependent. Emphasis in the former is on a mixture of interest, functional, and popular representation; and in the latter on popular and interest representation personified in a religious/ethical authority.

Although representation is treated here as an intervening variable, it does have several generalized subsystem characteristics. First,

---

[37] It is important to stress that quite often the role is created by the individual, i.e., a trusted lieutenant is made an administrator. If he, as occupant, can be replaced, but the role is retained, then role institutionalization has occurred and it is possible to consider the role independently of the occupant.

information is created through the functions of the elites. The greater the access to central control, goal specification, and institutional coherence by the elites, the more broadly is power distributed, the more likely are the elites to engage in competition to represent diverse groups, and the greater is the degree of information available to decision-making. When the system begins as a mobilization system, the competition among cities constitutes a disciplinary problem for government; elite functions are reduced and information is lost. The proposition that then emerges is: *When a society of the mobilization type is at the stage of late modernization or industrialization on the development continuum, it develops a multibonded/status social system. The competition for access by elites leads to decentralization of power but to no change in the principle of hierarchy, thus posing an authority problem for government likely to lead to coercion on the one hand and intrigue on the other.* Intrigue will be the main activity of the elites competing for access to central control, goal specification, and institutional coherence. In the absence of good information, coercion will be applied by government.

In reconciliation systems such competition among elites is likely to lead toward a greater degree of elite participation by wider sectors of the public, with two main tendencies emerging: representation on the basis of multibonded class, or *popular* representation; and representation on the basis of modern status, or *functional* representation. Competition among elites consists of conflicts over the role of experts versus politicians, with civil servants and technocrats among the former and elected representation among the latter. Such competition profoundly affects the effectiveness of participation by the public. Under conditions of high industrialization, a sense of powerlessness can lead to public feelings of alienation as well as to a decline in the overarching shared consummatory values of the system; so that the conversion of issues of value into conflicts of interest produces an excessive fractionalization of power which renders effective decision-makers impossible. Under the circumstances, free available information becomes unusable. *The proposition that emerges is that in reconciliation systems if the competition among elites for access to the elite functions and the differing claims to representation produce an excessive fractionalization of power, resulting in the privatization of wants and randomization of ends, then the rules of the system themselves become vulnerable. Such systems produce increasing amounts of information and little co-*

Notes for a Theory of Nondemocratic Representation

ercion; but the communications net is so overloaded, and the claims to participate in central control, goal specification, and institutional coherence are so competitive that the systems tend to be ineffective.

The conclusion to these notes is really to state a problem; namely, that the long-term process of industrialization polarizes social structure into groups that are counterposed against each other in a competition for representation that is imposed by the need for information. Although I believe this produces a long-run tendency toward a reconciliation system, the likely possibility is a "dialectic" between a modern form of the corporate state, with a high emphasis on functional representation, and a democratic state, with a high emphasis on popular and interest representation.

In sum, we have attempted to identify the types of representation that are functionally distributed to particular elites under conditions of variable access and growing need.

27

Shape-Shifting Representation
MICHAEL SAWARD

> *Shape-shifting representation is common in practice but largely shunned in theoretical and empirical analysis. This article resurrects, defines, and explores shape-shifting and closely linked concepts and practices such as shape-retaining. It generates new concepts of representative positioning and patterning in order to aid our understanding, and makes the case for placing this critical phenomenon front and center in the analysis of political representation. It examines crucial empirical and normative implications for our understanding of representation, including the argument that shape-shifting representation is not intrinsically undesirable. Developing the theory of shape-shifting representation can prompt a new level of analytical purchase on the challenge of explaining and evaluating representation's vitality and complexity.*

"Sadly, it is not the only Romney, as his campaign for the White House has made abundantly clear, first in his servile courtship of the tea party in order to win the nomination, and now as the party's shape-shifting nominee. From his embrace of the party's radical right wing, to subsequent portrayals of himself as a moderate champion of the middle class, Romney has raised the most frequently asked question of the campaign: 'Who is this guy, really, and what in the world does he truly believe?'" (Editorial, *The Salt Lake Tribune*, 22 October 2012)

Political representatives often need to be, or at least to appear to be, different things to different people. How they appear to others may be subject to their own choices, or deeply constrained by the choices of others or wider circumstances. This fact can work itself out in complex real-world patterns—at one extreme, representative claimants may put themselves across (or be put across) as different things to different people at different times in different spaces. As a comment on real-world politics, these ideas are not especially radical (as the quote from *The Salt Lake Tribune* suggests), but political science barely acknowledges their importance. There are strong grounds for arguing that, though he or she is not only a contemporary phenomenon, the shape-shifting representative is a crucial and perhaps the quintessential political figure in this era of increased media intensity, density, and differentiation (Helms 2012). Developing the theory of shape-shifting representation, and placing it front and center in analyses of political representation, can prompt a new level of analytical and empirical purchase on the challenge of explaining and evaluating representation's vitality and complexity.

I am grateful to Steven Forde for his editorial guidance, and to APSR's anonymous reviewers for their extensive and extremely helpful comments. I was fortunate to have the opportunity to present earlier versions in seminars and workshops at the universities of Geneva, Utrecht, and Warwick, along with the Universidade Federal de Minas Gerais, the European University Institute, and the London School of Economics. I benefited greatly from the chance to further develop my arguments on each occasion. My thanks to Cláudia Feres Faria, Mathias Koenig-Archibugi, Jane Mansbridge and Ed Page for particularly insightful comments and criticisms.

AN ABSENT PRESENCE: SHAPE-SHIFTING IN HISTORICAL AND CONTEMPORARY SCHOLARSHIP

The shape-shifting representative is a political actor who claims (or is claimed) to represent by shaping (or having shaped) strategically his persona and policy positions for certain constituencies and audiences. This figure *is* present in classical, theoretical, and empirical studies of representation, but only as a somewhat unnerving figure in the shadows. His or her troubling presence may reflect an abiding unease at the root of modern political theory, arguably above all in Machiavelli's *The Prince*. A prince, argues Machiavelli, "should have a flexible disposition, varying as fortune and circumstance dictate" (2004 [1532], 75). His power and his hold over his subjects may be in danger without cunning flexibility; he must "learn from the fox and the lion, because the lion is defenceless against traps and a fox is defenceless against wolves. Therefore one must be a fox in order to recognize traps, and a lion to frighten off wolves."

The figure of the Sovereign in Hobbes's *Leviathan* (1969 [1651]) is a "representer" with few restrictions on what he may do for or to his subjects. He is unpredictable, a vengeful and potentially deadly figure—a "monster" indeed (Kristiansson and Tralau 2014)—who may adopt forms or shapes favoring the reinforcement of legitimate sovereign control. From Locke (1924 [1640], 163) onwards ("to think that men are so foolish that they take care to avoid what mischiefs can be done them by polecats and foxes, but are content, nay, think it safety, to be devoured by lions"), the critical unease with which the Hobbesian vision has been greeted reflects the disturbing array of roles or actions that the Sovereign may adopt or perform, and the consequent and ever-present danger he poses. Mythological shape-shifting often involved human-animal and animal-animal transformations, a fact echoed directly in the classical writers' invocation of monstrosity and animal cunning.

From these deeper roots one can detect an underlying distrust of shape-shifting representatives which persists today. Arguably, a modern prioritizing of a negative normative framing of interpretations of shape-shifting in (for example) Machiavelli and Hobbes leads to the common sidelining of shape-shifting leadership

564 REPRESENTATION

Shape-Shifting Representation   November 2014

or representation. The persistent influence of this negative normative frame can be detected in contemporary approaches to the study of representation, promoting definitions and typologies valuing for example "isolated" and "separated" concepts (Rehfeld 2009, 221) *even where* the presence of the skewing normative frame is barely any longer visible. Contemporary normative frames stress singular and consistent roles of political actors or leaders, refusing for example to separate in any way means from ends. Is this framing defensible? Must the moral representative always be rigidly consistent? Being moral, or doing what needs to be done, may require *inconsistency*—shape-shifting—in a number of contexts. And good and moral ends may demand more flexible means, perhaps multiple role-playing.

For all its acknowledged virtues, Hanna Pitkin's contemporary classic *The Concept of Representation* (1967) adopts an analogous framing to the same ultimate effect—expunging shape-shifting from representation theory via a negative normative filtering of representation's meaning. In her thorough and complex account, Pitkin notes that the concept has been given many different meanings by different political philosophers. She finds beneath the great disagreements evidence of a common, underlying "correct definition": "the making present *in some sense* of something which is nevertheless *not* present literally or in fact" (1967, 8–9). Two points are especially noteworthy here. First, Pitkin seeks one, best or proper definition of representation. And second, a framing bias towards singular and consistent representation is crucial to this one definition.

This normative framing—asking what is "the proper relation between representative and constituents" (1967, 4)—in itself renders more urgent the perceived need to locate the one, correct definition. The proper relation unduly influences or frames the correct definition. For Pitkin, a good or proper representative, conforming to representation's true meaning, will play *one consistent role*, be it in terms of policy or character. Consider her approach to "the central classic controversy in the history of representation": "Should (must) a representative do what his constituents want, and be bound by mandates or instructions from them; or should (must) he be free to act as seems best to him in pursuit of their welfare?" (1967, 145). Her normative framing presses her to pose these questions in terms of "should" or "must". *One* role must be played by a representative; the only pressing question is which role this should be. Pitkin is certainly aware that representatives acting in different ways is compatible with her avowed search for "a consistent position about a representative's duties" (1967, 146). Nonetheless, she clearly favors a representative consistently pursuing one course or role, even if that view is as much a product of the style and framing of argument as its content.

Normative prejudgement, in this or another form, may be defensible. But it too hastily discounts alternative reasonable frames. The classic writers also provide accounts where shape-shifters may demonstrate or embody crucial leadership virtues; shape-shifting

may reflect intelligent, prudent, and flexible leadership, able to change strategies as circumstances demand. Machiavelli's prince may be a figure of unfixed and uncertain morality, for whom the maintenance of power is paramount. But Machiavelli does not prize amoral rulership for its own sake; its value lies in its capacity to achieve ends at least some of which are widely desirable: "Everyone realizes how praiseworthy it is for a prince to honour his word and to be straightforward rather than crafty in his dealings; none the less contemporary experience shows that princes who have achieved great things have been those who have given their word lightly..." (2004, 73). For Hobbes, of course, the overwhelming justification for the great scope and reach of the Sovereign's writ is the maintenance of order, or more viscerally the avoidance of bloody civil war. Machiavelli further argues that "Those who simply act like lions are stupid. So it follows that a prudent ruler cannot, and must not, honour his word when it places him at a disadvantage and when the reasons for which he made his promise no longer exist" (2004, 74). Shape-shifting may for example be essential to achieving great outcomes.

The most explicit contemporary account which in part escapes the impact of negative framing of definitions and therefore restrictive, singular understandings of roles is Eulau et al.'s account of the "politico":

> One can think of representation as a continuum, with the Trustee and Delegate orientations as poles, and a mid-point where the orientations tend to overlap and, within a range, give rise to a third role. Within this middle range the roles may be taken simultaneously, possibly making for conflict, or they may be taken serially, one after another as conditions call for. .... we shall speak of representatives who express both orientations, either simultaneously or serially, as Politicos. In general, then, the Politico as a representational role type differs from both the Trustee and the Delegate in that he is more sensitive to conflicting alternatives in role assumption, more flexible in the way he resolves the conflict of alternatives, and less dogmatic in his representational style as it is relevant to his decision-making behaviour. (1959, 750)

One can almost hear the voice of Machiavelli—the prince "should have a flexible disposition, varying as fortune and circumstance dictate". A representative who pursues one role or type with consistency, perhaps pursuing a clear moral vision, may in reality be dogmatic, insensitive, or inflexible. The politico is a theoretical forbear of the shape-shifting representative. Eulau et al. break through that part of the normative framing which dictates a consistent pursuit of a single role as being desirable normatively and (implicitly) correct in definitional terms. This important work—little acknowledged in recent years—begins to puncture overly restrictive framing. However, the politico is still defined by its pivoting between two fixed representative roles, trustee and delegate. The separation and opposition of the two defines the entire relevant field of representation (they form its two "poles"), on this account. This is unduly restrictive binary thinking,

REPRESENTATION

despite the partial breakthrough that the figure of the politico represents.

Important recent work by Mansbridge (2003; 2011) and Rehfeld (2009; 2011) productively unpacks, indeed to the breaking point, the pivotal place of the trustee-delegate binary framing of representation. In different ways—notably theorizing from empirical developments (Mansbridge) or defining representation separately from its democratic value (Rehfeld)—these writers also challenge restrictively skewed normative framing. Yet the focus on distinct, separate, and isolable roles or types persists; Rehfeld (2009, 221) for example places great weight on "isolating" representation's component parts. Although "amalgams" of a greater array of distinct types are entertained by breaking down the notions of trustee and delegate into varied component parts (Rehfeld 2009, 222), the strict separation and statis of the concepts constrains productive further analysis of innovative blurring and hybridizing of roles in and through practice.

In short, leading classical and contemporary theories provide resources to extend our thinking about representation by taking fully on board representation's movement as well as stasis. To account for the central but neglected figure of the shape-shifting representative, we need to exploit and develop these openings by (a) conceiving of representation as a dynamic and productive practice in context, rather than a phenomenon restricted to a grid of preconceived and acontextual categories; (b) suspending normative prejudgement in defining representation; (c) embracing the complexities of dynamic temporal and spatial aspects of representation; (d) considering the deeply relational and coconstitutive character of multiple representative roles, and (e) introducing normative assessment *of* shapeshifting representation (normative prejudgement, not normativity itself, is the problem).

To grasp the nature and importance of shape-shifting representation, the overarching task is to generate new concepts to extend the analytical and empirical purchase of our studies of representation. After defining and defending preferred conceptions of representation, I shall build on sophisticated recent accounts of representative types or roles (and typologies) to trace an analytical path from *representative roles to positioning* to *patterns of representative shape-shifting* as critical concepts for analyzing representation. The final section will turn to the normative question of the democratic legitimacy of claims to representation in the context of shape-shifting representation.

DYNAMIC REPRESENTATION: FROM ROLES TO SUBJECT POSITIONS

Representation roles

A core feature of contemporary analysis of political representation is the construction and use of typologies of representation. Often conceived as roles, not least those of trustee and delegate, they are also and variously conceived as views (Pitkin 1967), forms

(Mansbridge 2003), ideal-types (Rehfeld 2009), varieties (Pettit 2009), or conceptions (Disch 2011). The different terms reflect subtly different analytical starting points and perspectives. Representation "types" and "forms" reflect isolable, persisting, and distinct features of the political world; "ideal-types" are more abstract generalizations of such isolable, persisting, and distinct features; "roles" reflect isolable, persisting, and distinct practices in the political world (ways of doing representation); and (d) "views" and "conceptions" of representation are more explicitly situated (historical or contemporary) perspectives on what representation is or what it is for.[1]

The argument for identifying and analyzing the importance of shape-shifting representation is built upon the performative and constructivist definition of political representation as the contingent product of "representative claims."[2] According to this perspective, representation exists primarily by virtue of its being done—practiced, performed, claimed. Representative roles and relations gain a presence in our politics because myriad actors make claims to speak for others (and for themselves). Representation is a performative product in two linked senses: it is performed in the theatrical sense (i.e., it is both done and shown to be done (Schechner 2002)) and in the speech-act sense (it is a speech or other act which establishes, or contributes to establishing, a state of affairs) (Austin 1975; Butler 1997). A performative account initially emphasizes roles over types or forms because role emphasizes the crucial place of *practice*, or acts, in constituting representation. Political actors do not simply occupy or exemplify (for example) types or forms which exist independently of their actions; types do not have a practical existence outside their enactment as roles by agents. Inherent to the act of claiming—implicitly or explicitly[3]—to represent a constituency is a constituting or reinforcing of the social availability of that role.

The representative claim framework emphasizes the situated or contextual dynamics of producing relations of representation, rather than a wholesale break with a stress on typology construction (e.g., in the work of Mansbridge and Rehfeld). The emphasis on roles and practices highlights three features of representative politics which provide crucial underpinnings for the concept of the shape-shifting representative. First, it stresses representation's variability: it is a protean phenomenon that can be formal and informal, electoral and nonelectoral, national and transnational, potentially happening in multiple spaces and possessing many guises. Second, it stresses representation's

---

[1] Accounts of types, roles, etc., may also be distinguished according to whether they are products of inductive or deductive observation, or normative or explanatory intentions. My comments are intended to be indicative and not definitive.

[2] The representative claim is defined in Saward (2010, 38) as "a claim to represent or to know what represents the interests of someone or something."

[3] The actual words used in a representative claim may vary, but not just any discursive act will be a representative claim. Such a claim will always assert or imply a relation between two or more entities whereby one stands or speaks for other(s).

566 REPRESENTATION

contingency and dynamism: there's a lot "going on" in representation, a constant process of making, receiving, accepting, or rejecting representative claims. And third, this approach highlights representation's aesthetic and cultural character: would-be representatives need to "make representations" of their constituents (in the sense of artistic portrayals or depictions, such as candidates for office constantly using phrases such as "hard-working families," "strivers," or "battlers") to try to get the latter to recognize themselves in the claims being made (Saward 2010).[4]

Representation, on this account, is produced through the performance of roles. Consider a wide though not exhaustive snapshot of accounts of major representative roles (or types or forms that are best reinterpreted as roles) in the literature:

1. trustees and delegates (and politicos)
2. functional roles played in governmental systems[5]
3. promissory, surrogate, gyroscopic (Mansbridge 2003)
4. descriptive and substantive representation (e.g., Celis et al. 2008)
5. a politics of ideas and a politics of presence (Phillips 1995)
6. liberal and republican models of representation (Bellamy and Castiglione 2013)
7. conceptions of roles of the "good representative" (Dovi 2008)
8. formal or positional governmental roles (prime minister, member of parliament, etc.)
9. principals and agents
10. likeness and distinction (Chabal and Daloz 2006)
11. indicative and responsive (with the latter category divided into "directed" and "interpretive") (Pettit 2009)
12. modes of "informal" representation: e.g., stakeholder (Macdonald 2008), advocate, champion.

An extensive literature discusses derivations and applications of these examples, often spinning off Pitkin's (1967) extensive analysis. They vary greatly in their founding assumptions, political motivations, cultural and geographical reach, institutional focus, and empirical applications. But note that several categories in this rich list are primarily performative, ways of doing or carrying out representation, whether in specific, perhaps policy-to-policy terms (such as trustee, delegate, or directed-responsive), or in more general orientational terms (such as liberal, republican, gyroscopic,

substantive, or likeness). Others are more distinctly nominal (functional roles, such as senator or mayor), relational (principal and agent, ideas and presence, for example), or characteristic (such as descriptive).

However, *despite* those multidimensional variations each entry on the list can best be conceived as a representative role that can in principle be combined (in a number of ways, as we shall see) with a range of other entries. Arguably, even relational or characteristic categories of representation are parasitic on a performative or role-oriented conception of (for example) *acting as* a principal or a descriptive representative. A representative claimant plays the *role* of delegate, champion, descriptive representative, good or moral representative, and so on. In the practice of a would-be representative such roles can be mixed and matched outside and across their original theoretical or political points of derivation. For example: a representative may claim a descriptive likeness to the majority of members of his constituency ("I grew up in this town, and I know you can all recognize me as one of your own"), to be a trustee of constituency interests ("You can rely on me to do what's right for the town, even when that's not easy"), and claim the mantle of a good representative on the basis that he makes all of his decisions in a public and visible way ("With me, what you see is what you'll get"). In principle, a wide range of plausible examples can be gleaned by working the above list.

From role to subject position

These points add up to a reframing of representative roles as factors of *mobility* rather than *occupancy*, reflexive positioning rather than comparatively fixed positions. If we were to insist on describing shape-shifting representation as a "role," it would be a *meta-role*, a role of roles deploying shifting shades and aspects of a range of representative roles. The shape-shifting representative is not just one more role character alongside (e.g.) the trustee, the delegate, the surrogate, or the gyroscopic representative. The "role" of the shape-shifting representative is highly distinct; in theory and in practice it disrupts, conjoins, de- and re-attaches other, more familiar, roles. The shape-shifting representative is — they are — the linking mechanism, the creator of representative personas, the forger of hybrid roles of speaking and acting for, moving in and among a range of familiar roles.

However, importantly, these "roles" function most clearly as *resources* for representative claim-making. Indeed, it is at this point that the notion of a "role" becomes seriously strained, inadequate in its implied fixed or static status next to the need for concepts which can capture the more dynamic — and, I argue, for that reason more realistic — mobility and positioning work (betwixt and between "roles") that is central to claims of representation. Despite its superiority to "types" or "forms," the concept of role ultimately fails to capture the full importance *of the very attribute* which placed it above those alternatives; it can capture active practice of representation *within* the bounds of particular

---

[4] Although the constitutive character of representation is prominent in recent accounts focused on judgement (Urbinati 2011), reflexivity (Disch 2011), and aesthetics (Ankersmit 2002), it has deeper roots in the account of Bourdieu (1991) and, according to Disch in particular, in Pitkin (1967). Arguably, it goes all the way back to Hobbes: "For it is the unity of the representer, not the unity of the represented, that maketh the person one."

[5] According to Parkinson (2012), these are (1) representing experiences, opinions, and interests to other representatives; (2) making, checking, accepting, and challenging claims to represent; (3) communicating decisions and reasons to other members of society; and (4) making claims to public office and deciding between competing claimants.

REPRESENTATION 567

roles, but not for example when the performance of representative claims *breaks* those bounds, as a regular if not routine political phenomenon. Its more or less neutral, descriptive overtones deflect analytical attention from the very constitution of those roles through representative claim-making, and why this or that role is salient or prominent in a time and place. It cannot capture the wider subtleties of representative practice that are crucial to a more rounded understanding.

For these reasons, I propose displacing the concept of role in favor of *positioning*. Social psychologists made this productive move several years ago, arguing that "the concept of positioning can be used as a dynamic alternative to the more static concept of role" (Harré and van Langenhove 1991, 393). According to Henriksen (2008, 41), positioning theory's emphasis on "interactivity, movement and fluidity" has major advantages over "role-theory as a static tool for understanding social interaction." Just as the claim-making conception stresses representation's dynamism, so roles become (in principle) malleable resources for would-be representatives who *position* themselves to exploit those resources. In this light, for example, an election candidate, or a social movement figure, or a "shock-jock" talk show host, positions him or herself as a subject with respect to constituents, supporters, or listeners; in other words, they adopt *subject positions*. Subject positions are intersubjective, culturally and discursively constituted stances that are (differentially) available for adoption by actors. For example, the subject position of descriptive or sociological likeness, and another of trusteeship, is available to potential Western representative claimants (at least) as a social resource. If Chabal and Daloz (2006) are right, for instance, a claim such as "I can speak for you because I am like you an ordinary person, doing the things you do and concerned with the things that concern you" expresses a local cultural resource within which a Swedish politician may fruitfully position herself.

Subject-positioning occurs due to, and against a background of, a complex array of available resources in specific cultural-political landscapes (such as national, religious or linguistic communities). It fosters analysis of both stability and dynamic change, depending on how actors or subjects (are able to) deploy available cultural resources. Unlike with the concept of role, neither stable subject-positioning nor dynamic multior re-positioning is downgraded. Further, it introduces into work on representation an interactive dynamism: claims by representatives position themselves and their audience, and claims by the represented position both them and the representative. Representatives do not so much have or occupy roles as "pause at" or "move through" available subject-positional resources, which in turn they play a part in creating or reshaping. It is the relational and changeable array of such resources which defines the dynamic playground of political representation, including the situated capacities of wouldbe representatives to shape-shift, i.e., to reposition themselves among the array. Consider for example Fenno's view of "trustee" and "delegate" not as representative roles but as resources for congressmen to

use to justify their actions to constituents. Notions of trusteeship and delegacy are deployed in representatives' "presentational and explanatory activity" (2003, 168):

> If [House] members never had to legitimate any of their policy decisions back home, they would stop altogether talking in delegate or trustee language ... Unconnected to the explanatory part of the process, the concepts have little behavioural content (2003, 161–2).

POSITIONING AND PATTERNS OF REPRESENTATION: SHAPE-SHIFTING

I defined the shape-shifting representative as a political actor who claims to represent by shaping strategically (or having shaped) his persona and policy positions for certain constituencies and audiences. She does so by projecting images conforming to (adopting or adapting) familiar and hybrid representative resources, such as likeness or delegacy, and thus adopting (well or badly, for good or bad strategic reasons) subject positions such as delegate, or "champion" of marginalized interests. Variably constrained and enabled by her political-cultural context, she and her advisors attend to how she appears in different spaces and different times, and to modes of mediation of her style and persona, with an eye to strategic advantage for herself, and perhaps her party, faction, sponsors, and constituents.[6]

Bringing shape-shifting representation into focus can add an important dimension to recent advances in the theory of representation. To take the cutting-edge work of its type, note a further aspect of the dissection and reassembling of classic notions of trustee and delegate representation in Mansbridge (2003; 2011) and Rehfeld (2009; 2011). This work reinvigorates and expands our grasp of types of representation. Rehfeld writes of the sets of ideal-types debated by the two: "These ideal-types are meant to be just that—descriptions of conceptual points that are not necessarily realized in any pure form. In practice, representatives act in a way that mixes these forms" (2009, 220). This is the standard position, where the type-defining "conceptual point" allows us to retain analytical "pure forms." The latter, perhaps by their purity, remain the key analytical building blocks in understanding representation, and are presented as such in this exchange as elsewhere in the literature.

This is the approach I wish to turn around. It is not simply that the real world of representative politics complicates the ways in which ideal-types may be manifested. The "mix"—which most writers on representation would accept as a reality—is not a secondary fact to be noted in passing, but rather can be the key theoretical starting point; it is the mix which often *defines* the contingent, perhaps fleeting, roles, forms, or

---

[6] Representative claims are not only made by would-be representatives themselves. They can also be made about figures that may themselves be, or profess to be, reluctant to be seen as representatives. Groups or organizations may also reasonably be seen as potential claimants to representation, though individuals acting in the group or organization's name do the literal claiming.

types of which it is composed (as a network can define its nodes). This happens through subject-positioning. To consider the matter abstractly, representative role X (trustee, delegate, champion, etc.) gains its character *as* X by virtue of situated juxtaposition to roles or potential roles Y and Z. X-ness, as a position that the subject may adopt, perhaps because X-ness works well in context (it is a useful and available resource in that context), is constituted by its not-Y-ness, and not-Z-ness. For example, key to positioning oneself as a "delegate" is either (a) the ever-present potential to have positioned oneself otherwise (e.g., as a "trustee"), or (b) one's incapacity to position otherwise. In other words, whether or not an actor in a given context occupies consistently *or* traverses them, these positions are relational: co-defined or co-constituted in practice and in context.[7]

Patterns

Actual or potential movement through an array of culturally sensitive subject positions—shape-shifting—is critical to grasping the empirical and theoretical dynamics of representation. Crucially, this shape-shifting creates *patterns* of representation. It is not so much the separate types of representation that can provide purchase in explaining representative practices as the patterns of the worldly combination and recombination of subject positions. The most productive way in which to capture shape-shifting representation is through a novel shift in emphasis from role to contingent positioning and patterning. Together these concepts give us the practice and the outcomes of representation, where "role" runs together practice and outcome.

Consider a hypothetical example: a leader of a national trade union who claims to represent the substantive interests of his country on the basis of his union role speaking for significant numbers of workers. As that claim is challenged, he may shift to claiming representation by virtue of his likeness to ordinary people, not least by telling his story of rising through the union ranks from the shop floor. The decline of the trade union base prompts him to gain party support and to stand and win a parliamentary seat. Here, he adopts an outsider stance as champion of particular groups of low-wage and vulnerable workers, moving away from the "likeness" claims. Being a promise-keeping, unwavering good representative of the constituencies he cultivates becomes the core claim around which he functions. We have here a sequential pattern of subject positions: the actor offers himself as a representative by virtue of (a) substantive policy positions, then (b) on the basis of likeness or similarity to constituents, then (c) in terms of the champion of particular interests, and

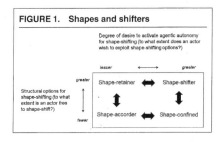

FIGURE 1. Shapes and shifters

finally (d) in terms of his moral consistency. Deploying concepts of positioning and patterning by would-be representatives presses us to take such dynamic trajectories seriously. Consider further the former president of Brazil, Luiz Inácio Lula da Silva, or more commonly Lula. From local union official to national union official, to co-organizer of the Workers Party to congressman, to multiple times presidential candidate to two-term president, Lula is noted for shifts from radicalism to reformism, and in styles of self-presentation. Of course, shape-shifting is not just sequential; as we shall see, time and space are more complexly deployed in the politics of representation. Such patterns and patterning of representation are crucial to our efforts to gain robust theoretical and empirical understanding of political representation.

"As fortune and circumstance dictate": Constraint and enablement

Are we dealing primarily with shapes or shifters, constraining structures, or enabling agency? Some actors may experience little choice as to which representative positions they adopt or in which they are placed— "delinquent youth," perhaps. Others may have much more choice as to whether they appear as a "champion" of certain interests, for example. Regarding subject positions as relationally defined opens up important questions of power and choice for would-be representatives, whether they occupy stable positions or shapes or move among them more actively. To explore patterns of shape-shifting representation, we need to understand two key dimensions: (a) structural options for shape-shifting, and (b) the degree to which would-be representatives activate the agentic opportunities available to them. The variations in shaping of representative roles which these two dimensions produce are set out in Figure 1.

Figure 1 captures key lines of variation of constraint and enablement. With respect to structural options for shape-shifting, aspects of socio-economic and political context will frame the extent and type of subject positions that representative claimants might be able to shape themselves for. For example, political parties in the U.S. remain more fluid ideologically than their European counterparts (despite the recent rise of more overtly partisan congressional politics). This fact can

---

[7] Mansbridge (2011) and Rehfeld agree that representation is relational, by which they mean that (e.g.) a surrogate model expresses a relation between the surrogate and the constituency. My sense of relational is wider: different representative roles gain definition or character in shifting modes of juxtaposition to each other, in a manner analogous to Bahktin's (1981) notion of the dialogical generation of meaning.

REPRESENTATION

569

foster greater opportunities to shape-shift among U.S. party politicians. Further, a pluralistic and multicultural society may offer greater repositioning options to greater numbers of representative claimants. On the other hand, actors may experience different degrees of desire (or, good reasons) to choose whether to shape-shift, i.e., the extent to which they activate opportunities for shape-shifting. So, for example, a context where an actor has little wish or need to shape-shift and there are few structural options for shape-shifting may lead to a "*shape-accordance*" pattern of representation.

A context where there are more structural options but strategic reasons for an agent not to shape-shift among representative roles may lead to a "*shape-retained*" pattern of representation (e.g., a strong and secure party leader who revels in her reputation for spotless consistency). The shape-retained pattern bears a close relation to Mansbridge's (2009) "selection model,", while emphasizing the degree of choice exercised by the would-be representative in how her representing is to be characterized and performed. This point underscores the utility of the shape-shifting approach; a representative may act in accordance with constituent preferences, whether by "selection" or "sanction" (Mansbridge 2009), but using a model that allows for consideration of the degree of choice he or she may have had in so doing adds important theoretical and empirical nuance. Positioning as a representative of sort A is one thing, but understanding how and why it is not B (or not-now B, or not-here B) can help us to begin to deepen our grasp via situated and relational analysis.

An agent who would wish to shape his or her representative claims to differing or changing positions, but faces fewer enabling structural resources, may give rise to a "*shape-confined*" pattern of representation. Similarly, a shape-confined pattern may arise where competitors or opponents claim that an actor stands for this or that goal or group, and the actor herself is unable to combat the claim effectively. Consider a challenge faced by President Obama five months before the U.S. presidential election of 2012:

> "With Election Day five months off, the campaign increasingly appears to consume Mr. Obama's days and his White House, shaping his schedule, his message and many of his decisions. He is running against himself as much as Mitt Romney, or rather two versions of himself—one the radical running the country the conservatives see, and the other the saviour of the country he promoted last time around and has struggled to live up to." (Peter Baker, "Obama finds campaigning rules clock," *New York Times*, 27 May 2012)

On this account, Obama recognized the dangers of shape-confinement—struggling to overcome strong characterizations of himself, not least from his opponents—and seeking the political space to shape-shift. The "*shape-shifting*" pattern in its strictest sense may arise where structural options for, and agentic choices and strategies favoring, shape-shifting among representative positions are both greater. To the question "what matters most, shapes or shifters, structure or agency?" the answer is: it depends. Attention to specific contexts and strategies is crucial.

The positions mapped in Figure 1 reinforce the idea that subject positions such as delegate, champion, and so on are adopted or traversed by actors, freely or reluctantly. This is one part of what it means to highlight positioning and patterns rather than roles in analyzing political representation. It is not simply that representatives may play a particular role; it is that certain contextual constraints and strategic opportunities and choices may lead to that "role" being played in the context of positioning and patterning behavior. Sometimes the shape-shifting is done by representatives out of strength, at others out of weakness; sometimes it is effectively imposed on representatives by others. The category of role tends to obscure agent choices and capacities—are they, for example, shape-confined or shape-retaining? The answer to *that* question is crucial to grasping the nature and force of their representative claims. There is only one box labelled shape shifter (in Figure 1), but each of the other three categories starts from the assumption that shape-shifting is normal, a core ingredient in the dynamics of politics across contexts.[8]

Dimensions and patterns of shape-shifting representation

Although just one of the four poles in Figure 1 is denoted "shape-shifter" strictly speaking, they all share a common conceptual space. They bleed into each other, and develop their texture only by virtue of the ever-presence of the others (i.e., relational). They all acknowledge the crucial place of (potential or actual) shape-shifting at the heart of our ideas and practices of representation. But what sort of shape-shifting? The two key dimensions to shape-shifting are the temporal and the spatial, key aspects in examining political representation which, despite for example the classic work of Fenno (2003) and Eulau et al. (1959), play little role in contemporary theories. I will comment on each in turn.

Among theorists of representation there is an underlying, and largely unspoken, assumption that representatives play one distinct representative role at a time. Likewise, there is a common linear assumption about time in representative politics—that any given moment in a passage of time is in principle equal in political significance and intensity to any other. Where issues of temporality are considered at all, they tend to be large-scale epochal ones, for example Pitkin's (1967) view of the period of the "fascist theory of representation." A focus on shape-shifting representation brings these assumptions into question. On one level, we have the importance of representatives being able to

---

[8] The types represented in Figure 1 are in principle independent of questions of who may be relatively powerful, or relatively powerless, political actors. A shape-retainer, for example, may retain his shape from a position of power; a shape-shifter may shift shape from a position of weakness.

"mark moments," to heighten or intensify the significance of particular times or junctures. We are familiar with the importance of election days and nights, for example, as key components of political "timescapes" (Goetz and Meyer-Sahling 2009). But more significant are the ways in which shape-shifting representative practice upsets common assumptions of temporal linearity and singularity. The shape-shifting representative may, for example:

1. offer representative claims on the basis of being one thing at one time, and other thing at another time — e.g., a delegate at one time and a trustee at another;
2. offer multiple representative claims at the same time, or in overlapping periods of time, to different (or even the same) audiences; or
3. offer claims to be, at one or at overlapping periods of time, one sort of representative (e.g., a descriptively representative delegate of a particular group) while in fact acting as a different sort (e.g., pursue a view of the common good while not subject to sanction).

Similar issues arise with respect to space and the closely linked notion of identity. Common assumptions among empirical and conceptual analysis of representation include the view that the electoral district and the nation-state (and little else) are the fixed and given "containers" of the primary issues, interests, and identities that may call for or require political representation.[9] Closely allied with this is the common view that the identity of the constituency or constituents is given (especially with regard to electoral representation).

Sometimes these assumptions will be accurate, but they do not go far enough. The significance of space(s) and place(s) and identities associated with them is a question of subjective and intersubjective perception, not an objectively given property of a system. Even a stable nation-state structure requires constant *evocation* through speeches, ceremonies, rituals, symbols, and so on (Rai 2010). And different "containers" of interests may be available for evocation by would-be representatives, many of them noncontiguous in their distribution: religious groups, cultural or identity groups, social classes, even nonhuman interests and intergenerational or future generation interests. A politically salient sense of what spaces and identities there are and how and why they matter (or need representing) is manipulable, with multiple possibilities in practice.

So we can combine an opened-up sense of both time and space to get a sense of the key dimensions of shape-shifting representation. A representative claimant may claim to be playing representation role A in one place (or to and for one group), and role B in another, at the same time. He may play roles C and D to a common or overlapping potential audience at the same time, perhaps by using dog-whistle tactics — "telling one group

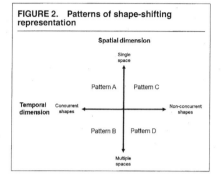

FIGURE 2. Patterns of shape-shifting representation

of voters one thing, while allowing or encouraging another group to believe another" (Goodin and Saward 2005). He may claim the reality of a little thought-of space in order to (try to) render it politically significant to his advantage — witness the Northern League in Italy, and in particular its leader Umberto Bossi, and his invocation of "Padania" as a would-be separate state from the rest of Italy (Giordano 1999).

Taking these two key dimensions, Figure 2 sets out four basic *patterns* of shape-shifting representation — I shall refer to these four as "level 1 patterns." Recall that shape-shifting refers to processes of positioning and repositioning the persona and the nature of his or her claims to audiences or constituencies. Where (in more conventional terms) roles reinforce roles, the argument here is that positioning creates and recreates patterns of representative practice. Each of the patterns A–D in Figure 2 are simplified snapshots of what in fact will be points on a spectrum, where for example the spectrum on the temporal dimension would cover varying degrees of (and shifts among) concurrency and non-concurrency of shape-shifting.

The example of the trade union leader as a shape-shifting representer outlined above offered a sequential shape-shifting. This is an instance of pattern D, where the actor shifts from claiming national-level representation to more specific spaces and groups (thus multiple spaces) through non-concurrent shaping of his persona (i.e., moving from one persona to another in a sequence). The example of President Lula of Brazil may exemplify Pattern C: sequential positions on policy and ideological orientation were adopted by Lula largely within (and for citizens within) one political space (the nation-state of Brazil).

The movement from roles to shapes and patterns of shape-shifting sets in train a continuing process of conceptual elaboration. If, as I have argued, shape-shifting representation ought to be a primary unit of analysis of political representation, then we need to pinpoint also the succeeding steps in the argument. Let us identify, then, three consequent key *levels* of patterning of shape-shifting representation.

---

[9] Notwithstanding extensive and growing numbers of studies of democracy in the European Union and at the global level. See Eriksen and Fossum (2012); Archibugi, Koenig-Archibugi and Marchetti (2012).

REPRESENTATION

Level 1 patterning—pattern A or B or C or D. The representative claimant positions herself, or is positioned, with respect to a number of representative "roles" (resources), and in so doing retains a particular (though complex) pattern of concurrency and spatial reference.

Level 2 patterning—A to B, or D to B, etc. The claimant moves from one pattern to another. For example, she moves from offering a range of representative personas in one space to acting likewise over a number of spaces or would-be constituencies (a move that may be advantageous because, in principle, a claimant might be judged unreliable or inconsistent if addressing the same group of people with different representative persona). Consider for example a member of parliament who is in favor of developing green energy technologies nationally, but in whose own constituency a major campaign opposed to the creation of a local wind farm has become popular. When he campaigns in his constituency, he softens his message, saying the technology might not be right for us, *here.* When campaigning elsewhere, he positions himself differently. This can be seen as a shift from pattern A to pattern B: from consistent positioning in all political spaces to differential positioning in different political spaces.

Level 3 patterning—A to B to C, or B to C to D, and so on. Here, the level of complexity of the patterning increases further.

In principle, of course, there will be a great many possible levels of patterning. Which patterns are discovered empirically will depend a good deal on political cultures of representation and the political positions that are being pursued or contested by representatives. For empirical analysis, this reconceptualization of political representation—from the prioritization of roles to the prioritization of patterns—can be expected to give rise to a number of distinct research questions. Detailed research can be expected to reveal an array of specific patterns, and their detection should tell us a good deal about the dynamics of political representation across geographical and political-cultural contexts. One might object that would-be representatives merely perform *ad hoc* or opportunistic shape-shifting. But, in my approach, *shape-retaining* for example may be just as "*ad hoc*" or "opportunistic" as shape-shifting proper. Further, we are not searching here for moral patterns—terms such as "opportunistic" unduly prejudge representation and overlook important structural reasons for, and patterns of, shape-shifting. Such objections beg the question: why take *this* opportunity to shape-shift, or indeed shape-retain, in this context, where another actor may not (be able to)? What are the patterns of constraint, enablement, and shape-shifting?

A number of questions may guide the generation of hypotheses about such patterns, not least for example:

1. Are identifiable patterns of shape-shifting representation correlated with different political actors (heads of state, members of parliament, interest group leaders, protest group leaders, and so on)?

2. Do specific countries or political cultures foster or in some way require distinctive adherence to certain patterns of representative claim-making?
3. Is there a relationship between shape-shifting or shape-retaining from a position of strength (or weakness) and a specific pattern (or level of pattern) of shape-shifting?
4. On a reasonable measure of political visibility, what pattern(s) in what contexts foster greater or lesser degrees of political transparency?

Let us take the final question by way of illustration. Surely, in cases of multiple, hidden, and (on the face of it) inconsistent claims by shape-shifting representatives, the latter will be "found out"? Political scientists have long offered evidence that American voters lack information about their political choices in the polling booth. They rely on cues from candidates, parties, and other actors which offer shortcuts (Popkin 1994). But even this view may rest on questionable assumptions about the ready availability of sufficient knowledge, or sources of knowledge, in addition to the problem that not enough people avail themselves of it. Amid contemporary tendencies to "narrowcasting" media, people get their information from limited sources, even when many further sources are feasibly available to them. Trends in access to and accessibility of knowledge of politics may underpin capacities for shape-shifting representation. With imperfect and differentiated distributions of perceptibility come opportunities to manipulate perceptions of political time, space, and identity. Capacities and opportunities for shape-shifting representation (and for example for shape-retaining representation) may increase where dense and divided modes of knowledge mediation form particular regimes of political visibility.[10]

Systemic representation

There remains a crucial issue with respect to space: where representation is understood to happen within a polity. Is it, for example, an instruction or practice relevant only to formal elective office? Recent innovations in thinking about political representation have, following one thread in Pitkin's work (1967), shifted their analytic and normative focus away from strictly dyadic relationships between represented and representative, and towards systemic views. Two factors underpin this move. First, in terms of defining representation, it is recognized that a range of actors, for example unelected as well as elected ones, may succeed in making effective representative claims (Montanaro 2012; Rehfeld 2006; Saward 2010, 82–110). Second, in terms of normative democratic criteria, it is the overall systemic quality of representation (however that quality

---

[10] Empirical hypotheses concerning developments in (at least) established modern liberal democracies facilitating shape-shifting representation may further take into account (a) uneven but increased social class mobility, (b) uneven but increased geographical mobility, and (c) a widening of the locations and opportunities for representative claim-making and reception.

572 REPRESENTATION

FIGURE 3. Dimensions of systemic representation

		Democratic legitimation	
		Dyadic	Systemic
Representation's domain	Systemic - governmental	A	B
	Systemic - societal	C	D

itself is assessed) which counts, however much dyadic instances of representation still matter, normatively. However, we need to question this new conventional wisdom and further unpack this distinction. It acts as cover for further important distinctions concerning the "systemic," and may obscure what is at stake in the linkages and mutual dependencies between dyadic and systemic representation. Consider Figure 3.

The *systemic-governmental* view holds that representation happens in the executive and legislature of a state, and perhaps in governmental and quasi-governmental international bodies. The *systemic-societal* view holds that representation occurs across society, including in governmental bodies but also for example in interest groups, social movements, and businesses. In terms of democratic legitimation, one can look to specified qualities of representative dyads within (box A), or within and beyond (box B), the governmental system. Without entering into a full defence here, I hold that boxes C and D in Figure 3 are the relevant ones to consider where the analysis of the quality of political representation is at issue.

Writers who advocate a "systemic" view of representation, notably Pitkin, Urbinati, and Mansbridge, especially as far as normative judgements are concerned, tend to assume that systemic = systemic-governmental. The key reasons behind my preferred systemic-societal interpretation include the argument that so-called "informal" representation—often located outside the state, often nonelective or informally or partially elective though still based on claim-making and reception—*is* political representation and is potentially democratic representation.[11] Representation is claimed or enacted by a wide array of local, national, and international groups

and individuals, elected or chosen or not-elected and rejected. Even democratic representation need not to be understood as confined to a set of statal institutions, but rather understood more broadly (and indeed more complexly) as a set of practices more or less present in a wide array of diffuse locations, including transnational contexts. On this basis, analysts should work with a systemic-societal basis of representation's domain, along with a dyadic+systemic view of representation's democratic quality. The key point is that the shape-shifting representative has in principle a wide and variegated societal playground (I return to the more strictly normative aspect of the argument below). Indeed, this framing rightly suggests that (shape-shifting) representation occurs throughout social, including personal and group, lives as well as in more conventionally political contexts. As Lloyd writes, "Humans are representing animals... Human life [...] is largely a cycle of making and interpreting representations" (cited in Slezak 2002). I acknowledge this fact and focus on the more clearly political aspects of shape-shifting representation.

A further crucial issue concerning the relationship between the dyadic and the societal-systemic arises in the specific context of shape-shifting representation. The "system" in this potentially broad systemic account is not a consistent, singular, or clearly bounded set of spaces, actors, or institutions. Nor do "dyadic" examples of representation exist in isolation from each other. Rather, shape-shifting representation itself *forges or enacts* the particular manifestations or experiences of the (societal) systemic. An instance of shape-shifting representation will characteristically involve a pattern of representative dyads. These patterns, in turn, enact the systemic. Urbinati (2011, 46) has written of the "... intricate network of interdependency between representatives and the represented." Unstable patterns of such networked interdependency result from (among other things) the activities and claims of shape-shifting representers. The latter, for example, may succeed in claiming to speak for several overlapping constituencies with respect to different sets of interests. That makes for a pattern of dyads that becomes in effect a patterned system of representative claim-making and reception. In this respect, the very distinction between the dyadic and the systemic views of representation begins to blur, or even to break down. The numbers, character, and timing of representative claims and their reception do not map at all neatly either onto a series of discrete dyads or a single clearly bounded conception of a system of representation. Shape-shifting representation challenges fundamentally such neat distinctions, just as it challenges unduly tight separations between types or roles of representation.

Patterns of shape-shifting representation shape in turn the character and boundaries of the larger representative system. Their claims to (patterns of) roles may suffer varied fates: fading, transforming, lingering, or being rendered effective or ineffective. Whichever fate they meet, their representative claims rest not on something that they *are*, but rather on what they *do*, and what constructions of the systemic

---

[11] It might be objected that states/governments still decide issues exclusively—they authoritatively allocate values not in the sense that they monopolize the authority to do so, but rather that their version of authority is decisive. In response, one can note the proliferation of more or less effective decision points and practices beyond and across states: devolved decision-making (for example through privatization of industries) gives powers to nonelective regulators as representatives of the public interest (see Keane 2011); formal "stakeholder" participation, as at the World Summit on Sustainable Development; the representative roles of varied UN agencies; the second set of rulers in a polyarchy, i.e., corporate leaders in the terms of Dahl (1985); think-tanks and interest groups and lobbies who draft legislation and regulations; and assorted modes of network governance (as in the European Union—Schmitter 2011).

REPRESENTATION

societal domain, persistent or ephemeral, their actions weave.

APPLYING THE FRAMEWORK: DEMOCRATIC LEGITIMATION AND THE SHAPE-SHIFTING REPRESENTATIVE

I have argued that conventional normative framing of the analysis of representation prejudges representation's meaning and value as *single* "proper" roles *consistently* performed—the (definitional) singularity and the (normative) consistency born of different but mutually reinforcing normative assumptions. The more dynamic and relational approach via subject-positioning *delays* normative questions about representation *in order to* foster more productive empirical investigation and theoretical understanding. It is an approach that "brings the politics back in" to both empirical and theoretical work. It does not, however, rule out normative assessment of representation.

Democratic legitimation of representation is a contingent product of the complex political play of claim and reception, an account of which requires that we draw on different traditions of thinking about democratic legitimacy. Democratic legitimation is most readily discussed in the context of electoral representation—free and fair voting is a relatively clear way for constituencies to signal acceptance or rejection of representative claims—but nonelective modes of representation may also achieve democratic legitimacy. The comments in this section pertain in principle to both elective and nonelective representative claims.[12]

On what I call the *procedural temporal* view, democratic legitimation is a specifically situated state of affairs whereby an instance of representation is regarded as democratically acceptable by, or is not rejected by, an appropriate constituency.[13] Pitkin's nonobjection principle is an important root of this point (see Runciman 2007), though acceptance (and for that matter rejection) is in principle more detectable and explicit than nonobjection. A range of norms may be used by members of an appropriate constituency. It starts with and from events, claims, and phenomena of representation. On a second, *substantive-snapshot* view, democratic legitimacy is a specific normative standard derived from a context-independent theory of legitimacy, allowing for more or less acontextual answers to the legitimacy question—so long as our concepts and theories are sharp enough and applied appropriately. Such substantive criteria may be understood or applied as a "regulative ideal."

We need to combine elements of both approaches. To the question "Are there actions which we can observe which infer or constitute legitimation?" (Barker 2001), my response is that democratic legitimation of representation concerns ongoing acceptance of representative claims by specific appropriate constituencies (the procedural-temporal) under certain conditions (the substantive snapshot). Thus we work from a procedural-temporal view in the first instance—in this or that specific context, does the appropriate constituency accept representative claims made on its behalf? How does the degree of acceptance change over time? More substantive elements enter our considerations as we step back from the fact or otherwise of acceptance to examine the conditions under which acceptance is given or withheld. Here, less case-specific criteria enter our assessments.

As we work from the inside out—from the situated procedural to the substantive—we also move from a more specific focus on dyadic instances of representation to more systemic-societal considerations. Bearing these points in mind—parallel shifts from the inside out, from dyadic to systemic, from cases to conditions—how might we specify the guiding questions to assess the democratic legitimacy of representative claims? I will first set out the approach that should apply to all representative claims. I will then consider particular issues that may arise in cases of shape-shifting representation.

1. For a specific dyad—a claim that A represents B—is there a sufficient degree of acceptance by the appropriate constituency?[14]
2. Are the conditions within which that acceptance is given conducive to open and uncoerced choices by member of the appropriate constituency?[15]
3. If we zoom out from specific instances and look at many such instances across society, to what extent are conditions conducive to uncoerced and open acceptance acts replicated across a diverse range of dyadic claims—at a systemic-governmental level or more broadly on a systemic-societal level?

The observer's priority even at the more systemic level should be on acts of acceptance or rejection by situated actors. This may necessarily involve detailed and perhaps difficult interpretations of specific cases where the relevant acts are not immediately detectable (see Scott 2012).

Moving further away from representative dyads, whether discrete or multiple, we may also reasonably

---

[12] Montanaro (2012) offers a detailed account of the democratic assessment of nonelective representative claims which resonates with features of the present account. Montanaro's approach is more geared to dyadic relationships and discrete claims, where my present focus is also concerned with more systemic factors and, of course, shape-shifting representation.

[13] For a definition of the "appropriate constituency," see Saward (2010, 145–51).

[14] The difficulties of specifying what a "sufficient degree" may mean do not invalidate this approach. As a general guide, acceptance, or at least nonrejection, by most or all members of the appropriate constituency without undue burdens being placed upon dissenters is an appropriate starting point.

[15] In practice we are dealing with a spectrum of possibilities here. A choice or acceptance may be uncoerced, but arguably none are entirely unconstrained in some way. Borrowing from Simmons' discussion of consent, it can be argued that acceptance must be given intentionally and voluntarily, and without threats of violence or undue burdens (Simmons 1976, 276–7).

574

REPRESENTATION

argue that fast-track (or shortcut) judgements about the democratic legitimacy of representative claims on a systemic level may be made by applying further general conditions to supplement those of case-based open and uncoerced judgements. These further general conditions are defined by additional questions:

4. To what extent is there a plurality of sites, moments, or opportunities for representative claim-making and reception (the extent of openness to many claims and their contestation)?
5. To what extent is there uncoerced equal access to subject-positional resources for claim-making in the given context?
6. To what degree is there variation in the nature and bases of representative claims in the given context (the extent of openness to different sorts of claims, by different sorts of claimant)?
7. To what extent is there reflexivity, in the sense that claim-makers are responsive, and contestation is encouraged (cf. Disch 2011)?

This set of more general conditions can reasonably be used as a second-best proxy for assessments of society-wide democratic legitimacy of representative politics. Plurality, equal access, variability, and reflexivity are key democratic ingredients in fields or systems of representation. A number of commentators regard the promotion of similarly conceived conditions as essential to the democratic or just character of representation (e.g., Garsten 2009, Hayward 2009, and Jung 2009). A greater prospect of democratic legitimation of a system of representation is broadly associated with more representative claims of more types and styles in a context of open contestation in a dense but open-ended network of claims. Lesser prospects of democratic legitimation of a system of representation are broadly associated with the dominance of a particular source or type of representative claim, with few openings for new types of claim from marginalised interests, and little opportunity for contestation of claims. Where opportunities for open and uncoerced constituency assessment of representative claims are not available, a further reasonable proxy judgement is to favor actors working to bring those conditions about, and who base their representative claims on the fact that they are fostering openness, plurality, etc.

It may be objected that this approach—acceptance under certain conditions—does not take a position on (or help to resolve) the important issue of the extent to which the opinions and preferences of citizens making these judgements are exogenous or endogenous to the political process. If preferences are endogenous, one might be concerned whether such preferences were "educated" (democratic?) or "manipulated" (undemocratic?) into their current state (Disch 2011; Mansbridge 2003). My approach does not resolve this question so much as *dissolve* it; if recipients of representative claims accept those claims (contingently or otherwise), then it is the fact of acceptance (or rejection) and not the provenance of the preferences involved that

matters. For example, as a voter I may regard health policy as the most vital issue, and my preferences on health policy as a voter may have been shaped significantly by the arguments of candidate or party A. *To the extent that* the context is one of pluralism, contestation, and alternative sources of information, the provenance of my preference *does not matter*. From a slightly different angle: in most contexts citizen preferences will be co-constituted in some form, and to some degree, by citizens and elites. This fact is insignificant compared to the conditions of plurality, contestation, and so on. I can accept as *my* preference an idea produced by another so long as I have had sufficient opportunity to do otherwise.

Let us now examine specifically shape-shifting representation in the light of this summary account of the democratic legitimation of representative claims.

As we have seen, the shape-shifting representative can operate across society (including making claims intended to carry beyond a polity's borders). His or her claims can take a great variety of hybrid and even seemingly contradictory forms. Here, the prevalence and dynamics of shape-shifting representation pose particular challenges. First, in addition to being involved in more-or-less discrete dyadic representative relationships, shape-shifting representers forge, or attempt to forge, patterns of multiple dyads which may be serial or nonsequential. As such, their actions may blur distinctions between different dyadic relationships, and between dyadic and systemic relationships. Shape-shifting may obscure or disrupt the basis upon which constituencies may accept or reject representative claims—it may, for example, undermine a clear sense of just what claims are to be accepted or rejected. By the same token, it may make representative claims more difficult to contest, in that shape-shifters may make a slippery, moveable, and complex set of claims that are difficult to "pin down."

Second, shape-shifting representation carries the danger of crowding out other representative claimants. This possibility may in practice pose a threat to a key aspect of the desirability of openness to variable claims made by different sorts of claimant. If the number of those who make representative claims (especially consequential ones) is smaller as a result of shape-shifters making a wide range of claims, this may reduce the opportunities for other would-be representative figures to voice their own claims, thus reducing the plurality of types of claimant.

As troubling as these two issues may be, they do not amount to a damning of shape-shifting representation. The difficulties with the first issue may mean that, specifically in cases of shape-shifting, certain systemic conditions may be particularly important to judgements about democratic legitimacy. A systemic perspective, encompassing conditions of openness across societies, may bring shape-shifters into public focus more than a perspective that examines discrete dyadic relationships. The second problem that may attend shape-shifting especially may be balanced by the fact that shape-shifting may be a phenomenon that

REPRESENTATION

American Political Science Review

facilitates more representative claims of greater variety, addressing hitherto dormant but important social interests.[16] There may be a trade-off here: shape-shifting may threaten to reduce the number of representative *claimants* in a given context, but equally it may facilitate a greater number of *claims*. The latter, in turn, may also help to foster uncoerced constituency assessments and their enabling conditions: plurality, equality, variability, and reflexivity.

So while some modes of shape-shifting representation may make some legitimacy judgements more difficult, and may crowd out some potentially representative actors, there is nothing *intrinsically* good or bad about shape-shifting representation. Shape-shifting may be a phenomenon born of political freedom and its exercise, and genuine efforts to knit together compromises between opposing interests; further, an absence of shape-shifting may in some circumstances represent a form of politics that is static and overly predictable. Overall, there is no strong case that norms of democratic legitimacy require that single representative claimants stick to single or small numbers of representative positions.

Admitting to being or aspiring to be a shape-shifting representer may paint a claimant as deceitful and manipulative, whereas to act in accordance with a more familiar type — a delegate or a surrogate, for instance — may be more acceptable. As we have seen, such implicit moral judgements may underpin both the absence and the haunting presence of the shape-shifter in theories of representation. It is true that shape-shifting representation is often regarded as negative by definition — see the *Salt Lake Tribune*'s emphatic case for not endorsing the candidacy of Mitt Romney for U.S. president in 2012. But there are plenty of contrasting examples. Consider a recent comment by Bill Keller in the *NYRB*: "Nelson Mandela was, at various times, a black nationalist and a nonracialist, an opponent of armed struggle and a practitioner of armed struggle, a close partner of the South African Communist Party and, in his presidency, a close partner of South Africa's powerful capitalists. In other words, he was whatever served his purpose of ending South Africa's particularly fiendish brand of minority rule."[17]

---

[16] It may be argued that a claimant being open about, and taking responsibility for, his or her shape-shifting can contribute to the legitimacy of their representative claims. Consider Edmund Burke's famous statement that "Your representative owes you, not his industry only, but his judgment; and he betrays, instead of serving you, if he sacrifices it to your opinion." Burke suggests that the content and framing of his representative activity may shift and change, but only in order to remain consistent with a larger ideal of what it means to represent. No doubt in many instances such openness will add to acceptance of claims by would-be constituents, but it remains the case that acceptance is the ultimate and most appropriate (democratic) arbiter.

[17] Alongside criteria of democratic legitimation, theorists may provide aides to citizen judgement. Citizens may for example consider (a) what shifts in a shape-shifter, character or policy? And (b) are shapes adopted or traversed compatible or incompatible with each other or previous positioning?

CONCLUSION

The shape-shifting representative may be an elected politician, a transnational governmental political actor, a social movement leader or dissident, a religious leader, a business or labor leader, or an artistic figure with a public profile (musician, film-maker, or actor). He adjusts and modifies his claims and seeks to influence the perceptions of constituencies and audiences (cf. Goffmann 1990 [1959]). He positions himself in and among the array of culturally available subject positions, perhaps strategically shape-retaining as well as shape-shifting as such, in order to make representative claims. He is not so much this-or-that type of representative, playing this-or-that type of representative role, but rather a liminal figure, more or less mobile betwixt and between subject positions. He reinforces traditional representative stances and resources by invoking them, and fosters the emergence of new and hybrid ones through creative claim-making and constituent information and cultivation. When successful, he conjures and summons publics.

In his claim-making, the shape-shifting representative takes care who he speaks to, and who he claims to speak for, at given moments. He watches how his words and claims transmit, and how and to whom they may be repeated. In this activity, the representative positions that he adopts or traverses are (as part of the same process) themselves adapted and reconfigured. His posture may at times be one of imposture, but it may be an imposture born of necessity in a differentiated and densely mediatized political world. The shape-shifting representative is an especially distinctive character in twenty-first century politics. To embrace the dynamics underlying political representation, political theory needs to embrace this enigmatic and sometimes troubling figure.

REFERENCES

Ankersmit, F. R. 2002. *Political Representation.* Stanford: Stanford University Press.

Archibugi, D., M. Koenig-Archibugi, and R. Marchetti, eds. 2012. *Global Democracy.* Cambridge: Cambridge University Press.

Austin, J. 1975. *How To Do Things With Words*, second edition, eds. J. O. Urmson and M. Sbisa. Oxford: Clarendon Press.

Bakhtin, M. 1981. *The Dialogic Imagination*, ed. M. Holquist, trans. by C. Emerson and M. Holquist. Austin: University of Texas Press.

Barker, R. 2001. *Legitimating Identities.* Cambridge: Cambridge University Press.

Bellamy, R., and D. Castiglione. 2013. "Three models of democracy, political community and representation in the EU." *Journal of European Public Policy* 20 (2): 206–23.

Bourdieu, P. 1991. *Language and Symbolic Power*, trans. by J. B. Thompson. Cambridge: Harvard University Press.

Butler, J. 1997. *Excitable Speech: Politics of the Performative.* London and New York: Routledge.

Celis, K., et al. 2008. "Rethinking Women's Substantive Representation." *Representation* 44 (2): 99–110.

Chabal, P., and J.-P. Daloz. 2006. *Culture Troubles: Politics and the Interpretation of Meaning.* London: Hurst & Co.

Dahl, R. A. 1985. *A Preface to Economic Democracy.* Chicago: University of Chicago Press.

Derrida, J. 1998. *Limited Inc.* Evanston IL: Northwestern University Press.

576 REPRESENTATION

Disch, L. 2011. "Toward a Mobilization Conception of Democratic Representation." *American Political Science Review* 105 (1): 100–14.

Dovi, S. 2008. *The Good Representative*. Malden, MA: Blackwell Publishing.

Eriksen, E.O., and J. E. Fossum. 2012. "Representation through Deliberation—The European Case." *Constellations* 19 (2): 325–39.

Eulau, H., J. C. Whalke, W. Buchanan, and L. C. Ferguson. 1959. "The Role of the Representative: Some Empirical Observations on the Theory of Edmund Burke." *American Political Science Review* 53 (3): 742–56.

Eulau, H., and P. D. Karps. 1977. "The Puzzle of Representation: Specifying Components of Responsiveness." *Legislative Studies Quarterly* 2 (3): 233–54.

Fenno, R. F., Jr, . 2003. *Home Style*. New York: Longman.

Garsten, B. 2009. "Representative Government and Popular Sovereignty." In *Political Representation*, eds. I. Shapiro et al. Cambridge: Cambridge University Press.

Giordano, B. 1999. "A Place Called Padania: The Lega Nord and the Political Representation of Northern Italy." *European Urban and Regional Studies* 6 (3): 215–30.

Goetz, H. H., and J.-H. Meyer-Sahling. 2009. "Political Time in the EU: Dimensions, Perspectives, Theories." *Journal of European Public Policy* 16 (2): 180–201.

Goffman, E. 1990 [1959]. *The Presentation of Self in Everyday Life*. London: Penguin.

Goodin, R. E., and M. Saward. 2005. "Dog Whistles and Democratic Mandates." *The Political Quarterly* 76 (4): 471–6.

Harré, R., and L. van Langenhove. 1991. "Varieties of Positioning." *Journal for the Theory of Social Behaviour* 21 (6): 393–407.

Hayward, C. R. 2009. "Making Interest: On Representation and Democratic Legitimacy." In *Political Representation*, eds. I. Shapiro et al. Cambridge: Cambridge University Press.

Helms, D. 2012. "Democratic Political Leadership in the New Media Age: A Farewell to Excellence?" *British Journal of Politics and International Relations* 14 (4): 651–70.

Henriksen, T. D. 2008. "Liquidating Roles and Crystallising Positions: Investigating the Road between Role and Positioning Theory." In *Global Conflict Resolution Through Positioning Analysis*, eds. F. M. Moghadden, R. Harré, and N. Lee. New York: Springer.

Hobbes, T. 1968 [1651]. *Leviathan*, edited and with an introduction by C. B. Macpherson. London: Penguin Books.

Jung, C. 2009. "Critical Liberalism." In *Political Representation*, eds. I. Shapiro et al. Cambridge: Cambridge University Press.

Keane, J. 2011. "Monitory Democracy?" In *The Future of Representative Democracy*, eds. S. Alonso, J. Keane, and W. Merkel. Cambridge: Cambridge University Press.

Kristiansson, M., and J. Tralau. 2014. "Hobbes's Hidden Monster: A New Interpretation of the Frontispiece of *Leviathan*." *European Journal of Political Theory* 13: 299–320.

Locke, J. 1924 [1690]. *Two Treatises of Government*. London: Dent.

Macdonald, T. 2008. *Global Stakeholder Democracy*. Oxford: Oxford University Press.

Machiavelli, N. 2004 [1532]. *The Prince* (trans. by G. Bull). London: Penguin.

Mansbridge, J. 2003. "Rethinking Representation." *American Political Science Review* 97 (4): 515–28.

Mansbridge, J. 2009. "A 'Selection Model' of Political Representation." *Journal of Political Philosophy* 17 (4): 369–98.

Mansbridge, J. 2011. "Clarifying the Concept of Representation." *American Political Science Review* 105 (3): 621–30.

Montanaro, L. 2012. "The Democratic Legitimacy of Self-appointed Representatives." *Journal of Politics* 74 (4): 1094–107.

Parkinson, J. R. 2012. *Democracy and Public Space*. Oxford: Oxford University Press.

Parkinson, J. R., and J. Mansbridge, eds. 2012. *Deliberative Systems*. Cambridge: Cambridge University Press.

Pettit, P. 2009. "Varieties of Public Representation." In *Political Representation*, eds. I. Shapiro et al. Cambridge: Cambridge University Press.

Phillips, A. 1995. *The Politics of Presence*. Oxford: Oxford University Press.

Pitkin, H. F. 1967. *The Concept of Representation*. Berkeley and Los Angeles: University of California Press.

Popkin, S. 1994. *The Reasoning Voter*, second edition. Chicago: University Of Chicago Press.

Rai, S. M. 2010. "Analysing Ceremony and Ritual in Parliament." *Journal of Legislative Studies* 16 (3): 284–97.

Rao, N. 1998. "Representation in Local Politics: A Reconsideration and Some New Evidence." *Political Studies* 46 (1): 19–35.

Rehfeld, A. 2009. "Representation Rethought: On Trustees, Delegates and Gyroscopes in the Study of Political Representation and Democracy." *American Political Science Review* 103 (2): 214–30.

Rehfeld, A. 2011. "The Concepts of Representation." *American Political Science Review* 105 (3): 631–41.

Runciman, D. 2007. "The Paradox of Political Representation." *Journal of Political Philosophy* 15 (1): 93–114.

Urbinati, N. 2011. "Representative Democracy and its Critics." In *The Future of Representative Democracy*, eds. S. Alonso, J. Keane, and W. Merkel. Cambridge: Cambridge University Press.

Saward, M. 2010. *The Representative Claim*. Oxford: Oxford University Press.

Schmitter, P. 2011. "Diagnosing and Designing Democracy in Europe." In *The Future of Representative Democracy*, eds. S. Alonso, J. Keane, and W. Merkel. Cambridge: Cambridge University Press.

Schechner, R. 2002. *Performance Studies: An Introduction*, second edition. New York and London: Routledge.

Scott, J. C. 2012. *Two Cheers for Anarchism*. Princeton: Princeton University Press.

Simmons, A. J. 1976. "Tacit Consent and Political Obligation." *Philosophy and Public Affairs* 5 (3): 274–91.

Slezak, P. 2002. "The Tripartite Model of Representation." *Philosophical Psychology* 15 (3): 239–70.

Young, I. M. 2000. *Inclusion and Democracy*. Oxford: Oxford University Press.

28

The Concept
of Representation
in Contemporary
Democratic Theory

Nadia Urbinati and Mark E. Warren

Abstract

Democratic theorists have paid increasing attention to problems
of political representation over the past two decades. Interest is
driven by (*a*) a political landscape within which electoral representation now competes with new and informal kinds of representation;
(*b*) interest in the fairness of electoral representation, particularly
for minorities and women; (*c*) a renewed focus on political judgment
within democratic theory; and (*d*) a new appreciation that participation and representation are complementary forms of citizenship. We
review recent innovations within democratic theory, focusing especially on problems of fairness, constituency definition, deliberative
political judgment, and new, nonelectoral forms of representation.

INTRODUCTION

The topic of political representation has become increasingly visible and important within contemporary democratic theory for two reasons. The first is a disjunction between the standard accounts of democratic representation, focused primarily on territorially based electoral representation, and an increasingly complex political terrain, which is less confined within state territoriality, more pluralized, and increasingly dependent on informal negotiation and deliberation to generate political legitimacy. These developments are driving renewed interest in the impact of electoral representation on broad patterns of inclusion and exclusion (Lijphart 1999; Powell 2000, 2004), as well as in the new forms of representation that are rapidly evolving in nonelectoral domains such as administrative policy development (Stephan 2004, Brown 2006, Fung 2006a), civil society advocacy (Alcoff 1991, Warren 2001, Strolovitch 2006), and global civil society (Keck & Sikkink 1998, Anheier et al. 2004, Grant & Keohane 2005, Held & Koenig-Archibugi 2005). Here we limit our attention to recent developments in democratic theory, which has been as much affected by these developments as other areas of political science.

The second reason is indigenous to democratic theory, which has tended to follow Jean-Jacques Rousseau in assuming that representative democracy is, at best, an instrumental substitute for stronger forms of democracy (Pateman 1976, Barber 1984). Until recently, participatory and deliberative democrats paid little attention to political representation, leaving the topic to neo-Schumpeterian theorists who viewed democracy as primarily about the selection and organization of political elites (Sartori 1987, Manin 1997; cf. Kateb 1992). This consensus division of labor began to unravel about 15 years ago at the hands of those interested in broad patterns of inclusions and exclusions in political representation, particularly of minorities and women (Phillips 1995, 1998; Williams 1998;

Mansbridge 1999; Young 2000; Dovi 2002). The turning point was clearly identified by David Plotke, who wrote in 1997 that "the opposite of representation is not participation. The opposite of representation is exclusion. And the opposite of participation is abstention.... Representation is not an unfortunate compromise between an ideal of direct democracy and messy modern realities. Representation is crucial in constituting democratic practices" (Plotke 1997, p. 19; see also Urbinati 2000). In addition, democratic theorists are increasingly appreciating the contributions of representation to the formation of public opinion and judgment, as well at its role in constituting multiple pathways of social influence within and often against the state. (Habermas 1989 [1962], 1996; Ankersmit 2002; Urbinati 2005, 2006). Importantly, these reassessments are leading an increasing number of democratic theorists both to reengage problems of electoral design (Beitz 1989, James 2004, Thompson 2004, Rehfeld 2005) and to think about democratic representation beyond the ballot (Saward 2006a,b; Warren 2008).

We review the concept of representation from the perspective of recent democratic theory. In the first section, we list the political and social reasons for rethinking democratic representation. In the second section, we review the background in democratic theory. In the third section, we comment on the developments that are sending democratic theorists back to "first things"—the nature of political representation itself. Next, we argue that constituency definition, long ignored in theories of representation, is among the most fundamental of first things because it establishes the frame—the inclusions and exclusions—within which issues are decided. From this perspective, we can appreciate the renewed interest in representative institutions within democratic theory, discussed in the fifth section. Last, we consider emerging nonelectoral forms of representation: new citizen forums and decision-making bodies, representative claims by civil society and advocacy groups,

REPRESENTATION

and other "voice entrepreneurs," for example. Nonelectoral forms of representation, we believe, are increasingly important to expanding and deepening democracy. But these developments challenge the existing conceptual and normative resources of democratic theory. Democratic theorists need to develop new tools and critical analyses that are sensitive to these new forms of political influence and indirect forms of power.

THE CHANGING POLITICAL LANDSCAPE OF DEMOCRATIC REPRESENTATION

Representative democracy as we know it today evolved from two key sources. First, during the twentieth century, the expansion of the franchise transformed liberal, constitutional regimes into mass democracies. Second, when structured through constitutionalism, electoral representation enabled a dynamic, if often fractious, balance between the rule of elites and the social and political democratization of society, with political parties displacing parliaments as the primary loci of representation. Until relatively recently, these two sources molded what we call, following D. Castiglione & M.E. Warren (unpublished manuscript), the "standard account" of representative democracy.

The standard account has four main features. First, representation is understood as a principal agent relationship, in which the principals—constituencies formed on a territorial basis—elect agents to stand for and act on their interests and opinions, thus separating the sources of legitimate power from those who exercise that power. Second, electoral representation identifies a space within which the sovereignty of the people is identified with state power. Third, electoral mechanisms ensure some measure of responsiveness to the people by representatives and political parties who speak and act in their name. Finally, the universal franchise endows electoral representation with an important element of political equality.

The complexities of the principal-agent relationship at the core of the standard account are well recognized (Pitkin 1967). The translation of votes into representation, for example, is mediated by varying electoral systems with more or less exclusionary characteristics. Parties, interest groups, and corporatist organizations set agendas, while public spheres, civil society advocacy, and the media form preferences and mold public opinion, as do debate and leadership within legislative bodies themselves (Habermas 1989). In addition, the principal-agent relationship between voters and representatives is notoriously difficult to maintain, for numerous reasons ranging from information deficits to the corruption of representative relationships (Bobbio 1987, Gargarella 1998).

These complexities remain, but they have been overtaken by new realities such that the very formulation of problems within the standard account is increasingly inadequate. Perhaps the most significant of these developments has been the dislocation, pluralization, and redefinition of constituencies. The central feature of the standard account is that constituencies are defined by territory; individuals are represented insofar as they are inhabitants of a place (Rehfeld 2005). Beginning with the formation of the modern state, territorial residence became the fundamental condition for political representation—a condition more inclusive than status- and corporate-based representation. Indeed, territory has had an important historical relationship to political equality that carried over into modern times. In ancient Athens, Cleisthenes changed the condition for counting as an Athenian citizen from family and clan identity to *demes* or village residence (Hansen 1993). In this way, Cleisthenes transformed the bare fact of residence into a sufficient condition for equal power-sharing, and laid the basis for the modern conception of constituency.

Yet territoriality, though historically essential to the evolution of democratic representation, identifies only one set of ways in which individuals are involved in, or affected by, collective structures and decisions. Issues such as migration, global trade, and environment, for example, are extraterritorial; they are not contained by any existing territorially organized polity (Benhabib 2004, Gould 2004, Held & Koenig-Archibugi 2005, Bohman 2007). Other issues are nonterritorial, particularly those involving identity, such as religion, ethnicity, nationalism, professional identity, recreation, gender identity, and many social movements. Such nonterritorial interests are not new to democratic theorists. The main object of disagreement in making and interpreting the democratic constitution of the Weimar Republic, for example, was whether representation should represent individuals or corporate interests. In modern constitutional democracies, however, the older corporatist views of parliaments and representation have given way to the representation of individuals whose only commonality is residence. Thus, legislatures attend to nonresidential constituencies only indirectly—not because citizens have equal shares of power assigned by territory, but rather because pressure and advocacy groups can organize territory-based votes along nonterritorial lines (Dahl 1956, 1971; cf. Mansbridge 2003). Other venues have emerged to represent other kinds of constituencies. The world is now populated with a very large number of transnational, extraterritorial, and nonterritorial actors, ranging from relatively formalized institutions built out of territorial units (such as the United Nations, the World Bank, the European Union, and numerous treaty organizations), to a multitude of nongovernmental organizations, transnational movements, associations, and social networks (Anheier et al. 2004, Saward 2006a), each making representative claims and serving representative functions.

Closely related, the sites of collective decision making are increasingly differentiated. In the developed democracies, markets and market-oriented entities are likely to continue to function as the dynamic sources of change. Governments are increasingly agile at channeling market forces and incentives, as are civil society organizations. In many cases, these developments dramatically shift the locus of collective decisions away from state-centric models of planning—those that can gather, as it were, sovereignty from the people in order to act in their name—and toward governance models. These issue-based and policy-driven networks of government actors and stakeholders are often more effective than bureaucracies accountable to legislatures, but they lack formal legitimacy and clear representative accountability to those affected by decisions.

The landscape of democratic representation is also clouded by the growing complexity of issues, which increasingly strains the powers of representative agents, and thus their capacities to stand for and act on the interests of those they represent. There is the familiar technical and scientific complexity that comes with the vast amounts of information and high levels of technology involved in most public decisions (Zolo 1992, Brown 2006, Beck 1997), which is often compounded by the political complexity that comes with multiple and overlapping constituencies (Andeweg 2003).

As a consequence of these developments, the standard account has been stretched to the breaking point. Among the most fundamental of problems, ironically, is the very element that ushered in democratic representation—residency-based electoral representation. The claim of any state to represent its citizens—its claim to sovereignty on behalf of the people—is contestable, not because states do not encompass peoples, but because collective issues only partially admit of this kind of constituency definition. Electoral representation continues to provide an ultimate reference for state power. But whereas Burke (1968, cf. Manin 1997) imagined that representatives could monopolize considered opinion about public purpose through the use of deliberative judgment, representative assemblies today must reach ever further to gather political legitimacy for their decisions. Judging by

REPRESENTATION

the declining trust in governments generally and legislative bodies in particular, representative claims based on territorial constituencies (under the standard model) continue to weaken (Pharr & Putnam 2000, Dalton 2004). Electoral representation remains crucial in constituting the will of the people, but the claims of elected officials to act in the name of the people are increasingly segmented by issues and subject to broader contestation and deliberation by actors and entities that likewise make representative claims. Political judgments that were once linked to state sovereignty through electoral representation are now much more widely dispersed, and the spaces for representative claims and discourses are now relatively wide open (Urbinati 2006). In complex and broadly democratic societies, representation is a target of competing claims.

THE NEW CONCEPTUAL DOMAINS OF DEMOCRATIC THEORY

Until recently, democratic theorists were not well positioned to respond to these developments, having divided their labors between those who work within the standard account of representation and those concerned with participation and inclusion. The division of labor followed the channels dug by Rousseau well over two centuries ago, which identified *res publica* with direct self-government and representative government with an aristocratic form of power. The English people, Rousseau famously claimed, are free only in the moment of their vote, after which they return to "slavery," to be governed by the will of another. "Sovereignty," Rousseau wrote, "cannot be represented for the same reason that it cannot be alienated. It consists essentially in the general will, and the will cannot be represented. The will is either itself or something else; no middle ground is possible. The deputies of the people, therefore, neither are nor can be its representatives; they are nothing else but its commissaries. They cannot con-

clude anything definitively" (Rousseau 1978 [1762] p. 198). Rousseau thus confined representation to the terms of principal-agent delegation while stripping the delegate of any role in forming the political will of the people. In legal usage, Rousseau understood political representation in terms of "imperative mandate": the delegate operates under a fiduciary contract that allows the principal (the citizens) to temporarily grant an agent their power to take specified actions but does not delegate the will to make decisions, which is retained by the principal.

Rousseau's distinction between legitimate government (or democratic government, in contemporary terminology) and representation built upon discourses with quite different historical roots. Democracy originated as direct democracy in ancient Greek city-states whereas representation originated in the medieval Christian church and the feudal relationships encompassed within the Holy Roman Empire, its monarchies, municipalities, and principalities (Pitkin 2004). In modern discourse, however, the concept of political representation evolved beyond this distinction, becoming something more complex and promising than the Rousseauian distinction between the (democratic) will of the people and the (aristocratic) judgments of political elites. Developing along with the constitutionalization of state powers, representation came to indicate the complex set of relationships that result in activating the "sovereign people" well beyond the formal act of electoral authorization. After Rousseau, representative politics is increasingly understood as having the potential to unify and connect the plural forms of association within civil society, in part by projecting the horizons of citizens beyond their immediate attachments, and in part by provoking citizens to reflect on future perspectives and conflicts in the process of devising national politics (see Hegel 1967). Political representation can function to focus without permanently solidifying the sovereignty of the people, while transforming their presence from formally sanctioning

www.annualreviews.org • Representation and Democratic Theory   391

(will) into political influence (political judgment). And importantly, political representation can confer on politics an idealizing dimension that can overcome the limits of territoriality and formal citizenship on political deliberation.

Rousseau's formulations, however, failed to shed light on these transformative potentials of political representation. Although he believed representatives to be necessary, he held to electoral selection rather than lottery or rotation—mechanisms traditionally associated with democracy. Whatever his innovations in other areas of democratic theory, with respect to representation he restated Montesquieu's idea that lottery is democratic whereas election is aristocratic. He concluded, with Aristotle, that whereas all positions requiring only good sense and the basic sentiment of justice should be open to all citizens, positions requiring "special talents" should be filled by election or performed by the few (Rousseau 1978, see Urbinati 2006).

The contemporary view that representative government is a mix of aristocracy and democratic authorization is the late child of Rousseau's model. "Realist" and "elite" democrats in the mold of Schumpeter (1976), Sartori (1965), and Luhmann (1990) replicated Rousseau's view that representation is essentially aristocratic, while viewing democratic participation in political judgment as utopian. Modern societies—with their bureaucratic concentrations of power, their scale, and their complexity—dictate that citizens are mostly passive, mobilized periodically by elections (see also Bobbio 1987, Sartori 1987, Zolo 1992; cf. Manin 1997). Although elite and realist democratic theorists have been widely criticized within democratic theory, it has not been for their account of representation as periodic selection, but rather for their portrayal of citizens as passive. Pluralist democratic theory, originated by Truman (1951) and Dahl (1956) in the 1950s, emphasized the many ways in which citizens of contemporary democracies can push their interests onto the political agenda

in addition to voting, owing to the porous design of liberal democracies. Participatory democratic theorists writing in the 1960s and 1970s pointed out that the many channels of representation in pluralist democracies were, in fact, filled by those with the most resources, particularly education and wealth. Pulling ideals from Aristotle, Rousseau, Marx, J.S. Mill, and Dewey, participatory democrats focused instead on those features of democracy most immediately connected with self-determination and self-development, while accepting Rousseau's view of representation as essentially nondemocratic (Pateman 1976, Macpherson 1977, Barber 1984; cf. Young 2000, Urbinati 2006).

Communitarians within democratic theory, borrowing from classical republicanism, have sometimes overlapped with participatory democrats owing to their focus on active citizenship. Although classical republicanism focused on institutional design—particularly checks and balances—these strains were absorbed by the standard account of representation, leaving contemporary communitarians to focus on closeness rather than distance, and direct engagement rather than indirectness (Arendt 2006; Wolin 2004; Held 1996, ch. 2).

Deliberative democratic theory, the third and most recent wave of contemporary democratic theory, is centered on inclusive political judgment. From this perspective, the standard account of representative democracy is suspect for its thin understanding of political will formation. The standard account, with its emphasis on elections, pressure groups, and political parties, suggested that political judgments are, in effect, aggregated preferences. Deliberative theories of democracy were spearheaded by Habermas in the mid-1980s and rapidly followed by parallel theories focused on judgment: Gutmann & Thompson (1996), Pettit (1999a), the later Rawls (2005), Richardson (2003), and others turned their attention to the formation of public opinion and judgment, the institutionalization of deliberation, and the relationship between inclusion and deliberation. Problems of representation,

REPRESENTATION

583

however, were bypassed by several strains of deliberative democratic theory, either because deliberation was conceived within a participatory framework (Cohen 1996) or because it was conceived within already established institutions (Rawls 2005).

For others, such as Habermas (1996), however, problems of representation reappeared in potentially productive ways. First in *The Structural Transformation of the Public Sphere* (1989 [1962]) and then more completely in *Between Facts and Norms* (1996), Habermas cast representative institutions as mediating between state and society via public spheres of judgment, such that representation is incomplete without the deliberative attentiveness of citizens mediated by public spheres, and the reflective transmission of public deliberations into the domain of representative institutions. Habermas was interested not only in the correlation between judgments emanating from the public sphere and institutionalized representation, but also in those moments of disjunction that generate extraparliamentary forms of representation, particularly through new social movements and other kinds of civil society associations. Importantly, these creative disjunctions are intrinsic to the functioning of representative democracy. In this way, Habermas opened a window on representation beyond the standard account.

Direct attention to representation within contemporary democratic theory has come from three other sources as well. The most broadly recognized of these, Pitkin's now classic *The Concept of Representation* (1967), came from within the standard account itself. Pitkin provided a comprehensive theory of representation, primarily within electoral contexts, just when participatory democracy had captured the imaginations of progressive democrats. Indeed, Pitkin herself turned to the participatory paradigm shortly after publication, returning to the topic only to note that the alliance between democracy and representation is "uneasy" owing to their distinct genealogies (Pitkin 1967, p. 2; Pitkin 2004; Williams 2000). If democracy is based on the presence of citizens, representation is at best a surrogate form of participation for citizens who are physically absent.

Nonetheless, Pitkin sketched out the generic features of political representation in constitutional democracy. For representatives to be "democratic," she argued, (*a*) they must be authorized to act; (*b*) they must act in a way that promotes the interests of the represented; and (*c*) people must have the means to hold their representatives accountable for their actions. Although Pitkin understood these features within the context of electoral democracy, they can in fact vary over a wide range of contexts and meanings, as we suggest below (D. Castiglione & M.E. Warren, unpublished manuscript).

Pitkin did not, however, inquire more broadly into the kind of political participation that representation brings about in a democratic society. Nor were her initial formulations further debated or developed. Instead, they stood as the last word on representation within democratic theory for three decades, until the appearance of Manin's *The Principles of Representative Government* (1997). Manin combined an elitist-realist approach to democracy with a deliberative approach, arguing that representative government is a unique form of government owing to the constitution of deliberative politics through election. Manin's work departed from the standard model by focusing on the deliberative qualities of representative institutions. But in other respects, he replicated the standard division between democracy and representation. In the spirit of Montesquieu, Manin viewed elections as a means of judging the characters of rulers. The value of democratic election is that the many are better than the few at recognizing competent individuals, though worse than the few at acting competently (Manin 1997, ch. 4). But electoral suffrage in itself, in Manin's view, produced no change in the practice and institution of representation, which are substantially the same today as they were when few citizens had the right to vote. Representative government is inevitably an

www.annualreviews.org • Representation and Democratic Theory   *393*

elected form of aristocracy because it discriminates among citizens and excludes some from the decision-making process. As de Malberg (1920, p. 208) put it, the very purpose of representative selection is to form an aristocratic regime. On this line of thinking, it follows that discourses that implicate representative institutions as exclusionary are simply incoherent. Such institutions cannot be something other than they are, namely, aristocratic entities that are at best constituted and contained by democratic elections. Thus, in this account, parliamentary sovereignty can be seen as an electoral transmutation of Rousseau's doctrine of the general will of the people, which, paradoxically, transforms the people into a passive body, with periodic capacities for selection but not voice (De la Bigne de Villeneuve 1929–1931, p. 32).

Important though these debates about active versus passive representative inclusion were, they glossed over the glaring fact that many groups within the established democracies lacked even passive inclusion. Although earlier participatory critics of the standard account had turned away from representation, by the early 1990s, theorists began to focus on the *representative* exclusion of marginalized groups—particularly those based on gender, ethnicity, and race—from the centers of political power. The initial questions were about injustices in the form of exclusion. But these questions went to the very heart of not only the meanings of representation, but also its mechanisms and functions. Kymlicka (1995) argued for group representation within the institutions of representative democracy, noting that the representation of individuals *qua* individuals is not sufficient to self-development, as self-identity depends on group relationships and resources. Phillips (1995) argued in *The Politics of Presence* that the "politics of ideas"— one in which interests, policy positions, and preferences are represented by agents within political institutions—fails to grasp that rightful inclusions require that diversities within society have represented presence, embodied within representatives who bring distinctive

perspectives into political institutions (see also Guinier 1994, Gould 1996, Mansbridge 1999, Young 2000, Dovi 2002).

Within this literature, Williams' (1998) *Voice, Trust, and Memory* most directly engaged the issue of marginalized groups in the language of representation, framing all of the classic issues of representation within the terms of the contemporary debate. "Liberal representation" of the kind descended from Locke, though promising formal equality, systematically underrepresents the historically marginalized. By treating individuals as individuals rather than as situated members of groups, Williams argues, liberal accounts of representation fail to conceptualize patterns of disadvantage that are based in group situations, and are often replicated within representative institutions. The liberal account (at least in its Lockean form) assumes a trustee relationship based on convergent majority interests, which does not in fact exist for disadvantaged groups. When such assumptions legitimate electoral systems that simply aggregate votes based on territorial constituency—particularly in the form of single-member districts—they serve to justify and stabilize existing patterns of disadvantage. For this reason, Williams argues, we need to think beyond principal-agent models of representation in which principals are presumed to be formally equal individuals. We need to understand representation as a relationship, mediated by group histories and experiences, through which relevant constituencies—particularly those related to fairness—come into existence. Finally, fair representation requires some relationship of trust between individuals and representatives, based on shared experiences, perspectives, and interests, and this is demonstrably not present for historically disadvantaged groups within residence-based systems of representation.

Still, the relationship between individual and group representation with respect to fairness remains ambiguous in Williams' argument. Disadvantages in society generate tensions between the formal equalities that lend

REPRESENTATION

legitimacy to representative institutions, and their results, which will often fail to reflect or address issues related to systematic group disadvantages. Clearly, for minorities whose claims consistently fail to be present within political institutions, representation based on formal equality also fails basic fairness. Yet the strongest historical argument for fair representation has not been based on group advantage or disadvantage, but rather the proportional representation of individual interests. If all individuals have an equal claim to representation, their representatives should have presence in representative institutions in proportion to the numbers of individuals who hold interests they wish to be represented. Indeed, as Mill argued, nonproportional counting as occurs in majoritarian systems is a violation of quantitative fairness, whereas proportional representation "secures a representation, in proportion to numbers, of every division of the electoral body: not two great parties alone" (Mill 1991, p. 310). Altering representative systems to increase their sensitivity to historical group disadvantage may trade off against the fairness embodied in quantitative proportionality, a tension that continues to deserve the attention of democratic theorists.

Although Williams' argument was focused on representing historically disadvantaged groups, she built on the emerging discourse of group representation to cast political representation as fundamentally about inclusion and exclusion—that is, about the basic problems of democratic theory and practice (cf. Phillips 1995, ch. 7). At the same time, the strain of thinking originated by Manin—that focusing on the relationship between representation and political judgment—increasingly intersected with deliberative democracy, drawing the "aristocratic" approach to representation closer to democratic problems of discursive inclusion (Plotke 1997, Young 2000, Ankersmit 2002, Urbinati 2005, cf. Williams 2000). Together, these lineages are now producing a new wave of democratic theory.

WHEN IS REPRESENTATION "DEMOCRATIC"?

If democratic representation is to be understood as more than a division of labor between political elites and citizens, we need to understand representation as an intrinsic part of what makes democracy possible. To do so, we must distinguish between generic norms of democracy and the institutions and practices through which the norms are realized. Much democratic theory has moved in this direction, conceiving democracy as any set of arrangements that instantiates the principle that all affected by collective decisions should have an opportunity to influence the outcome (see, e.g., Habermas 1996, p. 107; Dahl 1998, pp. 37–38; Held 1996, p. 324; Young 2000, p. 23; Gould 2004, pp. 175–78). Although there are important variations in the normative presuppositions embedded in this principle, most democratic theorists hold that (a) individuals are morally and legally equal and (b) individuals are equally capable of autonomy with respect to citizenship—that is, conscious self-determination—all other things begin equal. It follows that collective decisions affecting self-determination should include those affected.

The advantage of such a norm—call it democratic autonomy or simply collective self-government—is that it enables us to avoid reduction of "democracy" to any particular kind of institution or decision-making mechanism. It allows us to assess emerging institutions and imagine new ones by asking whether they fulfill the norm of democratic autonomy—a question we need to be able to ask, for example, of the many transnational regimes that increasingly affect the lives of individuals in ways the standard account of representative democracy cannot encompass, nor even conceive.

At the same time, without the relatively straightforward conceptual apparatus of the standard account, we need to formulate the concept of democratic representation with a rigor sufficient to identify and assess what has become a rich domain of representative relationships—a concern that increasingly drives the new literature (see, e.g., Williams 1998; Mansbridge 2003; Rehfeld 2006; Rubenstein 2007; D. Castiglione, A. Rehfeld, M.E. Warren, et al., unpublished manuscript).

We owe an initial formal specification to Pitkin, who—despite misgivings about formalizations—observed that democratic responsiveness includes, in one way or another, (*a*) authorization of a representative by those who would be represented, and (*b*) accountability of the representative to those represented. Building on Pitkin, D. Castiglione & M.E. Warren (unpublished manuscript; see also Rehfeld 2006) characterize these relationships as follows:

1. Political representation involves representative X being authorized by constituency Y to act with regard to good Z. Authorization means that there are procedures through which Y selects or directs X with respect to Z. Ultimate responsibility for the actions or decisions of X rests with Y.

2. Political representation involves representative X being held accountable to constituency Y with regard to good Z. Accountability means that X provides, or could provide, an account of his or her decisions or actions to Y with respect to Z, and that Y has a sanction over X with regard to Z.

These elements are generic; they specify only that a democratic relationship of representation is one of empowered inclusion of Y in the representations of X with respect to Z. Under this formula, the individuals or groups who are represented are not passive. There are points at which they assent to be represented, and the practices of assent—including communication—typically require multiple kinds of participation. For their part, if representatives are democratic, they are responsive to those they would represent, with respect to particular goods. A wide variety of actors may potentially fit these criteria: elected representatives, nongovernmental organizations, lay citizens, panels, committees, and other entities. A wide variety of goods may be formulated and represented: preferences, interests, identities, values. And, in principle, a wide variety of authorization and accountability mechanisms are possible. Along with elections, the possibilities include voice, deliberation, exit, oversight, and trust. This variety of relationships, entities, and mechanisms is close, we think, to encompassing the numerous kinds of representative relationships that inhabit contemporary democracies. Each should be parsed out and specified both in its own terms and in terms of its role within the broader political ecology.

CONSTITUENCY DEFINITION

Because it defines the initial terms of authorization and thus the nature of inclusion in representative relationships, the concept of constituency is receiving new attention. As Rehfeld (2005; see also Burnheim 1989, Pogge 2002) points out, the idea that constituencies should be defined by territorial districts has been all but unquestioned until very recently, although it has long been recognized that initial decisions about who is included in (or excluded from) "the people" constituted the domain of democracy (Dahl 1989, Held 1996).

But there is an even more fundamental issue. For the most part, the project of democratizing "democracies" has been conceived as a matter of progressively including more classes of individuals within territorial communities. But no matter how universal these inclusions, when represented geographically, the people are only a "demos" insofar as their primary interests and identities are geographical in nature. Nongeographical constituencies—those emerging from race, ethnicity, class, gender, environment, global trade, and so on—are represented only insofar as they intersect with the circumstances of location, producing only an accidental relationship between democratic autonomy

REPRESENTATION

587

(particularly the distributions of opportunities necessary for self-determination) and forms of representation (Bohman 2007; cf. Gould 2004, Held & Koenig-Archibugi 2005).

More generally, issues of justice raised by representation are issues of *isegoria*, or the equal chance each citizen should have to have his or her voice heard (Dworkin 2000, pp. 194–98). "Democratic representation is fair or just representation insofar as it involves issues of advocacy and representativity; issues of a meaningful presence, not simply presence alone, in the game of discord and agreement that is democracy" (Urbinati 2006, p. 42). Fraser (2007, pp. 313–14) has formulated the relationship between representation and justice quite precisely (see also Williams 1998, Fraser 2005, Rehfeld 2005, Saward 2006a):

> [R]epresentation furnishes the stage on which struggles over distribution and recognition are played out. Establishing criteria of political membership, it tells us who is included, and who excluded, from the circle of those entitled to a just distribution and reciprocal recognition.... Representation, accordingly, constitutes a third, political dimension of justice, alongside the (economic) dimension of redistribution and the (cultural) dimension of recognition.

From this perspective, the equality ensured by universal suffrage within nations is, simply, equality with respect to one of the very many dimensions that constitute "the people." Thus, from a normative perspective, geography-based constituency definition introduces an arbitrary criterion of inclusion/exclusion right at the start. Exclusions work not on *people*, who are, after all, universally included through residency-based franchise, but rather on *issues*, since residency-based constituencies define residency-based interests as most worthy of political conversation and decision—an effect that is arbitrary from the perspective of justice. Although the costs of territorial constituency defini-

tion are highest for disadvantaged groups, as suggested above, the theoretical point cuts even more broadly and deeply, as suggested by Fraser's formulation: Representation is a dimension of justice.

But territory is not entirely destiny, even when it is the starting point for constituency definition as well as the residence-based distribution of one vote to every citizen. The history of race-based districting in the United States can be understood as attempts to mold geographical constituencies in ways that encompass nongeographical issues, and to do so through the inclusion of racial minorities in decision-making bodies. Quotas and reserved seats also compensate for the inflexibilities of geography, although each arrangement comes with costs to other dimensions of representation (Guinier 1994; Williams 1998, chs. 3, 7; James 2004). Functional role adjustments, even if ad hoc, may sometime compensate. Mansbridge (2003) notes that empirical political scientists increasingly identify forms of representation that are not based on standard "promissory" mechanisms, whereby candidates make promises to voters and are then judged in subsequent elections by the results. In "surrogate representation," for example, a representative claims a constituency beyond his or her electoral district, as when Barney Frank (a member of the US House of Representatives from Massachusetts) represents gays beyond his district, or Bill Richardson (Governor of New Mexico) represents Latinos beyond his state. These functional adjustments testify not just to the inadequacies of territorial constituency, but also to its malleability. A key challenge for democratic theorists is to imagine how this malleability might be harnessed beyond the borders of nation-states.

RETHINKING ELECTORAL REPRESENTATION

Electoral democracy is that subset of representative relationships in which representatives are authorized through election to represent the citizens of a constituency to act on behalf of their interests, and then are held accountable in subsequent elections. These relationships have been examined and reexamined by political scientists during the postwar period (e.g., Eulau & Karps 1977). What is new is the reemergence of electoral representation as a topic within democratic theory.

Constitutional Design

Most fundamentally, electoral representation is established and molded by constitutional design—that is, the way in which political institutions form and formulate the patterns of inclusion to which they are subject. Again, this is an issue with an old pedigree. Contemporary interest is found primarily within the field of comparative politics—most notably, in debates about the democratic merits of presidential versus parliamentary forms of government. Here we highlight renewed interest within democratic theory, particularly in the impact of constitutional assignments of responsibility on the capacities of representatives for deliberation and political judgment.

Most generally, constitutions provide two concurrent forms of responsibility, one democratic (through elections) and the other hierarchical (appointment by superior organs of political power). The relationship between representation and political judgment is molded by choices between these forms. Consider, for example, the quite different ways in which the US and European constitutions locate the positions of judges, the clearest example of representatives assigned particular responsibilities of judgment. In the United States, many local and state judges are elected just like any other political representative and are therefore directly responsible to the people (see Kelsen 1999). In Europe, the judge is accountable only to the law and must not defer to the opinions of the people (Friedrich 1963, Kelsen 1992). In the US case, the role of the judge as representative of law often clashes with the political responsiveness required of an elected representative—which perhaps explains why many states seek to increase judges' independence by declaring elections to be nonpartisan (Thompson 1987), and certainly explains why higher courts are insulated from direct representative accountability. In the European case, however, the democratic legitimacy of judges is borrowed entirely from representative bodies that create the law, and judgment is viewed as limited to the application of law. In this way, European constitutions preserve the democratic element of representation within the judiciary, but at the cost of conceiving judges' powers of judgment as the application of rules.

The broader implication of this judicial example is that the ways in which constitutions assign responsibility and structure accountability affect representatives' capacities for judgment. Elections establish the nonindependence of the representative from the represented in principle, although in practice, representative institutions require enough autonomy to carry out their political functions, which will require bodies that can engage in deliberative political judgments (Bybee 1998). Accordingly, most constitutions forbid imperative mandate. But because political representation can only exist in the juridical form of a mandate that is not legally bounded, some other form of mandate is needed to check representatives, which is why almost all democratic constitutions delimit the responsibility of the representatives.

Electoral System Design

The central feature of democratic legitimacy, of course, resides in the electoral system. When we vote, we do two things at once: We contribute to forming a government or opposition, and we seek representation of our positions and preferences. This means that elections are not just a race that some win at the expense of others, but a way of participating in the creation of the representative body, as is suggested by Plotke's (1997) argument that the opposite of representation is not participation but exclusion.

REPRESENTATION

Although comparative analysis is beyond the scope of this essay (cf. Lijphart 1999, Powell 2000), it is worth noting here that different electoral systems empower this kind of participation quite differently, primarily by structuring the inclusiveness of the initial authorization and the strength of vote-based accountability (Urbinati 2006). The key design choice is between electoral systems based on single-member plurality (SMP) districts and those that seek proportional representation (PR) through multi-member districts (Farrell 2001, Przeworski et al. 1999, Powell 2004).

From the perspective of representing residence, it is worth noting that PR systems are inherently less geographical than SMP. Within the boundaries of a district (which may be the size of the entire state, as in the cases of Israel and the Netherlands), voters determine their constituency at the time of the vote (Duverger & Sartori 1988, Rehfeld 2005). In addition, because PR enables representation at lower thresholds (depending on the number of representatives within each district), PR systems tend to include a broader range of interests and identities than SMP systems. It is because of their greater inclusiveness and fairness that democratic theorists at least since Mill have favored PR over SMP systems. A government should reach decisions on the basis of debates among representatives of "every opinion which exists in the constituencies" in a body that reflects "its fair share of voices" (Mill 1991 [1861], pp. 448–50; see also Kelsen 1929, Friedrich 1968, Fishkin 1995). Democratic theorists concerned with the representation of disadvantaged groups also prefer PR, simply because its more inclusive logic increases the chances that disadvantaged groups will have representation (Amy 1996, Barber 2001). In addition, PR may result in more deliberative legislative bodies: Because the electoral system is less likely to produce governing majority parties, parliaments operating under PR are more likely to develop consensus forms of government (Sartori 1976, Lijphart 1999, Powell 2000, Steiner et al. 2005). For similar reasons, the design of local electoral systems—particularly municipal systems—is now back on the table (Guinier 1994).

Electoral systems that produce more inclusion may have costs to one feature of representation. They often produce coalition governments that can diffuse accountability, as party platforms that were authorized by voters are subsequently compromised for purposes of governing. Likewise, because they separate powers, presidential systems are often said to dampen responsiveness to citizens and diffuse accountability (Dahl 2003). In contrast, parliamentary arrangements based on SMP tend to provide citizens with stronger ex post accountability. These systems authorize governing majorities, which are then clearly responsible for governing as long as they retain the confidence of majority party members of the legislature.

It is not clear, however, that inclusiveness and accountability *necessarily* trade off against one another, given the variety of possible accountability mechanisms (Warren 2008). Some of these other forms of accountability are deliberative in nature, and depend on publics demanding that representatives provide accounts of their positions and decisions, even as they change (Mansbridge 2004, Urbinati 2006). This increasing attention to discursive accountability is yet another reason democratic theorists have paid more attention to the impact of constitutional design on deliberative judgment (Habermas 1996, Manin 1997, Elster 1998, Sunstein 2002, James 2004). These issues have returned also in contemporary debates over fair representation (Beitz 1989, Williams 1998, Thompson 2002). At this time, however, theories relating constitutional forms and electoral systems to new accounts of democratic representation remain underdeveloped.

Because of the normative importance of proportionality to the democracy-justice relationship, a small but growing number of theorists are becoming interested in representative bodies that are randomly constituted. Randomness would, on average, ensure that such assemblies would represent whatever issues are salient to the public at the moment of selection, not only in proportion to the numbers of individuals with interests in particular issues, but also in proportion to the intensity with which interests and opinions are held (Burnheim 1989, Fishkin 1995, Pogge 2002, Rehfeld 2005; cf. Dahl 1989, Warren & Pearse 2008). Closely related is the concept of randomly selected citizen representative bodies, discussed below.

Political Parties

Although democratic theorists have been reengaging questions of institutional design, they have ignored political parties (cf. Rosenblum 2008). No doubt the explanation for inattention mirrors the more general picture: Parties have been viewed as strategic organizations that are primarily instruments of political elites rather than venues of participation. Moreover, parties are, well, partisan— and thus do not provide a hospitable environment for reasoned deliberations about common ends, the preferred mode of political interaction for political philosophers from Plato to Rawls.

Yet if elections provide real choices for citizens—that is, if citizens are able to use the vote to authorize and to hold to account those who would represent them—parties will naturally form, structurally determined by the characteristics of electoral systems, the regulations that enable elections, and the constitutional form of government. As Rosenblum (2008) notes, in contrast to democratic theorists, most political scientists view democratic representation as unthinkable without parties. They are arguably the key representative bodies within representative government. Their representative functions include aggregating and deliberating interests and values, and linking issues through programmatic visions within political environments that are increasingly segmented. Because they perform these functions in ways that can be more or less inclusive and more or less deliberative, political parties should find their way

back onto the agenda of democratic theory (see Beitz 1989). Such integration, however, will require that we understand partisanship as an essential feature of deliberation. Parties as organizations are not to be confused with factions since they can and should transform particular forms of advocacy into more competing accounts of common goods and interests, and in this way structure public discourse (Urbinati 2006, pp. 37–38; Rosenblum 2008).

Ethical Obligations of Representatives

If representative roles are structured in part by institutional rules and inducements, they are also structured by the ethical duties of public office. Representatives are elected to do certain jobs, and their jobs come with obligations. The question of representative roles was famously conceived by Burke (1968), who argued that representatives should serve as trustees of the interests of those who elected them—"virtual representatives"—rather than serving as delegates. Representatives should not be bound by the preferences of constituents; they should use their autonomous judgment within the context of deliberative bodies to represent the public interest.

The notion that representatives are trustees is widely understood as a quasi-aristocratic understanding of representation: the best judgment of elites replaces the judgment of the people. This understanding of the delegate-trustee distinction crowds all "democratic" meanings of representation into the delegate model. The formulation drains the meaning from "democracy" and tells us nothing about how constituents' interests are converted into decisions within the context of a representative institution. That is, the concept of delegation provides no explanation of decision making and thus fails to provides an account of democratic rule. Pitkin (1967) offered more nuance when she noted that representatives cannot simply reflect their constituents' interests—in part because interests are often unformed (thus, it is unclear what

REPRESENTATION

591

should be represented) and in part because their jobs include making collective decisions that accord with democratic institutions. Instead, Pitkin argued, we should understand representatives as having the ethical obligation to be responsive to their constituents' interests. This formulation had the advantage of covering the complexities of the relationship, although it did not provide much more.

Ironically, perhaps, early incarnations of group representation arguments fell on the trustee side of the dichotomy, with its elitist leanings. If a representative is descriptively representative of a group, then the group's members must trust their representative, since descriptive similarity in itself implies no mechanisms for accountability—and, indeed, carries ambiguous role obligations. But working through the requirements for group representatives has put the problem of role ethics back on the agenda (Phillips 1995, Williams 1998, Mansbridge 1999, Young 2000, Dovi 2002). Interestingly, the category of trust has proved more fruitful than that of delegate, reconfigured so it is clear that, as a trustee, the representative is obligated to keep his or her constituents' interests in view (Dovi 2007, ch. 5). Mansbridge (2003) argues that much democratic representation is "gyroscopic": Voters select a representative because she holds values that converge with theirs. Voters then pay little attention to the representative, trusting her to do the right thing. They often "select" rather than "sanction"; they trust rather than monitor. On Mansbridge's view, there is nothing undemocratic about this strategy. Voters are, in effect, judging character rather than performance, but they retain their capacity to remove a representative should the bases of their trust be disappointed or betrayed (J. Mansbridge, unpublished manuscript).

Interest in the ethical obligations of representatives has also been fueled by problems of campaign finance and corruption (Beitz 1989, ch. 9; Thompson 1995; Stark 2000; Warren 2006). We are likely to see full theories of representative ethics in the near fu-

ture (cf. Dovi 2007; E. Beerbohm, unpublished manuscript).

Deliberation and Judgment

As we suggested above, one of the most important inspirations for rethinking political representation within electoral democracy has been the increasingly sophisticated emphasis on deliberation within democracy. From this perspective, representation induces and forms relationships of judgment that enable democracy, some of which may be formalized by election, and others of which may work through group advocacy, voice, the media, or indeed, representative claims by any number of actors from both within and outside institutionalized politics (Rosanvallon 1998). Intrinsic to these processes of judgment is what Urbinati (2006) calls indirectness in politics—the representation of citizens' judgments to them by their representative and vice versa—through which the demos reflects on itself and judges its laws, institutions, and leaders (see also Ankersmit 2002).

These reflexive relationships often go unnoticed, but they are essential to making political judgment work in complex, pluralistic, democratic societies. Representation functions to depersonalize claims and opinions, for example, which in turn allows citizens to mingle and associate without erasing the partisan spirit essential to free political competition. Representation serves to unify and connect citizens, while also pulling them out of the immediate present and projecting them into future-oriented perspectives. Representation, when intertwined with citizens' reflexivity and participation, evokes and focuses the natality of politics, through which individuals transcend the immediacy of their interests, biographical experience, and social and cultural attachments, and enlarge their political judgment on their own and others' opinions (Urbinati 2006; see Arendt 1989). Thus, even at its most divisive, in a democratic society representative institutions are never solely descriptive of social segmentations

www.annualreviews.org • Representation and Democratic Theory 401

592   REPRESENTATION

and identities. And at their best, they tend toward transcendence of the here and now in a process that is animated by a dialectic between what is and what can be or ought to be (Przeworski 1991, p. 19; cf. Hegel 1967). Finally, of course, representation also enables citizens to survey and discipline power holders, not only through the direct mechanisms of voting but also through the gathering and exposure of information by groups and the media who claim (not always credibly) to act as representatives of the public.

In short, we should think of representative democracy not as a pragmatic alternative to something we modern citizens can no longer have, namely direct democracy, but as an intrinsically modern way of intertwining participation, political judgment, and the constitution of demoi capable of self-rule. Understood in this way, elections are not an alternative to deliberation and participation, but rather structure and constitute both. Elections are not a discrete series of instants in which the sovereign will is authorized, but rather continuums of influence and power created and recreated by moments in which citizens can use the vote to select and judge representatives (Dahl 1971, pp. 20–21). Likewise, we should understand electoral representation as having an elective affinity with deliberative politics because it structures ongoing processes of action and reaction between institutions and society, between mistrust and legitimacy, and between sanctioned will and censuring judgment from below (Rosanvallon 2006).

THE NEW FRONTIER: NONELECTORAL DEMOCRATIC REPRESENTATION

As we argued above, there are limitations to a purely electoral rendering of democracy and representation. Some of these limitations are mutable in principle but unlikely to be changed in practice. The central organizing principle of territorial constituency, for example, is likely to remain, if only because it provides a transparent and practical basis for the distribution of votes to persons. But some of the primary virtues of electoral democracy are also limitations. Elections, for example, can and should be institutionalized in such a way that the rules are knowable and predictable, and accountability can be achieved over long periods of time (Thompson 2004). Yet the very stability of elected representatives and electoral institutions means that they are slow to respond to emerging or marginalized constituencies. Neither are elections very sensitive to information. Although the campaigns leading up to elections are, ideally, energetic periods of issue-focused deliberation, votes in themselves are information-poor. Elected representatives are left to rely on other means (polls, advice, focus groups, letters, petitions, and the like) to guess what voters intend them to represent—over what spectrum of issues, in what proportion, and with what intensity. Although electoral cycles of authorization and accountability provide a strong check against gross abuses of power, as representative devices they lack nuance and sensitivity (Dunn 1999). Stated more positively, insofar as electoral representation works, it does so in conjunction with a rich fabric of representative claimants and advocacy within society (Rosanvallon 2006, Urbinati 2006). This point was appreciated within early pluralist theory, though without the critical eye for the social and economic inequalities that group advocacy–based democracy usually entails (Truman 1951; Dahl 1956; cf. Held 1996, ch. 6).

Further limitations of electoral representation inhere in its partisan qualities, however necessary they are if elections are to serve as instruments of authorization and accountability (Urbinati 2006). This necessity trades off against others: If speech is always strategic, it will dampen or subvert deliberation oriented toward norm- or fact-based consensus (Chambers 2004, Mansbridge 2004). The deliberative elements of representation are likewise dampened by the fact that legislative institutions are responsible for decisions

REPRESENTATION

593

affecting the exercise of state power, meaning that they are poor venues for representing emerging agendas, which do much better in the less restricted give and take of deliberation in the public sphere (Habermas 1996).

In addition, these features of electoral representation—their inability to refract fine-grained representation into political institutions and their dampening effects on deliberation—fit poorly with the norms of citizenship evolving in the developed democracies. Dalton (2007) argues that new generations of citizens are voting less but engaging more. They want more choice; they want more direct impact. These are goods that electoral representation cannot provide. This fact alone should spur us to think about representation more broadly, including nonelectoral venues—not necessarily as competing forms of representation (though they can be), but possibly as complementary forms (Saward 2006a,b).

Finally, as we noted above (When is Representation "Democratic"?), the globalization of democratic norms and expectations simply does not fit with any electorally based constituencies at all—not only within the international domain but also in contexts that have weak or nonexistent electoral democracies.

Owing to these functional limitations of electoral representation, practices of democratic representation increasingly go beyond electoral venues, a phenomenon that testifies to the expansion and pluralization of spaces of political judgment in today's democracies. One of the most remarkable developments has been the proliferation of representative claims that cannot be tested by election. These claims come from at least two classes of representatives, discussed below. First, there are innumerable agents who, in effect, self-authorize: Advocacy organizations, interest groups, civil society groups, international nongovernmental organizations, philanthropic foundations, journalists, and other individuals, including elected officials functioning as surrogate representatives, claim to represent constituencies within public discourse and within collective decision-making bodies. Second, governments and other entities are increasingly designing "citizen representatives": new, non-elected forms of representative bodies such as citizen panels, polls, and deliberative forums (Warren 2008).

Self-Authorized Representatives

Self-authorized representatives are not new. Individuals and groups have always petitioned government and made representative claims on behalf of interests and values they believe should have an impact. Interest group liberalism and pluralism assume that this kind of representation does much, if not most, of the work of conveying substance (Dahl 1971; Held 1996, ch. 6). Moreover, history is replete with unelected leaders and groups making representative claims in the name of groups, peoples, or nations precisely because they are not formally represented. The constitutional revolutions of the seventeenth century were induced by groups such as the Levellers. In the French Revolution, Sieyes declared the existence of a "third class" that was the nation, and they proposed themselves as the speakers or representatives of this class, and thus for the nation.

It is not the existence of self-authorized representatives that is new, but rather their large number and diversity (Warren 2001). Collectively, self-authorized representatives organize what might be called the "negative power of the people" (Urbinati 2006) and can function as a "counter-politics" when institutionalized politics fails its representative purposes (Rosanvallon 2006). Groups claim to represent women, a particular ethnic group, victims of landmines, the impoverished and marginalized, parents, and children (Strolovitch 2006). They claim to represent a wide variety of goods: human rights and security, health, education, animals, rainforests, community, spirituality, safety, peace, economic development, and so on. They often claim to represent positions and arguments, functioning as "discursive"

www.annualreviews.org • Representation and Democratic Theory   *403*

representatives (Keck 2003; cf. Alcoff 1991, Dryzek 2000, ch. 4). So representation of this kind can be targeted and issue-specific; it can be flexible and respond to emerging issues, and particularly to constituencies that are not territorially anchored. The collectivities representatives seek to influence are increasingly diverse: not only governments and power holders but also public discourse and culture, as well as powerful market actors such as corporations. These kinds of representatives can and do function beyond borders. Not only do they have the potential to compensate for electoral inflexibilities—providing high levels of targeted, information-rich representation—but they also function in areas where no electoral democracy exists: in the global arena, and in authoritarian contexts (Dryzek 2000, ch. 5; Grant & Keohane 2005; Saward 2006b; Bohman 2007; Rubenstein 2007). Indeed, these representative functions are increasingly recognized by international organizations. For instance, the United Nations has begun recognizing civil society organizations within its programs as representative of groups that are not well represented by its member states. The challenges for democratic theory are to understand the nature of these representative claims and to assess which of them count as contributions to democracy and in what ways. It is now clear, for example, that self-authorized representation is not necessarily a precursor to formal, electoral inclusion but rather a representative phenomenon in its own right, which may contribute to democracy in ways that electoral representation cannot. But unlike electoral mechanisms, the arena of self-authorized representatives offers no discrete domain of institutional processes, and so identifying and assessing their democratic contributions will take imagination (D. Castiglione & M.E. Warren, unpublished manuscript).

One way to begin would be to ask the same generic questions asked of electoral representation, as suggested above: (*a*) How are the representatives authorized by those in whose name they act? (*b*) How are they held accountable by those they claim to represent? With respect to authorization, the nature of the representative agent will make a difference. Many self-authorized representatives are voluntary organizations with followings and memberships. In such cases, authorization might work through members' votes and voices. Other kinds of self-authorized representatives make claims on behalf of ascriptive, involuntary constituencies, such as racial or ethnic groups (Alcoff 1991, Strolovitch 2006). Then there are agents who claim to represent those with little or no voice, such as international human rights organizations, or organizations representing the interests of children or animals. Finally, there are many agents—nongovernmental organizations and foundations, for example—who claim missions on behalf of others, more or less formally (Grant & Keohane 2005, Saward 2006b). In these kinds of cases, initial authorization is inherently problematic; agents claim representative status and it is up to those who are claimed as "represented" to say yes or no or to offer alternative accounts. Authorization is, as it were, reflexive and retrospective at best. Where those who are represented are silent because of their context—or absent, as in the case of future generations—the analogy to electoral authorization breaks down altogether, and we are better off to look at generic norms and functions of democratic representation, and then to imagine nonelectoral devices that might serve these norms and functions (Rubenstein 2007).

No doubt because of the absence of formal authorization in most cases, the work relevant to these new forms of representation has focused primarily on accountability (Ebrahim 2003, Kuper 2004, Held & Koenig-Archibugi 2005, Castiglione 2006). There are several potential mechanisms of accountability. When membership-based voluntary organizations claim to represent their members, for example, members can either lend their names to the organization, or they can exit, producing market-like accountability

REPRESENTATION 595

(Goodin 2003). Groups without power may go public, gaining influence precisely because they can justify their representations (Warren 2001, ch. 4). A group may be held to account indirectly through "horizontal" policing by other groups, by boards, or by the media, often through comparisons between the group's representative claims (e.g., in its mission statement) and its actions (Grant & Keohane 2005). Devices such as performance indicators, audits, and surveys can add elements of accountability.

Of course, this list of possible ways and means of authorization and accountability only tells us that, in principle, we could develop theories that would stretch to the domain of self-authorized representatives. It is neither a theory in itself, nor a judgment as to whether or how this emerging domain contributes to democratic representation (cf. Warren 2001, ch. 7; 2003). But one key issue for democratic theory is increasingly clear, even in advance of well-developed theories. In the case of electoral representation, an abstract equality is achieved through the universal franchise. There is no equivalent equality of influence or voice in the nonelectoral domain, where the advantages of education, income, and other unequally distributed resources are more likely to translate into patterns of over- and underrepresentation (Warren 2001, Cain et al. 2003, Strolovitch 2006). The many advantages of self-authorized representation—and they are considerable—may also result in increasingly unequal representation.

Citizen Representatives

Self-authorized representation provides a possible frame for understanding the rapid evolution of what we call, following Warren (2008), "citizen representatives" (Rowe & Frewer 2000, Brown 2006). These forms involve nonelected, formally designed venues into which citizens are selected or self-selected for representative purposes. The oldest form of citizen representative is the court-

room jury, which represents the considered judgment of peers. We can now add more recent experiments with citizen juries and panels, advisory councils, stakeholder meetings, lay members of professional review boards, representations at public hearings, public submissions, citizen surveys, deliberative polling, deliberative forums, and focus groups (Pettit 1999b, Fung 2006b). Citizen representatives typically function not as alternatives but rather as supplements to elected representative bodies or administrative bodies in areas of functional weakness, usually related to communication, deliberation, legitimacy, governability, or attentiveness to public norms and common goods (Brown 2006, Warren 2008).

Although these representative forms are typically categorized as participatory democracy, direct democracy, or citizen engagement, these terms are misleading because only a tiny percentage of citizens are actively involved in any given venue. The more important properties of these forms of citizen participation, we think, are representative. A few citizens actively serve as representatives of other citizens. What is most interesting about these new forms is that they have the potential to represent discursively considered opinions and voices that are not necessarily represented either through electoral democracy or through the aggregate of self-authorized representatives in the public sphere. Fung (2003) highlights this unique representative function by referring to these new forms as "minipublics." They have the potential to capture opinions and voices that are not heard, not necessarily because of group-based disadvantage, but because the sum total of advocacy will often fail to represent unorganized interests and values. Minipublics can also represent considered public opinion, particularly opinions representing compromises and trade-offs in complex or fractious issue areas. Under the standard model, the work of deliberatively crafting policies belongs to the formal political institutions—and these institutions find it increasingly difficult to

www.annualreviews.org • Representation and Democratic Theory *405*

596 REPRESENTATION

represent considered, legitimate solutions before the public. Under the citizen representative model, venues are designed, as it were, to generate considered opinion. Deliberative polls, for example, involve a random selection of citizens who are convened for a weekend to discuss an issue such as health care policy. During this time, participants learn about the issue, deliberate, and then register their opinions (Fishkin 1995). The results should represent what informed public opinion would look like, were citizens to organize, become informed, and deliberate. Presumably, the results are not simply counterfactual; they represent a statistically representative snapshot of the existing but latent preferences of citizens—preferences that power holders seeking to represent "the people" should need to know.

For similar reasons, governments increasingly constitute citizen juries and panels charged with representing the views of citizens more generally, on a given issue (Brown 2006). In an unusual experiment in non-electoral representation, the government of British Columbia (BC) sought to assess the province's electoral system and recommend an alternative in the form of a referendum question. Rather than leaving the job to the legislature or an expert commission, the government constituted a "citizens' assembly" composed of 160 members, selected from voter rolls though a near-random process. The assembly met over a period of nine months, which included learning, public hearings, and deliberations. Professional representatives—in particular, organized advocates and professional politicians—were excluded. They were invited to speak with the assembly, but the designers assumed that the public interest would be represented only if stakeholder advocacy were separated from learning, listening, and deliberation (Warren & Pearse 2008). In short, because it combined authorization by an elected government, random selection, a deliberative format, and accountability through a referendum, the BC Citizens' Assembly was designed as a counter-balance to both electoral representation and self-authorized representation. Its democratic credentials stemmed from its initial constitution by elected representatives, its statistically representative makeup (so as to "look like the people of BC"), and its submission of its final recommendation directly to the people.

Randomly selected bodies represent a novel and potentially important new form of representative—or, more precisely, the rediscovery of an ancient form (Fishkin 1991, Lieb 2004). Should these forms grow, they will bring new challenges. Because any randomly selected deliberative body will inevitably generate opinions that differ from public opinion, for example, connecting them to broader publics will require new institutions, yet to be devised (cf. Fung 2003, Warren & Pearse 2008). At worst, randomly selected bodies might become tools that elites use to legitimate policies while bypassing electoral accountability, or they might substitute for broader citizen judgment and participation (Ackerman 1991, p. 181). At best, however, such bodies might function as an important supplement to existing forms of representation. They have the potential to link the judgments of political elites much more closely to public opinion, while correcting for the inequalities introduced by the rise of self-authorized representatives.

THE CHALLENGES AHEAD

If elections alone qualify as representative democracy, then it is hard to find good arguments against the critics of contemporary democracy who seek to unmask the role of the people as a mere myth, and point to the oligarchic degeneration and corruption of electoral democracy. Such criticism depends on an institutional history of representative government that has not been substantively edited since the eighteenth century. Moreover, the suggestion that we extend the meaning of democratic representation to include the informal, discursive character of a pluralistic public sphere of associations,

REPRESENTATION 597

political movements, and opinions risks looking like an ideological refurbishment, functional to the new legitimation strategies of political elites. Indeed, almost without exception, it remains the case that only an elected political elite has both deliberative and decision-making power, unlike the citizens, whose formal freedom to discuss and criticize proposals and policies does not ensure that their opinions will affect legislation and policy making.

Here, however, we draw attention to the important changes in representative institutions. These changes began with the adoption and extension of universal suffrage, which generated new forms of political life within society, in turn altering the nature and functions of representative institutions. Dahl's (2003) comment on the US case goes precisely to this point. "Even if some of the Framers leaned more toward the idea of an aristocratic republic than a democratic republic, they soon discovered that under the leadership of James Madison, among others, Americans would rapidly undertake to create a more democratic republic" (pp. 5–6). Given the complex and evolving landscape of democracy, however, neither the standard model of representation nor the participatory ideal can encompass the democratic ideal of inclusion of all affected by collective decisions. To move closer to this ideal, we shall need complex forms of representation—electoral representation and its various territorially based cousins, self-authorized representation, and new forms of representation that are capable of representing latent interests, transnational issues, broad values, and discursive positions.

DISCLOSURE STATEMENT

The authors are not aware of any biases that might be perceived as affecting the objectivity of this review.

ACKNOWLEDGMENTS

We thank Dario Castiglione and Nancy Rosenblum for their comments on previous drafts of this article.

LITERATURE CITED

Ackerman B. 1991. *We the People: Foundations*. Cambridge, UK: Cambridge Univ. Press

Alcoff L. 1991. The problem of speaking for others. *Cult. Crit.* 20:5–32

Amy D. 1996. *Real Choices/New Voices: The Case for Proportional Elections in the United States*. New York: Columbia Univ. Press

Andeweg RB. 2003. Beyond representativeness? Trends in political representation. *Eur. Rev.* 11(2):147–61

Anheier HK, Kaldor MH, Glasisu M, eds. 2004. *Global Civil Society 2004/5*. London: Sage

Ankersmit F. 2002. *Political Representation*. Stanford, CA: Stanford Univ. Press

Arendt H. 1989. *Lectures on Kant's Political Philosophy*, ed. R Beiner. Chicago: Univ. Chicago Press

Arendt H. 2006. *On Revolution*. London: Penguin

Barber B. 1984. *Strong Democracy*. Los Angeles: Univ. Calif. Press

Barber K. 2001. *A Right to Representation: Proportional Election Systems for the 21st Century*. Columbia: Ohio Univ. Press

Beck U. 1997. *The Reinvention of Politics*. Cambridge, UK: Polity

Beerbohm E. The ethics of democratic representation. See Castiglione et al., unpublished manuscript

598 REPRESENTATION

Benhabib S. 2004. *The Rights of Others: Aliens, Residents, and Citizens.* Cambridge, UK: Cambridge Univ. Press

Beitz CR. 1989. *Political Equality: An Essay in Democratic Theory.* Princeton, NJ: Princeton Univ. Press

Bobbio N. 1987. *The Future of Democracy.* Transl. R Griffen. Minneapolis: Univ. Minn. Press (from Italian)

Bohman J. 2007. *Democracy across Borders: From Dêmos to Dêmoi.* Cambridge, MA: MIT Press

Brown MB. 2006. Survey article: citizen panels and the concept of representation. *J. Polit. Philos.* 14(2):203–25

Burke E. 1968 (1790). *Reflections on the Revolution in France.* London: Penguin Books

Burnheim J. 1989. *Is Democracy Possible? The Alternative to Electoral Politics.* Berkeley: Univ. Calif. Press

Bybee KJ. 1998. *Mistaken Identity: The Supreme Court and the Politics of Minority Representation.* Princeton, NJ: Princeton Univ. Press

Cain B, Dalton R, Scarrow S. 2003. Democratic publics and democratic institutions. In *Democracy Transformed? Expanding Political Opportunities in Advanced Industrial Democracies*, ed. B Cain, R Dalton, S Scarrow, pp. 251–75. Oxford, UK: Oxford Univ. Press

Carré de Malberg R. 1920. *Contribution à la Théorie générale de l'État.* 2 vols. Paris: Sirey

Castiglione D. 2006. Accountability. In *Encyclopedia of Governance*, ed. M Bevir, pp. 1–7. Thousand Oaks, CA: Sage

Castiglione D, Warren ME. Rethinking democratic representation: eight theoretical issues. See Castiglione et al., unpublished manuscript

Castiglione D, Rehfeld A, Warren ME, eds. *Rethinking Democratic Representation.* Unpublished manuscript

Chambers S. 2004. Behind closed doors: publicity, secrecy, and the quality of deliberation. *J. Polit. Philos.* 12:389–410

Cohen J. 1996. Procedure and substance in deliberative democracy. In *Democracy and Difference: Contesting the Boundaries of the Political*, ed. S Benhabib, pp. 95–119. Princeton, NJ: Princeton Univ. Press

Dahl R. 1956. *A Preface to Democratic Theory.* Chicago: Univ. Chicago Press

Dahl R. 1971. *Polyarchy: Participation and Opposition.* New Haven, CT: Yale Univ. Press

Dahl R. 1989. *Democracy and Its Critics.* New Haven, CT: Yale Univ. Press

Dahl R. 1998. *On Democracy.* New Haven, CT: Yale Univ. Press

Dahl R. 2003. *How Democratic is the American Constitution?* New Haven, CT: Yale Univ. Press. 2nd ed.

Dalton R. 2004. *Democratic Challenges, Democratic Choices: The Erosion of Political Support in the Advanced Industrial Democracies.* Oxford, UK: Oxford Univ. Press

Dalton R. 2007. *The Good Citizen: How a Younger Generation is Reshaping American Politics.* Washington, DC: Congr. Q. Press

De la Bigne de Villeneuve M. 1929–1931. *Traité générale de l'Etat, Vol. 2.* Paris: Sirey

Dunn J. 1999. Situating democratic political accountability. See Przeworski et al. 1999, pp. 329–44

Duverger M, Sartori G. 1988. *Los sistemas electorales.* San José, Costa Rica: Inst. Interamericano de Derechos Humanos, Cent. Interamericano de Asesoría y Promoción Electoral

Dovi S. 2002. Preferable descriptive representatives: or will just any woman, black, or Latino do? *Am. Polit. Sci. Rev.* 96:745–54

Dovi S. 2007. *The Good Representative.* Oxford, UK: Blackwell

Dryzek JS. 2000. *Deliberative Democracy and Beyond: Liberals, Critics, Contestations.* Oxford, UK: Oxford Univ. Press

REPRESENTATION

Dworkin R. 2000. *Sovereign Virtue: The Theory and Practice of Equality*. Cambridge, MA: Harvard Univ. Press

Ebrahim A. 2003. *NGOs and Organizational Change: Discourse, Reporting, and Learning*. Cambridge, UK: Cambridge Univ. Press

Eulau H, Karps PD. 1977. The puzzle of representation: specifying components of responsiveness. *Legis. Stud. Q.* 2:233–54

Elster J. 1998. Deliberation and constitution-making. In *Deliberative Democracy*, ed. J Elster, pp. 97–122. Cambridge, UK: Cambridge Univ. Press

Farrell DM. 2001. *Electoral Systems*. New York: Palgrave

Fishkin J. 1991. *Democracy and Deliberation: New Directions for Democratic Reform*. New Haven, CT: Yale Univ. Press

Fishkin J. 1995. *The Voice of the People: Public Opinion and Democracy*. New Haven, CT: Yale Univ. Press

Fraser N. 2005. *Reframing Justice: The 2004 Spinoza Lectures*. Amsterdam: Van Gorcum

Fraser N. 2007. Identity, exclusion, and critique: a response to four critics. *Eur. J. Polit. Theor.* 6:305–38

Friedrich CJ. 1963. *Man and His Government: An Empirical Theory of Politics*. New York: McGraw

Friedrich CJ. 1968. *Constitutional Government and Democracy: Theory and Practice in Europe and America*. Waltham, MA: Blaisdell. 4th ed.

Fung A. 2003. Recipes for public spheres: eight institutional design choices and their consequences. *J. Polit. Philos.* 11:338–67

Fung A. 2006a. Democratizing the policy process. In *The Oxford Handbook of Public Policy*, ed. R Goodin, M Moran, M Rein, pp. 669–85. Oxford, UK: Oxford Univ. Press

Fung A. 2006b. Varieties of participation in complex governance. *Public Admin. Rev.* 66:66–75

Gargarella R. 1998. Full representation, deliberation, and impartiality. In *Deliberative Democracy*, ed. J Elster, pp. 260–80. Cambridge, UK: Cambridge Univ. Press

Goodin R. 2003. *Democratic accountability: the third sector and all*. Work. Pap. No. 19, The Hauser Center, Harvard Univ., Cambridge, MA

Gould C. 1996. Diversity and democracy: representing differences. In *Democracy and Difference: Contesting the Boundaries of the Political*, ed. S Benhabib, pp. 171–86. Princeton, NJ: Princeton Univ.

Gould C. 2004. *Globalizing Democracy and Human Rights*. Cambridge, UK: Cambridge Univ. Press

Grant R, Keohane RO. 2005. Accountability and abuses of power in world politics. *Am. Polit. Sci. Rev.* 99:29–44

Guinier L. 1994. *The Tyranny of the Majority: Fundamental Fairness in Representative Democracy*. New York: Free Press

Gutmann A, Thompson D. 1996. *Democracy and Disagreement: Why Moral Conflict Cannot Be Avoided in Politics and What Should Be Done About It*. Cambridge, MA: Harvard Univ. Press

Habermas J. 1989 (1962). *The Structural Transformation of the Public Sphere*. Transl. T Berger. Cambridge, MA: MIT Press (from German)

Habermas J. 1996. *Between Facts and Norms: Contributions to a Discourse Theory of Law and Democracy*. Transl. W Rehg. Cambridge, MA: MIT Press (from German)

Hansen MH. 1993. *The Athenian Democracy in the Age of Demosthenes*. Transl. JA Crook. Oxford: Blackwell (from Danish)

Hegel GWF. 1967 (1821). *Philosophy of Right*. Transl. TM Knox. Oxford, UK: Oxford Univ. Press (from German)

Held D. 1996. *Models of Democracy*. Stanford, CA: Stanford Univ. Press

600 REPRESENTATION

Held D, Koenig-Archibugi M. 2005. *Global Governance and Public Accountability*. Oxford, UK: Blackwell

James M. 2004. *Deliberative Democracy and the Plural Polity*. Lawrence: Univ. Press Kansas

Kateb G. 1992. *The Inner Ocean: Individualism and Democratic Culture*. Ithaca, NY: Cornell Univ. Press

Keck ME. 2003. Governance regimes and the politics of discursive representation. In *Transnational Activism in Asia: Problems of Power and Democracy*, ed. N Piper, A Uhlin, pp. 43–60. London: Routledge

Keck ME, Sikkink K. 1998. *Activists Beyond Borders: Advocacy Networks in International Politics*. Ithaca, NY: Cornell Univ. Press

Kelsen H. 1929. *Vom Wesen und Wert der Demokratie*. Tübingen, Ger.: Mohr

Kelsen H. 1992 (1934). *Introduction to the Problems of Legal Theory*. Transl. B Litschewski Paulson, SI Paulson. Oxford, UK: Clarendon (from German)

Kelsen H. 1999 (1945). *General Theory of Law and State*. Transl. A Wedberg. Union, NJ: Lawbook Exchange (from German)

Kuper A. 2004. *Democracy Beyond Borders: Justice and Representation in Global Institutions*. Oxford, UK: Oxford Univ. Press

Kymlicka W. 1995. *Multicultural Citizenship: A Liberal Theory of Minority Rights*. Oxford, UK: Oxford Univ. Press

Lieb E. 2004. *Deliberative Democracy in America: A Proposal for a Popular Branch of Government*. University Park: Penn. State Univ. Press

Lijphart A. 1999. *Patterns of Democracy: Government Forms and Performance in Thirty-Six Countries*. New Haven/London: Yale Univ. Press

Luhmann N. 1990. *Political Theory in the Welfare State*. Transl. J Bednarz, Jr. New York: Walter de Gruyter (from German)

Macpherson CB. 1977. *The Life and Times of Liberal Democracy*. Oxford, UK: Oxford Univ. Press

Manin B. 1997. *The Principles of Representative Government*. Cambridge, UK: Cambridge Univ. Press

Mansbridge J. 1999. Should blacks represent blacks and women represent women? A contingent "yes." *J. Polit.* 61:628–57

Mansbridge J. 2003. Rethinking representation. *Am. Polit. Sci. Rev.* 97:515–28

Mansbridge J. 2004. Representation revisited: introduction to the case against electoral accountability. *Democracy Soc.* 2(1):12–13

Mansbridge J. A "selection model" of political representation. See Castiglione et al., unpublished manuscript

Mill JS. 1991 (1861). Considerations on representative government. In *On Liberty and Other Essays*, ed. J Gray, pp. 205–470. Oxford, UK: Oxford Univ. Press

Pateman C. 1976. *Participation and Democratic Theory*. Cambridge, UK: Cambridge Univ. Press

Pettit P. 1999a. *Republicanism: A Theory of Freedom and Government*. Oxford, UK: Oxford Univ. Press

Pettit P. 1999b. Republican freedom and contestatory democracy. In *Democracy's Value*, ed. I Shapiro, C Hacker-Cordón, pp. 163–90. Cambridge, UK: Cambridge Univ. Press

Pharr SJ, Putnam RD, eds. 2000. *Disaffected Democracies: What's Troubling the Trilateral Countries?* Princeton, NJ: Princeton Univ. Press

Phillips A. 1995. *The Politics of Presence*. Oxford, UK: Oxford Univ. Press

Phillips A. 1998. Democracy and representation: or, why should it matter who our representatives are? In *Feminism and Politics*, ed. A Phillips, pp. 224–40. Oxford, UK: Oxford Univ.

REPRESENTATION

601

Pitkin HF. 1967. *The Concept of Representation*. Berkeley: Univ. Calif. Press

Pitkin HF. 2004. Representation and democracy: uneasy alliance. *Scand. Polit. Stud.* 27:335–42

Plotke D. 1997. Representation is democracy. *Constellations* 4:19–34

Pogge T. 2002. Self-constituting constituencies to enhance freedom, equality and participation in democratic procedures. *Theoria* 49:26–54

Powell GB Jr. 2000. *Elections as Instruments of Democracy: Majoritarian and Proportional Visions*. New Haven/London: Yale Univ. Press

Powell GB Jr. 2004. Political representation in comparative politics. *Annu. Rev. Polit. Sci.* 7:273–96

Przeworski A. 1991. *Democracy and the Market: Political and Economic Reforms in Eastern Europe and Latin America*. Cambridge, UK: Cambridge Univ. Press

Przeworski A, Stokes SC, Manin B, eds. 1999. *Democracy, Accountability, and Representation*. Cambridge, UK: Cambridge Univ. Press

Rawls J. 2005. *Political Liberalism: Expanded Edition*. New York: Columbia Univ. Press

Rehfeld A. 2005. *The Concept of Constituency: Political Representation, Democratic Legitimacy and Institutional Design*. Cambridge, UK: Cambridge Univ. Press

Rehfeld A. 2006. Towards a general theory of political representation. *J. Polit.* 68(1):1–21

Richardson H. 2003. *Democratic Autonomy: Public Reasoning about the Ends of Policy*. Oxford, UK: Oxford Univ. Press

Rosanvallon P. 1998. *Le peuple introuvable: histoire de la représentation démocratique en France*. Paris: Gallimard

Rosanvallon P. 2006. *La contre-démocratie: la politique à l'âge de la défiance*. Paris: Seuil

Rosenblum N. 2008. *On the Side of the Angels: An Appreciation of Parties and Partisanship*. Princeton, NJ: Princeton Univ. Press

Rousseau JJ. 1978 (1762). *The Social Contract*. Transl. J Masters, R Masters. New York: St. Martins (from French)

Rowe G, Frewer LJ. 2000. Public participation methods: a framework for evaluation. *Sci. Technol. Hum. Values* 25:3–29

Rubenstein J. 2007. Accountability in an unequal world. *J. Polit.* 69:616–32

Sartori G. 1965. *Democratic Theory*. New York: Praeger

Sartori G. 1976. *Parties and Party Systems: A Framework for Analysis*. Cambridge/New York: Cambridge Univ. Press

Sartori G. 1987. *The Theory of Democracy Revisited: Part One: The Contemporary Debate*. Chatham, NJ: Chatham House

Saward M. 2006a. Democracy and citizenship: expanding domains. In *The Oxford Handbook of Political Theory*, ed. JS Dryzek, B Honig, A Phillips, pp. 400–21. Oxford, UK: Oxford Univ. Press

Saward M. 2006b. Representation. In *Political Theory and the Ecological Challenge*, ed. A Dobson, R Eckersley, pp. 183–99. Cambridge, UK: Cambridge Univ. Press

Schumpeter J. 1976. *Capitalism, Socialism, and Democracy*. London: Allen & Unwin

Stark A. 2000. *Conflict of Interest in American Public Life*. Cambridge, MA: Harvard Univ. Press

Steiner J, Bachtiger A, Sporndli M, Steenbergen MR. 2005. *Deliberative Politics in Action: Analysing Parliamentary Discourse*. Cambridge, UK: Cambridge Univ. Press

Stephan M. 2004. Citizens as representatives: bridging the democratic theory divides. *Polit. Policy* 32(1):118–35

Strolovitch DZ. 2006. Do interest groups represent the disadvantaged? Advocacy at the intersections of race, class, and gender. *J. Polit.* 68:894–910

Sunstein C. 2002. *Designing Democracy: What Constitutions Do*. Oxford, UK: Oxford Univ. Press

602 REPRESENTATION

Thompson DF. 1987. *Political Ethics and Public Office*. Cambridge, MA: Harvard Univ. Press

Thompson DF. 1995. *Ethics in Congress: From Individual to Institutional Corruption*. Washington, DC: Brookings Inst.

Thompson DF. 2002. *Just Elections*. Chicago: Univ. Chicago Press

Thompson DF. 2004. Election time: normative implications of temporal properties of the electoral process in the United States. *Am. Polit. Sci. Rev.* 98(1):51–63

Truman DB. 1951. *The Governmental Process: Political Interests and Public Opinion*. New York: Knopf

Urbinati N. 2000. Representation as advocacy: a study of democratic deliberation. *Polit. Theory* 28(6):758–86

Urbinati N. 2005. Continuity and rupture: the power of judgment in democratic representation. *Constellations* 12:194–222

Urbinati N. 2006. *Representative Democracy: Principles and Genealogy*. Chicago: Univ. Chicago Press

Warren ME. 2001. *Democracy and Association*. Princeton, NJ: Princeton Univ. Press

Warren ME. 2003. What is the role of nonprofits in a democracy? *Society* 40:46–51

Warren ME. 2006. Democracy and deceit: regulating appearances of corruption. *Am. J. Polit. Sci.* 50:160–74

Warren ME. 2008. Citizen representatives. See Warren & Pearse 2008, pp. 50–69

Warren ME, Pearse H, eds. 2008. *Designing Deliberative Democracy: The British Columbia Citizens' Assembly*. Cambridge, UK: Cambridge Univ. Press

Williams MS. 1998. *Voice, Trust, and Memory: Marginalized Groups and the Failings of Liberal Representation*. Princeton, NJ: Princeton Univ. Press

Williams MS. 2000. The uneasy alliance of group representation and deliberative democracy. In *Citizenship in Culturally Diverse Societies*, ed. W Kymlicka, W Norman, pp. 124–53. Oxford, UK: Oxford Univ. Press

Wolin S. 2004. *Politics and Visions: Expanded Edition*. Princeton, NJ: Princeton Univ. Press

Young IM. 2000. *Inclusion and Democracy*. Oxford, UK: Oxford Univ. Press

Zolo D. 1992. *Democracy and Complexity: A Realist Approach*. University Park: Penn. State Press

29

The Transformation of Democratic Representation

BY MARK WARREN & DARIO CASTIGLIONE

Summary Report of the CDATS Workshop on "The Transformation of Democratic Representation" held at Georgetown University, 4-5 June 2004.

A. WHY REVISIT REPRESENTATION?

In the modern period, democracy was established in the form of representative democracy based on elections of political representatives and a universal franchise. Representative forms of democracy were based on two elements. First, the electoral form enabled democracy within large, integrated political units with large populations. Second, the electoral representative form established a viable if uneasy balance between the pressures of social and political democratization and the rule of professional political elites. Owing in part to these functions, we have come to understand democratic representation as having two key characteristics:

- Representation involves a principal-agent relationship (the representatives "stood for" and "acted for" the represented), mainly though not exclusively on a territorial and formal basis, so that democratic governments were responsive to the interests and opinions of the people.

- Democratic representation legitimatized political power so that it could be exercised responsibly and with a degree of accountability, while providing citizens some control over its deployment.

The standard form of democratic representation is that enacted through regular (territorially based) elections, which provide a mechanism for citizens to select their officials and entrust them with the running of public affairs. The assumption is that the representatives will (or should) faithfully carry on the business of government by reflecting (representing) the electors' interests, values and opinions. In fact, political representation has never been such a simple mechanism since it has always taken on a number of compensatory forms. The relationship between citizen and representative has been enabled and mediated by mass political parties, class-based groups, interest groups, and corporatist organizations. In addition, public spheres and civil society organizations have mediated public opinion so that mechanisms of representation have never simply aggregated citizens' preferences, but also formed and transformed them. Nonetheless, under the assumptions of the representative model of democracy, those political activities subject to democratic controls and input were focused on electoral-based representation.

Recent changes in patterns of politics, however, throw into question the adequacy of the representative model of democracy. Two of these changes involve the scale and complexity in processes of decision-making in modern society:

- Increasingly powerful transnational players and decision-making arenas tend to escape the reach of (nation-based) democratic representation.

- An increasing number of collective decision-making areas and issues, at both the national and supranational level, are now under the control of specialized and expert bodies with only loose connections to the traditional institutions of political representation.

> *Recent changes* IN PATTERNS OF POLITICS THROW INTO QUESTION THE ADEQUACY OF THE REPRESENTATIVE MODEL OF DEMOCRACY

Two other changes have to do with the ways people relate to their political community:

- The simple political egalitarianism on which the institutions and mechanisms of modern representative democracy were established has given way to increasing demands for group recognition as well as for forms of equality related directly to people's needs, characteristics, identities, and conditions. This has resulted in a more complex discourse of political and social representation for which simple egalitarian and "universalistic" standards seem no longer adequate.

- There has been a diffusion of more informal structures and opportunities for democratic representation and influence. This partly reflects the diminished role of formal political structures in social decision-making, but also the increasing diversification of the forms of association in modern societies as well as postmaterial ideals and culture.

Owing to these changes, it is no longer possible to represent and aggregate the interests, opinions, and values of the citizens through simple (territorially-based) electoral mechanisms. Nor does it seem likely that the standard model of representative democracy can describe and assess emerg-

Warren, *Continued on Page 20*

The Transformation of Democratic Representation WARREN & CASTIGLIONE

WARREN, *Continued from Page 5*

ing forms and meanings of political representation. These changes suggest a reconfiguration of the relationship between territory, function, and identity as the main vectors of democratic representation. They also imply a different balance between the political and the social, as well as between formal and informal representation.

B. CONCEPTUAL ISSUES

While there were many conceptual issues raised at the workshop, the following seem especially important to recall, revisit, or reconceptualize if the above challenges are to be met.

1. **Representation is a relationship.** Reconceptualizing representation as well as identifying emerging forms requires that we recall its generic features. Democratic representation involves a representative X being held accountable to constituency Y with regard to interest Z. Accountability means that X provides, or could provide, an account of his/her decisions or actions to Y with respect to Z, and that Y has a sanction over X with regard to Z. Democratic representation is, therefore, a *relationship*, specifiable in terms of a good.

2. **Input versus output representation.** In so far as representation is a relationship specifiable in terms of a good, it can be judged from both process and outcome perspectives. We should distinguish between the quality of representation within processes of collective decision-making—process representation—from the outcome or product of the process, which we might refer to as output representation or legitimacy. It is not necessarily the case that representation within a process will produce results that represent participants, however they judge the results. Or, possibly, we should simply ask whether, in particular cases, representation within the process results in good, fair, or legitimate outcomes.

3. **Representation as a political practice.** In the same way we think of representation as a relationship, we might also think of it as a *political practice*. Because democratic representation requires not only the development and expression of interests, but also accountability, it depends upon and includes participation by those represented. Thus, the traditional division between participatory and representative democracy is not, perhaps, helpful, and less so in modern democracies where participation and representation often intersect.

4. **Representation as constituted by/within political processes.** If we understand representation as *relational,* then objects of representation are *constituted within and by political processes.* This point allows us to understand repre-

sentation as something that is, in part, brought into being by institutions or groups which reflect social relationships, and evoke as well as formulate interests or identities within their more general understandings of the public good. The roles as well as the objects of representative relations are constituted through the political process. Citizens' education and representatives' qualifications both determine and are determined by the process of representation, so that citizens and representatives continuously contribute to each others' formation and transformation. For these reasons, issues such as political corruption and political communication are involved intrinsically in representative relationships.

5. **What is represented?** The common idea that *persons* or *characteristics of groups* are the objects of political representation is not exhaustive. The "goods" that may be represented might include any of the following:

Interests, values, identities: Representative relationships are not constituted among persons *qua* persons, but rather among the interests, values, and identities that are constitutive of persons. Each person is a complex of such attributes, any of which may be the object of political representation. "Groups" are stable complexes of attributes. But there are also latent interests or interests subject to collective action problems that may require representative leadership in order for the interests to have political representation.

Arguments, issues, ideas, public opinion: With the development of *influence* or *persuasion* as a kind of political force enabled by democracies, we may want to think about arguments, issues, and ideas as objects of representation. In this case, representatives function as agents of discursive force. Likewise, owing to the importance of expertise, we may wish to speak of *epistemic* representation—the professional representation of expert consensus within discourse or decision procedures.

Legal and political standing within political processes. With individual and group rights assuming a higher political profile and much political activity occurring within the courts, we may want to think of judicial systems and groups devoted to rights and citizenship issues as representatives of *standing* within political processes.

6. **Groups as representatives.** We may want to think not just of *persons* as representatives, but also *groups* and *institutions* insofar as they have mandates to represent, or are normatively constituted in such a way that they view themselves as representing constituents, arguments, positions, ideas, etc. The process of *selecting representatives* is a key element of representative systems: in formal institutions, we do so through elections. *Informal selection,* however, especially at the group level, occurs through group membership

REPRESENTATION

The Transformation of Democratic Representation WARREN & CASTIGLIONE

into administrative processes. Depending upon patterns of interaction between official and unofficial power; however, these forms of representation may shade into unwarranted forms of corporatism, and groups may be co-opted. A research project might focus on: (a) existing criteria for group representation within formal processes, and (b) whether criteria could be developed that would equalize representative opportunities, e.g., by requiring that groups themselves have a representative/democratic structure with respect to their representative claims, or that they develop broader coalitions in order to have access to formal processes.

6. **The representation of public opinion.** In deliberative accounts of democracy, public opinion has "force"—but it should count as "democratic" only when it develops a public quality—that is, when it is the result of public discourse. Opinion polls, deliberative polls, and the media make representative claims to public opinion, and seek authorization from it. What, exactly, can representation and accountability mean in this increasingly important context?

D. RESEARCH AND NETWORKING ACTIVITIES

The CDATS Workshop in June was meant as the first of a series of initiatives on the "Transformation of Representation". It is CDATS' intention to help promote other such initiatives, and encourage the formation of a network of researchers working in this area. At present, we suggest three ways of proceeding.

1. **Develop a loose network through the promotion of other initiatives.** By organizing other moments of discussion on issues of representation, we hope to carry on the conversation started at the June workshop. This would allow us, and other researchers who may want to participate in future initiatives, to verify if, as we originally suggested, there is a need for new studies on representation, reflecting important developments in our democratic practices and institutions. Andrew Rehfeld is organizing a series of panels on the topic at the Midwest Conference next April, and we hope this can be the first opportunity for some of us to carry on the discussion. We will also explore the possibility of connecting with other similar networks, such as the Collaborative Democracy Network, as suggested by Iris Young.

2. **Promote integrated research projects on representation.** One other aim is to promote empirical research that is theoretically informed. CDATS is particularly interested in setting up a research project on new regimes of accountability. In the short term, it is sponsoring, together with Virginia Tech, an Inter-University Workshop on Accountability and the Nonprofit Sector. In the medium-term, it aims to set up an in-depth research project on the same topic. We would hope that the Network may function as a place through which we can exchange ideas

and research results. To this end, CDATS' Website and its *Democracy and Society* Newsletter are open to contributions and information on research and initiatives on representation and accountability.

3. **Build a new theoretical agenda.** Following more directly from the June workshop, we would like to pursue the question of a "new theoretical agenda" for the study of democratic representation. We are therefore planning some other moments of discussion (including the panels organized by Andrew Rehfeld at MPSA) so that we can arrive at a publication outlining such a new theoretical agenda.

Contents

Page numbers in bold following some names indicate chapters
authored by those people.

accepting the charge 142–3
access, forms of 535–8, 540–1
accountability: aristocratic thesis
and 79–82; autonomy and 288;
British model of 290, 294; citizen
representatives and 512–19; for
decision-making 514, 516–17;
definition of 586; degree of 536;
delegates and 202–3; delegation
and 430; deliberative 334, 348–9,
497; democratic 21; descriptive
representatives and 184, 257;
discursive 496–8, 500, 514, 515–16,
589; discursive representation and
417–18, 419; elections/electoral
systems and 338, 505–6; forms of
513–14; freedom from 510; group
representation and 226–9, 240;
gyroscopic representation and 27–8;
institutional 516–18; institutional
complexity and 405; for interest and
value representation 514–15; internal
versus external 301; narrative 334,
348–9, 497; nonelectoral sources of
496–8; organizational 496–8; public
514, 517–18; representation and
287–303; selection model and 333–58;
self-appointed representatives and
490, 491, 495, 594–5; traditional
concept of 24; varieties of public
289–92
Achen, Christopher H. 297
Ackerman, Bruce 425–6
actor model 166
Adams, John 7
Addams 432, 440–1
adverse selection 85

advocacy, representation as 447–67
aesthetic representation 376, 386
affected interests standard 489, 490,
493–5
agencification 300
agency, problem of 75–6
agency fever 300
aggregation of interests and values 513
aggregative function of democracy
251–3
aggregative venues 522
agonistic model 463, 464
agora model 450, 456, 457–62
aims, shared 191–2, 195
Albericus de Rosciate 168
Alcoff, Linda 389
Al-Hajjaji, Najat Mehdi 131, 149–50
all affected interests principle 489
allocation responsiveness 43, 46–8
alternative control model 24
Althusser, Louis 481
ambassadors, congress of 176
Amy, Douglas J. 133
Anderson, Benedict 389
Ankersmit, Frank 6, 317, 390, 412, 413
anticipatory model of representation 11,
21, 22–6, 31, 279, 281–2, 314
Anti-Federalists 122, 351
Apter, David E. **523–62**
Arab caliphate 548–50
Arendt, Hannah 330, 481
Argarwal 435
aristocratic thesis: conclusions
regarding 102–3; democracy and
77–80, 113–14; elections or lotteries
and 97–102; introduction to 73–7;
policies and 93–7; political agency

and 84–8; representation and 80–3; representative government and 88–93

Aristotle 73, 74–5, 77, 78, 90, 91, 97–8, 319, 453–4, 458, 582

arithmetical democracy 460

Arnold, Douglas 23–4

audience: conditions for political representation and 141–5; definition of 135; institutional complexity and 404–7; mistakes of 143–5; recognition and 136–41; *see also* constituency

audience-creation 379

audience democracy 111, 116, 122, 124–6

Austen-Smith, David 95

Austrian social theory 116–18

authoritarian development 414–15

authorization: aristocratic thesis and 80–1; citizen representatives and 510–11; definition of 586; discursive 496, 499, 500; discursive representation and 417–18; elections/electoral systems and 505–6; group representation and 226–9, 240; interpretive responsiveness and 166; lack of 140, 141; nonelectoral sources of 495–6; organizational 496, 499; relationship of representation and 363; self-appointed representatives and 491–2, 495; statutory authorities and 368; transnational issues and 442–3; *see also* self-appointed/self-authorized representatives

authorization/accountability model 84

autonomy 8–9, 288

autonomy argument 186–7

Bachrach, Peter 23

Baldus de Ubaldis 168

Banks, Jeffery 95

Baratz, Morton 23

Barber, Benjamin 63–4

Barker, Rodney 385

Barry, John 414

Bartels, Larry M. 103, 297

Bartolus of Sassoferrato 168, 170

bedrock norm 309, 311, 312, 314, 318, 321

Bellamy, Richard 288

Benedict XVI 144

Benhabib, Seyla 412

Benson, Russell 111–12

Bentley, Arthur 129

Bernstein, Robert 27, 336–7, 341

Besley, Timothy 340–1, 347, 351

Bianco, William 26, 337, 341

Bickford, Susan 319

Bohman, James 133, 319, **423–45**, 494

Bono 400–1, 409, 489, 491, 492, 494

Boster, James S. 415

Bourdieu, Pierre 390

Bovens, Mark 291–2

Boynton, G. R. 40

Brennan, Geoffrey 339–40, 411

bribery 76

British model of accountability 290, 291, 294

Brown, Gordon 417

Brulle, Robert J. 415

Buchanan, James 340

bureaucratic systems 527, 536, 537, 538–40, 547–50, 560

Burke, Edmund: congress of ambassadors and 176; on deference to leaders 114; deliberative judgment and 580; elites and 108, 291, 351; indicative representation and 368; on interests 209; on responsibility of trustee 466; on role of representative 112–13, 590; trustees and 28, 350; virtual representation and 282–3

Burnheim, John 249

Bush, George H.W. 281, 282

Bush, George W. 122, 125, 132, 143–4, 146–7

Butler, Matthew 341

Bybee, Keith 133

Calhoun, John C. 114

Can the Subaltern Speak? (Spivak) 389

Capitalism, Socialism, and Democracy (Schumpeter) 107, 110

case work 45–6

caste 529, 531, 533, 550, 554, 555
Castells, Manuel 412
Castiglione, Dario 14, 411, 579, 586, **603–5**
CDATS 603–5
central control/government 116–18, 525, 527, 541, 544, 546, 550, 553, 555–8
Chabal, P. 567
Chamber of Discourses 409, 413–14, 416–17, 418, 419–20, 428
Chaplink example 278–9, 282
character, voter selection and 27
Chase, Samuel 122
chastened democracy 414–15
checkbook groups 418
'Chinese box' model 458
Chong, Dennis 311, 312, 321
Christiano, Thomas 165, 429
citizen activism 355–6
citizen-candidate models 101
citizen representative bodies 505, 510
citizen representatives 430–1, 503–22, 593, 595–6
Citizens' Assembly 367, 437, 505, 507, 512, 514–22, 596
citizenship 265–7, 397, 429, 431–5, 485, 524
citizens' jury/forum 426–7, 430, 437, 504, 596
Citizens' Summit 417
civic distrust 484, 485–6
civil rights disputes 171, 173
claims-making 14–15, 284
claims-making 2 400–7
class divisions 97–8, 100, 193–4, 529–31, 533–5, 554, 555, 558
Cleisthenes 579
Clinton, Bill 125–6, 129
Cloward, Richard 194
coercion/coercive power 25, 544–5, 561
Cohen 441
Cohen, Cathy 190, 192–3, 194–5
Cohen, Joshua 133, 239, 413
Cold War 57–60, 63
collective representation 28
collective self-government 585
comitology 301–2

Commission on Party Structure and Delegate Selection 202
committee memberships 47–8
communicative action 310, 313, 315, 318–19
communicative democracy 411
communicative freedom and power 425, 427–31, 435–6, 438–9, 440, 443, 444
communicative status 435, 443
Communism 57–61
communitarians 582
compensation, sorting and 347–8
complexity 62
concept formation 277
Concept of Law, The (Hart) 280
Concept of Representation, The (Pitkin) 184, 201, 375–7, 564, 583
concurrence 41–2, 44
Condit, Gary 125, 130
Condorcet 320–1
conflict management 516–17
conflict of conflicts 311–12
conflicts of interest 128–9
Congressmen's Voting Decisions (Kingdon) 336
Congress: The Electoral Connection (Mayhew) 336
congruence 32, 36–8, 40–3, 44, 315–16
Conover, Pamela 265
consensus 130, 462–3
Considerations on Representative Government (Mill) 118, 461
consociational systems 295–6, 436
Constant, Benjamin 447
constituency: constituting 389–90; control and influence of 35–8, 315, 336–7; definition of 586–7; dual 490, 491, 495; formation of 490, 491, 494, 579
constituent, services for 45–6
constituent-representative congruence 32
constitutional design 588
constitutive legitimacy 499
constraint 568–9
constructivist turn 311, 398, 477
contingency argument 186, 187

610 REPRESENTATION

control, assembly and 457, 461–2; *see also* central control/government
conventionally determined morality 126–8
corporate representation 556–7
corruption 466
crafted talk 310
crisis 478
crisis of electoral democracy 484–6
critical mass 253–4
Crockett, George 254
Crouch, Colin 484
cultural codes 387–8
cultural political representation 387
Cunningham, Frank 229

Dahl, Robert 7, 11, 22, 77, 130, 132, 220–1, 430, 451, 582, 597
Daloz, Jean-Pascal 382, 567
Dalton 506–7
Dalton, R. 593
Davies, B. B. 414–15
Dawson, Michael 190, 194
decisional status 436, 438–9, 441, 443
decision-making process 276, 299–303
Decision Rule 135, 137
decisions, justification for 9–10
de facto legitimacy 267–9
delegates 202–3, 276, 363, 376, 466, 564, 565, 567, 590–1
delegation model of accountability 497
deliberation 31, 312, 591–2
deliberation of interests and values 513
deliberative accountability 334, 348–9, 497
deliberative democracy 412–13, 462, 582–3
deliberative function of democracy 251–3
deliberative venues 522
de Malberg 584
demand-input model 40
democracy: accountability and 78; aristocratic thesis and 78–80; arithmetical 460; Athenian-style 73–4, 82, 87, 89–90, 93, 97–8, 327, 328, 451–2, 453, 455, 456–7, 579; crisis in

12; definitions of 77–8; deliberative 412–13, 462; deliberative systems and 425–8; direct 63–5, 73–4, 93–7, 220–1, 223; elections/electoral systems and 290; electoral 484–6; majoritarian forms of 3; method versus ideal 292–4; minimal 58–61; participatory 7; Pitkin on 325–32; preference-based 311–12; rationality and 410; representation as 57–71; representation as necessary for 8–10; representation before 4–7
democracy of appropriation 485–6
democratic accountability 21
democratic autonomy 585
democratic condition 79–80
democratic deficits 508–9
Democratic Legitimacy (Rosanvallon) 485–6
democratic legitimation 573–5; *see also* legitimacy
democratic representation 169–74, 498–9
democratic revolution 477, 478–9, 482–4
democratic state, hollowing out of 13–14
democratic theory, new conceptual domains of 581–5
demos, decline of 412
deputies 157, 164, 166, 169, 174, 364–5
Derrida, Jacques 185, 223–4, 313, 318
descriptive representatives 183–96, 201, 245–71, 290, 434; *see also* group representation
de-selection 345, 347, 354, 364
despotic governments 480–2
development process 528–9
Diamond, Irene 247
diamond model of political representation 336
différance 185, 222–6
difference principle 184
differentiated relationships 225
diffuse support 48
dilemma of democratic competence 310
Dillard, Angela 189
direct democracy 63–5, 73–4, 93–7, 220–1, 223

directed responsiveness 163–6
Disch, Lisa **309–23**
discipline, freedom and 526–7
discourses 428; *see also* discursive
representation
discursive accountability 496–8, 500,
514, 515–16, 589
discursive authorization 496, 499, 500
discursive exit 497, 498
discursive representation 409–20, 443
discussion, assembly and 457
disenfranchising of convicts 194
dispersion of influence 253–4
dispossessed subgroups 192–6
districts: boundaries of 240, 257,
269; group representation and 240;
homogeneous 352–6; indicative
representation and 366
distrust, contexts of 258–60
diversity 433
divine right 482–3
Dobson, A. 373
Dovi, Suzanne **183–97**
Downs, Anthony 93, 110
Druckman, James 311, 312, 313, 315,
316, 321
Dryzek, John 133, **409–21**, 412, 414,
427, 428, 436, 443
dual constituency 490, 491, 495
Dunn, John 9–10, 73, 293, 478
dyadic representation 571–2

Easton, David 48
Eckersley, R. 373, 375, 390
economic polarization 194
Economic Theory of Democracy, An
(Downs) 110
economic theory of politics 339
economic voting 297
economy of moral disagreement 417
Edelman, Murray 48
education 25, 310, 315, 481
egalitarian inclusiveness 511–12
ekklesia 451–2, 453–4
*Elections, Representation, and
Congressional Voting Behavior*
(Bernstein) 336

elections/electoral systems:
accountability and 290, 295–7,
338; aristocratic thesis and 97–102;
assumptions regarding 603;
authorization and accountability and
505–6; Canadian review of 367, 437,
505, 507; centrality of 5; citizenship
and 397; critique of 477; cultural
codes and 387; as defining feature
of democracy 77; design of 588–90;
discourses and 419; effects of 3–4; elite
selection and 91–3; *in European Union*
405–6; indicative representation and
160; minimal democracy and 58–9;
plurality versus proportional 298, 299;
policy formation and 341; political
equality and 9; problems with 507–8;
proportionality and 450; rethinking
587–92; standard accounts of
democratic representation and 492–3;
standard theories of representation
and 397; universal suffrage and 579;
voting as duty and 452
electoral democracy, crisis of 484–6
electoral political representation 386
elite representation 540–5, 546, 556–7,
561
elitism 282–3, 350
Elster, Jon 411
'embourgeoisement' 531–5, 539–40, 557,
558
empowered venues 522
empty place of power 479, 480
enablement 568–9
epistemic difference principle 433–4
epistemic representation 604
equality 9, 12, 461–2, 467, 482–4, 485,
486
Equal Rights Amendment (ERA)
259–60, 261–2
equilibrium policy 95
Erikson, Robert S. 283, 337, 341
essentialism 254–6
Estlund, David 433–4
ethical obligations 590–1
ethics, discursive representation and
411–12

etymological protocol 318
Eulau, Heinz **35–56**, 39, 40, 44, 46, 564, 569
European Union 300–3, 395–6, 397–8, 401–7, 423, 428, 431, 437, 440–4
exercise conception of deliberative representation 441
exit accountability 497–8
experiences, shared 245–6
expressive pressures 178

factor analysis 414
fallibility 461, 463
Farrakhan, Louis 189, 192
Fearon, James 338, 341
Fearon, Richard F., Jr. 27, 28
Federalist, The 328
Federalists 351
Fenno, Richard F. 47, 49, 111, 262, 343, 352, 567, 569
Ferejohn, John **73–105**
figuration 311
Finley, Moses I. 453
Fiorina, Morris P. 46, 47, 51, 52, 336
fiscal accountability 497
Fishkin, James S. 133
force 25
Ford, Gerald 262–3
formal representatives 518
Forward Studies Unit (FSU) 403
fourth 'popular' branch of government 414, 417
frames 312, 316, 319, 383
framing research 312
Frank, Barney 29
Fraser, Nancy 401, 587
Freed, Lee 189
freedom: discipline and 526–7; limitations on 5; representation and 8; of speech/expression 239
Friedrich, Carl 23
Function 135–6, 147–9
functionally determined morality 124–6
functional representation 524–5, 545–6, 561
Fung, A. 595

Gamson, William A. 311
Garsten, Bryan 319–20
Gay, Claudine 258
gender parity: justice argument for 204–8; overview of 199–204; paradoxes of representation and 219; quotas for 217; revitalized democracy argument for 212–14; women's interests and 208–12
general interest 463
general model, elite representation and 540–5
gerrymandering 278; *see also* districts
Gilens, Martin 103
globalisation 14
goal specification 525, 527, 541, 544, 546, 551, 553, 555, 556–7, 558
Goodin 433, 434
Goodin, Robert E. 373, 411
Gore, Al 125, 146–7, 498
Gouges, Olympe de 479–80
governance revolution 299–303
Gracchi 551, 552
Grant, Ruth 290, 497
Gray, William, III 253–4
Gresham, Jewell 194
Gresham's law 110–11
group polarization 410
group representation: authorization and accountability and 226–9, 240; *différance* and 222–6; discursive representation and 411; information selection and 604–5; introduction to 217–19; marginalized groups and 584; modes of representation and 229–37; new argument for 237–41; paradoxes of representation and 219–21; trustees and 591; *see also* descriptive representatives
Guinier, Lani 240
Gutmann, Amy 133, 417, 582
gyroscopic representation 21, 26–8, 31, 276, 277, 279, 282, 591

Habermas, Jurgen: accountability and 133; communicative and strategic action distinction and

310, 313, 315, 318–19; deliberative democratic theory and 412, 582, 583; parliamentary principle and 10; on public sphere 418, 430, 441; on rights 429; 'two-track' model of deliberation and 419
Hall, Stuart 387, 388
Hansen, Mogens Herman 451–2, 455
Hardin, Russell **107–30**
Hare, Thomas 449
Harrington, James 461
Hart, H.L.A. 280
Hartley, Jennifer A. 415
Hayek, F. A. 116–17
Haynes, Elizabeth 258
Hedlund, Ronald D. 40
Hegel, George W.F. 447, 449
Held, D. 373, 375
Helms, Jesse 263
Hendriks, Carolyn M. 418
Henriksen, T.D. 567
Héritier, Adrienne 405
heterarchy 300
hierarchical accountability 497
Hill, Anita 265
Hirschman, Albert 464, 497, 498
Hobbes, Thomas 5, 6, 132, 153, 166, 168–9, 170, 480, 563, 564
Hochschild, Jennifer 194, 415
Holmes, Leslie T. 414
Holmes, Stephen 455
homogeneity 352–6
horizontal accountability 349
Howard, Michael 379
human rights 327–8, 431, 483
Hume, David 107
Hunt, H. L. 126

Ibn Khaldūn 548
idealizing function of representation 449
ideas, politics of 193, 232
identity 6, 388–9
ignorance, representing 107–30
impeachment procedures 82, 129
implicit-explicit axis 384–5
inanimate objects as representatives 143
incumbency, extended 352–6

in-depth interviews 415–16
indicative representation 157, 158–63, 169, 363–70
indirectness 449, 450, 451–7, 591
individualism 458
influence 25–6
informalisation 300
informal representatives 518
informal structures of representation 603
Inner Ocean (Kateb) 448
institutional accountability 516–18
institutional coherence 525, 527, 541, 544, 546, 551, 553, 555–8
institutional complexity 404–7
institutional design, indivisibilities of 288, 297–9
'institutional' representation 28
institutional representation deficit 506
insufficiency of representative claims 404
interdependence 292–4
interest group representation 239
interest group theory 232–3
interest representation 70–1, 313, 524–5, 545–6
interests: definition of 493; overlooked 184, 188; representation of 231–2, 236–7, 238–9; uncrystallized 260–5
internal diversity 253–4
internal-external axis 385
interpretive representation 170
interpretive responsiveness 166–9
intrinsic motivation 342, 345, 348, 357
introspective representation 261–2
intuition 315
isegoria 467, 587
isopsephia 467
issue framing 311, 315

Jackson, John 28
Jacobs, Lawrence 310
James, Michael Rabinder 133
Jennings, M. Kent 46
Joerges, Christian 301
Johnson, James 25
Jones, Bill 112
Jones, Mack 266

judgment 276, 277–9, 591–2
'judgment' clause 316
judiciary 588
jury system 159, 504
Justice and Politics of Difference
   (Young) 186
justice argument 184, 203, 204–8
justification: formal and informal
   representation and 15; right to 293

Kant, Immanuel 74, 89
Karps, Paul D. **35–56**
Kateb, George 8, 448
Kempton, Willet 415
Kennedy, Ted 113
Keohane, Robert 290, 497
key lines of variation 382–5
Khrushchev, Nikita 132
Kilson, Martin 194
king: body of 479; power of 482–3
King, David 28
King, Deborah 194
Kingdon, John 27, 28, 336, 341
Kinshansky, Mark A. 454
Kishlansky, Mark 76
Klee, Paul 389
Knight, Jack 25
Kuper, Andrew 133
Kymlicka, Will 211, 247, 584

Laclau, Ernesto 65, 317, 494
Lasswell, Harold D. 48
Latour, B. 389, 390
League of Nations 443
Lee, David 341
Lefort, Claude 477, 478–80, 482, 484
legal accountability 82, 497
legislation, aim of 276
legitimacy: accountability and 603;
   audience and 145–7; constitutive
   499; de facto 267–9; discursive
   representation and 409, 412–13;
   elections/electoral systems and
   485–6; European Union and 513;
   lack of 133–4, 440; normative 133;
   rules of recognition and 148–50;
   self-appointed representatives and

489–501; shape-shifting representation
   and 573–5
Leib, Ethan J. 414, 417
Leland, Mickey 259
Leviathan (Hobbes) 563
Lewis, Bernard 548
Lewis-Beck, Michael 297
liberties, defense of 128
Lijphart, Arend 3
Lincoln, Abraham 327
Lindahl, Hans 480
Lindblom, Charles 410
linked fate 190
Lisbon Treaty 301, 402–3, 404, 406
Lloyd 572
lobby pressures 178
local pressures 178
Locke, John 170, 563
Loewenberg, Gerhard 40
Lomasky, Loren 411
Lord, Christopher **287–307**, **395–408**
Lorde, Audre 188
Lott, John 339
lottery 97–102, 121, 159, 247–50, 366,
   582
low-information rationality 110, 126
Luhmann, N. 582
Lukes, Stephen 23
Lula da Silva, Luiz Inácio 568, 570
Lupia, Arthur 312, 313, 319

Machiavelli, N. 461, 563, 564
MacKuen, Michael B. 283, 337, 341
Madison, James: accountability and
   277–8; on ambition 294; on Athenian-
   style democracy 74; common
   good and 97; on democracy and
   representation 328; on elections 91;
   elite representation and 75; interests
   and 291, 397; on qualifications
   of officeholders 121; on role of
   representation 4, 83, 88–9, 132
Madisonian representatives/lawmakers
   112–16, 124–5, 277–8
Magna Charta 132
Majone, Giandomenico 301, 405
majoritarian forms of democracy 3

majoritarianism 458–9, 585
makers of representative claims 378–81, 383–4, 398–9, 404–7
Mandela, Nelson 575
Manin, Bernard: accountability and 133; aristocratic thesis and 114, 133; on audience democracy 111; deliberative democracy and 461, 583, 585; elections/electoral systems and 91–3, 283; elites and 73; lottery and 97; predemocratic systems and 4; principle of distinction and 351; theories of 121–3; on truth 109
manipulation 25–6, 310, 319
Mansbridge, Jane: on accountability 497; anticipatory model of representation and 316; on deliberation/deliberative democracy 312, 412, 413; on descriptive representatives **245–74**; descriptive representatives and 187; on education and manipulation 310; group representation and 411; gyroscopic representation and 591; models of representation and 11; on political equality 460; on preference 313; on promissory representation 309; reflexivity and 311, 314–15; Rehfeld's response to 275–84; 'Rethinking Representation' 21–34; on rethinking representation **21–34**; on retrospective voting 314; on selection model **333–62**; selection model of representation and 406, 569; state of field and 374; surrogate representation and 587; systemic representation and 572; trustee-delegate framing and 565, 567
March, John 292
Margalit, Avishai 190
Marin, Louis 380–1
Marmor, Theodore 251
Marsilius of Padua 290
Mayhew, David 336
Mayo, Henry Bertram 275
McCubbins, Matthew 312, 319, 349
McGregor, Douglas 342

median voter models 94–7
Merriam, Charles E. 48
metaphors 410
Michels, Robert 91, 113–14, 129
microcosmic representation 248–9, 250
Mill 433, 434
Mill, James 208, 457–8
Mill, John Stuart: advocacy and 466–7; agora paradigm and 456, 457, 460; assembly and 454; on control of representative bodies 294–5; corruption and 466; criticism of 458; on deliberation 294; electoral representation and 165; on elites 115; on freedom of speech 455; on individual interests 109; on justification 10; on majority rule 293; political inequality and 126; proportionality and 367, 449–50, 585; rationality and 410; on role of representation 4, 132; on tasks of government 127; theory of democracy of 118–21, 457, 459–60, 463; on voting 452
Miller, Arthur 122–3
Miller, Dale 343
Miller, Warren E. 35–8, 40–1, 43, 44, 335–6, 337–8, 341
Miller-Stokes model 35–8
minidemoi 428, 435–40, 444–5
minimal democracy 58–61
minipublics 428, 430–1, 433, 434, 435–40, 444–5, 595
Mirabeau, Comte de 7, 159–60, 290, 366
mirror representation 222, 290–1, 458
misinformation 331
mission-orientation 347–8
Mitford, William 461
mixed government 75
mobilization 311, 315–18
mobilization systems 527, 536, 538–40, 545, 550, 555–9, 560
Modigliani, Andre 311
Mommsen, Theodore 551
monarchy 153, 478–9, 480–3
'monetary surrogacy' 29

money/wealth: dependence on 103;
  surrogate representation and 29
Montanaro, Laura 284, **489–502**
Montesquieu 74, 89, 121, 477–8, 480–2,
  483, 582
moral hazard 85
morality 107, 126–8
Moretti, Enrico 341
Morgan, Edmund 482
Morone, James 251
Moseley-Braun, Carol 263–4
motivation, intrinsic 342, 345, 348, 357
multiple self 411
Musharef, Pervez 145–6
mutual relationships 189–92, 195

Nagel, Jack 23, 25
Namier, Lewis 76
narrative accountability 334, 348–9,
  497
Näsström, Sofia **477–88**
National Assembly 320–1
nature of government 477–8, 480
needs: genesis of 528–9;
  instrumentalization of 532
negotiating allowance 138–9
network accountability 349
networked governance 412, 419
neutrality 3
Neyer, Jürgen 301
Nie, Norman H. 41–2, 44
Niemeyer, Simon **409–21**
non-citizens 431–2
nonelectoral democratic representation
  592–6
nonelectoral sources of accountability
  496–8
nonelectoral sources of authorization
  495–6
non-empowered venues 522
non-hierarchical selection 350–1
nonidentity 66, 69
non-objection criterion 316, 320, 321,
  573
normative criteria 31–2
normative framing 564–5
Norris 506–7

Obama, Barack 569
objectives, aligned 344–5, 358
Olsen, Johan 292
Olson, Mancur 302
O'Neill, Onora 343
'one person, one vote' 9, 10, 11–12, 30,
  251, 477, 524; *see also* voting
opinion formation 309, 310, 311–12, 313
opinions, representation of 232–3,
  236–7, 238–9
organizational accountability 496–8
organizational authorization 496, 499
overlooked interests 184, 188
Oxfam 489, 492, 499–500

Page, Benjamin 23
Paldam, Martin 297
Parkinson, John 426–7
parliamentary debate 109
parliamentary systems 297–9
partiality 390–1
participation, equality in 206–7
'participation explosion' 527–8
participation response, deficits in 508–9
participatory democracy 63, 206–7, 503,
  504, 582
participatory left 59–60
particular-general axis 383–4
particularity 429
'party discipline' model 27
Patterson, Samuel C. 40
Payne, Donald 258
Pennock, J.R. 7, 246
perspective, representation of 230,
  233–7, 238–9, 241, 432–5, 440
Pettit, Philip **153–81**, **363–71**, 582
Phillips, Anne 133, 165, 184, 185, 187,
  193, **199–215**, 232, 374, 461, 584
Phillips Griffiths, A. 200–1
Pitkin, Hanna: on composition of
  legislature 5; concerns of 484;
  constitutional democracy and 583;
  critique of 375–7; on definition of
  representation 65, 275, 289, 409, 564;
  on democratic responsiveness 586; on
  demos 412; descriptive representatives
  and 184, 201, 248, 249; differentiated

relationships and 226; fascist theory of representation and 569; mandate versus independence and 45; mobilization and 311, 315–18; non-objection criterion and 320, 321, 573; on participation 67; proportionality and 448; on representation and democracy **325–32**; responsiveness and 39–40, 42, 309; Rogowski on 150; on role of representative 590–1; on role playing 140; standard account of representation and 133; systemic representation and 572

Piven, Frances Fox 194

Plato 89, 277

Plotke, David **57–72**, 313, 314, 448, 578, 588

pluralism 539–40

pluralist democratic theory 582

plurality systems 298

plurality versus proportional 299

podesta 162–3

point d'appui 462

policy, in representative v. direct democracy 93–7

policy responsiveness 43, 44–5, 48

political agency 83–8, 95

political communities, challenges to 14

political equality 9, 12

political inequality 126

political learning 309, 310, 312

political parties/party theory 124–5, 232–3, 590

political systems, types of 535–8

politico 564

Politics (Aristotle) 75, 90

politics of presence 290, 414

Politics of Presence (Phillips) 584

Pollak, Johannes **287–307, 395–408**

polyarchy 300, 441

Polybius 75

Popkin, Samuel 110, 126, 262–3

Popper, Karl 410

popular power 479, 480

popular representation 524–5, 545–6, 561

populism 556–7

pork-barrel politics 46–7

portrait conception of representation 440–1

positioning 567–73

poverty 194

power 25, 479

Pratt, John 338–9, 341

predemocratic systems 525–6

pre-modern model of accountability 290

prepurchase knowledge model 339; *see also* selection model of representation

presence 68, 193, 207, 211–12, 290, 313

President, outreach efforts by 48–9

presidential systems 297–9

Prewitt, Kenneth 40, 46

primary assemblies 320–1

Prince, The (Machiavelli) 563, 564

principal-agent format 22, 68, 298–9, 315, 333, 338, 579, 603; *see also* role morality

principle (commitment) 480–2

principle of distinction 351

principle of equality 482–4, 485

Principles of Representative Government, The (Manin) 109, 121, 583

private attorneys general 369–70

private autonomy 288

Pro-Femmes/Twese Hamwe organization 499

promissory representation 22, 31, 279, 281–2, 309, 314

Proops, John 414

propaganda 331

proportionality 253–4, 267, 268, 269–70, 367–8, 410, 432, 448, 449, 450, 457–62, 465

proportional representation (PR) 589

proportional systems 298, 299

proportionate presence 211–12

Proposition 3 (California) 112

Proposition 184 (California) 111–12

protest tactics 194

proxies 157, 161, 162, 169, 364–5, 366

Przeworski, Adam 73

public accountability 514, 517–18

public appointees 161–3

public autonomy 288

618 REPRESENTATION

public choice method 340
public control 8–9
public debate 171–2
public deliberation 454
public discourse 449, 457
public good 115
publicity 495
public opinion 178–9, 605
public reasons 171, 173–4
public reputational accountability 497, 499
public speech 454
public will 517–18
Putnam, Robert 418

Q methodology 414–15, 417
Qualified Set 135, 136–7, 145–6

random sampling 158–9, 596
Ranney, Austin 202
rationality 410–11
Ratzinger, Joseph 144
Rauschmayer, F. 414–15
Rawls, John 126, 156, 171, 173, 184, 232, 299, 582
Raz, Joseph 190
reactionary antiliberalism 414–15
reading back 379–80
recognition, rules of 132, 135–47
reconciliation systems 527, 536, 538–40, 545, 550–5, 560, 561
reflexive constituency formation 494
reflexivity 314–15, 319–21, 449
Rehfeld, Andrew **131–51**, 160, **275–85**, 315, 366, 492, 493, 565, 567, 586, 605
relevant parties, illustration of 139
religious leaders 346
reparations 267
repraesentatio identitatis 290
re-presentation 317–19
representation: accountability and 287–303; as advocacy 447–67; aristocratic thesis and 73–103; basic continuities of 4; beyond election 477–86; beyond the state 16; as claims-making 14–15, 395–407; complexity and relational aspects

of 279–82; concepts of 275–84; conditions for political 141–5; in contemporary democratic theory 577–97; core democratic standards for 8–10; critique of 63–5; deferring group 217–41; definitions of 1, 65–6, 289; in deliberative system 423–45; before democracy 4–7; as democracy 57–71; democracy and 325–32; descriptive representatives and 183–96; discursive 409–20; elements of 65–8; formal and informal forms of 15–16; functions of 5; gender and 199–214; general theory of political 131–50; ignorance and 107–30; informal 13; mobilization concept of 309–23; models of 11; nondemocratic 131–2, 523–62; patterns of 567–73; 'rediscovery' of 313–15; responsive and indicative 363–70; responsiveness and 35–52; role of 2–3, 14, 525–8; selection model of 333–58; shape-shifting 563–75; theories of 10–17, 118–23, 396–400, 492–3; transformation of democratic 603–5; types of 1–2, 21; varieties of public 153–79
representational focus 49–50
representational model 545–7
representational theory, crisis in 38–40
representation roles 565–7
representative claims 317, 373–92, 398–9, 404–7, 477, 491, 494, 565
representative democracy 93–7
representative government, aristocratic rule and 88–93
Representatives, Roll Calls, and Constituencies (Fiorina) 336
representees, description of 156
representers, description of 154–6
republic 480–2, 483–4
republicanism 461
response, responsiveness versus 51–2
responsibility talk 485, 486
responsiveness: 'bedrock' norm and 309; components of 35–52; constituent preferences and 309–10; Pitkin and 317–18; service 43, 45–7, 48

responsive representation 157, 163–9, 363–70

retrospective voting 22, 314

revitalized democracy argument 184, 203, 212–14

revolutions 482, 483

rhetorical deliberation 319

Richardson 432, 433, 434

Richardson, H. 582

right to justification 293

Roemer, John 99, 100

Rogers, Joel 239

Rogowski, Ronald 150

role model argument 184, 203

role morality 107, 123–9

role playing 139–41

Roman Republic 551–3

Roosevelt, Franklin 123, 126

Rosanvallon, Pierre 12–13, 320, 478, 484, 485–6

Rosenblum, Nancy L. 313, 590

Rosenbluth, Frances **73–105**

Rousseau, Jean-Jacques: common interest and 355; direct democracy and 462; elites and 75; on freedom 5; on political representation 581–2; on representative democracy 123, 132, 329, 441; self-representation and 170; on silent deliberation 452–3, 454; Sparta as model for 461

Rubenstein, Jennifer 284

Ruggie 428

Runciman, David 316

Russia, political discourses in 414–15

Sabel 441

Sagoff, Mark 411

sanctions/sanctions model 276, 277–9, 333–5, 341, 342, 348, 356–7

Sapiro, Virginia 184, 266

Sartori, G. 582

Saward, Michael: on communicative freedom 430; on definition of representation 399; on legitimacy 409; representative claim and 14, 284, 302, 317, **373–94**, 396, 398, 405, 407, 477, 491; self-appointed representatives

and 400; shape-shifting representation and **563–76**

Schattschneider, Elmer Eric 311, 320–1

Schlafly, Phyllis 264

Schmitt, Carl 109, 112, 114, 119, 122, 123, 132, 389

Schmitt, Hermann 406

Schumpeter, Joseph 5, 58–9, 73, 78, 91, 96, 107, 119, 296, 350, 582

Schwartz, Thomas 349

Scott, James 117

secondary marginalization 192–3

second-class citizenship 265–7

Seitz, B. 390

Selden, John 328

Selection Agent 135, 137

selection model of representation 11, 282, 283, 333–58, 406, 569

selection processes 90–3

selective representation 249–51

self-appointed/self-authorized representatives 320, 489–501, 593–5

self-determination 493–4, 585

self-motivated agents 342–3, 358

self-representation 194

separation of powers 89

service responsiveness 43, 45–7, 48

shape-shifting representation 563–75

Shapiro, Robert J. 310

shared aims 191–2, 195

Sherlock, K. 414–15

Shotter, John 497

Sieyes, Emmanuel-Joseph 121, 351, 593

silencing 379, 380

single-member plurality (SMP) 589

single transferable vote (STV) 507

singular-multiple axis 383

skewed representation 499, 500

Skinner, Quentin 158, 365–6

Skjeie, Hege 211–12

slippery slope 201

Smith, Melanchton 159, 366

Smith, T.V. 48

social complexity 12–13

Social Contract, The (Rousseau) 453

social meaning, construction of 265–7

social mobility 529–31, 533–5

social positioning 233–4, 236
sorting, selection and 345–8, 357–8
Soullard, H.H. 552
Sovereign 563, 564
Speech and Phenomena (Derrida) 318
Spirit of Laws, The (Montesquieu)
477–8, 480–2
Spivak, G.C. 389
spokespersons 166, 167
Squires, Judith 314
standard accounts of democratic
representation 579–80
'standing participant' citizens 451–2,
453, 455, 456
Stanton, Cady 132
statistical representation 290
status deracialization 194
statutory authorities 368–70
stereotypes 346–7
Stimson, James A. 23–4, 27, 283, 337,
341
Stokes, Donald E. 35–8, 40–1, 43, 44,
335–6, 337–8, 341
strategic action 310, 313, 315, 318–19
stratification 529–31
Strolovitch, Dara 500
Strøm, Kaare 298
structural social locations 233–4, 236,
238
*Structural Transformation of the Public
Sphere, The* (Habermas) 583
subject positions 567–8, 573
suffrage: Mill on 120; unequal 120; *see
also* voting
Sunstein, Cass R. 410
supervisory accountability 497
support-input model 40, 49
surrogate accountability 284
surrogate representation 21, 28–31, 259,
279, 282–3, 499, 587
Swain, Carol 247, 257, 258, 259
symbolic representation 142–3, 376
symbolic responsiveness 43, 48–9
systemic representation 571–3

taxes, representation and 327
Taylor, Charles 268

term limits 28, 504
territoriality 579–80
Themistocles 79
theocratic systems 527, 536, 537, 538–40,
547–50, 560
Theory X and Theory Y 342
Thomas, Clarence 257–8, 265
Thomassen, Jacques 406
Thompson, Dennis 133, 373, 417, 419,
431–2, 582
three-strikes referendum 111–12
threshold presence 211–12
Thucydides 73–4, 89, 93, 457
Tocqueville, Alexis de 130, 330, 331,
457
totalitarianism 479
transnational discursive representation
419–20
transnational issues 432
transparency 348–50
treaty ratifications 405
Truman, David B. 189, 582
'trustee' form of representation 28
trustees 166–7, 176, 226, 276, 282, 350–1,
363, 376, 466, 564–5, 567, 590–1

unidirectionality 317–18, 321, 376, 380
universality 429
universal suffrage 479, 483, 579
unrepresented groups 431–2
Urbinati, Nadia: on concept of
representation **577–602**; Condorcet
and 320, 321; deliberation and
312, 318–19; on importance of
representation 424; indirectness
and 591; mobilization concept
of representation and 316; on
representation as advocacy 283,
447–75; on self rule 442; systemic
representation and 572
US model of accountability 290, 291,
294

values: intensity of 13; pluralities of 288
van Gunsteren 427
Verba, Sidney 41–2, 44
virtual representation 28, 282–3, 590

Voice, Trust, and Memory (Williams) 584

voice accountability 497, 498, 499

voter ignorance 110–12

voting: disenfranchising of convicts and 194; as duty 452; economic 297; Mill on 452; retrospective 22, 314; universal suffrage and 479, 483, 579

voting records 38

Wahlke, John C. 38, 40, 48

Warren, Mark E. 14, 411, 424, 430, 442, **503–22, 577–602, 603–5**

wars of independence 346

Washington model 174–6, 178

Weale, Albert 293

wealth distribution 100, 331

Weaver, Kimberlee 412

Weber, Max 22, 504

Weiler 423

Weissberg, Robert 28

Westminster model 176–8

Westminster parliament 155–6

whistle-blowers 163

Wilkerson, Margaret 194

Williams, Melissa S. 133, 184–5, 187, 194, 464, 584–5

will of the people 224–5, 227

Wilson, William Julius 194

Wolin, Sheldon 327, 484

women's interests argument 203, 208–12

Women's International League for Peace and Freedom (WILPF) 442–3

Wood, Gordon 76

World Trade Organization (WTO) 412, 439

Wycliffe, John 327

Xenophon 89–90

Yates, Robert 7

Young, Iris Marion: dialogue and 313–14; group representation and 133, 185–6, 195, **217–44**, 247, 374; on importance of representation 448–9; indirectness and 451; interests and 493; networks and 605; representation as identity and 283; social structure and 410–11, 434–5; veto power and 417

Zeckhauser, Richard 338–9, 341

Zeigler, L. Harmon 46